Feasting on the Word®

Editorial Board

Feasting on the Word®

Preaching the
Revised Common Lectionary

Year A, Volume 1

DAVID L. BARTLETT and **BARBARA BROWN TAYLOR**

General Editors

WESTMINSTER JOHN KNOX PRESS
LOUISVILLE • KENTUCKY

Unless otherwise indicated, Scripture quotations are from the New Revised Standard Version of the Bible, copyright © 1989 by the Division of Christian Education of the National Council of the Churches of Christ in the U.S.A., and are used by permission. All rights reserved. Scripture quotations marked JPS are from *The TANAKH: The New JPS Translation according to the Traditional Hebrew Text.* Copyright 1985 by the Jewish Publication Society. Used by permission. Scripture quotations marked NIV are from *The Holy Bible, New International Version.* Copyright © 1973, 1978, 1984 International Bible Society. Used by permission of Zondervan Bible Publishers.

Excerpts from Ron Ingram's, "'Holiness in the Hood' draws youth to neighborhood church celebration," by Ron Ingram, Herald&Review.com, July 21, 2008, are used by permission. Excerpts from an unpublished paper by the Rev. Doug King, Senior Associate Pastor, Brick Presbyterian Church, New York, presented to the Moveable Feast group in 2008 are used by permission. Excerpt from "A Christmas Hymn" in *Advice to a Prophet and Other Poems,* copyright © 1961 and renewed 1989 by Richard Wilbur, reprinted by permission of Houghton Mifflin Harcourt Publishing Company and Faber and Faber Ltd. Excerpts from *Remember Who You Are: Baptism, a Model for Christian Life,* by William H. Willimon, copyright 1980 by The Upper Room (Nashville, TN). Used by permission from the publisher.

Book design by Drew Stevens
Cover design by Lisa Buckley

2013 paperback edition
Originally published in hardback in the United States
by Westminster John Knox Press in 2010
Louisville, Kentucky

♾ This book is printed on acid-free paper that meets the American National Standards Institute Z39.48 standard.

16 17 18 19—10 9 8 7 6 5 4 3

Library of Congress Cataloging-in-Publication Data
Feasting on the Word : preaching the revised common lectionary / David L. Bartlett and Barbara Brown Taylor, general editors.
    p. cm.
    Includes index.
    ISBN 978-0-664-23107-1 (v. 12 alk. paper)
    ISBN 978-0-664-23106-4 (v. 11 alk. paper)
    ISBN 978-0-664-23105-7 (v. 10 alk. paper)
    ISBN 978-0-664-23104-0 (v. 9 alk. paper)
    ISBN 978-0-664-23103-3 (v. 8 alk. paper)
    ISBN 978-0-664-23102-6 (v. 7 alk. paper)
    ISBN 978-0-664-23101-9 (v. 6 alk. paper)
    ISBN 978-0-664-23100-2 (v. 5 alk. paper)
    ISBN 978-0-664-23099-9 (v. 4 alk. paper)
    ISBN 978-0-664-23098-2 (v. 3 alk. paper)
    ISBN 978-0-664-23097-5 (v. 2 alk. paper)
    ISBN 978-0-664-23096-8 (v. 1 alk. paper)
  1. Lectionary preaching. 2. Common lectionary (1992) I. Bartlett, David Lyon, 1941– II. Taylor, Barbara Brown.
    BV4235.L43F43 2008
    251'.6—dc22

                                                                                    2007047534

ISBN 978-0-664-23957-2 (v. 12 paperback)
ISBN 978-0-664-23954-1 (v. 11 paperback)
ISBN 978-0-664-23963-3 (v. 10 paperback)
ISBN 978-0-664-23960-2 (v. 9 paperback)
ISBN 978-0-664-23959-6 (v. 8 paperback)
ISBN 978-0-664-23956-5 (v. 7 paperback)
ISBN 978-0-664-23965-7 (v. 6 paperback)
ISBN 978-0-664-23962-6 (v. 5 paperback)
ISBN 978-0-664-23958-9 (v. 4 paperback)
ISBN 978-0-664-23955-8 (v. 3 paperback)
ISBN 978-0-664-23964-0 (v. 2 paperback)
ISBN 978-0-664-23961-9 (v. 1 paperback)

Contents

Publisher's Note

Feasting on the Word: Preaching the Revised Common Lectionary is an ambitious project that is offered to the Christian church as a resource for preaching and teaching.

The uniqueness of this approach in providing four perspectives on each preaching occasion from the Revised Common Lectionary sets this work apart from other lectionary materials. The theological, pastoral, exegetical, and homiletical dimensions of each biblical passage are explored with the hope that preachers will find much to inform and stimulate their preparations for preaching from this rich "feast" of materials.

This work could not have been undertaken without the deep commitments of those who have devoted countless hours to working on these tasks. Westminster John Knox Press would like to acknowledge the magnificent work of our general editors, David L. Bartlett and Barbara Brown Taylor. They are both gifted preachers with passionate concerns for the quality of preaching. They are also wonderful colleagues who embraced this huge task with vigor, excellence, and unfailing good humor. Our debt of gratitude to Barbara and David is great.

The fine support staff, project manager Joan Murchison and compiler Mary Lynn Darden, enabled all the thousands of "pieces" of the project to come together and form this impressive series. Without their strong competence and abiding persistence, these volumes could not have emerged.

The volume editors for this series are to be thanked as well. They used their superb skills as pastors and professors and ministers to work with writers and help craft their valuable insights into the highly useful entries that comprise this work.

The hundreds of writers who shared their expertise and insights to make this series possible are ones who deserve deep thanks indeed. They come from wide varieties of ministries. They have given their labors to provide a gift to benefit the whole church and to enrich preaching in our time.

Westminster John Knox would also like to express our appreciation to Columbia Theological Seminary for strong cooperation in enabling this work to begin and proceed. Dean of Faculty and Executive Vice President D. Cameron Murchison welcomed the project from the start and drew together everything we needed. His continuing efforts have been very valuable. Former President Laura S. Mendenhall provided splendid help as well. She made seminary resources and personnel available and encouraged us in this partnership with enthusiasm and all good grace. We thank her and look forward to working with Columbia's new president, Stephen Hayner.

It is a joy for Westminster John Knox Press to present *Feasting on the Word: Preaching the Revised Common Lectionary* to the church, its preachers, and its teachers. We believe rich resources can assist the church's ministries as the Word is proclaimed. We believe the varieties of insights found in these pages will nourish preachers who will "feast on the Word" and who will share its blessings with those who hear.

Westminster John Knox Press

Series Introduction

A preacher's work is never done. Teaching, offering pastoral care, leading worship, and administering congregational life are only a few of the responsibilities that can turn preaching into just one more task of pastoral ministry. Yet the Sunday sermon is how the preacher ministers to most of the people most of the time. The majority of those who listen are not in crisis. They live such busy lives that few take part in the church's educational programs. They wish they had more time to reflect on their faith, but they do not. Whether the sermon is five minutes long or forty-five, it is the congregation's one opportunity to hear directly from their pastor about what life in Christ means and why it matters.

Feasting on the Word offers pastors focused resources for sermon preparation, written by companions on the way. With four different essays on each of the four biblical texts assigned by the Revised Common Lectionary, this series offers preachers sixteen different ways into the proclamation of God's Word on any given occasion. For each reading, preachers will find brief essays on the exegetical, theological, homiletical, and pastoral challenges of the text. The page layout is unusual. By setting the biblical passage at the top of the page and placing the essays beneath it, we mean to suggest the interdependence of the four approaches without granting priority to any one of them. Some readers may decide to focus on the Gospel passage, for instance, by reading all four essays provided for that text. Others may decide to look for connections between the Hebrew Bible, Psalm, Gospel, and Epistle texts by reading the theological essays on each one.

Wherever they begin, preachers will find what they need in a single volume produced by writers from a wide variety of disciplines and religious traditions. These authors teach in colleges and seminaries. They lead congregations. They write scholarly books as well as columns for the local newspaper. They oversee denominations. In all of these capacities and more, they serve God's Word, joining the preacher in the ongoing challenge of bringing that Word to life.

We offer this print resource for the mainline church in full recognition that we do so in the digital age of the emerging church. Like our page layout, this decision honors the authority of the biblical text, which thrives on the page as well as in the ear. While the twelve volumes of this series follow the pattern of the Revised Common Lectionary, each volume contains an index of biblical passages so that all preachers may make full use of its contents.

We also recognize that this new series appears in a post-9/11, post-Katrina world. For this reason, we provide no shortcuts for those committed to the proclamation of God's Word. Among preachers, there are books known as "Monday books" because they need to be read thoughtfully at least a week ahead of time. There are also "Saturday books," so called because they supply sermon ideas on short notice. The books in this series are not Saturday books. Our aim is to help preachers go deeper, not faster, in a world that is in need of saving words.

A series of this scope calls forth the gifts of a great many people. We are grateful first of all to the staff of Westminster John Knox Press: Don McKim, Jack Keller, and Jon Berquist, who conceived this project; David Dobson, who worked diligently to bring the project to completion, with publisher Marc Lewis's strong support; and Julie Tonini, who has painstakingly guided each volume through the production process. We thank former President Laura Mendenhall and former Dean Cameron Murchison of Columbia Theological Seminary, who made our participation in this work possible. We thank President Steve Hayner and Dean Deborah Mullen for their continuing encouragement and support. Our editorial board is a hardworking board, without whose patient labor and good humor this series would not exist. From the start, Joan Murchison has been the brains of the operation, managing details of epic proportions with great human kindness. Mary Lynn Darden, Dilu Nicholas, Megan Hackler Denton, and John Shillingburg have supported both her and us with their administrative skills.

We have been honored to work with a multitude of gifted thinkers, writers, and editors. We present these essays as their offering—and ours—to the blessed ministry of preaching.

David L. Bartlett
Barbara Brown Taylor

A Note about the Lectionary

Feasting on the Word follows the Revised Common Lectionary (RCL) as developed by the Consultation on Common Texts, an ecumenical consultation of liturgical scholars and denominational representatives from the United States and Canada. The RCL provides a collection of readings from Scripture to be used during worship in a schedule that follows the seasons of the church year. In addition, it provides for a uniform set of readings to be used across denominations or other church bodies.

The RCL provides a reading from the Old Testament, a Psalm response to that reading, a Gospel, and an Epistle for each preaching occasion of the year. It is presented in a three-year cycle, with each year centered around one of the Synoptic Gospels. Year A is the year of Matthew, Year B is the year of Mark, and Year C is the year of Luke. John is read each year, especially during Advent, Lent, and Easter.

The RCL offers two tracks of Old Testament texts for the Season after Pentecost or Ordinary Time: a semicontinuous track, which moves through stories and characters in the Old Testament, and a complementary track, which ties the Old Testament texts to the theme of the Gospel texts for that day. Some denominational traditions favor one over the other. For instance, Presbyterians and Methodists generally follow the semicontinuous track, while Lutherans and Episcopalians generally follow the complementary track.

The print volumes of *Feasting on the Word* follow the complementary track for Year A, are split between the complementary and semicontinuous track for Year B, and cover the semicontinuous stream for Year C. Essays for Pentecost and the Season after Pentecost that are not covered in the print volumes are available on the *Feasting on the Word* Web site, www.feastingontheword.net.

For more information about the Revised Common Lectionary, visit the official RCL Web site at http://lectionary.library.vanderbilt.edu/ or see *The Revised Common Lectionary: The Consultation on Common Texts* (Nashville: Abingdon Press, 1992).

Feasting on the Word®

Isaiah 2:1-5

¹The word that Isaiah son of Amoz saw concerning Judah and Jerusalem.
²In days to come
   the mountain of the LORD's house
shall be established as the highest of the mountains,
   and shall be raised above the hills;
all the nations shall stream to it.
³ Many peoples shall come and say,
"Come, let us go up to the mountain of the LORD,
   to the house of the God of Jacob;
that he may teach us his ways
   and that we may walk in his paths."

Theological Perspective

We are accustomed to hearing words, and often we call on others to listen with us; but in dramatic fashion the prophet Isaiah speaks of "seeing the word." Seeing the word, a new idea for many of us, points to a new level of discernment. There is "a seeing beyond seeing," learning to see reality at its depth, as we learn that "there is often more there than meets the eye." In a profound sense the emphasis is not on human imagination or gifts of intellect, but on anticipation that the word concerning Judah and Jerusalem will be revealed by God. God's servants are expected to wait for God to reveal the word concerning their situation of faith. God shares the word with God's people, and they not only listen to the word, but also "behold the word."

Quite often in the Old Testament we are told that God's word is enacted. God's word does not return empty but accomplishes its intent. God's word happens as the word becomes deed. The word, as promise, is always looking toward fulfillment. "Then God said, 'Let there be light'; and there was light" (Gen. 1:3). Isaiah enables his community to see that the rich have been exploiting the poor and worshipers have been preoccupied with the scrupulosity of sacrifice and obedience; but he goes beyond that.

The genius of Isaiah is that he also paints a vivid picture of God's corrective message to the people and the new reality it will create. Along with his

Pastoral Perspective

By the time Advent comes around, we have already been primed by our culture for a Big Event. Catalogs arrive, showing us pictures of happy families in matching pajamas enjoying a quiet moment together. Commercials splash across the television screen, promising love and contentment in the form of new gadgets. Store displays evoke nostalgia for childhood wonder. We are invited to lean together toward the coming Big Event, when fantasies will be fulfilled, and dreams may yet come true.

In the face of such messages, we preachers have the task of articulating a message that is both faithful to our Scriptures and responsive to the deep, true needs of people who are longing for something Big. We fail when we take the easy road of simple assault against the cultural and commercial messages. Yes, our culture is celebrating a giddy overhyped pseudo-Christmas while we are attempting the more serious task of observing a holy Advent, but the reason the cultural messages are so powerful is that our human yearning is so real, and so profound.

Isaiah holds up a vision of the true. He takes us to a mountain and shows us what our hearts are actually tuned for. First, he shows that God's presence, by God's own initiative, will become more evident and compelling: the Lord's house will be established as the highest of the mountains, and the nations shall stream

For out of Zion shall go forth instruction,
    and the word of the Lord from Jerusalem.
⁴He shall judge between the nations,
    and shall arbitrate for many peoples;
they shall beat their swords into plowshares,
    and their spears into pruning hooks;
nation shall not lift up sword against nation,
    neither shall they learn war any more.

⁵O house of Jacob,
    come, let us walk
    in the light of the Lord!

Exegetical Perspective

This oracle is often called the "floating oracle of peace" because it also appears in Micah 4:1–3. It is apparently part of a general prophetic tradition that was available to both of these prophets as a promise of the eschatological fulfillment of God's kingdom. Presumably this is especially important in times of difficulty when present circumstances seem unpromising; confidence that the future belongs to God gives hope in the present. In Advent we anticipate the birth of Jesus into a world in need of light (v. 5). Every generation needs assurance that the powers of the world—whether the Romans of Jesus' time or the principalities and powers of our present age—do not determine the future.

In Isaiah's time the difficult present circumstances were probably associated with the Syro-Ephraimitic war, when the northern kingdom of Israel and the Aramaean kingdom of Damascus tried to force Judah into an unwise alliance in opposition to the Assyrian Empire. When these foes finally laid siege to Jerusalem, King Ahaz turned to the prophet Isaiah for advice and assurance.

In response, Isaiah offered a vision of promise that has a number of elements. The first is that regardless of where power seems to lie in the present, the day is coming when God's reign will be established for all humankind to see. God's dwelling on

Homiletical Perspective

As the Old Testament reading for the First Sunday of Advent, these lines from Isaiah are Scripture's first words to the church in Advent. They are, therefore, the very first words to be heard by the church as its new year begins. The curtain rises. A prophet walks onto the darkened stage in a circle of light. He begins to sing—of a mountain, and of nations streaming to it willing to hear holy instruction and be judged by it, willing also to make peace with each other. As the song is ending, another sound rises, the ringing sound of hammers striking metal. It fills the room. That sound is the first in the church's new year.

So vivid and appealing is the image of swords and spears beaten into plowshares and pruning hooks that we may be inclined to camp the whole sermon there. As usual, the preaching will likely be truer and richer if the larger sweep of the text is taken into account. So frame by frame, how does the vision proceed?

It begins by declaring that in God's future, the holiest ground becomes highest ground—above all other elevations will be the place of awe. From this place the Presence will call to the nations, who will flock to it. A new community is being gathered to the Holy, a multicultural, multiracial, multilingual convergence. Coming nearer, they urge each other on and call out to each other the longing that draws

Isaiah 2:1-5

Theological Perspective

contemporary Micah, he enjoins Judah that God requires justice, mercy, and even more, to walk with God. It is in this context that he articulates a theology of "the last days." The word of God provides the basis of a new future in which the temple of God becomes the focal point of the world. There is a break, a discontinuity, with the way things were. The good news is that tomorrow will be different from yesterday, because the future is based on the promises of God, which are always new.

There is no basis in the contextual situation of Judah for expecting or planning a new future. Without God's promise as basis and ground of hope, the future is bound to be a repetition of the past. With that promise, there is a new point of departure, because the future is based on the faithfulness of God. The new future that Isaiah offers as promise is that the temple of God will be lifted high above all the mountains and all people, including the Gentiles, will stream toward it. The promise comes in the midst of the waywardness and idolatry of the people. The promise is not consonant with the practice and the conduct of the people, but the prophet, who is able to "see beyond seeing" and somehow able to see God's hope for the people, articulates a message that transcends the reality on the ground.

Jews and Gentiles alike stream toward God's holy mountain. Why? What compels them? One insight that emerges here is that, at our core, human beings need instruction from YHWH. "Many peoples shall come and say, 'Come, let us go up to the mountain of the LORD, to the house of the God of Jacob; that he may teach us his ways and that we may walk in his paths'" (v. 3). The people are in need of instruction and direction at crucial junctures of life, but they are tired of false instruction and faulty directions from their culture's gods. So they set their gaze on the temple of YHWH atop the highest mountain, and together they become the pilgrim people of God.

There in the mountain of God they will encounter and meet God, who speaks not only in words but in acts. They will hear not only with their ears but with their hearts—and this God, whose actions they see and whose will they hear in their hearts, will be an all-welcoming God. The prophet offers a clue that the instruction of God revealed and hidden in the Torah is not only for Israel, but for all the nations. God's word, indeed God's law, is not the exclusive right of any particular people, but is "spoken" for all who stream toward the mountain of God.

God's word always comes as law and gospel. The law here comes not in an exhortation but in a

Pastoral Perspective

to it. People everywhere will be drawn to God, from all nations, all cultures, all races. They will converge out of a shared desire for divine instruction. Here is a revolutionary contrast to current complacency and cynicism. The preacher might find real fire for preaching if he or she simply contemplates how radical a promise this is—that we will all seek God together, and God will be present. Here Isaiah is declaring that one day we can quit trying to get by on scraps and remembrances of spiritual experiences. God's presence will be made manifest. God's house will be established, and we shall stream to it. We will press toward it together to be taught and to be changed.

Then the word of the Lord will go forth, and from that word will come justice; God will judge between the nations and settle disputes. The word of the Lord will make an actual difference in the way the world works: inequities will be balanced, shackles will be loosed, wrongs will be set right. Out of this justice will come transformation—weapons of violence will be turned into instruments for nourishment. The nations will put their swords down, and will not train for war anymore.

Consumerist visions of the good life may seem to prevail in our culture at this time of year, but Isaiah's prophecy will stand up to any of them. This picture of unity, of justice, of shared openness to the divine way, and of peace speaks to some of our deepest hopes. The preacher would do well to find ways to build bridges between the listeners' culturally driven anticipation and the deeper yearnings that lie beneath. How might the many pictures of happy families and yuletide gatherings actually speak to something real, like the desire for harmony across many divisions? How might the nostalgia for Christmases past and the idolization of childhood wonder represent our desire to believe again in things that seem impossible to us as adults—like peace on earth and goodwill for all?

Once tapped, these yearnings may reveal something raw and disillusioned. As much as we may long for a day when weapons are laid down, hearts are transformed, and peoples are drawn together, we find it hard to believe that such a day will actually come. Even to speak of the end of time, or of a time beyond time, when God will set everything right, is a stretch for many of us. Isaiah's vision may be even more preposterous than that. He announces that this remarkable transformation will take place "in days to come." "In days to come" may not be specific, but it does imply that such transformation will come within history.

4   *First Sunday of Advent*

Exegetical Perspective

Mount Zion will be central and elevated over all other claims to prominence or power (v. 2).

The temple on Mount Zion in Jerusalem was far more than a matter of local geography. It was the locus of God's presence in the midst of God's people. To envision Zion as elevated above all other mountains and the focus of pilgrimage by all peoples (vv. 2b–3a) is not so much a political claim by Jerusalem as a spiritual claim of God's presence as the true center to which all nations will eventually flow. Nations will always be in conflict unless God's reign is recognized beyond that of kings and God sits on Mount Zion enthroned above the ark of the covenant, reigning over all other claims to power. Already the prophet Isaiah understands God's ultimate purpose to bring salvation to all the nations and not simply to Israel. This universal quality is appropriate to Advent, where Christians celebrate the birth of the child proclaimed with the words "Peace on earth; goodwill to all people."

A part of that hoped-for future day is that all humanity will also recognize the need for God's direction in their lives. Verse 3 actually contains four synonyms that stress the ways in which the direction that comes from God will finally prevail: "he [will] teach us his ways," "we [will] walk in his paths," "out of Zion shall go forth the law;" "the word of the Lord [will come] from Jerusalem." Ways, paths, law, word—all express the direction that comes from God and counters the alternatives that tempt our allegiance in the world. The ways of this world are self-centered and idolatrous. This verse reorients the faithful to the alternative world created by covenant partnership with God. God is the true source of guidance in human life and community. In Advent, God's word incarnate is about to become flesh in our midst, countering the wisdom of this world. The Gospel of John expresses this hope in its profound claim that "the Word became flesh and lived among us" (1:14).

This new focus brings two results. The first is judgment. Nations and peoples are judged and rebuked (v. 4a). Those in the world who claim authority apart from God's reign are exposed and judged. The world is not the source of true authority, and it is not the source of hope for the future. The world is the source of conflict, the sword, the spear, the making of war.

In God's reign these implements of conflict will be transformed into tools of community (v. 4b). Swords will become plowshares and spears become pruning hooks. Nations will trade in their swords and war will not be the focus of nations. This

Homiletical Perspective

them toward a common center: to hear the instruction of God.

This instruction, it turns out, includes arbitration. The Holy One "shall judge between the nations, and shall arbitrate for many peoples." God, in other words, will not only speak, but will listen to the grievances, disputes, and concerns of the nations, and will adjudicate. These two words—"judge" and "arbitrate"—are the only active verbs assigned by the text to God. The nations and peoples are about to make peace, but the gift given by God is justice. The ending of inequity is ground for the ending of violence. The old assertion is true: there is no lasting peace without justice.

The nations accept God's judgments. One result, the only one named, is disarmament, inevitably leading to new capacities for tending the land and feeding the people. Since the reasons for envy, greed, resentment, retribution, and fear have been abolished, weapons are irrelevant. Since aggressions have been rendered absurd, resources once diverted for battle are available now for the provision of health, life, and communal growth. The text imagines *conversion* in its literal, material sense. Instruments of taking life are converted to implements for sustaining life. The economy is converted. The world's curriculum is converted from learning war to learning the ways of God.

Lest we get too dreamy about an idyllic future, the text hands us a present-tense invitation. Having pointed to a day when "the peoples" will say to each other, "Come, let us go to the mountain," the text now urges *us*: "Come, let us walk in the light." Whatever peaceable future there is to be, those who hear the promise are enjoined to go walking toward it "in the light of God."

Preachers face an odd challenge when a text points to the future of God. We are preaching a dream. In what way is the dream true, and in what realm? Isaiah is apparently proclaiming future wonders within human history. Real nations will bend their weapons toward the cultivation of the actual earth. On this First Sunday of Advent, preachers are not likely to declare that this vision will be historically and universally so.

Then what will we say? Strategically, it might be wise to say how absurd it all sounds. During the reading of the text, did no one in the room laugh out loud at the naiveté of it? Did no one smirk? Texts such as these cannot be preached effectively or truthfully without acknowledgment of the unbudging, bleak realities they claim will disappear. Sorrow and

Isaiah 2:1-5

Theological Perspective

proclamation: the people will make peace, as swords become plowshares and spears become pruning hooks. Once again the promise of peacemaking does not match the reality on the ground. The enemy is preparing for war, but the word goes forth that God's will is peace, and the people are called to join God in God's work of peacemaking. Because the prophet has his eyes on God and not merely on the situation—because he is focused on God's instruction and direction—he can actually see the word of God, the *promissio dei* in action. The word of encouragement for those who seek instruction at the house of God is not to focus on the present existential situation in such a way that they lose sight of the God who speaks and acts.

We are promised by God that as God's gift of peace becomes real among us, Jews and Gentiles alike will stream to the mountain of God to be instructed and directed by God. The people who are taught by God will seek peace and practice violence no more. Weapons of violence will be destroyed. To receive divine instruction is to share in a vision of a coming realm of peace in which God will judge among the nations, and nations will not learn war anymore. The way forward is to walk in the light of the Lord.

NOEL LEO ERSKINE

Pastoral Perspective

Herein lies another important pastoral insight. It is so much easier to pin our hopes on Christmas gifts and holiday feasts than it is to open ourselves to the possibility of believing in the seemingly impossible. We have been disappointed so many times by failed peace treaties abroad, and by divisions within our own culture, and by fractured relationships within our own lives. We know firsthand the destruction that conflict inflicts, even if we have never lifted an actual sword. It is important for the preacher to acknowledge the reality of disillusionment and disappointment, understanding that these apply not only to the lofty ideas of world peace, but also to some of the most intimate relationships in congregants' lives. As Christmas approaches, some in our churches will be feeling these losses acutely; it is important for the preacher to be honest about realities and attentive to the fact that happy visions of hope can make old wounds throb.

In the end, what Isaiah offers is not only a vision of global transformation, but an invitation to live toward that day. "O house of Jacob, come, let us walk in the light of the Lord!" However hard it may be to believe that a new and longed-for reality will take hold some day, there is power in walking in God's light now, one step at a time. Congregants may feel cynical or hopeless about the prospects of Isaiah's vision, but in his invitation lies enormous and practical power. The future belongs to God, but the first step toward that future belongs to those who have glimpsed God's light and are willing to trust that enough light lies ahead.

STACEY SIMPSON DUKE

Exegetical Perspective

transformational image has fueled the imagination of many generations. It is the inspiration for a large sculpture that stands outside the General Assembly tower at the United Nations headquarters in New York. The hope is that through the cooperation of nations, the tools of community can replace the weapons of war.

The occurrence of this same striking image in Micah 4:3 suggests that this was a common expression of hope within the wider prophetic movement during Isaiah's time. It moves beyond the particularities of immediate conflicts between peoples and nations to find unity in a common hope for the alternative world of God's reign. In Advent we lift our sight beyond the challenges and crises of our own time to participate with the generations since Isaiah in the hope for a world transformed by the final goal of peace and harmony toward which God is moving us.

In the end, the establishment of God's reign is a matter of walking "in the light of the LORD" (v. 5). Light is a strong image in the prophecies of Isaiah, in 9:2, where God's light gives the people hope, and in 42:6, where God's people are called to be a light to the nations. Light is also, of course, one of the primary symbols of Advent. This First Sunday finds the Advent community brimming with confidence. The light of the world is coming in Jesus Christ, and the world will be transformed. We light the candles of Advent as a foretaste of the light that is to come in the Christ child. The darkness of the world will not prevail. Conflict is replaced by community, and those who would oppose the advent of God's reign will be judged and overcome. God's light will not be denied. The reign of God will come.

BRUCE C. BIRCH

Homiletical Perspective

doubt need a voice in the room, or the promise is flippant. Advent proposes impossibilities. The fitting first response is bafflement. The season keeps giving us cause to blurt out the question of Mary: "How can this be?" (Luke 1:34).

We are in the presence of a mystery. God's own justice and peace will occur among the nations "in days to come." What days? How? Perhaps all we can say is that the vision describes what God is, in fact, at work in the world to do. It is what Jesus apparently meant by "the reign of God," which is already present and at work among us, though not yet in fullness. We saw it in Jesus, who converted fear to love, lunacy to sanity, enemies to friends. He died surrounded by swords; a spear stabbed him; nails tore him. They entered infinite love, which "melted them into light."[1]

Isaiah's vision should not be preached in the imperative. The text does not scold or admonish; it lifts a gleaming promise of what God will do in days to come. If the sermon blasts the nations or lectures congregants about being peacemakers, it violates the text's intention. True to the season, the sermon will express the deeps of human longing, and point to the dreams and promises of God for the world. In the end, the sermon will also be, as hope always is, invitational. "Come, let us walk in the light of the LORD." God's future casts its gleam into the present. We move toward God's future by making our choices—personal, relational, political, communal—in its light.

At St. Louis University is a small Jesuit chapel that is creatively lit. The light fixtures are made of twentieth-century cannon shells, converted. Emptied of their lethal contents, they now hold light for people to pray by. In such light we pray and live. And having laid our own weapons down, we bear witness to the promise of greater transformations in days to come.

PAUL SIMPSON DUKE

---

1. This image was used by George Arthur Buttrick in an unpublished sermon.

Psalm 122

¹I was glad when they said to me,
    "Let us go to the house of the Lord!"
²Our feet are standing
    within your gates, O Jerusalem.

³Jerusalem—built as a city
    that is bound firmly together.
⁴To it the tribes go up,
    the tribes of the Lord,
  as was decreed for Israel,
      to give thanks to the name of the Lord.

Theological Perspective

Beginning to read Psalm 122 leads to singing. The question is: "What song do you sing?" On the one hand, people might be drawn to the classical setting for organ and choir written by Sir Hubert Parry in 1902 for the coronation of King Edward VII of England. With ease that ought to worry us as much as it delights us, this music bespeaks the power of empires and their political, military, and religious elites all singing of the strong walls that enfold their peaceful and prosperous city. The divide is obvious, implicit throughout and made clear toward the end: prosperity to Jerusalem-lovers, but the hostile better keep their distance! This song is a song by and for the powerful.

What if those who are powerless sing the psalm? Can we hear it quite differently, less a theology of glory and more a theology of the cross? The song might begin with vibrant handclapping, Hammond organ, and drums, pulsing forth in a strong gospel style, such as the version by Joe Pace and the Colorado Mass Choir. The African American context insists that despite oppression, we have a mighty advocate fighting on our side, and in that one's house we have safety and protection. Rather than the power of empire and its elites, here we might find a safe house where we can exhale and gain strength for the struggles of life.

Pastoral Perspective

By the time Advent rolls around, most of North America is already thinking of Christmas. Carols are playing in the shopping malls, Christmas decorations are up, and the retail bonanza that drives our economy is well under way. The church comes late to the Christmas season. We are culturally out of step, emphasizing different themes, having different priorities. Psalm 122, a song of ascents or pilgrimage psalm, draws some attention to the different path we as Christians take toward Christmas, the celebration of the birth of Christ.

Verse 1 might be an interesting place to begin this discussion. "I was glad when they said to me, 'Let us go to the house of the Lord!'" I almost detect some ambivalence, here; the image is of people encouraging each other to go to worship, and the psalmist proclaims gladness at this—as opposed to some other prevalent emotions, perhaps? In my own context, people who proclaim an affinity for the church and for Christianity stay away from worship in droves. In the minds of some, it appears that "going to church" is indeed something that has been "decreed" (v. 4), an obligation that has been laid on us. We go to church not because we want to, but because we think we should. In the minds of many, also, are the images of a judgmental God and a judgmental church. Church can be the place where

^{5}For there the thrones for judgment were set up,
    the thrones of the house of David.

^{6}Pray for the peace of Jerusalem:
    "May they prosper who love you.
^{7}Peace be within your walls,
    and security within your towers."
^{8}For the sake of my relatives and friends
    I will say, "Peace be within you."
^{9}For the sake of the house of the LORD our God,
    I will seek your good.

Exegetical Perspective

The Psalter reading for this First Sunday of Advent is identified in its superscript (not included here) as "A Song of Ascents" (Heb. *shir hama'alot*)—one of fifteen psalms (Pss. 120–134) so identified. The Hebrew word *ma'aleh* usually appears as a geographical term describing rising terrain (Num. 34:4; Josh. 10:10; 1 Sam. 9:11) or as an architectural term meaning "step" (cf. Exod. 20:26; 1 Kgs. 10:19–20). While neither of these meanings is impossible in this context, the content of the psalms in this collection suggests another translation. All of these poems deal, in one way or another, with coming into or longing for God's presence in the temple. Since, in Hebrew idiom, going to the Jerusalem shrine always meant going *up*, the pilgrimage to Jerusalem was an ascent. Perhaps, then, we should read these psalms as the songs of those who ascend—as pilgrim songs.

The bulk of today's psalm deals with the city of Jerusalem. The poet rejoices to be at last within the city gates (v. 2). Jerusalem is praised for its stability ("built as a city that is bound firmly together;" v. 3), its political significance as a center for all the tribes (v. 4), and the justice enforced within it (v. 5). All of this is ensured by the king, descended from David, appointed by God (v. 5; see also 2 Sam. 7; Ps. 89:19–37). Because of these blessings brought by the city (as well as for the sake of family and friends

Homiletical Perspective

Advent, the beginning of the church year, is a time to begin our journey of faith afresh. Today's psalm captures in miniature the movement in the life of faith, that all of life should be one continual act of praise for God and service of neighbor. The psalmist creates a roadmap for peace that begins and ends in God (vv. 1, 9). This divine cartography propels the pilgrim's journey in acts of praise and prayer and purpose. When we journey to the heart of God, we become God's peace in the world.

Pilgrimage. The psalm invites the preacher to explore an itinerary for our Godward journey. We meet the psalmist, who is carried along by throngs of fellow pilgrims filled with joy about the impending journey. The psalmist exclaims, "I was glad when they said to me, 'Let us go to house of the LORD!'" (v. 1). Might we also detect a hint of hesitation and uncertainty? After all, one may be glad out of a sense of excitement, but one may also be glad out of a sense of relief.

That uncertainty seems true to the spirit of Advent, which, though filled with anticipation, is not devoid of dread. It causes us to question where we fear God's judgment, and where we need God's peace. We yearn for a world ordered according to God's purposes, but that is not the world we see. The

Psalm 122

Theological Perspective

The psalm itself has a theological argument about its meaning, Read through Joe Pace—that is, through the viewpoint of those on the underside of life—it subverts all we know about the violence that upholds empire and instead dreams of a city redeemed. What might such a reading of Psalm 122 imply? At least four things: a space for refuge-offering, a time for praise-making, a place for justice-doing, and a way for peace-living. Let me take each in turn.

Seen from the underside, the bold claim of space for *refuge-offering* is a theological claim, a declaration about the God whose house this is. The first and last verses of the psalm speak of the house of God, the one who made us, who brought us out of Egypt, and who desires for us good and not evil. We are, then, rejoicing as one rejoices in being where true joy lives. This is not simply happiness, the satisfaction that comes with a good meal or a lovely concert. The character of the moment is not subjective and emotional but, rather, objective and holistic. It is as if we could return to the womb, to our human place of origin. Here, people rejoice to come into the place where God dwells, the very house where God resides, from which all good things come to be. This house is a womb of the world, and our deep joy comes from being offered that deep and healing refuge.

In response to an overwhelming gift of healing refuge, the psalmist naturally turns to *praise-making*. The rejoicing at the psalm's beginning quickly moves through the doors and into the city, into the temple, where all go up to worship and give thanks to God. The centrality of praise to Israel's identity is directly related to their becoming a people in the first place. They are the people who were brought out of slavery. They are the people whose cry brings God's action through Moses, Aaron, and Miriam. The claim that giving thanks is what it means to be Israel, however, has to be held in tension with the story of how Jacob received the name "Israel." After wrestling through the night with the angel, asking for a blessing, Jacob received the blessing and a new name: Israel, one who has struggled with God (Gen. 32). The praise is ever entwined with the struggle.

Therefore, the time of praise-making finds its partner in a place for *justice-doing*. The God of Israel has always been both cosmos-creator God and committed-savior God, both transcendent and immanent in particular ways for us. Here the house of the Lord is described as having thrones, not for lording it over others, not for oppression and abuse, but for righteous judgment. This is the hope of the people, the long-ago promise that makes them glad:

Pastoral Perspective

"thrones for judgment [are] set up" (v. 5)—where we expect to be judged and made to feel guilty.

Why would anyone be *glad* to worship? In what way could those "thrones for judgment" be positive and life-giving for us? While the Christian path through Advent is different from the consumer one, and therefore challenging, it is also one that many people in our culture crave. While part of us delights in the materialism of the season, part of us yearns for something deeper. Who first invited you to church, and to faith? Are you glad they did? In what way has God's judgment (or, shall we say, God's fresh perspective on life, a new glimpse of the truth) transformed you, and brought you to new life? What truth, what depth, what gladness can we offer those who attend worship this Advent?

This psalm is also a prayer for Jerusalem, for its people and its allies. It is a prayer for peace, prosperity, and security—all fairly standard prayers, in almost every time and place. These prayers have particular force and poignancy in times of war, political turbulence, and/or economic difficulty. This, too, can be an entry point to consider the different paths taken by our culture and by the church of Jesus Christ.

It is worth noting that this psalm brings together worship, religion, and politics in a way that may be quite challenging to those of us who are reluctant to bring political issues explicitly into our worship and preaching. This will become even more clearly an issue in the psalms for the next two weeks. The thrones for judgment in Jerusalem are identified as the thrones of the house of David (v. 5). Images of divine and human kingship seem to shade into one another in a way that is probably quite scary for many of us (was it scary for the psalmist as well?). This presentation seems to raise the question: what is our relationship as church to the governance structures of our society? What is our relationship with our own "thrones for judgment," and with those who are judged?

A prayer for peace, security, and prosperity also raises the question of definitions. In what does peace consist? For whom are we praying? When the psalmist prays for Jerusalem, there is perhaps a tribal assumption in the background, in which the peace and prosperity of Jerusalem is lifted up as more important than the peace and prosperity of other competing nations and cities. Do we do this in our prayers? Are we praying for our own church or nation's peace and well-being over against that of others? Such a prayer does not seem consistent with

living within its walls, v. 8), the psalm instructs to all who read it:

> Pray for the peace of Jerusalem:
> "May they prosper who love you.
> Peace be within your walls,
>   and security within your towers."
> (Ps. 122:6–7)

The high view of Jerusalem expressed in this psalm was widely held in ancient Israel. The Old Testament lesson for today, Isaiah 2:1–5, expresses a longing for the day when Jerusalem will at last be revealed in its true glory and be recognized by the nations as the center of the world: "For out of Zion shall go forth instruction, and the word of the LORD from Jerusalem" (Isa. 2:3). Psalm 46:5 declares of Jerusalem, "God is in the midst of the city; it shall not be moved." In Psalm 48:12–14, the poet declares:

> Walk about Zion, go all around it,
>   count its towers,
> consider well its ramparts;
>   go through its citadels,
> that you may tell the next generation
>   that this is God,
> our God forever and ever.
>   He will be our guide forever.

For this ancient psalmist, a pilgrimage to Jerusalem was a journey into the very presence of the Divine. In other words, if you have seen Jerusalem, you have seen God.

The emphasis upon the peace and security of Jerusalem in today's pilgrim psalm is difficult, for, of course, Jerusalem would remain neither peaceful nor secure! The Babylonians destroyed the city in 587 BCE, bringing down its walls and bringing an end to David's line: no king in David's line would ever again sit on a throne in Jerusalem. In light of this disaster, the old "songs of Zion" became a mockery (for example, see Pss. 89:38–51; 137:1–4). Further, the prophets said that Jerusalem's destruction had come about because it was *not* a place of justice, that in fact it had become a city of violence, oppression, and idolatry (for example, see Jer. 7; Ezek. 8).

Eventually, the exile ended and the city was rebuilt, but then Jerusalem was destroyed again, by the Romans in 70 CE (see the text leading up to today's Gospel, esp. Matt. 24:1–2). Both destructions are commemorated by a fast in the Jewish year, on *Tish'ah Be'Ab* (that is, the Ninth of Av, which falls late in July or early in August). Through the long years of the Diaspora, prayer for the peace of

eschatological tension is inescapable, and it takes courage to have faith in the promises of God's peace and prosperity in a violent and broken world. It takes determination to begin afresh.

Whether a child heads off to kindergarten for the first time or an adult enters recovery from an addiction, change brings not only hope but also fear, and it requires courage to take that first step.

Praise. Even if there had been hesitation in the psalmist's intent to set out on pilgrimage, upon arrival the joy is unmistakable. The joyful homecoming to the Lord's house awakens gratitude (vv. 1, 4). Praise, honor, and thanksgiving are offered to God as the psalmist acknowledges God's sovereignty (v. 4).

So why is the psalmist moved to praise? It seems more reasonable that the psalmist might lament in the face of dire conditions and stark realities, since Jerusalem has been a place of strife and turmoil. Perhaps praise chases out the powers and principalities that threaten to take God's rightful place in our lives.

Praise may also come from the fact that despite difficulties in Jerusalem, the city was and is symbolic of a place that unites God's family. To come into Jerusalem's center is to spend time in the heart of God, who guides the pilgrim's journey. To come into God's presence reminds us of divine care for all creation, and so we offer praise.

Prayer. Though entering Jerusalem inspires praise, it also reminds us of the dual character of Advent—of the reality of violence and destruction as well as the hope for a world in which God's will is fulfilled. Nowhere was and is that tension more palpable than in Jerusalem, which is not only a center of God's presence but also a center of political and social instability. Although the psalmist extols the virtues of the city's political leadership, the historical record is less positive. So the psalmist is moved to pray for Jerusalem and for the consummation of God's reign of justice and peace.

We, then, are enjoined to reach beyond our singularity and into concern for others, for the cities and people where fulfillment is needed. In so doing, we escape our self-centeredness to experience our interconnectedness with one another, as well as our vulnerability.

Peace. Whenever we travel, the place we have been leaves a reminder, and we are transformed by its memory. In God's house, the residue is peace. The psalmist is inspired to take that peace to humanity

Psalm 122

Theological Perspective

that when they arrive in the house of the Lord they find a place for justice-doing.

Doing justice, in the biblical world, helps define a way of *peace-living* called shalom. Here prosperity is far from contemporary culture's consumer-driven definition. Living in peace includes duties and privileges, requires both well-doing and doing well. The psalm, as a whole, could be heard both as a declaration of what is and an invocation of what should be. At the end of the psalm, its character as invocation grows: the insistence that we should pray for Jerusalem's peace, that its peoples should live in peace, that the writer pledges to do the very best for "our God."

In fact, if one reads this psalm assuming the perspective of the oppressed, of those who struggle and depend on God's mercy and justice, the psalm seems to end as the flip side of a lament, one crying out against what is broken and the other crying out for what was and will be again when things are set right.

Jesus' lament over Jerusalem comes to mind as one way to come to this psalm. In Luke 19, Jesus enters the city to great crowds and enthusiastic praise. At Jerusalem's gate, Jesus weeps over the city before declaring that everything degraded and unjust will be broken down before a new and just city can arise. He himself begins the symbolic work in the temple, tossing over the tables of those making excessive profit on the backs of pious pilgrims.

In our cities and temples, where does this psalm leave us? Perhaps as we look at the sorrow of our world, its economic turmoil and ceaseless wars, we too join in Jesus' tears and moral outrage. Perhaps we too cry out for the promised house of God where we find refuge and an image of a new shalom that draws us into a life of well-doing as we seek to do well.

CHRISTIAN SCHAREN

Pastoral Perspective

Jesus' teaching to love and pray for our enemies (Matt. 5:43–48). In what does peace consist, in this world that has become in so many ways a global village?

Similarly, what is prosperity (v. 6)? Are we content to measure our prosperity in simply material terms, using our salaries or "net worth" as a guide? Are we content to measure the prosperity of our nation with a tool such as gross domestic product, which simply measures the amount of money spent in a given year? In that respect, the more we spend in a given Christmas season, the better the year— whether that spending is for gifts, feasting, alarm systems, or litigation for drunk driving. Is that how we see things? Or does prosperity have more to do with the *quality* of our life together?

The word "security" also brings with it a host of assumptions. Security typically brings to mind border guards and alarm systems (often euphemistically called "security systems"), airport checkpoints and military strength. Do these things make us secure, or are they testimony to our lack of security, to the divisions and injustices of our world? What would security for *all people* look like?

Finally, it seems important to pay attention to the form of our prayers, in light of this psalm. What are the assumptions behind our prayers? Do we pray as the privileged, for others who are disadvantaged? Do our prayers somehow imply a division between "us" and "them," somehow raising us and our interests to a place of greater importance?

Church and society approach Christmas ostensibly seeking the same things: celebration, peace, prosperity. Under the surface, though, there are profound differences. Society tends to focus on our own families and communities, and tends toward materialism (though longing for something deeper). The church is called to worship, to a wider community, and to a deeper and more widely shared prosperity. This purposeful hope is good news to a congregation of worshipers who are eager to say, "I was glad when they said to me, 'Let us go to the house of the LORD.'"

DAVID HOLMES

Exegetical Perspective

Jerusalem became in Judaism an expression of longing for deliverance from oppression, and of hope for unity and restoration.

In our own day, the land of Jerusalem is once more a battleground, as innocent victims on all sides of the conflict fall to Palestinian suicide bombers and Israeli tanks. Once more, Jerusalem has become for many a symbol, not of justice and peace, but of injustice and violence. This psalm read at this time of year requires us to ask, how should Christians respond? How shall we join our prayers with those of the ancients?

A vital feature of today's psalm saves it from being a jingoistic embrace of Jerusalem as a political power. The psalm begins and ends, not with the palace of David, but with the house of the Lord. The poem opens, "I was glad when they said to me, 'Let us go to the house of the Lord!'" (v. 1). The poet has come to Jerusalem in order to worship at the temple. Further, the last verse qualifies the prayer for Jerusalem's safety: "For the sake of the house of the Lord our God, I will seek your good" (v. 9). Jerusalem is prized, and its security is sought, not for the city's own sake, but because God's temple is there. Indeed, the tribes flow into Jerusalem "as was decreed for Israel, to give thanks to the name of the Lord" (v. 4). It is as the site of true worship that Jerusalem is praised in this psalm.

In our Gospel lesson, Jesus urges his hearers to be ready at any time for the inbreaking of God's kingdom. In Matthew, these words are followed by four parables that clarify what readiness means. The fourth, climactic parable in this series makes clear the standard of judgment in the world to come: "Truly I tell you, just as you did it to one of the least of these who are members of my family, you did it to me" (Matt. 25:40). So too, Jerusalem in our psalm stands for right worship and right living, for justice and mercy. Praying for the peace of Jerusalem, then, means praying for, and working for, the day when "nation shall not lift up sword against nation, neither shall they learn war any more" (Isa. 2:4).

STEVEN S. TUELL

Homiletical Perspective

(v. 9). As Easter people living in an Advent world, that too is our charge: to pray and work for God's peace and wellness for all nations.

Just as God is not bound by space to the temple, God's peace will be so expansive that it cannot be bound by the walls of any city. In the new Jerusalem, we see a radically new blueprint for the city, its proportions so expansive that even if fortifications can contain it, they will not be necessary, as God's glory will be its protection (Zech. 2:4, 5; Rev. 21:23). As the architect of creation seeks to bend our hostilities into peace, we are reminded of the many walls that have created forced separation of God's family for reasons of race, land, and political ideologies. Whether in Soweto, Gaza, or Berlin, in the Messiah we are promised that, even now, the dividing walls of hostility have been broken down by Christ, who is our peace (Eph. 2:14).

Purpose. Our purpose, then, is to become the peace with which we have been gifted and to return it to the world. When the psalmist writes that the people said, "Let us go to the house of the Lord," it reminds us that the first act of the psalm is an act of worship—an act of going to the temple to encounter the Lord, pray, and give praise. We can see then how, when one praises God, one begins to care about others, pray for them, and work on their behalf. That work becomes the work of peace, work that will shape the world into the hope God has for it.

Each time we approach our Advent pilgrimage anew, we are different. The end of one journey positions us to begin the next. Our yearly pilgrimage gives us once again an opportunity to reconsider the way we are living our lives. Through pilgrimage, praise, prayer, and purpose, the psalmist reminds us that we are always waiting in hope, always called to be light in the world and to work on behalf of God's reign of justice and peace. We are forever engaged in an act of new creation.

CAROL L. WADE

Romans 13:11-14

[11]Besides this, you know what time it is, how it is now the moment for you to wake from sleep. For salvation is nearer to us now than when we became believers; [12]the night is far gone, the day is near. Let us then lay aside the works of darkness and put on the armor of light; [13]let us live honorably as in the day, not in reveling and drunkenness, not in debauchery and licentiousness, not in quarreling and jealousy. [14]Instead, put on the Lord Jesus Christ, and make no provision for the flesh, to gratify its desires.

Theological Perspective

Paul's Letter to the Romans draws on a twofold image of people awakening from sleep and then putting on their clothes for the day.

It is time to get up. It is time to slough off the old life. It is time to wake up and live into the reality of the new age about to dawn. It is a wakeup call for Advent. For Paul, of course, this "time," this propitious moment, is the eschatological time, the time when the fullness of God's kingdom will be realized. The end times are ever nearer, so do not delay, do not procrastinate. Tomorrow is too late.

We are to awake from the darkness of sin and licentiousness into the new dawn brought about by Christ's life, death, and resurrection. We are to peel off the night clothes of selfishness and ignorance and to put on the new clothes of Christ, that is, "the armor of Christ."

These familiar Pauline metaphors are not external to who we are. They are the fabric of our transformation into Christ. The first metaphor evokes Ephesians 5:14: "Sleeper, awake! Rise from the dead," and the second echoes Galatians, "It is no longer I who live, but it is Christ who lives in me" (2:20). Pauline theology rests upon the reality that a new world is being born. The new man, the new woman, belongs radically to this new world, rather than to the old.

Pastoral Perspective

You *know* what time it is! Indeed we all do! Most of us who live in North America live under the tyranny of time. We consume it just as we do other products, and however much we "have" (as though one could ever really possess time), we never seem to have "enough." The lives of most American families are completely overwhelmed by the demands on their time: households must accommodate multiple work schedules, with school and extracurricular activities too numerous to count. The school calendar on the refrigerator can no longer manage the schedule a busy family keeps. Even finding time to coordinate multiple calendars can be a challenge! As the First Sunday of Advent brings the "holiday season" into full gear, time becomes a scarce commodity indeed.

The speed of communication in our world has only enhanced time's tyranny. Because we *can* communicate with anyone, anywhere, anytime, we increasingly feel that we *ought* to be connected 24–7 and that all of our electronic systems should be up and running at all times to make this possible. The world of instant communication has made us more accustomed to perceiving time in digital form—displayed as hour and minute (and sometimes seconds) that advance literally from moment to moment. In this format, we tend to see time as a series of discrete, disconnected units. What exists is the minute

Exegetical Perspective

The first verse of the stated lection, verse 11, is so clearly tied to what precedes it that we will need to consider larger boundaries of the passage, namely, verses 8–14 rather than simply verses 11–14. In its turn, verse 8 turns from a discussion of responsibility to the state (13:1–7) to a discussion of responsibility to the neighbor (13:8–14), providing further indication that verses 8–14 need to be considered as a unit.

The opening words of verse 8 have the form of an absolute imperative. It is a responsibility no Christian can avoid; one is to leave no legitimate obligation to another unfulfilled. The strong negative also indicates that this obligation is owed to all people, not just to fellow Christians. This obligation involves loving the neighbor, which in turn represents the fulfillment of God's law. Paul demonstrates this point in verse 9 with his citation of some of the commands from the "second tablet" of the Hebrew law, concluding that these and all other commands are fulfilled by loving one's neighbor. This surely reflects Jesus' words about the law in Matthew 22:34–40, although Paul gives no indication that he means his readers to know he is citing this particular saying. Verse 10 defines what loving one's neighbor means, namely, doing no wrong to a fellow human being.

The fact that verse 10 echoes verse 8 in its affirmation that love of neighbor is the fulfillment of the

Homiletical Perspective

During the Advent season, the church prepares for the coming of Christ. Even as we make ready for the baby to be born in Bethlehem, the lectionary this First Sunday of Advent takes us beyond the birth, life, death, and resurrection of Jesus to a new moment of expectancy as the Day of Christ approaches and the reign of God is made fully manifest. The Romans text suggests several different approaches for preaching.

What Time Is It? Paul reminds his readers that they already know what time it is; but do they really? Paul himself thought that he knew the correct time, but clearly he did not. His writings indicate that he believed Christ would return to earth during the lifetime of those to whom he wrote. That certainly did not happen; yet, theologically, Paul was not in error. He was right to believe that every moment in time is rich with divine possibility. He was right to urge his readers "to wake up from sleep"—to pay attention and be alert to the imminent inbreaking of eternity "within the flux of time," as Karl Barth put it.

How many people today "sleep" through their lives, utterly unaware that they are living on the frontier between the old order of things and the new order, where Jesus reigns and all that is wrong has been set right? Barth calls the age in which we live,

Romans 13:11-14

Theological Perspective

Within the context of the whole Epistle to the Romans, we of course hear Paul refining his earlier polemic against reliance on works of the law. As became clear in chapter 12, there is, after all, something to do. Shed your old clothes of darkness and ignorance and be clothed with the armor of Christ. In this new time, the Christian is swept up within a "solidarity in grace," dramatically more powerful than the solidarity in sin inherited from Adam. The gift of righteousness now pervades the heart and soul of the believer. It has also spread throughout the whole world.[1]

A Theology of Desire. So what is it that we are waking up to? For Paul, it was to the eschatological reality that Christ was coming. We might sense that it is our whole person, our deepest desires, the core of who we are that is waking up. Our deepest desires thus become a doorway to this spiritual reality of Christ's coming more fully into our lives. Catherine of Sienna, the great medieval Dominican mystic and spiritual theologian, said that it is only through our desires that we touch God, because God is infinite and it is only our desires that are infinite.[2]

One of a pastor's greatest challenges is to elicit from parishioners what it is that they really want. Asked, "What do you want to do?" often enough they respond, "Well, what do you think I should do?" If you can help them clear away the psychic debris, get them to claim what they want, tap into their passion, then they are already taking the first steps toward mental and spiritual health.

One of the leading causes of deadened desires is our determination to avoid pain at all costs. Several years ago the painkiller Mediprin ran a clever ad on TV. A guy with a hand-held pile driver rattled away on the streets of New York while chaos, stress, a noisy racket filled the air. The guy had a splitting headache. Then a sharp businesswoman rushed from meeting to meeting, conference call to conference call, not a second to spare. She too had a stunning headache. Then came a soothing voiceover: "Mediprin—when you don't have time for the pain."

If you "don't have time for the pain," you do not have time for desire either. You are deadening your body's normal responses. An awareness of suffering as a normal dimension of being born into flesh frees us up for a full human life. By dealing with suffering

Pastoral Perspective

(or second) displayed before you, and this moment will disappear from your eyes.

Something different happens when time is displayed on a clock face. As the hands move around, you not only see the moment as it passes. You can also visualize both future and past. It is two o'clock . . . three more hours until quitting time; two hours since you had lunch; thirty minutes until the big meeting; six hours since you kissed your partner good-bye this morning. This way of "counting" time is somewhat more like the experience of marking time by the movement of sun from dawn to dusk. We know (more or less) where we stand between the beginning and the end of day.

Paul is thinking about time more in this second way, in the sense of moving from past to future—but then he adds another dimension. When Paul calls his audience to remember "what time it is," he is not thinking about the daily or even yearly round of events and activities. Paul has a completely different horizon in mind. He believes that, just as time had a beginning at creation, so also time will have an end. Just as God brought all things into being, so also there will be a time when God will bring the history of this world to an end and usher in the promised new creation.

This "new creation" is compared to a new day. So Paul tells us what time it is: it is time to awake from sleep. It is time to get up out of bed and get ready dressed for the day. As Paul paints the picture, it is still dark outside when this theological alarm clock goes off; the day is "near" but not quite here. Perhaps it is that mysterious moment when the darkness of night begins to give way to shadows, and there is just enough light to know that morning is around the corner. This is a time of anticipation, and Paul urges his audience to action. It is time to get up and get dressed!

The clothing Paul wants us to put on is Jesus Christ: his life, his way of being are the garments that we are to put on as we get ready to meet the future. What concerns Paul here is that we adopt a new and more honorable way of life. Put aside partying and drunkenness—things that dull the senses or draw one's attention away from what is really going on. Put aside quarreling and jealousy—things that destroy community and injure relationships with others (v. 13). The new day that God is bringing is a time when God and humanity will be reconciled; when peace, justice, and integrity will be the hallmarks of human society. What Paul wants is for Christians to start living *now* as though this new day has already begun.

1. See Brendan Byrne, *Romans*, Sacra Pagina Series, ed. Daniel Harrington, S.J. (Collegeville, MN: Liturgical Press, 1996): 397–403.
2. See Patrick J. Howell, "Desiring: An Avenue to Mystery," in *A Spiritguide through Times of Darkness* (Kansas City, MO: Sheed & Ward, 1996), 35–50.

Exegetical Perspective

law forms an *inclusio*, an ancient rhetorical device that was used to indicate the boundaries of a thought unit, and to emphasize its major point. In defining the law in that way, Paul makes use here of an understanding of the law found throughout the New Testament, namely, that the ritual and dietary aspects of the Hebrew law were no longer valid. The ritual laws, designed to expiate sin through sacrifices, were eliminated by Christ's once-for-all sacrifice on the cross (e.g., Heb. 10:1–18). The dietary laws were rendered invalid by Christ's own reinterpretation of the true intent of the law with respect to what renders a person impure (e.g., Mark 7:14–19).

This means that to understand love as the basic requirement for the Christian who lives under the grace of Christ is to understand such Christian life as the fulfillment of the law God gave to Israel. As Christ is the one in whom the law found its culmination and hence its end (Rom. 10:4), so in the love that same Christ commanded (e.g., Mark 12:28–31), one is also to find the culmination and hence the end of the law.

The key here is a proper understanding of the word "love" as it is used in these verses. Our modern culture has so perverted the meaning of this word that it has come to mean at best a sheer sentimentality, at worst the kind of erotic feeling aroused when an attractive member of the opposite sex comes into view. Love as the New Testament uses it is not to be defined as an emotional state, as though when God loves us, he gets all warm and squishy inside. Rather, God loves us by doing something for our benefit, namely sending His Son to remove our sins. We know God loves us, therefore, not because of how he feels about us, but because of what he has done for us in Christ.

Love in the New Testament is thus based not on emotion, but on action. To love someone is actively to pursue that person's good, however we may feel about him or her emotionally. That also points to how we are to love our neighbor "as our self." The point is we are to do as little harm to our neighbor as we do to ourselves; emotional states are not involved here. Verse 9 makes clear that love means to cease actions that harm the neighbor. Verses 11–14 then are further examples of such love in action, given the current transition from the old age to the new age.

Verse 11 needs some sort of augmentation to convey the force of the opening two words, something like "And now do this, since you know the time . . ." Paul typically uses such language as waking

Homiletical Perspective

the time of "great positive possibility." Because divine love has already conquered, there is "this Moment— the *Now*—when past and future stand still. The former ceases its going, and the latter its coming."[1]

Christ was himself the turning point in time. The past might not be completely finished and gone, but the new has truly come. From this time forth, we are invited to dream along with God of a new heaven, a new earth, a new way of being human, reshaped into God's image as we were supposed to be from the beginning.

Eschatology and Ethics. Because "the night is far gone, the day is near" (v. 12a), we may now live and act toward one another in an ongoing state of love, even as God has loved us. Why would anyone want to cling to the old ways, now that a new day has come, now that we know how the story ends? We are able to move to higher ethical ground. To use Paul's imagery, we can "lay aside the works of darkness, and put on the armor of light" (v. 12b). An honorable life comes as a consequence of knowing what time it is. Some might think that knowing of God's ultimate victory over sin and evil gives us license to do what we please in the here and now. The opposite is true. Because the Day of Christ lies ahead, more is expected of us.

I cannot imagine any worse news than to be told that it does not matter what I do, what choices I make, how I treat other people. One of the most troubling characteristics of our culture today is that few people act as if character matters. People justify to themselves the most outrageous behavior and callous disregard for the well-being of others (see Paul's list of what we might call "vices of darkness"). Why? Because they do not believe any longer that anything is expected of them.

A few years ago, a member of my congregation wrote a meditation for the annual Advent devotional booklet:

> When I was an elementary school principal, I often walked the halls and visited the classrooms. . . . One day, outside one of the first grade rooms sat a troubled little boy. He had clearly been sent to the hallway by an irate teacher. As the child saw me approaching, it was obvious he was really working hard at figuring out what to say.
>
> Before I could speak, he stood up and hugged me around the waist and said, "Mr. Jones, I love you." I was disarmed but recovered sufficiently to

1. Karl Barth, *The Epistle to the Romans* (New York: Oxford University Press, 1968), 493 and 497.

Romans 13:11-14

we can start dealing with desire. A Mediprin society does not want to deal with those desires; it is too much to deal with all that passion. It could burst the straitjacket of a world driven by production.

Relationships. Subtly, all the appeals of these verses happen in the plural. Paul assumes community. Throughout the Epistle to the Romans he describes a healthy relationship to God, to the earth, to ourselves, and to others. In our contemporary language, we would call these sets of relationships our spirituality or even our spiritual ecology.

Scripture says *God is love.* We might say *God is relationship.* If God is relationship, then spirituality is about the caring for and building of genuine, true relationships. Spirituality and religion are two sides of the same coin. Without a personal spirituality, religion becomes formalistic and bound up in rules. It is driven by law. Without religion, that is, without relationship to a faith community, spirituality may become self-centered, even messianic—presuming to have all the answers.

If we recognize Mystery in our lives, if we live out of the Mystery of love, if we experience the transformation that comes through genuine relationships, then our own love flows spontaneously outward and reaches others. Once again we live out a "solidarity of grace."

Present and Future. Dag Hammarskjöld, the secretary general of the United Nations who died tragically in 1961 in a plane crash, wrote in his journal, "For all that has been—Thanks! To all that will be—Yes."[3] This terse synopsis is tremendous affirmation of both past and future. "Thanks" dissipates regrets and "Yes" dissipates fears. Hammarskjöld was a modern-day mystic because he had the capacity to see God in everyday life and could say "Yes" to the total reality of his life.

In today's epistle, Paul invites us in turn—in this urgent eschatological time when Christ is coming—to say "Yes" to all that will be.

PATRICK J. HOWELL

In the early years of the Christian movement, believers lived with a sense of real anticipation. The promises they read in the Hebrew Scriptures seemed tangible; the reign of God and all that it meant for cosmic "regime change" seemed close at hand. When they prayed (daily), "Thy kingdom come . . . on earth as it is in heaven," they were looking forward to that happening within their own lifetimes.

Two thousand years later, the sense of anticipation has diminished. From time to time, communities of Christians have developed a sense of urgency about the "end times"; some have even predicted precise dates for Christ's return, the beginning of "the end." For some branches of Christianity, the belief that God will bring a new day of justice and reconciliation figures prominently in preaching and church life. For many other Christians, however, the sense of anticipation that drives Paul's writing has diminished. To the extent that this is so, we may be the poorer for having lost this vision, because for Paul, this anticipation is not so much about circling a date on the calendar as it is about *hope.*

Paul really believes that the birth, death, and resurrection of Jesus is God's sign that all of those promises about life and wholeness prevailing over brokenness and death are true, and that God can be trusted to do what God has promised. Paul *knows* what time it is: it is time to wake up and look forward to what God will do in the future and what God is beginning to do now in your life and mine.

CYNTHIA M. CAMPBELL

---

3. Dag Hammarskjöld, *Markings*, trans. Leif Sjoberg and W. H. Auden (New York: Vintage Books, 1964), 89.

Exegetical Perspective

from sleep (v. 11) and the contrast between night and day, darkness and light (vv. 12–13a), to contrast the old and new aeons, thus giving a distinct eschatological flavor to the passage. There is also a sense of urgency: the night is about to end, the day is at hand, our (eschatological) salvation has drawn nearer than when we first accepted the Christian faith. As a result, we are to equip ourselves appropriately for the time: put off the actions that characterized our former life, and put on divine armor for the impending final battle between good and evil, a battle we already participate in with our loving deed to others. "Armor of light" (v. 12) is defined in verse 14, where the same verb ("put on") is used with the action of becoming Christlike.

The repeated use of words like "cast off" and "put on" reflects baptismal terminology when one casts off one's old garments/life and puts on the new garment/life of the newly baptized. One is to put one's baptism into practice now by abandoning one's old way of life, a way described here in verse 13b with three sets of two nouns. The first two pairs are plural, perhaps suggesting repetition, the third singular, perhaps describing them as results of the activities described in the first two pairs. The first pair points to excesses of drink (the first of those terms is derived from a word that originally identified a festival in honor of Bacchus, the god of wine); the second pair points to promiscuous sexual activity.

Verse 14 sums up the entire passage, contrasting Jesus Christ with "flesh," where flesh characterizes life apart from Christ, as demonstrated in verse 13b. The Greek of verse 14 is a bit convoluted; perhaps the best translation would be "But put on the Lord Jesus Christ, and don't be preoccupied with plans for gratifying the desires of the old aeon (=flesh)."

One last note: in verse 11b, Paul said salvation was nearer than when his readers first believed. Apparently he thought the Parousia (i.e., Christ's appearing) was imminent; but that means Paul's timetable was in error. Does that make what he says about the Parousia invalid? Yet Paul speaks of God's future—a future that already shines its light back into the present, showing us how to live in its light rather than in the darkness of the current age. The Christian thus lives in anticipation of God's fulfillment of his redemptive plan for all creation. It is the anticipation of that future the church celebrates in the Advent season.

PAUL J. ACHTEMEIER

Homiletical Perspective

tell the boy that good behavior was expected, and I asked him to return to the classroom and apologize to the teacher. My expression of love was to guide him into accepting responsibility.

The child settled down and had a good year. Each time he saw me in the cafeteria or on my rounds, he would smile and wave, and say, "Thank you, Mr. Jones."[2]

New Age Religion. Very few members of our congregations spend their time looking to the horizon for Christ to come again in glory. Too many centuries have passed, too many false messiahs have appeared, too much eschatological hope has evaporated into the atmosphere of our postmodern age. I remember a remark made several years ago by major-league baseball player Dan Quisenberry when his team was in a slump: "The future," he said, "is much like the present, only longer."

We who have been baptized into the promises of God ought to have a different outlook. We are already citizens of the new age. We have glimpsed in Christ the glorious future God has for the world when "the great positive possibility" has finally carried the day. We make the moral decision to live in hope, rather than despair. We stay awake because we know salvation could bathe our hurting world with healing grace any day now.

One winter morning, I was driving to work. The day was gray and dreary, as were my spirits as I negotiated my way through Atlanta's infamous traffic. All of a sudden, I felt a sudden warmth on my left hand as it gripped the steering wheel. I looked down and saw a thin shaft of light warming the back of my hand. "Impossible," I thought. "This is too drizzly and dark a day for the sun to shine!" Nevertheless, as I glanced over my left shoulder toward the eastern horizon, there it was—the sun, buttery, orange, gold, as big as the world.

Let us pray for the dawning of the Day of Christ; and until it comes, let us dress ourselves in his light every morning.

JOANNA M. ADAMS

2. Robert S. Jones, from an Advent booklet produced by Trinity Presbyterian Church, Atlanta, GA, in the 1990s.

Matthew 24:36-44

36"But about that day and hour no one knows, neither the angels of heaven, nor the Son, but only the Father. 37For as the days of Noah were, so will be the coming of the Son of Man. 38For as in those days before the flood they were eating and drinking, marrying and giving in marriage, until the day Noah entered the ark, 39and they knew nothing until the flood came and swept them all away, so too will be the coming of the Son of Man. 40Then two will be in the field; one will be taken and one will be left. 41Two women will be grinding meal together; one will be taken and one will be left. 42Keep awake therefore, for you do not know on what day your Lord is coming. 43But understand this: if the owner of the house had known in what part of the night the thief was coming, he would have stayed awake and would not have let his house be broken into. 44Therefore you also must be ready, for the Son of Man is coming at an unexpected hour."

Theological Perspective

In contrast to some Eastern religions that view time as an endless cycle of birth, death, and rebirth, Christianity with its Judaic roots is a deeply historical religion. This history begins with God's creation of the world and ends with God's judgment and re-creation of it. Christians look backward, remembering God's mighty acts of salvation over the generations, and forward, anticipating the vindication of God's ways in a new heaven and a new earth. They live, as Karl Barth said, "between the times."

The season of Advent invites us to consider again the character of Christian existence "between the times." On the one hand, Advent reminds us of God's promises to Israel of Immanuel. God comes in human flesh to deliver God's people from sin and evil. On the other hand, Advent calls us to anticipate the day on which this Immanuel will return as King of kings and Lord of lords. He will put all that resists him, even death itself, under his feet. Living between the times, we give thanks to God for the Christ child, even as we plead with God to realize, once and for all, the kingdom that Jesus declared to be at hand.

Matthew 24:36–44 stands in a series of sayings and parables about a day of judgment that will inaugurate this kingdom to come. Jesus warns that this day will take the world by surprise. As in Noah's time, people will be going about their everyday

Pastoral Perspective

The advent of Advent with its emphasis on the coming of the Son of Man produces two quite different reactions among congregants.

Some Christians think that the whole emphasis on Christ's Parousia (i.e., appearing) is much ado about nothing, or at least much ado about nothing believable. If they are faithful churchgoers, they endure the annual Advent apocalyptic texts and look forward to next week, when John the Baptist, that tangible historical figure, helps us look forward to Jesus.

Some Christians think that Christ's second coming is the heart of the gospel. As Karl Barth is supposed to have enjoined, they start the day with the Bible in one hand and the newspaper in the other, but their hermeneutical strategy is often quite different from Barth's. They search the Bible for signs of the end times, and they search the newspaper to see if those signs are yet in view.

Those Christians who are agnostic about last things are tempted to fall into a state of perpetual apathy. Those Christians who are focused on last things are tempted to fall into a state of perpetual anxiety. Our passage encourages faith rather than apathy and hope rather than anxiety.

The Advent Community of Faith. The passage from Matthew calls us away from historical apathy. I once

Exegetical Perspective

The season of Advent usually begins with an eschatological text, as a way of framing Advent as the end of an old order and the birth of a new era. Matthew's eschatological text can be outlined as follows:

24:36   theme: watchfulness amid uncertainty
24:37–39   illustration of theme (days of Noah)
24:40–41   two further illustrations of the theme (men and women)
24:42   repetition of theme frames parable (application 1)
24:43   parable as illustration of theme
24:44   repetition of theme frames parable (application 2)

The passage we are studying comes from Matthew's fifth discourse, which deals with eschatological matters and judgment (Matt. 24:1–25:46).

The theme of this section of Matthew's discourse is the necessity for watchfulness in light of the uncertainty surrounding the coming (Parousia) of Jesus. Verse 36 makes a startling claim: "neither the angels of heaven nor the Son" know when "that day" will occur. It is remarkable how many interpreters seem to believe that they can accomplish what the Son confesses he cannot do. This view of the limit of the Son's knowledge is entirely compatible with passages like the *kenōsis* hymn in Philippians 2:5–11, so the statement should not surprise us so much as it

Homiletical Perspective

Upon noticing the Gospel reading assigned for the First Sunday of Advent, more than one preacher may wince, if not grimace with pain. That facial expression is an outward and visible sign of an inward and spiritual struggle between going where a text wants to go and staying where the people think they want to be.

Typically, the Advent I congregation already has Christmas on its mind and is tilting toward December 25. Hanging the greens, decking the halls, and already caroling Christmas seem high on the list of congregational expectations.

The Advent I Gospel reading is at odds with this congregational expectation because it tilts toward a different day altogether. Matthew and the Jesus he presents seem not at all interested in Christmas, but are focused instead on an apocalyptic day in the unknown future, when the Son of Man will suddenly return and lives will be suddenly and surprisingly changed. This "shall come again" language of Scripture and the Apostles' Creed are enough to give more than a few of our people the creeps, and many would prefer that it be "left behind." One need not lean very far to the theological left to be prone to dismiss this line of thinking as somewhere way out there to the right.

When, then, the preacher sits down in the study with the Gospel lection for the First Sunday of

Matthew 24:36-44

Theological Perspective

business—eating and drinking, marrying and giving in marriage—with no awareness of God's impending judgment. They will be like a householder who fails to anticipate the hour at which the thief will break in. Not even the angels or the Son know the day or hour. The point is that we must be ready for the Lord at any time. When he finally appears, those who are ready will be saved, and those who are not ready will perish.

Jesus reiterates these themes in three parables in the following chapter (Matt. 25). The first tells of ten bridesmaids who wait for a bridegroom. When he finally arrives in the middle of the night, he receives the five who wisely kept oil in their lamps but shuts the door to the five who foolishly let theirs run out. The second tells of a master who, leaving on a long journey, entrusts his servants with his money. When he returns, he commends two servants who made wise investments, but condemns the one who only buried his portion in the ground. The third parable, like the first two, warns of a day of judgment that will divide humanity into two groups. Those ("the sheep") who fed and clothed "the least of these" also fed and clothed the Lord, though they knew it not; those ("the goats") who failed to feed and clothe them failed to feed and clothe the Lord, though they too knew it not. All three parables explicate the point in Matthew 24:44: "Therefore you also must be ready, for the Son of Man is coming at an unexpected hour."

Christians have long debated when and how this day of judgment will take place. One line of thinking has combined Matthew 24:36–44 with other apocalyptic passages in the Hebrew Bible and New Testament to work out a timeline of events that are already underway or soon to transpire. Representative of this position is Hal Lindsey's *The Late, Great Planet Earth* (a bestseller in the 1970s) or more recently Tim LaHaye and Jerry Jenkins's *Left Behind* novels. Like other American fundamentalists, these authors anticipate a day on which God's elect will be raptured—that is, lifted up in their physical bodies to the Lord—while the reprobate are "left behind" to incur God's wrath. We must get ready, because these things may take place yet in our lifetime.

A second line of thinking has seen the day of judgment not at the end of human history but at the time of each individual's death. Each of us will stand before God's judgment seat as soon as we have taken our last breath. We will have to give an accounting of our life and be weighed in the Lord's balance. Again, the lesson is clear: we dare not put off doing what

Pastoral Perspective

heard the distinguished New Testament scholar and bishop Krister Stendahl say that we misread our congregations if we think they are most often puzzling about the eternal life of each individual. On the contrary, said Stendahl, contemporary Christians are most often puzzling about whether history has any significance.

The passage from Matthew reminds us of the profound biblical faith that God is sovereign over all of human history. However metaphorically, however mythologically, Jesus tells us in this discourse that the God who created history at the beginning is not only history's goad but history's goal.

Pastoral attention to the themes of Advent requires a major counterproposal to Macbeth's cynical apathy: "Life is a tale told by an idiot, full of sound and fury, signifying nothing."[1] For the Bible and for the church, life is a tale told by a strong and sovereign God, enacted according to God's pleasure. It is full of both judgment and grace, and it moves toward the time when God will make all things new.

For Advent especially we attend to liturgy, music, pastoral care, and Christian education that help assure God's people that we *are* God's people, and that the history in which we live is God's story, moving from God to God.

The Advent Community of Hope. Today's passage calls us away from historical anxiety. Of course it is full of signs of the end, but the initial warning steers us away from the temptation to keep apocalyptic calendars on the kitchen wall: "But about that day and hour no one knows, neither the angels of heaven, nor the Son, but only the Father" (v. 36). The serenity prayer, usually attributed to Reinhold Niebuhr, asks us to accept the things that we cannot change. Sometimes it is even harder to acknowledge the facts that we cannot know; yet with that acceptance can come a kind of eschatologically sensitive serenity. If Jesus is hopeful as he waits for a consummation he himself does not fully understand, surely we can learn our hope from him.

In pastoral care and in religious formation, one of the gifts we most desire is for people to be able to trust in the future without controlling or even knowing the details of what is yet to come. All our hope is founded in God.

The Advent Community of Memory. Today's passage helps us look forward without apathy or anxiety

---

1. William Shakespeare, *Macbeth*, act 5, scene 5.

Exegetical Perspective

may induce a certain humility into our efforts to discern God's will.

Three examples follow in verses 37–39, 40–41. The first (vv. 37–39) draws on the days of Noah. The figure of Noah has been variously interpreted in biblical traditions. In Hebrews 11:7, Noah heeds God's warning of impending catastrophic judgment and so builds an ark that saves his family, but his faith condemns the world. In 1 Peter 3:20, Noah's rescuing his family from the flood serves as a metaphor for baptism that saves us through water. In 2 Peter 2:5, the writer notes that God did not spare the world from judgment but saved Noah, "a herald of righteousness." The prophet Ezekiel groups Noah together with Daniel and Job to indicate that God's judgment is so great that even their presence would save themselves but no one else (14:14, 20). Finally, Isaiah speaks of "the days of Noah" (54:9) to reaffirm the covenant with Jerusalem.

The saying about the days of Noah in our Advent passage belongs to Q (Luke 17:26–36 // Matt. 24:36–44). What makes this saying so unusual is that it focuses on those who failed to prepare themselves, not on the righteousness of Noah. The "herald of righteousness" fades into the background, and the heedless and thoughtless step onto center stage. The point of the sayings is to emphasize that people were just doing business as usual while the specter of judgment hung over their heads unnoticed. "Eating and drinking" do not refer to drunkenness and gluttony, just everyday meals, and "marrying and giving in marriage" indicate that people presumed that there would be a future, assuming there was time for another generation to be born. Then all this came crashing down upon them, and they were swept away.

The next two illustrations make a similar point but indicate the two-sided nature of judgment, namely, that some are saved and others are not. The universality of judgment is indicated by the fact that the first two are men, and the second pair are women. In each case, they are involved in gender-specific behavior in Jesus' culture. The men are in a field, and the women are in the courtyard shared by several houses using a common grinding wheel. Both are well-chosen illustrations to indicate the extent of judgment and its invasion of domestic space and fields alike. In both instances, the figures are engaged in their normal, everyday activities.

This reading raises an interesting and sometimes overlooked question. Is the one taken being saved or being snatched up for judgment? What is the fate of the one left behind? Based on the use of the two

Homiletical Perspective

Advent, there is both the powerful push toward Christmas and the equally powerful pull away from apocalyptic eschatology. Still, in spite of this push and pull, there is the press of the text, just as powerful and commanding.

If the preacher lets the text win in this push, pull, and press, the initial wince can open into the soft smile of a growing insight. The insight comes when one is suddenly taken by the idea that there is no reason why the first part of this text should not be taken literally. While the text may tilt toward a mysterious future day, it actually remains firmly put in an ordinary present day. This present day is characterized by uncertainty, by a perplexity that extends all the way to the angels and even to the Son. Since we know we are confused much of the time, there is ample reason and evidence to take this part of the text literally. If we begin here, our people might stop pushing toward Christmas and pulling away from apocalypticism, and start listening to a sermon about today.

Most people know they are perplexed. They also know they want to be persons of faith. Along with all the problems associated with their perplexity is the problem posed by the spoken or unspoken assumption that persons with real faith are not perplexed but clear. Instead, the faith of our listeners does not bring everything into focus. What God would have them do in regard to their daily decisions—much less their daunting difficulties—is far from certain. They have neither chapter nor verse nor the foggiest notion how to figure these deep matters through.

Since many of them, like many of us, are good at guilt, they assume they are baffled because they are at fault, because their faith is flawed and weak. Our text presents a splendid opportunity to show them that uncertainty is a condition of even the best biblical faith. This does not solve any of the unanswered questions, of course, but it may begin to bring our people a kind of rapture of relief because it takes the pressure off. It is a relief to know Christ does not expect us to know everything.

We are not expected to know everything, but we are expected to do something. The Jesus of the verses before us calls persons to a life of work in a spirit of wakefulness. Work in this sense means activity here and now. Biblical faith as Jesus envisions it is not so concerned with otherworldly matters that it neglects this world's affairs. Matthew's Jesus has an eye on what is to come and believes something decisive is going to happen in the future, but he keeps attention focused on the present day and the needs of the hour. We find this in the manner in which he directs people

Matthew 24:36-44

Theological Perspective

Jesus has commanded. None of us can know when death will overtake us, and then it will be too late.

A third understanding of this passage emphasizes the symbolic character of Jesus' language. The point is not to speculate about a day of judgment sometime in the future, whether at the end of all humanity or at the death of each individual, but rather to confront us with God's radical claims on us here and now. Each day is a day of judgment, so I should always be asking myself, Am I living in the way of Christ? Am I trusting in him alone? Have I allowed myself to be distracted by selfish cares?

Other Christians have combined aspects of these positions, or have developed variations on them. None of these interpretations will be true to the gospel, however, unless they keep the day of judgment firmly in relationship to the new day that has already dawned in the life, death, and resurrection of Jesus Christ. We live between the times! A theology of the coming kingdom is most faithful to the biblical witness when it reminds us that the Christ who judges us is also the Christ who endured judgment for our sake; that God's judgment never contradicts or overrides God's grace; and that the readiness to which Jesus calls us is shaped not by fear of the future, but rather by gratitude for life in the kingdom that Christ already offers us.

To live between the times is, above all, to trust and hope that God has begun, and will continue, to transform us more and more into the stature of Christ, in whom all of God's mercy and loving-kindness becomes manifest. Advent calls us into a continuing history of relationship with the Christ who meets us whichever way we turn, whether toward the past, the present, or the future.

JOHN P. BURGESS

Pastoral Perspective

because it is not afraid to look back. What this particular passage looks back on is the time of Noah. The tale is a cautionary reminder that we ignore the judgment and power of God at great cost. The tale is also a helpful reminder that sometimes by looking back at what God has done we can have confidence in what God will do, in God's own time.

Part of the power of Scripture is that it provides the stories that are foreshadowings (not blueprints) for what God is doing in our own time and will do. Part of the power of community is that we can look back together at the moments in our past where God was present to chasten and to bless, and find there hope and admonition for the future.

Liturgy is the great remembering. Surrounding the sermon are the hymns and prayers and readings that recall what God has done for God's people and for God's world. It is bad faith to come to Advent services as if we had no idea that God has come to us in Jesus Christ. We wait in hope because we wait in memory.

While pastoral care is by no means confined to pastoral psychology, we have learned over these past decades that looking back can be essential to moving ahead. Think about Noah, we say to the parishioner. Think about the stories in your own life that showed forth the judgment and the promises of God. Move forward in that light.

The Advent Community of Alertness. One major function of our apocalyptic text is to remind us to keep awake. Faith, hope, and memory all help draw us toward Christian responsibility. We respond to the God who acted in Jesus Christ, who acts now, and who will act in the consummation of history.

As the next chapter of Matthew's Gospel will make abundantly clear, we also keep awake to the needs of others (see Matt. 25:31–46). One day Jesus may appear in the clouds, suddenly, like a thief in the night. But before that—as Matthew reminds us—Jesus will appear just around the corner, suddenly, like a hungry person, or a neighbor ill-clothed, or someone sick or imprisoned.

"Therefore [we] also must be ready" (v. 44).

DAVID L. BARTLETT

verbs (taken=*paralambanō* and left=*aphiēmi*) in Matthew, it would appear that the one taken is the fortunate and watchful disciple who remains undistracted by the signs of the times enumerated in Matthew 24:3–28. In the birth narrative, the verb "taken" is used four times (2:13, 14, 20, 21) to indicate taking the child to safety. In 20:17 and 26:37, Jesus "takes" the disciples aside. In the "days of Noah" saying, those who are taken in the ark are saved while those who are left perish. So, in Matthew's vocabulary, "taken" (*paralambanō*) seems to refer to being redeemed from danger, while being left behind (*aphiēmi*) carries the sense of being forsaken or abandoned.

The "days of Noah" illustration and the paired scenes of judgment share a common theme. Because the day of the "Son of Man" will come unexpectedly and cannot be anticipated, one must develop the art of watchful living. Daily work in the field and in the courtyard is necessary to maintain life, but one must always peer through the ordinary days to discern the coming of that extraordinary day. However, one is not to waste time on wild speculations over the claims of false messiahs (24:3–14). The coming judgment will separate the redeemed from the lost.

The parable of the Thief in the Night (v. 43) is surrounded by two applications (vv. 42, 44), both of which make the same point. However, the surprising depiction of the coming of the Son of Man as a thief raises a question. To whom might the reign of heaven and the coming Son of Man be seen as a threat? Whose hegemony would be undermined? Which "strong man's house" would be "plunder[ed of] his property"(12:28–29)?

Amos could say to an Israel eagerly anticipating the coming day of the Lord, "Why do you want the day of the LORD? It is darkness, not light" (Amos 5:18–20). Jesus' comments here may indicate that he shares a view of the Day of the Lord much like Amos's. The master of the house is simply the negative counterpart of the watchful disciple. For what is the disciple being watchful?

A new advent!

WILLIAM R. HERZOG II

to the field, the mill, the daily grind, the ordinary places of human endeavor where life is lived. This region of the mundane is where faithfulness happens, and it is not to be neglected. Biblical faith knows it does not know everything, but it does know it is called to do something here and now. Whatever else Christians may be, they are a work force in the world.

The work the Christian does is to be accomplished in a spirit of wakefulness or watchfulness. The key element for Jesus is not the work, important as it is. The indispensable part of faithful work is the awareness or sensitivity Jesus names as watchfulness or wakefulness. He does not define this awareness with clarity, spelling out its details—more uncertainty!—but indications are it at least means that work is not all there is. Work will not do everything and cannot do everything. Hope will come—the deepest, best, and highest shall come—not from our work but from somewhere outside and beyond it.

So the sermon has brought another moment of rapture, has it not? If the first rapture of relief came when the people were taken up by the idea that they need not know everything, the second comes when they are taken up by the idea that they need not do everything—to work their or anyone else's salvation. The voice of Jesus has assured them: if they do what they can in a spirit of hope and trust, they will do enough.

MARK E. YURS

Isaiah 11:1-10

¹A shoot shall come out from the stump of Jesse,
  and a branch shall grow out of his roots.
²The spirit of the Lord shall rest on him,
  the spirit of wisdom and understanding,
  the spirit of counsel and might,
  the spirit of knowledge and the fear of the Lord.
³His delight shall be in the fear of the Lord.

He shall not judge by what his eyes see,
  or decide by what his ears hear;
⁴but with righteousness he shall judge the poor,
  and decide with equity for the meek of the earth;
he shall strike the earth with the rod of his mouth,
  and with the breath of his lips he shall kill the wicked.
⁵Righteousness shall be the belt around his waist,
  and faithfulness the belt around his loins.

Theological Perspective

One of the essential differences between the Old Testament prophets and the writers of the New Testament has to do with their views concerning the realm of God. The OT is generally couched in the future tense. "The spirit of the Lord shall rest on him" (v. 2) or "The wolf shall live with the lamb" (v. 6). In the NT the tense changes: "The Spirit of the Lord is upon me" (Luke 4:18); "the kingdom of God has come near; repent, and believe in the good news" (Mark 1:15). While this contrast can be exaggerated (see, e.g., Mark 14:25 and Luke 22:30, where God's kingdom is a future reality), this lection appears during Advent for a reason: the earliest Christians heard echoes of this prophecy in the life of Jesus.

With a future tense organizing his thought, Isaiah in this chapter highlights themes of hope and a coming prince of peace. Taking his cue from the concrete and current situation, he indicates that Assyria will fall like a tree that will never sprout again. The scene changes when he turns to the house of David. Although David's house is falling, also like a tree, from its roots a branch will sprout. All is not lost for the people of Judah, because from the Davidic line will emerge a king of peace whose reign will be one of peace and righteousness. A second David will emerge from the line of his ancestors to usher in a time of peace.

Pastoral Perspective

With the exception of the white dove, it would be difficult to come up with a more iconic image of future peace than that of a lion lying down with a lamb. Though Isaiah never actually portrays this pairing, it has been depicted so often as to be emblazoned on our collective conscious. The idea of predator lying down with prey has the power to thrill us, to move and delight us. We send each other videos of a rat who rides on the back of a cat who rides on the back of a dog, or pictures of a tiger nursing piglets, or articles about a lioness adopting antelope calves.

Our fascination with such oddities surely has to do with more than our love of the cute and fascination with the bizarre. We recognize something profound in these reports. They signify hope. If even animals can override bloody instinct, how might we humans do the same?

These pictures strike us because they are so rare. If every lion took care of baby antelopes, it would not be news. Likewise, the parade of animal friends Isaiah shows us is remarkable because of its absurdity: wolf with lamb, leopard with kid, calf and lion, cow and bear, and little children playing without fear. Even snakes do not bite. Is this a prophecy or a fairy tale?

Isaiah's declaration stands in direct contrast to the terror and brutality that pervade our world and

⁶The wolf shall live with the lamb,
   the leopard shall lie down with the kid,
   the calf and the lion and the fatling together,
   and a little child shall lead them.
⁷The cow and the bear shall graze,
   their young shall lie down together;
   and the lion shall eat straw like the ox.
⁸The nursing child shall play over the hole of the asp,
   and the weaned child shall put its hand on the adder's den.
⁹They will not hurt or destroy
   on all my holy mountain;
   for the earth will be full of the knowledge of the LORD
   as the waters cover the sea.

¹⁰On that day the root of Jesse shall stand as a signal to the peoples; the nations shall inquire of him, and his dwelling shall be glorious.

Exegetical Perspective

This passage falls into two distinct parts, both dealing with Israel's future hope for the coming of God's kingdom. The first part reflects the hope for a righteous ruler in the line of David (vv. 1–5); the second expresses the hope for an age of harmony and peace (vv. 6–9). The first of these hopes makes the second possible.

The context for this oracle is the difficult period of tensions around the Syro-Ephraimitic war in 733, when the northern kingdom of Israel and the Aramaeans of Damascus tried to force Judah and King Ahaz to join their rebellion against Assyria. On Isaiah's advice, Ahaz refused; but then, instead of joining the rebel alliance, he called Assyria to intervene. This they did with devastating impact, eventually leading to the destruction of Samaria and the end of the northern kingdom in 721. Isaiah objected to this dangerous move by Ahaz, but he was hopeful that the young Hezekiah who would follow Ahaz might be the righteous Davidic ruler long hoped for. This hopeful passage may reflect that rising hope in Hezekiah as God's righteous king (vv. 1–5, 10) ushering in the peaceable kingdom (vv. 6–9).

This passage is one of three texts in the book of Isaiah thought of as messianic oracles. Messiah, a title that means "anointed one," was used of Israel's Davidic kings. The prophet Isaiah has several

Homiletical Perspective

The text is a hinged pair of paintings. The panel on our left shows a young king. He exudes vitality and strength, severity and a brilliance of joy; deep wisdom is in his eyes. On a distant hill behind him, cruel-faced monarchs lie dead. Nearer to him is a gathering of the poor, whose faces are lifted and radiant. The panel on the right is a fantastic bestiary. There are sleek, beautiful carnivores—leopard, wolf, lion, bear; and there are domestic animals—calf, lamb, ox, goat. The predators and their edible counterparts are lounging together. A child sings to them while toddlers play by the nests of quite peaceable rattlesnakes. Beneath each panel of the diptych is an inscription: the first reads *Justice*, the second says *Peace*.

Each scene may be taken as freestanding and more than rich enough to be preached on its own. The two are purposefully set side by side, however, and letting them inform each other may yield a more interesting and insightful sermon. No transformation of nature can be envisioned apart from a new righteousness in human affairs, and the gift of a real Messiah will extend beyond redemption for humans to the emerging of a new creation. The intention of God moves, as Julian of Norwich understood, from "all shall be well" to "all manner of things shall be well."

Isaiah 11:1-10

Theological Perspective

The renewal of the Davidic reign is not merely a human possibility but a divine gift, because this will be effected by the spirit of YHWH. As great as David was, the hope that God will renew Judah is not limited to the Davidic line but is rooted in the new life that the spirit of YHWH makes possible. A king will emerge from Bethlehem who will lead his people with "wisdom and understanding," "counsel and might," "knowledge and the fear of the Lord" (v. 2). The clue here is to be found in these gifts that are endowed by YHWH. The coming one, the promised prince of peace, will be the bearer of the spirit of YHWH.

In the coming one resides the salvation toward which the children of Israel look. The hope of the people is expressed in Psalm 72:1–2: "Give the king your justice, O God, and your righteousness to a king's son. May he judge your people with righteousness, and your poor with justice." Like Solomon the new leader will be skilled in knowledge and the gift of discernment (1 Kgs. 3:9). Knowledge must be coupled with the fear of God. Knowledge must never be for its own sake; it must always point to the acknowledgment of YHWH and the superiority of the ways of YHWH. The promise that the king of peace will embody and make possible is one in which the whole creation will participate. The sign and signal of the new day will be the appearance of this new king who will restore the Davidic line, ushering in the eschatological realm in which God's knowledge will cover the earth "as the waters cover the sea" (v. 9).

Andrew, the brother of Simon Peter, illustrates for us the force of the messianic promise and how this shaped Jewish expectation. After a day with Jesus, he returns home and says to his elder brother Peter, "We have found the Messiah" (John 1:41). John's Gospel does not let us in on what Jesus said or did to warrant this identification, but in the Messiah resides hope of salvation and the prospect for the dawning of a new day, when "the wolf shall live with the lamb, the leopard shall lie down with the kid, the calf and the lion and the fatling together, and a little child shall lead them" (Isa. 11:6). This hope looks larger and more obviously divine than a monarchy in Judah. The promised salvation will not come through human intervention but through divine action, in which the rights of the poor and the frail members of society will be respected.

In this wonderful vision of peace inaugurated by the Messiah, the entire creation participates. The place of peace will be the holy mountain of God, and the land will be filled with the knowledge of God.

Pastoral Perspective

inform our decisions, both personal and corporate. Our congregants, whatever their circumstance, are acquainted with fear and violence. News of terrorism, war, economic collapse, and climate catastrophe can instill a deep sense of anxiety even among the very young. Some in our congregations may be acquainted by experience with violence we can scarcely imagine. It is important for the pastor to speak honestly and with sensitivity about the power of violence to wreck lives. We might search for ways to name the more insidious forms of abuse and destruction in our lives. What lions have ravaged those in the congregation? What snakes coil hidden in their lives, threatening to strike?

Our fear for children's safety and future is especially acute. Some in our congregations may have had the tragic experience of a child's death; they may be particularly fragile when it comes to Isaiah's images of vulnerable children living and playing in safety. That grief may not be confined to those who have suffered the loss of near ones. We are intimately acquainted with suffering children through heartbreaking images broadcast via the electronic media. This produces its own brand of grief. Isaiah's word is for all, but the pastor must be sensitive to the grief in the room. Isaiah promises future security; how might this be a word of hope for those from whom security has already been stolen? Answers are not easy, but the pastor who wants to care for congregants in grief will want to wrestle with the question.

How is Isaiah's word also a word of security for *now*, for people living in unstable and frightening times, and not just a word about a secure future? According to Isaiah, the transformation from a culture of fear to a world at peace begins with a stump. Out of something that appears finished, lifeless, left behind, comes the sign of new life—a green sprig.

This is how hope gets its start—it emerges as a tiny tendril in an unexpected place. Listeners might be asked to examine where the stumps are in their own lives; where do they feel cut off? Can they imagine or believe that even now God might be nurturing the growth of something new and good from their old, dead dreams? They might consider what areas of their lives most need the promise of new life, and how they might become open to such newness. Isaiah's promise is not just a future one; even now there are tiny signs of hope and life in places that look dead and discarded.

Of course Isaiah's promise is not meant as a merely personal one. He proclaims the coming reign of God, which we read through our Christian lens as the

Exegetical Perspective

passages that seem to reflect the hope for a righteous king in the context of his own time. In the first two of these passages (7:14–16; 9:2–7), the prophet seems hopeful that such a righteous ruler might be near at hand in Israel's future. Some think that today's passage from chapter 11 reflects Isaiah's growing sense that such a righteous ruler might be in the future beyond his own lifetime. The peaceable kingdom (vv. 6–9) represents the final consummation of God's kingdom, not something Isaiah himself would expect to see.

The passage opens (vv. 1–5) with the metaphor of a tree base (not really a stump, since it is not cut off) from which branches grow. The trunk and roots of this tree are named Jesse, but our attention is directed to the stem or branch that represents new growth. Jesse, of course, is the name of David's father (1 Sam. 16:1), so we begin to see that this growing tree is the house of David. It is literally a family tree, and this passage is the source of the popular devotional and worship device of a Jesse Tree used during Advent in many churches as an Advent calendar. Our attention is being directed to a new branch, and subsequent verses go on to describe this hoped-for new stem from the house of Jesse/David.

The coming king will receive the spirit of the Lord. In 1 Samuel, both Saul and David are anointed by the prophet Samuel and immediately receive God's spirit (1 Sam. 10:10; 16:13). Being possessed of God's spirit is a mark of God's anointed one. Verse 2 goes on to expose to the reader various attributes of this empowerment by God's spirit. These include association with "wisdom and understanding," with "counsel and might," and with "knowledge and the fear of the LORD." These are attributes to be highly desired in a hoped-for ruler. The sense of reverence toward God is underlined by beginning verse 3 with a statement that the expected one delights "in the fear of the LORD."

Such an expected one will not rely solely on the immediate impression of his senses (v. 3, eyes and ears), but will rely on the qualities of covenant commitment, righteousness and equity (v. 4a). This theme of covenant qualities continues in verse 5 with the image that the anointed one will be clothed in righteousness and faithfulness. The beneficiaries of these covenant commitments will be the poor and the meek (v. 4a), and the wicked of the earth will be laid low by the mouth and lips of his judging word.

Verses 2–5 paint a powerful portrait of one to come in the line of David who is empowered by God's spirit, equipped with the qualities of covenant

Homiletical Perspective

What are we to make of this king? We notice that he is a surprise. The royal family tree is finished, yet from its stump he nonetheless appears—and is unlike all others. Our kings and executives are not possessed of these depths of reverence, wisdom, righteousness, and effectiveness in righting the world. Such a ruler does not evolve from among us. This is a new and miraculous sovereign presence, stepping forward from the mystery of God.

Is this a promise of the coming of Christ? For us it is. We cannot hear these lines without seeing Jesus among the poor and victimized, confronting procurators and priests, and in solitary places praying. Of course, he redefines our notion of king, just as Isaiah has already done. There is no throne for him, "no place to lay his head." What is more, he invites others to join him in this messianic spirit and work. The world still languishes for the embodied wisdom, discernment, compassion, and fidelity envisioned by Isaiah. The messianic enterprise foreseen by our text invites us to ask not only about Jesus, but about ourselves. The sermon, however briefly, could ask: can a shoot come out from the stump of the church?

With or without us, God will accomplish a new creation. Having raised up the righteous leader, the Creator will make a new paradise of the earth. Enter the animals. Imagine—baby goats are best friends with grizzlies; a lamb and a wolf enjoy conversing over a breakfast of clover. Imagining such unlikely friendships between ex-predators and prey invites a little fun, but we should guard against getting too cute. The text has its eye on the deadly aggressions and fears that sicken the world, the ending of which can be envisioned only in a far-future tense. A thoroughly healed creation is imagined, nothing less than Eden remade. We notice that there is not much of a human presence in it— only a few little children are there.

We would not be wrong to reflect here on the dreadful abundance of human predators in the world. Predator nations, individuals, institutions, and societies live by destroying the vulnerable. Do these predators need destroying, as the messiah kills the wicked (v. 4c) in the first vision? Are miraculous transformations possible, as with these lions and wolves? Or are both visions true? New creation will not likely occur without some further dying among us; painful endings precede the great breathing wonders of harmony.

Such visions are not easy to trust, and it would be best to say so. All around us, fangs are bared. Nations and factions are snapping and snarling. We are at each other's throats. Edward Hicks, a

Isaiah 11:1-10

Theological Perspective

The peace of God expected will include human beings, animals, and the land. The promise is reconciliation and restoration for all of God's creation. It is a beautiful vision that, in the day of salvation, the animals and the land will be included. Little children will be able to play with snakes.

What of the Christian church and its vision of the coming one and the coming realm? The church points to Luke 10:24, "For I tell you that many prophets and kings desired to see what you see, but did not see it, and to hear what you hear, but did not hear it." The kingdom is in our midst and belongs to all who are willing to see the word of God enacted. Eschatology has become history. The secret of the church and its mission are in relationship to the kingdom.

The church is not the kingdom of God, but its relationship to the kingdom signals its mission. The realm of God shines through the witness and mission of the church as the poor have good news preached to them and are judged with righteousness and equity. The Messiah awaits the church in a future of righteousness marked off by the gifts of wisdom and understanding, counsel and might, knowledge and the fear of God, beckoning the church to a new future not of its own making but one made possible by YHWH. The challenge is not to be stuck in the traditions of the past but to be open to the new realm in which the proud will be punished, the humble will be exalted, and the practice of justice will be the order of a new day.

NOEL LEO ERSKINE

Pastoral Perspective

coming of Christ. The little shoot will rise to be a new kind of king, one who judges with righteousness and brings justice for the poor and the meek. He manifests a power unlike any other, and his power is for the weak. From this declaration proceeds the vivid vision of the peaceable kingdom, a compelling portrayal of both aggression and weakness overturned.

Most of us can relate to feelings of both weakness and aggression. Most of us have felt preyed upon at one time or another; most of us have sometimes been the predator as well. Though Isaiah speaks of a future time when predator and prey will feast and rest together, his vision can have transformative implications now, if we allow the possibility of conversion in our own lives. The pastor might invite listeners to give some thought to those areas in their lives where they feel weak, as well as those areas where they may be prone to aggression or even violence. Advent is a good time for reexamining our old assumptions and definitions, including how we think of and use power. In Christ, power has been reinterpreted. How might our own lives be reinterpreted in his light? How might our own lives be remade—so that the wolf and the lamb within us live together in a new kind of harmony? Our own lives can become peaceable kingdoms when subjected to the judgment and transformation of Christ.

Isaiah is clear that we are not the ones who usher in a new era; it is God who brings it forth. Some would therefore say that Isaiah's call is a call not to action but to hope; but hope, in the end, *is* action, with the power to overturn old assumptions and sad cynicism, to give us new eyes, and to heal our warring hearts.

STACEY SIMPSON DUKE

Exegetical Perspective

commitment, and directed to the welfare of the most defenseless and marginal. This is a model of hoped-for leadership in any generation; early Christians saw it completely fulfilled in Jesus by the testimony of New Testament Gospel narrative.

The vision of harmony in verses 6–10 is often referred to as the vision of "the peaceable kingdom." Edward Hicks's paintings of this scene, with William Penn's treaty with Native tribes in the background, is the visual image that comes into mind for many. The image is of a return to Eden when God's reign is finally consummated. When the anointed one described in earlier verses ushers it in, broken creation becomes the completely harmonious creation God intended.

Wolf, leopard, lion, and bear will live harmoniously with the domestic animals lamb, calf, kid, and cow (vv. 6–7). Lions will now eat straw like oxen, and a small child will play over the holes of poisonous snakes (v. 8). These seemingly natural adversaries will live in harmony with no thought of hurt or destruction. Indeed the earth will now be filled with the "knowledge of the LORD" (v. 9). This Hebrew term for knowledge is more than cognitive information; it is the full entering into and experiencing of what is known. So the earth will be infused with the reality of God, and it shall be as comprehensive as the waters of the sea (v. 9).

In verse 10 the passage returns to the hope for a descendant of David who will usher in the full reign of God's kingdom. Further, this kingdom will encompass not simply the future of God's people but the Gentiles of all nations as well. This is a very universal and comprehensive vision of hope for the future. We read this text in Advent as a new generation that lives between two times: we celebrate the coming of an anointed son of David in Jesus Christ, and we look forward to the promised final consummation of God's peaceable kingdom yet to come.

BRUCE C. BIRCH

Homiletical Perspective

nineteenth-century Quaker artist and minister, painted Isaiah's vision of "The Peaceable Kingdom" at least sixty-two times. All the animals are there, and a child among them, and in the background a delegation of Quakers in peaceful conversation with some Native Americans. Over time, the paintings changed. Hicks grew increasingly discouraged by the conflicts of his time, especially within his religious community, and began to make the predators in his paintings more terribly ferocious.[1] So we who preach this text should take care to make its claws and teeth sharp enough.

Are the predators the only ones to be transformed? Why not also their former victims? The predators have lost all interest in eating them, having crossed over to join them in a congenial vegetarianism; but does conversion apply only to the powerful? The first vision speaks more of gifts for the poor and meek than of consequences for the mighty. So why not imagine a purring lion beside a calf who has learned to roar, and a wolf wagging its tail in the company of a brave, lion-hearted lamb?

What of the "little child" who leads them? Shall Christians think of Jesus again? We should not make this move too quickly. Like the calf, lamb, kid, and ox, the child stands for the vulnerable, and is joined by others even younger and more vulnerable, happily playing in a safe world at last. Why is it the child who leads the whole bleating, mooing, yipping, snuffling, roaring, giggling company? The new creation wants a human presence—new, bright, undefended, and free—to love and care for it all.

This, of course, is the child we seek in Christ, in whom the lion of Judah and the lamb of God are one. In this Child we meet the divine vulnerability and the divine strength. In this Christ comes a halting of aggression and a banishing of fear—the justice of God, the peace of God, together.

PAUL SIMPSON DUKE

---

1. John Dillenberger, *The Visual Arts in America* (Chico, CA: Scholars Press, 1984), 130–32.

Psalm 72:1-7, 18-19

[1]Give the king your justice, O God,
   and your righteousness to a king's son.
[2]May he judge your people with righteousness,
   and your poor with justice.
[3]May the mountains yield prosperity for the people,
   and the hills, in righteousness.
[4]May he defend the cause of the poor of the people,
   give deliverance to the needy,
   and crush the oppressor.

Theological Perspective

Psalm 72 represents a longing in the midst of broken political realities.

"We want a king!" they had said, so we can be like other nations (1 Sam. 8). Did they really know what they were asking for, these elders of Israel, gathered about Samuel? Ever since the people of Israel escaped Egypt and were thereby made a people by YHWH, they had been struggling to learn and live a new form of life dependent upon the Lord alone. They had escaped the idolatry and oppression of archaic empire. When they asked for a king, Samuel knew they had sold out their own liberation and were rejecting God.

God told Samuel to describe clearly the realities people would face under kingly rule, and it is was not a pretty sight. Kings needed armies, and conscription would surely take their sons away to war. Kings needed workers to support their lavish lifestyle, so people could expect a large group to be forced into labor for the king. On top of that labor, their production would be taxed to support the king's court nobles, the priests, and a large standing army. Before long, Samuel warned, the people would cry out against the oppression of their king.

Israel's trouble with kings emerged right away, beginning with Saul's paranoia and David's lust and murder. Solomon, David's son, made a good start by

Pastoral Perspective

On this Second Sunday of Advent the church is invited to consider the political ramifications of the coming of the Lord—both as the child Jesus and as the returning Lord. What implications does the coming of Christ have for the way we order our society?

The pastorally aware preacher will also move beyond ideas about justice and into the specific lived lives of the diverse collective she faces when she speaks. In that sanctuary each listener from every place on the social, economic, and political spectrum will be offered a next step forward toward the just participation this psalm describes.

Psalm 72 is simply a prayer for the king, concluding with a blessing to God. Most churches, as part of their Sunday liturgies, can safely and usefully pray for the political and governmental authorities. It seems a worthwhile thing to do, since governments are responsible for shaping and ordering our common life, our society. The government sets the goals toward which we strive, establishes the priorities of our culture, and guards the values and peace we hold dear . . . does it not? On the other hand, we are not powerless subjects of a remote monarchy. We live in democracies, which means we are a part of the political authority for which we pray. Interestingly, Psalm 72 is presented in the Bible (in the superscription, not printed above) as a psalm of Solomon—a prayer

^{5}May he live while the sun endures,
   and as long as the moon, throughout all generations.
^{6}May he be like rain that falls on the mown grass,
   like showers that water the earth.
^{7}In his days may righteousness flourish
   and peace abound, until the moon is no more.
....
^{18}Blessed be the LORD, the God of Israel,
   who alone does wondrous things.
^{19}Blessed be his glorious name forever;
   may his glory fill the whole earth.
      Amen and Amen.

Exegetical Perspective

Today's psalm is one of only two ascribed to Solomon; the other is Psalm 127. In each case, the reason for this traditional attribution by the scribes is easy to discern. Psalm 127 is a wisdom psalm (for Solomon's association with wisdom, see 1 Kgs. 3:1–15//2 Chr. 1:1–13; 1 Kgs. 3:16–28; 4:29–34; 1 Kgs. 10:1–13//2 Chr. 9:1–9; Prov. 1:1; 10:1; 25:1; and Eccl. 1:1) that begins with reference to building, calling to mind Solomon's role as temple builder (Ps 127:1; cf. 1 Kgs. 6:1–30; 7:15–51//2 Chr. 3:1–5:1). Psalm 72 deals with the rightful duties of the king, calling to mind Solomon's prayer for just such guidance ("Give your servant therefore an understanding mind to govern your people," 1 Kgs. 3:9//2 Chr. 1:10).

Likely too, the reference to the "king's son" in verse 1 reminded the scribes of Solomon, son of David. Psalm 72 is further distinguished by the role that it plays in the Psalter. The book of Psalms is divided into five parts, each concluding with a doxology (see Pss. 41:13; 72:18–19; 89:52; and 106:48; Book 5 apparently concludes with Psalms 146–150, a series of "hallelujah" psalms). Today's psalm comes at the end of Book 2. Psalm 72 ends with the only explicit editorial note in the Psalter, "The prayers of David son of Jesse are ended" (v. 20). This note relates well both to the content of Books 1 and 2 (most of the psalms ascribed to David in the Hebrew

Homiletical Perspective

The psalm opens with a petition that God will give Jerusalem a king beyond all their imaginings, who will bring a reign of justice and prosperity for all. This all-encompassing plea asks for a ruler empowered by God who will serve the common good. In Advent, Christians are also waiting—waiting not only for personal rebirth but also for the consummation of our world in the coming of the Messiah's reign of peace and justice.

Power, peace, and justice are the abiding themes for the psalmist, who explores the definitions of dominion ranging from Israel's king to God's reign in the world. These ideals are predicated upon the notion of righteousness, or in Hebrew *tzedakah*, a complicated noun that might best be translated in this way: "What *tzedakah* signifies," writes Jonathan Sacks, "is what is often called 'social justice', meaning that no one should be without the basic requirements of existence."[1] So what kind of image does the psalmist ultimately offer of power, peace, justice, and righteousness?

Attributes of Kingship. The psalmist shows that the king is representative of God's glory and goodness.

1. Jonathan Sacks, *The Dignity of Difference: How to Avoid the Clash of Civilizations* (New York: Continuum, 2003), 114.

Psalm 72:1-7, 18-19

Theological Perspective

asking God for wisdom to judge with justice, a request echoed in the first line of this psalm; but his syncretism and greed led to a life of pleasures lived on the backs of his subjects. His reign foreshadowed many more severe departures from God's ways with future kings in the years that followed.

The gift of wisdom to judge with justice seemed to do little good, given the sorry story of corrupt kings stretching down through Israel's history, through exile and return, culminating in a horrific yet symbolic way with Herod the Great. It was this latter king who, according to tradition, was willing to kill all the baby boys in his territory rather than abide the word of the magi that a new king had been born who would finally fulfill the old longing for a king like the Lord.

What is the character of such a king? One can hear in the imperative voice of the first verse the desperation of those struggling to survive, who know the injustice of social arrangements that benefit the few rich at the expense of the many poor. The verse has the tone of a strong pleading, of an intense cry that by its very guttural nature hopes to confect the reality for which it cries.

The initial cry gives way to a murmuring prayer of invocation rooted in a longing for hope and history to rhyme. The job description is uncompromising in its utopian aim. It has to be, since the model king is the Lord, the maker of heaven and earth, the liberator of the oppressed, the one who bears the ragtag people as a mother bears her child when the child's exhaustion means not one step further.

This invocation, modeled after God's rule and reign, asks for justice and righteousness as the foundation. Upon that firm foundation a dual theme unfolds to guide the new king in defense of the poor against oppression and toward its opposite—a downpour of blessings upon the people so that their lives flourish and grow as a verdant garden. Here we see the dream that is later unfolded in Isaiah and Revelation, of a place with no tears or sorrows, a rule founded on shalom for all.

The worst moments in the long history of God's people across history come to pass when leaders throw their lot with the politically powerful. Solomon and Herod are obvious examples, but so are church leaders in Germany during National Socialism or in Chile during the reign of Augusto Pinochet. Year after year, people watch their rulers again succumb to corruption, greed, and power— some more, some less. Tension grows between the vision and reality. It is this gap, wearing on the

Pastoral Perspective

by the king *for* the king—so he would be expected to become a part of the answer to his own prayer. Are we in a similar position? In what way can our practice further our prayer?

Psalm 72 does more than simply offer support and blessing to the existing authorities, however. The particulars of the prayer also hold the governing authorities to account; *what is prayed for the king* clearly indicates what the king's power is to be used *for.* Justice, righteousness, prosperity, and peace are to be the hallmarks of good government. This is hardly a list that would be disputed anywhere! However, there are two notions present in this psalm that seem particularly challenging to the way our own society is ordered.

The first is that the poor and needy are the key population to watch in assessing the king's justice and righteousness. Is this how we judge the political effectiveness of our own leaders—by how well they "defend the cause of the poor" and "give deliverance to the needy" (v. 4)? What would be different if the acid test for the world's economic policy was improvement in the lives of the poorest people of the earth? What would change if our "bottom line" was the quality of life for First Nations in North America? Here the pastorally aware preacher will know that "the poor" are not an abstract concept, but include real people who will be listening to the sermon that very day. What if those poorer people were seen to be the people who matter *most*—first in our congregations, then in our land?

Not long ago, Mohammad Yunus was given a Nobel Peace Prize for his work in microcredit, with the Grameen Bank. The Grameen Bank (as do several other microcredit organizations) turns conventional banking policy on its head by giving very small, unsecured loans to very poor people. These loans pay very little interest, but they do enable very poor people to improve their lives, build small businesses, and rise out of the depths of poverty. Microcredit may be one example of the kind of economic policy that results from paying attention to the lives of the poor.

The second challenging notion is found in verse 3: "May the mountains yield prosperity for the people, and the hills, *in righteousness*" (emphasis added). In this verse, prosperity and righteousness are held together in a way that they do not seem to be in our own society. What does *righteousness* mean when applied to prosperity from the earth? Does it imply sustainability—that we are not plundering the earth, enjoying our prosperity at the expense of future

Exegetical Perspective

text fall in these two books, suggesting a preliminary collection of "David" psalms) and to the content of Psalm 72, which deals with the dignity and responsibility of the Davidic king.

Many of us come, of course, from a culture *without* kings—indeed, a society formed in rebellion against monarchy! Even in ancient Israel, the confident hope that the king might "live while the sun endures, and as long as the moon, throughout all generations" (v. 5; cf. Ps. 89:36–37) proved unrealistic. Davidic kingship ended when Jerusalem fell. Clearly, this meant that God's everlasting covenant with David needed to be understood in new ways. In the Psalms, kingship increasingly comes to belong not to any human, but to God (see the "enthronement songs," Pss. 24, 29, 47, 93, 96, 97, 98, 99). James Luther Mays writes, "The psalms are the poetry of the reign of God. They are the praise and proclamation and prayer of those who believe that the confession 'The LORD reigns' states the basic truth about the world and life lived in it."[1]

In the prophets of the exile, the Davidic covenant was democratized, reinterpreted as being not between David and the Lord, but between the Lord and the entire people Israel (Jer. 32:40; 50:5; Ezek. 16:60; and esp. 37:25–26). For example, in Isaiah 55:3–5, the only mention of David or David's line in Second Isaiah, God swears an everlasting covenant with *Israel*: "I will make with you an everlasting covenant, my steadfast, sure love for David." Israel is to be to the nations what David had been to Israel; now the restored, reborn people become the leaders and commanders of all the nations of the earth, to bring them into the light of the Lord.

Of course, for Christian readers, the covenant with David and the image of kingship apply particularly to Jesus. As Mays writes, "Christians have always known that they can pray the psalm in its fullness only for the heir of David who was Jesus of Nazareth."[2] Read in this way, the psalm's focus on the poor and oppressed takes on even greater significance.

According to the universal witness of the Hebrew Bible (and in keeping with ancient Near Eastern ideals of kingship), the king was primarily responsible for rightly administering justice, particularly for those persons who had no one else to stand for them: the widow, the orphan, and the stranger (for the king as enforcing justice and righteousness, see, e.g., Ps. 99:4; Isa. 9:7; Jer. 22:15; 23:5; 33:15; Ezek.

1. James Luther Mays, *Psalms*, Interpretation series (Louisville, KY: John Knox Press, 1994), 30–31.
2. Ibid., 238.

Homiletical Perspective

In many ways, the king is depicted as an agent of God's righteousness. The hope is that the king sees the world as God sees it, defending the world's most vulnerable and bringing deliverance to the needy (v. 4). This may include offering professions, providing shelter, and cultivating useful skills or meaningful work. This is the hope that Israel had for its kings—that the power of the Spirit would rest upon them (Isa. 11:2).

The psalmist envisions a king who will crush oppressors and dismantle the sinful structures that keep God's people from flourishing. The ruler will maintain determination in enduring hardships and sacrifice to overcome evil with good. These things will be done for all times and all generations (v. 5). The fruit of the king's labors will be days when righteousness flourishes and peace abounds (v. 7). All that the sovereign is and does shall be life giving to the people, a source of refreshment and renewal for the whole of creation. It is a herculean task, is it not?

Indeed it is. The writer of 1 and 2 Kings reminds us that it was only David, Solomon, Josiah, and Hezekiah who were deemed great rulers, and even they were less than perfect.

Contemporary Leaders. So what does this say about our mandate for living with power and authority today? We do continue to hold our current elected officials and other leaders to a higher standard. We hope that they will provide us with a rubric for ethical living. We also hope that the actions our leaders take will provide a habitat where justice, hope, adequate shelter, and a more environmentally friendly world prevail. We imbue these leaders with expectations as we place many of our hopes and dreams for our world on their promises to deliver.

It is important to remember not to place too much trust or authority in such figures, because they, like us, are only human. Rather, our need for an exemplar such as the one Psalm 72 imagines reinforces our need for a Messiah, for Jesus, who never fails or forsakes us. As Christians, we look to Jesus as our ultimate moral exemplar, not to our earthly leaders.

John the Baptist recognizes this division between earthly leaders and the Messiah, remarking that he is not worthy to carry Jesus' sandals and that one more powerful than he is coming (Matt. 3:11). Nonetheless, John recognizes that we are not impotent; rather, we are called to "bear fruit worthy of repentance" (Matt. 3:8). So, following in John's humility, we may not be worthy to carry Jesus' sandals, but we

Psalm 72:1-7, 18-19

Theological Perspective

faithful over time, that gave way to a hope for one who would come to fulfill this vision and rule as God in flesh, one with God's vocation. This hope is for a son of David unlike Solomon, who both asks for wisdom to rule with justice and does so truly, for the flourishing of all creation.

Carefully looking at the world as it is, while praying this psalm during the season of Advent, suggests a number of directions for Christians today. First, while acknowledging the psalm's vision of the kind of leadership that God desires for us and that we hope for ourselves, we can and ought to pray for rulers today: good, bad, and ugly. After all, if we take Jesus at his word in Matthew 5, God rains blessings on the nice and the nasty, and we are called to love and bless like God. How then can we pray only for those political leaders who hold the views and enact the policies with which we agree?

Second, it is finally one, and one alone, upon whom we can fully pray this prayer. He is the one hoped for in Isaiah's words about a shoot from the stump of Jesse (Isa. 11:1), the one whose life and death and resurrection have already begun a reign that embodies God's very life, transforming the life of the world. In him we finally find a "king" whose spirit is of the Lord, who will rule with justice and righteousness for all the earth.

CHRISTIAN SCHAREN

Pastoral Perspective

generations? Does it imply a lack of oppressive or exploitative business practices? Does it imply a fair or equitable distribution of the earth's bounty?

The way we envision and measure prosperity and progress sets the economic course for our society. In the Western world, we typically measure prosperity in economic terms, using gross domestic product (GDP) as our primary indicator. GDP is simply a measure of all the money spent in a given year. What an odd measure of economic success! Already in 1968, Robert Kennedy eloquently named the shortcomings of this method of accounting:

> Too much and too long, we seemed to have surrendered personal excellence and community values in the mere accumulation of material things. Our Gross National Product . . .—if we should judge America by that—. . . counts air pollution and cigarette advertising, and ambulances to clear our highways of carnage. It counts special locks for our doors and the jails for the people who break them. It counts the destruction of the redwood and the loss of our natural wonder in chaotic sprawl. . . . Yet the gross national product does not allow for the health of our children, the quality of their education or the joy of their play. It does not include the beauty of our poetry or the strength of our marriages, the intelligence of our public debate or the integrity of our public officials. It measures . . . everything in short, except that which makes life worthwhile.[1]

What would it mean for us to seek prosperity *in righteousness*? What kind of prosperity *really matters*, in our eyes and in God's?

The incarnation is all about God becoming a part of earthly, human life. Therefore, this psalm challenges us to see that in political and economic terms—to give our prayer support to our leaders, to be sure, but also to hold our leaders (and our own political participation) to account. Pastorally aware preachers will also hope that justice starts in the room, with a renewed sense that everyone worshiping with them that morning matters.

DAVID HOLMES

---

1. Robert Kennedy, Remarks at the University of Kansas, March 18, 1968, quoted in Mark Anielski, *The Economics of Happiness* (Gabriola Island, British Columbia: New Society Publishers, 2007), 27.

45:9). In today's Old Testament reading, this high view of the king is on prominent display:

> He shall not judge by what his eyes see,
> or decide by what his ears hear;
> but with righteousness he shall judge the poor,
> and decide with equity for the meek of the earth.
> (Isa. 11:3b–4)

However, it is the Lord, who "loves righteousness and justice" (Ps. 33:5; see also Isa. 5:16; 28:17; 33:5; Jer. 4:2; 9:24; Mic. 7:9; Pss. 36:6; 103:6; 106:3; Job 37:23), who is ultimately responsible for guaranteeing the rights of the powerless. Psalm 72 takes that idea a step further, referring to the needy as "your [that is, *God's*] poor" (v. 2). This radical concept is found elsewhere only in Psalm 74:19 ("do not forget the life of your poor forever") and Isaiah 49:13, which calls upon heaven and earth to sing praises: "For the LORD has comforted his people, and will have compassion on his suffering ones [in Hebrew, the same term translated as "poor" in Ps. 72:2]." Far from being God-forsaken, the poor are here described as God's own possession. No wonder the psalmist says of the king,

> May he defend the cause of the poor of the people,
> give deliverance to the needy,
> and crush the oppressor.
> (v. 4)

In an address to representatives of some of America's largest United Methodist churches, Bishop Peter Storey of South Africa placed the church's mission to the poor on an unexpected level: "Those Methodist churches struggling in places of poverty and injustice are fortunate—they are already where Jesus is. Those who have become prosperous must find Him again."[3] We misunderstand ourselves, and our God, if we believe that we are *taking* Christ to the world's poor. Instead, now as when he walked the hills of Galilee, it is among the poor that we will find our Lord. Heeding John the Baptist's call to repent, may we resolve today to "Bear fruit worthy of repentance" (Matt. 3:8).

STEVEN S. TUELL

are worthy to carry on the work of empowering those who are poor and needy.

Our Servant Leadership. Our leaders—both earthly and divine—provide models for us, but what we look for in others we might also need to find in ourselves. The psalmist inspires us to action: to give, judge, yield, defend, uphold, and know God. Just as the king in the Davidic monarchy strove to embody God's righteousness, so too do we attempt to take on that mantle of righteousness; we seek to be instilled with the power of God's Spirit.

Like the leaders about whom the psalmist writes, preachers are also held accountable to our communities. As servant leaders in an impoverished world, we strive to bring liberty to the oppressed and the captive. We must not only carry a message of liberation; we must also work to see that it is implemented in a way that empowers others. Education is a key component here—to be good citizens, we all need access to the knowledge and skills that will enable us to work for and with others.

As Jonathan Sacks writes, "The highest form of aid is one that enables the individual to dispense with aid. Humanitarian relief is essential in the short term, but in the long run, job creation and the promotion of employment are more important. . . . As an African proverb puts it: the hand that gives is always uppermost; the hand that receives is always lower."[2]

Ultimately, the psalmist reminds us that it is "the God of Israel, who alone does wondrous things" (v. 18). However, we are called to participate in that work as well. It is our vocation to work for a world ordered by God's good purposes, where justice, righteousness, and peace reign for all. That work may include serving on juries, speaking out against inequality, volunteering at soup kitchens, making charitable contributions, or tutoring in elementary schools. Whatever form ministry takes, it is our hope to be cloaked with God's righteousness to do God's will and to enable flourishing for all.

CAROL L. WADE

---

3. From Peter Storey, "Making a World of Difference," an address at the Large Churches Initiative of the United Methodist Church in Orlando, FL, January 20, 2008.

2. Ibid., 120.

Romans 15:4-13

⁴For whatever was written in former days was written for our instruction, so that by steadfastness and by the encouragement of the scriptures we might have hope. ⁵May the God of steadfastness and encouragement grant you to live in harmony with one another, in accordance with Christ Jesus, ⁶so that together you may with one voice glorify the God and Father of our Lord Jesus Christ. ⁷Welcome one another, therefore, just as Christ has welcomed you, for the glory of God. ⁸For I tell you that Christ has become a servant of the circumcised on behalf of the truth of God in order that he might confirm the promises given to the patriarchs, ⁹and in order that the Gentiles might glorify God for his mercy. As it is written,

"Therefore I will confess you among the Gentiles,
and sing praises to your name";

Theological Perspective

The search for God begins with our acceptance of the human. Christians believe this, says the pastoral theologian John Heagle, "Because it is in the stable of humanity that God has come in search of us."[1] In this season of anticipating the birth of Christ, a theology of incarnation enlivens, enables, and encourages us to live as Christ did. "Accept one another, therefore, as Christ has accepted you" (v. 7, my trans.).

The Jesuit theologian Peter van Breemen wonderfully develops this theme of acceptance, this theology of God's radical love. One of the deepest needs of the human heart, he says, is to be accepted and valued. Every human being wants to be loved, but there is an even deeper love, a love of acceptance. Every human being craves to be accepted, accepted for who one is, not for what one has done or achieved or merited.

"'A friend is someone who knows everything about you and still accepts you,'" van Breemen says, quoting Augustine. "That is the dream we all share: that one day I may meet the person with whom I can really talk, who understands me and the words I say—who can listen and even hear what is left

1. See *Advent Sourcebook*, ed. Thomas O'Gorman (Chicago: Liturgy Training Publications, 1988), 66.

Pastoral Perspective

Hope is the theme that forms an envelope around this concluding section of Paul's long letter to the community of believers in Rome. In 4 he urges that they find in "the scriptures" (that is, the Hebrew Bible) the encouragement that will produce hope. Verse 13 is one of Paul's "benedictions": "May the God of *hope* fill you with all joy and peace in believing, so that you may abound in *hope* by the power of the Holy Spirit."

Hope may seem illusive in the modern world. "A thing with feathers that perches in the soul," Emily Dickinson called it. For many of us, hope may be something of a court of last resort: it is what we do after all our planning and preparing is done; it is what we do if we cannot fix whatever the problem is. Such a perspective puts us at the center of the universe, of course, and God is what is there to take up the slack.

For others, hope is buying a lottery ticket or going to the casino. It is imagining that there is some force in the universe that will come to our rescue and give us what we think we want. We may call this "luck" or "fate" or "chance." Whatever it is, it depends on the random event that falls our way and that just maybe will change our lives for the better.

Neither of these meanings fits with Paul's intention in this passage. For Paul, "hope" is more like

Second Sunday of Advent

^{10}and again he says,
  "Rejoice, O Gentiles, with his people";
^{11}and again,
  "Praise the Lord, all you Gentiles,
    and let all the peoples praise him";
^{12}and again Isaiah says,
  "The root of Jesse shall come,
    the one who rises to rule the Gentiles;
  in him the Gentiles shall hope."

^{13}May the God of hope fill you with all joy and peace in believing, so that you may abound in hope by the power of the Holy Spirit.

Exegetical Perspective

The general point of this passage, with its quotations from the OT, is that God's decision, enabled in Christ, to unite Jews and Gentiles into one people of God is not a recent divine decision, but was a part of God's plan for a chosen people from the beginning. To that end 15:1–3, which must be considered a part of this passage, summarizes Paul's discussion of the need for weak and strong to accept each other (Rom. 14), as Christ accepted all, not doing what he wanted but what God wanted: unify all people by bearing their sin (15:3). Through such a unity of weak and strong, the Christian community may face its future with hope.

This passage is divided into two units, verses 1–6 and 7–13. Each of these two parts quotes the OT, each points to the accomplishments of the historical Jesus, each contains paraenetic, didactic, and doxological elements, and each ends with a prayer wish.

In verse 4, it is not clear whether the "endurance" (NIV; NRSV "steadfastness") mentioned refers to our own endurance or that of Christ. It is probably the latter, with the point growing out of the reference to Christ not pleasing himself, but enduring the reproaches aimed at others. This scriptural citation from Psalm 69:9b then prompts Paul to say such Scripture was written for our instruction, so that through the steadfastness Christ exhibited, and the

Homiletical Perspective

On the Second Sunday of Advent, the Epistle lesson reminds us of two of the most precious gifts we receive from God. In much of North America, culture's Christmas is all about what we buy and wrap and give to one another, but these gifts Paul knows can be neither bought with money nor made by human hands. Our human minds have a difficult time even imagining they exist; yet they are ours for the taking, priceless treasures from the realm of God's redeeming love. Our job as preachers is to make room in hearts of people, helping them to wait expectantly for gifts only God can give, two of the most valuable of which are *hope* and *harmony*.

Hope. Paul brackets this passage with a twofold reminder that hope is at the heart of the gospel of salvation. He begins by maintaining that everything "written in former days was written . . . [so that] we might have hope." He is referring, not to some generalized emotion that ignores reality and insists that everything will turn out fine, but to a core kind of trust that relies on the steadfastness of God and enables us to be steadfast, no matter how dire the situation.

Paul concludes the passage with a benediction that not only sums up what he has just been trying to say about why the Gentiles are now able to live in

Romans 15:4-13

Theological Perspective

unsaid, and then really accepts me. God is the ultimate fulfillment of this dream."[2]

Nothing is so crippling, van Breemen goes on, as the experience of not being fully accepted. When I am not accepted, a deep, unnamed emptiness pervades my being. A baby who is not welcomed is ruined at the roots. A young athlete who is not accepted by the coach performs poorly.

Acceptance means that my friends and family give me a feeling of self-esteem, a feeling of being worthwhile. They are happy that I am simply as I am. Acceptance means that I can grow at my own pace. I am encouraged and supported, but not forced.[3]

The craving for acceptance can absorb all our creative energies. It is comparable to the physical craving caused by rickets, a softening of the bones due to a deficiency of vitamin D. Children with rickets, over a century ago, would scratch the lime out from the walls to feed their bones. Likewise, people who are not accepted attempt to scratch out acceptance from others. They may develop rigidity because of their lack of security, or they may resort to boasting, a not-so-subtle way to provide themselves with the praise they so badly crave.

The twentieth-century theologian Paul Tillich claims that *faith is the courage to accept acceptance.* I am accepted by God as I am, not as I should be. However, this requires an act of faith. It requires the courage to embrace Acceptance, that is, God's very self. God absolutely, fully accepts me and intimately knows my name: "See, I have inscribed you on the palms of my hands" (Isa. 49:16).

It is one thing to know I am accepted and quite another to embrace it. It takes a long time to believe that I am accepted by God as I am. The basic faith is that I know myself to be accepted by God. Self-acceptance can never be based on my own self, my own qualities, or my own herculean efforts. Such a foundation would collapse. Self-acceptance is an act of faith. When God loves me, I must accept myself as well. I cannot be more demanding than God, can I?

Our reading proclaims that *Christ accepted you for the glorification of God* (vv. 7, 9). The glorification of God will be possible only if the acceptance enacted by Christ flows through to mutual acceptance of one another, in particular those "weak in faith." Whatever one has received from God is bound to spread to others.

2. Peter van Breemen, SJ, *As Bread That Is Broken* (Denville, NJ): Dimension Books, 1974), 15.
3. See Patrick Howell, "The Courage to Accept Love," in *A Spiritguide through Times of Darkness* (Kansas City, MO: Sheed & Ward, 1996), 70–81.

Pastoral Perspective

"trust." The ground for hope is neither the last resort nor random chance. The ground is *God*: the God of "steadfastness and encouragement," the "God of hope." Because God is the guarantor of whatever is promised, the believer may live with complete confidence. What God has said, is what *will* be.

Paul's exhortation to hope comes in a particular context that turns this from a well-meaning bromide into a critically important word for the church today. Paul is writing to a community of believers in Rome made up of both Jews and pagans or Gentiles. They are together because Paul and others have been preaching a gospel whose message is that the promises that God made long ago to God's people Israel are now open to all because of the life, death, and resurrection of Jesus. The first eleven chapters of Romans are Paul's explanation of how this works theologically. Then, in chapter 12, he spells out what the theological vision means for how this community is supposed to live, in particular, how they are to live with their very real differences and live into their new unity in Christ Jesus.

The summary of all he has said in chapters 12–14 comes in 15:7: "Welcome one another, therefore, just as Christ has welcomed you, for the glory of God." In order to give glory and praise to God, Paul says, Christ extended his welcome to all—Jew and Gentile alike. In order to fulfill God's promises, Christ embodied God's intention to widen the circle of divine love. *Therefore* (Paul's favorite word for making the transition from theology to ethics), if God has welcomed you—*all of you*—you are to be imitators of God. Life in Christian community is to be shaped by the practice of extending a welcome, of opening one's home and life, of giving hospitality to the "other." Each side is to welcome *the other*. There is no longer insider and outsider. Now all are hosts and all are guests, because all have been welcomed by the infinite expanse of divine love.

Living as we do in a world that draws boundaries all the time and in every possible way, it is impossible to preach this message too frequently. From the time we are old enough to be in school, we know all too well the patterns of forming "in-groups" and "outcasts." There are people who are cool and those who are not; there are those who get power and influence because of good looks or athletic prowess; there are those who grab power by being bullies. We learn this as children, and we can see the effects of this behavior in almost every aspect of adult life—in business, education, politics, and even the church.

Second Sunday of Advent

encouragement (or comfort, or exhortation; the Gk. word *paraklēsis* also has such meanings) Christians find in Hebrew Scriptures, they may have hope. Hope is mentioned twice in verse 13, showing its importance for this passage. Unless there is trust in God, there can be no hope; but unless God is faithful, there can be no trust. It is therefore the faithfulness of God, demonstrated in Christ, upon which our hope is based. Paul will return to this theme in verses 8–9a.

Verses 5–6, the prayer wish by which Paul closes this first section, take up the ideas of patience and exhortation/comfort once again, this time making clear their source is God himself. The language found here reminds one of Philippians 2:2–4 and represents the kind of vocabulary Paul uses when Christian unity is uppermost in his mind. Unity is of course, here as in Philippians 2, the purpose for which Christ became incarnate and died, namely, to break down the barrier between Jew and Gentile.

The "therefore" with which verse 7 begins in the Greek now introduces the concluding paragraph of this section of Romans. What has been said in 14:1–15:6 is summed up in the command: receive one another because Christ has received you, to the glory of God. There are two minor questions here. The first is whether the reading is Christ welcomed "us," or welcomed "you." While both readings have strong support in ancient manuscripts, "you" is probably the original, since unlike verse 1, where Paul is addressing the strong, among whom he includes himself, in verse 7 he is addressing the whole Christian community, weak and strong together. The "you" is the more inclusive and is thus the preferred reading.

The second question is the construal of the phrase "for the glory of God." Its placement in the Greek sentence is such that it could refer either to the command that Christians welcome one another, or to the statement that Christ welcomed you. Given its position in the sentence, Paul may have wanted it to refer to both. Hence, both Christ's mission and our response are done for the glory of God.

The "For" with which verse 8 begins connects it to verse 7 as a further development of verse 7, giving additional support to the command to welcome one another. The Greek structure of verses 8b–9 is not entirely clear. The parallelism of some grammatical constructions, and Paul's tendency in the second part of such constructions to omit words repeated from the first part, could indicate that Paul meant the following: Christ became a servant for the circumcised (Jews) for the sake of God's truth, to

hope, but describes magnificently what the Letter to the Romans has to say and what life in Christ is all about: "May the God of hope fill you with all joy and peace in believing, so that you may abound in hope *by the power of the Holy Spirit*" (emphasis added). Clearly, hope is not a human accomplishment, but the gift of our gracious God.

The hope of which Paul writes is not a pie-in-the-sky kind of optimism. Neither is it a cheery denial of the painful realities of life and death, injustice and suffering. Paul has wagered his life on a hope that is grounded in the promises of God and looks forward to the reality to which the gospel of Jesus Christ bears witness. Hope is the undaunted force that comes from the Holy Spirit, getting into our human spirits and drawing us beyond the darkness of today and toward the light of the new tomorrow. Encouraged by the marvelous things God has already done, we abide in hope for what is not yet but will surely come to be.

Like the members of the Christian movement in ancient Rome, we who live in today's troubled times have every reason not to hope. One thinks of the world Matthew Arnold pictures, which "Hath really neither joy nor love, nor light / Nor certitude, nor peace, nor help for pain; / And we are here as on a darkling plain / Swept with confused alarms of struggle and flight, Where ignorant armies clash by night."[1]

Taking the long view, Paul knows that the church, if it is to have a future, must be hopeful and share hope abroad. Every Advent, we look again to Christ, not only for our own salvation, but for the redemption of the world. We renew our hope that God will come among us to heal and to save. We discover anew that "the hopes and fears of all the years" are met in a stable in Bethlehem, the place where God became flesh among us, and the whole world had new reason to hope.

I love these glad lines written by the poet Rainer Maria Rilke: "My eyes already touch the sunny hill, / going far ahead of the road I have begun. / So we are grasped by what we cannot grasp; / it has its inner light, even from a distance— / and changes us, even if we do not reach it, / into something else, which, hardly sensing it, we already are."[2]

Hope is the light that draws us onward toward the peace and harmony that only God can give.

---

1. "Dover Beach," *The New Oxford Book of English Verse* (New York: Oxford University Press, 1972), 703.
2. Rainer Maria Rilke, "A Walk," quoted by Robert Bly, *Iron Man* (Cambridge, MA: DaCapo Press, 2004), 49.

Romans 15:4-13

Theological Perspective

Israel understood its call this way: "The LORD your God has chosen you out of all the peoples on earth to be his people, his treasured possession. It was not because you were more numerous than any other people that the LORD set his heart on you and chose you.... It was because the LORD loved you" (Deut. 7:6–8).

This deeper, divine acceptance leads to harmony in the community and to glorifying God "together" and "with one voice" (v. 6). Granting their differences, Paul prays that they may nonetheless have joy and peace with each other.

Our gospel speaks of a God who accepts us as we are. We are capable of accepting others because Christ has accepted us. Barriers are down. We belong.

We are all slow learners in the church. In the "school for sinners," most of us are in the remedial class, but the first and absolute necessity is that we accept that we are accepted. To grow in that awareness is to grow into the potential of truly accepting others. "Love your neighbor as yourself," says God (Lev. 19:18; Mark 12:31).

The great medieval monk Bernard of Clairvaux explained that there are four stages of growth in Christian maturity: (1) love of self for self's sake; (2) love of God for self's sake; (3) love of God for God's sake; (4) love of self for God's sake. God emptied himself so that he might become flesh like us (see Phil. 2:5–11).

Much of the self-help literature and world of advertising asserts, by way of contrast, that you must "love yourself," that "you deserve to be pampered," that the first love is "love of self." This basic love is certainly critical, but it can also be quite self-deceiving and illusory.

The challenge of our reading today is that ultimately love reaches out to the other, expands the boundaries of self, even empties the self of all self-seeking, for the sake of Christ, because that is precisely what God has already done. Imagining such free giving of selves to one another, it is not surprising that the last word Paul speaks in this passage is one of hope.

PATRICK J. HOWELL

Pastoral Perspective

Paul calls Christians to another way of living, another way of relating: Welcome one another. It is a model of gracious reciprocity based on the most profound of theological insights: God has already welcomed *all*—and so there is no longer slave or free, Jew or Greek, male and female (Gal. 3:28). We, of course, must translate: no longer rich or poor, black or white or Hispanic or Asian, no longer gay or straight, no longer evangelical or progressive, no longer free-market capitalist or socialist or libertarian. God has welcomed us all . . . just as we are . . . into God's embrace.

Paul wants to make sure that his audience knows that he is not just making this up, that this is not the result of some wild-eyed idea he has come up with all by himself. No, God's intention to make known this plan of wide embrace is already there in "whatever was written in former days" (v. 4). The clues to God's intentions have been there all along, Paul says. It is now, in the light of Christ, that we can see the true meaning of these texts. So Paul brings out four citations of Hebrew Scripture that point to the inclusion of the Gentiles (the "other," from the point of view of Paul and his community). "Rejoice, O Gentiles. . . . praise the Lord, all you Gentiles!" (vv. 10–11) He saves the best for last, a word that believers were coming to see as a foretelling of the birth of Jesus: "The root of Jesse shall come . . . in him the Gentiles shall hope" (v. 12). Something new has happened that has brought into the world God's ancient promise: *all are welcome*—so welcome one another.

CYNTHIA M. CAMPBELL

confirm the promises made to the ancestors, and became a servant with respect to the Gentiles for the sake of God's mercy, so that they would glorify God. In its current form, without taking such parallelisms into account, perhaps the best translation would be: "Christ became a servant for the circumcised for the sake of God's truth, to confirm the promises made to the fathers, and with respect to the Gentiles on behalf of mercy to glorify God."

However one construes the structure, the point seems clear: Christ's coming shows God was truthful to the patriarchs when God promised that through them all humankind would be blessed (Gen. 12:1–3). Therefore Jews can trust God and in that trust welcome others. Christ's coming also shows God's mercy in that Gentiles—now also included in God's people—can praise God. On the basis of that mercy, Gentiles can also now welcome others because God in Christ has shown himself to be merciful.

The citations from Scripture in verses 9b–12, each of which includes the word "Gentile," are drawn from all three parts of the OT: Law (*torah*), Prophets (*nebiim*), and Writings (*ketubim*). Paul apparently intends to show that the whole of Hebrew Scriptures bears witness to God's original plan to include both Gentiles and Jews in one elect people.

Paul may have seen in the quotation in verse 9b a prediction of his mission to the Gentiles. Verses 10b–11 emphasize the inclusiveness of God's call— no one is to be excluded from the people of God who praise God. Verse 12 points to the fact that the unity of Jews and Gentiles is due to the Messiah who is a Jew, yet who represents the hope of the Gentiles.

The word "hope" then becomes the key concept in the prayer wish in verse 13 that concludes the entire passage. Only the power of God, working through the Holy Spirit, can grant both Jew and Gentile joy, peace, faith, and hope. "Hope" is the key word, a hope possible because God controls the future and has given a glimpse of that future by sending Christ. Advent is thus for Christians a time of expectation and joy, of waiting and fulfillment.

PAUL J. ACHTEMEIER

Harmony. Paul's next prayer is that God give the Romans "harmony with one another, in accordance with Jesus Christ" (v. 5). What is the point of such harmony? It is not peace for the sake of peace, but "so that together you may with one voice glorify the God and Father of our Lord Jesus Christ" (v. 6). Our world has forgotten that we human creatures exist, not for the fulfillment of ourselves, but for the glory of God. The text goes on to encourage believers to "welcome one another, just as Christ has welcomed you" (v. 7). Whom did Christ not welcome? The children, the outcasts, the foreigners were all his people, the sheep of his pasture.

No one who has lived for a time in our fractured, fractious world or held membership in the often fractured, fractious church can deny that peace and unity are conditions to which we are not naturally inclined, at least not since the exit from Eden. Paul reminds us that regardless of our natural inclinations to look down upon "the other," God has a different idea in mind for the human race. At one time, the Gentiles were perceived to be outsiders, but now both Gentiles and Jews are included in the covenant God made with "the patriarchs" (v. 8). God expands the covenant. Unity comes, not because somebody had the big idea to be inclusive, but because that is the way God wants us to be, intended us to be in the first place.

"Peace on earth, goodwill among those whom God favors": this is the message the angels will sing, come Christmas Eve. Until then, may the church be the demonstration project of the peaceable kingdom God intends.

In *Seasons of Celebration,* Thomas Merton wrote, "The Advent mystery is the beginning of the end of all in us that is not yet Christ."[3] Until then, may harmony mark our holidays, and may the peace of Christ calm and correct our divided world.

JOANNA M. ADAMS

---

3. Thomas Merton, *Seasons of Celebration: Meditations on the Cycle of Liturgical Feasts* (Notre Dame, IN: Ave Marie Press, 2009), 77.

Matthew 3:1-12

¹In those days John the Baptist appeared in the wilderness of Judea, proclaiming, ²"Repent, for the kingdom of heaven has come near." ³This is the one of whom the prophet Isaiah spoke when he said,

"The voice of one crying out in the wilderness:
'Prepare the way of the Lord,
   make his paths straight.'"

⁴Now John wore clothing of camel's hair with a leather belt around his waist, and his food was locusts and wild honey. ⁵Then the people of Jerusalem and all Judea were going out to him, and all the region along the Jordan, ⁶and they were baptized by him in the river Jordan, confessing their sins.

Theological Perspective

Advent has traditionally been a season of preparation. The church over the centuries has come to understand that Christians need to set aside regular times of the year to consider again the full significance of what God has done for us in Jesus Christ. The meaning and joy of Christmas will easily elude us unless we make a focused effort to dwell ahead of time on all the promises of God that have come to fulfillment in Jesus' birth.

The church's traditional Advent practice stands in tension with contemporary culture. The rhythms of a secular, consumer society have displaced the church year. In that society, preparations for Christmas have been reduced to hanging twinkling Christmas lights, listening to cheery holiday music, and gazing at an abundance of material goods for the buying, all of which we hope will evoke in us a sense of magical, childlike wonder and goodwill. Not the promises of God, but our own ideals and longings, have become the focus.

How different is the preparation to which John the Baptist calls the people of Israel! The promises of God that are coming to fulfillment in Christ should compel people to confess their sins. John asks us to examine ourselves, rather than bask in holiday wonder. We should bear good fruit, rather than worry about material things to get or give. John is almost a

Pastoral Perspective

Here is what we do not want in our church lives—especially at Advent.

We do not want judgment.

And we do not want nostalgia.

We Do Not Want Judgment at Advent. Every congregation I have served as pastor has been populated in large measure by Christians recovering from Christian judgment. Christian spouses who are divorced and have remarried are recovering from churches that provide unbending interpretations of Mark 10:11–12.

Gay and lesbian Christians are recovering from churches that provide implausible interpretations of 1 Corinthians 6:9, where Paul says that *malakoi* and *arsenokoitai* will not inherit the kingdom, though no one knows for sure what these Greek words mean.

Inquiring Christians are recovering from churches that read 2 Timothy 3:16 ("All scripture is inspired by God") as the place where Paul requires a literal interpretation of Scripture, though it may well be that Paul did not "literally" write this letter.

So Christians quite appropriately come to accepting churches where they will feel at home.

Then here comes John the Baptist: "You brood of vipers! Who warned you to flee from the wrath to come? . . . [Jesus'] winnowing fork is in his hand,

[7]But when he saw many Pharisees and Sadducees coming for baptism, he said to them, "You brood of vipers! Who warned you to flee from the wrath to come? [8]Bear fruit worthy of repentance. [9]Do not presume to say to yourselves, 'We have Abraham as our ancestor'; for I tell you, God is able from these stones to raise up children to Abraham. [10]Even now the ax is lying at the root of the trees; every tree therefore that does not bear good fruit is cut down and thrown into the fire.

[11]"I baptize you with water for repentance, but one who is more powerful than I is coming after me; I am not worthy to carry his sandals. He will baptize you with the Holy Spirit and fire. [12]His winnowing fork is in his hand, and he will clear his threshing floor and will gather his wheat into the granary; but the chaff he will burn with unquenchable fire."

Exegetical Perspective

Advent not only marks a new beginning, but it defines a time of transition, and this may be why John the Baptizer is the focus for the Second Sunday of Advent. John has one foot in the old age that is coming to a close and the other foot in the new age that is being born. No less than Samuel, John is a bridge between eras in Israel's history. The sources for Matthew's construction of this picture of John the Baptizer are at least Mark and Q (the sayings source composed of sayings found in Matthew and Luke but not in Mark). A quick review of the sources of Matthew's narrative will reveal his compositional control: Verses 1–2, 4–6, and 11 are drawn from Mark. Verses 3, 7–10, and 12 are drawn from Q.

The passage can be outlined as follows: (1) "John's prophetic witness" and "life on the margins" (vv. 1–6); (2) the "same old, same old" and "the empire strikes back" (vv. 7–10); and (3) "hope springs eternal" (vv. 11–12). It may be helpful to examine each section more closely.

In verses 1–6, something unusual is happening. In the ancient world, power was concentrated in central cities, where the temples and imperial buildings witnessed to the power of the current regime. In the center were located the bureaucracies that collected tribute and other direct and indirect taxes. As a general rule, if people wanted to get something or get

Homiletical Perspective

The person of John the Baptist attracts immediate attention as a tough-minded, straightforward, no-nonsense preacher. John may have been like Alexander Whyte (1836–1921), noted preacher at Free St. George's Church in Edinburgh. It was said that Whyte could be so direct and penetrating that to hear him preach was to take your life in your hands.[1] Whether they knew it or not, those who went into the wilderness to hear John did the same thing. His example leads to one of the toughest questions that can be asked about our preaching: Is anything really at stake when people listen to us? Do persons have to take their lives in their hands when they come to hear us?

John's wilderness preaching brings to mind a memorable line from Stanley Hauerwas and William H. Willimon. Without confessing which of the two thinks it, they write, "Indeed, one of us is tempted to think there is not much wrong with the church that could not be cured by God calling about a hundred really insensitive, uncaring, and offensive people into ministry."[2] If they overstate the case, it is not by much. Since John here seems to qualify as one of the

1. John Kelman, "Whyte of St. George's," in *The Best of Alexander Whyte*, ed. Ralph G. Turnbull (1958; reprint, Grand Rapids: Baker, 1968), 26.
2. Stanley Hauerwas and William H. Willimon, *Resident Aliens* (Nashville: Abingdon Press, 1989), 167.

Matthew 3:1-12

Theological Perspective

comical figure, dressed in camel's hair and eating locusts and wild honey, but his message is hard-hitting: "Repent, for the kingdom of heaven is at hand."

Repentance is a confusing concept to many Christians today. Does it mean feeling sorry for our mistakes? Is it a matter of trying to be a better person? Is repentance something that we even need to do, if our lives are now hidden with Christ, our Savior? For some Christians, language of repentance dredges up feelings of guilt and unworthiness, and may even evoke a deathly fear of a day of judgment, when God will separate the wheat from the chaff. For them, the question soon becomes, Can I ever be sure enough that I will experience God's mercy rather than God's wrath?

What John—and Advent—remind us is that repentance is not primarily about our standards of moral worthiness, but rather about God's desire to realign us to accord with Christ's life. Repentance is not so much about our guilt feelings as about God's power to transform us into Christ's image. For Matthew, John's strange clothes and harsh sayings are necessary aspects of communicating the full meaning of the gospel. While warm and fuzzy feelings at Christmastime are not all wrong, they fail to capture the full picture of what God has done for us in becoming human flesh.

Matthew uses several key images to enlarge our vision. One important image is the *wilderness*; John preaches in the wilderness and is a voice crying out in the wilderness. Wilderness evokes memories of the joyous yet troubled history of Israel. God led the people of Israel out of bondage into the wilderness, yet they feared that God had brought them there to die. They sinned and rebelled against God in the wilderness, yet also learned to trust and obey God there. The repentance that befits the church's observance of Advent will have similar dynamics. We will remember and affirm that Christ has brought each of us out of bondage and has fundamentally reoriented our life. Our own wanderings in the Christian life will not be without wilderness hesitancy and resistance, yet God promises to keep pointing the way ahead.

A second key image for Matthew is *baptism*. John baptizes people in the Jordan as they confess their sins. This baptism, says John, points forward to a more radical baptism in Christ and by the power of the Holy Spirit. This new baptism will be much more than a symbol of our own efforts to live according to God's will, for it will represent God's act of fully claiming us for new life in Christ. Advent

Pastoral Perspective

and he will clear his threshing floor and . . . the chaff he will burn with unquenchable fire."

It is easy to hope that John had only scribes and Pharisees in mind when he pronounced such judgment, but the larger context of the chapter and the entire context of Matthew's Gospel make clear that we all need to be on our toes. Because John, and the Jesus he announces, arrive with the most astonishing combination of acceptance and admonition. We all discover this Advent, not only that we are cherished for who we are, but that we are responsible for what we do.

That can be good Advent news, because if God does not care about what I do, I will begin to suspect that God does not actually care about me. If God loves me enough to welcome me into Christ's family, then God loves me enough to expect something of me. (What God expects, it need hardly be said, is not necessarily what churches that specialize in judgment expect; see Matt. 7:1–2.)

William Muehl underlines this point in an appropriately Adventesque story:

> One December afternoon . . . a group of parents stood in the lobby of a nursery school waiting to claim their children after the last pre-Christmas class session. As the youngsters ran from their lockers, each one carried in his hands the "surprise," the brightly wrapped package on which he had been working diligently for weeks. One small boy, trying to run, put on his coat, and wave to his parents, all at the same time, slipped and fell. The "surprise" flew from his grasp, landed on the floor and broke with an obvious ceramic crash.
>
> The child . . . began to cry inconsolably. His father, trying to minimize the incident and comfort the boy, patted his head and murmured, "Now, that's all right son. It doesn't matter. It really doesn't matter at all."
>
> But the child's mother, somewhat wiser in such situations, swept the boy into her arms and said, "Oh, but it does matter. It matters a great deal." And she wept with her son.[1]

It does matter. Our Advent worship, Advent hymns, Advent expectations, and Advent comforts require the reminder that John the Baptist makes so clear. It does matter. We do matter.

Perhaps the church can give up on judgment, but we cannot give up on responsibility.

We Do Not Want Nostalgia at Advent. Our people may want nostalgia, but we do not. They are ready to

---

1. William Muehl, *Why Preach? Why Listen?* (Philadelphia: Fortress Press, 1986), 82.

something done, they would travel to a center city. The margins came to the center, but not the reverse.

In this portrayal of an obscure wilderness prophet, a peripheral prophet, John remains on the margins, and the center comes to him. In this passage, people from Jerusalem (a central city), "all Judea," and "all the region along the Jordan" (areas under the control of Jerusalem) came to John. Of course, the "all" is hyperbole, but its effect is to emphasize the extent of John's surprising influence.

John "appears" on the margins, the "wilderness of Judea," proclaiming the coming of an empire profoundly different from the Roman Empire and the client kingdom of Herod Antipas. The wilderness (*erēmia*) was in Israel's history the place of renewal where the revelation of the Torah was given, and it was a place of judgment where a hardhearted generation perished for lack of faith. The echoes of Isaiah 40:3 (v. 3) indicate that Matthew may be invoking the theme of new creation and new exodus so deeply embedded in Second Isaiah. So also for Matthew, the wilderness will be a place of both judgment and redemption.

John is clearly described as a prophetic figure speaking with a prophetic voice and performing a prophetic symbolic action—baptism. He stands in the tradition of Second Isaiah, who announced the need for someone to show the people how to find a "way" in the "wilderness." John's words are as important as his symbolic action. Note that the description of John as Elijah (v. 4; see 2 Kgs. 1:8) follows directly the quote from Isaiah. John will not be a prophet with connections to the centers of power (as Isaiah had been) but will live on the periphery. His food will be the food of the poor (locusts with whatever honey he can find), and his clothing will be the clothing of the poor, the common camel's hair smock of the bedouins.

This strongly ascetic prophet was admired and, as the Gospel traditions indicate, his baptism was considered to be from heaven (Matt. 21:23–27). Living on the margins did not render John marginalized; it provided him with a prophetic distance from the issues of his day. Perhaps it would be better to say that John created "liminality" through his proclaiming and baptizing. It is difficult for us to realize what a challenge his prophetic witness was to the authorities who came from the center, Jerusalem, and the temple in Judea. John was baptizing those who were confessing their sins, a redemptive activity usually reserved for the temple and the sacrificial system controlled by the high priests and the priestly caste.

hundred, no sermon true to this text can avoid at least some edginess.

The image of the wilderness is as appealing as John himself, and there is value in thinking about the wilderness as the location of *our* preaching and not just John's. How and to what extent do preaching and church life take place in a wilderness today? Every wise and sincere congregation works hard to be warm, friendly, inviting, and do all it can to make persons feel at home. Nevertheless, worship is always something of a wilderness where people think their lives through and wonder about all that is unknown and frightening and causes them to double- and triple-check their holds on what is reassuring. No matter how beautiful the sanctuary, the pew where people sit with their fears, worries, responsibilities, and all the rest is a kind of wilderness place where people confront the howling winds, thorny brambles, and lonely emptinesses of their lives. All this is the stuff of life, and the stuff of the preaching moment.

Verses 5 and 6 give us license to think the harshest wilderness is within the hearer. Matthew tells us people went out to John to confess their sins. Few topics are more "churchy" and religious than that; so, fearing the subject is trite, some pulpits may be led away from taking it up as a theme. Other pulpits may shy away from the subject of sin for fear of appearing prudish or moralistic. Matthew's text may contain hyperbole, but these verses remind us that pews rush in where pulpits fear to tread. Persons in the pews before us may have no doctrine of sin but they have the experience of it and the desire to be rid of it. They at least know that they have themselves to contend with and that, in all their relationships and undertakings, they are their own worst enemies and do not seem to be able to get out of their own way. Whatever else they may be dealing with in their lives when they come to worship, they are dealing with this.

What kind of preaching is needed in the wilderness today? John's methods supply ample materials for a lesson in wilderness homiletics. If we want to give him a theological label, we could call him a kind of liberal evangelical. He is somehow both at the same time. He challenges the conservatism of his day, which seeks entitlement in bloodlines and position; yet he does not use new ideas or theologies but ones from the very heart of tradition, such as sin, judgment, and repentance.

John's wilderness sermon addresses the persons who are before him. When he sees particular people in the congregation (here the Pharisees and Sadducees) he does not trim his message to please them,

Matthew 3:1-12

Theological Perspective

has similar meanings. We repent as we remember and affirm the new identity given us in baptism. We have been buried and raised with Christ, and have been adopted into the family of God.

Other key images evoke God's judgment and wrath. The ax is being laid to the root of the trees; every tree without good fruit will be thrown into the fire; Christ has a winnowing fork to thresh the grain; the chaff will be burned with an unquenchable fire. Matthew wants to make clear that the kingdom of God brings about a fundamental break with the past. The world no longer goes about its normal business. Human ideals and longings have been shaken to the core. At the same time, God's judgment is essentially related to God's promises: the old is passing away, in Christ the new has come. Similarly, in Advent the church practices repentance as it remembers and affirms that this world no longer has the last word, and that we live instead by hope in a new heaven and earth.

The preparation to which John calls Israel, like the preparation to which Advent calls the church, happens not primarily as self-purification but rather by way of a radical trust that Christ himself is working to purify us and the world around us to become a dwelling place fit for himself. Remembrance of God's promises nurtures this trust, and faithful service to the world affirms it. We need the space that Advent provides for remembering and affirming Christ's incarnation and all that it means for us.

The church's rediscovery of Advent will come in small steps, such as when we learn the difference between Advent hymns and Christmas carols, recover ancient practices of Advent fasting and waiting, or pray the daily lectionary of Advent with its themes of judgment and purification. These Advent disciplines prepare us for Christmas joy and feasting (including holiday lights, music, and presents!) when they finally arrive. But this Advent preparation also does something more. It rehearses us in the way of life that should flow out of Christmas, a life marked by a steady confidence that God's kingdom is indeed at hand.

JOHN P. BURGESS

Pastoral Perspective

pull out "O Little Town of Bethlehem" and "Silent Night" by the Second Sunday of Advent, but we have the good sense to know that there are still four stanzas of "O Come, O Come, Immanuel" to go before we light that final candle.

They want the Christmas pageant to be just the same as it was last year and the sixty-two years before that, preferably in the King James Version; and God forbid that we depart from the traditional poinsettias by introducing red chrysanthemums for this holy season. Because Advent is about looking back, they think. Feeling good about what used to be.

"Advent is about looking ahead," we pray and preach and teach, "waiting expectantly for what is to come."

Then here comes John the Baptist, dressed up in such a way as to remind us of old Elijah and speaking words taken directly from old Isaiah. "The voice of one crying out in the wilderness: 'Prepare the way of the Lord, make his paths straight.'"

Here comes John the Baptist to remind us that in the odd economy of God's grace—as we find it in Scripture—we look forward only by looking back. The Jesus we wait for in our future was already planned for in God's past.

Maybe our people are not as hopeless as we thought. Looking back on Advent past they find the courage to trust in Advent present and wait for Advent to come. Those ghosts who made Scrooge look back before he could look ahead had a point.

Nostalgia is memory filtered through disproportionate emotion. Faith is memory filtered through appropriate gratitude.

We sometimes use our liturgies and our prayers and our sermons and even our pastoral care to play make-believe with our people. "Move toward the future and make believe you have no past." "Wait for Jesus to come and pretend that you do not already know how the story turns out, so that when we sing 'Joy to the World' you can try to be not only grateful, but astonished."

It is an exercise in false piety to come to the manger without remembering the cross, and it is an exercise in false liturgical correctness to read Isaiah's "for unto us a child is born" while pretending that we do not know what George Frideric Handel and the church have made of that promise.

Perhaps for Advent we can give up on nostalgia, but we cannot give up on memory.

So, go ahead and sing "O Little Town of Bethlehem" this week.

DAVID L. BARTLETT

Exegetical Perspective

In verses 7–10 we see that, if the peripheral prophet would not travel to the center, then the center would journey to the margins to assess the significance of the challenge and the danger it posed. A good deal hinges on the meaning of a preposition (*epi*), which can mean either "coming for (*epi*) baptism" or "coming against (*epi*) baptism." The latter reading fits the context better than the first reading. The Pharisees were a political interest group with a holiness agenda for Israel, and they promoted their program by aligning themselves with factions in the powerful ruling class (both lay and priestly). Though they differed in many and significant ways, both Pharisees and Sadducees would perceive John as a threat to their interests, especially any attempt to reduce the sphere of influence of the temple through an appeal to John's "baptism from heaven" (Matt. 21:25–26).

Their opposition also explains John's immediate hostile reaction to their appearance. He knows that they oppose what he is doing, and, like any honorable man, he will attack his opponents rather than wait for their verbal assaults. The images are strong: vipers slithering ahead of a rapidly spreading fire. Snakes were, of course, unclean animals, so John is adding insult to injury. John then turns his attack to their inevitable appeal to special status through relationship with Abraham. The appeal is an attempt to define insiders (the elite of Abraham's offspring and covenant community) and outsiders (John's desert community) and, in this context, a reminder that they are the insiders.

John responds by mixing images of judgment (ax; cut down; thrown into the fire; winnowing fork; burn chaff; vv. 10, 12) and hope (one more powerful than I; baptize with fire and Holy Spirit; gather wheat into God's granary; vv. 11–12). Note that fire relates to judgment and hope. The passage looks forward to the grand transition: the advent of a new age that can be reached only by finding a way through the wilderness and living through judgment into hope.

WILLIAM R. HERZOG II

Homiletical Perspective

but rather speaks in a way that reaches them. How many sermons delivered on any given Sunday miss the mark because they do not speak to the people present?

John Ames, the main character in Marilynne Robinson's *Gilead*, tells of once scrapping an antiwar sermon that pleased him very much. He scrapped it because the only ones who would be present to hear it were a handful of old people who agreed with him already and who had no power. "Mirabelle Mercer," he concluded, "was not Pontius Pilate, and she was not Woodrow Wilson, either."[3] Like John Ames, John the Baptist directs his words to persons who are present rather than far away.

John's wilderness sermon is, for the most part, in the present tense. The matter seems to hinge almost entirely on what God is doing now, or is about to do. He reports on what he sees to be true now. We who preach may love history and the inner workings and plots of texts. The stories of old are, indeed, key to our theology and preaching; but those sermons that tell what God is doing today have the best chance to be interesting and make a difference. To see how this can happen, take an old sermon and change the tense of the verbs from the past to the present. See how much a simple change like this brings life, movement, and interest to what was otherwise true but flat.

John's wilderness sermon points beyond himself to God. Whatever our message is going to be, it is not going to be found in ourselves. We are not the message. The church is not the gospel. The community of faith is not the savior. Preaching worthy of the name strives to point ever and always to Jesus. He should increase in every sermon, and the preacher, and even the church, should decrease.

MARK E. YURS

---

3. Marilynne Robinson, *Gilead* (New York: Farrar, Straus & Giroux, 2004), 43.

Isaiah 35:1-10

[1]The wilderness and the dry land shall be glad,
    the desert shall rejoice and blossom;
    like the crocus [2]it shall blossom abundantly,
    and rejoice with joy and singing.
The glory of Lebanon shall be given to it,
    the majesty of Carmel and Sharon.
They shall see the glory of the LORD,
    the majesty of our God.

[3]Strengthen the weak hands,
    and make firm the feeble knees.
[4]Say to those who are of a fearful heart,
    "Be strong, do not fear!
Here is your God.
    He will come with vengeance,
with terrible recompense.
    He will come and save you."

[5]Then the eyes of the blind shall be opened,
    and the ears of the deaf unstopped;

Theological Perspective

We are accustomed to read in sacred Scriptures that the people of God are to rejoice. Many a psalm makes this point. But in this chapter, as the prophet shares God's vision for Judah, even the desert—the dry places and the wilderness—is seen rejoicing in God's glory. The created order shares in the divine glory and in the work of reconciliation: "The wilderness and the dry land shall be glad, the desert shall rejoice and blossom; like the crocus it shall blossom abundantly, and rejoice with joy and singing" (vv. 1–2). A land that was scorched by the enemy in war will be renewed and restored as the people are reminded that they and the land belong to God. God's grace is not limited to human beings but reaches to all of creation.

The lectionary offers this scriptural text during the Third Sunday of Advent as we are reminded that God prepares the way for the coming of the Messiah. The good news of Advent is: "Behold your God is coming." The promise of divine presence means that judgment makes room for salvation. God's graciousness and generosity are expressed to all of creation. God has not given up on God's original purpose for creation; the intrusions and breaks that are caused by sin are met with God's judgment as the way is prepared for salvation. The God of creation is faithful and will bring all things to their rightful end.

Pastoral Perspective

In some churches, each Sunday of Advent is represented with a particular word: Hope for the first Sunday, then Peace, Joy, and finally Love. Whether or not we are in churches that observe these themes explicitly, it is worth noting that this text from Isaiah is an extraordinary match to the traditional theme of Gaudete (Rejoice) Sunday, the Third Sunday of Advent. Joy pulses through Isaiah 35 from the first line, with its glad lands and blossoming deserts, to the last, when a ransomed people come home singing.

The transformation promised in the previous Isaiah texts for Advent glistens here in every line; redemptive reversals will be dramatic and complete. What kind of changes do worshipers in Advent seek? What do they sigh for, what sorrows have brought them to tears? We may not know what haunts each heart in the room, but we can take a cue from Isaiah, who speaks in detail of how the world looks now, and what it will be when God has saved it. Just as the prophet wrote for a scattered people, we too speak to people living fragmented lives in a fractured world, with torn-apart families and broken hearts.

The text speaks concretely of wholeness: the blind will see, the deaf will hear, the lame will leap, the mute will sing. Surely this promise goes deeper than the physical, to the spiritual. Such healing also has a communal dimension, since disability, like disease,

⁶then the lame shall leap like a deer,
  and the tongue of the speechless sing for joy.
For waters shall break forth in the wilderness,
  and streams in the desert;
⁷the burning sand shall become a pool,
  and the thirsty ground springs of water;
the haunt of jackals shall become a swamp,
  the grass shall become reeds and rushes.

⁸A highway shall be there,
  and it shall be called the Holy Way;
the unclean shall not travel on it,
  but it shall be for God's people;
no traveler, not even fools, shall go astray.
⁹No lion shall be there,
  nor shall any ravenous beast come up on it;
they shall not be found there,
  but the redeemed shall walk there.
¹⁰And the ransomed of the Lord shall return,
  and come to Zion with singing;
everlasting joy shall be upon their heads;
  they shall obtain joy and gladness,
  and sorrow and sighing shall flee away.

Exegetical Perspective

Most scholars believe that this passage (as well as chap. 34) is displaced from the section of the book of Isaiah called Second Isaiah, chapters 40–55. It shares with that second portion of Isaiah a background of Babylonian exile (587–539 BCE). This oracle in chapter 35 is a promise to the exiles that God will redeem his people from exile and bring them once again to Mount Zion. Its tone of promise and restoration sits out of place in the context of chapters from the eighth-century prophet Isaiah, who calls Judah to repentance in the hope of avoiding judgment and exile. It may well be that the editorial insertion of narrative material from the book of 2 Kings (to become Isa. 36–39) was clumsily handled and inserted after Isaiah 35 instead of after Isaiah 33. This earlier placement would have made what is now chapters 34–35 the opening lines of Second Isaiah.

The central image of this oracle of promise is that of the people's return through the wilderness once again to the land of promise. The journey of exodus is repeated, only this journey through the wildness is begun with a picture of the wilderness blossoming and flourishing with life. In verses 1–2 the wilderness is no longer a fearsome place of trial and testing, struggle and suffering. Instead, it is a place of joy and singing (v. 2a) and the revealing of the glory and majesty of God (v. 2b). This is a familiar theme in

Homiletical Perspective

All four Old Testament readings for Advent in Year A are from Isaiah, but the first three are sisters, sharing some distinctive qualities that are absent in the fourth. Each is a poem. Each envisions fantastic transformations. Each pertains to massive numbers of people. Each involves changes in creation itself. Each describes the ultimate future of the world under God. If we preach all three texts, we might effectively, if briefly, now trace their continuities and point to how this week's text extends them.

While the first two texts celebrate coming transformations of weapons, economies, social orders, and animals, Isaiah 35 announces coming transformations of land and of human disabilities, locations, emotions, and destinies. It sings of liberations, jubilant homecomings, and the end of all sorrow and sighing. It replaces deserts with acres of bright blossoms, streams, pools, marshes. More exuberant than the preceding texts, it reports leaping, singing, rejoicing, gladness, and "everlasting joy." Our text is finer poetry too. Isaiah 35 has the feel of a culmination: a cascade of bright images, a ringing of many bells.

Which makes it a challenge to preach. What does one do with such a swirl of happy glimmers from a dream? Where do we focus? What do we leave out? How can the sermon find movement? As always with such texts, how do we translate these extravagantly

Isaiah 35:1-10

Theological Perspective

If this prophecy imagines God's reach beyond humanity on to all creation, humanity can also take heart that it is included in God's care for all creation. The good news at Advent is that God has not taken off on a retreat but that the God who cares for the dry and barren places cares for each and all of us. God shows up even in the desert and barren places of life to await us in renewal, restoration, and salvation. The God who cares for the earth also cares for us, offering change not only for the wild and barren places but also for those who are faint in heart and weak at the knees. According to the prophet, "sinking hands and tottering knees" are to be strengthened. In anticipation of the God who awaits us in a new future, we are challenged "to be strong and of good courage."

The circumstances on the ground that confront God's people on a daily basis are similar to the desert and the wilderness, but the God who awaits us is faithful and has prepared a new future for the covenant people. Hope includes a new confidence that the barren and dry places will be made verdant. The presence of God provides courage and strength for all who are timid and afraid of tomorrow.

There are rational and genuine reasons why Judah is scared. Enemies are real and powerful. In their own strength and efforts, the people would be made like the dry places and barren land, but the God who has covenanted to restore creation is faithful and will come to save them. This is the interpretive key: God is their salvation. It is God who saves. It is the promise of divine presence that strengthens sinking hands and failing knees. From a physical point of view, Judah is no match for Assyria; but all creation, including the dry and barren places, can give glory to God because God is on the way to save God's people. "Behold, your God is coming" in liberation and salvation.

It is important to note in this passage that when God shows up, God comes with vengeance—on the one hand, to thwart all that would impede the return of God's people to God and, on the other hand, to provide a new future for Judah. God always comes in judgment and salvation. Whatever separates God's creation and God's people from God's purpose must come under the divine judgment. Obstacles will be removed and the covenant restored as people and the created order enter the sphere of salvation.

The divine presence means deliverance from sin, separation, and all its consequences. The prophet points to the marks of salvation in the new future that awaits God's people. "Then the eyes of the blind shall be opened, and the ears of the deaf unstopped; then the lame shall leap like a deer; and the tongue

Pastoral Perspective

would render a person "unclean" and therefore excluded from the community. Preachers of this text should name contemporary equivalents of such brokenness—personal, communal, global.

Though Isaiah's vision of healing is intended as a joyful promise, contemporary understandings of disabilities call for sensitivity on the part of the preacher dealing with such texts. Some people reject the term "disabled" for the phrase "differently abled," under the conviction that what we typically call "disabilities" might instead be understood better as a difference in human experience. In deaf culture, for instance, deafness is not viewed as a condition requiring fixing; it is embraced as a distinctive characteristic.

This sentiment may not be articulated as strongly from other communities of people with disabilities, but the resistance to old clinical and charitable understandings is growing. To preach this passage (which resonates with themes throughout Scripture, including Jesus' own healings) in the context of people living with physical limitations can be a powerful experience, but the pastor should first consider how hearers may feel about their own "disabilities." The elderly person struggling with macular degeneration or the person living with a spinal cord injury may receive the news from Isaiah very differently from the young adult who accepts her deafness as an essential and positive part of her identity.

How might a pastor be attentive to the true good news of the reversals God offers—the transformation and wholeness of both body and spirit—while honoring these different understandings of disability? How does the preacher attend to the spiritual realities of blindness, deafness, lameness, and muteness, without reducing the people who live with those physical realities to something pitiable or subnormal? Our preaching should guard against further isolating people who have already endured too much isolation.[1]

The sense of marginalization that accompanies disability can be acute; this text offers rich possibilities for preaching toward inclusion and communal wholeness, and not simply for those who have suffered isolation because of disability. The accent of

---

1. For further theological and pastoral reflections on disability, see: Thomas E. Reynolds, *Vulnerable Communion: A Theology of Disability and Hospitality* (Grand Rapids: Brazos Press, 2008); Amos Yong, *Theology and Down Syndrome: Reimagining Disability in Late Modernity* (Waco, TX: Baylor University Press, 2007); Hans S. Reinders, *Receiving the Gift of Friendship: Profound Disability, Theological Anthropology, and Ethics* (Grand Rapids: Eerdmans, 2008); Nancy Eisland, *The Disabled God: Toward a Liberatory Theology of Disability* (Nashville: Abingdon Press, 1994).

Third Sunday of Advent

the chapters we call Second Isaiah (e.g., 41:18–19; 51:3) and is designed to bring hope to exiles in Babylon.

The transformed way through the wilderness is also the sign of God's impending new age, when all that is less than whole is restored and made new. Broken creation becomes new creation, and the *shalom* that God intended in creation becomes reality once again. As elsewhere in Scripture, the coming of God's kingdom is signaled by reversals in the world's priorities and understanding. This is why this text has become an Advent reading. In verses 3–4 the weak are given strength, the fearful given courage. The feeble are made firm, and the coming of the Lord brings salvation. Hearing such reversals in Advent readings cannot help but remind us of the many such reversals in worldly notions of power signaled by Mary's Magnificat in Luke 1:46–55.

In verses 5–6a these reversals border on the miraculous, because the vision of this oracle promises that those who suffer disabilities will be made whole. The blind, the deaf, the lame, and the speechless shall be given the same powers given those who do not suffer such disabilities. We should remember the context of these verses in speaking to Babylonian exiles. They are the captives of war and as such have been wounded, maimed, even intentionally blinded, as was King Zedekiah (2 Kgs. 25:7). These marks of war and its suffering will be overcome and all made new and whole.

Even nature will participate in the great reversals of God's new age of deliverance and hope. In verses 6b–7a the wilderness, normally characterized as a parched and dry wilderness, becomes a place of water, pools, and streams. The "haunt of jackals" (barren and rocky desert) becomes a land of marshes and swamps in verse 7b.

Verses 8–9 introduce the theme of a remarkable highway through the desert, where the redeemed people of God may travel in safety and confidence. It will be called the Holy Way and represents the way into a future for exiles who lacked confidence that the future was open or hopeful. Herein lies the significance of this passage for Advent. God's coming signals a future for those who have given in to hopelessness and sorrow. In God, wilderness becomes not a journey of struggle but of hope, and the Advent season rekindles this hope for a way through the wilderness anew each year.

Of course, this is a common image for the passages we identify as Second Isaiah. The most famous is Isaiah 40:3–4, a text heard often in the Advent season

imagined hopes for long-ago Israel into meaningful hopes for current conditions anywhere or everywhere, for present and/or future, for others and/or ourselves, for concrete historical realities and/or for possibilities somehow beyond or deeper than measurable time?

This is exactly the difficulty being dealt with in our text: the problem of connecting old hopes with the need for new ones. Isaiah 35 understands that though certain of the old promises came true, their fulfillments were somehow unfinished, not altogether satisfying, and are in need of new expression. In specific, the promise of a wilderness highway for exiles had already come and gone. Captives from Babylon had returned to Zion long ago, but disappointments met them. Judah was a prolonged devastation; new oppressions overtook it. Now, in the far extended bleakness, this poet chooses, of all things, to retrieve the old vision of a highway in the desert. The promise will be fulfilled once more, says the prophet, but its meaning will be broader, deeper, and more finally true. From everywhere on earth, the "ransomed" will return to Zion. All the scattered promises will be joined in fulfillment together, as in a dance—earth renewed, bodies remade, freedoms conferred, the city reclaimed, new joys bestowed, and sorrow and sighing banished.

The text, in other words, is doing what good preaching must do. It is claiming old texts for new situations, extending their trajectories, suggesting new convergences, re-visioning God's dominion, future and present. This is the move that Advent in particular requires us to make. The promised Immanuel already came and is surely still among us—so why on earth are we singing "O come, O come, Immanuel"? Because Immanuel's visitation among us is an unsatisfied fulfillment. Real captives and refugees suffer in the present; the earth is a burning desert; bodies are broken; cities are joyless; and human hearts everywhere, including our own, are sighing.

It will not always be so, say the text and the sermon. We will seek to stir memories of liberation and glad homecomings, the healing of the broken, the blossoming of joy. Glimpses of Jesus working such wonders would be fitting. We might then turn to the grim realities of refugees and captives in our time, and of bodies and lives broken, and of inconsolable grief. Strikingly, every image in our text of God's ultimate gifts is the exact reverse of what human beings systematically do to the earth and to each other. The prophet declares that desolation,

Isaiah 35:1-10

Theological Perspective

of the speechless sing for joy" (vv. 5–6). All creation will witness to the glory of God that shall cover the earth "as the waters cover the sea" (Isa. 11:9).

The healing of those with physical disabilities is a messianic sign. It is a sign of the time of salvation ushered in by the one who is expected. Our Lord witnesses to this when, in today's Gospel, John the Baptist sends to ask Jesus if he is the expected one. "Go and tell John what you hear and see: the blind receive their sight, the lame walk, the lepers are cleansed, the deaf hear, the dead are raised, the poor have good news brought to them" (Matt. 11:4–5).

Although the people are in a place of desolation, God will prepare a highway for them to the holy city. There is a way from the barren and dry places to this new space and place that God has prepared for the people of God. It will be a highway, indeed a holy way, in the desert for them to travel into God's new future for them. God excels "in making a way out of no way." Like the barren and dry places, God's people shall burst forth in singing and praises to God as they return home to Zion. Behold your God! God shall be your guide.

NOEL LEO ERSKINE

Pastoral Perspective

the text falls on the happy homecoming of those who have been liberated. A highway cuts through the now blooming desert, and God's people travel it without threat, singing on their way home. Isaiah speaks of them as the "redeemed" and the "ransomed of the LORD."

Christians have applied these terms to the experience of salvation; we have sometimes become so facile with such words that we have lost both their history and their depth. In addition to offering the contextual understanding of these words—that Isaiah is writing about those who have actually been brought out of physical, economic, and political slavery by God—the pastor may want to reflect on what bondage looks like in contemporary terms. What economic, political, spiritual, emotional, relational, and religious captivities do congregants struggle under? For the promise of redemption to speak with its full power, the pastor should articulate in concrete terms the many varieties of bondage contemporary listeners face.

How would freedom from such domination appear to the senses? In Isaiah's poem, it looks like coming home, and it sounds like singing. Though Isaiah's endnote is one of joy, our songs and hymns about going home often have a twinge of melancholy in them. Consider some of the old Southern folk hymns: "I'm just a poor wayfaring stranger, I'm traveling through this world of woe; But there's no sickness, toil, or danger In that sweet home to which I go." "When I can read my title clear to mansions in the skies, I bid farewell to every fear and wipe my weeping eyes. I feel like . . . I'm on my journey home."[2] To sing such songs is to acknowledge the same thing we realize when we read Isaiah's words of promise: we still sorrow, and we still sigh, we are not yet home.

This text does what Advent does: it points backward to old promises, which point forward to a fuller, future joy. We still live in the in-between time, as this prophet's people did. We are asked to take heart. God will come and save; we will find our Holy Way toward home, and our mouths will be filled with no more sighing, only song.

STACEY SIMPSON DUKE

2. For an exceptional Advent compilation of Sacred Harp hymns and sermons, consult Fred Craddock and Steven Darsey, *Southern Folk Advent* audio CD (Meridian Herald, 2000).

Exegetical Perspective

because of its use in Handel's *Messiah* and associated in the Gospels with John the Baptist (cf. also Isa. 42:16). In verse 9 we are told that travelers on this highway need not fear ravenous beasts or lions, and those who walk there are the "redeemed" of God.

For a note of irony or humor, those who go to this passage for a hopeful Advent note may take particular comfort that verse 8b promises that not even a fool can go astray on this way of hope. Most of us need this promise at times.

The climactic verse 10 is an exact duplicate of Isaiah 51:11, which is, of course, one of the strong arguments for seeing chapters 34–35 as part of Second Isaiah and addressed to Babylonian exiles. This verse leaves little doubt as to the identity of the addressees, for it promises return to Zion with singing and joy. Zion is the holy mountain on which the temple stood, and the Babylonians had reduced the temple to rubble and carried the citizens in captivity to Babylon. The final word of this verse is one more reversal in this passage of divinely wrought reversals. The "sorrow and sighing" of destruction and despair when Zion was desolated "shall flee away," replaced by "everlasting joy." Exile is replaced by return. The despair of those who were cut off from the future is replaced by the joy of those who see a new and unexpected future become possible.

What a marvelous Advent theme this ending makes! Advent celebrates the story of Jesus' coming—a promised and promising baby born into a Jewish people held in captivity under Rome, despairing about the future. This promise is of return, of restoration, of new ways into the future, and finally of "joy to the world."

BRUCE C. BIRCH

Homiletical Perspective

disability, grief, and sighing for home will all be swept away, overtaken by luxuriance, liberation, health, strength, safety, and multitudes, fools included, singing their way home—and God will send us flowers on the way!

Not everyone gets them. The promises celebrated here include God's "vengeance" and "terrible recompense" (v. 4); and "the unclean shall not travel" the highway home (v. 8). Who are the "unclean" that are barred from the pilgrimage? The first recipients of the text did not likely have to wonder, but perhaps we should, and make our confession, and seek the newness granted to the blind, the deaf, the lame, the mute.

All such wonders can occur because the Lord "will come and save." This is precisely the language of Advent—its longing, its prayer, its horizon—that the Lord will come and save.

With such language, as usual, comes a bracing command. In this poem it holds a prominent place—not as preliminary summons or concluding invitation, but in four strong lines of imperative within the vision itself: Strengthen weak hands! Straighten feeble knees! Tell the fearful-hearted: be strong! do not fear! (vv. 3–4). So the promises are not dreamy, but insist on real consequence in human action and spirit. The vision wants an incarnation in lips, hands, knees, and unterrified hearts. Whatever shape the sermon takes, these words should be sounded with clarity and strength, for they speak both to our mission of expressing good news for a languishing world, and to our own terror, weakness, and lost hopes.

The final words are poignant. "Sorrow and sighing shall flee away" (v. 10b). We are not surprised to hear that sorrow will vanish, but sighing? Beyond sorrow, we sigh with weariness and regret; we sigh for beauty we cannot reach and for understanding beyond our grasp; we sigh in our aching desire for union and love, and in our longing for what we do not even know how to name.

Perhaps in the end it is all a sighing for home. Perhaps it is the sighing of the earth itself—and if biblical faith is true, it is the sighing of God. It will not always be so. The Lord will come and save. The ransomed will come home singing with gladness; and sorrow and sighing, all sighing, will flee away.

PAUL SIMPSON DUKE

Psalm 146:5-10

⁵Happy are those whose help is the God of Jacob,
   whose hope is in the LORD their God,
⁶who made heaven and earth,
   the sea, and all that is in them;
 who keeps faith forever;
⁷ who executes justice for the oppressed;
   who gives food to the hungry.

The LORD sets the prisoners free;
⁸ the LORD opens the eyes of the blind.
The LORD lifts up those who are bowed down;
   the LORD loves the righteous.
⁹The LORD watches over the strangers;
   he upholds the orphan and the widow,
   but the way of the wicked he brings to ruin.

¹⁰The LORD will reign forever,
   your God, O Zion, for all generations.
 Praise the LORD!

Theological Perspective

Psalm 146 is one of the so-called Hallelujah psalms that wrap up the Psalms. While the verse is not in this lection, the text begins with "Hallelujah!" This one word sums up all human response of praise to the God who has created, as Martin Luther put it, "me and all things." Its music gives birth to many songs. For many, "Hallelujah" will bring to mind the chorus from George Frideric Handel's *Messiah*. However, the version that resonates with contemporary people both inside and outside the church is Leonard Cohen's song "Hallelujah."

Cohen's version has been covered by more than 100 other artists, including Jeff Buckley, Rufus Wainwright, k. d. lang, U2, and Bob Dylan, to name just a few of the more famous artists. Why does Cohen's poem-psalm resonate so broadly in popular culture today? In part, the song allows for complexity, acknowledging both the glorious heights of the "holy hallelujah" and our failings that make necessary a "broken hallelujah." Finally, despite all the brokenness of our lives, Cohen claims the bold stance of standing before the Lord of song and singing his praise to the Lord of song. It is as if the promise rings out in the midst of brokenness. God's will for good, for a life of shalom, of both well-doing and doing well, evokes praise, and in the praise arises hope.

Pastoral Perspective

On the Third Sunday of Advent, we are approaching in earnest the celebration of the incarnation. Whereas the second week looks at the political implications of the coming of the Lord, this third week lifts up the very fundamentals of the Christian faith. In Psalm 146 we are counselled to put our trust not in political leaders or mortal human beings, but rather in God. God is described as compassionate and just, trustworthy, and active in the world. The question before the preacher this week is a faith-shaking one: Are these things *really true* in our experience, both preacher and parishioner? Can we trust God to act with justice and compassion in the real world and our real worlds?

This psalm draws a particular picture of God in the mind of the hearer. God is the creator of heaven, earth, and sea—and is therefore ultimately powerful in the world. God is faithful, just, and generous. God pays particular attention to those in need—giving food to the hungry, freedom to the prisoners, sight to the blind, safety and support to the vulnerable, a hand up for those who are bowed down. For judgment, the psalm says that God "loves the righteous" (v. 8) and brings "*the way of the wicked . . . to ruin*" (v. 9, my emphasis). On the one hand, this picture of God surprises no one. God is expected to wear the white hat, to be the embodiment of everything that

Exegetical Perspective

In Hebrew, the book of Psalms is called *Tehillim*, or praises: an odd choice, given that there are far more prayers for help in the Psalter than songs of praise. However, as we saw last week, the Psalms are divided into five parts by four doxologies, so that the book is punctuated with praise. Moreover, the book of Psalms concludes with a series of five rollicking songs of praise, beginning with the psalm for today, all incorporating the shout of praise *halleluyah* (rendered "Praise the LORD" in the NRSV; see 146:1, 10).[1] In this way, the last word of the book (quite literally; see Ps. 150:6!) becomes a word of praise, spoken in the face of trouble, need, and disaster.[2]

Although this psalm begins and ends with hallelujahs (vv. 1 and 10), it moves quickly to a contrast between earthly kings and the heavenly king. In sharp contrast to last week's psalm, which in keeping with ancient Near Eastern traditions as well as biblical precedent regarded the king as guarantor of justice for the oppressed, Psalm 146 offers a warning:

---

1. Gerald H. Wilson, "The Shape of the Book of Psalms," *Interpretation* 46 (1992): 132–33.
2. Jerome Creach writes that lament "gives evidence of faith worked out in the midst of hardship, hurt and loss. Perhaps this is the reason the editors of the Psalter labeled the book 'Praises,' even though it is dominated by the lament genre" ("Between Text and Sermon: Psalm 70," *Interpretation* 60 [2006]: 64).

Homiletical Perspective

The Third Sunday of Advent is traditionally called Gaudete Sunday or Joy Sunday, the day when we turn from preparation and judgment toward expectations of joy and fulfillment. That expectation will only continue to grow as we approach the celebration of the Christ's birth, and today's psalm captures that ebullient spirit.

The psalm reveals how joy is found through reliance on God. The psalmist's words are flung aloft in high hopes for the help that God brings, and we see this demonstrated in swelling praises of God's *shalom*. The exalted words of happiness and the ensuing divine deeds are surely a testament that the psalmist's hope is well founded.

The key components of the psalm are hope, help, and happiness. They invite the preacher to reflect on the mutually influencing aspects of these powerful antidotes to a world in need of redemption.

Hope. There is no doubt that our world is a broken and hurting one—poverty ravages billions globally, preventing them from receiving proper nutrition, medical care, vaccinations, or shelter. Those oppressed by personal or societal injustice experience prejudice, discrimination, violence, or persecution, while others facing physical or psychological illness must struggle to find hope for personal comfort or restitution.

Psalm 146:5-10

Theological Perspective

What sense does it make to speak of a broken hallelujah when the text clearly says, "happy are those whose help is in the LORD" (v. 5)? "Happy," as Bob Dylan once remarked, is a yuppie word. In the first instance, this text, despite the translation of its first word, is not about happiness. At least it is not about happiness in the sense shared by most people in the developed nations of the West, oriented as they are to individuals rationally pursuing "life, liberty, and . . . happiness." No, happiness here is about flourishing. From ancient times, the stark choice has been set before the people of God: walk the way of life or the way of death. This psalm is about walking the way of life. Deep gladness may get at the sensibility of life lived in response to the God described in this psalm.

So when one hears about hope in the Lord as this reading unfolds, by association it is easy to hear the opposite, the broken hope that comes when we put trust in leaders. This psalm, and many like it, rises from the tension between the broken and the holy hallelujah. The biblical witness is not that leaders should be automatically opposed; in fact, they are desperately needed. The issue is rather in trusting rightly, and passage after passage witnesses to the trustworthiness of God rather than human leaders. In fact, one could say that the season of Advent as a whole arises from the tension between the broken realities of actual leadership and the holy trustworthiness of God.

This section of the psalm (and similar texts such as Isa. 35 and Matt. 11, both assigned for this day) offers what one might call a resume of what we can expect when we trust in God. Put better, these few verses offer us a testimony to the basis of God's trustworthiness. That basis begins in a claim of power. This is emphatically not the God of any one tribe or nation, not the pet deity of any prosperity seeker or power grabber. This god is God of all creation, maker of sky, earth, water, and all that lives in them. There is, to paraphrase the Reformed theologian and former prime minister of the Netherlands Abraham Kuyper, not one square inch of all creation over which the Lord does not say, "Mine!"

The creator of all has power beyond measure, yet its exercise does not take the form or character of a tyrant, someone whom we must bribe for our petitions and prayers to be answered. Rather, this powerful God has already taken sides in history, responding to the cries of those in great need, responding with great mercy and transforming love.

The litany is familiar and deeply comforting to all who feel pressed down by the broken power and

Pastoral Perspective

we consider to be good. On the other hand, though, this picture stands in contrast to the way God is often viewed in the culture at large and, truth be told, in the depths of our own Christian hearts.

Richard Dawkins overstates the case, but likely speaks for many, when he writes:

> The God of the Old Testament is arguably the most unpleasant character in all fiction: jealous and proud of it; a petty, unjust, unforgiving control-freak; a vindictive, bloodthirsty ethnic cleanser; a misogynistic, homophobic, racist, infanticidal, genocidal, filicidal, pestilential, megalomaniacal, sadomasochistic, capriciously malevolent bully.[1]

On this Third Sunday of Advent, many in our pews do *not*, in their heart of hearts, believe that God is truly compassionate and just. A woman had just given birth to twins; one of them was stillborn and the other was in intensive care, balanced between life and death. Her first desperate question to her pastor was, "Was there something I did to deserve this?" Many fear God's judgment. Many carry guilt and assume that they are not good enough to be loved by God. Many, in the depths of their hearts, believe that they must be more righteous than they are in order to be loved by God, and that oppression, imprisonment, blindness, loneliness, and suffering are not occasions for God's care but the thin edge of God's condemnation.

Neither Dawkins nor the general populace pulls that harsh image of God out of thin air; suffering and injustice are very real, and the pictures of God presented in the Bible and by the church are, to say the least, complex. Contradictory images of God struggle in the depths of many, and perhaps most, of those who will hear Advent sermons this year. This psalm, so soon before we celebrate the out-of-wedlock stable birth (or the refugee flight) of the Messiah, presents an opportunity to present the good news of unconditional love, and a judgment that falls not upon the person of the wicked, but upon the *way of the wicked*.

That said, this psalm raises an even more troubling question. There are many in this world—and in our own pews on this Third Advent Sunday!—who find themselves in exactly the situations described here. The blind, the widowed, the hungry, the oppressed are called upon to trust God. Is God truly trustworthy? Does God act in tangible ways, bringing grace to the point of our need? Our people are asking that this Sunday.

---

1. Richard Dawkins, *The God Delusion* (Boston: Mariner Books, 2008), 51.

Exegetical Perspective

Do not put your trust in princes,
   in mortals, in whom there is no help.
When their breath departs, they return to the earth;
   on that very day their plans perish.

(vv. 3–4)

However exalted his station, the king remains mortal. Therefore, the institution of kingship is fundamentally flawed. Even assuming that his intentions are good, the king is subject to human weakness and failure; indeed, ultimately, every king *will* fail, because ultimately he will die, and his plans, for good or ill, will be left in the hands of others. To put it another way, kingship cannot bear the weight of ultimacy; no human institution can.

However, God does what the kings either could not, or would not, do. It is the Lord "who executes justice for the oppressed; who gives food to the hungry" (v. 7a). God's reign means freedom for the imprisoned, sight for the blind, exaltation for the humiliated (vv. 7b–8). It is God, not the king, who truly regards the plight of those without advocates—orphans, widows, refugees—and guarantees justice for them (vv. 8–9a). God is *willing* to act because "the Lord loves the righteous . . . but the way of the wicked he brings to ruin" (vv. 8b–9). God is *able* to act because he is the world's creator (v. 6). Unlike the mortal kings of David's line, God's rule is eternal. God can bear the weight of our trust and ultimate regard, for it is the Lord "who keeps faith forever" (v. 6b). Therefore, the psalmist acclaims God's rule:

The Lord will reign forever,
   your God, O Zion, for all generations.

(v. 10)

It is likely that Psalm 146 reflects the reconsideration of God's eternal covenant with David (see 2 Sam. 23:5; cf. also 2 Sam. 7:11b–16) in the time after the exile. Previously, it had been thought that the promise guaranteed the political survival of David's line forever (see, e.g., Ps. 89:35–37). Then Jerusalem fell to the Babylonians, and the succession ended with Zedekiah. Never again would a son of David sit on a throne in Jerusalem.

How was Israel to cope with this disaster? The Psalms respond theologically, by affirming God's reign over any and every false claim to authority over this world (see esp. the enthronement songs, Pss. 24, 29, 47, 93, 96, 97, 98, 99). Psalm 146 stands as a rebuke to the naiveté that had ascribed to the human institution of kingship an ultimacy that even the best and most noble king could not bear.

Homiletical Perspective

The psalmist reminds us that God recognizes the devastating effects of these realities and envisions a world reordered. Hence, we are told that justice is being rendered, prisoners released, the hungry fed, the sick healed, and society's most vulnerable sheltered (vv. 7–9). In the advent of Christ, that work has begun anew. So, looking to our world, we see the manifestations of it. In the abolitionist movement, slaves were freed because of the work of activists like Harriet Tubman, Harriet Beecher Stowe, and William Wilberforce; in the struggle against apartheid, racial equality began to be restored in South Africa because of leaders like Nelson Mandela and Desmond Tutu; and with the advent of medications such as the tuberculosis and polio vaccines, millions of lives have been saved.

Help. For us as Christians, empathy for the global problems that we face comes easily, but so does feeling overwhelmed. An empathic response is true to our nature, and yet we often feel helpless as individuals. What can we do that will make a difference?

It is perhaps most important for us to remember that this work must be accomplished not just at a personal level but at a communal one as well, and that our greatest strength is in numbers. After all, earth holds six billion people, and two billion consider themselves Christians—that's one-third of the global population. Together we can make a difference; the work of alleviating global poverty, oppression, and illness must be done not alone but in community.

One of the frustrating aspects of engaging in this work is that we often will not see the fruit of such labors in our lifetime. This makes it easy to believe that our work is for naught. Nevertheless it is our hope that our efforts will benefit those who come after us, a hope that rests in God, who "will reign forever . . . for all generations" (v. 10). In the meantime, there are many things that we can agree upon across belief systems to work toward the eradication of extreme poverty for the good of God's global family.

Tangible goals will help our hearers hope along with the psalmist. Many faith families have embraced the Millennium Development Goals (MDGs) as helpful tools to work toward God's vision of our world restored. These goals offer a series of poverty reduction targets that can help organize our action. Participating in programs that empower women and girls, support education, build healthy infrastructures, fund research for devastating diseases, and promote environmental sustainability can all help to build the reign the psalmist envisions.

Psalm 146:5-10

Theological Perspective

untrustworthy leadership of this world. The oppressed will finally receive justice; the hungry will be fed; those held in bondage will be freed; the blind will find new sight; those broken down by the weight of their worries will find their load lifted; and the righteous, often despised by the world, will find the Lord of all creation present to them in overwhelming love. If this were not clear enough evidence in the courtroom, offering a witness to the character of this God of power and majesty, we find that this God tends those most marginal, most vulnerable: the stranger, the orphan, the widow. Today, it might be a lonely AIDS orphan in Ethiopia or an illegal immigrant sweating in a hot restaurant kitchen in New York or a scorching field in California.

While God loves the poor, caring for them in particularly tender and specific ways, God also has a strong word for the wicked. Wicked lives are brought to ruin in many ways, but the most significant may be the tears of recognition at the end of life, when one faces the inhumanity of one's own privilege. It is a wretched ruin when one sees, as does Dickens's Scrooge, how stone-hearted hoarding creates its own hell.

More people fall into this hell today than we care to admit. Thus it can be argued that this psalm comes as a critique of leaders, of those in power, of those with wealth and success, asking them how their use of power matches up to God's own character. Does their leadership bend toward mercy as does that of the Lord of space and time? As well, it asks all of us to assess our trust making—even with leaders who seem very noble. If our trust is placed in the Lord alone, we can continue to press our leaders to be trustworthy measured against the picture of God's desired shalom, our longed-for hope in the midst of this broken not-yet time.

CHRISTIAN SCHAREN

Pastoral Perspective

It is all too easy for Richard Dawkins and his many sympathizers in and out of churches to say that God does *not* intervene in the lives of humanity. For examples, they bring up all those hungry who are *not* given food, all those vulnerable who are *not* protected, all those who are bowed down and *not* lifted up. The point is undeniable. Many in this world look to God for help, and the looked-for help never comes. Probably all of us know this experience at some level. Even Jesus knew this experience, on the cross. How can we honestly say that God is faithful and just, and *trustworthy*? If God is *not* pulling puppet strings or interfering with the laws of nature to rescue humanity in time of need, what *is* God doing? How does grace really operate in this real world?

Finally, there seems to be a challenge—and a promise—to our incarnational faith in this psalm, given the time of year. In what way does the church—the body of Christ—incarnate this grace and trustworthiness of God? Where once people could find healing by reaching out to touch the hem of Jesus' garment (Mark 5:25–34) can they now find healing by touching the community of the church?[2] Profoundly, is this true—not just for the masses who suffer out there, around the world, but for those who suffer right here in our midst in this place on this Sunday?

Psalm 146 is a powerful lead-in to the great surprise of Christmas, the birth of the Messiah in a stable, into poverty and oppression. It confronts us with the conflict and contradiction in our images of God. It forces us to look honestly and deeply for the grace of God, the true ways in which God is trustworthy, just, and compassionate. It asks us, as the gospel so often does, to be the change we hope to see in the world. It prepares us for the surprise that God's grace will find us in the places where we are least deserving, and most in need.

DAVID HOLMES

2. For a very helpful discussion of this idea, see Ronald Rolheiser, *The Holy Longing* (New York: Doubleday, 1999).

Exegetical Perspective

Sadly, this temptation is still with us. Too often, Christians have identified the gospel unambiguously with some political party or movement, forgetting that faith's proper role is to critique all human authorities in light of the God made manifest in Jesus. Inevitably, such mistaken investitures of faith end in disillusionment and disappointment. Only God can, and ought to, bear the weight of our ultimate faith and commitment.

The alternate reading for today's Psalter is Luke's Magnificat (Luke 1:46b–55). Like that well-known poem, Psalm 146 is an expression of God's passion for justice and special concern for the poor. Although it lacks the explicit reversals set forth in Mary's song, today's psalm involves an implicit reversal of status, through its contrast between untrustworthy princes and the trustworthy God. In Psalm 146, the righteous, however humble and oppressed, have God's care and regard, while the wicked, however powerful, earn God's enmity (v. 9).

The description of God's work for justice in Psalm 146:7–9 sounds much like the description of Jesus' ministry in the Gospel for today. Indeed, this parallel points us toward another solution to the problem posed by the end of Davidic kingship in Israel: the hope that one day, God would raise up a future descendant of David as Messiah, to usher in God's kingdom. The Christian confession that Jesus is Christ (the Greek *christos* is the equivalent of the Hebrew *mashiach*, or messiah) embraces this idea, though paradoxically: Jesus' identity is revealed through humble service, not through kingly pomp. So, when John the Baptist sends from prison for confirmation that Jesus truly is that promised one, the proof comes in Jesus' care for the needy: "the blind receive their sight, the lame walk, the lepers are cleansed, the deaf hear, the dead are raised, and the poor have good news brought to them" (Matt. 11:5).

It is likely that both the Matthew passage and our psalm are drawn from the vision of a new world of justice and peace in today's Old Testament lesson (see especially Isa. 35:5–6). God's reign means justice and deliverance, particularly for the least and forgotten. When we care for the needy, we act as the hands of Christ in our world and participate in God's coming kingdom here and now.

STEVEN S. TUELL

Homiletical Perspective

To become part of God's work means being part of a biblical ethic in which God "loves the righteous" and the wicked are brought to ruin (vv. 8b, 9b). As J. Clinton McCann Jr. writes, "To be righteous is to trust that one's life fundamentally depends on God. . . . To be wicked means fundamentally to be self-ruled rather than God-ruled. In Biblical terms, wickedness means to be autonomous, which means literally to be a 'law unto oneself.'"[1] Wickedness becomes essentially a question of allegiance: in whom or in what do we trust? In the advent of Christ, radical dependence is writ large in the poverty of the stable, just as it is in the agony of a garden. However, this kind of radical dependence on God and our community is counterintuitive in Western cultures that prize autonomy and independence.

Our mission, then, is one of interdependence in which we strive to participate with one another in God's mission. The work is not ours alone, nor can it be accomplished by us alone. In Africa this kind of interdependence is called *ubuntu*, which Desmond Tutu's words translate: "A person is a person *through* other persons."[2] As persons uniquely created in the image of God, we are truly ourselves only in relationship with others.

Happiness. Our happiness comes in recognizing our total dependence on God, and when we rely on God, joining in the global community working to alleviate poverty and other ills becomes easier. When we partner with our global family near or afar, we not only begin to combat our world's great problems; we also are enriched by the gifts of our neighbors, discover our interconnectedness, and come to know strangers as friends.

Finally, when we rely on God, joy is the result. Empowered by God, we can go into the world, engaging in right relationship with God and neighbor. We can therefore live in a reality that is both God-centered and other-centered. This rightful ordering of our relationships and our place in creation allows us to say yes to the life and labors before us. Therein lies our happiness.

CAROL L. WADE

1. J. Clinton McCann Jr., "Preaching on Psalms for Advent," *Journal for Preachers* 16, no. 4 (1992): 14–15.
2. Desmond Tutu, *God Has a Dream: A Vision of Hope for Our Time* (New York: Random House, 2004), 25.

James 5:7-10

⁷Be patient, therefore, beloved, until the coming of the Lord. The farmer waits for the precious crop from the earth, being patient with it until it receives the early and the late rains. ⁸You also must be patient. Strengthen your hearts, for the coming of the Lord is near. ⁹Beloved, do not grumble against one another, so that you may not be judged. See, the Judge is standing at the doors! ¹⁰As an example of suffering and patience, beloved, take the prophets who spoke in the name of the Lord.

Theological Perspective

The contrast between the first and second readings on this Third Sunday of Advent could not be stronger. Isaiah paints a picture of the parched land exulting, the desert land blooming, and the whole earth rejoicing. In counterpoint, James encourages the early Christians, probably Jewish Christians, to stand firm, not to judge one another, but to bear each other's faults and failings with patience. Isaiah has a theology of exuberance, James a theology of patient endurance.

As Christians, we are invited to live fully into both these realities. We are invited into the paradoxical place of joy and sorrow, of a grace-filled vocation and the daily grind of duty; of the earth bursting with abundance and the dry-as-dust times when the farmer can barely eke out a living.

Traditionally, the Third Sunday of Advent is known as Gaudete Sunday, a command to "rejoice." Even in this penitential season of preparation and expectation, we are commanded to rejoice. Do not get too serious about your ascetical practices; do not cling to your fasts and your prayers, because the birth of Christ is just around the corner. Listen to James, but do not take him too seriously. So rejoice, which is a healthy antidote to the theology of striving found in James.

The mature Christian lives into this paradoxical tension of penance and rejoicing, of expectation and

Pastoral Perspective

Many of us grew up with the adage "Patience is a virtue." It comes to mind as we read the opening words of the text from James: "Be patient, therefore, beloved, until the coming of the Lord." The author compares the patience he encourages to the patience of the farmer who waits for "the early and the late rains." Then, as the passage ends at verse 10, the author connects patience with suffering: "As an example of suffering and patience, beloved, take the prophets who spoke in the name of the Lord." What do patience, suffering, and farming have to do with one another and with the season of Advent?

First of all, the text raises the very pastoral question: In what circumstances is it appropriate to urge people to be patient? When is patience a virtue? Certain kinds of work require patience. The woodworker refinishing a piece of furniture, the jewelry repairer fixing a broken clasp, the quilter carefully stitching fabric, the accountant running trial balances to make sure all records are accurate: all of these must work carefully and patiently, because precision and accuracy are demanded by the work they do. Learning various things often requires patience: years of finger exercises precede playing Bach or Mozart; time on the driving range is needed to master a good golf swing; memorization and repetition are required to learn any new language. All of us

Exegetical Perspective

After condemning the heartless conduct of the rich (5:1–6) toward those who suffer from such conduct, the writer now urges his fellow Christians who also suffer such humiliation to exercise patience, since the Lord is coming as judge. Discussion of such patience extends through verse 11, so it will be included along with verses 7–10.

This epistle has not enjoyed great favor in the church. That can be seen, for example, from Eusebius's fourth-century report that its canonical status was "disputed," as well as from Luther's famous judgment that it was an "epistle of straw" because "it does not show you Christ." The author identifies himself only as James, and the Greek stamp of both language and ideas makes it difficult to ascribe it to Jesus' brother, a Galilean peasant. Although he is often accused of being more Jewish than Christian, the "royal law" of which James writes is not concerned with circumcision, food, or purity regulations. Like Jesus, the author reduces the law basically to loving God and neighbor. Like Paul (e.g., Gal. 5:6) he is convinced that the Christian faith must express itself in works of love (e.g., 1:22–27; 2:14–26).

Our passage is remarkable in two ways. The first is the omission of any reference to the passion of Jesus as an example of patient endurance while suffering (see such references in 1 Pet. 2:21; Heb. 12:3;

Homiletical Perspective

On this Third Sunday of Advent, with Christmas fast approaching, the desire is particularly tempting to throw over the traces of anticipation and preparation to head straightaway for the manger. Happily, James 5:7–10 counters the magnet force of Christmas with compellingly direct rhetoric that pleads for patience "until the coming of the Lord." Using the very down-to-earth image of a farmer waiting patiently for his "precious crop" to grow until "it receives the early and the late rains" (v. 7), the writer implies that the Lord's return will not be just any day now, but will occur when what is needed for his return has fully taken place. The crop can break forth fully only after the second rain.

Facing James's double exhortation to be patient, the problem is that not many of us are farmers, who willingly subject themselves to timetables not of their own making, specifically, the utterly not-under-our-control seasons of nature. Most of us do not have an innate inclination to patience, either. I remember once standing in a line to buy a ticket for a movie when the person in front of me asked everyone in earshot, "Which moves faster—a glacier or this line?"

Of course, there is an important difference between a movie ticket and the return of the Lord. The movie might be sold out when your turn at the

James 5:7-10

Theological Perspective

fulfillment, without collapsing the polarities. It is precisely in this tension that we find our life with Christ, the same Christ who died a hideous death and rose in glory, who welcomed the poor leper and dined with the rich Pharisee, who preached in both the temple courtyard of Jerusalem and on the country hillside of Galilee. Christ, fully human and fully divine, continues to invite us to live life to the full, in all its suffering and sorrow, and to share in his glorification for all eternity.

Orthodox theology through the centuries has insisted, according to G. K. Chesterton, on this paradox "that Christ was not a being apart from God and humans, like an elf, nor yet a being half human and half not, like a centaur, but both things at once and both things thoroughly, very human and very God."[1]

This paradox lies at the heart of Christianity. Christianity did not combine opposites into some kind of favorable blend; rather it holds all dimensions of the human, all the dimensions of the divine in vibrant and furious tension. The church goes in for dangerous ideas. She is a lion tamer. Chesterton adds a final caution, "The idea of birth through a Holy Spirit, of the death of a divine being, of the forgiveness of sins are ideas which, any one can see, need but a touch to turn them into something blasphemous or ferocious."[2]

In his helpful article on biblical paradoxes, Richard Hansen explains, "Paradox is the wild territory within which most ministers live and work. We see unseen things. We conquer by yielding. We find rest under a yoke. We reign by serving. We are made great by becoming small. We become wise by being fools for Christ's sake."[3] Our readings hold this tension together. Each corrects and supplements the other.

Unless we recognize this tension, we can easily read the Epistle of James as a bundle of "straw," as Martin Luther did. Luther, rightly scandalized by the papal sale of indulgences, believed that James emphasized "works" to the exclusion of God's saving, redemptive mercy. The Epistle of James, Luther contended, burdened the human spirit by laying out what we had to do, rather than what we gratuitously received through the sheer mercy of God.

Ignatius of Loyola, a contemporary of Luther, would certainly have agreed with Luther on the priority of God's gratuitous love, but he also urged the

1. G. K. Chesterton, *Orthodoxy: The Romance of Faith* (San Francisco: St. Ignatius Press, 1995), 68.
2. Ibid., 74.
3. Richard Hansen, "Making the Most of Biblical Paradoxes," *PreachingToday.com* (2008): 1–4, http://www.preachtoday.com/skills/artcraft/117–hansen.html.

Pastoral Perspective

understand this kind of patience—the "practice-makes-perfect" kind.

Patience can also be a virtue in situations where waiting is required and where one is essentially powerless to change the circumstances: sitting in the car on the freeway during rush hour, standing in the seemingly interminable security line at the airport, waiting in the checkout line at the grocery store at 5:00 p.m. with a checker who is learning how to run the cash register. In these situations, there is an unavoidable delay. Try as we may, we can exert no control over some important factors in our lives. You can either get angry and fret and feel your blood pressure rise, or you can be patient. This aggravating wait will be familiar to everyone as well.

The example that the author of James uses is a patience more like this second type. The author is thinking of dry-land farming in Palestine before the modern invention of drip irrigation that has turned this semiarid region into productive farmland. In classic dry-land farming (such as the way wheat is grown in the central United States), whether or not there is a crop depends almost entirely on how much moisture falls, in what form, and at what time. There must be rain when the crop is put in to germinate the seed and then rains later to nourish the crop. However, when rain (or worse yet, hail) comes just before harvest, the results can be disastrous. Since there is nothing the farmer can do about this, you learn one way or the other how to wait.

In other situations, however, counseling patience is absolutely the wrong thing to do; it is not a virtue but rather a form of oppression. When one partner in a relationship is being physically or mentally abused by the other, advising the victim to "be patient" is itself a form of abuse. When women and people of color of the United States were seeking the legal right and actual access to vote, they were often urged to "be patient," that these things take time. But as we now recognize, justice delayed is justice denied. In his "I Have a Dream" speech, Martin Luther King famously called this kind of waiting "the tranquilizing pill of gradualism." Patience in the face of unjust circumstances that can be changed is not a virtue; patience with injustice is complicity in the evil that holds the upper hand.

If patience is sometimes but not always virtuous, how does it relate to suffering? We assume that the author is not thinking about individual suffering in the sense of facing illness, disability, or death. Probably the author is thinking about the suffering of the early Christian community as it was dealing with

Acts 7:52, among many others). Such an omission in 5:10–11 is difficult to account for, and has led some to judge the letter as essentially a Jewish writing with a thin Christian veneer. Such a judgment is called into question, however, by the second remarkable feature of the passage. Like the remainder of James, many of the exhortations here show similarities to sayings of Jesus preserved in the Gospels. It is difficult to account for two such different characteristics in the same passage.

Verse 7, with its admonition to patience, reflects the basic theme of the entire epistle (e.g., 1:3–4). It also repeats the exhortation to wait patiently for the return of Jesus (cf. 1:6; 5:17–18). The example of patience here is the farmer who must wait both for the early rain (to soften the ground for planting) as well as for the late rain (to allow grain to ripen) before he can harvest his crop. Such reference to rain (often thought of as a gift of a kindly creator, e.g., Ps. 65:9–11) reflects Deuteronomy 11:14, where early and late rains are signs of God's faithfulness to his people. Such patience is frequently mentioned also by Paul. It is one of the fruits of the Spirit (Gal. 5:22), a characteristic of Christian love in dealing with others (1 Cor. 13:4), and one of the marks of a truly Christian character (Col. 3:12; cf. Eph. 4:2). Being patient "until the coming of the Lord" (a common phrase for the Parousia; cf. Matt. 24:27; 1 Thess. 3:13; 2 Pet. 3:4; 1 John 2:28) points out that although God is patient with the faults and faithlessness of human beings, God's coming divine judgment shows God will not finally ignore the wrongdoings of wicked people.

Verse 8 rounds out the thought of verse 7 and ends with the emphasis on patience and the Parousia (i.e., appearing) of the Lord with which verse 7 began. Such a rhetorical rounding-out prepares for the shift of emphasis contained in verse 9. In Jesus' parables, his return is compared to the harvest (e.g., Matt. 13:39), a comparison implied by the content of verses 7–8. The verb "is at hand," describing the Parousia, is the same word used in Mark 1:15 to summarize Jesus' preaching: "The kingdom of God *is at hand*" (emphasis added).

In verse 9, the emphasis shifts from patience toward outsiders (cf. 5:1–6) to patience toward fellow Christians. The Greek word for "grumble" refers to feelings of a grudge against another. The warning that such judgmental activity will itself be judged reflects Jesus' saying about judgment in Matthew 7:1. That the judge is standing at the door reflects a similar saying of Jesus (e.g., Mark 13:29; Matt. 24:33; Luke 12:36; cf.

ticket counter finally comes, whereas you know that if the Lord has made a promise, supply will not run out. You can bet your life it will come true. Second, like the tiny shoots of green that appear in the soil after the first rain, there are signs all around that what has been promised is already being fulfilled. In the faith communities to whom James writes, "prayers of faith" are saving the sick "and anyone who has committed sins will be forgiven" (5:15). Signs of the nearness of salvation are visible already.

In addition to practicing patience, James prescribes a second spiritual exercise: "Strengthen your hearts," he urges; the reason is the same as the reason for patience: "The Lord is near" (v. 8). By now, we realize that the word "near" in an eschatological sense does not mean "soon," as we think of soon. In his book *Time's Arrow, Time's Cycle*, Stephen Jay Gould tried to capture in words the incalculable dimensions of time: "Consider the earth's history as the old measure of the English yard, the distance from the King's nose to the tip of his outstretched hand. One stroke of a nail file on the king's finger erases human history."[1]

Whatever the length of time believers have to wait, heart strength will be essential to their survival. The Letter of James was addressed to communities who, like ours, lived in a culture that gave little heed to the values of the Christian tradition or to the good news of Jesus Christ. If having a strong heart spiritually is in any way comparable to having a healthy cardiovascular system in one's physical body, then exercise must be a part of it. You cannot stand against the forces of evil, indifference, or oppression with flaccid faith, puny hope, or on-again-off-again love.

One way you strengthen your heart is to avoid "grumbling against one another." What an odd and yet appropriate exhortation. Survival over the long haul requires patience, not only with the Lord who will return in God's own good time, but with each other, lest you destroy the community that holds you up during the waiting.

Another reason not to grumble is that others will judge you and, in you, the Christ whom you claim to serve. In these between times, how do people know what Christ is like, if not through you? There is only the body of Christ to witness to his lordship and his love.

The most important reason not to grumble, however, is that God will judge you for it. As a matter of

1. Stephen Jay Gould, *Time's Arrow, Time's Cycle: Myth and Metaphor in the Discovery of Geological Time*, The Jerusalem-Harvard Lectures (London: Penguin, 1988), 3.

James 5:7-10

Theological Perspective

paradox that "we pray as if everything depended on God, and . . . work as if everything depended on us."

Modern biblical exegetes explain that the Epistle of James is an ethical and religious treatise cast in the form of a letter. The addressees were Jewish Christians of the Diaspora who endured poverty and oppression in their lives among the pagans of Syria and Cilicia. The letter is modeled on the Wisdom books of the Hebrew Scriptures. Exhortations, instructions, and practical norms for the everyday life of a Christian are loosely strung together.

If we simply let the author speak his own mind in his own way and to his own purpose, then the book can be appreciated for what it really is: an answer to questions that are important to our lived lives. What does a Christian do about his or her faith (Jas. 2:14–26)? What should be one's attitudes toward the rich and the poor (Jas. 2:1–7)? The new law for James is a paradox, worthy of Paul. Christians are subject to "the perfect law . . . of liberty" (Jas. 1:25; 2:12), which culminates in the "royal law" of love of one's neighbor (Jas. 2:8).

The Jews who have become Christians must take their faith seriously in their daily lives. They must translate their faith into action. What is the use of faith that does not bear fruit? It is an empty show.

In these days of Advent, the readings keep us aware of the multiple paradoxes of our faith: A God who is wholly other, yet born to an adolescent mother who is engaged but not married yet. A God who reveals God's self as the unsurpassed mystery born as a child in a cave outside an obscure village in Judea. How else than through paradox do we invite contemporary people to touch this Mystery?

Could it be that the eternal Light wishes to illumine our inner darkness, to give healing and light we had dared not even hope for? The Christian tradition evokes this paradoxical, redemptive hope. It makes external and practical fatherly care and motherly love—a gift so sacred that it could only be a visitation of the Divine.

PATRICK J. HOWELL

Pastoral Perspective

persecution, poverty, and marginalization. In all probability, the community was so small that resistance was impractical; patience was an appropriate stance only because the situation was truly beyond their control. This text is not a proof text for submission to injustice but, rather, advice for how to wait out the immediate situation of injustice.

When the author combines suffering and patience, he does so by pointing to "the prophets who spoke in the name of the Lord." If anything, this must be an example of "impatient patience." Think of the deep yearning of Isaiah for days of renewal for Israel or the longing of the psalmists who cry out, "How long, O Lord!" While the prophets who called Israel to repent in the face of oncoming disaster were not anxious to see the destruction of their people, they were not content to be "patient" while the people ignored their calls to repent and reform. Whether the "Day of the Lord" was a day of judgment or redemption, the prophets of Israel waited with impatient patience even in the midst of suffering, knowing that, whatever it brought, that day would be "the Lord's."

Similarly, the author urges those who wait to keep in mind the "long view." The end point is the "coming of the Lord." This author is filled with anticipation that God will keep God's promise to renew and restore creation, to vindicate and redeem God's people, to set right all that is wrong—and that God will do this soon, within the lifetime of both author and readers. Centuries have passed and the end of days has not come, but the season of Advent is the time when the church chooses to keep alive the hope that God is not finished either with creation or with human history, that God is present and active in our lives and in the life of the world to bring about the purposes that God intends.

CYNTHIA M. CAMPBELL

Exegetical Perspective

also the saying of Jesus recorded in Rev. 3:20). Judging is also associated with the return of Christ in 2 Timothy 4:1 (cf. John 3:19, Matt. 25:31–32).

In the phrase "suffering and patience" (NRSV) describing the prophets in verse 10, the Greek noun translated "suffering" has more the connotation of "endurance." The two words are probably a hendiadys (two words expressing one concept) and mean "patient endurance" with the implication of enduring evil visited upon them. The prophets as examples of such conduct are cited in sayings of Jesus (Matt. 5:12; cf. 23:37) as well as in other places in the NT (e.g., Acts 7:52; Heb. 11:32). The point is that obeying God by speaking in God's name did not give the prophets immunity from persecution. On the contrary, such faithfulness to the Lord actually involved them in suffering. The implication here is that Christians also will suffer in an evil society, precisely because they too are faithful to the Lord's will.

Verse 11 sums up this point: those who are steadfast in the face of suffering are blessed. The same word for patience is used in the same situation by Jesus (e.g., Matt. 10:22; 24:13; Luke 21:19). James cites Job as another example of endurance. Job is associated in this respect with the prophets (cf. Ezek. 14:14, 20). The phrase "purpose of the Lord" (Gk. *telos kyriou*) is a Hebraism and means the goal that the Lord has set. That goal is compassion and mercy, often ascribed to God in the Psalms (e.g., Ps. 103:8, paraphrased here in James; cf. also Pss. 78:38; 86:15; 111:4; 112:4; 145:8) and to Jesus in the NT (cf. Matt. 15:32; 20:34; Mark 5:19; Luke 7:13). Such mercy may be hidden, but as Christ shows, it is God's final purpose for his creatures. It is a fitting note to sound during the Advent season.

PAUL J. ACHTEMEIER

Homiletical Perspective

fact, "the Judge is standing at the doors!" (v. 9). If you do not want to be judged by the Judge, you had best leave judgment of others to the Judge as well. The day of salvation is near, and when that day comes, the Lord will take care of everything and everybody. Until then, the thing for you to do is to attend to the sinner who lives under your own hat.

Finally, the writer advises the people to allow the prophets of old to be their role models in "suffering and patience." He is not suggesting suffering for the sake of suffering, but suffering as the often-inevitable consequence of being true to God in an alien or indifferent environment. If the prophets had to pay through suffering, then let the same be so with you. There are some things worse than suffering, and even death. One of them is losing your soul.

Members of our congregations are not likely to be stoned, beheaded, or burned at the stake any time soon, but today's believers live as much under the imperative of faithfulness as did our courageous ancestors whom we know from Scripture, history, and, in many instances, the stories our families tell. My grandfather worked for justice and once risked his life for a black friend in the segregated South. He had been dead for decades when the civil rights laws were finally passed, but when he was on this earth, he made sure his heart was strong and did what he could to see that little shoots of hope grew in the rocky, red clay soil of his time. His memory genuinely inspires me and teaches me that there really is a kingdom coming in which all God's people are worthy of respect.

I once heard about a woman who had, in spite of a hard life and virtually no resources except her stamina and the strength of her faith, raised six fine children and sent them all to college. Asked how she did it, she replied, "I saw a new world coming."

Let us hold on to the vision and live in love until the Lord comes again.

JOANNA M. ADAMS

Matthew 11:2-11

²When John heard in prison what the Messiah was doing, he sent word by his disciples ³and said to him, "Are you the one who is to come, or are we to wait for another?" ⁴Jesus answered them, "Go and tell John what you hear and see: ⁵the blind receive their sight, the lame walk, the lepers are cleansed, the deaf hear, the dead are raised, and the poor have good news brought to them. ⁶And blessed is anyone who takes no offense at me."

⁷As they went away, Jesus began to speak to the crowds about John: "What did you go out into the wilderness to look at? A reed shaken by the wind? ⁸What then did you go out to see? Someone dressed in soft robes? Look, those who wear soft robes are in royal palaces. ⁹What then did you go out to see? A prophet? Yes, I tell you, and more than a prophet. ¹⁰This is the one about whom it is written,

'See, I am sending my messenger ahead of you,
    who will prepare your way before you.'

¹¹Truly I tell you, among those born of women no one has arisen greater than John the Baptist; yet the least in the kingdom of heaven is greater than he."

Theological Perspective

The great iconostases of the Russian Orthodox Church include a special row of icons dedicated to Christ and those saints who lead the church in worshiping and adoring him. In the middle of this row hangs a large icon of Christ as the one who has saved humanity and now rules the earth from on high. The first icon to his right is of Mary, his mother; to his left hangs the icon of John the Baptist. Both Mary and John are standing. Both look and lean toward Jesus, as though their whole existence is bound up with his.

The Gospels report that those who encountered Jesus were regularly confused about who he really was. Jesus himself eventually asked his disciples, "Who do people say that I am?" (Matt. 16:13). Those whose existence is bound up with that of Jesus' end up posing the same question about themselves: Who am I really? Such questions of identity come to the fore in Matthew 11:2–11. John wonders who Jesus really is, and Jesus notes that the crowd wonders who John really is. Jesus alone can bring clarity to both questions.

The Gospels depict John as the first of Jesus' contemporaries to recognize him as Israel's long-awaited Messiah. Like the ancient prophets, John had borne witness to Christ without first seeing him. Unlike the other prophets, John lived to see the one of whom he

Pastoral Perspective

The Gospel passage for the Third Sunday of Advent is really a pericope and a half.

The first pericope is Matthew 11:2–6—John's query from prison and Jesus' response. The pericope that follows is Matthew 11:7–14. The Revised Common Lectionary breaks off at 11:11, relieving the preacher and pastor of having to puzzle about the relationship between the kingdom of heaven and violence on the one hand, and between John the Baptist and Elijah on the other.

The assigned pericope and a half give plenty of room for pastoral practice and reflection.

John's Query from Prison (vv. 2–6). Homiletically and exegetically we can ponder why Matthew places John's question at this place in his Gospel. Theologically John seems to have understood Jesus correctly in chapter 3, so why the puzzle now?

Pastorally the puzzle is not hard to understand. As our story tells it, this prophet has seen in Jesus the one who is bringing God's judgment, to gather the wheat and scatter the chaff (Matt. 3:12). Now it is John who is being treated like chaff—thrown into prison while Herod's power grows and flourishes. No wonder John asks, "Are you (really) the one who is to come, or are we to wait for another?" (11:3).

Exegetical Perspective

On this Third Sunday of Advent, the emphasis continues to be on John the Baptizer, who embodies the advent of a new age while remaining embedded in the old age.

John is imprisoned, a stark reminder of how his prophetic witness has been received. In the first century, prison was a way station but not a final destination. People were kept in prison awaiting trial until they were exonerated, exiled, or executed. During their incarceration, prisoners could have contact with supporters and so picked up the news of the day. It is even possible that John was imprisoned with people he knew as part of the repentance movement. All of this is to say that John could have heard of Jesus' activities from his disciples who conveyed his question to Jesus and eventually Jesus' response back to John. In any case, for Matthew, its narrative purpose is to address the identity of John and Jesus.

The question would seem to be a simple one, "Are you the one who is to come, or are we to wait for another?" As is so often the case, Jesus responds to John's question indirectly. More to the point, Jesus' response enlarges the scope of the question, with echoes from Isaiah and Second Isaiah that provide glimpses of a new age in which the wounds of Israel will be healed.

Homiletical Perspective

It is a relief when someone else asks our question. We are doubly helped when the one who does the asking is the brightest kid in class. If the one with all the answers does not know the answer, then we do not feel so bad about not knowing it ourselves.

Here someone else asks Jesus our question. "Are you the one who is to come, or are we to wait for another?" This question occurs to just about every person in the church, including the strongest Christians. Is Jesus the real thing? Is there anything to our religion? Has the church really gotten hold of something that matters, or is this business of Christmas and its Christ only a fanciful tale, charming, but ultimately worthless and powerless against forces that dampen hopes and deaden dreams?

Since the question is so dangerous, particularly in terms of its implications about the questioner, it is not one we tend to ask openly. We do not want our hands to be the ones in the air when someone assumes that persons of real faith and spiritual depth never ask anything like this. The question, we fear, implies weakness, dullness, and doubt at the core. To ask it, we suppose, is to appear faithless.

Strong help comes when we notice through the text whose hand is in the air. It is the hand of the smartest kid in class. John is the one who said wonderful things about Jesus. Earlier in Matthew he said,

Matthew 11:2-11

Theological Perspective

spoke. One day Jesus followed the crowds into the wilderness along the Jordan, where John was preaching, and asked John to baptize him, even though John protested that Jesus should baptize him (Matt. 3:14). God's prophecies to Israel came to fulfillment before John's very eyes.

Matthew 11:2–11 further explores this unique relationship between John and Jesus. John is now in prison and sends his disciples to ask Jesus if he is truly the one promised to Israel. The question brings us up short, since John had clearly witnessed to Jesus as the Messiah at the time of Jesus' baptism. In Matthew's narrative, John seems to raise his question because of his own imprisonment under Herod, but something else has profoundly changed in the meantime. John is now no longer the predecessor and preparer, no longer the messenger who goes before Christ's face (v. 10). Rather, the one who now testifies to Christ is no less than Christ himself. Christ himself prepares the witness that John must receive. John must hear for himself that in Christ the blind see, the lame walk, lepers are cleansed, the deaf hear, the dead are raised up, and the poor have good news preached to them (v. 5). He must become a disciple.

The crowds that had gone into the wilderness to behold John had not really understood that John's identity was wrapped up with that of Jesus. So, Jesus asks them what they had expected to find. A reed shaken by the wind, like an emaciated holy man? A man dressed in fine, soft robes, like a king? Or a prophet? Jesus declares that John is indeed a prophet (a new Elijah, he will later say in verse 14), yet even "prophet" does not adequately describe John. As one preparing the way for Christ, John has surpassed the great prophets. In the whole history of Israel, he has no equal. Among those born of woman, truly no one rises above him. Nevertheless, as one who must still learn to become a disciple, John is least of those in the kingdom of heaven (v. 11). John who had preceded Jesus must now learn to follow him; the one who prepared the way for Jesus must now receive him. The first will be last, and the last will be first.

The question of what constitutes true discipleship has haunted Christians ever since Jesus began to call people to follow him. Their model has sometimes been the holy man or woman who abandons civilization to practice solitary, ascetic disciplines in the wilderness. At other times, the Christian king, czar, or ruler has been regarded as the true disciple, as though worldly power and riches bring a person closer to God. Yet another candidate for exemplary discipleship has been the prophet, the person who

Pastoral Perspective

Clergy have learned to set aside extra time for pastoral conversations during Advent, and to make time for visits to people who may seem, metaphorically at least, imprisoned. (For some of our people, in institutions of all kinds, the metaphor is not all that metaphorical.) Not only our churches but the media and the entire consumer culture assure us that if this is not the messianic age, then it is still time for tidings of comfort and joy. For those who are neither comfortable nor joyful, the announcement that Jesus is the one to come—and Advent is the time to get excited about his coming—may simply seem cruel.

Jesus' response is of course right on the mark theologically, but it does not help John pastorally: "Go and tell John what you hear and see: the blind receive their sight, the lame walk, the lepers are cleansed, the deaf hear, the dead are raised, and the poor have good news brought to them" (vv. 4–5).

John, on his way to being a saint, probably gets that word and thinks: "Lovely." The rest of us, in John's situation, would be more apt to say, "Good for the blind, the lame, the lepers, the deaf, and the temporarily dead. You may notice, however, Jesus, that *I* am still in prison."

We have noticed that it does not necessarily contribute to the comfort of the lonely to see how others are surrounded by loving family. Sadly it does not entirely comfort the people in the nursing home or the hospital ward when all those cheery youth group members come through, singing "Joy to the World" and shouting "Merry Christmas" as they head out to Christmases that at least appear to be merry beyond the residents' imaginings.

Pastors, think about these people as Advent comes. You may not be able to bring them tidings of joy, but find ways to bring them tidings of comfort.

It is great for the youth group to carol the lonely and then head back to church for hot cider and donuts. How about asking members of the youth group, one by one, to adopt a shut-in, or a person in hospital, or someone in a nursing home? How about inviting the youth to sit and talk for awhile—and even better, to sit and listen for awhile?

Jesus is fundamentally right, of course, but John the Baptist has a point.

Jesus' Testimony about John (vv. 7–11).
There is a word here about appropriate expectation, and there is a word here about who is in church.

One reason people find Advent and Christmas depressing is because they have good reason to be depressed. Another reason people find Advent and

Exegetical Perspective

The following parallels will illustrate Matthew's indebtedness to Isaiah: The blind see in Matthew 9:27–31 and in Isaiah 29:18; 35:5; the lame walk in Matthew 9:2–8 and Isaiah 35:6; the lepers are cleansed in Matthew 8:1–4 and are not in Isaiah's language; the deaf hear in Matthew 9:32–34 and Isaiah 35:5; the dead are raised in Matthew 9:18–19, 23–26 and Isaiah 26:19; the poor are cared for in Matthew 9:35–38 and Isaiah 29:19; 61:1–2; 42:7.

Taken together, these activities define a profile of expectations and portray an Israel in crisis, at least for the peasant villages and the rural poor. Their wounds call for healing, exactly the role Jesus assumes as healer and exorcist. While Isaiah anticipates this wide-scale benefaction, he does not link it to the coming messiah. In fact, there appear to be no distinctive documents that specifically depicted the messiah fulfilling these roles; so Jesus either breaks the mold (if there is one) or introduces unexpected complications to the conversations of the day.

Perhaps the most intriguing member of the list is the final entry, "the poor have good news brought to them" (11:5). The poor (*ptōchoi*) refers to the destitute, the down and out, the desperate. It is interesting that Jesus culminates his response to John with a reference to the poor. In the age to come, the poor will have good news brought to them. Their wounds will be healed by a true healer, not a phony physician. "They have treated the wound of my people carelessly, saying, 'Peace, peace,' when there is no peace" (Jer. 6:14).

The poor are always the test case of the covenant. If the Torah's communal covenant is kept, then the promises of Deuteronomy 15 will come to pass. The reference to the poor as a group, rather than as people with individual needs, suggests a systemic concern for the injustice and oppression visited upon the poor by the rulers, whether Caesar, Herod Antipas in Galilee, or the high-priestly families in Jerusalem.

It is in this context that we can understand the beatitude with which Jesus concludes his remarks, "blessed is anyone who takes no offense at me." The issue is pointed. Jesus is not talking about an amiable disagreement in a policy debate by saying, blessed are the analysts and courtiers. Jesus knows that differences will be face-to-face personal contests and challenges. The emphasis is on "me." John and Jesus share one crucial characteristic: they are both willing to risk entering the public arena against well-prepared opponents, even when it means speaking truth to those in power, a very dangerous occupation

Homiletical Perspective

"One who is more powerful than I is coming after me; I am not worthy to carry his sandals" (Matt. 3:11). Pointing to Jesus in John's Gospel, he said, "Here is the Lamb of God who takes away the sin of the world!" (John 1:29). Perhaps his shining moment came when, a little later in John, he said of Jesus, "He must increase, but I must decrease" (John 3:30). John the Baptist had the answers. He had the conviction. He had the clarity that told him Jesus was the real thing and second to none.

Now he asks of this same Jesus, "Are you really the one we have been waiting for?" What has happened?

For one thing, a prison has happened. He has been arrested and jailed as a political enemy of King Herod. Prison can put doubt into anybody's heart. It is easy to believe in God in the bright sunlight when all is joyful and free, but let the iron doors of difficulty slam shut, and doubt is there in the darkness. "Are you for real, Jesus?" "Can religion matter in my case, in my condition, with my concerns, or has it reached the end of its usefulness?" Hard experiences, like John's prison bars, press such questions upon us.

It was not a prison alone that made John ask his question and ours. It was something about Jesus himself. Something did not add up. Matthew puts it this way: "When John heard . . . what the Messiah was doing, he sent word . . . and said to him, 'Are you the one who is to come, or are we to wait for another?'" (Matt. 11:2–3). Something that Jesus was doing did not seem quite right to John. Jesus did not fit his idea of a Messiah. He was not acting the way John thought a Savior would act. The lamb of God who takes away the sin of the world was not taking Herod's sin away. Jesus was not fitting John's theology. So John wondered. There is comfort in the idea that faith as strong as John's is capable of doubt as strong as ours.

Pass now from the prisoner's question to the Savior's answer. How does Jesus answer John? He says, in effect, "I cannot answer for you. You have to decide on your own whether I am for real. Look at the evidence. What do you see?"

Christ's answer is exactly the same when we ask the question. Persons have to decide for themselves on the basis of the evidence they see. Whether the preacher's role is perceived as pastoral, prophetic, or evangelistic, part of the task is to report on and name the evidence that can be seen today. What evidence is there that Jesus is for real? The best path at this point may be that of personal testimony.

For example, I am moved to confess Jesus is for real when I realize some of the best minds the world

Matthew 11:2-11

Theological Perspective

declares God's will, preaches God's word, and warns the world of God's coming day of judgment. Even ministers sometimes succumb to the temptation of believing that they have moved closer to the front of the line in the kingdom of heaven because they have proclaimed prophetic words in service of God and the church.

These answers fall short, just like each of the crowds' speculations about John. True discipleship is never first a question of our efforts to make Christ known to ourselves or others. The focus never falls first on our ascetic achievements, worldly ambitions, or prophetic diatribes. A true disciple knows how easily we substitute the vain imaginations of our heart in place of the living Christ. A true disciple knows that he or she is still learning how to follow Jesus.

The twentieth-century Protestant theologian Karl Barth regarded John the Baptist as the prototype of Christian discipleship. Over Barth's desk in Basel, Switzerland, hung a reproduction of the Isenheim altarpiece (executed by Matthias Grünewald, ca. 1515). To the left, John the beloved disciple holds Mary, Jesus' mother, as she looks in horror at the bloody, pierced body of her Son on the cross. To the right, John the Baptist, in bare feet and camel's hair cloak, holds a book in one hand and with the other raises his long bony index finger toward Jesus on the cross. That, says Barth, is true discipleship: simply to point to all that God has done for us in Christ.

"Who am I?" asked Dietrich Bonhoeffer, Barth's contemporary, in a poem from prison only a few months before the Nazis hanged him. Despite all his efforts to live faithfully, he wondered whether he was just a hypocrite or a weakling. "Who am I?" every Christian sometimes asks. In John the Baptist, we find an answer: to be a disciple is no longer to look at oneself, but rather to look at Christ. In pointing to him alone, the disciple's own identity finally becomes clear: "Whoever I am, thou knowest, O God, I am thine."[1]

JOHN P. BURGESS

Pastoral Perspective

Christmas depressing is because they may be looking for the wrong thing.

No one is quite clear what Jesus means by wondering whether the people went into the wilderness to see a reed shaken by the wind. If this is a tribute to John, then it may be a way of saying that he remained steadfastly unshaken, even into prison (narratively) and to his death (historically). If so, he becomes an example to the church at Advent and throughout the year that the kingdom is not negotiable or subject to ratification by popularity polls. Soon enough we will see how the baby we welcome will become unshakable and broken too. Advent preaching, teaching, and singing always remembers John's prison and Jesus' cross.

As to the contrast between those who wear soft robes in royal palaces and John the Baptist, God's servant, the point is clear enough. It is the contrast between the miracle on 34th Street and the miracle in Bethlehem—between the benefits of Macy's and the wonders of God's love.

One reason we try to encourage simple Christmases in our homes and in our congregations is because the event we are awaiting has its own simplicity. John the Baptist foreshadows the poverty of Christ by the simplicity of his own life. The only rich people to show up for Christmas in Matthew's Gospel are the magi, and they bow down and then give up their gifts.

Here is a thought: could we try a simple Christmas in church as a model for a simple Christmas at home? What about *not* paying $200 for the brass choir and giving the money to the local food pantry instead? What about doing what many churches already do, asking members to send one card to the church to be displayed for the entire congregation, and sending the money that otherwise would have gone to Hallmark to the Salvation Army? We love soft robes and palaces, especially at this season, but the kingdom is about something else.

As to who is in church, they are the "least in the kingdom of heaven." In Matthew's Gospel the least, the little ones, are the sheep of God's fold. In God's eyes they are as great as John the Baptist, and they are entrusted to our care.

DAVID L. BARTLETT

---

1. See Dietrich Bonhoeffer, *Letters and Papers from Prison*, ed. Eberhard Bethge (New York: Macmillan, 1971), 347–48.

that can land the prophet in prison or on a cross. All of this speaks about how the old age continues to operate. Those in power stay in power. The powerful exploit the powerless. It is a vicious cycle that only an advent can change. Both John and Jesus are part of that advent as it struggles to come to life.

In Matthew 11:7–11, Jesus shifts the focus to John and away from himself. His comments use three sharp images: a reed shaken by the wind (v. 7), a soft-robed courtier (v. 8), and more than a prophet (vv. 9–11). The reed image may reflect the fact that Herod Antipas placed the image of reeds on the coins he minted. The saying may also be a wry commentary on the fact that Antipas is just a reed (client king) blown about by every wind emanating from Rome.

One other reading sees in the reed a reference to the exodus through the Reed Sea while the winds held back the waves. If the first reading is likely, then Jesus is engaged in a form of dissembling and indirect commentary on Herod Antipas's precarious existence as a vassal of Rome. If this is a reference to exodus, then the saying embodies a theology of hope, a look to a liberated future.

The third image—prophet and more than a prophet—is attested by the compound quotation (Exod. 23:20; Mal. 3:1). This is a complex section. At one moment, John is greater than any other person born of woman. The next moment, the least in the reign of heaven is greater than John the Baptizer. What gives? John is both the culmination of prophecy and its conclusion, for he is a bridge between this age and the age to come.

One way to understand this quagmire is to take verses 9–11 as a way of saying that "just when you think you have measured the magnitude of this advent of heaven's reign, you discover that you have not begun to capture the dimensions and magnitude of this advent." As the reign of heaven comes into focus, John suddenly diminishes in importance; yet, even though he is least, he still belongs. Something about the advent of the reign of heaven simply cannot be measured or comprehended. Perhaps that is why we return to the mystery every year.

WILLIAM R. HERZOG II

has known have believed in Jesus. Solid minds have looked away from him, but minds just as clear have believed in him strongly even after putting the matter to the strictest of tests. It is possible some of these people were mistaken, but it is very unlikely all of them were.[1] The sermon can make this point by way of some quick biographies telling of persons such as Saul of Tarsus, Augustine of Hippo, Calvin of Geneva, Lewis of Oxford, or another whose biography the preacher knows and loves.

The sermon can be brought closer to home with persons who have been nearer in time, space, and heart. I am moved to confess that Jesus is for real when I realize some of the best souls I have known belonged to persons who believed in Jesus and were committed to his cause.

A kind of climax to the message can come when the preacher helps people think of their own experiences and not just those of others. Some of the deepest moments we have known have been rooted in Christ. The preaching task at this point is to identify experiences of this kind and name them as experiences of Christ and his ability to be present and active. Those with eyes to see will find that Christ is present in word and song and fellowship and in the quietness of the heart as it sits in the pew and ponders life.

MARK E. YURS

---

1. Elton Trueblood, *Robert Barclay* (New York: Harper & Row, 1968), 146.

Isaiah 7:10-16

[10]Again the Lord spoke to Ahaz, saying, [11]Ask a sign of the Lord your God; let it be deep as Sheol or high as heaven. [12]But Ahaz said, I will not ask, and I will not put the Lord to the test. [13]Then Isaiah said: "Hear then, O house of David! Is it too little for you to weary mortals, that you weary my God also? [14]Therefore the Lord himself will give you a sign. Look, the young woman is with child and shall bear a son, and shall name him Immanuel. [15]He shall eat curds and honey by the time he knows how to refuse the evil and choose the good. [16]For before the child knows how to refuse the evil and choose the good, the land before whose two kings you are in dread will be deserted."

Theological Perspective

The four Sundays of Advent are like great tympani beats sounding a prophetic word of yearning and hope. In the Fourth Sunday, Isaiah brings us round to the great sign of God's promise: a young woman will give birth to a son whose name will be Immanuel, "God with us." The church's overfamiliarity with words about a virgin conceiving and bearing a son may lead many to take this claim for granted. Theologically speaking, we expect this in Advent. Yet others, outside the church and unfamiliar with the language of Zion, may be mystified. What can keep us from either presumption or incredulity about the prophet's Advent proclamation of this sign? Perhaps the strangeness of the setting in Isaiah can help us.

Here is a twist: Isaiah comes to reassure King Ahaz that Jerusalem will not be captured by the coalition ranged against him. The divine intention mediated through the prophet is to thwart the enemies of Jerusalem. Ahaz is offered a sign from God if he but ask for it, whether "deep as Sheol or high as heaven" (v. 11). Ahaz refuses, with the excuse that he does not wish to tempt God. This rejection of God's offer betrays his fear and his lack of trust. Even so, Isaiah declares that God himself will give a sign anyway—a woman pregnant with a child of promise. Devastation will come to the land of those who threaten Ahaz. As it turns out, the child is also a sign

Pastoral Perspective

On this last Sunday of Advent a pastor might be aware of higher than usual attendance in worship and take opportunity to address the concerns of some of those whose attendance is more occasional than regular. Chief among them is often the challenge of their assumptions about *belief*, and especially their assumptions as to what constitutes *right* belief. They may love the pageantry and familiarity of Christmas, but are often suspending disbelief in order to enjoy familiar music, be with family, enjoy children singing or a host of other possibilities.

Isaiah's prophecy of Immanuel as born to a young woman provides a way into discussing the doctrine of the virgin birth of Jesus and various approaches we might take toward it. Alongside a literal adherence to the claim, these include the story as expression of divine identity; a matter of faith in the power of God; an articulation of what function the birth narratives took for the authors of the Gospels; a more general discussion of the use of creeds in worship.

The young woman might be the wife of the prophet or a concubine of Ahaz. In any event, the import of the older translation as "virgin" does not need to mean "a woman who has never known a man." In all likelihood the young woman was already with child at the time of Isaiah's prophecy. Matthew (and possibly Luke) later suggests that Jesus' birth is a

Exegetical Perspective

Isaiah 7:10–17 is the second part of a story about an encounter between the prophet Isaiah and the Judean king Ahaz. Because of its later association with the birth of Christ in Matthew 1:22–23, this text has received much attention throughout the history of Christian biblical interpretation. It remains a powerful witness to God's work in the world in its own right, however, enriched by its connections to the NT without being exhausted by them.

The beginning of Isaiah 7 locates the story during the Syro-Ephraimite conflict of 734–733 BCE, when the kings of Israel (also called Ephraim) and Aram attempted to invade Jerusalem and replace Ahaz with a puppet ruler who would support their coalition against Assyria (Isa. 7:1, 5–6; cf. 2 Kgs. 16:5–9). Although we learn immediately that the invasion was unsuccessful (Isa. 7:1), the events of the story take place before its outcome is known. Ahaz and his subjects are terrified at the impending attack (v. 2), which threatens not only the survival of the nation but also the promise that a descendant of David would always reign in Jerusalem (2 Sam. 7:11–16). In this time of national terror, YHWH sends Isaiah to reassure Ahaz of divine protection.

In verse 10, YHWH again speaks to Ahaz through Isaiah. It is not clear how much time, if any, has elapsed since verses 1–9, but Ahaz apparently has not

Homiletical Perspective

When you read them together, the texts for this Sunday point toward Jesus' birth as the fulfillment of prophecy. In Matthew's birth narrative, the evangelist quotes Isaiah: "Look, the virgin shall conceive and bear a son, and they shall name him Emmanuel" (Matt. 1:23). By focusing attention on Isaiah's prophecy to Ahaz, you and your congregation may gain a fresh and challenging perspective on both the first and second coming of the Messiah. One of the immediate challenges will be to interpret this familiar text in its own context before exploring its implications for our understanding of Jesus Christ.

From a literary perspective, the opening verse of the passage is connected to the preceding text. The allied forces of Aram and Ephraim are attempting to attack Jerusalem, and King Ahaz is deeply afraid. In verse 10, God offers Ahaz a sign—any sign he wants—to convince him to trust in God; but Ahaz refuses the sign, saying that he will not test the Lord. God immediately brushes aside his objection and gives Ahaz a sign nevertheless. Isaiah says to the king, "Hear then, O house of David! Is it too little for you to weary mortals, that you weary my God also? Therefore the Lord himself will give you a sign" (vv. 13–14a). By giving the sign despite the king's refusal, God shows Israel steadfast faithfulness and grace.

Isaiah 7:10-16

Theological Perspective

of the Assyrian invasion that will devastate Jerusalem. What a strange and disorienting sign to the prophet's hearers!

Could it be that the Christian community's easy access to the meaning of Immanuel and our confident images of the nativity need to encounter this ambiguity in the sign God is giving us? Could it be that the easy skepticism about God derived from culturally popular images of Christian faith needs to be shaken by a different sense of historical complexity? Here then we encounter a hidden depth in the meaning of the sign of incarnation.

In our contemporary situation it is problematic to claim that God characteristically operates by raising up and destroying armies, though vestiges of that theological viewpoint are real. This Advent sign raises the question of how God enters and acts within the world of time and space. The idea that God becomes human and therefore we are saved from participation in history is at least astoundingly naive. It is more likely that we come to understand God to be at work in the ambiguities, the twists, and the ironies of human history, as Reinhold Niebuhr long since has observed. This passage in Isaiah, occurring as it does in the Fourth Sunday of Advent, provokes a certain disturbing wonder at such a sign. The hope for the coming of a child of destiny is certainly still alive in secular society. In complicated times—politically, socially, economically—the yearning for some sign of promise and hope in the form of a new leader is still very much with us. This is true both outside and inside our churches.

The particular sign God gives in Isaiah arouses hope. At the same time it opens up the gap between what the world is and what it ought to be. Such a sign focuses the contrast between the forces ranged *against* the good, and the hope for salvation from all that is violent and destructive. Awareness of the gap between the *world's actuality* and God's *ought-to-be* of the world kindles the prophetic spirit in every age. As in Isaiah's circumstances, so too in our own. The vulnerability and the unexpected future of a child borne in a womb and birthed into this world are indispensable features of this sign given in Isaiah's prophecy. On the one hand, vulnerability: a child as such is subject to growing up—coming to know evil and good. The apparent weakness of a child plays against the hope. As the words of Johann Rist's chorale, "Break Forth O Beauteous Heavenly Light" (used by J. S. Bach in his *Christmas Oratorio*) express it: "This child, now weak in infancy, our joy and confidence shall be." The hearers too are vulnerable to the circumstances that

Pastoral Perspective

fulfillment of this ancient expectation and hope (Matt. 1:23). Both Matthew and Luke add to "Immanuel" other titles, like "Son of Man," "Son of God," "Messiah," and other such titles pointing toward divine provenance and quintessential humanity.

Preachers who would suggest that the young woman of Isaiah's prophecy is on some level predictive of Mary might want to encourage the skeptical to suspend disbelief and focus on the trustworthiness of God in history. This trustworthiness may be sought in Israel's history prior to the Bethlehem moment—perhaps in the ultimate fate of Ahaz (also known as Jehoahaz), who engaged pagan customs, sacrificed his own son, and established a pagan altar in the temple (2 Kgs. 16). He was denounced by Hosea and Micah in addition to Isaiah of Jerusalem, before making an alliance with Assyria, turning Judah into a vassal state.

The Immanuel prophecy might serve to introduce the idea that Matthew and Luke were telling a story of Jesus' birth directly counter to the stories of Greek gods, who were well known to take on the guise of humans, come down from Mount Olympus, and cause great mischief, leading to heartache and brokenness among humans. Those who have difficulty believing the medical details of the Gospel might find some way of appreciating the birth stories as polemical use of Isaiah to contrast this birth with the actions of those foreign gods. While some Christians might use the story to emphasize Jesus' divine nature, Matthew and Luke were, at least in part, using the story to make clear that Jesus was not a Greek god, but a child born of a woman with all the bloody and fleshly reality of full humanity.

Finally, addressing the concerns of those who have difficulty "swallowing the mumbo jumbo" (as one parishioner put it) might be offered a way into the community of faith by a discussion of the creeds and their purpose. To those who choke on the words "born of the virgin Mary," it might be helpful to discuss the import of *credo* as being less "I give intellectual assent to the following propositions" and more "I place my trust in God, creator of heaven and earth."

The history of the development of the creeds and their use in the life of the Christian community across the world and down the ages has included their use with the intent of making assent to right doctrine the precondition for admission to the Table of Christ; however, they have also served more generally as a bare-bones outline of the story of our faith, the story that in some sense "authors" us, or has authority for us as that which shapes our

Exegetical Perspective

demonstrated the faith that Isaiah had demanded. As a result, the prophet offers him a sign to bolster his confidence. The lack of restrictions on the sign ("deep as Sheol or high as heaven," v. 11) suggests that God will stop at nothing to secure the king's faith. Ahaz refuses, ostensibly on pious grounds, and a frustrated Isaiah responds that YHWH will give him a sign anyway: the birth of a child, by the time of whose weaning the threat against Jerusalem will have passed (vv. 14–16). The child will be born to a "young woman" (Heb. 'almah) who is already pregnant and will give birth in the near future, as suggested by the Hebrew construction *harah weyoledet* ("is with child and shall give birth," v. 14).

The child's name, Immanuel ("God is with us"), reinforces the divine promise to deliver the nation from its enemies; a brief prophetic oracle in Isaiah 8:9–10, likely connected to the same events, develops the implications of the name. Note that Isaiah is accompanied by his similarly symbolically named son Shear-jashub ("a remnant will return") during the encounter in verses 1–9 and perhaps in verses 10–17 as well. The prophet Hosea also had children with symbolic names (Hos. 1:2–9).

In the Septuagint, an ancient Greek translation of the OT, the term 'almah in v. 14 was translated with a word meaning "virgin" (*parthenos*). Reading this translation, the author of Matthew understood the verse as a prediction of the birth of Jesus to the virgin Mary, a move consistent with interpretive practices of his time. Within the story told in Isaiah 7, however, an event many centuries later would have offered little hope in the face of an imminent military threat. The Hebrew term 'almah, moreover, simply denotes a woman of marriageable age, without any suggestion of her sexual experience (e.g., Gen. 24:43; Exod. 2:8). If the author had wanted to indicate that the woman was a virgin, the Hebrew term *betulah* ("virgin") would more likely have been used.

Who, then, is this woman? Some biblical scholars think that she is Ahaz's wife and her son is, perhaps, the future king Hezekiah.[1] Others more persuasively identify her as the wife of Isaiah, referred to in Isaiah 8:3 as a prophetess.[2] As noted, Isaiah already has one child with a symbolic name, and Isaiah 8:1–4 recounts the birth of another such child named Maher-shalal-hash-baz ("swift to the spoil, quick to

1. See Christopher R. Seitz, *Isaiah 1–39*, Interpretation series (Louisville, KY: John Knox Press, 1993), 60–75.
2. See J. J. M. Roberts, "Isaiah and His Children," in *Biblical and Related Studies Presented to Samuel Iwry*, ed. A. Kort and S. Morschauser (Winona Lake, IN: Eisenbrauns, 1985), 193–203.

Homiletical Perspective

To reflect homiletically on this, consider what signs of faithfulness God is giving today—to your congregation, to your community, and to the world. Where can God be seen and known? Where is God breaking into the world? By naming these signs in the sermon, you help the congregation begin to recognize God's gracious activity in their lives and in the world. You could also explore possible theological connections to the sacraments, since they are signs in which God promises to be present to us and with us. As with Ahaz, God gives these signs and fulfills these promises with steadfast faithfulness and grace, sometimes even despite our objections.

Another homiletical possibility you could pursue is the flip side of God's gracious offer to Ahaz: the king's refusal. His refusal is particularly interesting because of the reason he gives. When God instructs Ahaz to ask for a sign, Ahaz responds: "I will not ask and I will not put the LORD to the test" (v. 12). At first, it seems that Ahaz is piously following the law of God, but, as Isaiah makes clear, the king is missing the point of God's offer entirely. Ahaz does not test God if he accepts God's free offer; rather God is testing Ahaz. When Ahaz refuses the sign, he is actually refusing to trust in the living God who is speaking to him.

This is an opportunity for you and the congregation to reflect on your own encounters with and responses to the living God. How does God meet you in unexpected ways, with unexpected grace? Can you think of pieties that sound righteous but are actually refusals of God's grace? Even more to the point, consider the challenge that God presents to Ahaz: How do you respond with trust to the living God—to God with us? Indeed, part of the focus of Advent is to prepare for the second coming of Immanuel.

Of course, to say that the child who shall be called Immanuel is Jesus the son of Mary is to make a Christian confession. When interpreted in its own context, Isaiah's prophecy concerning the child is much more vague. We are not told the identity of the mother, we do not know why it matters that she is a young woman, and we do not know how the sign of the child relates to the given name of Immanuel. Perhaps most disturbing, the sign appears to cut both ways by bringing both good news and bad news. In short, the sign is frustratingly ambiguous. Perhaps this very ambiguity can serve a purpose: to summon us to trust in the one thing that is plain: the promise that God is with us.

This sure promise, among much ambiguity, offers another homiletical angle from which to approach the sermon. Christmas seems like a time when we

Isaiah 7:10-16

Theological Perspective

challenge their very existence in the world as it is. Thus an element of "fear and trembling" must accompany the receiving of such a sign.

The idea of a child who grows over time into the promise of a world made right is a remarkable image for any idea of human salvation. Living into a future that has not yet come to be is living into the unexpected. Human individuals and societies characteristically require more certainty than this sign seems to offer. This was true of the situation that Isaiah addressed; but it is true always of the historical situation into which every Advent brings us. The church is called by Advent to face the vulnerabilities of time and place. The very sign by which God promises to world and to church, "I will be with you," evokes the unexpected hope. When Advent falls in the midst of severe human travail—as it has fallen and will fall again—it is hope against all the evidence.

The sign of a child is to be seen and heard against our deepest fears, but also our desires that the world be transformed. As in the great Advent hymn "O Come, O Come, Immanuel," the ancient biblical images of what God has promised stir us beyond our clichés and our presumptions. The sign God gives, despite our own refusals and our self-interests in deliverance, goes beyond our ambivalences to God's eternal self-consistency. God's covenant with the creation is to redeem it from the inside out. The promise of a Messiah is grounded in God's intention to restore us and to transform the world as we have come to make it into our own image. The divine promise is thus deeply hidden in God's own being, just as the child is hidden in the mother's womb.

DON E. SALIERS

Pastoral Perspective

discovery of meaning and purpose as we begin to know ourselves beloved of God.

The prophecy of Isaiah also allows a pastor to look forward to the blessings of Christmas and the birth of Jesus through a discussion of the nature and purpose of prophetic actions like the one Isaiah performed when he foretold the birth of Immanuel. He also named his other children as signs, with Shear-jashub meaning "a remnant shall return" (Isa. 7:3) and Maher-shalal-hash-baz meaning "spoil speeds, prey hastes" (Isa. 8:3). These are prophetic signs as much as when Jeremiah watched the potter reworking a clay jar and made a prophecy to the house of Israel. Such signs were understood to effect what was prophesied.

In other words, the signs were not understood as analogy (it will be like . . .) but as action bringing about the thing prophesied (as this child is named, so is God with us as judgment and hope). This prophetic sign is like the pronouncing of blessing or absolution in some Christian traditions, in which blessing or absolution is understood as effected, rather than requested, through prayer or plea. It might help some worshipers to know that there is a difference between asking or begging God's blessing and the sacramental or prophetic proclamation of blessing in the midst of the people. The blessings of Christmas then are less about good times with family or friends, and more about the prophetic traditions of forgiveness, reconciliation, peace on earth, righteousness or right relationship, and the like.

Finally, a pastor may wish to address the challenge of knowing or otherwise experiencing the presence of God in our lives. "Immanuel" means "God with us"; so it may be worth reminding those in attendance of the gratuitous nature of grace, that there is nothing we can do to force or guarantee some particular experience of God's grace and power in our lives. We all do well to manage our expectations of Christmas accordingly.

GEOFFREY M. ST.J. HOARE

the prey"). As with Immanuel, the birth and name of this child are connected to the Syro-Ephraimite conflict, but there seems to be sufficient time between the births for the children to have the same mother. In Isaiah 8:18, Isaiah refers to his children as "signs . . . from the LORD," using the same Hebrew word for "sign" (*'ot*) that appears in Isaiah 7:11, 14.

The very birth of a child could have evoked hope in a time of national duress. During the Assyrian siege of Jerusalem some twenty years later, by contrast, Hezekiah would lament that "children have come to the birth, and there is no strength to bring them forth" (2 Kgs. 19:3; Isa. 37:3). More to the point, Isaiah uses the birth to designate a specific time by which Jerusalem would be delivered from the threatened invasion. Verse 15 refers to the time when the child "knows how to refuse the evil (*ra'*) and choose the good," which probably means the capacity to choose between edible and inedible food rather than the development of moral agency; the Hebrew term *ra'* can describe something of bad quality without ethical connotations (Lev. 27:9–12; 2 Kgs. 2:19; Jer. 24:2–3; etc.).

Siege warfare usually resulted in severe food shortages and starvation, with small children disproportionately affected (e.g., 2 Kgs. 6:25–30; Lam. 2:11–12, 20). By the time of this child's weaning, though—perhaps as soon as three or four years— "curds and honey" will be readily available (v. 15), implying that Jerusalem will no longer be under siege. Isaiah makes the point clear in verse 16, declaring that the nations threatening Jerusalem will themselves have been defeated by this time. Continuing this message of hope, verse 17 promises that Judah will soon enjoy a period of national resurgence unlike anything since the kingdom was divided after Solomon's death (1 Kgs. 12:1–19). The reference to the king of Assyria in the final phrase, however, which many scholars think was added later, ends the passage on a more ambiguous, if not ominous, note. This surprising ending remind us that God's ways ultimately remain mysterious, even when, as the text powerfully insists, God is "with us."

J. BLAKE COUEY

are all brimming with faithful confidence, but serious doubts and questions about life and faith are often just beneath the surface. Explore your own uncertainties that arise at this time of year, and consider those of your congregation. Can Isaiah's oracle offer you a chance to name these doubts, and perhaps affirm them? Like this ambiguous sign of the child, the incarnation of Christ and the promise of Christ's return call forth faith in God's presence with us even when all the details are not clear. What is it like to trust in God's living presence in murky and sometimes frightening situations?

In his novel *Silence*, Shusaku Endo offers a profound understanding of God's gracious and unexpected presence with us. He writes a fictional account of the persecution of Christians in seventeenth-century Japan. In order to prove they are not Christians, those who are suspected are required to trample on a *fumie*, a carved likeness of Christ. If they do not trample the image, they will be brutally killed. Those who do trample it in order to save their lives live with deep shame. As the story climaxes, a young Jesuit missionary has been betrayed to the officials, and he is staring at a *fumie*. The face he sees in the carving is filled with exhaustion and sorrow. As the young missionary continues to stare at the *fumie*, the voice of Christ speaks to him. With astonishing grace, Christ tells him to trample the image, because to be trampled on is why Christ is there.

In this fictional account, Endo poses the same question that arises from Isaiah's encounter with Ahaz: How do we respond with trust to the gracious and unexpected presence of the living God with us?

PATRICK W. T. JOHNSON

Psalm 80:1-7, 17-19

¹Give ear, O Shepherd of Israel,
   you who lead Joseph like a flock!
You who are enthroned upon the cherubim, shine forth
²   before Ephraim and Benjamin and Manasseh.
   Stir up your might,
      and come to save us!

³Restore us, O God;
   let your face shine, that we may be saved.

⁴O LORD God of hosts,
   how long will you be angry with your people's prayers?
⁵You have fed them with the bread of tears,
   and given them tears to drink in full measure.

Theological Perspective

Compared with other lections for Advent and Christmas, Psalm 80 is strangely desperate, more like the pathos of Good Friday than the confident hope nourished by Advent. God is addressed as "Shepherd of Israel," recalling the quiet trust embodied in Psalm 23, but this is a communal lament reminding all, even God, that the essential divine task is to care for the sheep: to provide food, drink, and protection in horrific circumstances, including the plunder and mockery of enemies. The psalm becomes intensely personal, baring the soul of the community before God, pleading for restoration and wholeness while exhibiting anger, despair, and even desire for vengeance. It contrasts sharply with the joyful odes in Psalms 96 and 98, the readings for Christmas Eve and Christmas Day.

Psalm 80 reflects an experience that Jews, ancient and modern, have described as *hester panim*, the "hiding of God's face" or the "eclipse of God." The refrain of the psalm (vv. 3, 7, 19) pleads for the return of God's countenance: "Restore us, O God; let your face shine, that we may be saved." The refrain recalls the much-beloved priestly benediction in Numbers 6:24–26, which associates God's shining countenance with well-being; it also recalls prophetic warning in Deuteronomy 31:17–18, which links the hiding of God's face to the Israelites' turn to other

Pastoral Perspective

Worship has begun, and the congregation pauses for what is undoubtedly the most honest moment of the hour. It is the prayer of confession . . . a time for acknowledgment of our corporate guilt as well as our personal brokenness. It is a moment of sincere and truthful expression.

The prayer comes to an end, and the liturgist prepares to express the triumphant assurance of pardon. The worship leader takes a breath, and pauses before proclaiming the good news. It is in that pause that much of our life is lived. It is in that pause, hanging between our guilt and our forgiveness, that Psalm 80 gives voice to our cries. The prayer of confession is a time of honest admission of our longing for God's grace. The assurance of pardon is the joyful announcement that in the person of Jesus, that grace has arrived. The pause of our worship leader connects our longing with God's arrival.

With that pause, there is a great deal of expectation. What if God's grace is not given? What if the pardon does not come? What will become of us if our confessional prayer is nothing more than a cathartic outpouring of guilt? The liturgist pauses, and the congregation waits in anticipation and expectation.

The Fourth Sunday of Advent is a final step in a season of expectation. The celebration of Christmas

⁶You make us the scorn of our neighbors;
    our enemies laugh among themselves.

⁷Restore us, O God of hosts;
    let your face shine, that we may be saved.
. . . .
¹⁷But let your hand be upon the one at your right hand,
    the one whom you made strong for yourself.
¹⁸Then we will never turn back from you;
    give us life, and we will call on your name.

¹⁹Restore us, O Lᴏʀᴅ God of hosts;
    let your face shine, that we may be saved.

Exegetical Perspective

Psalm 80 is a communal prayer that arises from intense yearnings for a new beginning. Petitions for God to restore the people punctuate the psalm (vv. 1, 3, 7, 14, 17, 19), and these expressions of potent longing make it a most suitable reading for the last Sunday of Advent. The text also gives voice to our hopeful waiting during the Advent season because it refers to "the one at your right hand" who will become the agent of Israel's redemption (v. 17). This "one" at God's right hand probably refers to Israel's king, but Christians interpret the one to be Jesus, whose coming we anticipate this week.

    The deep desires this prayer expresses emerge from the tangled roots of human life, from the physical, social, and profoundly theological needs of a people in deep distress. Today's reading draws only from the beginning and end of the psalm, but the omitted verses at its center (vv. 8–16) provide clues to the source of the community's yearning, expressed in language of metaphor. In these middle verses, the people appeal to God directly ("you") by speaking about their common past. They are the "vine" whom God brought from Egypt and planted to become fruitful and prosperous in the land. Wild beasts have ravaged the vine, now burned and cut down. The vine is Israel destroyed by foreign nations, probably Assyria in particular, who invaded the northern

Homiletical Perspective

In this psalm the community laments the absence of God, petitioning God to "stir up your might" (v. 2). The psalmist describes the community as a beautiful vine ravaged by wild animals (vv. 8–13, sadly not included in the lectionary). They see no signs of God's presence in the midst of this disaster, which appears to be the demise of the northern kingdom (v. 2). To the worshipers, God appears distant or inactive. As the psalmist and this community gather to worship, they do not shirk from exposing the whole range of raw emotions they feel, including hurt, anger, and grief (vv. 4–6). When injustice prevails, God's people lament. Corporate worship is too important to pretend that God is in heaven and all is right with the world when it is not.

    Contemporary worshipers struggle with the pressure to put on a façade, to suppress their hurts and negative feelings and cover them over with our Sunday best. The lyrics from the song "Stained Glass Masquerade" express this struggle: "Am I the only one in church today feelin' so small?"[1] The song looks at the ways in which our devotion has become "plastic"— synthetic—and yet holds out hope for a more genuine faith on the other side of brokenness. Communal

---

1. Casting Crowns, "Stained Glass Masquerade," August 30, 2005, *Lifesong*, Reunion.

Psalm 80:1-7, 17-19

Theological Perspective

gods. The community has not simply fallen on hard times. It is experiencing God's temporary absence or, perhaps worse, a permanent absence or—as Job feared—God's sinister delight in tormenting him.

The theologian must tread carefully here and avoid the example of Job's friends, who confuse theological reflection with pastoral care. Job's friends seek to comfort Job by offering reasons for his suffering: It is punishment for Job's sins, it is a test of his faith, it is a character-building exercise that will leave him stronger and spiritually mature. Job rebuffs his friends, suggesting insightfully they are defending not God but their own views of how the world works. "Who that was innocent ever perished?" asks Eliphaz, who concludes emphatically that Job must be guilty, for the contrary is unthinkable. If Job is innocent, then Eliphaz and his associates are also vulnerable to catastrophe "for no reason" (Job 2:3).

As "faith seeking understanding," theology is a second-order discourse, moving away from the intensely personal language of Psalm 80 to a more rational, objective language that tries to explain the reasons for the psalmist's sufferings. Perhaps later the psalmist will be able to reflect theologically on his or her suffering, but theology is not a substitute for pastoral care. Immersed in grief and anger, the psalmist needs the consoling embrace of a friend, not a sermon or lecture on why he is suffering.

The horrors of the twentieth century have led many Jewish and Christian thinkers to "anti-theodicy," the surrender of all attempts to justify God of such horrendous suffering. The logically satisfying theodicies—that suffering is punishment for sin, a test of faith, or a character-building exercise—may hold true in some instances, and the psalmist suggests in verse 18 that some degree of punishment was deserved. These theodicies become sacrilege when advanced as explanations for the Holocaust and similar instances of genocide and oppression. Psalm 80 embraces a theodicy of protest, which cries out to God and insists that God must bear some responsibility for evil.

There is a strong tendency in Christianity to think that one should suffer in silence before almighty God and to be suspicious of any protest that does not end with an affirmation of insight and a return to faith. One might argue, however, that the protest of Psalm 80 is rooted in an affirmation of faith. The psalm is addressed, not to a mute unmoved mover, but to the God who speaks and acts in the life of Israel. The psalmist has not been ren-

Pastoral Perspective

is just days away. Families have been awaiting the arrival of loved ones. College students, home for the holidays, have been catching up with hometown friends. Children have been eyeing the pile of presents with enthralled anticipation. Recent widows have been looking to the coming of Christmas with questions, wondering how to make it through the season that now seems so different. Christmas Day is almost here . . . but it has not yet come. There is still a time of waiting and hoping and wondering. So on this Fourth Sunday of Advent, worshipers pause, offering to God their hopes and then, with anticipation and expectation, looking forward to the fulfillment of those dreams.

In a much grander way, all of life is lived in that moment. For years people have tried to make a better world, and in some small ways there have been measures of success. A few more mouths are being fed. Fleeting signs of justice emerge around the globe. Every once in a while people actually seem to do the right thing. Racial divides are broken down; marriage vows are honored; people are treated with dignity; and for a few shining moments it looks as if humanity is going to pull it off. A better world is going to be built.

Then the world rears its ugly head, and the morning headlines proclaim the reality of this broken world. Keeping up with the neighbors becomes an obsession. Rampant consumerism drives people to extend their credit cards to the maximum. Fears about losing our own precious health insurance keep us from advocating for those who have none. Internet pornography offers an unsatisfying but unending answer to the lure of lust. Suddenly, optimism and naiveté give way to a more realistic assessment. Left to our own devices, we have made a mess of things.

We have strategized; we have planned; we have held hearings; we have hosted meetings; we have read and we have studied. Still, on our own, we have not found the key to peace or the solution to the animosity that divides us. We have come to a moment of honest confession.

So, both together in the name of all humanity and individually in an expression of personal sin that entangles us all, the congregation offers its prayer of confession and waits for the assurance of God's grace and God's forgiveness.

It is in that waiting, in that pause, that the cry of Psalm 80 becomes real. Three times (vv. 3, 7, 19) the psalmist cries out, "Restore us, O God let your face shine, that we may be saved." The implication is clear. If God's face does not shine, then we are lost in

Exegetical Perspective

kingdom of Israel in 721 BCE and displaced its people. According to this prayer, however, the angry God of Israel is the primary agent of the destruction.

Today's reading contains petitions that frame these words about the nation's predicament. The reading divides into three parts: petition for attention and action (vv. 1–3), complaint (vv. 4–7), and petition and promise (vv. 17–19). Each unit ends with a refrain, asking God to restore them (vv. 3, 7, and 19).

Petition for Attention and Action (vv. 1–3). The communal speaker begs God, the Shepherd of Israel, to hear the people. This first request of the text is perhaps the most essential. It seeks what all suffering people seek, to be heard, and later to be seen, in their suffering (v. 14). Their primary desire is for God to recognize their plight and attend to their pain. They assume that if God could see the situation, God would surely do something about it.

The Shepherd to whom they appeal is God as King, but addressed in more tender terms as the one who cares for and nurtures the flock. This Shepherd King is enthroned on a dais beyond ordinary royal expectations. God is enthroned on the ark of the covenant and supported by the cherubim. The ark is the visible, portable shrine upon which the invisible God accompanied Israel through its travails in the wilderness. God is before them again, "shining forth" before the three tribes who also appear in procession through the desert in front of the ark (Num 2:32–34). Here they are probably stand-ins for all Israel, portrayed as the worshiping community that it is at the root of its identity and desires to be again. The speaker relies on divine power and urges God to "stir up your might," because God alone can save them.

Then the speaker's voice heightens the people's petition with two clauses that illuminate one another and form a refrain across the psalm: "Restore us, O God" and "Let your face shine" (v. 3). The Hebrew of these lines allows for several nuances. The verb "restore" also means to "return," "bring back." The plea, then, is for more than the political restoration of the nation. That concrete hope is interlocked with the deep desire to be brought back to God or to be returned to their former relationship. The second clause confirms this nuance. When it begs, "Let your face shine," it asks for divine presence, for the light of God's own being to spread over them (cf. Num 6:25). The final words of this refrain underscore the consequences of such blessing; when the people renew relationship with God, they will be saved, but that has not yet happened.

Homiletical Perspective

laments like Psalm 80 invite worshipers to express their own disillusions with life and with God.

How do you preach lament to relatively comfortable and secure congregations? We may not be oppressed, but the neighborhoods and urban communities in which many of us live are. We are a part of larger communities; when our communities hurt, we hurt along with them.

As a corporate lament, this psalm presents an occasion for the church to name the places in our neighborhoods, communities, and country where God seems absent. Preachers will do well to ask, Where is love neglected? What vineyards have been abandoned and ravaged (vv. 12–13)? What communities have been devastated?

As I think about the city of Memphis, where my church community lives, we have much about which to lament. We lament because Memphis has the highest infant mortality rate of any major city in the country; babies are buried in mass unmarked graves every Tuesday and Thursday in a cemetery nicknamed Babyland.[2] We lament that in 2008, about 9,000 out of the 15,000 children born were born to single mothers. We lament that the 2007 FBI report lists Memphis as the second most violent city in the country. We lament because our community remains one of the poorest urban centers in the United States.

Yes, we have plenty about which to lament. Most importantly, as a church we lament our neglect and indifference to our communities. The book *Blue Like Jazz* tells how a few Christian students at Reed College in Portland, Oregon, set up a "Confession Booth" during a particularly wild weekend festival on campus, knowing that plenty of sinning will occur.[3] However, there is a twist. As curious students walk by and enter the booth to inquire what this is all about, they discover that they are not expected to confess to the Christians, but that the Christians confess to them! The Christians confess their lack of love and their bitterness. They apologize for the televangelists, for neglecting the poor and the lonely. They express sorrow for having misrepresented Jesus on campus. The Christian students ask for forgiveness. Quite a refreshing irony!

The spirit of this psalm calls on churches to lament with neighbors our own role in making God absent: our neglect of the urban plight, our disengagement from our neighborhoods, our flight from cities to suburbs. This psalm invites us to accept vicariously

2. See "Babyland," on ABC's *20/20*, August 22, 2008.
3. Donald Miller, *Blue Like Jazz* (Nashville: Thomas Nelson, 2003), 116–27.

Psalm 80:1-7, 17-19

Theological Perspective

dered mute by the experience of suffering, which would suggest surrender, a withdrawal from community, perhaps even the loss of one's capacity for empathy. Perhaps this protest gives voice to others whose trauma has been far worse, effectively rendering them unable to speak.

The cry of protest is an expression of grief, the affirmation that things are not right. This honest protest saves the psalmist from hypocrisy and despair. It saves the psalmist from hypocrisy because the psalm is not a glib affirmation of faith that subverts the protest of the psalm and may be understood as an attempt to bargain with God. It saves the psalmist from despair because it is an attempt to communicate with God and with fellow human beings, harboring the hope that change is possible and seeking the formation of a community of solidarity that will work for change. The psalmist's "dark night of the soul" should be instructive to Christians celebrating Advent and Christmas. It bids us to recognize just how thick our darkness is, and it invites us to empathize with the cries of protest from all over our world, especially at Christmas.

The protest of Psalm 80 also prompts a question: Does protest belong to Christmas? Is Christmas a response to this theodicy of protest? Matthew's birth story is clearly modeled on the exodus, a time when God was moved by the cries and groans of the Israelite slaves: "I have observed the misery of my people who are in Egypt; I have heard their cry on account of their taskmasters. Indeed, I know their sufferings, and I have come down to deliver them from the Egyptians" (Exod. 3:7–8). If we take seriously the claim of incarnation, is it too much to suggest that Christmas marks another time when God hears the cries of suffering and comes down in solidarity to share that suffering, joining the protest against violence, oppression, and deception? The birth stories in Matthew and Luke are themselves signs of protest against powerful agents of violence and oppression, including King Herod and his Roman supporters. The violent opposition of Herod and those serving him provokes yet another protest: Mothers and fathers weeping for their slaughtered babies, refusing to be consoled (Matt. 2:16–18). How can such evil possibly be defeated?

JOHN C. SHELLEY

Pastoral Perspective

our sin. Salvation will be but a distant dream and an empty hope. We will be, as Paul later wrote to the Corinthians, "of all people most to be pitied" (1 Cor. 15:19). We have tried to make it on our own, but our efforts have proven fruitless. They have brought us to this point of desperate honesty.

Like all of the psalms, this Eightieth Psalm expresses the raw, honest emotion of a person of faith. It is a plaintive and hopeful cry, voiced by one who has tried and come up short. Standing in the footsteps of the psalmist is not a popular place to be. To arrive at this point has required an honest admission of guilt and even failure. Standing with the psalmist has meant speaking the truth about one's own inadequacies. It is a not a pleasant place to stand.

To stand in the place of the psalmist is also to stand in a place of hopeful anticipation. Having admitted a need for salvation, the psalmist stands waiting for God's answer. It is a place of hope, a place of anticipation, a place of new beginnings.

The prayer of confession has been completed, and the worship leader pauses before continuing. In the next breath, it will be Christmas morning, and the "hopes and fears of all the years" will be met in the one who is born in that manger. In the next breath, it will be the culmination of all of human history, and Jesus will return as "King of kings and Lord of lords." In the next breath, it will be that triumphant moment expressed in the book of Revelation when God "will wipe every tear from their eyes. Death will be no more; mourning and crying and pain will be no more" (Rev. 21:4).

The people pour out their confession, expressing their deepest needs. "Restore us, O God; let your face shine, that we may be saved." The liturgist stands to speak, and in the next breath proclaims these triumphant words: "In Jesus Christ, we are forgiven!" It is this hope that sustains us on even the darkest bleak midwinter day.

E. LANE ALDERMAN JR.

Exegetical Perspective

Complaint (vv. 4–7). The hopeful petition for restoration does not express quiet submission to win divine approval. Instead, the speaker rebukes God with the familiar complaint "How long?" According to this psalm, the problem does not rest with the people; the problem is God, who is angry at the people's prayers. How else can the present turmoil be understood? Rather than nourishing them with the bread of life, God has served them tears for food and drink and made them objects of scorn and laughter among their neighbors (vv. 5–6). Verse 7 repeats the refrain of verse 3, calling for God to restore, renew, shed light, and be present, so they may be saved.

Petition and Promise (vv. 17–19). The final section asks for God to strengthen Israel's political king, the one at God's right hand, "the one you made strong for yourself." Although the hope for a strong king will never be realized for the northern kingdom, the prayer takes the shape of messianic expectations for Christians, who see it fulfilled in the birth of Jesus. When God does answer their prayer—when God does give them life—the people promise they will never turn away from God. The life that the community seeks is to survive, to have a future, and to live in restored relationship with God. That possibility rests in divine hands. The psalm closes with the repetition of the refrain that Christians can pray with full hearts. The Christ is the one at God's right hand, the one who saves the people. "Restore us, O Lord God . . . ; let your face shine, that we may be saved." With Jewish brothers and sisters, Christians await salvation through the one at God's right hand. We too wait for God's face to shine upon us and for God to satisfy our deepest longings, so that we may live as the worshiping people we are.

KATHLEEN M. O'CONNOR

Homiletical Perspective

the suffering of our community, to express our agony and grief to God in worship, and then to take action that will demonstrate God's presence.

Psalm 80 is assigned to the season of Advent. In the midst of the lament, the psalmist cries out to God to remain absent no longer but to come, intervene, and rescue: "Restore us, O God of hosts; let your face shine, that we may be saved." This refrain is repeated throughout the psalm (vv. 3, 7, 19; cf. v. 14). The psalmist recalls with fond memories the exodus, when God delivered Israel from oppression. The psalmist does not replay the historical facts about the exodus. Rather, by use of imagination, the psalmist evokes the emotions of the worshipers and recreates the exodus experience as a story about a weak and dying vine (vv. 8–11). God rescues the vine and carefully transplants it in the rich and fertile soil of Canaan, where it grows into a vibrant beautiful plant. (Preachers would do well to find ways to implement such imaginative reframing in their preaching.) Now Israel pleads with God to do it again (vv. 14–15). Israel believes with all its being that God can rescue it from its miserable state.

During Advent, the church pleads to God on behalf of the city to come, to restore health and vigor to the vine, to rescue the city from its plight. As the church worships, we believe in God's power and love to save the city. Little by little, as the church repents of our former neglect, we look for ways to become authentic representatives of God in the community. The church can no longer masquerade as "happy plastic people under shiny plastic steeples" ("Stained Glass Masquerade"). Only when we take responsibility will God be able to intervene and restore. Only then will we witness the glory of the coming of the Lord.

DAVE BLAND

Romans 1:1-7

¹Paul, a servant of Jesus Christ, called to be an apostle, set apart for the gospel of God, ²which he promised beforehand through his prophets in the holy scriptures, ³the gospel concerning his Son, who was descended from David according to the flesh ⁴and was declared to be Son of God with power according to the spirit of holiness by resurrection from the dead, Jesus Christ our Lord, ⁵through whom we have received grace and apostleship to bring about the obedience of faith among all the Gentiles for the sake of his name, ⁶including yourselves who are called to belong to Jesus Christ,
⁷To all God's beloved in Rome, who are called to be saints:
Grace to you and peace from God our Father and the Lord Jesus Christ.

Theological Perspective

Before the gospel story is narrated in Advent 4, the epistle provides some theological foundation in a series of key words. These trigger reflection on a range of themes centered on the salvation event of God in Jesus and our response to that event. Both foci are prominent here: Paul writes concisely of God in Jesus and of his own and his addressees' response, in a typical letter opening reinforced by what looks like an early creed.

Writing to a city he had not yet visited and where some believers probably distrusted him, Paul may have counted on this Jewish Christian confession of faith to provide reassurance in terms that foreshadow the later christological orthodoxy summarized in four words: truly human, truly God. Davidic descent (v. 3) refers to Jesus' royal messiahship. This was soon weakened by Gentile Christians to little more than the name Christ, but it strongly underlines the humanity of Jesus, and his Jewish particularity. The Christmas celebration encourages reflection on the holy child's dependent humanity, corresponding to his vulnerability on the cross, and that calls for more reflection than is common on his Jewishness and Palestinian context. This and his royal messiahship will again be highlighted by the inscription on the cross (Matt. 27:37; Mark 15:26; John 19:19–22).

Pastoral Perspective

It is always a strained day, this Fourth Sunday of Advent. The liturgically faithful cling tenaciously to the waning season of Advent and its songs and themes of waiting, patience, anticipation, and expectation. Meanwhile, those fully immersed in the flow (which includes just about all of us) of consumer culture are feeling strongly the urge to let loose a carol or two. Here we are with Paul's salutation to his Christian sisters and brothers in Rome. It is tempting to set this text aside and take up the Gospel lesson from Matthew 1, which commends itself to the Christmas-hungry crowd; or the Old Testament lesson from Isaiah 7, which plays well with those inclined to toe the Advent line. For those willing to venture beyond the obvious choices, I encourage you to spend some time with these opening verses from Romans 1.

Salutations are something we spend less time with these days in our written communications. Many e-mails I receive no longer have any salutation at all. Never a "greetings from" sentence or two and often not even a "Dear David." We live in an age of promiscuous communication—more messages and less meaning. We have lost the art of the salutation. Perhaps our lives have lost the gravity necessary to construct a meaningful salutation.

Paul chooses his opening words with great care. As is often the case in his letter writing, Paul's

Exegetical Perspective

The opening greeting of Paul's letter to the Romans is unique among all his letters in the NT. Typically, he follows a simple pattern adapted from ordinary Greek letter writing: the name of the sender(s) and recipients, followed by a brief prayer for grace and peace. Each letter has its own developments, but only Romans has such an elaborate declaration about Jesus Christ. The reason for this is to be found in the twice-repeated word "gospel."

Paul identifies himself as one called to be an apostle and then defines "apostle" as one "set apart for the gospel of God" (cf. Jer. 1:5). He then describes this gospel in terms of two significant aspects: its foretelling in prophetic Scripture and its content concerning Jesus. Paul then brings the subject back around to his apostleship and its consequences: he received this apostleship through Jesus, and the result has been "the obedience of faith among all the Gentiles" (v. 5), including the first readers of the letter. The christological elaboration is meant to show Jesus Christ as both the content and the source of the gospel that Paul, as an apostle, preaches.

By first relating the gospel to the prophets, Paul makes an appropriate introduction to the christological material that follows, for in early Christian thinking both Jesus' descent from David and his resurrection were understood to be the fulfillment of ancient divine

Homiletical Perspective

"Called"—Paul makes it sound so simple and straightforward! Three times in the space of his letter's *long* first sentence, Paul tosses off the term without hesitation, qualification, or seeming awareness of how debatable his claim might be. Especially since this "call" is supposedly from *God*, and asserted to apply to his *listeners* as well, anyone within the reach of Paul's voice might be pardoned for raising an eyebrow!

Calls from God are notorious—mental institutions are full of folks who "hear" them. Calls from God can be noxious—untold numbers of innocent victims are maimed or murdered because true believers follow through on a mission inspired by an unquestioned call.

Amid all the pitches that are pressed upon us at this time of the year (Buy *this*! Give to *that*!); amid all the internal impulses that surge to consciousness during the days before Christmas (I *must have* this! I *should do* that!)—how do we discern *to what* we are "called," and *by whom*?

What seems a clear trumpet one day can, on the following day, be muted, distant, silent. What is unmistakable and incontrovertible to one side of a political or religious debate is just not heard by the other. It is hard enough to get clear on one's own call. What gives anyone the assurance (to say nothing of the authority) to lay claim to the call of another?

Romans 1:1-7

Theological Perspective

The particularity of the incarnation makes the Old Testament and Judaism part of every Christian's heritage and makes us mindful of our relationship with our fellow worshipers of God in the synagogue. This link with Abraham has grown in potential as our relationship with Islam and the political turmoil involving Jews, Christians, and Muslims in the Middle East have again become urgent. Our shared heritage has to become a bridge, not a continuation of family feuds. The messiahship of Jesus remains a bone of contention, but one to be chewed over together by believers who have much in common, including varying degrees of reverence for Jesus himself.

The early creed echoed here could suggest an "adoptionist" perspective on Jesus, as though he were promoted to divine status at the resurrection. That is not Paul's view and his introductory "concerning his Son" (v. 3) prefaces the reference to his human origin with a hint of preexistence. Who Jesus is and was, he must presumably have always been. As the saving revelation of God, he is appropriately thought of as eternally in the presence of the Father. The Nicene Creed draws out implications of this New Testament witness in philosophical language from its own day. It has remained a normative expression of Christian truth and retained its doxological solemnity even for generations that no longer share its modes of thought. The exalted title "Son of God," prominent throughout the New Testament, is now naturally read in the light of that subsequent doctrinal development.

The liturgical celebration of Christmas makes ample room for the imagination, but the doctrinal language of incarnation holds Christian reflection to the divine meaning and status of Jesus, even when referring without narrative elaboration to his human birth, and alluding through the word "gospel" to his death. The early creed roots our celebration in the resurrection (through the agency of God's Spirit), which is foundational to all Christian discourse about Jesus, and Paul prefaces it with something else: a strong affirmation of the Old Testament promise (included in a creed at 1 Cor. 15:3–5). This reinforces Christian talk of God, because religious talk of God is regularly based on earlier religious traditions being understood in new ways in the light of new revelation.

Talk of God also speaks of the humans who receive and are changed by this revelation. Christology therefore has soteriological and ecclesiological dimensions. The Davidic echo here thus points to God's agent rescuing or redeeming God's people. "Son of God" also has messianic overtones (Ps. 2:7) and in addition evokes political hopes of salvation in

Pastoral Perspective

salutations lay the groundwork for the content to follow. This salutation here in Romans is his longest. What comes through is a strong and clear sense of his personal identity and purpose. His life is entirely shaped by his commitment and devotion to Jesus Christ.

First, Paul begins by naming his commitment and devotion to Christ as servant. He sees himself, first and foremost, in terms of service to Christ. Paul does not begin with his social location—as a child, a parent, a spouse, or a worker of one kind or another. He begins with his relation to Christ. The point of reference for Paul is not a doctrinal tradition, a set of laws, a series of practices. He identifies himself with a person—not an idea or an abstraction. It is a way of life that he lives in response to the grace he has personally received.

Second, he names his commitment and devotion to the "gospel of God" as an apostle. This apostleship is not of his own making—to this he has been called, and for this he has been set apart. In this context, Paul elaborates the "gospel" in which his calling is embedded and from which it derives its legitimacy. This gospel is not abstract or impersonal for Paul; neither is it purely subjective or experiential. It is grounded in the "holy scriptures," the historical appearing of Jesus in the flesh, the revelation of Christ as Lord through the event of resurrection, and the particular experience of grace he has known in his own life. Paul situates himself squarely and unambiguously in the story of God's unfolding purpose in the world. It is, from start to finish, a story of redemption and inclusion.

Third, Paul names his commitment and devotion to all those "called to belong to Jesus Christ" (v. 6), especially the Gentiles—a particular expression of his apostleship. It is the fact that he belongs to Christ that frees him to belong to and with others. One cannot read Paul's letters without coming away with a strong sense for his profound devotion to individuals and communities. He had never visited the church in Rome, but already he shared a bond with them because of their common bond in Christ.

Paul's salutation frames for us a life lived in light of the coming of Christ. Who among us does not yearn for this kind of clarity of identity and purpose in life? Surely the culminating call of the Advent season is a call to renew our commitment and devotion to Christ and his purposes for us in and for the world. There is a crucial reminder to be heard and heeded as we turn the corner to the familiar tunes and tales of Christmas.

promises, foretold in Scripture (Matt. 2:5–6; 1 Cor. 15:4). Paul's claim that the Gentiles who have converted through his preaching include the believers at Rome is a little surprising, since he has never preached there (Rom. 1:10–15). He is evidently speaking inclusively as the one who "had been entrusted with the gospel for the uncircumcised" (Gal. 2:7).

In fact, the whole reason for this elaboration of the content of his gospel is precisely that the Roman believers had not heard him preach. He is planning to come to them, and he wants their support for the continuation of his mission, this time in Spain (Rom. 15:23–29). If they are to support his preaching of the gospel, they will need to know what it is firsthand, rather than relying on rumors (3:8). A major part of Paul's reason for writing this letter is to introduce his gospel to the Roman Christians whose backing he desires for his mission. He begins this introduction already in his opening greeting: Paul the called and set-apart apostle preaches the gospel to bring Gentiles to faith, and this is what that gospel is.

The declarations about Jesus, then, are in some sense the essence of Paul's gospel message. According to many scholars, they are not an original composition on Paul's part, but a very early formulation of Christian belief, a kind of primitive creed or confession that was already traditional when Paul wrote. The core formulation in verses 3–4 mentions only two facts about Jesus, his descent from Israel's ancient King David and his resurrection from the dead. The latter, however, is also associated with his being declared Son of God. Jesus thus has a double "sonship," human and divine.

Correspondingly, these two things are said to be "according to the flesh" (v. 3) and "according to the spirit of holiness" (v. 4; a Hebraic way of saying "Holy Spirit") respectively. That is to say, Jesus' Davidic descent came about in the normal course of human events, while his being Son of God was the result of an extraordinary intervention "with power" (v. 4) by God's own Spirit. Both kinds of sonship are ways of designating Jesus as the expected Messiah, descended from David and enthroned at his resurrection as God's royal Son (connected with such texts as Ps. 2:7; 2 Sam. 7:8–16).

The most surprising feature of this ancient formulation may be the way it presents the claim that Jesus is God's Son (which has to do more with messianic than with Trinitarian ideas here). This early Christian confession of Jesus as Son of God associates that claim with his resurrection, rather than with his birth. Jesus' birth is said to be "according to

As a noun (a "call") or a past-tense verb ("called"), the word carries connotations of fixed and final—something issued and uttered (and answered, ignored, or declined), rather than an unsettled, ambiguous, open-ended process of dawning, discovery, and development (as in "a calling").

While Paul does not seem (at first hearing, anyway) to address such questions and concerns in his introduction to the Christians in Romans, they cannot help but be live for us. (They would surely also be in play for Joseph in the dream narrative with which Matthew commences his Gospel. The God who speaks to him in a disturbing dream is, after all, the same God who has given the law Joseph is attempting to honor in relation to Mary—not slavishly obeying, but sensitively applying it.)

The more that is at stake in a call, the more urgent these questions become. Advent is not just about *awaiting* a clearly anticipated call; it is also about seeking a space in the midst of a cacophony, for discerning what *is* call, here and now; and what response is called for and feasible at this particular point. Rhetorical ruffles and flourishes about "answering the call" ("Paul and Joseph *did*, so the Romans and we *should!*") will inevitably founder as abstractions—inappropriate theologically and ineffective homiletically.

There is more than meets the ear in an initial hearing of this letter's opening. Paul, in fact, *does* have our concerns in mind. The call he experienced, according to his own account (and that of his biographer Luke), was a long time coming, and one that continued to address him throughout his life. His Damascus road experience was but one focal point in a journey of discernment. His Epistle to the Romans is a sustained invitation to vocational adventure of which these words are but the overture.

As Paul will later say, "the gifts and the calling of God are irrevocable" (Rom. 11:29), but honing in on *who* is calling—and *how*—is, for Jew and Greek alike, a protracted, even tortuous journey, a story of God's attempting to engage the broken stories of human beings who constantly respond to a myriad of tempting, deceptive calls.

Here, at the outset of the letter to the Romans, Paul makes a "called" claim concerning himself, "to make a long story short." He offers a deft, summary sketch of an extended continuing calling process. The claim that his listeners are also called is not a manifestation of manipulative religious marketing; rather, it is an expression of trust in a God who keeps on calling until the divine voice is, at long last, deeply heard and faithfully obeyed.

Romans 1:1-7

Theological Perspective

the Roman world, as does Paul's third prominent christological title, "Lord" (v. 4). Even the word "gospel" has a secular background, suggesting salvation in Roman imperial ideology. All these cultural echoes are redirected by Paul to point to Jesus.

Paul's characteristic word "gospel" (*euangelion*), repeated in verse 9 ("of his Son") and verse 16 ("of God"), recalls the verb, which is prominent in Second Isaiah, quoted at Romans 10:15 and by Handel. It encapsulates his oral proclamation of the still-contemporary event of Christ's death and resurrection. According to Paul, the only appropriate response is "faith," here qualified as "obedience" (v. 5; cf. Rom. 15:18) but including trust in God, hope in God, and the thankful confession of God's involvement in the world in and through Jesus.

What this involves will be unfolded as the letter continues. Those who have heard it read and reread will have their memories jogged by some twenty key words in this passage. "Grace" is part of the greeting in verse 7, but in verse 5 refers to the power and gift of God mediated in the gospel. Paul himself is an apostle, sent with a particular mission to the Gentile world of which his Roman recipients are a notable part, but God's call is not limited to those with some special role, nor is God's grace limited to those whose special task requires special gifts. All believers are called to some vocation and ministry, and all are empowered. Labeling his hearers "saints" or "holy ones," Paul indicates that as he is "set apart" (v. 1) for his apostolic task, so they are no less set apart, dedicated, holy.

The recipients in Rome are also defined as called "of" (taken as "belonging to") Jesus Christ (v. 6). This too unfolds what is meant by "faith," the identity marker of the Christian. It is defined by its double object, God and Christ. We are oriented to God, whom we know through Christ in his death and resurrection, which events remain as central to Christian remembrance at Christmas as in all other seasons.

We are also (and most aware of this at Christmas) united in him with all who call upon his name, beloved of God. The greeting to "all" Christians in Rome contains a hint of the separation of the different house churches in Rome, and probable divisions between Jewish and Gentile believers that Paul is perhaps hoping to help overcome by his letter. The unity of Christians in one body is as basic to Christian faith as membership in that body itself.

ROBERT C. MORGAN

Pastoral Perspective

For Paul, creed is not a detached recitation of doctrine, to prove right thinking or to establish orthodox credentials. Creed (and this is what commentators believe was being employed by Paul in this text) is nothing less than a template for a way of life. Here he weaves together in seamless fashion the story of Christ and his own story. He does not conflate the two—Christ remains primary in every way. However, the work of Christ works its way out in the specific purpose and calling that shapes his daily existence. Paul makes clear that this is not the case for him alone. This is the way it is for all who "are called to belong to Jesus Christ" (v. 6).

Having begun his salutation by grounding his identity in a relationship, Paul ends it by grounding the Roman Christians' identity in one as well. Some in our midst are lonely and lost during this mandatorily joyful season. Preachers will do well to let Paul address them, as he did their ancient brothers and sisters, as all those who are beloved by God (v. 7).

Perhaps in the context of this culminating Advent Sunday, it is appropriate to press the question of how our way of life could be identified in relation to the creed that is most familiar to the congregation at hand. What connections between the identity of Christ and the identity of the confessor could be readily made? Does the creed amplify one's sense of purpose and calling? Does it help to situate one in time and in relation to the world? Does the creed hover above one's life as an abstraction, or does it supply, in some sense, the form and orientation for one's daily existence? These are by no means simple questions to answer, but they remind us that the beliefs we hold are to hold us and mold us into saints and servants of God.

As we prepare for the season in which we celebrate the Word become flesh, Paul's salutation provides the perfect segue.

DAVID J. WOOD

Exegetical Perspective

the flesh," not the result of a supernatural conception; at any rate, no such conception is mentioned. Especially in Advent, this presents difficulties for the theologically more advanced or "higher" understanding of Jesus as Son of God from his birth. It is a reminder that even the NT is not perfectly uniform in the details of its Christology, and that the claim that Jesus is the Son of God (found throughout the NT) developed in various ways as the earliest Christians reflected on their memories of him and their experiences of him both before and after his resurrection. This may be an encouragement for Christian communities today who find themselves in situations of theological diversity or disagreement.

The christological formulation or confession, which may well have been familiar to the Roman Christians independently of Paul's letter, lets Paul identify his gospel message with an understanding of Jesus that was widely accepted in the early church. It focuses on Jesus as Messiah, the eschatological (end time) king and bringer of redemption, whose coming inaugurates the eschatological or messianic age. He fulfills the promises of the prophets as the Messiah descended from David, enthroned as God's royal Son at his resurrection. The powerful intervention of God's Spirit was also expected in the end time, and by bringing about the resurrection of Jesus, it opens the door to the general resurrection of the dead, a key feature of messianic expectation.

This passage thus connects to Advent themes of Christ's coming to fulfill God's promises of redemption, and of hope for the full and final redemption yet to come. By declaring Jesus to be God's chosen ruler and lord, the subject of a gospel (*euangelion*, proclamation of good news, often made about Roman emperors), it also contrasts him with Caesar and implies that God's eschatological ruler trumps even the power of the world's greatest empire. Paul's own mission was part of God's eschatological action (v. 5), and by continuing it today the church continues to offer redemption and hope as an alternative to oppressive powers.

DAVID RENSBERGER

Homiletical Perspective

The "gospel of God" (v. 1) itself unfolds, Paul says, in a sweeping, spacious trajectory, rather than coming as a cold, sudden blare. It is initially promised through the "prophets in the holy scriptures" (v. 2). The impact and implications of the call, as concentrated in Jesus Christ, become apparent only in a revelatory arc that moves from a human birth as a descendant of David (v. 3), through a divine certification by way of resurrection (v. 4), to a commissioning of human apostles for extending God's calling to the ends of the earth. Paul is setting both himself and his listeners within the surrounding sweep of a cosmic symphony. When such glorious music is playing all around us, how can we keep from singing?

This does not, of course, answer all the legitimate questions about bogus calls that are beamed in our direction, or misguided hearings of calls God is trying to send us. It will not provide us with easy escape routes from making hard calls concerning these calls. In the immediately following verses (vv. 11–14), however, Paul declares himself to be a "debtor" to all kinds of people, and as eager to be strengthened and challenged by the call of God as it comes to him through the Romans as he is to offer such strength and challenge to them through what he says and does. The listening process, in other words, is ongoing. While it is surely sorely tempting to shut down our attention during the frenetic run-up to Christmas ("All I want is some peace and quiet!"), we are in a better position to home in on our calling if we are open to the record of how God *has* spoken over time (in history and in Scripture) and how God *may be* speaking here and now (in dialogue with fellow Christians and the wider world)—that is, if we undertake Advent listening.

DAVID J. SCHLAFER

Matthew 1:18-25

[18]Now the birth of Jesus the Messiah took place in this way. When his mother Mary had been engaged to Joseph, but before they lived together, she was found to be with child from the Holy Spirit. [19]Her husband Joseph, being a righteous man and unwilling to expose her to public disgrace, planned to dismiss her quietly. [20]But just when he had resolved to do this, an angel of the Lord appeared to him in a dream and said, "Joseph, son of David, do not be afraid to take Mary as your wife, for the child conceived in her is from the Holy Spirit. [21]She will bear a son, and you are to name him Jesus, for he will save his people from their sins." [22]All this took place to fulfill what had been spoken by the Lord through the prophet:

[23]"Look, the virgin shall conceive and bear a son,
    and they shall name him Emmanuel,"

which means, "God is with us." [24]When Joseph awoke from sleep, he did as the angel of the Lord commanded him; he took her as his wife, [25]but had no marital relations with her until she had borne a son; and he named him Jesus.

Theological Perspective

Jan Milič Lochman (1922–2004), the gently provocative Czech theologian who taught in Basel for many years, frequently noted the way both the communist East and the capitalist West fostered "one-dimensional" views of reality. Truth is reduced to fact, and fact denotes what fits into the reigning economy, with its ideals of production and consumption and its corresponding ways of measuring and controlling reality. For Lochman, Christian faith involves a deliverance from that sort of impoverished perception—or, rather, lack of perception.

Christian preaching can open eyes and ears to a fuller awareness of reality in its God-relatedness, and can equip us to become doers as well as hearers of a more adequate and life-giving truth. Christian preaching can do so, that is, provided that preachers are not themselves so captivated by the dominant order of things—the *kosmos* of which the Fourth Gospel speaks—that their preaching simply reinforces it rather than challenging it at its base.

This familiar nativity text in Matthew provides an opportunity for preachers to examine themselves on this score, and then to help their congregations receive a similar gift of vision. Lochman's treatment of the relevant passages in the Apostles' Creed—"conceived by the Holy Spirit, born of the Virgin

Pastoral Perspective

American culture and media both load Christmas with false expectations of family harmony and good cheer. These images and expectations allow Hallmark and the shopping mall catalog to define the "perfect Christmas." In the weeks before Christmas, many who worship in our congregations invest a great deal of time and energy trying to achieve that picture-perfect Christmas. Others feel emptiness or sadness that their lives and families prevent them from having the sort of Christmas they believe they should have.

In today's story of Mary and Joseph, God's work often upsets comfortable social expectations and conventions. The first Christmas was not produced by a flawless lead-up and elaborate preparations dictated by convention. Certainly most people would not expect the incarnation to happen through the life of the young virgin girl, Mary. Many in our congregations forget just what a scandal the incarnation and the virgin birth really were, that behind the pretty nativity scene lies both a wonder and a scandal.

Invite people to think about their own experience—the ways in which they have failed to live up to the notion of the "perfect Christmas" and the ways that, despite that failure, they ended up finding themselves more graced and more faithful than they might have otherwise been.

Exegetical Perspective

The long genealogy presented in Matthew 1:1–16 ends with a problem. The first verse indicates that the following genealogy intends to show that Jesus Messiah is the son of David, yet when the report reaches Joseph, we do not read, "and Joseph fathered Jesus." Instead we get the genealogically awkward, "Joseph the husband of Mary, of whom Jesus was born" (v. 16).

The central function of verses 18–25, therefore, is to deal with this problem. Mary's miraculous conception is announced as a fact without explanation: "she was found to be with child from the Holy Spirit" (v. 18). Since Joseph does not know the cause of her pregnancy, he fears she has been unfaithful. Betrothal was equivalent to marriage; infidelity counted as adultery. The marriage was completed when the groom took his betrothed to his own home. In the interval she remained in her father's house, and sexual intercourse was not permitted.

Joseph is described as a righteous man. This means that he must divorce his unfaithful wife; the law does not allow him to "forgive and forget." His righteousness, however, is more than legal; he does not want to humiliate Mary with a public divorce proclaiming her adultery. He plans to divorce her quietly. Before he carries out this plan, he has a

Homiletical Perspective

Our congregations on this Fourth Sunday of Advent will expect us to preach the good news that the savior is near. Even if they already know the *answer* that Immanuel is near, might we wonder if they are asking the *right questions*? Do contemporary believers still need a savior? What does a savior save us from? What does a savior save us for? Perhaps today's preaching could help people ask those questions. The sermon might also focus on Joseph in his act of profound *trust* that God will provide marvelous answers through Mary, his young bride.

Asking the Right Questions. Perhaps you have had a teacher or professor who somehow always seemed to miss the question. She or he barely catches a word before immediately launching into a lengthy answer to a question that the student did not ask. The answers are often interesting, but not to the point, and therefore not especially helpful. Preachers too often answer questions that the congregation has not asked. As Christmas approaches, we might be tempted to proclaim that the long-awaited savior is near, before first helping believers ask whether they know that they really need a savior.

Isaiah's people knew they needed a savior. At key moments in their salvation history, believers knew

Matthew 1:18-25

Theological Perspective

Mary"—can be of substantial help here.[1] Lochman observed how the meaning of these passages, and of the Gospel text behind them, is lost when they are subjected to the kind of reductive reading our one-dimensional worldviews seem to force upon us.

On the North American scene, the modernist-fundamentalist controversy of a century ago may have represented a low point in this process, but its effects are still with us. Many Christians, to say nothing of the wider population, seem agreed that the intent of these passages is to assert a factual claim, a biological/historical claim, about the parentage of Jesus. Jesus had a human mother, Mary, but no human father. Mary was somehow impregnated (supernaturally) by God, so that the child was both divine and human. The question, then, is whether this affirmation is properly part of Christian faith—perhaps an essential part thereof—or rather a legend that somehow became part of the early tradition and is at best harmless.

To deny the claim seems to amount to a denial of the incarnation—Jesus is simply an ordinary human being, with two ordinary human parents—but to affirm the claim may be equally problematic. It too amounts to a denial of the incarnation, at least as Christians have come to articulate its meaning. A being with one divine parent and one human parent is most readily construed by the modern "one-dimensional" mind as a hybrid, a demigod. This is not the copresence of full divinity and full humanity in Jesus that the church, following the Council of Chalcedon, confesses: one person in two natures, "complete in his deity and complete—the very same—in his humanity."[2]

The Chalcedonian "definition" speaks of Jesus' divine and human origins, but not in a way that raises questions about his DNA. "As to his deity," it affirms, "he was born from the Father before the ages, but as to his humanity, the very same one was born in the last days from the Virgin Mary, the Mother of God, for our sake and the sake of our salvation."[3] The translator's "born from the Father" / "born . . . from the Virgin Mary" reflects the fact that there is one verb, *gennēthenta*, applied here both to the eternal generation of the Son and to the Son's incarnation. The Father's "begetting" of the Son refers not to a temporal event some months prior to

Pastoral Perspective

Today's text reminds us that the preparations for the first Christmas were anything but conventional and were far from "proper." Joseph, whom the text calls a righteous man, discovers that his soon-to-be-wife is pregnant. The narrator knows that it is a child of the Holy Spirit, but such things are unheard of at this point to the characters in the story. To Joseph, the pregnancy is a violation of social convention and ethics for an unmarried woman. He decides to divorce Mary, the more humane of his customary legal options. Perhaps out of kindness, or regret, he will do this quietly in order not to shame her, and he realizes that things are not going to go as planned or as convention would have it. Mary has simply violated the important moral rule that she should not be pregnant when they were married.

We are all like Joseph at times, are we not? We go about our business and do not want to make trouble; we just handle things quietly and without a fuss. Perhaps this text reminds us that things we want to do loudly should be done quietly.

In light of this story it is helpful to think about the ways that the faithful thing to do and the faithful way to be are sometimes at odds with social convention. This is a difficult truth to learn. Joseph did not violate convention to be politically rebellious, or even to know his own goodness. He violated convention and remained faithful to Mary because God, as God often does, intervened in an unexpected way. God sent an angel to appear to Joseph in a dream. The angel basically said, "I know this is not what you expected, Joseph, but it is going to be OK. God is about to do something wonderful, despite the fact that according to Jewish custom and law you are in a rather socially unacceptable situation."

That is the message part of this text brings—that unexpected things, things outside of convention can often be wonderful signs that God is at work. Amid all our less-than-picture-perfect Christmases, the Christmas trees that are not quite as perfect as we want them to be, the lives that are not as perfect as we want them to be, God does something new.

Somehow Joseph has to trust this strange news: that this child is from the Holy Spirit; that he already has a name, Jesus; and that he will save people from their sins. One needs to think about what it means to be saved from sins by an infant who lies in a manger. Often we think too theologically about salvation, getting caught up in later debates about exactly how Jesus makes the forgiveness of sins possible. All that comes later.

1. Jan Milič Lochman, *The Faith We Confess: An Ecumenical Dogmatics*, trans. David Lewis (Philadelphia: Fortress Press, 1984), 101–14.
2. From the "Definition of the Faith" of the Council of Chalcedon, in *The Christological Controversy*, ed. and trans. Richard A. Norris Jr. (Philadelphia: Fortress Press, 1980), 159.
3. Ibid.

dream in which an angel explains to him that Mary's pregnancy is of divine origin.

The angel addresses him as "son of David," reminding the readers of the genealogical problem. Jesus can be son of David only through Joseph, yet Joseph is not his biological father. This problem is solved by the angel in verse 21: "you shall name him Jesus." By naming the baby, Joseph acknowledges him as his son; in effect, Joseph adopts Jesus, and thus incorporates him legally into David's genealogy.

Twice in this chapter Matthew uses the word *genesis* with reference to Jesus. Verse 1 may be a title for the genealogy, or perhaps for the birth narratives of chapters 1–2: "Book of the *genesis* of Jesus Messiah." The word recurs in verse 18: "Now of Jesus Messiah the *genesis* was thus." Since another word was available for "birth," one cannot help but wonder whether Matthew is thinking of the first book of the Bible, which in his Greek Bible, as in our Bibles, was called "Genesis." Is Matthew hinting at the role of Jesus in the new creation? (See 2 Cor. 5:17.)

Matthew's play on words in verse 21 would have been missed by most of his Gentile readers. "Jesus" is the Greek form of the Hebrew name Joshua. The Hebrew and Aramaic forms of this name reminded Jews of the Hebrew word for salvation. Matthew has twice identified Jesus as "Messiah" (vv. 1, 18). It was popularly believed that the Messiah would bring salvation to Israel by defeating its Gentile foes. Matthew begins his Jesus story by reminding his readers that Jesus brought a very different kind of salvation. The theme reappears in 20:28, "just as the Son of Man came not to be served but to serve, and to give his life a ransom for many," and in 26:28, "for this is my blood of the covenant, which is poured out for many for the forgiveness of sins."

"His people" refers very naturally to Israel, but Gentile converts understood that by faith in Jesus they had been incorporated into the Messiah's people (see Rom. 11:17).

In verses 22–23 we encounter the first of Matthew's frequent "formula quotations," in which he confirms the truth or the significance of something he is reporting by referring to Scripture. Here he finds support for Mary's miraculous conception in Isaiah 7:14.

In the Hebrew version of this verse, *'almah* refers to a young woman, either married or unmarried. The context in Isaiah does not suggest a miraculous birth. When Isaiah was translated into Greek in Alexandria, the Jewish translators chose the word *parthenos*, which means "virgin," and retained the

they needed a savior. The angel in today's Gospel recalls one of those dark moments when the people must have wanted to yell out for deliverance. It was during the time when God's people had been taken captive in Babylon. We can see those ancient faces reflected in the plight of contemporary exiles we see during the evening television news. We are familiar with the face of the refugee woman as she prepares a tiny meal for her five children living with her in their small tent pitched far from home and security. Sometimes the faces on the news belong to homeless men and women from our own city streets who sleep in shelters or above heating grates. When we have seen those exiles on television, we have seen the faces of God's people living in Babylon. The Gospel echoes the wonderful news that Isaiah had for these people in exile. God would send them Immanuel. Dianne Bergant reminds us that Immanuel, that is, "with us is God," is more of a title than a personal name. Our ancestors in the faith believed that kings were either gods in human form or at least men descended from the gods. There were many immanuels in their midst from time to time. The church reads this ancient prophecy, first uttered to King Ahaz, as referring to an Immanuel beyond our wildest imaginations.[1]

Do We Still Need a Savior? Does an ancient promise of Immanuel, made to a specific group of political exiles and then to another specific group of early Christians, really matter to those who listen to our sermon today? The old promise will matter if contemporary believers reflect on our own moments of exile. The plight of Isaiah's people, as well as the images of contemporary exiles, reminds us that most of us have our own exile moments. We can identify those exile moments by asking, "Am I truly happy? If not, what seems unfilled in my life? What do I need to be truly happy?"

Certainly there are some very happy and contented people around who believe that they have all they need. They have a good income, they love their families, and they enjoy life in general. This is fine as far as it goes. Have they ever asked, "Why was I created? What is the purpose of my being here? Where will I go at the end of this life?" Anyone who asks those questions will know that we need more from our lives. Even the most contented humanist will be restless if he or she asks, "What is my life really all about?" That is the beginning of knowing why we need a savior.

1. Dianne Bergant, "What's in a Name?" *America* (December 13, 2004), 22.

Matthew 1:18-25

Theological Perspective

the nativity of Jesus, but rather to the distinctive relation of Father and Son within the divine reality.

When our Gospel text speaks of God's involvement in the conception and birth of Jesus, it speaks of God not as Father but as Spirit. Mary "was found to be with child from the Holy Spirit" (v. 18), and Joseph is told that "the child conceived in her is from the Holy Spirit" (v. 20). This way of speaking may be the most important clue to a theologically appropriate reading of our text—one that might lead us out of one-dimensionality and on to a fuller apprehension of the context of our lives.

It does so by bringing the story out of the realm of Hellenistic mythology and relating it decisively to the history of God's involvement with Israel. Throughout that history, God's Spirit is the catalyst of the new; the Spirit is (as the Nicaeo-Constantinopolitan Creed puts it) "the Lord, the giver of life." To say that Mary's child is "from the Holy Spirit" is to say that this is a radically new beginning and, furthermore, that it is God's doing, not ours. In this context, Joseph's noninvolvement in the conception—which pointedly sets aside the carefully constructed genealogy in the preceding seventeen verses of the opening chapter of Matthew, intended to establish Jesus' royal descent through Joseph—indicates that this advent is something for which human beings, no matter how worthy or highly credentialed, can claim no credit.

These reflections have followed the suggestion of J. M. Lochman that we think of the virgin birth as an "interpretative dogma." It is not an "article of faith" in itself. Perhaps the extent to which it became one among some Christians around a century ago (and was just as vehemently denied by others) is a symptom of our need for a rebirth of vision. It is best construed as a pointer to a more central and truly indispensable affirmation, namely, that in Jesus, God has assumed our humanity. That is the gracious mystery conveyed in our text and in the event for which Advent has us so expectantly waiting.

CHARLES M. WOOD

Pastoral Perspective

What begins here—what God announces—is a human being who will somehow show us a different way to be. It might be helpful to ask people to think about the ways someone has saved them—through love or intervention—from doing something they regretted doing. How many times has the wisdom or love of another shaped our action? Try to think about salvation in a different way—in humility, instead of in the arrogance that comes with pronouncements in some traditions that one is "saved" while others are not.

The news catches Joseph off guard. At this point in the story, he is totally unaware of the journey that will take the one he will call Jesus from Bethlehem to Jerusalem, from the temple to the cross to the empty tomb. If Joseph were told all of that, the news might overwhelm him even more than the news he has received. So many times God opens a door for us, or gives us a vision, beckoning us to trust and follow.

As you think of such times in your own ministry, invite those who hear you preach to think about the times in their own lives when God has called them to do something strange and unexpected, and you or they just went. As the poet David Whyte notes, for most of us "the call will not come so grandly, so biblically, but intimately, in the face of the one you know you have to love."[1]

Those are the small steps God calls us to. As Mary and Joseph journeyed to the first Christmas, they did not know where God would take them; all they knew was that something wonderful had been promised and that they had been beckoned to follow. So too the text calls us to rise and follow God's call, not knowing where the journey will take us, or the path that God has set before us.

AARON KLINK

1. David Whyte, "The True Love," from *The House of Belonging* (Langley, WA: Many Rivers Press, 1997).

definite article, "the virgin." Why did they translate in this way? A helpful clue is provided in the prophets' use of "virgin" with reference to Israel (Isa. 37:22; Jer. 14:17; 18:13; 31:4, 21; Lam. 1:15; 2:13; Amos 5:2). We can conjecture that this verse was of special importance to Matthew because it was already considered a messianic proof text by Greek-speaking Jews. The translators saw here a prophecy (by inserting a future tense, "shall conceive") that virgin Israel would give birth to the Messiah. This messianic hope was reinforced by the text's statement that the virgin's son would be called Immanuel, a Hebrew phrase meaning "with-us-God." By applying this text to Mary, Matthew not only defends the tradition that Jesus was the child of the Holy Spirit, but also presents Mary as the essence of virgin Israel.

There are two very different ways of understanding Immanuel, "God [is] with us" (there is no verb either in the Hebrew or in the Greek), representing a "low christology" and a "high christology." There is no hint in Isaiah that the baby about to be born will have supernatural significance. In fact, no role of any kind is assigned to him. His name is simply a "sign," like the names that Hosea gives his three children (Hos. 1:4–8). The name "Immanuel" is a divine promise that God will be with the nation in the midst of international crises. If the Alexandrian translators took this as a messianic text, they would undoubtedly have taken "Immanuel" as meaning that God would stand beside the Messiah and empower him. For Jews, the Messiah was not a divine figure. Some propose that this was also Matthew's view. He calls Jesus "Son of God," but this did not always mean "divine Son." In 2 Samuel 7:14, God refers to Solomon as his son: "I will be a father to him, and he shall be a son to me."

There is evidence in Matthew of a "higher christology," however. After the resurrection Jesus' disciples *worship* him, and Jesus declares, "All authority in *heaven* and on earth has been given to me." He orders that converts be baptized "in the name of the Father and of *the Son* and of the Holy Spirit," and promises to be with them always (28:17–20). Consequently, to Matthew, "Immanuel" probably means "Jesus is God-with-us."

DOUGLAS R. A. HARE

Once we start asking the real questions about our lives, we enter risky territory. The right questions will usually demand that we change. On a radio talk show, a recovering drug addict told the story about the day he began his road to recovery. He had locked himself in a hotel room to take care of his $600-a-day habit as usual. This time he finally realized that whenever he turned to chemicals to achieve a sense of happiness, he went off to be alone. He isolated himself from others.

This is a powerful image of what sin looks like in our lives. Sin is the choice to minister to ourselves, rather than allow the savior to minister to us; and often we preclude that divine help by removing ourselves from community. Some people choose to minister to themselves through chemical dependency, others through acquiring money, shopping, gambling, addiction to work, or simply going it alone. The Christmas season invites us to ask whether we have managed to save ourselves in any of these ways. That is a risky question. Can we trust Jesus truly to fulfill that emptiness that we know is within us?

The Call to Trust. Joseph shows us a profound trust in today's Gospel. God does not appear to Joseph when he is wide awake and at prayer. There is no assurance of a burning bush or parting clouds on the mountaintop. There is only a dream. Can we trust dreams? Do we not quickly dismiss dreams if we can even recall them a few moments after we awake? The dream, however, was enough for Joseph. He had been asking many questions. "What should I do about Mary? What does the law demand? What does my heart tell me?" The dream answered these big questions. As preachers, we may wish to help people ask the big questions on this last Sunday before Christmas. If we have the right questions, we will be ready to hear Jesus as the answer.

DANIEL HARRIS

Isaiah 9:2–7

> [2]The people who walked in darkness
>   have seen a great light;
> those who lived in a land of deep darkness—
>   on them light has shined.
> [3]You have multiplied the nation,
>   you have increased its joy;
> they rejoice before you
>   as with joy at the harvest,
>   as people exult when dividing plunder.
> [4]For the yoke of their burden,
>   and the bar across their shoulders,
>   the rod of their oppressor,
>   you have broken as on the day of Midian.

Theological Perspective

For many, Christmas Eve services are not to be missed. Music and candlelight mark the experience and the memories. Because many come to worship who are infrequently present through the movement of the liturgical year, the readings from Scripture can easily be heard in a kind of sentimental haze. Here is Isaiah again, with an astounding claim: God has come to the world in the form of a boy child born of a young woman. It is no wonder that this reading has been associated with Christmas through the centuries. It is no wonder that this reading is also heard as the culmination of prophetic desire for a Messiah. The announcement of a world-transforming reign of righteousness and justice now begun is not a sentimental set of feeling states. It is a radical prophetic claim.

As with the passage from Isaiah 7, these words are familiar to the faithful worshiper. They also contain phrases that have been planted deeply in the Western mind, whether Christian or not, by Handel's *Messiah*: "For unto us a child is born . . . a son is given." One can almost hear the music by looking at the words. The stunning messianic titles are set side by side by Handel's musical genius: "Wonderful Counselor, Mighty God, Everlasting Father, Prince of Peace." To someone on the edges of the Christian faith, this may seem impossibly hopeful, even naive.

Pastoral Perspective

For many who worship on Christmas Eve the prophecy of Isaiah is inextricably connected with the celebration of Jesus' birth. Handel's *Messiah* has made it so. At first, though, this paean was for the accession of a king to the throne, quite possibly that of good King Hezekiah, in contrast to the dreaded and dreadful Ahaz. This passage is placed in the lectionary as fulfillment of the Immanuel prophecy heard last Sunday (Isa. 7:10–16).

People will grasp a political setting: Isaiah expresses the kind of hope that sometimes, but not always, accompanies new governments promising new directions for a people suffering from oppression or malaise. He sings of light overcoming darkness (v. 2), an increase of joy (v. 3), the breaking of the rod of the oppressor that would have been used to beat and subjugate the people of the land (vv. 4–5), and the promise of peace upheld with justice and righteousness (v. 7).

At Christmas a pastor may want to be aware that many people who desire change in their lives or in the world have a generalized wish that things might be different and a vague hope that they will not have to do anything but welcome the change. Many of us have a functional theology or hidden expectation that assumes an all-powerful God is supposed to fix problems. The worshiper may lapse into a spectator's

⁵For all the boots of the tramping warriors
    and all the garments rolled in blood
    shall be burned as fuel for the fire.
⁶For a child has been born for us,
    a son given to us;
    authority rests upon his shoulders;
    and he is named
    Wonderful Counselor, Mighty God,
    Everlasting Father, Prince of Peace.
⁷His authority shall grow continually,
    and there shall be endless peace
for the throne of David and his kingdom.
    He will establish and uphold it
with justice and with righteousness
    from this time onward and forevermore.
The zeal of the LORD of hosts will do this.

Exegetical Perspective

The prophetic poem in Isaiah 9:2–7 brings together two themes: the end of military oppression (vv. 2–5) and the accession of a new king (vv. 6–7). Although the lectionary reading does not include it, verse 1 (Isa. 8:23 in Hebrew) may also belong to this textual unit. If so, the geographic names in this verse—northern territories that had been captured by the Assyrian king Tiglath-pileser III in 732 BCE—ground the text in a particular historical situation. Isaiah's words are not abstractions divorced from reality; rather, they are concrete promises delivered to real, suffering human beings. Many biblical scholars think that this text originally celebrated the coronation of Hezekiah, who ruled the kingdom of Judah 715–687 BCE. It gives voice to profound hope for the reign of this descendant of David, at a time when Judah faced the harsh realities of Assyrian dominance.

In contrast to their recent humiliation, the prophet envisions a glorious future for the territories named in verse 1. Verse 2 develops the note of reversal with imagery of darkness and light. The vivid language conveys the depth of the people's despair: they had "walked in darkness" and "lived in a land of deep darkness" (*tsalmavet*; cf. Ps. 23:4; Job 3:5; 28:3; etc.). The next verse attributes this change in national fortune to God, who has "increased its joy." A pair of similes underscores the magnitude of

Homiletical Perspective

On Christmas Day 1531, Martin Luther preached from the Christmas story at the morning service and from Isaiah 9:6 at the afternoon service. He began the afternoon sermon by quickly recalling that the congregation had heard the Christmas story earlier in the day. He told them that they would not hear it again; rather, they would learn how to make use of it. Luther then turned to the words of the prophet Isaiah, "For a child has been born for us, a son given to us."

As you reflect on this text for Christmas Eve, you may wish to begin with Luther's insight and explore what Isaiah's prophecy says about the significance of Christ's birth for us. Isaiah works with a rich mixture of metaphors and patches them together like a quilt of images: light shining in darkness, tramping boots and bloody garments, a child who is a father and a prince. Let Isaiah's images play in your mind. Perhaps think of them as swings that take you back and forth between the text and your context.

Consider first the "land of deep darkness." For Isaiah, the story behind the image is the Assyrian conquest of the northern kingdom. This defeat, which led to exile, offers context and depth for your exploration of what the "land of deep darkness" means. For instance, initially you may be tempted to interpret darkness in personal terms, and specifically as personal sin that darkens our spiritual lives. Yet

Isaiah 9:2–7

Theological Perspective

"Endless peace"? Really? "Justice with righteousness" (vv. 7a, 7b)? Where? As the world turns from one age to the next, these questions ought also to be raised by the Christmas gospel.

In order to understand what is being prophesied and sung, the promises require entering into the yearning that stands in the background of Isaiah and of all the other prophetic hopes gathered in the Christmas herald. Entering the darkness of which the opening of this passage speaks is more than coming out after dark. This is solidarity with the immense history of suffering that longs for deliverance. Such solidarity comes from having heard and known the larger pattern of biblical stories. It also comes from having become aware of the gap between the *is* of the world and God's desired *ought to be* of the world.

The power of this reading depends on our understanding something of the captivity of God's people in Babylon, yet these words speak to more than the remembered suffering of the children of Israel. Anyone held in captivity as a prisoner of war knows something of the anguish and darkness as well. For Isaiah, the announcement of having seen a great light also speaks to those who consult their gods, their "ghosts and the familiar spirits that chirp and mutter" (8:19). When we fall back on our idols and neglect to desire and to wait in hope for God, then gloom and darkness fall upon us. Consulting our own devices and projected fantasies is itself a form of captivity.

The divine humanity in the form of the child casts light in the midst of the darkness of such human captivities. This is a light that breaks the grip of death and nothingness. To speak of light shining in the darkness is to speak of the divine persistence. In the ancient night prayer the antiphon sounded: "Jesus Christ is the Light of the world, a Light no darkness can extinguish." So this is indeed a reading that sounds the contrasts between deep darkness and the joyful light. In many Christian traditions, the symbol of the Christ candle is lit at evening prayer to the singing of the ancient Greek hymn, the *phōs hilaron* ("Hail, gladdening light").

On the eve of nativity we see how Isaiah's tense changes. What has been promised in the sign of a child is *now* to be received as gift. This *now*—figured in the prayers, hymns, and symbols of Christmas Eve—is yet paradoxically still about the future. What must have been nearly impossible for the first hearers of Isaiah's time to comprehend is here and now in this Christmas assembly equally astonishing.

Pastoral Perspective

passivity. Christmas Eve can be a time to refocus the celebration of Jesus' birth as the birth of one who will honor the extraordinary freedom we have been granted in creation, and whose work is not carried out by swooping in and sorting out problems for us.

It could be helpful therefore to say something about the shape of this peace Isaiah announces in the "Prince of Peace." It is God's peace, which "surpasses all understanding" (Phil. 4:7). Peace or *shalom* is that condition that becomes apparent when God is present. It cannot be other than part and parcel of a just world. Peace is dependent on right relationship or righteousness, and so is both a gift and fruit of the Holy Spirit (Gal. 5:22).[1] Right relationship is bound up with forgiveness, grace, and the ever-present possibility of a new start in life. The light that shines in the darkness might signal the dawn, but congregants know from experience that it does not vanquish the deep darkness all at once.

We might suggest that Søren Kierkegaard's "leap of faith" points less to the conclusion of an intellectual process beyond which there is no certainty, and more to the beginning of a journey of faith in which the content of the gift is to be filled out, explored, and understood in days and years to come as we appropriate the gift of Christmas. Faith or trust in the transforming possibilities of the newborn king is, perhaps, a gift of the season. Isaiah's paean on the accession of a king is less a celebration of the end of challenge, and more a celebration that the conditions for newness of life are upon or among us.

It can be difficult to grasp or recognize some of the ways in which God does address the reality of our lives or is present to us. Isaiah can help us come to terms with this pastoral challenge as well. Isaiah's God is concerned both with what we identify as personal matters (counselor, father) and also with societal realities (prince, governor). There is, however, no hint of coercion in any of these titles. The new government of this new king will increase without end, partly as a result of his zeal for righteousness or right relationship.

We might miss the birth of a child in a far-flung and relatively unimportant corner of an empire; we might also miss the presence or action of God nearer to hand. God will often address us obliquely or at a tangent or parabola (as in parable). Examples from the life of the preacher or preacher's community will

---

1. Preachers in communities that include a passing of the peace in worship have a practice that will help anchor these contemplations of peace. One could point out that this is a prayer we offer one another as well as a recognition of the presence of God, even when we do not feel or experience it at the moment.

that joy, comparing it first to the celebration that usually accompanies the harvest. In an agrarian economy like that of ancient Judah, the quality of life, if not survival, depended upon consistent food production. As a result, successful harvests were occasions for festivity, accompanied by dancing, shouting, and wine drinking (Judg. 9:27; Pss. 4:7; 126:6; etc.). The second simile likens the nation's joy to the jubilation of soldiers who divvy up spoils after a victorious battle (1 Sam. 30:16; Ps. 119:162). For an audience that in recent years had experienced only defeat, the comparison must have been bittersweet.

While the poetic language is highly evocative, it does not specify the cause for this joy, which heightens the audience's sense of anticipation. That information comes in verses 4–6, which all begin with the word "for" (*ki*), indicating that they explain the preceding material. In verse 4, the phrases "yoke of their burden" and "bar across their shoulders" refer to Judah's status as an Assyrian vassal, comparing it to the labor of a pack animal. The term "rod" (*shevet*)—in this context, the goad used on such an animal—occurs elsewhere in Isaiah 1–39 as an image for the dominance of one nation over another (Isa. 10:5, 15; 11:4; 14:29; etc.).

Isaiah declares that YHWH has now shattered these instruments of cruelty "as on the day of Midian," most likely an allusion to Gideon's miraculous victory over the Midianites in Judges 7. Verse 5 evokes the horrors of war with its concrete references to the boots and bloodstained garments of soldiers, but the anticipated destruction of these objects signifies a more hopeful future. The combination of figurative imagery in verse 4 and more literal imagery in verse 5 powerfully makes the point that Assyrian oppression will soon come to an end. In retrospect, it becomes clear that the mention of plunder in verse 3 ironically foreshadowed this development.

The climactic moment of the poem occurs in verse 6 with the arrival of the new ruler, who will bring about this glorious new era. In the Hebrew text, the prominent repetition of certain sounds draws attention to these lines and emphasizes the importance of their content. Although the verse speaks of the birth of a royal child, it probably refers instead to the coronation of the king. In the royal ideology of ancient Judah, the Davidic monarch became a son of YHWH at his coronation, as suggested by Psalm 2:7: "He said to me, 'You are my son; today I have begotten you" (cf. 2 Sam. 7:14). The placement of "authority" on the king's "shoulders"

the historical context of the image turns the focus to a more corporate kind of darkness: social sin, national tragedy, and corrupt social infrastructure. Since this kind of darkness forms the background of the text, it may also form an illuminative background for the sermon.

Against the background of darkness, the prophet heralds the dawning of light. In this light, people are celebrating as if they have won the battle. Their yoke is thrown off, and the oppressive rod is broken; the instruments of war are being thrown into the fire. The prophet uses these images to elaborate on the dawning of light, the birth of the child, and what this means for the people in darkness.

What emotions do these images evoke for you, and what experiences do they recall? What emotions and experiences might these images evoke for your congregation? As you consider your congregation and your community, where do you see light dawning? What rods of oppression are broken? What is thrown into the fire? Specific answers to these questions will help you proclaim Isaiah's good news in images and metaphors that are fitted to your context.

In proclaiming this good news, though, we must be completely honest about the darkness of the world. There are many rods of oppression that seem unbreakable, and the boots of war are rarely fuel for the fire. Can you imagine someone in your congregation telling you that this prophecy sounds more like a pipe dream than a real hope? What would you say to them? As you reflect on the persistence of the darkness, consider the text from an eschatological perspective. In other words, look at the oracle as a vision of God's future reality breaking into our present reality. Isaiah is envisioning the future, and this text points to signs of this future even amid the darkness.

Think of it as seeing with spiritual bifocals: in one lens you see the harsh reality of the world, and in the other lens you see God's kingdom breaking into the world. Take time to explore this image. What darkness do you see in the one lens, and what light do you see in the other? What are the signs of God's inbreaking kingdom that you see around your congregation? The challenge will be to help the congregation see with this dual vision. By identifying concrete instances of God's activity, the congregation can see the signs of God's reign and live as those who rejoice before the harvest.

At the core of Isaiah's prophecy is the reason for rejoicing: the birth of the Messiah, which inaugurates God's coming kingdom. This messianic hope bursts into full view as Isaiah describes the child with titles

Isaiah 9:2-7

Theological Perspective

Given the violence of our world, with all the tramping warriors and bloody garments still reported, the gospel of a child born to Mary transforms the violence. The images of violence are themselves subverted by the child. This proclamation turns darkness into an illumination of the way of justice, peace, and righteousness. It strikes at the heart of human distress and calls out to all our captivities: "The people who walked in darkness have seen a great light" (v. 2).

What kind of sign is this that has been fulfilled? What a vulnerable sign—utterly human in its appearance, but with the power to alter human destiny! The poetic prophecy of Isaiah comingles with songs of birth and joy. This is the divine counterpoint to all human powers and principalities. Here is the wonder of divine agency at work in the midst of confusions and vagaries. Here is hope incarnate.

We look around us at the clash of nations and peoples, of the death dealing, of "ignorant armies that clash at night" and we wonder: is God aware, can God be said to act at all? To all this "nothingness," God says a definitive Word; *becomes* the definitive Word made flesh. How is this possible? Not by merely human engineering. Only by the very passion of God, as Isaiah asserts, the "zeal of the LORD of hosts" will do this. It is still to be completed. Isaiah here speaks of future events in the past tense, but this is how the eternal intention to save comes to this temporal world. That God's coming to dwell in solidarity with the human race is accomplished, means precisely that the promises will yet be so. This "Wonderful Counselor, Mighty God, Everlasting Father, Prince of Peace" is for all time and will be the light until all manner of things shall be well.

This is why we read Isaiah with the Gospel the eve of the Feast of the Nativity.

DON E. SALIERS

Pastoral Perspective

be specific to that person or community. What they will have in common, however, is the respect of God for the freedom we are granted in creation. The word is not an indisputable word, but a Word made flesh that addresses our personal and societal situations.

Another pastoral reality to which Isaiah might speak at Christmas is the reality of abundance in a world where we are too rarely reminded of scarcity on a regular basis. Many will know the experience of the ambivalence felt on receiving a generous gift. This might attend a sense of some perceived obligation to the giver that comes with being the recipient of generosity; or maybe the experience is one of guilt at the knowledge that we have not been as generous to the one who has blessed us.

A preacher might explore the way we react to the image of the mutual joy that comes at the end of a harvest when the crop is shared (v. 3), possibly in contrast to our reactions when the boots and clothes of the warrior will be burned as fuel for the fire (v. 5). Is it possible that we could enjoy a share of abundance without jealousy, rancor, obligation, or guilt? In one perspective, it is inconceivable that the infant of Bethlehem could be sufficient for the salvation of the world. In God's perspective, however, this birth signals enough and more than enough, the possibility of unalloyed joy, rather than all of those other emotions and feelings that can so often accompany giving and receiving in our lives.

GEOFFREY M. ST.J. HOARE

recalls the removal of "the bar" from Judah's "shoulders" in verse 4. Following an ancient Egyptian tradition, the king receives a series of royal titles at the beginning of his reign, and these titles reflect the people's high expectations for their new leader. "Wonderful Counselor" praises the king's wisdom in making decisions.

Although it may seem blasphemous to us to assign the title "Mighty God" to a human ruler, Psalm 45:6 indicates that kings in ancient Judah could be called "god," which is consistent with the view that the king is God's son. The word translated "mighty" (*gibbor*) specifically denotes military prowess. The parental language of "Everlasting Father" refers to the king's care and provision for his subjects (cf. Isa. 22:21). Finally, "Prince of Peace" (*shalom*) envisions the absence of military conflict during his reign, as affirmed in the next verse. Isaiah 2:1–4 and 11:1–10 likewise imagine a future state of international peace centered upon the Davidic king in Jerusalem.

The final verse of the poem looks forward to an endless period of peaceful rule by the Davidic dynasty. Its language echoes God's promises to David in 2 Samuel 7:11–17, in particular the verb "establish" (*kwn*) and the terms "throne" and "kingdom." This new era will be characterized by "justice" (*mishpat*) and "righteousness" (*tsedaqah*). Although God demands these qualities from all persons throughout the OT—especially in the prophetic literature (Isa. 5:1–7; Amos 5:24; etc.)—the king bears special responsibility for enacting them in society (Ps. 72:1–2; Isa. 32:1; etc.).

Despite the poem's strong emphasis on the role of human authority in its vision of the future, the final lines affirm that it is YHWH who ultimately makes these events possible, as a result of divine zeal (*qin'ah*; cf. Exod. 20:5; 34:14; Deut. 4:24; Zech. 1:14; etc.). Although this text reflects the specific features of its historical setting, its demand for an end to oppression, its expression of longing for peace, and its vision of just leadership resonate with people from every time and place, who continue to hope with Isaiah that "the zeal of the LORD of hosts will do this" (v. 7). Set in a Christmas Eve service, Isaiah 9 injects its profound hopefulness into the story of that Bethlehem birth.

J. BLAKE COUEY

that pile greatness upon greatness. He paints a portrait of a perfect ruler whose kingdom will last forever, whose reign will be marked by endless peace, by justice and righteousness. It may be nearly impossible for you to hear these titles without Handel's *Messiah* in the back of your mind! How familiar is your congregation with this part of Isaiah's prophecy? Often a comfortable familiarity can take away from the startling impact of the proclamation.

Consider how you can help the congregation see Isaiah's vision with new insight. Think of metaphors and images that are native to your context and social location. What images would help your congregation grasp the perfection and promise of this child? If your congregation painted a picture of endless peace, of justice and righteousness, what would it look like? What metaphors capture the life-changing promise of the text for you and your community?

These images, from the text and from your context, are bursting with homiletical possibilities. Explore them with patience, and allow your spiritual imagination to range freely. When you settle on the homiletical idea you want to develop, you will want to consider the form and language you will use in the sermon. For instance, if you decide to focus only on Isaiah, you could follow the literary form of the text by doing what Isaiah does: describe the inbreaking of God's reign in the specific terms of your context, and craft your sermon with metaphors and poetic images that evoke the experience of overwhelming joy.

Alternatively, if you decide to bring Isaiah's text into conversation with the Christmas story, you could travel across the centuries to Christmas 1531 and follow Luther's insight by using metaphors and images that communicate what the child who is born to Mary means for us.

PATRICK W. T. JOHNSON

Psalm 96

¹O sing to the LORD a new song;
  sing to the LORD, all the earth.
²Sing to the LORD, bless his name;
  tell of his salvation from day to day.
³Declare his glory among the nations,
  his marvelous works among all the peoples.
⁴For great is the LORD, and greatly to be praised;
  he is to be revered above all gods.
⁵For all the gods of the peoples are idols,
  but the LORD made the heavens.
⁶Honor and majesty are before him;
  strength and beauty are in his sanctuary.

⁷Ascribe to the LORD, O families of the peoples,
  ascribe to the LORD glory and strength.

Theological Perspective

Psalm 96 celebrates the reign of God as a past, present, and future reality. Clearly, something has happened to bring joy to the heart of this psalmist, perhaps the decree of Cyrus permitting the Jews to return to Zion (2 Chr. 36:22–23); and he invites the whole earth to join the new song of praise to God the king. The psalm, read on Christmas Eve in all three lectionary cycles, is important for obvious reasons: Jesus is for Christians the messianic king who proclaimed and embodied the coming reign of God.

The reign of God is one of the great themes of the Bible, a crucial part of the promissory structure of both testaments. The Bible is not a treatise explicating the divine attributes but a collection of stories about covenants, promises, and fulfillment. One thinks, for example, of Noah, Abraham, Moses and the Israelites at Sinai, David, and Jewish refugees in Babylon. The promise becomes ever more inclusive, drawing in all peoples and the whole of nature, as in Psalm 96, and eventually stretching beyond death (Jer. 31, for example, and the resurrection of the crucified Jesus).

The reign of God is the ultimate biblical metaphor of salvation. Protestant Christians have preferred other images, such as justification, sanctification, reconciliation, and eternal life. These remain important, but divorced from the reign of God, they

Pastoral Perspective

Worship is not scheduled to begin for another fifteen minutes, but already the pews are full. The ushers are scrambling to find seats for those still arriving. The lights in the sanctuary are dim, and the conversations are hushed. Those who study these sorts of things tell us that this is the most attended day of worship in the country. More people will be in our pews on this day than any other. It is Christmas Eve.

They have come to sing the familiar carols; to hear the well-known story of a birth in a manger. They have come to be nostalgically transported to a time that may exist only in their dreams . . . a time of sentimental memories of Christmases past. They have come to escape the world in which they currently reside. They have come to get away from paychecks that never seem to pay all the bills; from fears that next year's economy may be worse than that of the year now ending; from worries about the medical test that was taken just last week; from concerns about the neighborhood violence reported in yesterday's news. They have come to escape and to get away. It is Christmas Eve.

The preacher rises to read the lesson for the day, and she begins with a psalm: "O sing to the LORD a new song." One thing they have not come to do is to sing a new song. This is Christmas Eve, a time for the well-known and oft recycled old songs of our

⁸Ascribe to the Lord the glory due his name;
    bring an offering, and come into his courts.
⁹Worship the Lord in holy splendor;
    tremble before him, all the earth.

¹⁰Say among the nations, "The Lord is king!
    The world is firmly established; it shall never be moved.
    He will judge the peoples with equity."
¹¹Let the heavens be glad, and let the earth rejoice;
    let the sea roar, and all that fills it;
¹² let the field exult, and everything in it.
    Then shall all the trees of the forest sing for joy
¹³ before the Lord; for he is coming,
    for he is coming to judge the earth.
    He will judge the world with righteousness,
    and the peoples with his truth.

Exegetical Perspective

Psalm 96 is called a royal psalm because its purpose is to praise God as the king of the cosmos. The royal psalms probably emerge from the inauguration of Israel's kings, events filled with joy and hope that finally, after a long line of corrupt and faithless rulers, a king will govern the people in justice and truthfulness. The ecstatic praise of this prayer, however, looks beyond human rulers to the coming of the one King who will rule the world with justice. Human kings are but God's agents. That God alone is king makes relative the glory and strength of human rulers and sets them under a far greater authority than their own. The psalm therefore conveys an implicit critique of human governors and implies that they should use their power as God would, in service of the earth and all its peoples.

From a Christian perspective, Psalm 96 is ideally suited for recitation or, better still, for singing during Christmas liturgy. In clear theological terms, this royal psalm interprets the humble Gospel narrative of Jesus' birth and points to its transcendent meaning. When the second person of the Trinity takes on human flesh, he comes among us as the ruler of the world, bringing justice, righteousness, and truth, and is worthy of all praise. This psalm invites the whole cosmos to join in worship and praise of the King. The one born this night is no ordinary human ruler

Homiletical Perspective

This psalm of praise and celebration to God is assigned to the liturgy for Christmas Eve and provides the theological center of the worship. The psalmist announces the coming of the Lord (v. 13) and the establishment of God's reign (v. 10). Each of the three major parts of the psalm begins with admonitions to praise God (v. 1; vv. 7–8a; vv. 11–12a).

Paradoxically, however, on a night famed for its harmony, the music produced by this psalm brings dissonant sounds. The psalmist speaks of singing to the Lord (vv. 1–3) and the judgment of the Lord (vv. 10, 13) in the same song. Singing and judgment resonate discord rather than harmony; they sound like clanging cymbals. However, the preacher can capitalize on the tension between these two themes by playing one off the other and, as a result, engaging the listeners more deeply.

The sermon might begin by helping the congregation experience the emotive power of singing. The preacher could recreate occasions when the singing of a hymn was an especially inspiring and memorable moment. There are occasions when I have been moved by such hymns. In the opening scene of the delightful movie *Trip to Bountiful* (1985), a mother runs after her son in an open field and in the background one hears the singing of "Softly and Tenderly Jesus Is Calling." To hear the hymn in that context is

Psalm 96

Theological Perspective

become susceptible to otherworldly and individualistic distortions, reducing salvation to a change of heart and the soul's ascending to heaven at death. The reign of God captures better the social and ecological dimensions of human life. Modern human and natural sciences demonstrate the importance of relationships for understanding who we are, supporting the notion that salvation must include not only a change of heart but transformation of the social, political, and economic orders, as well as our relationship to nature.

The reign of God is subject to distortion, of course, as is true of any metaphor. Imaging God as "king" carries risks because we inevitably transfer to God characteristics of human kings. Most earthly kings, for example, are more concerned with personal privilege than citizens' welfare, with power than compassion, with grandeur than moral substance. The Bible, including Psalm 96, seeks to deconstruct or unmask the pretensions of human kings (and other gods). Israel's God is one who establishes justice, extends hospitality to the stranger, welcomes the poor and others on the margins, and exposes the presumption of the rich and powerful. No wonder the anticipation of God's coming is an occasion for a new song.

The theological question that emerges here is an ethical one: How does the promise of the reign of God shape the lives of Christians? Many Christians over the centuries have identified the reign of God with the church or reduced the reach of the image to an otherworldly, individualistic reality, a synonym for traditional conceptions of heaven. This often nurtures a quietistic existence focusing on "spiritual" matters and devoid of specific concern for the social order. If, however, the reign of God is understood in relational terms as the ultimate will of God, the image opens up possibilities for change here and now and becomes a protest against those conditions that contradict the justice of God's reign. The coming reign of God enters into our present as a new way of construing the world, as an alternative story about how one should live.

Most human beings seek coherence in their lives by consulting a script that tells us what to aspire to, with whom to associate, how to spend money and time—in essence, a sketch as to what really matters. The reign of God may be conceived as an alternative script competing with dozens of others. Jesus' teachings, especially the parables, draw together the basic features of the reign of God. Most scripts give priority to oneself; Jesus bids us to seek first the reign of

Pastoral Perspective

past. Singing a new song on a day like this will bring only discontent and grumbling among the ranks of the worshipers.

Perhaps, if they can hang in there long enough to hear this new song, these sentimental worshipers will encounter a word of good news breaking through the nostalgic shell with which they have surrounded themselves on this night. This word of good news invites them first to confront their lives with honesty. "All the gods of the peoples are idols" (v. 5). In our more lucid moments we know the truth of that statement. The gods of this world have brought momentary relief, but the worries, the fears, the anxious moments have always returned. The "gods of the peoples" have been unable to deliver on the promises they make.

Singing this new song on Christmas Eve invites the worshipers to hear a longer-lasting word of good news. This king whose birth is celebrated will establish a kingdom that will bring order and stability into our lives and into this world. The roller-coaster on which the worshipers live their lives will come to an end. The constant ups and downs that are subject to the changing whims of the world will be over. Life will be grounded in a kingdom that is firm and solid. The changing fortunes of the workplace, the ups and downs of the stock market, the shifting state of their health, the emotionally wrenching stories on the news will not send them shooting around like the ball in a pinball machine, aimlessly driven by the turbulent world in which they live. The world into which these worshipers are being invited is a world that "is firmly established; it shall never be moved" (v. 10).

Singing this new song on Christmas Eve is not so bad after all. In fact, for a moment, our Christmas Eve worshipers find themselves transported to that sentimental place of their dreams . . . away from the hurts and the struggles of this world. Singing this new song is helping them escape into the nostalgic world of all those familiar songs that they have come to sing on this Christmas Eve. The invitation of the psalmist to "worship the LORD in holy splendor" (v. 9) is one to which they can respond. On this night, with the familiar music and the softly glowing candles, it is easy to "ascribe to the LORD the glory due his name." Even to "bring an offering" (v. 8) on a night like this makes sense. For a few quiet moments, there is escape. God is in charge, and all is right with the world.

Then the preacher gets to the end of the psalm, and suddenly our worshipers are awakened from their nostalgic escape. "He will judge the world with

Exegetical Perspective

who sees with warped vision, accepts bribes, or benefits the elites. Nor does this King care for one people or group to the exclusion of others. This is the King who rules the cosmos with justice and judges with righteousness.

The psalm divides thematically into four parts, reaching a dramatic climax in the last unit: Sing (vv. 1–3); Reasons to Sing (vv. 4–6); Ascribe Glory (vv. 7–9); Reasons to Ascribe Glory (vv. 10–13). Imperative speech abounds in the psalm, but the commands and invitations are not addressed to God. Instead, the psalmist urges everyone to join in worshipful praise of the just King.

Sing (vv. 1–3). Three exuberant commands—"sing," "sing," "sing"—open the psalm. The triple repetition creates a rhythm that, for Christians, calls forth Christmas joy. The song to be sung is "a new song," and the one called to burst forth in song is no less than "all the earth" (v. 1). The lyrics of the song appear in the following two verses. "Sing to the LORD, bless his name; tell of his salvation from day to day" (v. 2). The impetus for the singing is the joyous news that God saves "from day to day." Salvation occurs on this day, in this specific set of events, and then again tomorrow, in its specific set of events. Sing, because God's salvation is specific and continuous.

The verb shifts in verse 3 from the command to "sing" to the command to "declare," because the song itself is to announce the good news and teach the listeners about the inbreaking of salvation. This time the ones commanded to give voice are the nations who will learn of God's "marvelous works among all the peoples." The King is not simply Israel's ruler, but the ruler of all peoples, the one greatly to be praised. This psalmist clearly understands that the reign of the glorious King extends to the broadest possible horizon and bears significance for all created reality.

Reasons to Sing (vv. 4–6). Exuberance continues as the psalmist tries to motivate the audience, perhaps gathered in the temple, to praise God. "Great is the LORD . . . greatly to be praised . . . to be revered above all gods" (v. 4). In a move toward monotheism akin to the words of Second Isaiah, the psalmist asserts that this God is superior to any other god. Honor and majesty belong to God; strength and beauty reside in God's sanctuary. So far, the psalmist speaks abstractly, as if so awed by the ruler of the cosmos as to be unable to name the qualities that characterize the divine Ruler. The psalm focuses on glory around the King rather than on the person.

Homiletical Perspective

moving. In the past, when I heard the beautiful voices of my parents blend together to sing "How Great Thou Art," it was sheer delight. Music inspires us as nothing else does. Singing evokes out of us a well of deep emotions, feelings, and memories. Singing has the power to move us deeper into relationship with God.

However, there is discord in this psalm. The singing that is produced comes in the context of the Lord's judgment! How can singing and judgment stand together in the same psalm? The next part of the sermon might explore the theme of judgment and the tension experienced when judgment is placed alongside singing.

The typical images that come to mind when we think of the judgment of God revolve around punishment, anger, and fear. In addition, we sometimes associate human judgment with one who is judgmental—that is, one who is critical, harsh, and unloving in evaluating others.

We also know that human judgment is often impaired, prejudiced, and partial. This is precisely the problem the Lord has with the way in which the gods practice justice in Psalm 82. Psalm 82 serves as a commentary on verses 4–5 of Psalm 96. Psalm 82 connects judgment to the relationship between the Lord and the gods. The gods are found wanting by YHWH because they judge with partiality and favoritism. They show little concern for the weak, the orphan, the lowly, and the destitute. They favor the rich and the powerful (82:1–4). Thus in 96:4–5 we understand better why the Lord stands in judgment over the gods, who are nothing more than idols; their judgment, like human judgment, is faulty. Substitute human judges for the gods, and it is understandable why we have a bad taste in our mouth when it comes to the word "judgment." We witness its abuse all around us.

To understand further the tension between justice and singing to the Lord, the preacher would do well to read Amos's words of judgment to the people when he condemns Israel's worship and singing: "Take away from me the noise of your songs; I will not listen to the melody of your harps" (Amos 5:23; cf. 6:5). God hates it when Israel sings to the Lord! Why? Because what they sang inside the worship assembly clashed with the injustices they practiced outside. What the Lord really desires is for justice to flow through the land (Amos 5:24).

Amos, however, is not condemning Israel's singing per se. He is condemning their singing because injustice reigns in Israel. When justice

Psalm 96

Theological Perspective

God. Most scripts extol the pleasures of vanity; Jesus says, "Blessed are the peacemakers." Most scripts ignore those on the margins; Jesus invites the "tax collectors and sinners" to dinner. Most scripts seek ways of defeating, even crushing, one's enemies; Jesus bids his followers to love their enemies and seek their good.

Even so brief a sketch highlights the importance of relationships in the reign of God. Terms such as justice and righteousness do not name primarily personal attributes of human beings, or even God. God is the one who establishes justice or sets things right. Justice is a situation of being rightly related to God, to one's fellow human beings, to nature. What emerges is a vision of justice that can enrich and enlarge our Enlightenment model of justice, a relatively minimal social morality concerned with identifying and protecting human rights and enforcing equal opportunities.

The more relational view of justice found in the reign of God sees oppression and domination not simply as abuse of human rights but as the poisoning of a whole web of relationships, including the relationship between oppressed and oppressor. Poisoned relationships are a malignancy that metastasizes to and among groups and institutions. Justice in this view is not simply a matter of restoring rights or recalibrating equality to find the right mix of freedom and equality. It is, rather, like the healing of a wound, the restoration of relationship, the renewal of the capacity of perpetrator and victim to see each other as fellow human beings. Justice is not opposed to mercy, but serves the ends of reconciliation and the restoration of relationship.

As the future of history, the reign of God is subject to distortions that tempt Christians in two very different ways: despair and presumption. Despair is the sin of resignation in the face of injustice and oppression, the surrender of hope that real change is possible in our social and political order. Presumption, a particularly insidious form of pride, is the sin of identifying my commitments, my efforts, my party, my nation as the embodiment of the reign of God. So the Christian life must be lived in the tension between the already and the not yet, between the recognition that new possibilities abound and the humble acknowledgment that the reign of God is ultimately the reign of *God*.

JOHN C. SHELLEY

Pastoral Perspective

righteousness, and the peoples with his truth" (v. 13). Sentimental dreams are shattered, and the congregation is taken back into the world of family quarrels and backstabbing coworkers and leaders who too often play on the fears and the worries that divide us. Suddenly, the calm peace of Christmas Eve is shattered by the reality of today. The Lord may be king, but the powers and principalities of this world are still very much alive.

The psalmist ends with a word of challenge that our worshiper dare not miss on this Christmas Eve. God calls us to a life of righteousness and truth, a life of faithfulness. It is not enough merely to escape into dreams of the perfect world that is to come. God's people are called to live in this imperfect world with confidence that YHWH is not merely one of the "gods of the peoples" (v. 5), but is the one who desires justice and equity for all the people of the world. The psalmist calls the worshiper out of a nostalgic dream of the future and brings a challenge to live faithfully today with the truth of that future. God's people look forward to this new world that is just over the horizon. In fact, they will continue to sing the "new song" of this kingdom that is breaking forth, but they will sing this new song in this foreign land, constantly challenged by God's call to righteousness and truth.

It is Christmas Eve, and the pews are full of worshipers who have come to sing the comfortable old songs of their past. Into the quiet of this night has come a new song. It brings an invitation of grace. "The LORD is king! The world is firmly established" (v. 10). It brings a call to faithfulness as well. "He will judge the world with righteousness, and the peoples with his truth" (v. 13).

E. LANE ALDERMAN JR.

Christmas Eve

Exegetical Perspective

Ascribe Glory (vv. 7–9). This unit repeats the rhythm of the psalm's opening verse by beginning with three repetitions of the verb "ascribe." To ascribe glory means to say out loud, to publish, to broadcast, the glory due to YHWH. Those commanded to ascribe glory are here more particular than the whole earth (v. 1); they are "families of the peoples" (v. 7), the tribal and national gatherings that make up the human population. The psalm envisions the unity of the earth's people and invites everyone to give glory to God's name, make offerings in God's courts, and tremble before the Holy One.

Reasons to Ascribe Glory (vv. 10–13). As if the psalmist finally comes down from a worshipful "high," specific reasons to ascribe glory to God appear in the last poetic unit to create the psalm's climax. "Say among the nations, "The LORD is king!'" (v. 10) The kingship of YHWH is uniquely a rule of right judgment and justice. The King will judge the peoples of the earth "with equity" (v. 10). Because the Lord is King the earth is firm, established, stable, and given a solid foundation.

In these final verses, the psalm offers a great swelling symphony of praise, of singing, rejoicing, and loud joy uttered by all of the created world. The coming of such a ruler is surprising and marvelous good news, so the whole of the cosmos is encouraged to "be glad" and "rejoice" (v. 11). The heavens, the earth, the sea in its roaring praise, the creatures that fill the sea, the fields, and whatever grows in them, and all the trees of the forest are to be joyous. The cause of this hubbub of delight is "joy before the LORD; for he is coming" (vv. 12–13) to rule the earth with righteousness and the peoples with truth. This is the source of Christian joy; it is what Christians celebrate on this holy day and what we are summoned to embody throughout the year.

KATHLEEN M. O'CONNOR

Homiletical Perspective

begins to flow through the land, then the singing these worshipers offer becomes a sweet melody to the Lord. Amos can then proclaim with the psalmist: "Sing to the LORD a new song" (v. 1). Singing to the Lord activates within us a desire to practice the Lord's justice. We are called to practice what we sing. Neither Amos nor the psalmist knows of any divide between social justice and worshipful singing. The two are one and the same.

The basis for singing a new song, however, begins not with us but with God's justice in the world (vv. 10, 13). No, we are not inclined to rejoice at the prospect of judgment, yet this psalm calls us to do so. The judgment of the Lord is an occasion for joyful singing because the Lord's judgment, unlike that of the gods, is righteous. God's judgment is relational. It is about restoring relationships between individuals, between spouses torn apart by conflict, and between family members at odds with one another. It is about restoring security in neighborhoods riddled with crime.

As we follow the trajectory of God's justice then, we sing to the Lord because God's justice is revealed through God's people. God's goodness is revealed wherever people are treated with love and respect. When singing moves us to say a kind word to those who are discouraged, we sing to the Lord a new song. When singing causes us to stand up for those who are mistreated, God's justice flows through the land. When we reach out to our neighborhood and show them we care, when we invest ourselves in their lives, we activate God's justice. The judgment of the Lord is an occasion for joy because God's judgment is righteous. It sets all our relationships right again. As a result, all of creation breaks forth in song: "Joy to the world, the Savior reigns! Let all their songs employ [v. 10]; . . . While fields and floods, rocks, hills and plains, repeat the sounding joy" (vv. 11–12).[1] God's judgment is an occasion for cosmic singing and celebration!

DAVE BLAND

---

1. Words by Isaac Watts (1719).

Titus 2:11-14

[11]For the grace of God has appeared, bringing salvation to all, [12]training us to renounce impiety and worldly passions, and in the present age to live lives that are self-controlled, upright, and godly, [13]while we wait for the blessed hope and the manifestation of the glory of our great God and Savior, Jesus Christ. [14]He it is who gave himself for us that he might redeem us from all iniquity and purify for himself a people of his own who are zealous for good deeds.

Theological Perspective

In this (and the next) set of Christmas Day readings, the weight falls on the prophetic proclamations from Isaiah and part of the Christmas story from Luke. The Epistle lection is a short interlude providing foundation and strong theological support for the Christmas message celebrated and retold in prophetic and narrative terms. The exalted language of this passage strikes christological, soteriological, eschatological, and ecclesiological chords. In the original context of Titus, these all support the moral message pressed here in verse 12 and also present in the rounding off of the extract in verse 14. Taken out of that literary context and given a new setting in the liturgy, the ethical exhortation is subordinate to the focus on the Christmas message.

The passage is linked ("For") to a preceding reference to "the doctrine of God our Savior" (v. 10), a central Old Testament idea repeated in the Lukan canticles in the birth narrative (Luke 1:77, cf. 1:69–71; 2:30) and made the central christological title for the infant in the Gospel reading that follows (Luke 2:11). The ascription is also common in Greek religion and in the emperor cult, and that Hellenistic and Roman background is more prominent in the Pastoral Epistles on account of the combination of "Savior" with references to the "epiphany," that is, appearance, manifestation, revelation of a god

Pastoral Perspective

What a wonderful call to worship for Christmas Eve: "For the grace of God has appeared, bringing salvation to all!" (v. 11). It echoes the angelic announcements found in the reading from Luke. However, the text takes a turn we are not used to taking on Christmas Eve: "training us to renounce impiety and worldly passions, and in the present age to live lives that are self-controlled, upright, and godly" (v. 12). The reading from Titus reminds us that the salvation being announced has direct and immediate implications for our lives. The offer of a good life is intrinsic to the appearance of this grace.

In Khaled Hosseini's bestseller *The Kite Runner*,[1] there is a phrase that stirs the heart and drives the plot: "There is a way to be good again." The central character, Amir, betrays his boyhood friend, Hassan, in a way that leads to tragedy and suffering. The knowledge of his transgression plagues him throughout his life. As an adult, he receives a note from an old family friend who knew something of his transgression. The note contains the simple words: "There is a way to be good again." This eventually leads him on a journey on behalf of Hassan who, with his wife, was murdered several years before. At great risk to his own life, Amir locates and rescues Hassan's son.

1. Khaled Hosseini, *The Kite Runner* (New York: Riverhead Books, 2003).

Exegetical Perspective

This reflection on the meaning of Jesus' coming derives from a context in which the teaching of Jesus, his welcoming of sinners and social outsiders, and even Paul's gospel of God's free and liberating grace, were fading into the background. For the Pastoral Epistles (written in Paul's name, but most likely by followers of his a generation after his death), to be Christian essentially means "to renounce impiety and worldly passions" and "live lives that are self-controlled, upright, and godly" (v. 12), values that were shared with many other religious and moral philosophies of the time.

Passions or desires (*epithymiai*) were generally recognized as problematic qualities that needed to be curbed. Self-control (*sōphrosynē*; also translated "moderation" or "temperance") and uprightness (*dikaiosynē*; more often translated "justice") were two of the four cardinal virtues widely recognized by philosophers, the other two being prudence (*phronēsis*) and courage (*andreia*). The godliness urged by this writer (*eusebeia*, the opposite of *asebeia*, "impiety") was important in the wider Greco-Roman context as piety toward any god, not specifically the Christian or Jewish God.

This passage contains language that may reflect the thinking of Paul as well as early Christian liturgy that drew on the Jewish Scriptures (God's transforming

Homiletical Perspective

Poor Titus! The Revised Common Lectionary only lets him out for public reading once a year—always on Christmas Eve, when he is sure to be upstaged by Luke's shepherds, angels, and baby lying in a manger! Add candlelight and carols, plus the inevitably high excitement of the occasion, and Titus hardly has a chance. (When was the last time you heard a Titus-based sermon on Christmas Eve?) Granted, Titus also appears in a third set of appointed lessons for Christmas Day; in the unlikely event that both lectionary options are exercised in the same year, how many people would turn out to hear him twice?

Perhaps it is just as well that Titus gets no more press than he does. While everyone else is singing "Glory to God and peace on earth," he is holding forth about "impiety and worldly passions," solemnly exhorting his listeners to "self-control" (v. 12). Really, now, is this the fellow you want sitting next to you at Christmas dinner?

Maybe Titus is the victim of an unfortunate sound-bite selection? No! His moralizing is completely in context. Titus has just unburdened himself of a lengthy string of admonitions to old women, young men, and slaves—those who are at the low end of a highly patriarchal pecking order. His advice to all of them sounds like: "Keep your head down,

Titus 2:11-14

Theological Perspective

("appeared," v. 11; "manifestation," v. 13). Drawing on the resonances words have in the surrounding culture and discovering new meanings in the traditional language is essential to Christian communication.

The passage contains no explicit reference to the birth of Christ, though "epiphany" could refer to the birthday of a god in the cult. Associating God's saving act with the birth of Jesus as well as his death and resurrection was a fourth-century development. The Western church's celebration of the Epiphany as "the manifestation of Christ to the Gentiles" is in tune with the universal scope of the revelation "to all" here (v. 11).

The title "Savior" has sometimes acquired an individualistic flavor in accord with its personal and existential character. The word is related to healing and wholeness and naturally refers to personal well-being. That is not to be undervalued, but it needs a corrective emphasis on the corporate and political dimensions of salvation. The background and usage of the word in the Pastoral Epistles can help us to preserve a proper balance, as can the Lukan canticles. God saves, God rescues, and most of what we need to be saved from is social and cosmic, not simply personal and individual. The word includes the public sphere, where it can motivate our political engagement.

Both God and Jesus Christ are called Savior in the parallel passage Titus 3:4–7, as here in 2:10 and 13. In the NRSV translation of verse 13 this leads to Jesus himself being called God, as in the near contemporary epistles of Ignatius. It would also be possible to translate the phrase (in accord with other phrases in the Pastorals) "of the great God, and our Savior Jesus Christ," but the advance from divine attributes to divinity is small, and in nondogmatic contexts Jesus was soon called God as well as Lord and Savior.

In hearing the good news and being faced with Jesus, we are confronted by and respond to God our Savior, not simply a messenger. The same "thinking together" of God and Jesus Christ is apparent in Paul's epistles, especially in the title "Lord," which is replaced by "Savior" in this epistle (1:4). The most exalted language available is needed to articulate that experience and conviction. It is God with whom we have to do in Christ, and that knowledge of God in Christ maintained by and in the Spirit pressed Christian thought into developing Trinitarian theology. Understanding God as the triune God has its roots in New Testament Christology and soteriology.

Pastoral Perspective

"There is a way to be good again." This is an evocative phrase. It is not simply about exploiting an overactive conscience. It taps into that deep yearning we have to be better than we are. It also reveals the deep doubt we harbor that there is no real hope of becoming other than what and who we have become.

For many who take their seats in the Christmas Eve service, there exists an inarticulate yearning to hear the words, "There is a way to be good again." It is a night uniquely suited to being caught up in the possibility that there is something to the outrageous, mysterious claim that God in Christ has made a way for redemption. There will be many listening, more deeply than they want to admit, for a way to be good again—straining under the weight of accumulated lost opportunities, betrayals, broken promises, and failed love.

All that sorrow, grief, shame, and sin is not out of view this night. It all belongs here. It finds a place amid the candlelight, amid all the talk of cattle lowing, babies waking, stars shining, and shepherds watching. Our lives are called out from the shadows and into the light of this night.

We here on earth sing "Glory to God in the highest" from the foot of the cross, from the mouth of the tomb. We sing in the midst of suffering and pain, of the evil we have done and the evil that has been done unto us, of a life that is indeed filled with the knowledge of both good and evil. "Glory to God in the highest." We sing in the night; but morning is promised, and is coming. "Glory to God in the highest."[2]

So there is hope to be proclaimed—a hope that stems not from the possibility of pulling ourselves up by our own bootstraps, but from the fact that Jesus "gave himself for us that he might redeem us from all iniquity and purify for himself a people of his own who are zealous for good deeds" (v. 14). We embody this hope in our lives by identifying what we need to say no to and giving ourselves to what is good. M. Shawn Copeland reminds us that as blessed as this effort may be, it is no short-term undertaking:

> Learning when and how, to what, and to whom to give our yes or our no is a lifelong project. It is learning to live not merely in dull balance or tedious moderation but in passionate, disciplined choice and action. It is learning to find support and challenge, courage and correction, as we live out our choices. Sustaining and realizing our yes from day to day is only possible when negative and destructive behaviors are supplanted by positive

2. David Johnson, "Making Theology Come Alive in the Parish," *Pro Ecclesia* 3, no. 4 (Fall 1994): 402.

grace, eschatological hope, Christ's redemptive self-giving). This language is blended, however, with commonplace exhortations to virtuous living that are solidly anchored in the pagan culture of their time. It is hard to connect these exhortations with Paul's joyous insistence that the Christian life is a life of radical love (Rom. 12:9–21) lived by the power of the Spirit of God, not by moral striving (Rom. 8:1–13; Gal. 5:22–23). It seems an even longer stretch back to the teacher who welcomed all to his company, regardless of social standing or spiritual and ethical attainment; who was crucified for asserting the claims of God against those of society's conservative rulers; and who was born into such insecurity that he literally had no place to lay his head.

One thread in this passage may help us make those connections. The passions or desires that the author desires his readers to renounce are called *worldly* passions, which was not the normal philosophical way of describing them. The term "worldly" (*kosmikos*) commonly meant "having to do with the universe" in a spiritually neutral way. For early Christians, however, "the world" came to mean more specifically *human* systems structured in self-centered opposition to God, so that God's people find themselves in a hostile relationship to "the world" (John 17:14–16; 1 John 2:15–17; 1 Cor. 2:12; Gal. 6:14; Col. 2:20).

Thus in opposing "worldly" passions—desires associated with the world that opposes God's will for human beings—the author of Titus remains in continuity with the sense of Christianity as something radically different and marked off from the status quo of human society and culture. The Pastoral Epistles seem to expect their readers to work out a manner of living that is not "of the world," even as they remain firmly anchored "in the world."

Although their language is unblushingly derived from the high moral aspirations of the surrounding culture, the Pastorals see this as something that strengthens believers in their obedience to the God who has intervened in cultural and religious history to save and transform them. This intervention is called the *appearance* of God's grace, using another common piece of ancient religious terminology. The verb used, *epiphainō*, is the source of the term "epiphany," which names the liturgical season following Christmas that celebrates the manifestation of Christ to the world. Indeed, that very Greek word, *epiphaneia*, is used in verse 13 (NRSV "manifestation") to refer to Christ's second coming.

The Pastoral Epistles are among the earliest texts to use these terms to refer to the coming of Christ

your nose clean! And whatever you do, don't rock the boat! The reign of God will be best advanced if you acquiesce to the rule of men!"

"Be submissive!" he counsels women and slaves.

"Self-control!" is his injunction for the young of both sexes.

Small wonder that the lectionary framers allow Titus a limited appearance—an awkward, fleeting interlude between the well-beloved celebration songs and stories of Isaiah and Luke—a grudging inclusion perhaps justified by a single line: "the grace of God has appeared, bringing salvation to all" (v. 11).

Added to these oddities in the Titus passage (and what precedes and follows it), there is another: a curious juxtaposition of "self-control" (v. 12), on the one hand, and a people, redeemed and purified, who are "zealous for good deeds" (v. 14) on the other. What should we make of that?

The driving purpose behind this author's exhortation, apparently, is not buttoned-down behavior. He is seeking not to *repress* passions, but to *redirect* them. What Titus has most deeply in mind is a release of redemptive energy, a full-voiced celebration of communal service—a celebration that will build a bridge in space and time between "the grace of God [that] has appeared, bringing salvation to all" (v. 11) and "the blessed hope and the manifestation of the glory of our great God and Savior, Jesus Christ," that we "wait for" (v. 13).

Are we any more comfortable with the notion of zealous good-deed-doers than that of those who are "self-controlled" (especially in the way that Titus seems to enjoin)?

The word *zealous* is often held captive to the connotations surrounding "zealot"—"a fanatical partisan." "Zealous" is better understood, however, in relation to its other noun cognate: "zeal"—"eagerness and ardent interest in pursuit of something." Still, how is Titus's claim that Christ Jesus gave himself to redeem us from impurity, and to purify a people "who are zealous for good deeds" (v. 14) compatible with his previous threefold injunction to "self-control" (2:5, 6, 12, and several similar moralizing adjectives punctuating 2:2–9)?

Think of Christmas celebrations that are blowouts—orgies of food, drink, and bacchanalian behavior. Recall images of holiday debris tossed out for trash collection before the sun has even set. Think of the all-consuming, highly competitive consumer frenzy that so often characterizes the run-up to Christmas Day. Expand the imaginational horizon still more broadly: envision the orgies of self-assertive

Titus 2:11-14

Theological Perspective

Neither God nor Jesus can be spoken of in Christianity without constant reference to salvation, the future hope, and morality. The soteriological dimension is underlined here (and at 3:7) in Pauline language. Jesus gave himself for us (cf. Gal. 2:20), but the eschatology is weakened. Christians still wait in hope for the future coming of Christ. "Epiphany" in verse 13 now refers to the Parousia: the revelation of God our Savior in Christ awaits its consummation. All Christian life is lived in hope between these two poles, conditioned by what the incarnation inaugurated and the cross and resurrection achieved, but lived realistically in a world not yet redeemed. Where Paul sees the cross as setting us free from the present evil age (Gal. 1:4), the author of Titus gives this a moral emphasis, seeing it as redeeming us from iniquity as we continue the moral struggle in the present age (v. 12).

The ecclesiological note is closely connected with this moral emphasis. The purity of the community, equally important for Paul, is evoked here in the language of Deuteronomy. The people of God is a people for God's own possession, as at 1 Peter 2:9. The writer was not himself writing for the celebration of Christmas. However, by bundling together most of the main themes of Christian doctrine in speaking of the incarnation (the Spirit and baptism occur in the parallel passage in the next chapter), he reminds us to relate our reflection on Christmas to the central themes of Christian faith, in particular the cross.

The passage set to be read here is placed under the title "the revelation of the grace of God" (v. 11), speaking of God's gift and power. Single words can evoke the whole Christian symbolic world of doctrine and practice, provided that those who hear the lection are adequately instructed. Without that, the passage may yet be persuasive rhetoric, but will not reinforce the "sound doctrine" that the writer is keen to preserve. The gift of grace is communicated at Christmas in the birth of a powerless child, and that points also to the saving event in the self-giving of Christ on the cross. The community he calls remembers that above all, even at Christmas, and knows itself called by this grace to lives worthy of our calling.

ROBERT C. MORGAN

Pastoral Perspective

and generative ones, when we redeem the routines of our daily lives, when we choose and carry out commitments that give and support life.[3]

Tonight is the night to rekindle the hope that there is a way to be good again. There is a way to be freed from the entanglements of our failings and fallings. It is not that they do not matter—it is that they do not have to determine or predict the flow of our lives. The life in view here is a flourishing, impassioned, graceful, contented, purposeful life.

This night *is*, not just *was*, a turning point. Tonight we are all called to become a part of that turning. I am reminded of Dan Wakefield's *Returning: A Spiritual Journey* (New York: Doubleday, 1988), in which he recounts his journey back to faith—a journey that began when he wandered into King's Chapel in Boston for the Christmas Eve service. That was the night his life turned.

It is tempting on Christmas Eve to look out upon the congregation (often brimming with twice-a-year visitors) and feel that there is not much of salvific significance to be accomplished in the next hour or so. Resist that temptation, and speak the good news. You never know who may have wandered in.

For the celebration of Christmas to be faithful, it must remind us of where we stand in relation to God's intentions for each of us. This is to be heard not as threat, but as promise, even as a blessed hope. There is a way to be good again!

DAVID J. WOOD

---

3. M. Shawn Copeland, "Saying Yes and Saying No," in *Practicing Our Faith: A Way of Life for a Searching People*, ed. Dorothy C. Bass (San Francisco, CA: Jossey-Bass, 1997), 67–68.

Exegetical Perspective

(for the first coming, see also 2 Tim. 1:10; Titus 3:4; for the second coming see 1 Tim. 6:14; 2 Tim. 4:1, 8). *Epiphaneia* was already in common use for the appearance or revelation of pagan deities by vision, word, or deed. The Septuagint uses this terminology to refer to manifestations of Israel's God (Gen. 35:7; Num. 6:25; Deut. 33:2; and Psalm passages related to it; see esp. 2 Macc. 3:24, 30; 3 Macc. 5:8, 51).

Here again there is some tension in the way the Pastoral Epistles use the shared religious language of Hellenistic culture to refer to acts of God that stand apart from that culture and may even threaten it. The epiphanies of Greek deities took place within the accepted religious framework of ancient society. Indeed, our passage is set in a context that urges the readers to maintain social hierarchies. The appearance of God's saving grace in Jesus is of a different order from that of the Greek deities and has the potential to challenge that agreed-upon social framework. Certainly the ultimate manifestation of his glory (v. 13) will transcend everything that currently exists and bring it to an end.

The Pastoral Epistles seem to struggle between two currents. They want Christians to live in positive dialogue with their cultural surroundings; yet they believe that God has sent the Messiah as a revelation of the divine will that is both redeeming and transformative. Thus they offer an example—sometimes a sobering example—for churches enmeshed in modern and postmodern cultures today. How can we "renounce . . . worldly passions," including the passion for security, power, and dominance, while still interacting with a culture that is devoted to those things? The goal of God's grace is to bring "salvation to all" (v. 11), and it is the church's responsibility somehow to let all know about the manifestation of this grace in the coming of Christ, without falling into fatal compromises in the process.

The writer of the Pastorals hopes that behavior that reinforces widely held social values will help to commend the Christian gospel to that society (see also Titus 2:5, 8, 10). When the gospel is commended in this fashion, how can it keep its authenticity and its power to challenge dominant values that conflict with the way of Jesus?

DAVID RENSBERGER

Homiletical Perspective

self-protection that have been conducted in recent years to exercise more "control" with regard to national security. Are any of these behaviors zealous? In the "zealot" sense, perhaps. Are they expressions of "self-control"? Doubtful.

Imagine now an alternative universe: Christmas dinners planned with patient, attentive, professional care—with eyes alert to making every participant fully welcome. Allow your memory to be flooded with senses of Christmas Eve services where disciplined musicians offer festal sounds filling sanctuaries exquisitely decorated with artistic splendor. In that setting, envision communal feasting on the Word, orchestrated as choruses of different voices—readers, preachers, liturgical leaders—each one of them lovingly and thoroughly prepared. "Zealous"? Such occasions are surely that! And consummate expressions of self-control as well.

Now think back in time—and think ahead as well (Titus clearly has!). Think of the well-focused zeal that energizes the actions of shepherds and angels, Mary and Joseph. Recall again the soaring poetry of Isaiah (set to music by Handel and any number of other disciplined, passionate musicians). Now dream of history's far horizon: "the manifestation of the glory of our great God and Savior Jesus Christ" (v. 13), toward which creation moves and longs. What measures of "self-control" are called for in preparation for such a celebration? How might those become festive means of channeling anticipatory zeal? How, in other words, can our *preparation* for such glory be a *participation* in it? Such "good-deed-doing" would not be so much *duty* as *delight*—a "keeping of Christmas all the year" (as Charles Dickens puts it in *A Christmas Carol*).

Yes, but what about all that "submission" stuff that Titus has gone on about? We might well discern that, in our time and place, "zealous good deeds" permit (even require) the resisting of certain social structures, rather than unquestioning submission to them. If we undertake the work of social transformation as *zealots*—as "fanatical partisans" only—we may not, in fact, be exercising the kind of self-control that is in character with the redemptive work of the one who has already "appeared, bringing salvation to all," and the full manifestation of whose glory we still, in hope, await.

DAVID J. SCHLAFER

Luke 2:1-14 (15-20)

¹In those days a decree went out from Emperor Augustus that all the world should be registered. ²This was the first registration and was taken while Quirinius was governor of Syria. ³All went to their own towns to be registered. ⁴Joseph also went from the town of Nazareth in Galilee to Judea, to the city of David called Bethlehem, because he was descended from the house and family of David. ⁵He went to be registered with Mary, to whom he was engaged and who was expecting a child. ⁶While they were there, the time came for her to deliver her child. ⁷And she gave birth to her firstborn son and wrapped him in bands of cloth, and laid him in a manger, because there was no place for them in the inn.

⁸In that region there were shepherds living in the fields, keeping watch over their flock by night. ⁹Then an angel of the Lord stood before them, and the glory of the Lord shone around them, and they were terrified. ¹⁰But the angel said to them, "Do not be afraid; for see—I am bringing you good news of great joy for all the people: ¹¹to you is born this day in the city of David a Savior, who

Theological Perspective

This text, with its heavenly evangelist, specializes in the kind of direct personal address that Luther saw as a hallmark of genuine gospel proclamation: The angel says, "I am bringing you good news (*euangelizomai humin*) . . . to you is born this day. . . . This will be a sign for you" (vv. 10, 11, 12). Luther notes, "He [the angel] does not simply say: 'Christ is born,' but: '*for you* he is born.'"[1] "What good would it do me, if he were born a thousand times and if this were sung to me every day with the loveliest airs, if I should not hear that there was something in it for me and that it should be my own?"[2]

To whom is this good news addressed? This question merits some attention. Not only are there various answers to it in the text itself, but differences in translation—for example, between the King James Version (whose rendering of the Christmas stories still shapes our common memory) and the New Revised Standard Version—raise further issues. Before jumping to the conclusion that "you" simply means *us*—us hearers, whoever we might be—it might behoove us to investigate.

1. Martin Luther, *Luther's Works*, vol. 52, *Sermons, II*, ed. Hans J. Hillerbrand (Philadelphia: Fortress Press, 1974), 15.
2. Ibid., 21.

Pastoral Perspective

The Gospel text for Christmas Eve reminds us again of the wonder and surprising nature of God's incarnation. The preparation for God's coming into the world in Christ happens amid the requirements of daily life and the requirements of imperial politics, which is to say, amid citizenship in the "earthly kingdom." Even as politics, economics, and other forces try to "name and number the entire world," God will establish a counterpolitics that will place kingly rule not in the imperial palace but in a manger, whose culmination will be not conquest but a cross. Thinking about the political, economic, and social forces that shape our lives and hearts makes this passage relevant. Around Christmas, those forces ask us to buy more presents, put up a fancy tree.

Amid Hallmark trivialities, we must not lose the scandal of God's incarnation as an infant, outside of town, to a yet-to-be-married couple. These are model outsiders! How many churches would turn this pair away if they came knocking at our church doors today? Amid the power of the Roman emperor, few questioned the government's ability to "name time." It might be helpful to use this text to have individuals think about their citizenship in the multiple kingdoms of jobs, work, family, church, and

is the Messiah, the Lord. [12]This will be a sign for you: you will find a child wrapped in bands of cloth and lying in a manger." [13]And suddenly there was with the angel a multitude of the heavenly host, praising God and saying,

[14]"Glory to God in the highest heaven,
    and on earth peace among those whom he favors!"

[15]When the angels had left them and gone into heaven, the shepherds said to one another, "Let us go now to Bethlehem and see this thing that has taken place, which the Lord has made known to us." [16]So they went with haste and found Mary and Joseph, and the child lying in the manger. [17]When they saw this, they made known what had been told them about this child; [18]and all who heard it were amazed at what the shepherds told them. [19]But Mary treasured all these words and pondered them in her heart. [20]The shepherds returned, glorifying and praising God for all they had heard and seen, as it had been told them.

Exegetical Perspective

Like Matthew, Luke places Jesus' birth in the time of Herod the Great, but he is intent on providing a wider framework for this world-historical event: it occurred when Augustus Caesar was undisputed ruler of the Mediterranean world. By naming Augustus, Luke sets up an implicit contrast between the Roman emperor and Mary's baby, God's Messiah, who will be ruler over all peoples. The contrast is between military power and God's power.

Luke tells his readers that the birth occurred during a census ordered by the emperor. The Gospel writer exaggerates; there was no empirewide census under Augustus. Moreover, he has the time wrong; Quirinius was not governor of Syria until 6 CE. There is little support for his hypothesis that a census would require people to return to their ancestral homes in order to be counted. The historicity of his proposal does not undercut Luke's understanding of its theological significance, however. During Quirinius's census there was a rebellion, led by Judas the Galilean, who "got people to follow him" (Acts 5:37). Subtly, Luke suggests to readers who know about the political unrest occasioned by the census that in just such a time God's Messiah was born. There is here an implicit contrast between the weakness of the baby and the violent strength of the

Homiletical Perspective

A Flood of Feelings. It should be easy to preach on Christmas Eve, should it not? Luke's account of Jesus' birth is familiar and so very eloquent. Many feelings rush in on us and our congregations on Christmas Eve. Ah, those pesky feelings! For weeks television advertisements have told us how we ought to feel this night. We ought to feel warm and loving, especially if we have spent a small fortune on gifts for our family and friends. We hope that most in our congregations this night do feel great peace and joy, but let us take care not to presume. Some may come to church this night dealing with the death of a loved one, worrying about mounting financial debts, or struggling with tensions in their relationships. The good news from the Scriptures this night is more powerful than the pain that some may bring. Our preaching this night announces that the real king of peace is among us.

The Real King of Peace. Luke begins this account by telling us that the wonders of this night take place during the reign of Caesar Augustus. That is an important detail, because Caesar was praised as the great king of peace. In fact, he was the object of a cult; the one whose *Pax Augusta* would bring an end

Luke 2:1-14 (15-20)

Theological Perspective

In the account itself, of course, the good news is addressed first of all to some shepherds outside Bethlehem. Some commentators indicate that, in the context in which this account originated, the shepherds would be understood as representatives of the people. Others have suggested that shepherds, living away from settled communities, would have been regarded with some suspicion by respectable folk and might better be taken to represent the marginalized or outsiders, the sorts of people with whom Jesus would come to associate in his ministry. Luther, while identifying the shepherds with ordinary people, pointedly observes that the angel did not appear to kings or prelates.

The news is not just for the shepherds. "I am bringing you good news of great joy for all the people" (v. 10). "For all people," reads the King James Version; the NRSV, with other older and more recent translations, retains the definite article of the original Greek: "for all the people." There is a difference. "*The* people" normally implies a distinction, and often a contrast: some particular people, the people of *x* as distinct from other people, or perhaps "the people" as distinct from "the rulers" or "the clergy." It may be tempting to side with the friendly, all-embracing version, and simply avoid whatever distinction might be implied in the more literal (and probably more appropriate) NRSV rendition of *panti tō laō*. That way, the beneficiaries of the good news would certainly include "us"—no questions asked.

It is well to remember, however, that it is in Luke's Gospel that Jesus identifies himself as the one "anointed," in the words of Isaiah, "to bring good news to the poor, . . . to proclaim release to the captives" (Luke 4:18). At first blush, this is not good news to the captors, nor to those who have profited by the poverty of the poor. (Poverty, in this Gospel and in the prophetic tradition on which it draws, is neither a natural state nor an unfortunate accident, but rather the result of deliberate social policy.) Indeed, this is the Gospel of a rich fool (12:13–21), the rich man who neglects Lazarus to his peril (16:19–31), and the all-too-direct words of Jesus, "Woe to you who are rich, for you have received your consolation" (Luke 6:24). However we construe the referent of "all the people" in the angel's promise, these indications of a more complicated, conflicted reception of Jesus and his message should not be ignored.

To whom, then, is the good news addressed? Our question arises again when we come to the words of the heavenly host in verse 14. Here, differences involving the transcription and proper construal of

Pastoral Perspective

community. Making those conflicting demands apparent will connect them to this story.

Joseph traveled to Bethlehem for a census registration, not a vacation. He had to obey the rulers of his day, even as God's plans were beginning to unfold a different kingdom. It is helpful, especially in these days dominated by politics and responsibility, to think with our congregations about how God's work unfolds, not despite life's other tasks, but in the midst of them. How can we look for God's unfolding power in the midst of our daily lives?

On Christmas Eve, many know what it is like to leave new homes and return to the town or the family of their birth. Others wish they could have that experience but do not, because other rulers demand their time. Some undertake the journey home with trepidation, others with joy, some out of obligation, some by choice. Like Mary and Joseph, they undertake it in the midst of life's other challenges and events. They go to particular places, sometimes to the home of their birth, to join a gathering of people that is, or in some cases will become, soaked with memory. It is in those specific places, not in some abstract place, that God's work unfolds. Think about the ways you can guide people to reflect on how God unfolds in their particular lives and particular places. Place shapes how God is experienced.

Often politics does not bend to our needs, as contemporary events make all too clear. Think about the latest struggles for justice in your community, over any one of a number of issues. Mary sought shelter to give birth for her child but there was no room. Those who swarmed back for the census earlier had taken the rooms already, leaving Mary without a place. Some in our congregations feel there is no room for them in the places they were born either. They feel as if they are relegated to outsider status, that they too have to enter by the back door or sleep down the street. It would be helpful to have congregants think of times they have been shut out of the inn, and what that felt like. Most people have some memory of exclusion. Then have them think of ways God's work might have been done in the midst of that exclusion.

Even if things did not go as planned, new life breaks forth. Jesus, God's work, arrived in the midst of political events and no vacancies. The important message of Christmas is that even when things do not go as planned, God arrives. We forget the scary nature of the first Christmas—that it was all about things that were unexpected, in places unsought. Christ arrived in a manger, in a cattle stall. If the Son

Exegetical Perspective

insurrectionists. One is reminded of Paul's comment that "God's weakness is stronger than human strength" (1 Cor. 1:25).

Jesus and Augustus are contrasted implicitly again in verse 11, when the angel announces that this Messiah is both Savior and Lord. In many Greek inscriptions, Augustus was hailed as "savior of the whole world." One declares that his birthday "has marked the beginning of the good news through him for the world."[1] The emperor also bore the title of *kyrios*, "Lord." Luke employs this usage in Acts 25:26, "But I have nothing definite to write to our sovereign [literally: to the *kyrios*] about him" (Note: Not *a* lord but *the* lord, the supreme lord of the Roman Empire). In the birth narrative Luke implies that Jesus bears the titles of Savior and Lord more authentically than Augustus.

There is another contrast between the two world rulers. Augustus was hailed as savior because of his vigorous policy of putting down minor local wars and suppressing piracy on the seas and brigandage on the land. As a result, people spoke glowingly of the *Pax Augusta,* or the *Pax Romana*, the worldwide peace established by Augustus. In Luke 2 the angelic chorus announces that Messiah's birth brings peace to the world, but a peace very different from the *Pax Romana*: "and on earth peace among those whom he favors."

The Greek of this line is difficult and gave rise to many variant readings in the ancient manuscripts, including the one on which the KJV is based, "good will toward men." The reading now preferred by scholars, which underlies the NRSV, is "among people of *eudokia*." This word *eudokia* refers to human goodwill in Philippians 1:15, "Some proclaim Christ . . . from goodwill." Hence it is possible that the angelic song promises peace to people of good intentions. The use of *eudokia* in the Greek Old Testament, however, makes it much more likely that the word here refers to God's favor. The divine favor seems to be dependent not on human behavior but on God's gracious will. We should think here of the history of salvation. God willed to effect salvation through his chosen people, Israel. There is thus a connection between "peace among those whom he favors" in verse 14 and verse 10, "a great joy which will be to the whole people" (my trans.), that is, Israel.

This uncaesar's parentage is not august. At his dedication in the temple, they will offer the

1. See Joseph A. Fitzmyer, *The Gospel according to Luke (I–IX)*, Anchor Bible 28 (Garden City, NY: Doubleday, 1981), 394.

Homiletical Perspective

to war.[1] We do not need to be history students to know how many wars Caesar Augustus fought and how many have taken place since his reign. The Gospel announces the arrival of the true king of peace. Christ brings a peace that no earthly king will ever achieve. This Christmas Eve Gospel first of all shows us the true king of peace, who enters our lives even if we have come to church this night with pain in our hearts. Christ brings peace this night especially to those with broken hearts.

The Angels' **Inclusio.** The angels certainly know that this new child is the genuine king who has come to bring peace. In verse 14 they pronounce blessed those on whom the peace of this new king will rest. This is not the last time Luke's readers will hear that proclamation. When Jesus makes his triumphal entry into Jerusalem near the end of his mission, the crowds will echo this Christmas proclamation as they shout out that this great king brings peace in heaven and glory in the highest (19:38). The literary device *inclusio*, the repetition of an idea or phrase, is meant to alert readers to what the author considers to be especially important. The great humorist Mark Twain was fond of pointing out that he was born when Halley's Comet appeared in 1835, and predicted that he would exit life when this same comet returned on its seventy-six-year cycle. True to his promise, Twain died one day after the comet made its reappearance in 1910. Readers often allude to this celestial *inclusio* as a testament to Twain's special place within the literary community. Luke's artful use of his *inclusio* helps the believer focus on a central message of this night; that Jesus is the true king who brings us lasting peace.[2] With all that will be said and sung this Christmas Eve, Luke wants us to know that the king of peace is here.

The Angels Visit Shepherds. Preachers may also want to point out that shepherds were the first to hear this angelic news bulletin. If there is a crèche in your church, you might mention how artists usually depict these poor but humble men standing on the edge of the scene with their heads bowed. Perhaps a few sheep from Central Casting are resting nearby. The Gospel does not want us to see shepherds this way. The scandal of this night is that shepherds in this culture were at the bottom of the social ladder.

1. Robert J. Karris, OFM, "The Gospel according to Luke," in *The New Jerome Biblical Commentary,* ed. Raymond Brown, Joseph Fitzmyer, and Roland Murphy (Englewood Cliffs, NJ: Prentice-Hall, 1990, 1968), 683.
2. Ibid.

Luke 2:1-14 (15-20)

Theological Perspective

the final word of the Greek text (*eudokia* or *eudokias*) have led to three divergent options in rendering the sense of the passage. One is represented by the King James Version: "Glory to God in the highest, and on earth peace, good will toward men." The second is represented by the Douay-Rheims Bible, following the Vulgate: ". . . and on earth peace to men of good will." The third option is represented by our NRSV: ". . . and on earth peace among those whom he favors!" The varying options stem in part from differing manuscript traditions, but theological motives or predispositions also have played some role in the processes through which they have been developed and sustained. In the end, none may be adequate.

The key term at issue here, *eudokia*, is often translated "good pleasure" (or "well-pleased-ness"). Elsewhere in Luke, *eudokia* and the verb *eudokeō* "always denote the divine will to save."[3] The angels are not announcing that peace is at hand for those who have pleased God, but rather that the peace to be realized—the earthly counterpart of God's own heavenly glory—is God's gracious gift, bestowed at God's good pleasure. Not far from the angels' message, either textually or theologically, is that of another voice from heaven, this time at Jesus' baptism: "You are my Son, the Beloved; with you [literally: in you] I am well pleased" (Luke 3:22).

Christmas Eve is liminal time, liturgically. It is the culmination of the Advent season, and we are crossing over from that time of self-examination and preparation to the Christmas time of thankful receiving. We are not there yet. It is fitting that this Gospel text include both the story of Jesus' birth and the first proclamation of its significance, in a form that leads us to ponder how this news relates to us, and what it might mean concretely in our own lives to receive this gift.

CHARLES M. WOOD

Pastoral Perspective

of God can arrive in such circumstances, so can truth. So can joy.

The Gospel reminds us that God appears to the less than perfect and less than powerful. Too often congregants think God will not speak to them, because they do not go to church, or because they are aware of their sin, or because they think their lives are less than holy, or because the church has told them so. By appearing to shepherds, God showed God's willingness to appear to any who will listen. God came unexpectedly, at night, to those who were simply going about their daily occupations. The shepherds had not withdrawn from the world to seek holiness; they were simply going about their task, and God appeared. Too often we look for God in the beautiful, in the times and places we set out to seek God. It is also important to remember that God seeks us. Think about the ways that you have seen God move unexpectedly, a moment that you were least expecting the Holy but found the Holy.

The shepherds were probably tired, tending sheep at night. Then, unexpectedly, and intrusively, God's messenger appeared. The angels terrified them. They had apparently not been waiting or praying for a message. Rather, God's message interrupted them right where they were in order to announce God's work. It is helpful to remind people to think about how God shows up, even in small and ordinary ways in the midst of what they do. At Christmas, the awe-inspiring and terrifying God whom Moses had to veil his face to see, appeared as an infant. In times like ours, when angels are celebrated as friendly and sentimental characters, it may be difficult to picture what powerful and unsettling creatures angels can be. God whispers, "Do not be afraid; . . . I am bringing you good news of great joy" (v. 10). This is the same call that Jesus will echo in the Gospels: "Fear not."

Finally, we have a blessing of peace. God sends us peace. God does not desire huge festivals, frantic preparations, or wish us boundless energy to do everything. Rather, God wishes us peace.

AARON KLINK

3. François Bovon, *Luke 1: A Commentary on the Gospel of Luke 1:1 to 9:50*, trans. Christine M. Thomas (Minneapolis: Augsburg Fortress Press, 2002), 91.

Exegetical Perspective

turtledove of the poor (Luke 2:24). No scandal is seen in the fact that Mary is pregnant prior to a formal marriage, as might be suggested by the English "engaged" (2:5). Matthew 1:19 calls Joseph Mary's husband, and says that he considers divorcing Mary, not breaking the engagement, as in our culture.

Their lodging is not regal. The word translated "inn" in most versions does not bear this meaning in Greek (a different word appears in Luke 10:34). In Luke 22:11 the NRSV has "guest room." The word had as its general meaning "lodging." Moreover, it seems unlikely that a small village would have had an inn. Here the word may refer to an empty room in a private house, where travelers could spend the night. In Palestine it was common for animals to be housed in a part of the house. Perhaps Joseph and Mary were permitted to sleep in the animal portion of a house whose "guest room" was filled. Although Luke mentions a manger, there is no reference to the animals so beloved in modern representations of the manger scene. It has been proposed that the presence of animals was suggested by Isaiah 1:3, "The ox knows its owner, and the donkey its master's crib."[2]

Do the attendants at this birth suggest royalty? No hint is given concerning why shepherds were chosen to receive the revelation concerning Messiah's birth. It has been proposed that the shepherds reflect Luke's concern for the poor ("poor" occurs eleven times in this Gospel). It is true that many shepherds were simply hired hands and as such were at the bottom of the social scale (see John 10:12–13). Here the shepherds seem to be owners of the sheep; they are guarding their own sheep. Perhaps the shepherds represent Israel's rulers, as in Ezekiel 34. Another possibility is that the shepherds are meant to remind us of a more famous Bethlehem shepherd, David (1 Sam. 16:11).

It is not clear why Mary is said to ponder "all these words," or perhaps "all these happenings." since Gabriel has already announced that her baby will be Israel's king forever (Luke 1:26–33). Perhaps Luke is reminding his readers that it was by no means obvious how Jesus would replace Augustus.

DOUGLAS R. A. HARE

Homiletical Perspective

They were dirty and smelly from living out in the fields. When I lived near Los Angeles, I would often see men standing in small groups on street corners waiting for someone to drive by and pick them up for a day job. Perhaps they would be hired to mow the lawn on a wealthy estate or sweep the factory floor. These hardworking immigrants would do a good job; if they were undocumented, it was all the better, since they could be hired for less than minimum wage. How could they complain to the authorities? These are the shepherds. Did the angels take a wrong turn that first Christmas night? Had they intended to announce the king of peace to movers and shakers, the important people? The angels knew exactly what they were doing, of course. The new king born this night has brought peace to all men and women, but especially to the poor.

Silent Night. We might conclude the sermon by recalling an event that took place on Christmas Eve in the little Church of St. Nicholas in Oberndorf, Austria. A few days before Christmas, the parish organist informed the pastor that the aging church organ was broken and could not be fixed by midnight services. The organist said that he could play his guitar that night if the pastor thought that would be appropriate. The pastor agreed to the guitar music and added that he had written a simple poem that the musician might be able to set to music. So that night in 1818, in St. Nicholas Church, the world heard in German for the first time "Silent Night." We still sing this simple, but very noble song many years later. The song captures well the spirit of this night. The appearance of Jesus went unnoticed by so many, but the shepherds noticed. Perhaps we might arrange for a musician to play "Silent Night" softly under the final words of our sermon. When the preaching concludes, the choir and/or congregation could sing the hymn. In the silence, we notice!

DANIEL HARRIS

2. Ibid., 406.

Isaiah 52:7-10

> ⁷How beautiful upon the mountains
>   are the feet of the messenger who announces peace,
> who brings good news,
>   who announces salvation,
>   who says to Zion, "Your God reigns."
> ⁸Listen! Your sentinels lift up their voices,
>   together they sing for joy;
> for in plain sight they see
>   the return of the LORD to Zion.
> ⁹Break forth together into singing,
>   you ruins of Jerusalem;
> for the LORD has comforted his people,
>   he has redeemed Jerusalem.
> ¹⁰The LORD has bared his holy arm
>   before the eyes of all the nations;
> and all the ends of the earth shall see
>   the salvation of our God.

Theological Perspective

No one can miss the sheer exuberance of this reading from Isaiah. This day breaks into singing just as the birds do at dawning of daylight. Now the images of light and hope and the sign of a child to be born all converge. Isaiah bids Jerusalem to wake up and to put on beautiful garments. Now is grim captivity put behind, and the dawning of a new day comes. There is something so real about God's act of deliverance that the very cosmos bursts into song.

This resonates with Luke's Gospel, where the story of Christ's birth is told and unfolded in such a way that Luke cannot make it through two chapters without breaking into song four times: Mary, Zechariah, old Simeon, and the hosts of heaven. Those canticles sound forth from earth and the *Gloria in excelsis Deo* sounds from heaven. The first three are prophetic acclamations, and the angels' song reflects the glory of God. The glory, which marks the inner life of God, is now shed abroad on the earth—all this because what the prophets of old desired and longed for has come to pass.

For Isaiah there is nothing ambivalent or obscure about the reason for this exultation. The return of the exiles is real. This event in the history of God's people demonstrates the faithfulness of the Holy One of Israel to the ancient promises. For the Christian community, this passage echoes with

Pastoral Perspective

Those congregations that offer worship on Christmas Day are usually doing so in addition to their offerings of Christmas Eve. The people who attend will not usually have attended on the previous evening and are frequently looking for a quieter celebration than is often the case on the night before. The pastor may want to help them connect with a more interior sense of the magnificence of the occasion they celebrate, and the prophecy from Second Isaiah can be a great help in that task of preaching on this day.

In this song a messenger is approaching Jerusalem with extraordinary news, namely, that the king is on his way to the city (v. 8) because YHWH has defeated the Babylonians and Jerusalem is saved (v. 9). The messenger is approaching and the preacher could build a sermon around the image of each proclamation: the announcement of peace, the bringing of good news, and the announcement of salvation (v. 7). It is as though the members of the congregation are the sentinels or watchers who begin to grasp what is being said and together sing for joy (v. 8).

Peace here is not only the end of warfare but the presence of God and all the conditions that inhere when God is present: justice, right relationship, forgiveness, and newness of life. The good news is that all of these things are now made possible in our day as God is present in Jesus and the Word has become

Exegetical Perspective

A sense of anticipation runs throughout the prophetic poetry of Isaiah 40–55, a section of the book of Isaiah dating to the end of the Babylonian exile (587–538 BCE). Following the destruction of Jerusalem and its temple and the decades spent in Babylon, many exiled Judahites concluded that their God had abandoned them (Isa. 40:27; 49:14). Second Isaiah—the scholarly designation for the prophet(s) behind these chapters—insists that YHWH is about to move decisively, despite the recent appearance of inactivity, to bring the exiles home and restore Israel's glory. Nowhere is this sense of anticipation more immediate than in Isaiah 52:7–10, which declares that the nation's salvation is "in plain sight" (v. 8). This vividness of presence makes these verses especially apt readings for Christmas Day worship.

These verses form part of a larger poem about the future of Jerusalem, also referred to as Zion, in Isaiah 51:17–52:12, which in turn belongs to a series of alternating poems about the servant of YHWH and Jerusalem/Zion in Isaiah 49–54. The passage brings together a number of important themes and characteristic terminology from Isaiah 40–55, which indicates its important place within these chapters.

Verse 7 opens with an exclamation, "How beautiful!" The term "beautiful" (*n'h*) appears in Song of Solomon as an expression of physical attraction to

Homiletical Perspective

Hearing this text at Christmas may call to mind the hymn "Joy to the World": it is a rousing invitation to join together in full-voiced praise of God. In the oracle, the prophet imagines heralds proclaiming good news to the city of Zion and envisions the joyful response of the people, and of the city itself, to God's saving action.

Have you ever thought of your preaching as doxological—as an act of praise to God? Have you ever considered that your preaching leads into the doxology of the congregation—that it inspires the congregation to praise? This joyful text provides you with a perfect opportunity to explore these homiletical possibilities. The prophet imagines that sentinels are on the city walls singing for joy, and then tells Zion to break into song. The prophet's call echoes Psalm 98:4, which is also assigned for this day: "Make a joyful noise to the Lord, all the earth; break forth into joyous song and sing praises." It is as if the prophet is seeing the fulfillment of the psalmist's hope and proclaiming to the city, "It's happening! Start up the band!"

To reflect on the preaching possibilities of this call to praise, you could start by considering various ways in which people praise God. One way is through testimony, through stories of God's activity in their lives. What stories of God's reign and victory can be told from the life of your congregation and

Isaiah 52:7-10

Theological Perspective

something both in history and beyond. As the ruined Jerusalem is to be restored, so the whole of humanity is embraced by the ingression of divine love, righteousness, and peace. The great titles the earlier Isaiah used to speak of the long-expected child—titles befitting divinity—are now in the human world because of this birth.

Even here there is a future orientation of this joy and song. While the Lord God has acted so that all the nations see the return from captivity, it still cannot be exhausted in the event itself. Just as the deliverance lives into time, so the birth of Jesus Christ must unfold in time and over time. Thus the concluding phrase announces, "All the ends of the earth shall see the salvation of our God" (v. 10). Built into the song of nativity is a palpable but mysterious "future present." This rejoicing has consequences well beyond the marking of a birth, however miraculous or unexpected. This rejoicing gathers to itself what is yet to come from the life of Christ. Let joy be unbounded in how God has acted, but also let the prophecy of Isaiah continue. There is suffering and death and resurrection yet to come that will shed light upon the meaning of this birth. T. S. Eliot's "Journey of the Magi" speaks of how birth and death come together. This birth signals the death of the old ways.

No one can claim to understand fully the meaning of this message of peace and good news that says "Your God reigns" (v. 7). In fact, the more we trace the implications of the birth, the more astounding is the mystery of the divine act of incarnation at Bethlehem. Tracing backward, we note how the desire for deliverance pervades the biblical witness. All the prophets teach us to yearn with them. Isaiah is especially prominent, but by no means alone. Each year Advent features different aspects of Messianic desire. Human history also teaches us this longing for peace and reconciliation.

Tracing forward, we encounter the fact that the child will embrace the whole of the human drama—life, suffering, and death. Because the wood of the cross and the wood of the manger are the same, and the grave clothes left at the resurrection were also the material of Christ's swaddling clothes, we cannot understand the birth until we enter the whole of his story. The traces go on to encompass his risen presence, the community called out by his Spirit, and on to the promise Julian of Norwich knew, that "all manner of things shall be well."

We can say that the exultation hinted at in Isaiah is itself both in time and about time itself. In short, the song of earth and heaven at nativity is already an

Pastoral Perspective

flesh. Salvation might be understood as what happens in us as well as in the world, as we respond to and appropriate this good news. Perhaps the messenger comes in and out of view as he or she approaches and in the end offers a cry of triumph, "Your God reigns," and the sentinels take up the cry singing for joy, for they see the king returning to Zion.

There will be, inevitably, some people present for whom joy is the furthest thing from their experience at the moment. While it is wise not to dwell on all the problems of the world and the problems in our lives in a Christmas Day sermon, Isaiah affords the opportunity to acknowledge the reality of brokenness. The exiles this prophet addresses know that Jerusalem has been conquered and is a city of rubble.

When the prophet calls on "you ruins of Jerusalem" to "break forth together into singing" (v. 9), the prophet's audience likely does not feel like singing along. There are times, though, when faith requires action before we have fully thought through or lived into the consequences of our actions. The celebration of Christmas over and against what we may feel and experience some of the time may be one such action. In his 1915 story *The Happy Hypocrite*,[1] Max Beerbohm tells of a ruffian who puts on the mask of a saint in order to woo a saintly girl. He succeeds in his quest, only to run into his former villainous friends some years later. They set about trying to unmask him and reveal his true character as a hypocrite. As they tear off the saintly mask, they are amazed to discover that this former villain's face has conformed to the mask and that he now has the visage of a saint himself. He has acted himself into a new way of being.

Such decisive action as singing with joy, even if our feelings have not yet fully conformed themselves to the sentiment we express, reflects the decisive action of YHWH, who "has bared his holy arm before the eyes of all the nations" (v. 10). The baring of the arm is probably a reference to drawing the arm from a breast fold or removing it from under a cloak as a precursor to taking action and as a display of power.

That display takes place before the eyes of all the nations. Some in attendance will find it pastorally helpful to hear something that helps them make sense of the claims of Christian faith to universal significance. By the time of the exile and these prophecies, the God of Israel had progressed from being understood as one God among many, to being a

---

1. Max Beerbohm, *The Happy Hypocrite* (London: John Lane Co., 1915).

one's lover, often referring to a particular body part like the cheeks or mouth (Song 1:5, 10; 2:14; 4:3; 6:4). The target of the description here is also a body part, but a surprisingly mundane one: the feet. Although hardly attractive in themselves, these feet prove beautiful because they belong to a "messenger" (*mebasser*) who has traveled over great distance and difficult terrain ("upon the mountains") with an important announcement. While the messenger's identity is unimportant for the meaning of the passage, commentators have variously identified the figure as a prophet or an angel, while Paul reinterprets the verse as a reference to early Christian missionaries to the Gentiles (Rom. 10:15).

In Isaiah 40:9, Jerusalem/Zion itself is called a "herald of good tidings" (*mebassret*), the feminine counterpart of the term translated "messenger" here in Isaiah 52:7, where Zion is clearly the recipient of the message. Successive phrases characterize the messenger as one "who announces peace," "brings good news," and "announces salvation." These vague but suggestive descriptions heighten suspense before the content of the message is revealed at the end of the verse: "Your God reigns."

The notion of God's kingship finds expression throughout the OT, with the specific declaration "God/YHWH reigns" occurring primarily in the Psalms (Pss. 47:9; 93:1; 96:10; etc.). This confession gains new significance in the exilic context of Isaiah 51 as a counterclaim to Babylonian belief in the superiority of their supreme deity, Marduk. Note especially the statement "Marduk is king!" in the Babylonian creation myth (*Enuma Elish* 4.28).[1]

Verse 8 describes the reaction to this message. Sentinels were an important part of a city's defense, standing watch for threats from the vantage of the city's fortifications (2 Sam. 18:24–27; 2 Kgs. 9:17–20; Ezek. 33:2–6; etc.). Instead of the expected cry of warning, these sentinels respond to the messenger's appearance with enthusiastic song, more like a choir than a military unit. Their joy results from their recognition of "the return of the LORD to Zion." As vividly depicted in Ezekiel 10, many Judahites believed that YHWH had abandoned Jerusalem during the exile. The proclamation of God's return to the city follows from the earlier confession of divine kingship, since Jerusalem was viewed as the earthly locus of God's reign (Pss. 48:1–2; 87:1–3; 146:10; etc.). The phrase "in plain sight" literally means "eye

community? Perhaps you could share the stories of others as part of your sermon, or maybe they could share their testimony themselves. These testimonies point to the ongoing work of God, who bares "his holy arm before the eyes of all the nations" (v. 10). You could also draw on another mode of praise, which is in the text: singing. What songs of praise are familiar and loved in your congregation? Could the words of these songs be woven into the sermon, or could the congregation sing a song of praise as part of the sermon? Singing songs of praise is a way in which the community participates in the continuing joyful doxology of all creation.

The call for praise in the text takes on deeper meaning when we reflect on the place and the people from which the song will arise. In an act of profoundly faithful imagination, the prophet takes his exiles with him to the broken walls of Jerusalem. The prophet hears the sentinels on the walls, and says to the people in the city, "Break forth together into singing, you ruins of Jerusalem" (v. 9). The city that is crumbling under foreign occupation can now rejoice: God is returning, the city will be restored, and the community will be made whole. The prophet describes this future with certainty, as an accomplished fact, a fact that calls for songs of praise.

This is an opportunity for you to consider the social location of the congregation. Do ruins surround your congregation? What are they? What songs of praise can you all imagine arising from this place? It might seem incongruent for those who live in fear of violence and in grinding poverty, with broken homes and communities, to sing praise—but these are they to whom the prophet cries, "Sing!" The child who is born and the promise of God's coming kingdom are for all who live among ruins.

So far we have been imagining the congregation as those who live in the ruined city. You could also picture the congregation as the sentinels who call to the city. In the oracle, the prophet sees a messenger running across the mountains bringing good news. Sentinels are posted along the city walls, listening to hear the messengers announce the king's arrival, and watching to glimpse the returning of the king. In the text, the sentinels hear the messenger and "lift up their voices, together they sing for joy" (v. 8). Their singing is a proclamation of good news to the city, calling forth songs of praise.

Imagine the members of your congregation as sentinels, standing watch in the community, looking and listening for signs of God's reign breaking into the world. Where do you see God working in your

---

1. See "Epic of Creation," trans. Benjamin R. Foster, in *The Context of Scripture*, ed. W. W. Hallo, 3 vols. (Boston: Brill, 2003), 1.111:390–402.

Isaiah 52:7-10

Theological Perspective

eschatological song. The promises and the faithfulness of God are real, but our participation in them is never completed in one season or in a particular historical epoch.

All this in Isaiah 52 is made even more mysterious and powerful by what follows—the "suffering servant" passages of Isaiah 53. Christmas carols sing joyfully, but they are about far more than "Happy birthday." They sound the fact, not only that salvation is to be in actual human history, but also that "all the ends of the earth" will see it. This seeing and hearing and singing is for all eternity. This is no mere extension of what we already know. God is born into solidarity with us in all times and places, until history itself shall find its true consummation. Christmas itself is already but not yet. As long as human history goes on, the struggle against evil and all that would rob this birth of its joy continues. God has acted despite us, even beyond our expectations.

The words of poet Robert Southwell, set to music by Benjamin Britten in his *Ceremony of Carols*, express this well: "This little babe, so few days old, has come to rifle Satan's fold."[1] Yes, this child "now weak in infancy, our confidence and joy shall be, the power of Satan breaking, our peace eternal making."[2] The humanity of God is found at Bethlehem. God became one of us that we (all, not just some) may become restored in God's likeness.

DON E. SALIERS

Pastoral Perspective

tribal god over against the gods of other nations, to being one who has universal significance.

Some will say that this progressive unfolding or revelation of the nature of God through history brings us to a point at which this story should be definitive and decisive for all people who desire salvation. Others will say that the prophet's vision is less one of the ultimate triumph of his vision over against all others, and more a vindication of fidelity in the face of hardship, as we hold fast the identity that has been given us by God. Christmas Day does not lend itself to an argument one way or the other about universal salvation, but the prophet does provide a way for the preacher to make an existential appeal for commitment to a particular way of faith, whether that way is understood as one among many or not.

At Christmas we see the salvation of God as having universal significance in the birth of Jesus, and a preacher can point to the long tradition of seeing this birth as the fulfillment of ancient prophecy. A brief excursion into the prophetic tradition may be pastorally helpful to many who are troubled by the idea of prophecy as prediction, which appears in popular culture as wildly apocalyptic and scary. The preacher might mention how those in the prophetic tradition were almost symphonic in the way they applied and reapplied prophetic insight to changing circumstance. By proclaiming the birth of Jesus as the dawn of the time of salvation, the good news of God's decisive action, and a source of true joy in the presence of God, we are standing firmly and properly within that tradition.

GEOFFREY M. ST.J. HOARE

---

1. The stanza appears as "This Little Babe" in Britten's *Ceremony of Carols*. It is from a poem titled "New Heaven, New War," which was published in *The Poetical Works of the Rev. Robert Southwell*, ed. W. B. Turnbull (London: John Russell Smith, 1856), 100.
2. Johann Rist, "Break Forth, O Beauteous Heavenly Light," trans. John Troutbeck.

to eye" (*'ayin be'ayin*), and this body language—along with references to the messenger's feet in verse 7 and God's arm in verse 10—imparts an air of physicality to the poem.

In verse 9a, the prophet commands the personified ruins of the city to join the sentinels in their jubilation, repeating the words "break forth . . . into singing" (*rnn*) and "together" (*yahdaw*) from verse 8. Similar calls to praise are common in biblical hymns (e.g., Ps. 100), as is the verb *rnn*, and the occurrence of these features here evokes the atmosphere of that genre. The imperative verbs directed toward Jerusalem continue a string of such verbs in the larger poem (Isa. 51:17; 52:1–2). Even as the text looks forward to Jerusalem's imminent restoration, the use of the term "ruins" acknowledges the devastated state of a city not yet rebuilt, and belies the reference to sentinels in the previous verse as a bold act of poetic imagination.

Having depicted YHWH's activity largely from the perspective of its observers in verses 7–9, Second Isaiah now describes it directly. Verse 9b provides the motivation for the preceding call to praise. The statement that YHWH "has comforted [*nhm*] his people" marks the fulfillment of Isaiah 40:1 ("Comfort, O comfort my people"), and the verb "redeem" (*g'l*) occurs frequently in Isaiah 40–55 (Isa. 41:14; 44:22–23; 48:20; etc.). Although these actions remain in the future, the verbs appear in the perfect tense in Hebrew, as indicated by their translation in the NRSV, reflecting the prophet's certainty that they will happen. The baring of God's "holy arm" in verse 10 is a display of divine power. This motif recalls the opening vision of Second Isaiah (Isa. 40:10) and anticipates the fourth Servant Song, which almost immediately follows this passage (Isa. 52:13–53:12). Alluding to the exodus, with which the motif of the divine arm is frequently associated in the OT (Exod. 6:6; Deut. 5:15; Ps. 136:12; etc.), the prophet had called upon "the arm of the LORD" to "awake" and "put on strength . . . as in days of old" in the previous chapter (Isa. 51:9).

That prayer has now been answered. This display of power takes place "before the eyes of all the nations" (v. 10), continuing the emphasis upon vision in these verses. Just as the other nations witnessed Jerusalem's humiliation in its defeat and exile, they will soon see its restoration and the return of its people. This unprecedented marvel will provide powerful evidence of God's rule over the entire world, which these verses both announce and call God's people to celebrate.

J. BLAKE COUEY

community and in the world? Are there testimonies of God's activity that you could incorporate into the sermon? How can the sermon inspire the congregation to praise God? For whom is your congregation a sentinel, and for whom might the congregation's praise be good news? This text can help form the congregation as witnesses to the world, sentinels who sing of the God they have seen and heard in Jesus Christ.

As you conclude your reflections on the text and begin to move toward the sermon, you will need to consider what form the sermon will take, and what kind of language you will use. Since the text is poetry, one possibility is to follow the text by crafting a poetic sermon that does what the text does. You could invite the congregation to sing a song of praise to God, as those who dwell in the city to which God is returning, and to sing so that others will sing as well.

In his moving history *There Is a River: The Black Struggle for Freedom in America*, Vincent Harding tells a story that may prompt you to reflect further on the scene of rejoicing in the text. He recounts the celebration of freed slaves in Richmond, Virginia, at the sight of black and white Union troops after the surrender of the city near the end of the American Civil War. As songs and shouts echoed back and forth between marching troops and cascading crowds, the multitude descended upon Richmond's infamous slave market. There, on the ruins of oppression, they proclaimed freedom to all people in a scene that Harding imagines could have evoked a turning point in history.[1]

Can you envision this scene: songs and shouts echoing in the war-torn city, the jubilant proclamation of those who are free? Allow it to open your imagination as a sign and foretaste of the celebration envisioned by the prophet: God is returning to God's holy city, and all will be freed to worship and praise God forevermore.

PATRICK W. T. JOHNSON

---

1. Vincent Harding, *There Is a River: The Black Struggle for Freedom in America* (New York: Harcourt Brace Jovanovich, 1981), 275.

Psalm 98

¹O sing to the LORD a new song,
   for he has done marvelous things.
His right hand and his holy arm
   have gotten him victory.
²The LORD has made known his victory;
   he has revealed his vindication in the sight of the nations.
³He has remembered his steadfast love and faithfulness
   to the house of Israel.
All the ends of the earth have seen
   the victory of our God.

⁴Make a joyful noise to the LORD, all the earth;
   break forth into joyous song and sing praises.

Theological Perspective

Surely Psalm 98—with Psalm 96, the reading for Christmas Eve—is right to suggest that the natural and appropriate response to the reign of God, in both memory and anticipation, is to burst into song. In Christian communities, Christmas is that time of year most closely associated with music—carols, cantatas, oratorios—joyful music celebrating the birth of Jesus, incarnation, the beginning of a new chapter in God's reign.

It is precisely here that Christmas presents comfortable, affluent Christians with a peculiar dilemma: How can we welcome the birth of Jesus with joyful singing in the midst of a world marked by violence, exploitation, oppression, and hunger? The reign of God seems impotent; Christmas tidings ring hollow. Perhaps Karl Marx is right to suggest that Christian joy is a delusion. How is it possible to welcome the joyful singing of Christmas without ignoring the cries of distress all around us? The prophet Amos is quite blunt about the sinfulness of singing that ignores or suppresses the cries and silences of those who suffer: "Take away from me the noise of your songs; I will not listen to the melody of your harps. But let justice roll down like waters, and righteousness like an ever-flowing stream" (Amos 5:23–24).

Richard Wilbur wrestles with this dilemma in his haunting carol "A Stable Lamp Is Lighted," now set

Pastoral Perspective

With especially triumphant voices, the small but enthusiastic congregation belts out the final verse: "He rules the world with truth and grace, and makes the nations prove the glories of his righteousness and wonders of his love."[1] As the sound of the organ fades away, a brief moment of silence in the Christmas morning worship is punctuated by the scream of an ambulance roaring by the front of the church. Our worshiper is suddenly drawn to another place. For someone, perhaps not so far away, this Christmas morning is not such a joyful time. Is it a heart attack at a nearby home? An automobile accident? Our Christmas worshiper wonders.

The sound of the ambulance has been enough to break the mood, and now his mind is wandering. He is remembering the morning news show that was on while they opened presents just a few hours ago. There was laughter and fun in his den, but those troops in faraway places did not seem to be having so much joy. Images of young men and women away from their families on Christmas for the very first time are spinning through his mind.

He tries to refocus as the preacher stands to read the text of the day. She is reading Psalm 98, the traditional psalm for Christmas Day. He wants to pay

1. Isaac Watts, "Joy to the World," 1719.

^{5}Sing praises to the Lord with the lyre,
    with the lyre and the sound of melody.
^{6}With trumpets and the sound of the horn
    make a joyful noise before the King, the Lord.

^{7}Let the sea roar, and all that fills it;
    the world and those who live in it.
^{8}Let the floods clap their hands;
    let the hills sing together for joy
^{9}at the presence of the Lord, for he is coming
    to judge the earth.
He will judge the world with righteousness,
    and the peoples with equity.

Exegetical Perspective

Psalm 98 celebrates the coming of God's presence into the world. The psalm is a hymn about music, words about a great symphony, unimaginably beautiful and harmonious, and of cosmic import. The musical celebrates God's coming as the Just Judge who will rule with justice and equity. For these reasons, it is perfectly suited for Christmas liturgy. Its theme interprets the Gospel story of Christmas, pressing beyond the simple narratives of manger and birth, shepherds and magi, to point to the transcendent meaning of those events. For Christians on this day, the event of Jesus' birth brings the joyous hymn of praise to fulfillment. The presence of God as Just Judge is revealed in Jesus.

The psalm divides into three stanzas: Sing for the Victory (vv. 1–3); Make Joyful Noise (vv. 4–6); Let the Cosmic Orchestra Play (vv. 7–9). All three stanzas begin with imperatives, urging the people and the world to break forth in enthusiastic praise for God's victory on their behalf. With exuberant joy, it celebrates this unspecified victory. God appears in the psalm as victorious warrior who brings justice to an oppressed people and, in so doing, sets the world in right order.

Sing for the Victory (vv. 1–3). The song to be sung is "a new song," one not sung before, but newly

Homiletical Perspective

This psalm overflows with exuberance and is thus an appropriate psalm for the celebration of Christmas. The psalm is both an exhortation to praise and an offering of praise. The psalm moves in an ever-expanding mode as it broadens its scope of praise. The first part of the psalm describes the praise, the new song, sung as a result of the salvation God has brought to Israel (vv. 1–3). God saves Israel so that the nations can see God's love and power and stand in awe. In the second part, the psalmist calls on the whole earth to pay homage to God (vv. 4–6). Here one feels the enthusiasm of the psalmist intensify. In the final stanza the psalmist widens the scope of praise. All of creation harmonizes its beauty and voices of praise to God (vv. 7–9). Because of God's victory and saving activity, the whole universe sings the Hallelujah chorus. This psalm echoes the message of the whole Psalter: God reigns.

One suggestion for preaching this psalm is to allow the sermon to follow the psalm's movement and emotional crescendo. The sermon could begin by exploring Israel's love for singing and rejoicing. Israel did not need much of an excuse for breaking forth in song. Singing was a part of the routine of life: "This is the day that the Lord has made; let us rejoice and be glad in it" (Ps. 118:24). Israelite women and men sang beautiful songs to express

Psalm 98

Theological Perspective

to an equally haunting tune by David Hurd. The first stanza offers arresting images inspired by Luke's birth narrative, but these are easily recognized as a Christmas carol. The second stanza looks ahead to another occasion of joy, Jesus' triumphal entry into Jerusalem on Palm Sunday. The third verse, however, struggles with the pathos of Good Friday and the violent opposition to the reign of God:

> Yet he shall be forsaken, and yielded up to die;
> The sky shall groan and darken, and every stone shall cry.
> And every stone shall cry, for stony hearts of men;
> God's blood upon the spearhead, God's love refused again.[1]

In the fourth and final stanza Wilbur returns to the celebration of Christmas while alluding to Jesus' resurrection, a harbinger of the consummation of God's reign. Beyond the manger lie the cross and the resurrection! The carol suggests that the joy of Christmas is not compromised but actually deepened by the acknowledgment that the reign of God provokes powerful opposition. We sing, therefore, in gratitude for what God has done and is doing and in anticipation of what God has promised. We also sing in protest of all that stands in opposition to the reign of God.

The birth stories in Matthew and Luke feature opposition between Jesus, on the one hand, and Herod and his Roman benefactors, on the other, marking Christmas as a protest against the violent rule of Herod and the life-crushing taxes of Rome. Even modern dictators know that Christmas songs can be a powerful protest. In 1983 the military junta ruling Argentina prohibited the singing of the *Magnificat* during the Christmas season. Mary's song was just too radical: "He has brought down the powerful from their thrones, and lifted up the lowly; he has filled the hungry with good things, and sent the rich away empty" (Luke 1:52–53). The spirituals, composed and sung by slaves, were songs of protest against white slave masters, a refusal to accept slavery as their essential condition. Songs of protest, such as Psalm 80, the Psalter reading for the Fourth Sunday of Advent, often have the paradoxical result of bolstering one's courage and discerning reasons for hope against unbelievable odds.

Psalm 98 begins with the particular experience of Israel and concludes with a vision of the reign of God encompassing all people and nations, indeed the

Pastoral Perspective

attention, but he keeps looking around at the other worshipers. Mary and Tom have smiles on their faces, but he knows they have been trying for so long to have a baby, and one more Christmas has now passed without a child of their own to share the day. There is Mrs. Carter, sitting alone as a widow after more than fifty years of marriage; he wonders what is going on in her mind. Steve is just a couple of rows in front of him, sitting by himself as well; the divorce has just become final, and it appears that Linda has the children for this Christmas morning.

"O sing to the LORD a new song, for he has done marvelous things. . . . He has remembered his steadfast love and faithfulness to the house of Israel. All the ends of the earth have seen the victory of our God" (vv. 1, 3). Our worshiper wonders to himself, "All the ends of the earth?" He wonders if those who called the ambulance, or those young troops so far away, or even those hurting people sitting around him would agree.

It is Christmas, a time to sing and rejoice. Years before the birth of our Savior, the psalmist sang of a great victory on the part of YHWH. It was reason to rejoice. It seemed as if all of creation was joining into the celebration. All the earth was gathering to "make a joyful noise before the King, the LORD" (v. 6). From the days of the early church, Christians have looked to this psalm as an expression of the joy experienced at the birth of Jesus. In its words Isaac Watts found the inspiration for his familiar carol "Joy to the World."

It is Christmas Day, the day to celebrate that YHWH is not a distant, impersonal God who ignores the groans of creation. This is a God who has come into this real world, born as a real flesh-and-blood baby, entering into creation at a particular point in history, living and teaching among real people, and loving humanity even to the point of death. This is a God who cares and who loves.

The birth of Jesus signals the arrival of a new kingdom, a kingdom punctuated by the justice and the righteousness of this loving God who stands among creation. The birth of Jesus announces the triumphant promise of God to bring righteousness and equity to all the peoples of the earth. The birth of Jesus is a day of victory. It is a day to sing and to offer praises. Isaac Watts knew it, and our worshipers gathered on this holy day know it as well.

Except that ambulances still roar by, and troops are still stationed in faraway places, and funeral homes are still in business. We may join the psalmist in singing that "The LORD has made known his

---

1. Richard Wilbur, "A Christmas Hymn," in *Advice to a Prophet and Other Poems* (New York: Harcourt, Brace & World, 1961), 62–63.

emerging. This implies that God has done something new to evoke this praise. God has worked wonders because God is strong of hand and arm, mighty and victorious. The historical victory is not named, perhaps because when Israel first sang the song, everyone knew the specific event the psalmist had in view. Perhaps the psalm is anticipatory in its praise, built upon the sure confidence that God will win the victory. The lack of historical detail opens the hymn to include all victories of God that amaze and astound the community of believers. Its openness also invites every generation to sing this hymn in continuing appreciation of God's victories on our behalf.

In these verses, God's victory is a vindication of God, as if divine power and strength were in doubt until this moment. Now the nations see this victory and recognize in it who God is. This God is one who remembers steadfast love and faithfulness to Israel, as if for a time those loyal qualities were forgotten. Steadfast love, or loving-kindness (*hesed*), and faithfulness are covenant terms that speak of God's intimate fidelity and care for Israel. These qualities motivate God's victory and reveal the victory to the whole earth. The call to sing arises from more than one act of deliverance. Praise springs forth because the divine victory reveals to the whole world God's profound relationship with Israel.

Make Joyful Noise (vv. 4–6). Because God's victory in the first stanza reveals to all the world who this loving, strong God is, the second stanza invites all the earth to make a joyful noise. The invitation to musical rejoicing is so emphatic that it is repeated in the last line of the stanza to form a frame around exuberant repetitions of the invitation. The earth is to "break forth into joyous song," and twice to "sing praises, sing praises to the LORD." They are to sing with instruments to create a symphony of praise: the lyre, the lyre with the sound of melody, trumpets, and the horn all together are to make "a joyful noise before the King." The victory of God's loving-kindness to Israel now emerges as the victory of the King of the whole earth.

Let the Cosmic Orchestra Play (vv. 7–9). In a rising climax of beautiful sound, the final stanza expands the number and kind of musicians and musical instruments into a symphony performed by the earth itself. Let the volume of praise increase and the whole cosmos vibrate as the sea and everything in it roars, accompanied by the world and all its inhabitants. The floods are to "clap their hands" and the

their love and affection for one another (Song of Solomon). In the midst of the daily uncertainties of life, Ecclesiastes calls for God's people to rejoice (Eccl. 7:14; 9:7–10; 11:9). Israel sang when lost lambs, possessions, and people were found (Luke 15). They sang frequently and spontaneously.

Even in the most difficult of circumstances, Israel sang. They sang songs of lament, many of which are preserved in the first half of the Psalter. While their captors taunted them in exile (Ps. 137:1–3), they still could not keep Israel from singing (Ps. 137:4–6). With the variety of psalms found in the Psalter, it is significant that the book is entitled "Praises," because regardless of psalm type, in one way or another all of the psalms honor the one Lord. When Paul and Silas were in chains and imprisoned, they sang (Acts 16:25). During the Passover meal as Jesus faced imminent suffering and death, he sang (Matt. 26:30).

Israel also sang to celebrate those special moments and victories in life. After escaping the Egyptians on the shores of the Red Sea, Israel broke forth in praise to God (Exod. 15). When they returned from Babylonian captivity, they returned with songs on their lips (Isa. 52:7–10). They sang before they entered into battle and after they returned victorious (1 Sam. 18:6–7; 2 Sam. 22). Mary composed a song to announce the birth of the Messiah (Luke 1:46–55).

So it comes as no surprise that Psalm 98 exhorts Israel to sing to the Lord. Israel is exhorted to sing a *new* song. There is nothing new about Israel singing. There is nothing new about the lyrics or the music. What is new is the new way of life and the new creation breaking in because of the victory and salvation God brings (vv. 1–3).

The psalmist, however, exhorts not only Israel but the whole earth to sing (vv. 4–6). The nations see the glory of the Lord and how God showered upon Israel steadfast love and faithfulness (v. 3); so Israel, the nations, and all living creatures are invited to "make a joyful noise to the LORD" (vv. 4, 6). They are encouraged to use all the resources available to do so: the voice, the lyre, the trumpet.

Finally, as the psalm concludes, all of creation, animate and inanimate, enters into the chorus to sing the new song. The rivers and oceans, the mountains and valleys come alive with the sound of music. This is not like a scene from a Disney movie, where all of nature becomes animated out of its own willpower and sings just for the sheer joy of singing. In this psalm, creation responds out of awe at the work and power of the Creator. As Paul says, both

Psalm 98

Theological Perspective

whole of nature. What should Christians make of this invitation to a universal orchestra and chorus? Is it significant that the invitation is to sing or play an instrument, not to join in the recitation of a creed? In an earlier time, this would be read as a call to convert all peoples and nations to Christianity. For many Christians in the twenty-first century, the call to convert has become a problem in a world of religious pluralism. How can a religious tradition maintain its distinctive commitments and engage with honesty and compassion those of another tradition? Psalm 98 and Christmas invite us to take a cue from music.

Charles Ives, one of the great American composers of the twentieth century and a devoted Christian, hoped that music would one day become the universal language of human beings, a universal confession of faith. When we confess our faith simply with words, as in the great creeds and confessions, the thoughts often seem cold, hard, and rigid, effacing the eternal mystery of God and drawing boundaries that easily divide. Set to music, however, the language of faith is often transformed into poetry, images imbued with grace and warmth that point toward the eternal mystery that transcends our language and thought. It invites rather than divides.

Ives goes further and offers a sort of musical parable for the "problem" of "religious pluralism." Ives sought to expand our taste for harmony, moving beyond our pedestrian notions of what sounds right and seeking ways to incorporate dissonance into the beauty of some larger whole. Ives attributed this vision to his boyhood experience of attending camp meetings that featured vigorous singing of gospel songs. According to James McClendon, Ives learned from his father, a bandmaster, "not to despise the 'wrong' notes some singers sang, or the unconscious key changes entire congregations, exalted, sometimes made, but to accept these as contributions to the larger musical whole." This is exactly what we find in many of Ives's compositions, says McClendon: "His music [had] a unity, not one achieved through an orderly progression of key changes and back home again by the book, but through a rugged plurality mightily heaped together so that its unity reflected nothing smaller than the grand plural unity of the cosmos. In such unity 'disharmonies' were overcome, not by filtering them out but by enclosing them in a whole perhaps not fully or finally seen."[2]

JOHN C. SHELLEY

Pastoral Perspective

victory" (v. 2), but reality forces us to admit that the victory has not yet been fulfilled. The promise of the psalmist has not yet been completed.

It will be, however. For that reason alone, this is a day to celebrate! Christmas Day is an opportunity for the people of God to look forward to the promise that one day God's victory will be completed once and for all. One day we will be able to say that "all the ends of the earth have seen the victory of our God" (v. 3). That day may have not yet arrived, but Christians live with the promise that it is coming, and that promise gives hope and sustenance in the current struggles of life. That promise brings joy even in the midst of pain.

Our Christmas worship ends with a triumphant benediction, and the congregation begins to make its way out of the sanctuary. Friends surround Mrs. Carter, and there are smiles all around. Steve is leaving with a family to go have Christmas lunch. Tom and Mary are down on the floor playing with some of the children of the congregation and learning about the new toys they have brought.

The kingdom has not yet come, but for a moment there is a glimpse of God's victorious hand at work. It is enough of a glimpse to keep our worshiper filled with promise. It is enough to send our worshiper back to work next week with renewed hope and energy. It is enough to keep our worshiper committed to the calling of our Lord and looking to the future with confidence and with assurance. It is enough to keep God's people singing, "Joy to the world, the Lord is come. Let earth receive her king!"

E. LANE ALDERMAN JR.

---

2. James Wm. McClendon Jr., *Biography as Theology* (Philadelphia: Trinity Press Int., 1990), 144–45.

Exegetical Perspective

hills to sing for joy. The cause of all this musical commotion and glorious uproar is the "presence of the LORD." God is coming to be present in the world, to judge it, to rule it, and to bring righteousness and equity to the people. The psalm exuberantly summons the people and the world to joyous expressions of gratitude, love, and praise for the wonders performed by this Just Judge, the King who rules in righteousness.

Besides trying mightily to motivate praise and express it in highly enthusiastic terms, the psalm makes strong theological claims. It asserts that the God of Israel is not the possession of Israel alone but God of all the earth, the Creator worthy of all praise, silent and vocal, of every living being. This is the God beyond all gods, the King of kings, and Lord of lords, who comes among us this day, who is present here and now and who beckons us to lives of joy.

If it should seem on this Christmas Day that this presence is not available to us, that this victory is not yet won, or that the Christmas event is but a tale to make children happy and merchandisers rich, then the psalm is an invitation to sing anyway. It is a call to open our hearts, minds, and eyes to the world around us and to the possibility of a victory so wondrous as to be unthinkable, so unimaginable as to be hidden still from our comprehension. Singing this new song together can increase hope and build among us a new perception of divine presence. It can instill faith, because singing the song creates faith and imprints hope in our souls. This new song can reveal our already-given connections to the sea and all that is in it, to the earth and all its peoples, and to the floods that clap their hands in joy. The psalm reveals the presence of God in the events of the earth, of relationships among nations, of our own participation in this glorious, cosmic symphony of life over which rules the King of the universe. This is most assuredly one of the meanings of Christmas.

KATHLEEN M. O'CONNOR

Homiletical Perspective

humans and nature groan in anticipating the coming of the new creation (see also Rom. 8:18–23).

In the midst of a world ravaged by tragedy, infected by disease, and plagued by war, creation breaks forth in impatient celebration at the thought of God's salvation. We imagine the new creation ushered in by God that is described by the familiar hymn "This Is My Father's World":

> . . . All nature sings, and round me rings
> The music of the spheres. . . .
> This is my Father's world; O let me ne'er forget
> That though the wrong seems oft so strong,
> God is the ruler yet.
> This is my Father's world; the battle is not done;
> Jesus, who died, shall be satisfied,
> And earth and heaven be one.[1]

God reigns. That is a Christmas celebration!

If everything in the universe is designed to praise, then praise is not something humans do only now and then. It is the primary way in which we communicate with God. Extract from a person's life a healthy dose of song, and you reduce that person to something less than a human—even less than the rest of God's song-singing creation. Regardless of our situation or our context, however rich or poor, encouraged or discouraged, we find ways to sing. There is restorative power in singing, power that is released to those who praise God.

Psalm 98 is the psalm for Christmas Day. As this psalm, alluding to the exodus and the return from exile, celebrates these significant moments in Israel's history, so we celebrate the ultimate inbreaking of God in the birth of Jesus. It is a day to rejoice, a day to "sing to the LORD a new song!"

> And heaven and nature sing,
> And heaven and nature sing,
> And heaven, and heaven, and nature sing.[2]

DAVE BLAND

---

1. Maltbie D. Babcock, 1901.
2. Isaac Watts, "Joy to the World," 1719.

Hebrews 1:1-4 (5-12)

¹Long ago God spoke to our ancestors in many and various ways by the prophets, ²but in these last days he has spoken to us by a Son, whom he appointed heir of all things, through whom he also created the worlds. ³He is the reflection of God's glory and the exact imprint of God's very being, and he sustains all things by his powerful word. When he had made purification for sins, he sat down at the right hand of the Majesty on high, ⁴having become as much superior to angels as the name he has inherited is more excellent than theirs.

⁵For to which of the angels did God ever say,
"You are my Son;
today I have begotten you"?

Or again,

"I will be his Father,
and he will be my Son"?
⁶And again, when he brings the firstborn into the world, he says,
"Let all God's angels worship him."

Theological Perspective

The traditional Epistle and Gospel for this day both proclaim the divine status of Christ in solemn and exalted language. The lection from Hebrews draws on the Old Testament and the later Septuagint Wisdom of Solomon, to speak of the cosmic scope of Jesus and what in him God has achieved for human salvation, the destiny of those who persevere in their faith. The rhetorical strategy throughout this "word of exhortation" (Heb. 13:22) is to contrast what has been done here, and especially who did it, with the old dispensation. This introduction also works rhetorically by a contrast, insisting on the superiority of Jesus, the anointed Son of God, to the angels. Some christological interpretation of Scripture, and other passages from the Psalms that give angels a subordinate role, provide the vehicle.

Christian talk of God is dependent on the older Jewish religious tradition interpreted in the light of what Hebrews will call "the confession." Jesus' atoning death and exaltation in verse 3 anticipates the lengthy discussions of priesthood and sacrifice. The Psalm 110:1 testimony to the vindication of Jesus ("sat down at the right hand," Heb. 1:3b) presumably triggers the author's imagining Jesus as the "priest forever according to the order of Melchizedek." Psalm 110:4 is quoted in chapter 5 and "priest" stretched to high priest (5:10) to make the typological connection

Pastoral Perspective

Once a year, on this day, the birth of Jesus is placed front and center. Incarnation is singled out for celebration. In contrast, from its earliest days, the church made it (at least) a *weekly* habit to remember the death of Christ. Learning to behold the face of a newborn comes naturally. It takes a lot more practice to take in the fullness of meaning when we stand before the casket of a loved one.

Reading these opening verses of Hebrews on Christmas Day helps us to see the full meaning of the incarnation. While this day may stand out on the calendar, both liturgical and cultural, it must never stand apart from the larger and long story of all that is disclosed to us in Christ—in birth, life, death, atonement, resurrection, and glorification. The breadth of this birth story is breathtaking.

Having said that, I want to zero in on the central claim of the text before us—an astounding claim about the connection between God and flesh, body and spirit, the universal and the particular, the temporal and the eternal. It comes in verse 3: "He is the reflection of God's glory and the exact imprint of God's very being." It is tempting to elaborate on this text in terms of its high Christology and to expound upon its unambiguous proclamation of the deity of Christ. Without diminishing the importance of Christology, pastors must not miss the implied

⁷Of the angels he says,
  "He makes his angels winds,
    and his servants flames of fire."
⁸But of the Son he says,
  "Your throne, O God, is forever and ever,
    and the righteous scepter is the scepter of your kingdom.
⁹ You have loved righteousness and hated wickedness;
    therefore God, your God, has anointed you
      with the oil of gladness beyond your companions."
¹⁰And,
  "In the beginning, Lord, you founded the earth,
    and the heavens are the work of your hands;
¹¹they will perish, but you remain;
    they will all wear out like clothing;
¹²like a cloak you will roll them up,
    and like clothing they will be changed.
  But you are the same,
    and your years will never end."

Exegetical Perspective

In this prologue, the author of Hebrews contrasts Jesus with prophets at the beginning and angels at the end. Hebrews does not regard the prophetic Jewish Scriptures as defective or dispensable, but as an imperfect foreshadowing of the ultimate revelation in Christ, who both fulfills and transcends them. Angels were regarded as mediators of that former revelation, especially the law (Heb. 2:2; Gal. 3:19), so that Christ transcends them as well. Exalted as they are, they are but servants of God for the sake of those saved by Christ (1:14). Thus Hebrews 1:5–12 goes on to show how the revelation in Christ fulfills Scripture in being superior to the angels and their ministry.

More significantly, this prologue also expresses much the same understanding of Christ as the more famous prologue to the Gospel of John (1:1–18), reminding us that this understanding is not unique to John in the NT (Col. 1:15–20 offers another example). In this understanding, Jesus is not only a teacher, prophet, and miracle worker; he is also closely connected to the very reality of God. He is the one through whom God created the universe, who nevertheless came into the world as a human being to bring eternal salvation and the ultimate revelation of God.

Although each text uses distinctive terminology, Hebrews, John, and Colossians all speak of Jesus' uniquely intimate and eternal relationship with God,

Homiletical Perspective

Much ado about angels! As is often observed, Jesus gets very high billing at the outset of the text we call Hebrews: "appointed heir of all things" (v. 2), critical agent in creation, "reflection of God's glory and the exact imprint of God's very being" (v. 3), creation's ultimate sustaining "speech act," the world's pollution purifier, the sole and supreme coregent with "the Majesty on high" (v. 3). An impressive resume Jesus has, indeed!

However, those whom Jesus is "superior to" or "more excellent than" (v. 4) receive greater air time than Jesus does in this sermon's opening move. If the angels are of such relatively inferior importance to the Son, why does the preacher go on so long about them? Perhaps because, one way or another, angels have a way of stealing the show (even if that is not really their fault).

It is well and good to describe Jesus in sweeping cosmic terms (as the writer of the Fourth Gospel also does), but the cosmos is hard to observe with the naked eye. So it is perhaps not surprising that celestial creatures more strikingly depicted can be more attention grabbing—particularly since God's exalted "Last Word" (as the preacher soon will say) nevertheless looks pretty ordinary under the best of human circumstances, and ends up looking not at all pretty.

Hebrews 1:1-4 (5-12)

Theological Perspective

with the Son's making "purification for sins." This creedal summary of the gospel on Christmas Day centers Christians' remembrance of Jesus on his death and vindication by God, a reality described metaphorically as resurrection or exaltation.

The lection ends before the quotation of the testimony in verse 13, but the christological confession of the death and vindication of Jesus "according to the scriptures" (cf. 1 Cor. 15:3–5) is the seed for all that follows in Hebrews. This magnificent evocation of God's word throughout the history of salvation—reaching its climax in God's revelation in these last days in his Son—includes that, but the emphasis on the word of God in revelation, and the brief mention (v. 2) and final celebration (v. 10) of God the creator also prepare modern worshipers for the Johannine prologue that follows. Other liturgical language in the New Testament also relates the incarnation to God's good creation (Col. 1:15–20). This became a central theme of Christian theology in Irenaeus's opposition to the gnostics' dualism.

Orthodoxy's insistence on the one God's plan of salvation is anticipated here and in the Johannine prologue by echoes of what the tradition says about divine Wisdom. That goes back to Proverbs 8:22–31, but here key phrases from Wisdom of Solomon 7:26 are quoted. This introduces a theological and christological theme that many find suggestive today. Even though modern writers who develop Wisdom Christologies do so quite differently from the early Christian hymns' and this author's acclamation of Jesus' divinity, one approach corresponds to the theological emphasis of Hebrews on Jesus' humanity.

In his ministry Jesus was recognized as a wise teacher (Mark 6:2). His sayings were probably collected, and he perhaps began to be seen as himself the Wisdom of God incarnate, a motif comparable to the Johannine Logos. The feminine gender of "wisdom" in Hebrew, Greek, and Latin was probably an obstacle to this Christology, but that is now widely welcomed as helping balance the gender imagery used in speaking of God as personal. This extraordinary christological affirmation may thus have roots in the community's memory and experience of Jesus.

Most believers accept that, in having to do with Jesus, we have to do with God[1] and therefore associate Jesus with God as closely as is conceivable. The existential dimension of all human talk of God is also preserved, however weakly. This passage

1. On this, cf. Barth's *Church Dogmatics*, II/1, first part, "The Veracity of Humans' Knowledge of God," ed. G. W. Bromiley and T. F. Torrance, trans. T. H. L. Parker et al. (Edinburgh: T. & T. Clark, 1957), 204–54.

Pastoral Perspective

anthropology in this text. Approaching this text as a witness to the full meaning of incarnation frames not only our knowledge of God, but our knowledge of ourselves and of the theological significance of our bodily existence.

To proclaim that in Jesus the glory of God was revealed and that Jesus (in body and spirit) was nothing less than "the exact imprint of God's very being," is to declare that flesh can no longer define existence that is not-God. Flesh is God's territory no less than spirit. The world of bodies, time, and space is God's world through and through.

When beholding the face of an infant, most of us feel we are not far from the glory of God. It is the faces aged by innocence long lost, including our own, that challenge our capacity to see the reflection of God's glory. Christology at its highest reveals the mystery of a God who bridges height and depth, temporality and eternity, flesh and spirit, divinity and humanity. It is the truth of incarnation that keeps us awake and alert to the possibility of the glory of God in the flesh of humanity—even our own.

For all our talk about spirit and spirituality, it is bodily life that preoccupies much of our attention. The prayers offered in worship on any given Sunday reveal our yearning to know God's grace and presence in relation to the experience of our bodies. This is a principal theme to be developed in later passages in the Letter to the Hebrews: "Since, therefore, the children share flesh and blood, he himself likewise shared the same things" (Heb. 2:14). "Therefore he had to become like his brothers and sisters in every respect, so that he might be a merciful and faithful high priest" (Heb. 2:17). "For we do not have a high priest who is unable to sympathize with our weaknesses" (Heb. 4:15).

I remember clearly the Christmas morning we gathered for worship a few years back in the Baptist congregation I was serving at the time. In Baptist life, when Christmas Day falls on a Sunday, it is experienced as an intrusion on the tradition of Christmas! Worship attendance is as low as it gets. As we gathered in the front several pews, there among the faithful remnant from the overflowing crowds of the night before was Truman. He had to retire from ministry, a life he loved, in his early sixties after he was diagnosed with Parkinson's disease. He had been suffering for several years, declining month by month. He recently had had to give up his driver's license.

As I elaborated on the text from Hebrews, I found myself more conscious than ever of his presence and of his daily struggle to live with his deteriorating

and of his role in creation. John speaks of the Word (Logos) who was with God in the beginning and yet also *was* God (John 1:1–2). For Colossians, "He is the image of the invisible God" (Col. 1:15). Hebrews, rather similarly, calls him "the reflection [or "radiance," NIV] of God's glory and the exact imprint of God's very being" (Heb. 1:3). The concept is of a being so close to God as to bear the nature or essence of God, through whom the light of God's presence emanates to all things. (Though masculine personal pronouns may occur, it is clear that such a being, as an "exact representation" [NIV] of the divine nature, is beyond gender.) It was this being, these three texts declare, who in Jesus of Nazareth took human flesh and even accepted human death to make known and put into effect God's saving purposes.

This being, so intimately related to God, is God's agent in the creation of the universe. The striking similarity of the formulations in Hebrews, John, and Colossians, in three otherwise unrelated texts, suggests that they may be drawn from a common source, not necessarily a written document, but some fairly early Christian reflection on Jesus conditioned by Hellenistic Jewish wisdom traditions. Already in Proverbs 8:22–31, Lady Wisdom is pictured as God's companion and helper in creation. Assisted by the concept of Logos (a divine intelligence pervading the universe and giving it rational order) developed in Stoic philosophy, Jewish thinkers writing in Greek developed a theology of Wisdom as mediator between the transcendent God and the material world.

A typical example comes from the apocryphal Wisdom of Solomon, written in Alexandria perhaps just before or just after the birth of Christ: "Wisdom [is] the fashioner of all things. . . . There is in her a spirit that is intelligent, holy, unique, manifold, subtle . . . all-powerful, overseeing all, and penetrating through all spirits. . . . For wisdom . . . pervades and penetrates all things. For she is a breath of the power of God, and a pure emanation of the glory of the Almighty. . . . For she is a reflection of eternal light, a spotless mirror of the working of God, and an image of his goodness" (Wis. 7:22–26). Within a monotheistic system, this theology made room for God's Wisdom as a semi-independent mediator of divine order to creation.

There can be little doubt that as Christians in the first century pondered whom they had encountered in Jesus and what the meaning of that encounter might be, they found their way to wisdom traditions such as this. They came to see in Jesus not only the

It will not do to pass off this preacher's preoccupation with preventing angel gazing as driven by an outdated and irrelevant concern over myth and superstition. Angel gazing is always alive and well—a thriving business, both commercially and spiritually. Take an image count from Christmas cards, wrapping paper, holiday displays, and seasonal carols. Angels almost always come out on top. (The majority of Holy Family images are bedecked with angelic halos!) Take a survey of how much Christmas sermon message language (beginning with Scripture) relies on angels (or stars), in proportion (if not preference) to the factors and features of the mundane life the Son comes to inhabit.

Who knows whether angels were really being "worshiped" by members of this sermon's original audience—or how relevant such information would be if available? Explicit idolatry is always the easiest to identify and exorcise; distraction is quite sufficient—probably more "effective" for undermining convictions and commitments in tired and dispirited communities of faith!

Angels (of whatever sort) can be energizing (in an entertaining sort of way); they can seem to be sources of the life for which they are only ministers.

So . . . let us assume that angels have gotten their due in song, story, and visual description at last night's Christmas Eve service. Nothing wrong with that! Luke gives them a prominent place; the author of Hebrews has high regard for them also: "Are not all angels spirits in the divine service, sent to serve for the sake of those who are to inherit salvation?" (v. 14).

Let us *not* assume, however, that, by exercising the option allowed us by the lectionary loppers—to excise the "angel" verses (5–14)—we will thereby manage to avoid the issue (on the chance, or in the hope that, if ignored, the angels will just "go away"). Instead, contemporary preachers can (perhaps should) set themselves to the discerning task of *naming the angels*—identifying those meaning bearers that might, by virtue of their compelling brightness, cloud our vision of what God, through the gift of the incarnation, most wants us to apprehend.

Taking our cue from the preacher, therefore: what serve, for us, as "spirits in the divine service, sent to serve for the sake of [us] who are to inherit salvation"? On that criterion, all the "Christmas angels" that flutter about our holiday celebrations probably do not make the cut. (Which does not mean they are incapable of functioning as serious distractions!) Far more is at stake here than a secularization of Christmas. What, is, literally, "angelic" (in the

Hebrews 1:1-4 (5-12)

Theological Perspective

includes believers at the outset (vv. 1–2), and their salvation is the last word of the chapter (v. 14). That God has spoken to us in his Son will be elucidated imaginatively as the sermon unfolds in a web of images from the now superannuated cult, but first the crucified and exalted Jesus is introduced as God's Son, superior even to the angels. A variant in the Greek translation of Psalm 45:6 (LXX 44:7) even allows the writer by implication to call the royal Messiah "God" (Heb. 1:8).

In confirming that Jesus is Son of God, these quotations conform to the axiom for all New Testament theology that Christian talk of God is rooted in the Old Testament witness of faith. What is said about Jesus needs to relate him to God by being similarly rooted. The subsequent philosophical development of Christology makes neither testament redundant. It was intended to sharpen the witness of Scripture. Making the Old Testament imagery persuasive in Christology is difficult when most interest in Jesus is focused on his historical reality.

For theology, what matters most is who God is: the God and Father of our Lord Jesus Christ. Typology affirms this claim that in Judaism God is known. It proves nothing but is devotionally fruitful. Relating Old Testament ideas and images to Jesus stimulates the imagination and reinforces the basic conviction that it is the "God who spoke in many and various ways" (v. 1) in Israel's history who now addresses us in his Son. The angels who play a positive role in the Christmas story are a negative foil here, but beyond the initial contrast subordinating them to the Son, they have a positive role in worship and can help us reenact the enchantment of Christmas. We join them in singing Luke's "Glory to God in the highest and peace on earth," drawn into acknowledging the Son of God and Word incarnate.

The lectionary gives ministers the option of stopping at verse 4 or continuing through verse 12. One might argue for throwing more weight on the Gospel by an even shorter Epistle. Verses 1–3 contain enough theological substance for any liturgical occasion. Verse 4 has its place only as a bridge to the succeeding verses, which labor a point already made most powerfully and effectively. This loss of theological density allows hearers time and rhythm to respond to the revelation proclaimed. Listening to God speaking of the Son in verses 5 through 14, we can be caught up in the psalmist's celebration of God's eternity.

ROBERT C. MORGAN

Pastoral Perspective

condition. In that moment, I understood the importance of naming the presence of God in relation to our bodies and how that presence is celebrated on the feast day of incarnation. Moments later we shared the body and blood of Christ—an incarnational moment to be sure.

In his book of essays entitled *Mortal Lessons: Notes on the Art of Surgery*, Richard Selzer recalls a story from his surgical practice. The case involved a young woman, newly married. A tumor embedded in her cheek had to be removed. Its removal required that a nerve controlling the muscles to her mouth be severed. Upon regaining consciousness after surgery, her husband by her side, the woman saw for the first time her mouth, irrevocably "twisted in palsy." Selzer tells us what happens next:

> "Will my mouth always be like this?" she asks.
> "Yes," I say, "it will. It is because the nerve was cut."
> She nods, and is silent. But the young man smiles.
> "I like it," he says, "It is kind of cute."
> All at once I know who he is. I understand, and I lower my gaze. One is not bold in an encounter with a god. Unmindful, he bends to kiss her crooked mouth, and I so close I can see how he twists his own lips to accommodate to hers, to show her that their kiss still works.[1]

Selzer is right to identify this act of love as a glimpse of divinity in the flesh. It is to identify the existence of God in the acts and movements of everyday life. To see and know God in the flesh, in our own flesh—this is the miracle and the mystery of Christmas.

DAVID J. WOOD

---

1. Richard Selzer, *Mortal Lessons: Notes on the Art of Surgery* (New York: Simon & Schuster, 1976), 45–46.

Christmas Day

Exegetical Perspective

fulfillment of messianic prophecies but much more: the unique embodiment of divine Wisdom. Jewish philosophers, like their pagan counterparts, had understood the human intellect or Logos to be a share of this divine Wisdom present in every person, identifying it as the image of God (Gen. 1:26–27). Early Jewish Christians, familiar with this line of thought, apparently took it in a new direction by identifying Jesus as the incarnation (in John's terms) of the creative divine Logos/Wisdom in a way that distinguished him from any other human being.

This passage in Hebrews invites us to think more broadly and more deeply about Jesus and our own encounter with him. We may be used to acknowledging him as teacher, savior, example, or friend. When we also think of him as giver of existence and order, as ever-present sustainer of each detail of the created world since time began, new horizons open up both in our ideas about him and in our relationship with him. To celebrate his coming into the world is to recognize the world's Creator entering into it in a new and unexpected way, as one of us, united with us creatures in life and in death. In an era of ecological crisis, there is also a powerful resource here for the construction of a fully and authentically Christian approach to reordering human relations with the rest of creation.

In the last clauses of verse 3, the unknown author encompasses much of what Hebrews will go on to say in later chapters. The divine Son, imprint of God's being and sustainer of creation, became fully and utterly human, and so was able to offer himself as an appropriate sacrifice for our salvation (Heb. 2:9–18). Having done so, he entered the true sanctuary in heaven, the very presence of God, as high priest (4:14–16; 9:11–15, 24–28). This profound and complex Christology, presented more in imagery and scriptural interpretation than by systematic exposition, is fully incarnational, and challenges any theology that considers Christ too divine to be really human or too human to be really divine.

DAVID RENSBERGER

Homiletical Perspective

author's sense), that can, by the brightness of its illumination, obscure the one true Light?

Close personal relationships, perhaps? Not the dysfunctional ones, but those that are the healthiest, even the most holy. Compelling theological visions, those in light of which we recognize God and understand ourselves? Deeply nourishing spiritual practices by means of which we find strength and comfort? Social commitments that represent our highest ideals and call forth our most costly sacrifices?

To pose such possibilities is to encounter an immediate and understandable objection. Since (as the preacher readily acknowledges) God has spoken and does speak to us in these "many and various ways," how (we might rightly wonder) would God "get through" to us above and beyond them? Even our appropriations of the saving inheritance given us in Jesus Christ are sometimes, often, even always mediated through the ministry of such "angels."

The answer to this concern is not contained in the text for the day, but requires journeying with the preacher through the entire argument that constitutes the sermon. It will involve, in the end, an embrace of the exalted Son as both suffering servant and great high priest. The celebration of Christmas Day, in other words, is incomplete—perhaps of limited "angel" value—unless/until it culminates in the celebration of Good Friday, and the down-to-earth injunctions that the preacher advances at the very end of the sermon (Heb. 13): such practices as mutual love, hospitality to strangers, standing with those who are in prison and are being tortured, marital faithfulness, discipline with regard to finances, respectful imitation of credible leaders. Mundane though they be, it is through them that we meet Jesus "outside the camp"—by not neglecting "to do good and to share what you have" (13:13, 16).

All of these are "sacrifices of praise" that, without in any way denigrating the existence and agency of angels, keep them in their proper place. Does any of this necessarily undercut the joyful celebration of this day? Of course not! Today is not just for announcing glory to God in the songs of angels; it is giving and receiving the whole cradle-to-cross Gift they come to announce.

DAVID J. SCHLAFER

John 1:1-14

¹In the beginning was the Word, and the Word was with God, and the Word was God. ²He was in the beginning with God. ³All things came into being through him, and without him not one thing came into being. What has come into being ⁴in him was life, and the life was the light of all people. ⁵The light shines in the darkness, and the darkness did not overcome it.

⁶There was a man sent from God, whose name was John. ⁷He came as a witness to testify to the light, so that all might believe through him. ⁸He himself was not the light, but he came to testify to the light. ⁹The true light, which enlightens everyone, was coming into the world.

¹⁰He was in the world, and the world came into being through him; yet the world did not know him. ¹¹He came to what was his own, and his own people did not accept him. ¹²But to all who received him, who believed in his name, he gave power to become children of God, ¹³who were born, not of blood or of the will of the flesh or of the will of man, but of God.

¹⁴And the Word became flesh and lived among us, and we have seen his glory, the glory as of a father's only son, full of grace and truth.

Theological Perspective

"But, as a matter of fact, another part of my trade, too, made me sure you weren't a priest."

"What?" asked the thief, almost gaping.

"You attacked reason," said Father Brown. "It's bad theology."[1]

The thief disguised as a priest had been trying to convince Father Brown—G. K. Chesterton's priest-detective—of his priestly credentials by disparaging reason. Evidently he thought it was the religious thing to do: to gaze reverently at the heavens and claim not merely that the mysteries of the universe exceeded our understanding but that they made reason itself "utterly unreasonable." Father Brown knew better. "Reason and justice," he affirmed, "grip the remotest and the loneliest star."[2]

Our text, constituting most of the prologue to the Fourth Gospel, is one of several sources in Christian Scripture to which he might have appealed in support of that affirmation. (Others frequently cited in conjunction with this text are Ps. 33:6, Prov. 8, Col. 1:16–17, and Heb. 1:2.) All creation is imbued with the Logos, the Word and Wisdom of God. All creation bears witness to the primordial, sense-making

1. G. K. Chesterton, "The Blue Cross," in *The Innocence of Father Brown* (New York: Penguin Books, 1975), 29.
2. Ibid., 24.

Pastoral Perspective

John's prologue is quoted in the debates over Christology that many pastors encounter in seminary. To most congregants these debates are impenetrable or uninteresting and seem distant from their lives, questions, and loves. However, those christological debates may matter for the power of this passage, which establishes the nature of the world in which we live as people of faith, and God's intention toward that world. God's will and Christ are revealed as being eternal, and hence unable to be easily bound to any current political or economic program. So many are eager to claim God. Pastorally the prologue helps readers understand the length and breadth and depth of God's providence and existence. In the beginning are not our wishes, hopes, dreams, and plans, but God, and God's Word, and God's love toward the world that God chooses to create.

This text reminds its readers that, amid life's chaos, the world belongs to God. The prologue asserts that Christ always was, as if to reveal that God's love and intention for humanity was not simply the result of human sin, but part of God's intention and love for the world from the start. That news and that person are here called "light." Even at Christmastime, which in much of the Northern Hemisphere is cold and dark, Christ's light shines. In the midst of the worries of the world, of illness, sickness, and doubt, Christ's

Exegetical Perspective

In contrast to Matthew and Luke, Mark and John write nothing about Jesus' birth, but instead begin the story about Jesus with John the Baptist. John the evangelist, however, prefaces the earthly story with a heavenly story: "In the beginning was the Word, and the Word was with God, and the Word was God. . . . All things came into being through [the Word; NRSV "him"]" (vv. 1, 3a).

The Greek pronoun translated "him" in verse 3 is ambiguous; it can also mean "it." "Word" is an abstract noun; it does not designate a heavenly person. These verses echo Genesis 1:1, "In the beginning God created . . ." John is not saying that the Word created, but that God created through God's Word. In Genesis 1, God creates by *speaking*: "God *said*, 'Let there be light,' and there was light" (Gen. 1:3). The Word is not a heavenly being distinct from God but a function of God in creation. There is a parallel in Isaiah 55:11: "so shall my word be that goes out from my mouth; it shall not return to me empty, but it shall accomplish that which I purpose."

In Proverbs, Wisdom is assigned a role in God's creation: "The LORD by wisdom founded the earth" (Prov. 3:19; see also Wis. 7:22, "wisdom, the fashioner of all things"). The personification of God's Wisdom is carried much further in Sirach 24. Since the word for "wisdom" in Hebrew and in Greek is

Homiletical Perspective

The Gospel for Christmas Day says nothing of crèches and shepherds; those peaceful images were offered in the Christmas Eve narrative. This morning John tells us that Jesus is word and light. In this age of the Internet's ever-expanding barrage of words, as well as high-definition televisions that bathe our living rooms in multicolored light, preachers may find it helpful to stress that *word* and *light* can still convey the wonder of God with us at Christmas.

Merry Christmas. How many times have we said "Merry Christmas" already this morning? We will repeat those words many more times as the day goes on. It is important that we use these words. It would sound strange to hear "Joyful Christmas" or any other variation that would mean almost the same thing. While other words would convey the spirit of the greeting, we have canonized the words "Merry Christmas" through years of custom. Words still matter to us, at least on special occasions, but Barbara Brown Taylor reminds us that words have also fallen on hard times. Our words are impoverished by advertisers who use them to make empty promises to consumers; the words in our newspapers and magazines that convey seemingly important information are quickly bundled up and discarded before we can read them all; and of course there is

John 1:1-14

Theological Perspective

Word through which it has come to be and in which it finds its coherence. Thanks to this formative and informing Wisdom, creation is not only intelligible but intelligent, sense-seeking, and sense-honoring. Creaturely reality is marked by a lively participation—in ways appropriate to various, finite, contingent, sojourning creatures—in the Truth that is with God, and that is God.

All this is affirmed by Christian traditions generally, but the affirmation is accompanied by a sober acknowledgment that, however it may be with the remotest star, we human creatures, at least, have seriously strayed from our calling to honor reason and justice. Having long ago exchanged the truth for a lie (Rom. 1:25), we seem intent on leaving reason and justice behind, while busily making up our own substitutes and giving those substitutes the name of the real thing. What often passes for reason with us is a truncated form of this capacity, sometimes called "instrumental rationality": the ability to manipulate and control things (and persons) as objects, for our own purposes. What often passes for justice is the arrangement of laws and legal systems by the powerful to serve the interests of the powerful. This is "the wisdom of this world" that is indeed "foolishness with God" (1 Cor. 3:19). It should not be confused with the genuine article.

When discussing human beings' rational capacity, our theological forebears sometimes made a sober and useful distinction between *created* reason and *fallen* reason. Created reason—the human mind as it was meant to be, and as it was thought by these writers to have been exercised by Adam and Eve in the original human "state of integrity" in the garden of Eden—participated rightly in the Logos that informs reality. What we know and experience now in our post-Edenic state is fallen reason, reason that is corrupt and corrupting, and a twin to injustice. (Recall how close is the tie between injustice and the willing misrepresentation of reality: "Ah, you who call evil good and good evil, who put darkness for light and light for darkness, who put bitter for sweet and sweet for bitter!" [Isa. 5:20].) This latter form of reason (if it can be called that) deserves all the censure it has received at the hands of Paul and subsequent generations of Christian thinkers, so long as it is clear that the target of censure is this distortion and corruption of a created good, and not reason as such.

Unfortunately, that has not always been made clear. Christians have at times indulged in assaults on reason itself, contrasting it to faith. The sometimes popular tendency to associate Christianity

Pastoral Perspective

light shines. How do we see and show that light to others? It may be as simple as welcoming the stranger who appears in church around the holidays; it may mean buying a cup of coffee for a homeless person on the street; it may mean protesting an injustice at a rally.

The text is ecological as well. Some read Genesis 1 as a license to take "kingly" dominion over the rest of creation. John tells us that all of life on earth is God's handiwork. In a world too often divided and ecologically fragile, John's vision starts with all things being created by and through God. It might be helpful to remind our parishioners to think for a moment about what it would be like to live in a world where we respected God's creation of each and every living thing. Take a look outside. Go for a hike in the mountains, or take a walk on the shore. Have these experiences not shown us the beauty of God's creation? Have we not, in the midst of that creation, felt the wonder? All creatures were made by God, according to John—even society's outcasts, along with those whose age, disability, or intellectual capacity may make others in the congregation see them as "less than human" or imperfect.

Our churches urge us to be Christlike. However, most days this task seems impossible in our sinful and busy lives. Many who sit in our congregations wonder and worry if they are being "good enough Christians." This text reminds us that we are not called to be Christ. We are called to be John the Baptists, whose lives testify to God's light and love in the world.

How can we, like John, point to Christ? There are many ways we can do so, depending on the character and experience of the congregation and the preacher. The ways we speak and act can either point others to God's grace in Christ or turn others away from the community of the church. Do we greet the stranger, visit the sick, and care for the needy in ways that show our lives have been changed by God's love for us, by the light that banishes our darkness? Have we taken the time to call the elderly parent, to go out of our way for a struggling coworker, or to do something for the important people in our lives that would say, "You are God's gift, and I see God's light in you"?

Thoughts about light and darkness can be misused, but all people understand, on a personal and social level, about the darkness of the world. John notes that Christ and Christ's message were not well received in his time. They are similarly not always well received in ours. This is partly due to the way

feminine, Wisdom is personified as a female person: "Wisdom praises herself, and tells of her glory" (v. 1); yet Sirach shrinks from presenting Wisdom as a goddess: "I came forth from the mouth of the Most High" (v. 3). John was perhaps influenced by this wisdom tradition, which attributed a role in creation to Wisdom, but in anticipation of verse 14, he preferred to use "Word," because in Greek this word is masculine.

The NRSV footnote offers an alternate translation of verse 9: "He was the true light that enlightens everyone coming into the world." This seems preferable to the standard translation, "The true light . . . was coming into the world," which suggests that the incarnation was an extended process. The illumination of everyone may then refer not to religious enlightenment but to the philosophical idea that all human beings possess reason as a divine gift. It is thus possible to see verses 9 and 10 as speaking about the preincarnational activity of God's Word. Verses 11–13, however, are postincarnational; they look back to the incarnation that has already occurred.

"He came to what was his own," or "to his own home," refers to the historical location of the incarnation in Jewish Palestine; "his own people" emphasizes the specific human context of the incarnation: Israel. Here the refusal of most Jews to accept Jesus is presented as a fact without any negative comment; later in the Gospel the mutual hostility of "Jews" and Christians becomes a major theme (see esp. chap. 8). Verse 12 implies that those who did not accept Jesus had no right to consider themselves children of God, despite the fact that they called God "Father" (Isa. 63:16, 64:8; see John 8:41–42).

The time implied by verses 12–13 is not clear: "all who received him" could refer to those who believed in Jesus prior to the crucifixion, or it could include all those who came to faith subsequently (John 20:29). The reference in verse 13 to being born of God anticipates 3:7, "You must be born from above."

The climax of the passage, of the whole Gospel— one might even dare to say of the whole New Testament—comes in verse 14: "And the Word became flesh and lived among us." It is the chief foundation stone of the doctrine of the Trinity.

Christian interpreters have become so comfortable with this text that it no longer shocks us. It does, however, shock Jews and Muslims, because it seems sacrilegiously to blur the distinction between God and human beings. It shocks Unitarians, who see it as a fatal breach of monotheism. It can even be a source of discomfort to Christians as they ponder

the sheer number of words added to our vocabulary every day.[1] Words sometimes lose their power even in our churches. I heard a preacher describe how he was trying to help a group of teenagers appreciate something Jesus had taught. Evidently the young folks found the words difficult to hear. One of the boys said, "Well, that's just Jesus' opinion."

Words Still Have Power. On this Christmas morning when we hear the Gospel proclaim that "in the beginning was the Word," and this "Word was God," we might ask if words still matter. Consider the constantly growing number of Internet blogs that might make us wonder if words still have the power to persuade and enlighten. One commentator quipped that the readers of most blogs are the authors and their mothers, yet in this sea of words there have been words that truly matter. Older folks in the congregation may remember the comforting words of Franklin D. Roosevelt as he assured a worried nation through his fireside chats on the radio. The stirring words of Dr. Martin Luther King proclaimed that he had a dream of equality for all God's children. Couples who have spoken those solemn words, "I do," at their weddings know that some words truly matter.

Jesus Is the Word. Words mattered a great deal to those who first heard our Gospel. John wrote to first-century Greek Christians who inherited a rich philosophical tradition. They knew of the Logos that helped them see how all of creation is ordered. It was a small step for them to go from the Logos to Jesus as the Word. In the very beginning was Jesus the Word. These ancestors in the faith would also know of the Hebrew word *dabar*, how the word has the power to enact what it conveys. They would recall that when the world was created, God did not wave a magic wand, nor did God *think* creation into existence. God uttered the Word.

Jesus the Light. Jesus is also the light. We know how important lights are to Christmas. We put lights on the Christmas tree; perhaps we even cover the outside of our homes with lights. There are lights in the stores and in our churches. Once I asked in a sermon, when we look at the lights on our Christmas tree, in addition to simply enjoying the beauty, might we let the lights remind us how Jesus has become the light in our lives? Several years after that

---

1. Barbara Brown Taylor, *When God Is Silent* (Cambridge: Cowley Publications, 1998), 9–11.

John 1:1-14

Theological Perspective

with anti-intellectualism, opposition to scientific knowledge, and authoritarian thought control gains support from such undiscriminating talk. That is not the message of the gospel. Christ, the one Paul calls "the wisdom of God" (1 Cor. 1:24) and whom our Johannine author knows as Word and Light, came not to destroy reason but to restore us to it: to bring us to our senses.

Our forebears spoke not only of "created" and "fallen" reason but also of *regenerate* reason, reason reborn. One aspect of the "second birth" that Christ brings to the sons and daughters of earth is a rebirth of understanding: the onset of a recovery of the human capacity to honor the truth. "The Word became flesh and lived among us" (v. 14). The Wisdom of God seeks friendship with us, in tangible, vulnerable, human form. (Making a connection with 2 Cor. 8:9, Gustavo Gutiérrez and others have suggested that the most apt contemporary equivalent to "the Word became flesh" may be "the Word became poor."[3]) This gracious disclosure of reality not only unmasks our own current pitiful practices of "reason" and "justice," but sets us on a different path, toward the renewing of our minds (Rom. 12:2).

We are embarked on a journey of transformation. We are not there yet. There is much to unlearn, as well as much to learn, as we are led into the truth under the guidance of the Spirit of truth of whose coming Jesus spoke (John 16:13). One of the constant themes of the Fourth Gospel is the importance of the community of faith, both as a context for growth in understanding and as a witness to the power of Truth incarnate. The work of Christ and the work of the Spirit are inseparable in this process through which, together, we are renewed through the one whose coming to dwell among us we celebrate this day.

CHARLES M. WOOD

Pastoral Perspective

that would-be purveyors of light sometimes work darkness instead. One only needs to think about the ways the Christian message has been used to justify slavery, or to oppress those whom society or the church has seen as outcast, to know that even those who claim to "get the Bible" do not always understand how God's light came into the world. Too often, we do not want to know God's light; it is simply too disruptive.

The last verse calls hearers to reflect on the amazing proposition that we have a God who is not distant but present among us, made known to us in real flesh. That present God's walk among us is attested to by Scripture and, in certain traditions, by the sacraments. We believe in God as Christians because we have seen God in Christ. In Christ's love, compassion, and honest speech about the world, we have seen that God. Martin Luther calls Christ the "mirror of the Father's heart."[1] It is important to stress just how distinctive the notion that "the Word became flesh and dwelt among us" really is.

The most central claim of the Christian faith, one that should scandalize us from time to time, is that God became incarnate, one of us, that we might know God's nature and God's love for us. In what ways have you beheld God's glory? Perhaps in a huge cathedral, or a magnificent worship service in your own church, or through events that seem miraculous or particularly providential. John is claiming that those who know Jesus see God's glory in him.

John's Gospel paints a picture of Jesus as full of grace and truth. How we define that truth is of course a matter of theological debate, but it is important to remember that John begins with grace. It is that graciousness that we are to embody amid the business of Christmas, bearing witness to the light we have seen.

AARON KLINK

---

3. Gustavo Gutiérrez, "God's Revelation and Proclamation in History," in *The Power of the Poor in History*, trans. Robert R. Barr (Maryknoll, NY: Orbis Books, 1983), 12–13.

1. Martin Luther, *The Large Catechism* (Minneapolis: Augsburg Fortress, 1986), 63.

the question, Was Jesus a real human being or not? In what ways was he divine, in what ways was he human?

In the second century, Marcion promoted a revised version of Christianity. He taught that Jesus, a heavenly messenger of the highest god, arrived in Galilee having the appearance of a fully grown man. He taught that humans could escape the material world created by the evil god of the Jews and rise to the realm of pure spirit. His crucifixion and resurrection were pure charades. Some lines in John's Gospel may have encouraged Marcion, such as 6:38, "For I have come down from heaven." However, the Fourth Gospel, like the other three, is focused on Jesus' death as the central event in God's redemptive history. The crucifixion is no charade; the real death of a real man is involved.

John 1:14 does not teach us that Jesus was part God and part human. It is essential that we recognize that the divinity of Jesus, however we understand it, did not compromise his humanity. He did not know everything; he could not do everything. Jesus related to God the way we do: through prayer. In chapter 17 John presents Jesus as praying fervently to God on behalf of his followers. He pleads, "As you, Father, are in me and I am in you, may they also be in us" (v. 21). This verse offers another way of looking at the incarnation. It reminds us of Paul's statement, "In Christ God was reconciling" (2 Cor. 5:19).

It is best to take John's daring incarnational language dynamically rather than statically; that is, he did not intend to instruct his readers about "the two natures of Christ," still less, about the Son "being of one substance with the Father," as the Nicene Creed avers. He was concerned rather with what God accomplished through the unique relationship of Father and Son. John was saying that Jesus of Nazareth was yoked to God as no other human being ever was. Jesus' dying was a very human dying, but God and Jesus were one in his dying.

DOUGLAS R. A. HARE

sermon, a woman in the parish told me how her children still remembered that challenge. John tells us in verses 4 and 5 that Jesus is the light who has overcome the darkness. For that good news to have meaning for today, we might consider the contemporary experiences of darkness that need the light of Jesus. Christmas sermons may not be the most appropriate times to focus on the wars, illnesses, and crimes that represent some of the darkness in our present world. Instead, we might simply invite the congregation to ask whether they could use a bit of Christmas light. We might ask, "As we hear this Gospel proclaim that Jesus the light is more powerful than any darkness, is there something going on in our life right now that needs the Lord's light?" Unless we have some sense of what darkness looks like for us, we really do not need Jesus the light. What can Jesus the light do in our lives this Christmas Day?

Children of God. Visual images can be powerful and lasting. Since our culture bombards us with holiday sights, sounds, and smells, we might reflect on a few images that we could place before our congregations. One image that speaks loudly from today's Gospel comes from verse 12, which tells us that those who accepted Jesus were made children of God. On Christmas Day children are the center of attention. We adults enjoy watching their sense of excitement and wonder as they bask in the special foods, decorations, and gifts this day. Are we able to remember that far back? One of my earliest Christmas memories was about waiting. In our house, we opened our gifts after dinner on Christmas Eve. The afternoon dragged on as we children waited for Dad to come home from work. We urged the adults to rush through dinner; we demonstrated how quickly people could eat if only their put their minds to it! At last it was time; the long wait was over. We preachers might look into our past experiences of Christmas for images that would speak to the Gospel's proclamation that Jesus has made us God's children. My own experience of Christmas Eve anticipation helps me appreciate how I am called as an adult to yearn for the Word and the Light here and now.

DANIEL HARRIS

Isaiah 63:7-9

⁷I will recount the gracious deeds of the Lᴏʀᴅ,
  the praiseworthy acts of the Lᴏʀᴅ,
 because of all that the Lᴏʀᴅ has done for us,
  and the great favor to the house of Israel
 that he has shown them according to his mercy,
  according to the abundance of his steadfast love.
⁸For he said, "Surely they are my people,
  children who will not deal falsely";
 and he became their savior
⁹ in all their distress.
 It was no messenger or angel
  but his presence that saved them;
 in his love and in his pity he redeemed them;
  he lifted them up and carried them all the days of old.

Theological Perspective

By the time chapters 56–66 appear in the Book of Isaiah, Cyrus has allowed the return of those who desire it from Babylonian exile. They have come back to a life in Jerusalem that they believe will be joyous and bountiful, as depicted in Second Isaiah, only to find a life of extreme hardship. The prophet is thus speaking to these disillusioned people in apocalyptic language, reminding them of the powerful works of God who has already and will again make things right for them. In this brief section, Isaiah describes the ways God delivered them from Egyptian captivity. Two themes stand out in this passage: the character of God as a parent to humankind and God's concern for the liberation of the enslaved.

God as Parent. On this First Sunday after Christmas, after the birth of the Son of God, this passage from Isaiah reminds us about how we might imagine the parenthood of God, as parent to all God's children. Hebrew biblical scholar and theologian Walter Brueggemann asks the reader to consider God's attributes in Isaiah as both motherly and fatherly; that is, the fierce God of Isaiah 63:1–6 gives way to traditionally maternal imagery in verses 7–9. Here, in God's care and concern for Israel, the prophet tells us that God "lifted them up and carried them all the days of old" (v. 9). This imagery of bearing Israel has

Pastoral Perspective

Good preachers and good pastors pay attention to context. They notice what is being said, who is saying it, how they say it, and what is left unsaid. They notice those who are waving their hands for recognition and those who with heads lowered are ducking behind their desks. They not only read the bold print, but take the time to make sense of the fine print as well. Good preachers and good pastors pay attention to context.

For all its contributions to the worship and educational life of the church, the lectionary tempts those who teach and preach *not* to do what good preachers and good pastors know they must do. Barbara Brown Taylor opens the homiletical perspective on this text by naming this temptation, "Preachers who turn to Isaiah for a comforting word this Sunday will have to ignore everything they learned in seminary about interpreting a text in context, for these three verses are airlifted out of a chapter thick with divine wrath and human despair."

In addition to the three verses in today's lection, Isaiah 63 is known for its final verse, "O that you would tear open the heavens and come down" (64:1 in NRSV), a verse that will play a pivotal role in Mark's baptismal and crucifixion theology. To focus only on the final verse or the three verses from today's lection set apart from their meaning within

Exegetical Perspective

These verses present a poignant and tender picture of God. Because the lectionary committee isolates these three verses from a much longer unit, the contrast with what comes before and after these verses highlights the theological insight and depth of these lines. This theological insight is a consistent but understated and often neglected theme in the biblical understanding of God.

Verse 7 obviously begins a new unit, in great contrast to the first six verses of the chapter. In verses 1–6 God speaks in first person, recounting acts of judgment against foreign enemies. This is the divine Warrior who fights on behalf of the chosen people. With no transition a new speaker emerges in verse 7, announcing the intention to recount the gracious deeds of the Lord. Isaiah 63:7–64:12 is one long poem with a complex structure, covering a range of responses from gratitude to lament to confession to intercession. The poem may have originated in the early part of the exile as a lament over the destruction of Jerusalem and the deportation into Babylon. It may later have been adapted by the prophet scholars have come to call Third Isaiah (chaps. 56–66, although these chapters may be composite) to reflect the despair felt by those who had returned from exile but were facing repeated frustrations in the attempt to rebuild community, structures, and liturgical practice.

Homiletical Perspective

Preachers who turn to Isaiah for a comforting word this Sunday will have to ignore everything they learned in seminary about interpreting a text in context, for these three verses are airlifted out of a chapter thick with divine wrath and human despair. In the verse preceding today's lection, God declares, "I trampled down peoples in my anger" (v. 6). In the verse following, God is the enemy of those who have grieved God's holy spirit and "fought against them" (v. 10). The three verses planted between these judgments rise like tender shoots among sharp briars.

Chapter 63 reads like a play script with parts for at least two players. The first voice opens the chapter with two questions. The second voice enters at the end of verse 1, using language that leaves little question of the speaker's identity. This is God the holy warrior, whose clothing is red with the blood of those whose desertion has provoked his deadly anger (v. 3). When God looked around for someone to help with the work of redemption, no one was there. No one was on God's side; "there was no one to sustain me; so my own arm brought me victory, and my wrath sustained me" (v. 5). God crushed the people in anger, pouring their lifeblood on the ground (v. 6).

The firsts voice enters again at verse 7 while this awful speech is still ringing in the ear. "I will recount the gracious deeds of the Lord," the prophet says, as

Isaiah 63:7-9

Theological Perspective

precedence in Isaiah 46:3–4, in which God reminds the remnant that they have "been borne by me from your birth, carried from the womb."[1] God is with God's children like a mother who carries her children in her womb and then, once they have been delivered, lifts her children up to her hip to keep them out of harm's way. This God deals with them tenderly, in an "abundance of steadfast love" (v. 7c), looking on God's lost children with love and pity (v. 9b).

Brueggemann's insight into the nature of parenthood, by way of the divine Parent, is instructive here. Rather than considering God as *either* father or mother or *simultaneously* mother and father, in interpreting Isaiah, Brueggemann asks us to expand our understanding of the capacities of one parent so that a single parent (male or female) can be both fierce and tender, angry and pitying. Such an understanding of the capacities of a parent of whatever gender, as derived from the capacities of God as parent, liberates earthly fathers and mothers from restrictive (earthly) models of what a "real" mother or "real" father is like. Following God as described in Isaiah, the capacities of a parent are vast.

In considering the female imagery for God alongside the language and images of God as male, Carol Myers reminds us that we cannot know whether or not ancient people understood these literally. Rather, this language offered the faithful imagery to attempt to "grasp aspects of the fundamentally nonhuman character of God."[2] The language we use is our human effort to grasp that which always exceeds our grasp. God defies every human attempt to compartmentalize God. Religious language is our attempt to speak of a reality that ultimately cannot be contained by the limits of language. The good news is that being faithful to God means being willing to leave behind the thought ruts and language ruts we fall into to express our sense of the Divine, and to imagine God ever new, as Isaiah does when he describes a God who bears God's children as a mother. As those imprinted with the divine image, breaking through all of our easy assumptions about God means we will break through easy assumptions about ourselves and others as well.

God's Concern for the Enslaved. This passage also speaks of a God who has delivered and will again

---

1. Walter Brueggemann, *Theology of the Old Testament* (Minneapolis: Fortress Press, 1997), 258.
2. Carol Myers, "Female Images of the Hebrew God," in Carol Myers, Toni Craven, and Ross Kraemer, eds., *Women in Scripture* (Grand Rapids: Eerdmans, 2000), 527–28.

Pastoral Perspective

this substantial chapter is to contribute to the church's neglect of Hebrew Scripture and to risk thinking that Scripture functions like a fortune cookie—"airlifting" favorite passages from their context for the church's reading pleasure. One hopes, on this First Sunday after Christmas, that those who teach and preach will not fall prey to the lectionary temptation to focus only on verses 7–9, but will see this lection as an invitation to pay close attention to chapter 63 in its entirety.

Still lingering from the afterglow of Christmas cheer and after the Christmas crowds have thinned out, Isaiah sings, "I will recount the gracious deeds of the LORD, the praiseworthy acts of the LORD, because of all that the LORD has done for us" (v. 7). The challenge facing pastors and preachers is that for many who sit in post-Christmas congregations, the profound feeling in the air does not reflect what Isaiah chants in these verses. Fatigue and financial woes, dashed expectations and lingering doubt are often the lyrics of the unsung song of post-Christmas congregations, rather than gratitude and praise.

Reading all of Isaiah 63 can give voice to the complexity of post-Christmas emotions, as well as provide the necessary context to hear verses 7–9 in all their fullness. In the first six verses of Isaiah 63, we hear the voice of fatigue and disillusionment, but it is not a human voice. In these first verses of chapter 63, we hear the voice of God, who is fatigued and disillusioned with the so-called "people of God." In verse 6, God cries aloud, "I trampled down peoples in my anger, I crushed them in my wrath"—not exactly a dose of Christmas cheer and obviously an easy verse for the lectionary to omit. It is an unfortunate omission, though, because this verse gives voice to a God who cares profoundly about "my people" (v. 8a).

So much about Christmas in and out of the church suffers from shallow sentimentality and hollow theology. "Be of good cheer" masks the reality that much of the time life is anything but cheery. Throughout Advent and Christmas, popular culture bleeds over into the church's theology as baby Jesus rides with Santa on the way to battle the Grinch. Pre- or post-Christmas, congregations hear far too little about the God who cares deeply enough for the world to enter the human fray and to be encountered by the horrors of Herod. As chapter 63 opens, Isaiah speaks first in the voice of an angry and disillusioned God who is not interested in spiritual sentimentality but in a community of the faithful who will live in covenant fidelity despite their circumstances.

Exegetical Perspective

Although the poem has a form consistent with use as a community lament, it is longer than most pieces used for ancient community worship. Nevertheless, it conveys the gamut of responses of the community to its situation. In its full length, the poem praises God for divine grace (63:7–9), confesses sin (63:10, 64:7a), laments the current situation (63:11–14, 18b; 64:7b, 10–11), and appeals plaintively to God to act (63:15ff.). Contemporary use of the full oracle could enable the community to experience this full journey through a variety of stances toward God.

The effect of isolating the three verses for one Sunday puts the emphasis on God's grace, so that the contemporary worshiping community can explore deeply the theological affirmation of this introduction to the whole poem. The prophet begins by announcing his intention to extol God's grace. His first assertion is that God reveals grace through God's deeds. God demonstrates grace through the election of Israel, and definitively through the exodus event (63:11–12) and the provision of land (63:14). The prophet uses the familiar terms "favor," "mercy," and "steadfast love." These terms allude to God's choice to make Israel a special part of the divine plan for the redemption of the world and of God's compassion and dependability. This assertion is a typical way for biblical writers to convey God's grace. One can infer God's character through God's actions.

Verse 8 may move into a quite remarkable assumption for the prophet. When the prophet recounts the words of God ("For he said,"), he seems to delve into God's very thoughts. To whom did God say the line that follows ("Surely they are my people, children who will not deal falsely")? Was this God's inner reflection, speaking only to Godself? In any case, verse 8 reveals a vulnerable, perhaps even naive God, who simply assumes that the people will respond to the acts of divine grace. At the very least, this is a God who trusts the people to act faithfully. Even if one cannot say that the God of verse 8 is naive, one can say that this God gives the people the benefit of the doubt, at least in the beginning.

The term "my people" can carry a number of connotations. It can imply obligation on the part of the people. It can convey God's decision to act through the people. Here, it seems to imply that God assumes the people will learn to identify with God's character. The people will choose to be God's people. Verse 9 continues the idea of God's vulnerability. Although the NRSV transmits this idea only in the footnote, verse 9 declares that God experienced the anguish

Homiletical Perspective

shocking in his mildness as the Lord was in fury. Then he goes on to praise God's favor, mercy, pity, and love. Moses-like, the prophet stands between a furious God and a feckless people, reminding both of their truest identity in relationship with one another.

Do you remember, God, when you claimed this people as your children? (v. 8)

Do you remember, Israel, when God lifted you and carried you around? (v. 9)

With language like this, the prophet seeks to remind both parties of the days of old, calling each back to the memory of God's intimate, saving presence with God's people. A little later he will appeal to God as Father (v. 16), directly challenging the God who is acting like a soldier instead. The chapter ends with the prophet's boldest shot of all, pleading with God to repent ("turn back") to the people, whose only hope is to hear God call them once again by name (v. 19).

Before deciding whether to ignore this difficult context or to make use of it, preachers will do well to read the exegetical, theological, and pastoral perspectives on this passage. They will also take the liturgical context into account, along with the other readings appointed for the day.

In the reading from Hebrews, Jesus—the pioneer of salvation made perfect through suffering—echoes the speech of Isaiah 63:7–9. Both the pioneer and the prophet praise God in spite of everything they have seen and suffered, witnessing to a trust in God that transcends their own comfort levels. Psalm 148 picks up the same theme, calling all creation (sea monsters along with flying birds) to praise God. In the reading from Matthew, Herod is the one with blood on his hands, not God. While there is no replacing the children lost to Herod's fury (2:18), a brave dreamer named Joseph acts to protect his wife and her child from harm. Who needs a GPS system when he has angels of the Lord?

While the First Sunday after Christmas may not seem the best timing for any of today's readings, there may be no better day to confront the truth that neither God's presence nor Christ's birth rids the world of horror and death. Even the most sheltered parishioner may have noticed a sharp dip in holiday cheerfulness over the past week, as both neighbors and news media buckle their seat belts for the new year. Any gospel that seeks to avoid the realities of sea monsters, murderous political leaders, dead children, wailing mothers—and yes, even the chilling image of an angry God—is not a gospel big enough for human life.

Isaiah 63:7-9

Theological Perspective

deliver God's people from exile. In remembering the actions of God in the Egyptian captivity, Isaiah reminds us that God desires freedom for humankind. God stands with humankind to work for our liberation; love and mercy characterize God's engagement with us. Important for us in this text is the realization that God's people were living in physically limiting conditions contributing to their spiritual diminishment, and it was from all of these that God released them.

To what extent should we work for the ends that God desires? What can/should our roles be in the liberation of others? Latin American liberation theologian Gustavo Gutiérrez tells us that care for others is the task of faith. "If faith is a commitment to God and human beings, it is not possible to live in today's world without a commitment to the process of liberation. That is what constitutes a commitment today."[3]

The passage also tells us that it was "no messenger or angel but his presence that saved them" (v. 9a). God did not give Godself to the captives secondarily through an intermediary, but was present to them in their suffering and in their release. It may be that in working for God's ends, in this case the liberation of those in captivity, we must be there in person. It was, the prophet tells us, God's being with them in love that "redeemed them." The work of liberation may require that we go to the places of enslavement, where people are not free, and work, through love, to aid in their release. Where are the people who are captive? Where are God's people who will work in love and mercy to aid God's desired end for humankind, which is freedom?

EMILY ASKEW

Pastoral Perspective

Surely, if ever the church is to sing of God's saving grace, it is on the Sunday after the boxes are unwrapped and the tree has dropped its needles. So, often the church laments, "Where was God when we needed God the most?" Here in chapter 63, God laments the unfaithfulness and ingratitude of "my people." In verse 5, God grieves, "I looked, but there was no helper." The faithful covenant people of God were nowhere to be found, and so God grieves. Listening to all of chapter 63 on the First Sunday after Christmas will call the church to a long memory of God's faithfulness and the people's fickleness. Even more importantly—and unlike the human tendency to give up on those who disappoint and anger us—Isaiah calls the church to remember the one who maintains covenants, even when "my people" do not: "He became their savior in all their distress. It was no messenger or angel but his presence that saved them; in his love and in his pity, he redeemed them" (vv. 8–9).

As the church enters a new calendar year and approaches the celebration of Epiphany, perhaps one gift of this lection is a resolution worthy of a church-wide effort to keep. Instead of pledging ourselves to exercise every day in the coming year or to lose all the Christmas fat or to watch less TV and read more books, maybe this lection invites the community of God's people to a new posture of prayer and a new way to live in the world. What if, even when the world is harsh and ugly and severe, the people of God awoke each day to utter and then live this prayer: "I will recount the gracious deeds of the LORD, the praiseworthy acts of the LORD, because of all that the LORD has done for us" (v. 7)?

I suspect this prayer would extend Christmas far beyond its twelve days and would remind us that Christmas is always far more about God than about us.

GARY W. CHARLES

---

3. James Nickoloff, ed., *Gustavo Gutiérrez: Essential Writings* (Minneapolis: Fortress Press, 1996), 25.

Exegetical Perspective

and distress of the people. Even the NRSV translation conveys that God cared deeply about the hurts and suffering of the people, and acted to save them. What a contrast to the bloody God of verses 1–6!

The appeals to God later in the same poem (64:1–2) are a desperate attempt to persuade God to stop ignoring the plight of the people. The overall effect of the editor placing this poem after the material that precedes it is to portray a God capable of great power (even violence) but predisposed to mercy and steadfast love. What comes after the verses assigned by the lectionary also fleshes out the understanding of God's grace. The love of this God cannot be taken for granted or presumed upon. The people who have betrayed the trust of this God can implore God to return. That God seems to have turned away is not cause for hopeless despair. The God who once acted, who once chose to give the benefit of the doubt, is amenable to the pleas of the people.

This message of the vulnerability of God, emphasized by the isolation of these verses from the rest of the poem, is an important affirmation for contemporary proclamation. The contemporary understanding of God often swings between God as angry and judgmental and God as overindulgent. Verse 8 presents a God willing to assume the best of the people and willing to risk being hurt by that assumption. Chapter 11 of Hosea presents a similar understanding of God's vulnerability. This message is especially appropriate for the season after Christmas, a time marked by excessive sentimentality. This passage reinforces the vulnerability of a God who comes to earth not as mighty warrior (vv. 1–6) but as a helpless child. This vulnerability has the capacity to disarm the view of God as judgmental and to shame the view of God as overindulgent. This vulnerable God has come to save and to draw out the assumed goodness of the people.

CHARLES L. AARON

Homiletical Perspective

Here, then, is one possible theme for the sermon. In all of the readings for today, God's faithful ones persist in praising God—or at least in trusting God—through all that befalls them. This trust does not save them by helping them float above the sufferings of the world; it saves them by helping them endure. In the case of Isaiah, memory is key. Recalling the gracious deeds of the Lord to the whole house of Israel, the prophet aids his listeners in two important ways.

First, he rescues them from the isolation of their individual experience. Recounting "all that the LORD has done for us" (v. 7), the prophet sticks with plural pronouns throughout. No one who hears him can indulge in the fantasy of being an only child. God's love and pity are focused on "people," "children," "the house of Israel." Even when a child of God prays the Lord's Prayer all alone, the first word is "Our."

Second, the prophet rescues his listeners from the prison of the present. By recalling how God has acted toward the people in the past, he reminds them that the way things are is not the way they have always been. There was a time when God saved them from their distress (v. 8). There was a time when God lifted them up and carried them (v. 9). By extension, the people may imagine that there may be more such times in the future. While their present distress is not to be denied, it is not the whole of their lives. The God of their present is also the God of their past and of their future.

Another theme present in all four readings is God's eagerness for partners in the divine work of redemption. In Isaiah 63:8, God counts on "children who will not deal falsely." Psalm 148 calls all creation to the work of praise. Matthew 2 testifies to the saving work of Joseph in preserving his family's life, while Hebrews 2 praises the pioneer Jesus, who also serves as high priest. Skillful preachers will make sure that this long list of God's helpers includes those who have come to worship God today.

BARBARA BROWN TAYLOR

Psalm 148

[1]Praise the LORD!
  Praise the LORD from the heavens;
    praise him in the heights!
[2]Praise him, all his angels;
    praise him, all his host!

[3]Praise him, sun and moon;
    praise him, all you shining stars!
[4]Praise him, you highest heavens,
    and you waters above the heavens!

[5]Let them praise the name of the LORD,
    for he commanded and they were created.
[6]He established them forever and ever;
    he fixed their bounds, which cannot be passed.

[7]Praise the LORD from the earth,
    you sea monsters and all deeps,

Theological Perspective

On the occasion of the First Sunday after Christmas, it is appropriate that the congregation recall the basics of their faith in Jesus Christ, the incarnate Son of God. Psalm 148 does not disappoint. Indeed, it calls all creation to praise God and reiterates the heart of the Psalter: it is the sovereign God who reigns, and all creation is to praise the Lord with jubilation.

Theologically, we can see that the greatest of God's "gifts" is the second person of the Trinity.[1] Thus it is right to acknowledge, especially at this season of the church's year, that incarnation and creation are linked. All creation emanated from Creator/Redeemer/Sustainer and exhibited the grace of YHWH. All creation was designed by grace to return to Creator/Redeemer/ Sustainer. The incarnation revealed the grace that was planted in creation and in ourselves as the objects of God's continuing love. The linkage of creation and redemption is a central feature of many Christian heritages.

It is virtually impossible to imagine any piece of literature that is more universal and expansive in its praise and adoration of God and God's creation than Psalm 148. Indeed, one can only call this an ecological hymn of praise. For those concerned with

1. Indeed, can we call the Son or, for that matter, the Spirit a "gift"? Does that suggest hierarchy, and ranking? That is not my intention.

Pastoral Perspective

The other readings for this day are so appealing that a preacher might not view the psalm as a sermon text. Consider, though, the mood of the congregation just days after the hoopla of Christmas. To regular worshipers, the swelled ranks of the choir, the alleluias and trumpet blasts of a midnight mass might seem more theatrical than worshipful, especially with so many relative strangers in the pews.

Home festivities rarely live up to our desires. Many parents have been dismayed at the wide-eyed materialism that rips open packages and jumps from one gift to the next with barely a thank-you in between. Some Sunday morning might find it difficult to discern the incarnate Lord in the midst of too much *stuff* onto which we pile lofty expectations. "Family" is the new socially approved idol in which we invest our hopes for happiness, and "family" often boils down to "children." Parents organize their schedules around soccer practice, piano lessons, and dance classes, and many in church overspent their Christmas budgets for toys and electronic gadgets. The outreach committee of my parish has a special line item that provides funds specifically so that nearby families "can make sure their children have Christmas." I think our hearts are in the right place, but we do have an exalted idea of what a few dollars can buy.

^{8}fire and hail, snow and frost,
　　stormy wind fulfilling his command!

^{9}Mountains and all hills,
　　fruit trees and all cedars!
^{10}Wild animals and all cattle,
　　creeping things and flying birds!

^{11}Kings of the earth and all peoples,
　　princes and all rulers of the earth!
^{12}Young men and women alike,
　　old and young together!

^{13}Let them praise the name of the LORD,
　　for his name alone is exalted;
　　his glory is above earth and heaven.
^{14}He has raised up a horn for his people,
　　praise for all his faithful,
　　for the people of Israel who are close to him.
Praise the LORD!

Exegetical Perspective

Psalm 148 is one of a cluster of five hymns at the end of the book, which all repeatedly use "Praise the LORD!" They appear to be liturgical pieces from the postexilic period.

The Hebrew expression *hallelu-yah*, which constitutes the central refrain of Psalm 148, moved beyond native Hebrew speakers to become part of the basic vocabulary of Jewish and Christian worship in many languages. Already the ancient Greek Bible translation, the Septuagint, sometimes transliterated it as *alleluia*. Still today, nothing seems to express the intensely joyful celebration of God as sharply as the simple exclamation "Hallelujah!" It actually is a plural imperative of a verb that means to cheer or cry out in praise or boasting. The "jah" ending is a short form of the personal name of Israel's God, YHWH. To utter "Hallelujah" is to command some group energetically to praise the God of the Bible. A few modern Bible translations actually use "Hallelujah," but most, like the NRSV, translate it "Praise the LORD."

Although this verb literally denotes a command to praise, it also functions as an exclamation of praise. As Augustine aptly observed, when people say, "Praise the Lord," by that very utterance they are doing exactly what they are telling others to do.[1] This verb occurs

Homiletical Perspective

Psalm 148 is an exuberant song of praise sung by the entire universe! The joyful chorus is in strong contrast to the sorrowful tone of the accompanying Gospel text telling of the slaughter of the innocents so soon after Jesus' birth. In Psalm 148, there is no hint of the pain, anger, fear, or cruelty found in Matthew's story of Herod's infanticide.

Kathleen Norris, in her chapter "The Paradox of the Psalms," lends the preacher helpful insight on the disparity between the extreme gladness expressed in the psalm and the extreme sadness over the slaughter of young children around Bethlehem. Echoing Calvin and quoting Emily Dickinson, she writes that paradoxically in the Psalms " 'Pain—is missed—in Praise,' but in a way that takes pain fully into account" rather than avoiding or dismissing it.[1]

On this Sunday when the Gospel focuses on human cruelty, the psalm, with its personification of all of nature joining humankind in praise, might seem at first glance like some kind of denial or flight from reality. However, as Norris points out, the "psalms demand that we recognize that praise does not spring from a delusion that things are better than they are, but rather from the human capacity for joy. Only when we see this can we understand

1. Augustine, *Expositions on the Psalms 121–150*, trans. Maria Boulding, ed. Boniface Ramsey, 6 vols. (Hyde Park, NY: New City Press, 2004), 6:477.

1. Kathleen Norris, *The Cloister Walk* (New York: G.P. Putnam's Sons, 1996), 93.

Psalm 148

Theological Perspective

ecojustice, climate change, and the health of the earth community as a whole, Psalm 148 stands in counterpoint to those who claim that Christianity and Judaism are anthropocentric or antinature; the same rebuttal is present in Genesis 1:1–2:4a, which emphasizes the goodness of God's creation, and in Psalm 104, which images YHWH as playing with whales.

Though the forms of the verb for "praise" vary from the imperative to the jussive and back again, the tone of the psalm is quite clear. The praise that is called for is natural and uncoerced, almost spontaneous or automatic. In fact, the call to universal praise is itself praise, rather than something that the "heavenly host" or "wild animals" or "kings of the earth" need to be reminded of. This is universal sovereignty, an inclusion of all of God's beloved heavenly and earthly creatures.

Note the order of the roll call: first, from the heavens: heights, angels, and other heavenly hosts (vv. 1, 2), then celestial bodies (sun, moon, stars, highest heavens, and "waters above the skies"). *Next* in order of praise are earth beings: sea creatures and ocean depths, fire and hail, snow and frost, stormy winds, mountains, hills, fruit trees, cedar, wild animals, all cattle, small creatures, and flying birds. Included are many of the elements in Genesis 1–2. Also taking their place among the earth creatures are kings, all nations, princes, rulers, and all people, young and old alike. The question is whether humankind is a culmination or only part of the web. Placed as it is after the hail and frost, the human species just might be a bit more humble than it usually is (we usually are).

While I could make too much of this ordering by seeing it as hierarchical in reverse, my theological point lies elsewhere. The psalmist is calling attention to the ecological whole; we of the earth community are included together to emphasize the sovereign providence and grace of God. Anything less than universal praise is human arrogance and the beginning of ecosinfulness. The psalmist's aim is to indicate the majesty of the Lord that the heavens and all earth are designed to glorify and enjoy forever. It is YHWH's name alone that is to be exalted (v. 13), and God's splendor that is to be celebrated unstintingly.

The conclusion of the psalm, while continuing the praise imagery, focuses especially on Israel. What in the world might "raising up a horn for [YHWH's] people" mean? If we accept that the horn is a symbol of protection and continuing care, which is consonant with the foregoing emphasis on providence, then that suggests another reason for praise. Who or what is this horn? Three possibilities come to the fore. One is

Pastoral Perspective

W. H. Auden, in his verse play *For the Time Being*, describes the post-Christmas letdown this way:

> There are enough
> Left-overs to do, warmed-up, for the rest of the week—
> Not that we have much appetite, having drunk such a lot,
> Stayed up so late, attempted—quite unsuccessfully—
> To love all of our relatives, and in general
> Grossly overestimated our powers.[1]

Auden hits a nerve and we might wince at the recognition of ourselves. As hard as we have shopped, baked, and overscheduled, an outside observer might suppose that we believe our own work makes Christmas happen. That Christmas is about happy, well-fed crowds and lots of *stuff*, rather than a child in a drafty stable chased into exile by a brutal despot.

Preachers might complain that our secular culture has hijacked the Feast of the Nativity and rendered it meaningless beyond cutesy angels and Santa Claus. The great thing about our commercial celebration, however, is that it all takes place in Advent. It is a time of preparation for the real thing, when we might be full of hope but cannot know exactly how things will work out. The Christmas season as it is celebrated in church—after the fact—is ignored by commerce.

For those for whom shopping the sales is not the most important post-Christmas activity, for that faithful few who come to church, a reflective doxology might be just what they need. The psalmist calls on all of creation in heaven and earth to sing God's praise. Angels and hosts, sun, moon, and stars are convened as the heavenly choir. From the earth they are joined by sea monsters, fire and hail, wind, and wild animals, men and women, young and old. The psalmist seems to be summoning God's praises from just about everywhere except the marketplace and the temple! That might square perfectly with our own deepest wisdom.

There is a possible direction here. God first makes the divine Presence known not so much in the things we think of as religious as in the things of creation. In Psalm 148 "all you shining stars . . . you highest heavens . . . you sea monsters and all deeps" (vv. 3, 4, 7) are partners in giving praise to God.

So who will be in the pews this Sunday? What will be their experience leading up to this Sunday after Christmas? As on most Sundays, there will be a mix of people. Younger parents may be weary, yet hopeful for a deeper awareness of Immanuel, of God-with-us. They may even wonder how to communicate that awareness to their children. Others,

---

1. W. H. Auden, *Collected Longer Poems* (New York: Random House, 1969), 195.

twelve times in Psalm 148; this repetition creates the feeling that the whole world is indeed praising God.

The psalm is structured symmetrically, dividing the universe into two sections as it commands all the various elements to praise God. Assuming the same hierarchical, prescientific view of the cosmos that is reflected elsewhere in the Hebrew Bible (e.g., Gen. 1), it begins in verses 1–5 with the highest region, the heavenly places and their occupants: angels, sun, moon, stars, and atmospheric water. Then, in verses 7–12, it shifts to earth, giving a strikingly detailed list of its occupants: sea monsters, ocean deeps, fire, hail, snow, frost, storm wind, mountains and hills, fruit and cedar trees, wild animals, domestic animals, creeping animals (i.e., things that move in swarms or in a scampering fashion), birds, and human beings, both royal and common, male and female, young and old.

This elaborate list echoes a kind of wisdom text known in ancient Egyptian and Mesopotamian cultures that contains a long compendium of names for plants, animals, stones, and so forth. Such "nature wisdom" must have been cultivated also in Israel, for Solomon is described as speaking of trees, animals, birds, reptiles, and fish (1 Kgs. 4:33), and Job (chaps. 38–39), Psalm 104, and Sirach 43 all suggest similar catalogs of natural phenomena.

This psalm does not find concentration on the person of God to be a motive for devaluing the material world. Just the opposite: exuberant exaltation of YHWH enhances fascination with the interesting details of both heaven and earth. The animals called upon here to praise YHWH include many which the Priestly code forbids as food or altar sacrifices. The categories of clean and unclean served important functions in Israelite religion, but such distinctions were bracketed by the broader belief that all of creation was the good work of God, fascinating and worthy of attention.

Each section concludes with a statement of *why* praise of God is warranted: "for he commanded and they were created" in verse 5, and "for his name alone is exalted" in verse 13. The concept of creation by divine word in verse 5 echoes the narrative in Genesis 1, but the emphasis here is not on the process but on the result. The sheer immensity and complex but unfailing order of the world prompt praise of the Lord, who alone brought it into being. "He fixed their bounds" in verse 6b is a skillful rendering. The preposition "their" may refer back specifically to "waters" in verse 4, an allusion to the ancient image of God subduing the watery forces of chaos and imposing on them permanent boundaries

that both lamentation and exultation can be forms of praise." Neither should be denied; each ought to be held in tension with the other, accurately expressing true experiences known to every one of us. The ability to hold conflicting feelings of joy and despair or disappointment and hope at the same is a sign of an individual's spiritual and psychological maturity.

Communities of worshipers also need to acknowledge both the beauty and the terror of our world. A resounding reading and interpretation of Psalm 148 along with the Gospel text serves that necessity. Our joy at the birth of Jesus can then continue to be felt, even as the dark theme of the day and the dark days of the North American winter season try to shroud us in gloom. The church is equipped with faith in the light that shines into even the darkest, most death dealing of places.

Like the personified heavens, elements, and creatures that join in the chorus of praise, we human beings sing praises by the design of our Maker. The psalmist helps us understand that even though all of creation has suffered the ravages of reckless human behavior and sin, praise still springs forth. Praise cannot be stopped; creation pulses with the power to say yes to life and to the Creator, despite anything that would point to the contrary.

Nevertheless, such spontaneous praise by the trees, hills, sea monsters, creeping things, and all peoples is in need of encouragement in our time, when we are so prone to depression over injustices and violence of every sort. We glimpsed our innate capacity for praise in the exuberance and joy that sprang from the election of the first African American U.S. president. Whether on the winning or the losing side, we rejoiced together, recognizing that the prophets' dream of equal opportunity had finally come true. Spontaneous celebrations of joy burst forth on election night, despite the fact that our country was fighting two wars, businesses were failing, and the economic forecast was dreadful. The Spirit could not be squelched.

This means that the preacher has the possibility to juxtapose the Gospel lesson and the psalm to teach the valuable lesson that pain and grief are not meant to be discounted, and neither is joy. We praise despite the pain. Again, Norris notes that life's painful images are essential for praise, for without them praise is meaningless. When we try to protect ourselves by censoring difficult readings like the slaughter of the innocents, we are preaching an incomplete, inaccurate picture of our world. Both the pain and the praise have their rightful places if we are to worship in spirit and in truth.

Psalm 148

Theological Perspective

the continuation of the monarchy, but if this psalm is postexilic, that is unlikely. The second is that the rulership of Israel has passed or returned to YHWH and to all God's faithful, maybe even beyond the people of Israel. Perhaps there is a special role for Israel. Israel is one among the participants in the praising of God; "its unique role, perhaps, is to articulate intelligibly the unspoken praise of the rest of creation."[2] The third possibility is that the horn that YHWH has raised up was quite outside the Psalter's grasp (or maybe not). Perhaps, the hymn is referring to the messianic hope, which Christians recognize in the kingship or reign of Jesus Christ. That would seem to be at least theologically appropriate to acknowledge during the First Sunday of Christmastide.

One other point bears investigation: What is the purpose or nature of praise? In some instances, praising someone means little more than complimenting him or her. That is far more external to the identity of the one doing the complimenting than is entailed here. Instead, the praise here is an acknowledgment of *one's own* identity. To praise the Lord as universal sovereign is to proclaim one's own ultimate loyalty as the foundation of one's being. *That is what is being called for.*

Thus, to praise the Lord is to show forth God's glory by being the creatures that God designed them and us to be. Israel and the other beings are to mirror their creation as YHWH's creatures and also those whom YHWH has redeemed. The creation and redemption are joined for Christians. We honor God and witness to God's power and steadfast love by praising God in our lives. God rules the cosmos, and all beings join in an ecological hymn of praise. All God's beings—angels, sea creatures, humankind, and rulers—participate in this exultant hallelujah! Especially at Christmas.

L. SHANNON JUNG

Pastoral Perspective

perhaps older or solitary, may be glad for a low Sunday with people they recognize from week to week. All are there to be fed with something more substantial than festive roasts and seasonal pies.

The monks of seventh-century Ireland had a practice of "listening for the heartbeat of God."[2] Not listening *to* the heartbeat, as if it were obvious, but listening *for* it, concealed within all that is around us. That is the faith proclaimed in Psalm 148; all creation echoes the presence and praise of God. "Mountains and all hills, fruit trees and all cedars! . . . All cattle, creeping things and flying birds!" (vv. 9–10)

So the preacher may challenge the congregation to discern where they could have heard the heartbeat of God through the rustle of gift wrap and beneath laughter around a dinner table. Perhaps more importantly, how might the heartbeat have been heard in the grief of a woman passing her first Christmas as a widow? On battlefields crying out for peace? In hungry children looking out at us accusingly from the pages of a magazine? Look for God's presence, not in the intentional practices of our faith, but in improbable places and in the accidents that we can neither control nor predict.

As today's congregation listens for the heartbeat in the midst of their post-Christmas reflections, Psalm 148 invites them to join all creation in celebration. As Eugene Peterson translates verse 13:

> Let them praise the name of God—
> it's the only Name worth praising.
> His radiance exceeds anything in earth and sky;
> he's built a monument—his very own people![3]

Those in church today already know Christmas may not be reduced to nostalgia about an event that happened a long time ago. Today's congregation deserves the joy of knowing they are agents of God's ongoing presence in the world. They have joined heavenly hosts, stars, mountains, wild animals, and kings in reflecting God's radiance. Psalm 148 mirrors the picture of angels, shepherds, and sages attending the child in the manger. The heartbeat of God was born not only into Bethlehem's stable but into today's faithful too. "Young men and women alike, old and young together . . . Praise the LORD!"

MARTIN G. TOWNSEND

2. J. Clinton McCann Jr., "The Book of Psalms," in *The New Interpreter's Bible,* vol. 4, ed. Leander Keck (Nashville: Abingdon Press, 1996), 1272.

2. J. Philip Newell, *Listening for the Heartbeat of God* (New York: Paulist Press, 1997), 7.
3. Eugene H. Peterson, *The Message* (Colorado Springs, CO: Navpress, 2002), 1091.

Exegetical Perspective

so that the world could come into existence (cf. Pss. 74:17; 104:5–9).

In verse 13, everyone on earth, like everyone in heaven in verse 5, is admonished to praise the *name* of the Lord. This probably does not mean only the sacred divine name, YHWH, but is a reference generally to the name of God as a symbol of God's being. Contrary to modern practice, personal names in Israel were thought somehow to epitomize an individual's very self. To know someone's name was to gain a kind of access to him or her (cf. Gen. 32:27–29). This concept is applied to God in the book of Deuteronomy, so that God's presence in the Jerusalem temple is described as putting God's *name* there (Deut. 12:5, 11). Psalm 148 here employs God's name as a representation of God's very self. Thus, one could paraphrase verse 13: "Let them praise the Lord, for he alone is exalted."

The psalm's language is straining to express the sublime "otherness" of God. The physical splendor of a richly robed human king is the literal meaning of the word translated "glory." It evokes the magnificence of the state robes of a wealthy monarch, which both dazzle and delight onlookers, yet God's "glory" is not something physical. "His name" and "his glory" are in parallelism in verse 13; God's self has a splendor beyond anything humans know in the created world.

This rather abstract idea is not, in fact, the climax of the psalm. Verse 14 proceeds to expound verse 13 by a recollection that God has saved the covenant people in some concrete way. Using the image of a horned animal, the expression to "raise the horn(s)" means to restore or increase the dignity or power of someone. "All the horns of the wicked I will cut off, but the horns of the righteous shall be exalted" (Ps. 75:10; cf. 92:10). Clearly YHWH has performed some major, though unidentified, act for Israel.

Psalm 148 celebrates the God who created and the God who has saved. Its exuberant praise is rooted in informed wonder at the intricacies of creation and in clear remembrance of an experience of God's saving power.

ROBERT J. OWENS

Homiletical Perspective

We preachers can learn from poets—and the psalmist—who ably express our creaturely nature for praise, even as they focus on the brokenness in and around us. A prime example is in *The Divine Comedy*, in which Dante shows how right praise is not an optional extra in life, but is the fundamental condition of happiness and for staying in harmony with reality. Praise abounds in paradise; God is not praised in hell. Ellen Davis points out that "the main reason to preach Psalms is not the bare fact that they contain great lines or great metaphors. Rather, it is because the poets who composed them thought differently about God than we do, and more deeply."[2]

Psalm 148 speaks deeply about the abundance of God's love. This First Sunday after Christmas the church ought to join in its exuberant chorus of praise, for Jesus Christ is God's gift of love to restore and fulfill all creation, as expressed in this hymn text by Rosamond E. Herklots:

May that great love our lives control . . .
Till, . . . we share your pain and find your joy.[3]

DEAN MCDONALD

---

2. Daniel Hardy and David Ford, *Praising and Knowing God* (Philadelphia: Westminster Press, 1985), 48–52 on Dante; Ellen Davis, *Wondrous Depth: Preaching the Old Testament* (Louisville. KY: Westminster John Knox Press, 2005), 26.
3. Rosamond E. Herklots, "In Bethlehem a Newborn Boy," in *The Presbyterian Hymnal* (Louisville, KY: Westminster/John Knox Press, 1990), 35.

Hebrews 2:10-18

[10]It was fitting that God, for whom and through whom all things exist, in bringing many children to glory, should make the pioneer of their salvation perfect through sufferings. [11]For the one who sanctifies and those who are sanctified all have one Father. For this reason Jesus is not ashamed to call them brothers and sisters, [12]saying,

"I will proclaim your name to my brothers and sisters,
    in the midst of the congregation I will praise you."
[13]And again,
    "I will put my trust in him."
And again,
    "Here am I and the children whom God has given me."

Theological Perspective

The Cost of Redemption. After the pageantry and celebration of Christmas Day, with all that it brings, what do the life and suffering of Jesus Christ mean for each of us today? How do we begin to make sense of the ways in which believers are sanctified through the beauty of salvation? Indeed, these are critical questions about which all Christians, at some point or other, have struggled. During this time of transition, as thoughts of the new year begin to form, these questions become more prominent. Often the challenges of the new year seem overwhelming as vestiges of the past year's struggles continue. In Hebrews, we find an engaging look into the nature of salvation and the ways in which Christians not only share in the redemptive sufferings of Jesus Christ but also are sanctified and made whole by those sufferings.

As indicated in Hebrews 2:11, "For the one who sanctifies and those who are sanctified all have one Father." There is a sense in which the life of Jesus creates the space for envisioning new realities of peace, healing, wholeness, and community for the present moment and the months ahead. Jesus, as depicted in this passage, is the "author, leader, and in their very ranks the captain of their salvation."[1] The mere

1. Fred B. Craddock, *The Interpreter's Bible* (New York: Abingdon Press, 1955), 11:614.

Pastoral Perspective

The First Sunday after Christmas we find ourselves in the heart of the twelve-day celebration of the incarnation of our Lord. Our attention has shifted from the manger, the star, the shepherds, the baby. Now we are able truly to marinate in the glory and the mystery of the incarnation: "The Word became flesh and lived among us" (John 1:14).

These verses from the Letter to the Hebrews do as much as any other text to help us to know the meaning of this holy mystery:
—In Christ, God became one of us.
—In Christ, God is with us in our suffering.
—In Christ, we have been freed from the fear of death.
Three theologically packed facets of our faith, all in nine verses!

First, in Christ, God became one of us. Knowing that we all share the same spiritual Father, Jesus joined us in being born of a human mother. In doing so, he "was not ashamed" to call us his brothers and sisters.

It is remarkable, really, that God would choose to become a human being and not be ashamed to do so. Given our history of rejecting God's way and choosing instead to follow the lure of the tempter; given our history of violence, abuse of creation, pride, and vainglory; there are plenty of good reasons for Jesus to be

¹⁴Since, therefore, the children share flesh and blood, he himself likewise shared the same things, so that through death he might destroy the one who has the power of death, that is, the devil, ¹⁵and free those who all their lives were held in slavery by the fear of death. ¹⁶For it is clear that he did not come to help angels, but the descendants of Abraham. ¹⁷Therefore he had to become like his brothers and sisters in every respect, so that he might be a merciful and faithful high priest in the service of God, to make a sacrifice of atonement for the sins of the people. ¹⁸Because he himself was tested by what he suffered, he is able to help those who are being tested.

Exegetical Perspective

Incarnation. How fitting that Hebrews 2:10–18 should be the Epistle reading for the First Sunday after Christmas. This is a proclamation on the incarnation writ large! The very fact that it comes to us in a book called Letter to the *Hebrews* (this letter reads more like a sermon) reminds the reader of Jesus' Jewish background. More than that, the author of Hebrews pushes the incarnation beyond Judaism to the very foundations of human history, back to the primal creative act—"Let us make humankind" (Gen. 1:26).

In order to gain some perspective, let us set this passage in its literary context. The first portion of the book of Hebrews offers several comparisons: between Jesus and the angels, between Jesus and Moses (through whom came the law), and between Jesus and Aaron (through whom came the priesthood). In each case, the author argues, Jesus is superior.

The structure of this lectionary passage is reminiscent of the descent and ascent of Jesus in Paul's hymn to Christ in Philippians 2:5–11. The book of Hebrews begins with "the Son" in the heavenly realm as "the reflection of God's glory and the exact imprint of God's very being, . . . [seated] at the right hand of the Majesty on high" (1:3). Jesus leaves the heavenly realm to become a human being (2:9–16). After completing his liberating work, God returns

Homiletical Perspective

A man said to the universe:
"Sir I exist!"
However," replied the universe,
"The fact has not created in me
A sense of obligation."[1]

It is a cruel world, and when we are under great stress or harsh suffering, we are prone to feel abandoned by God. We cry out for help, and none seems to come. We are caught between the extravagant promises of God as found in the Bible and the reality of our own painful situation. Human suffering by innocent people is a baffling experience and tests the faith of the believer to the core. The fact of human suffering is used as a major argument against the existence of God. *"How can a loving God allow . . . ?"* has been thrown in the face of more than one pastor or teacher.

Although this lection does not give a complete answer to the question, it does give us some help in living with the issue. For whatever reason, suffering does exist in this cold, impersonal, fallen world. The believer is not exempt from it. Diseases attack our bodies, friends betray us, and in the face of temptation we find we cannot resist and succumb. Evil

1. Stephen Crane, "A Man Said to the Universe," in *War Is Kind, and Other Poems* (Mineola, NY: Dover Publications, 1998), 43.

Hebrews 2:10-18

Theological Perspective

notion that human beings have divine companionship as we live out our day-to-day lives is a dramatic occasion for pause. It is recognition that we are not alone, that in our daily affairs there are both visible and invisible forces guiding the climate of our experiences.

In these passages, the writer's primary concern was to prevent Jewish Christians from embracing the temptation to retreat to Judaism and allow its influences to overwhelm their new lives as followers of Jesus Christ. The passage starts by emphasizing the finality and perfection of God's revelation in Christ. Because Jesus Christ is in fact the Son of God, made evident by his redemptive work as priest, we as believers can have confidence in the salvation made possible through Christ. In the passage, we see a preview of Jesus' ministry of salvation.

Classical theologians described this work of salvation as the atonement. It has been the quintessential event where God has removed the enmity between God and humanity. It is a God event. God in Christ is solely responsible for making this salvation possible and creating the conditions under which human beings may live free from the inevitability of death. Christ is, as Marcus Dods observes, "the strong swimmer who carries the rope ashore and so not only secures His own position but makes rescue for all who will follow."[2] By making salvation possible for human beings, every person now has the capacity to participate in the activity of God in the world or to experience the goodness of God as healing, wholeness, and community.

Life is filled with so much fragmentation and brokenness. The uncontrollable madness of the entertainment industry and nonstop infotainment with all of its sensationalism contributes to a growing sense of fragmentation all around us. The essence of salvation, in the other hand, is unity with God and others. The distinctive factor in understanding the nature of this salvation is the identify of Christ, as perhaps distinguished from the Old Testament vision of the Messiah, yet building on this theme. Jesus, like the Messiah, had to be both divine and human—divine, because as sinful creatures human beings are incapable of saving themselves. The depth of human sin and evil in the world provides compelling evidence that human beings are in need of salvation from a source beyond our ranks. Christ is also human. The experiences of Christ were as fully human as those of any other person.

2. Marcus Dods, in Wm. Robertson Nicole, *Expositor's Greek Testament* (1897; repr., Grand Rapids: Eerdmans, 1967), 4:265.

Pastoral Perspective

ashamed to become "one of us." Instead of seeing our differentness from him, Jesus chooses to see our common spiritual heritage. Not only is he not ashamed; he is ready, like the psalmist, to proclaim his kinship with us publicly, in the middle of the public assembly. Just as God proclaimed at the baptism of Jesus, "This is my Son" (Mark 1:11), God the Son is ready to proclaim of us, "Here is my brother; there is my sister."

God has become a human being, which means that, in a strange and wonderful and unprecedented way, God is with us. God did not become a puppy dog, or a dolphin, or even an angel. God became one of the descendants of Abraham who are numerous as the stars. While Christmas may be a lonely time of year for many, in the celebration of the incarnation we are never alone. God in Christ is with us, and is even pleased to be so.

Second, the writer of the Letter to the Hebrews proclaims that Christ is the "pioneer of [our] salvation," made perfect in suffering (v. 10). Through the incarnation, the One who suffered on the cross is one with God and one with us in our suffering. God is therefore with us in the midst of our sorrow: in the midst of earthquake, fire, and flood; in the midst of our illness, our pain, our grief. God is with us, and we are with God. This is good news indeed.

Through the prophet Isaiah, God speaks: "Do not fear, for I have redeemed you; I have called you by name, you are mine. When you pass through the waters, I will be with you; and through the rivers, they shall not overwhelm you; when you walk through fire you shall not be burned, and the flame shall not consume you" (Isa. 43:1b–2).

God became incarnate in Jesus, became human like us—not that suffering would be removed from us, but that suffering could be embraced head-on, fully embraced by Christ. Jesus fulfills his role as our Savior and Redeemer by suffering completely, even to the point of death. This is how he becomes the "pioneer," going ahead of us and clearing the way.

"Because he himself was tested by what he suffered, he is able to help those who are being tested" (v. 18). No longer is our suffering something that we endure alone; Christ is in it with us. Just as Christ embraced his own suffering, he now embraces us in ours. Just as suffering was a means through which Christ became "perfect" or complete, so too can our suffering become the means though which we are united more fully with Christ, and are therefore made more complete or whole ourselves.

This does not mean that our suffering ends—far from it. Neither does it mean that we should go out

Exegetical Perspective

him to his eternal service as heavenly high priest (2:17–18).

Jesus Our Brother; The Journey Down (vv. 10–17a). The author of Hebrews reflects the general thought world of first-century Hellenistic theologians. In the divine hierarchy of being, God sits at the top, angels are a category lower, and human beings are "lower than the angels" (Heb. 2:7 quoting Ps. 8:5 [8:6 LXX]). In this passage our author explains how it is that Jesus is an eternal heavenly high priest *and* a mere mortal like us. This same Jesus who is higher in the heavenly hierarchy than the angels was also "for a little while . . . lower than the angels" (v. 9). The author engages the reader in one of the early christological discussions about the humanity and divinity of Christ. In verse 9, the author for the first time refers to Jesus by his human name. Jesus' humanity is for the author of Hebrews the starting point for any christological discussion. As we shall see, it is a starting point with layers of meaning.

Verse 10 is the christological key to this passage. While the Greek text does not mention God (perhaps a bit of first-century Jewish reticence regarding the Divine), it is clear from the context that the Creator, who brings all things into being, picked the right historical moment to recreate Adam, a man in God's image. The reader is reminded of Genesis 1–2, with an added value. Paradoxically, Jesus is the latter-day *archēgos* (translators do not know quite what to do with this word: "captain" [KJV], "author" [NASB], "leader" [NAB], "pioneer" [NRSV]). One might simply understand this word as a reference to creation—the *archē*, origin of all that is (also see Prov. 8:22ff.). God has offered us, in Jesus, a new beginning—a new creation. Irenaeus of Lyon (ca. 185 CE) describes this incarnational Christology in an elegantly succinct phrase: "Our Lord Jesus Christ . . . became what we are, that he might bring us to be even what he is himself."[1]

In verses 12–13 the author emphasizes Jesus' humanity by identifying us as his brothers and sisters and undergirds this with references to Psalm 22:22 and Isaiah 8:17–18. Furthermore, this is not just a platonic affinity, a sharing of some human essence, but a genuine (non-gnostic) sharing of "flesh and blood" (v. 14). The only way Jesus' triumph over death could be effective was to die as a real flesh-and-blood human being. By leading the way through death to

1. Irenaeus, *Against Heresies*, in *Ante-Nicene Fathers*, ed. Alexander Roberts and James Donaldson, 10 vols. (Buffalo: The Christian Literature Publishing Co., 1885–96), book 5, preface.

Homiletical Perspective

governments perpetrate holocausts, and institutions crush the many for the benefit of a few. The righteous do not always prevail, and evil persons triumph.

Trouble and difficulty will come, and all of us will have very serious bumps on the road. We are given guidance and help in this text for the times when trouble comes . . . and it will. If you have blood in your veins and flesh on your bone, life will have its share of pain.

This lection delivers us from the misconception that would have us believe that God's goal for us is to be happy in this life. God's concern is not to make pampered children by attending to our every whim. God is infinitely more concerned with our holiness than with our happiness, and with giving us help at the point of pain than with delivering us from the pain.

Note how the writer references Jesus "pioneer of [our] salvation," being made "perfect through sufferings" (v. 10). It is in this suffering that we best experience God's relationship with humankind. The writer of this passage is seeking to vivify the complete identification of Christ with humankind, including human suffering. Jesus does not bend a little from heaven to beckon us, nor does he move among us without being touched by us. Remember that he stood with the disciples and sang a hymn before Gethsemane. He too put his trust in God. He is in every sense one of us and is not ashamed to call us brothers and sisters.

Being truly our brother means that he must share our bitterest defeat. Since he is the author of our salvation, he must do something about our greatest enemy, death. In order to share in flesh and blood with his brothers and sisters, he too must face death. Here, also, he has been faithful. He too died. This is perhaps the strongest part of the lection.

The avoidance of death is a phenomenon of American life. The American way of death is carefully manipulated, with silence, denial, and avoidance as the major tools. Death is no longer a part of God's purpose but is now a logical problem to be solved by those who deal with it—doctors, funeral directors, clergy, and lawyers. Death is a taboo in conversation. Instead, we prefer "passed away," "gone from us," or "promoted to the church triumphant." We hide from its reality with false grass at the cemetery and a cosmetically prepared body. Death is a reality. Also, the fear of death is aggravated by the fear of what comes after death.

If the fact of death were ever admitted to be a reality in America, we would also have to admit that

Hebrews 2:10-18

Theological Perspective

In his humanity, Christ has shown humanity the way to salvation, and in his death and resurrection he has conquered what Paul called the enemies—sin and death. By taking on the weight of human sin, Christ serves as capitulation or surrogate for results of human sin in the world. As fully human, Jesus Christ addresses humanity's greatest threat—death. As Paul writes in 1 Corinthians, "The sting of death is sin, and the power of sin is the law" (1 Cor. 15:56). This was even forecast in the book of Hosea, "I will ransom them from the power of the grave; O Death, I will be your plagues! O Sheol, I will be your destruction!"(Hos. 13:14, note). With all the monumental achievements of humanity, the inevitability of death and human suffering has been undeniable. By confronting and overcoming the forces of sin and death, Christ has demonstrated his faithfulness and obedience for the sake of humanity and the formation of a new redeemed community.

Redemption does not come without a cost. Dietrich Bonhoeffer, a theologian in Germany during Adolf Hitler's Third Reich, remarked in his classic book *The Cost of Discipleship* that salvation is costly because it cost a man his life. Bonhoeffer recognized that salvation is properly understood in the context of community, when individuals gather together to work out their faith with love and responsibility toward others. Often the only way this faithfulness and responsibility get exposed is when we find ourselves engaged in meaningful relationships with others. Service, which is central to the process of sanctification and at the heart of Jesus' ministry, involves a persistent commitment to advancing the well-being of those around us. This is extremely difficult in our contemporary culture, which is obsessed with self-gratification, indulgence, and personal autonomy. If we were dependent on our own capacities, it indeed would appear quite overwhelming. Here, in this Hebrews passage, the theme of God in Christ working to bring about the salvation of humanity is the assurance believers need to overcome the challenges, pitfalls, and burdens the new year may bring.

JOHNNY B. HILL

Pastoral Perspective

and look for ways to suffer in order to be closer to Jesus. We really do not have to; there is plenty of suffering to be had in life. It *does* mean that in suffering we may find ourselves closer to Jesus, and more grateful for the way that he makes known.

Third, the writer of Hebrews proclaims that in Christ—the merciful and faithful high priest—we have been liberated from the fear of death. Christ endured suffering to death on the cross. His subsequent resurrection and ascension make plain that death was not the final victor, though. Through our oneness with him, death no longer holds the power over us that it did before.

Certainly we still yearn to live, we still cherish the gift of life, and we still work hard to support and protect the lives of all. Because Jesus has allowed himself to suffer and to die a painful death, all of suffering and death are now transformed for us. While we still are tempted to live in fear of it, we need to fear no longer.

Analogies are frail, but if we know and see a peer endure an illness or a frightening episode with dignity and courage, we are then more able to endure it ourselves. When the one who suffers ahead of us is human, we are inspired. When the one who suffers ahead of us, and dies, is fully God *and* fully human, that suffering and that death are transformed, and we are free from whatever bonds of fear we had before.

Jesus, in his holy incarnation, has become like us in every way—flesh and blood, child of God, born of a woman, tempted and in pain. Jesus, in his suffering and death, has made known to the daughters and sons of Abraham the pure compassion and mercy of God, for whom and through whom all things exist. We are free.

LISA G. FISCHBECK

life, Jesus frees us from the fear every human being harbors—"the fear of death" (v. 15). (Our author notes that "the one who has the power of death" is the devil—the personification of deceit, who tests us to our human limits; another allusion to the creation story in Genesis.) Through his own death Christ has come face to face with the unknown and makes the unknown known to his followers. In doing so, he renders the devil and death impotent.

In a move that reminds the contemporary reader of the preacher's Jewish background, he declares to his congregation that Jesus did not come to aid angels, but to help "the descendants of Abraham" (v. 16). To further emphasize Jesus' Jewishness, he adds, "Therefore he had to become *like his brothers* [NRSV adds "and sisters"] *in every respect*" (v. 17a).

Jesus Our High Priest; The Journey Up (vv. 17b–18). The author of Hebrews returns to the theme of Jesus the "merciful and faithful high priest in the service of God" (v. 17b). The third part of this important verse offers a hint of how this heavenly high priest functions. As our high priest, Jesus makes "a sacrifice of atonement [*to hilaskesthai*] for the sins of the people" (v. 17c). Once again, translators have offered a variety of ways to think about the weighty term *hilaskomai.* The RSV offers the term "expiation," removing sin. The NASB reads "propitiation," turning away divine wrath. The NRSV suggests a process: "make a sacrifice of atonement." The KJV appears to offer a theologically comprehensive way to understand this term: "to make reconciliation."

In a final reminder of Jesus' solidarity with us, the preacher says, "Because [Jesus] himself was tested by what he suffered, he is able to help those who are being tested" (v. 18). We are in this together, Jesus and we. This is the paradox of Christmas. Because of the incarnation, this helpless infant in the cradle will carry us through our most severe times of testing.

PAUL WALASKAY

the United States is not the earthly paradise that it is deemed to be.[2]

Prior to the twentieth century, rural, quiet America faced death openly as an inevitable consequence of our mortality. Death was spoken of freely. A religious framework explained its meaning as a part of the purposes of God. People believed that when the earthly pilgrimage ended, they would awaken to find themselves in the presence of God.

Jesus frees us from this fear of death by gentle contempt, "Do not fear those who kill the body" (Luke 12:4), and also by his own brave facing of it. Our writer in verses 14–15 emphasizes that "through death" (his own death), Jesus destroyed the one who has the power of death, the devil, and delivered all those who through fear of death were subject to lifelong bondage. For the Christian, death does not mean separation from God but access to God. This assertion frees us from bondage to the fear of death.

In this lection Jesus has been introduced, his identity with the Father has been maintained, and his service to humankind has been outlined. The author has moved from the heavenly to the earthly. The author's assertion is that God's final word has been spoken through God's Son, who shared God's nature and was the agent of creation. Jesus, the great high priest of the universe, entered into the experience of humankind through his temptation, suffering, and death.

The preacher of this passage will want to note the assurance given at the end of verse 18: "He is able." *He is able* to help us in our moment of fierce temptation. *He is able* to save those who seek him (7:25). *He is able* to do far more for us than we would dare to pray for or think about (Eph. 3:20). *He is able* to keep us from spiritual collapse (Jude 24–25).

However great the pressures, these assurances should encourage us to deeper trust and renewed confidence in God's ability not only to see us through the troubles, but to make us more than conquerors over them (Rom. 8:37).

WILLIAM L. SELF

---

2. Arnold Toynbee, ed., *Man's Concern with Death* (New York: McGraw-Hill Book Co., 1968), 131.

Matthew 2:13-23

¹³Now after they had left, an angel of the Lord appeared to Joseph in a dream and said, "Get up, take the child and his mother, and flee to Egypt, and remain there until I tell you; for Herod is about to search for the child, to destroy him." ¹⁴Then Joseph got up, took the child and his mother by night, and went to Egypt, ¹⁵and remained there until the death of Herod. This was to fulfill what had been spoken by the Lord through the prophet, "Out of Egypt I have called my son."

¹⁶When Herod saw that he had been tricked by the wise men, he was infuriated, and he sent and killed all the children in and around Bethlehem who were two years old or under, according to the time that he had learned from the wise men. ¹⁷Then was fulfilled what had been spoken through the prophet Jeremiah:

Theological Perspective

This portion of Matthew's infancy narrative follows the departure of the magi to their own country. Preaching on this text signifies a departure from festival preaching and a return to the Sunday-by-Sunday unfolding of the gospel. The pericope falls into three sections, each dependent on a command that generates the activities of the following verses: an angel's command, a ruler's command, and again an angel's command. All sections conclude with a quote from Hebrew Scripture.

In order for the preacher to translate Matthew's words into an effective sermon, it is crucial to note two major textual facts: Matthew's overall theological intentions within the context of the entire Gospel and how these form his construction of individual episodes. For example, the narrative action of this text depicts a departure-return motif from Israel to Egypt. In turn this emphasizes the overall Matthean understanding of Jesus as the new Moses, the new and final lawgiver. The very didactic nature and arrangement of Matthew's Gospel underscore this fact.

Second, Matthew uses Hebrew Scripture to emphasize prophetic fulfillment. He does this with a Christian midrashic focus on the Hebrew Scriptures he quotes; in doing so, he employs the literary mechanism of typology. In these authorial moves

Pastoral Perspective

God's Protection in Uncertain Times. In the aftermath of the 2008 international economic meltdown, we can all agree that we are living in uncertain times. Not since the 1930s and the Great Depression have we seen such social and economic upheaval: massive layoffs and mounting unemployment, companies closing that we would have never dreamed would close, stock-market turmoil where many are losing money that it has taken years to accumulate, and with even more uncertainty ahead. In the midst of all this, families are having a hard time.

In an article in *USA Today,* mental health experts said the financial stress of these times is taking a toll on people and the family: "The struggling economy is hurting many Americans' mental health: anxiety, depression, sleep problems, and money-rooted marital conflicts." The article quoted Joy Browne, a psychologist in New York with a radio network talk show, who says that she "has been hearing from working class listeners who have been beset by layoffs and hair-trigger tempers at home." Even upper-middle-class people are taking a hit to their well-being. "They expected to retire and cannot," Browne said. "They're being asked to take care of their grandchildren's education. They have homes they cannot sell and they cannot travel." People are more agitated, anxious, and angry. Layoffs, job

18"A voice was heard in Ramah,
    wailing and loud lamentation,
    Rachel weeping for her children;
    she refused to be consoled, because they are no more."

¹⁹When Herod died, an angel of the Lord suddenly appeared in a dream to Joseph in Egypt and said, ²⁰"Get up, take the child and his mother, and go to the land of Israel, for those who were seeking the child's life are dead." ²¹Then Joseph got up, took the child and his mother, and went to the land of Israel. ²²But when he heard that Archelaus was ruling over Judea in place of his father Herod, he was afraid to go there. And after being warned in a dream, he went away to the district of Galilee. ²³There he made his home in a town called Nazareth, so that what had been spoken through the prophets might be fulfilled, "He will be called a Nazorean."

Exegetical Perspective

This Gospel lesson unfolds in three movements: (A) the flight to Egypt (vv. 13–15), (B) the slaughter of the infants (vv. 16–18), and (A′) the return from Egypt (vv. 19–23). It continues Matthew's evocation of Moses parallels, demonstrating the fulfillment of the Scriptures in the birth of Jesus. Five dreams propel the action (Matt. 1:20; 2:12, 13, 19, 22), as it was assumed that dreams were often means of revelation or divine guidance. Like his Old Testament namesake, Joseph is a dreamer.

God's warning to Joseph to flee from Judea raises problems of providence and theodicy. Why did God not warn the other parents in Bethlehem? Although the Gospel shows no sensitivity to the issue, the revelation is embedded in a specific and connected context apart from which others would presumably have had no opportunity to grasp it. Joseph knew that Jesus was the promised Messiah, and that the magi had asked Herod's court where the "king of the Jews" was to be born. No other parents in Bethlehem had the context for understanding the imminent danger.

Herod the Great (who ruled 37–4 BCE) was an Idumean, not a Jew, and was appointed by the Romans. He had to fight for several years (40–37 BCE) to take control of his kingdom, so he never felt secure. He maintained a private security force and built fortresses at Jerusalem, Sebaste, Caesarea,

Homiletical Perspective

Are the three dreams that Joseph has after the magi depart good dreams or bad? It is tempting to interpret the first dream as a good dream because an angel appears to Joseph with an urgent message. Even so, the dream is a nightmare: Herod is out to kill the newborn child, and he has the authority and the means to do it and, furthermore, to do it with impunity. That is a dream terrifying enough to make any human break into a cold sweat, to set the heart beating furiously, to constrict the breath, to make the whole body quiver with the question: will we escape in time?

The infant has just received extravagant gifts from exotic visitors. The meaning of his birth, the promise of his life seemed in that bright and shining moment so momentous, so filled with hope, and now this nightmare. Joseph moves from promise to terror with the dreaming of one dream.

The nightmare does not end when Joseph awakes. There is a frenzy of activity: stuffing together whatever they have, walking down the street and out the gate onto the main road to get to Egypt as fast as possible, the child crying, the mother exhausted, Joseph's heart clutching in his throat every time he sees a soldier. The nightmare does not end when they get to their place of refuge. It grows greater, spreading beyond Joseph and the new family, pervading the region they have left behind as the blood

Matthew 2:13-23

Theological Perspective

Matthew is less concerned with "how it happened" than with "what it means."

Why are the midrashic and typological elements important? Since parishioners hear Luke and Matthew's infancy narratives varying significantly in detail, it becomes important for the preacher to preach the larger questions of Matthew's theological intentions, rather than dwell only on the geography of the text. Matthew's midrashic fix on the cited prophetic materials reveals God's guiding purposes. The typological lens affords him more leeway to interpret Jesus in the context of Israel's past and future hopes than does the use of a tighter one-to-one set of correspondences as with allegory. Using Matthew's meta-approach enables the preacher to avoid the pitfalls of preaching this text literally, which often results in sentimentalizing and trivializing Matthew's theology.

This approach is well served if the preacher finds a way to focus on the following features of the text. First, the central feature is that God's actions initiate all human activity. This includes the sending of the angels, the actions of Joseph and his family, and the decisions of Herod and other agents of political unrest.

Second, Mathew's typology includes the elements of Jesus and Moses and the escape to and from Egypt with its evocation of the exodus (paradoxically making Jesus both redeemed and redeemer). It is clear that Matthew wanted his community to understand that God is functioning in the earliest events of Jesus' life to signify fulfillment of the prophets' words and redemption, regardless of the world's activities to the contrary.

With these larger textual matters in mind, how might these be brought into sermonic form? First, it is important to proceed with caution in utilizing the Hebrew Scripture references Matthew uses. Each is laden with a significant number of doctrinal interpretations and ambiguities. Matthew's scriptural citations have multiple possible references. In one instance (v. 23), it is unclear as to the source and meanings of the final prophetic quote, "He will be called a Nazorean." This could refer to the lineage of Jesus or to Jewish sect membership or have Greek language resonances resembling the name of the town of Nazareth (which is never mentioned in the Old Testament).

Several sermonic approaches are open to the preacher's work in terms of his or her own context. One suggested threefold framework based on the text's three sections can assist the preacher in

Pastoral Perspective

insecurity, college expenses, bills that cannot be paid: the article said sleep problems are soaring—"they lay awake at night and worry."[1]

These are uncertain times, but our text suggests that God provides protection in uncertain times. God demonstrates God's providential care in uncertain times. The loss of the "innocents" was an overwhelming cruelty, but we see a more hopeful vision in the way that God protected the Messiah child, and we can pray for God to protect each of us in uncertain times.

Matthew 2:13–23 is clear that God would act to protect the Messiah, God's Son, from the dangers of life in this world. Herod waited to hear from the magi, who had come from the East, following the star that announced the birth of the one born king of the Jews. He had instructed them that when they found the child, they should return and let him know, so that he could worship as well. In a dream, it was revealed to the magi that they should not go back to Herod but should return to their country by another route. When Herod realized that they had tricked him, he was angry, and in his jealous rage he gave orders that all the boys in Bethlehem and vicinity that were two years old and under were to be killed.

An angel of the Lord appeared to Joseph in a dream, instructed Joseph that Herod was seeking to kill the child, and that they were to go to Egypt and stay there until receiving further instructions. Egypt, under Roman control, was outside of Herod's jurisdiction, and the child would be safe there. Herod went forth with his diabolical plan, and the weeping of mothers was heard throughout Bethlehem. The grief was so large that the women refused to be comforted. One commentator suggests that despite the weeping of mothers, the blessing and hope was that the Messiah escaped, and because the Messiah escaped, eventually the people would be comforted. In the Messiah's escape, everyone, even mothers who lost their sons, would be comforted. The Messiah would reign one day, and there would be no such murder and violence.[2]

Some scholars argue that in several places this text is exegetically problematic. The main area of difficulty is with Matthew's mention in these verses that an act was to fulfill prophecy. There are four places where an act in the text is said to fulfill Old Testament prophecy. First, we are told that Jesus' birth in Bethlehem was a fulfillment of Scripture

---

1. *USA Today,* July 2, 2008, 1.
2. Robert H. Gundry, *Matthew: A Commentary on His Literary and Theological Art* (Grand Rapids: Eerdmans, 1981), 34–37.

Machaerus, the Herodium, Masada, and elsewhere so he would never be far from a defensible refuge. He killed descendants of the Hasmoneans so he would have no rival. When he suspected intrigue in his own family, he killed his wife Mariamne and one of his sons. Before he died he commanded that at his death political prisoners should be killed so that there would be mourning throughout the land. While there is no other record of the slaughter of the innocents at Bethlehem, it is nevertheless consistent with what we know about Herod. We do not know how many children were killed, but Bethlehem was a small village, so the number would not have been over twenty.

Herod died in 4 BCE, so Jesus was probably born about 6 BCE. The years of the Common Era were not calculated until 533 CE, when Dionysius Exiguus (Denis the Short) calculated the date of Jesus' birth from the founding of Rome; but he concluded that Herod died in 754 after the founding of Rome, when in fact he died in 750.

The flight to Egypt serves two purposes: it delivers the Christ child from Herod's wrath, and it sets up the recapitulation of the history of Israel with an exodus from Egypt (cf. Hos. 11:1). Two dreams finish the dream sequence in Matthew 1–2. First, Joseph is told that Herod has died, and the danger to his family is over, so they can return to the land of Israel. The concept of the land is so important that it is repeated in verses 20 and 21. When they return, however, they are told that Judea is under the rule of Archelaus, who is so brutal that he is later removed from power by the Romans—who were not usually intolerant of brutality!

In the final dream, Joseph is instructed to take the family to Galilee, which is ruled by Herod Antipas. So it is that they come to Nazareth and Jesus comes to be called a Nazorean. The Scripture is not quoted, but the reference in verse 23 appears to be a conflation of Isaiah 4:3 and Judges 16:17. The flight to Egypt therefore serves yet another function in the Gospel tradition: it explains how Jesus was born in Bethlehem and grew up in Nazareth. Alternatively, Luke reports that Joseph and Mary traveled to Bethlehem because of the census. So, whereas Matthew explains how the family from Bethlehem came to Nazareth, Luke explains how the family from Nazareth gave birth to a child in Bethlehem.

Matthew's account of the birth and infancy of Jesus is so grounded in historical events, real geographical locations, the history of Israel, and the fulfillment of Scripture that one cannot understand it apart from them. By weaving this rich tapestry of

of baby children darkens the earth, and their inconsolable mothers set the land echoing with "wailing and loud lamentation" (v. 18).

How swiftly and how far we have traveled from "gold, frankincense, and myrrh" to the homes drenched with the blood of children because a tyrant fears any potential challenge to his power and authority! The intense compression of Matthew's story, from the magi to the slaughter in eighteen brief verses, reveals the truth of the human situation. It shows us to be capable of a passionate desire to search for, to find, to adore, to lavish our gifts upon the gift of God, while with equal realism it portrays the massive weight of our intransigence to grace, not only in the human heart, but also in our systems of military and political power that repress our highest and holiest yearnings with brutal violence.

The next two dreams in the passage continue this oscillating pattern between hope and nightmare. The second dream is a dream of relief: Herod is dead, the tyrant out of the way, the immediate threat removed. The family can head home. Home! After dealing with a strange language and different food and customs and the ambiguous status of being refugees, if not illegal immigrants, they can go home, home to the food and the local talk and the neighborhoods that have become only more precious as they remembered them from far away.

No sooner do they arrive than the old nightmare returns. This time Joseph does not even have to dream it. Herod is gone, but Archelaus his son, a man who takes after his father's cruelty, is ruling over Judea. Perhaps because of his experience with Herod, Joseph is immediately on edge and "afraid to go there" (v. 22). His fear is confirmed by his third dream, so that he and the family head further north to Galilee. There will be no homecoming after all, no return to the old neighborhood.

According to Matthew then, Jesus starts his childhood as a refugee: fleeing from Judea to Egypt, then briefly from Egypt to Judea, and finally from Judea to Galilee. Jesus' early childhood gives witness to the truth that Matthew will later have Jesus summarize in his own words: "Foxes have holes, and birds of the air have nests; but the Son of Man has nowhere to lay his head" (Matt. 8:20). The infant Jesus has nowhere to lay his head from the day he is born. The Holy Family is a refugee family.

It is the custom in most homes and churches that set up manger scenes to take them down after Christmas and store them until the season returns the next year. Matthew's account of the Holy Family's

Matthew 2:13-23

Theological Perspective

working through the theological beauties and diffi-culties of this text: I. God's Call; II. God's Politics; III. God's Provision.

God's Call. Section one of the text, God's call, features the angel of the Lord directing Joseph and his family to life in a foreign land, one with many associations connected to the history of Israel. The preacher can enumerate these connections for the listeners as a prelude to the next two sections by exploring such motifs as the unexpected change of human plans when God calls; God as an escape artist (on a more poetic note); and the thematic role of the exodus in proving the identity of Jesus as the Messiah.

God's Politics. In section two, God's politics, a type of "meanwhile, back at the ranch" scene, returns to Israel and Herod's retaliatory actions. Herod's directive demonstrates his obsession with the now-departed magi and their astrological predictions. Here Matthew informs the reader retrospectively of what God's flight plans really mean for Joseph and his family. Jesus is sheltered by God from death itself. In Christian his-tory, this text is associated with the commemoration of the Holy Innocents. This is an area of theology that is difficult to negotiate, since it raises the question of why the innocent suffer. It bleakly points to the fact that the birth of the Messiah brings in its wake death and tragedy. The preacher may wish to focus on the reality that the world our Redeemer, the Messiah, comes to is one fallen and riddled with the violence and the actions and consequences of sin.

God's Provision. Section three, God's provision, finds Joseph and his family leaving the land of Egypt and returning to their home country, but not the locale of Bethlehem. The preacher can talk about God's hiding of Jesus in a remote area, one in which he will pass the next few decades before reappearing definitively on the public scene. The district of Galilee is God's provi-sion of a place and time of interlude, preparation, and shelter for the child Jesus. Since the Gospels tell us almost nothing of the years following this text before Jesus appears as an adult, the preacher can speak of the long-term nurture that God extends to Jesus, and the role of preparation in his life as he grows to adult-hood and his unfolding life as God's Messiah.

SUSAN HEDAHL

Pastoral Perspective

(2:5–6); second, Jesus' return from Egypt fulfills the Old Testament text that refers to the exodus (2:15); third, the weeping of the mothers of Bethlehem ful-fills Jeremiah's reference to Rachel weeping for her children in Rama; finally, Jesus' move to Nazareth ful-fills "what had been spoken through the prophets" even though no specific text is in mind (2:23). The scholarly commentary on the fulfillment of prophecy is voluminous, but Matthew is writing to a primarily Jewish audience and therefore labors to demonstrate that the unfolding events are connected to Old Testament prophecy. Old Testament prophecy is a warrant that legitimates the child who is the Messiah.

Despite wanting to kill the child, Herod died. Upon the death of Herod, the angel of the Lord appeared again, and Joseph was instructed to take the child home, because the one who wanted to take the child's life was dead. Joseph heard that Herod's son was reigning in place of Herod; therefore, according to another dream, he withdrew to Galilee and lived in a town called Nazareth. Nazareth was a despised place. Old Testament prophets foretold that the Messiah was to be despised (Pss. 22:6–8, 13; 69:8; Isa. 49:7; 53:2–3, 8; Dan. 9:26). The point is that God can protect the Messiah from hurt, harm, and dan-ger, from even the most despicable people in the most despised places.

The text alludes to God's protective care and power in uncertain times. As God protected the Messiah from the threat of death, so will God pro-vide protection in our times of job loss, bad news, falling stock prices, and unprecedented social and economic uncertainty. Faithfulness and trust in God will yield protective care. God will protect us in uncertain times and hide us in secret places. The Messiah was looked after, provided for, and placed in an environment where he could be nurtured and grow, even in the midst of dangerous and violent cir-cumstances. God will do the same for us.

FRANK A. THOMAS

Exegetical Perspective

allusions, Matthew effectively designates Jesus as the Son of God and the expected prophet like Moses (Deut. 18:15, 18) who will deliver Israel through a new exodus. There is nothing sentimental about Matthew's "Christmas story," however. It is set in the turbulence and terror of a violent history. Tyrants kill children, and families flee in middle of the night. No shepherds come to see the wonder, and no heavenly choir sings, "Glory to God in the highest, and peace on earth, goodwill" (Luke 2:14). Instead, there is a provident God over all who guides a devout and compassionate, dreaming and trusting father so that a child will be able to grow to become the Savior of his people and of generations to come.

Matthew therefore calls for all who observe Jesus' birth to renew their hope. Even if there are no apparent reasons to believe in a provident God, the birth and infancy, life and preaching, death and resurrection of Jesus are signs enough. At Jesus' birth, violent forces seek his life, just as violent forces had sought the life of Moses. The violent forces at his birth foreshadow the violence that will eventually lead to his crucifixion. Nevertheless, he is delivered from Herod's murderous intent, just as the people of God were delivered from Pharaoh. Even more so, Jesus will eventually be delivered from death itself. Matthew dares to see things as they are and still affirm that God is working, even in the worst that we can do. Let us declare the real joy of Christmas this year: nothing can defeat God's promise of Immanuel, God with us. Even when we cannot celebrate peace on earth, therefore, we can celebrate Immanuel, and hence the love of God and the promise of peace.

R. ALAN CULPEPPER

Homiletical Perspective

trials suggests that this is wrong. Perhaps we should put away the shepherds (Luke) because they returned to their fields, and put away the magi because they returned to their distant home, but we should keep out Jesus, Mary, and Joseph. Just the three of them, all alone, facing the terrors of a brutal despot. No visitors. No sheltering barn. No cuddly looking sheep. No friendly oxen. Then we should move the Holy Family to another location in our church or our home. Perhaps to a window looking out on the larger world, the world where there is still violence and repression and terror, and where there are refugees fleeing, needing protection, human beings in whom the Christ is crying to us for protection.

I imagine a sermon or even a sermon series on Jesus the refugee. Preachers could augment Matthew's account with stories from denominational communications about refugees, as well as material from online sites and the news. The sermon could incorporate the dismantling of the manger scene. As each group of characters departs, the congregation might sing a verse from an appropriate carol. Then the sermon would focus on the Holy Family and their perilous situation.

Finally, having reviewed Joseph's nightmares, the preacher might ask the congregation to imagine the dream they wish Joseph could have, the dream of a world where, instead of having to flee, the refugee family would find itself at last welcome and secure. Imagine what the Christmas carols would sound like if we brought that dream alive. How would "Silent Night, Holy Night" sound in our hearts if we had helped to create a world in which baby Jesus would never again be refugee Jesus?

THOMAS H. TROEGER

Sirach 24:1-12

[1]Wisdom praises herself,
   and tells of her glory in the midst of her people.
[2]In the assembly of the Most High she opens her mouth,
   and in the presence of his hosts she tells of her glory:
[3]"I came forth from the mouth of the Most High,
   and covered the earth like a mist.
[4]I dwelt in the highest heavens,
   and my throne was in a pillar of cloud.
[5]Alone I compassed the vault of heaven
   and traversed the depths of the abyss.
[6]Over waves of the sea, over all the earth,
   and over every people and nation I have held sway.
[7]Among all these I sought a resting place;
   in whose territory should I abide?

Theological Perspective

In this text from the Wisdom writer Jesus ben Sira, the Wisdom of God is named as female and speaks of herself in the first person. Wisdom tells her story of being sent by the Creator from the heavens to be housed in Zion. From her resting place on earth she describes her thriving in terms of stately, fragrant, and fruitful flora. She will share this abundance with all those who seek her and follow her teachings.

Theologians squabble over *how* to consider Wisdom female. Eileen Schuler in *The Women's Bible Commentary* reminds the reader that while Wisdom herself is highly honored, human women in the book of Sirach as a whole are not. She writes that the book as a whole "provide[s] some of the most positive as well as the most negative statements about women in the tradition."[1] For instance, just two chapters earlier Ben Sira advises his male pupils, "It is a disgrace to be the father of an undisciplined son, and the birth of a daughter is a loss" (Sir. 22:3). In the midst of this ambiguity interpreters committed to revealing the voices of women in Scripture use the gendered noun "Wisdom" as representative of a feminine attribute of God. Thus closely tied to the Father God is the female Wisdom, in Greek "Sophia."

---

1. Eileen Schuler, "The Apocrypha," in Carol Newsom and Sharon Ringe, eds., *The Women's Bible Commentary* (Louisville, KY: Westminster/John Knox Press, 1992), 237–38.

Pastoral Perspective

From an exegetical and theological perspective, one can see why this passage from Sirach is combined with the passage from the prologue to John's Gospel. Many scholars believe that the background for John's great claim that the Word was present at God's creation of the world can be found in Jewish Wisdom literature. In Sirach, Lady Wisdom sings a paean to herself and notes that she was present before the creation of the earth. Like John's divine Logos, she came forth from the mouth of God and held her sway over sea and dry land, heaven, earth and the abyss. Moreover, the climax of John's song, "The Word became flesh and tented among us" (John 1:14, my trans.), seems to echo Wisdom's song as well: "Then the Creator of all things gave me a command, and my Creator chose the place for my tent. He said, 'Make your dwelling place in Jacob, and in Israel receive your inheritance"(v. 8).

For Sirach, Wisdom is the transcendent majesty of God that becomes immanent in the world, and especially in Israel. For John, the Word is the transcendent majesty of God who becomes immanent in the world—and at first, at least, especially in Israel. To use traditional theological language, in Sirach, Wisdom is God's instrument both of creation and of redemption. In John, the Word is God's instrument of creation, and Jesus, the Word incarnate, is the instrument of redemption.

> ^{8}"Then the Creator of all things gave me a command,
>   and my Creator chose the place for my tent.
> He said, 'Make your dwelling in Jacob,
>   and in Israel receive your inheritance.'
> ^{9}Before the ages, in the beginning, he created me,
>   and for all the ages I shall not cease to be.
> ^{10}In the holy tent I ministered before him,
>   and so I was established in Zion.
> ^{11}Thus in the beloved city he gave me a resting place,
>   and in Jerusalem was my domain.
> ^{12}I took root in an honored people,
>   in the portion of the Lord, his heritage."

Exegetical Perspective

As one of only a few readings in the lectionary from what Protestants call the Apocrypha, this poem is obscure and unfamiliar to both pastors and laity. Worshipers in both church and synagogue should become familiar with it, however. Its sheer beauty and elegance alone commend it for public reading. The important place that the poem holds in the development of biblical thinking also deserves attention from the worshiping community. The way in which these verses prepare for certain christological affirmations in the New Testament presents a third reason for study and reflection. The lectionary committee cuts the reading of the poem in the middle. The remarks in this essay will concentrate on the verses assigned, but will take the full poem into consideration.

The poem presents a first-person speech by personified Wisdom herself. This technique interprets Wisdom as an active, intentional, relational entity rather than an abstraction. All of the sages of Israel wanted to portray wisdom in a winsome, attractive way, seeking to engage the reader in the pursuit of wisdom. Personification is an effective way to invite dialogue. Not only is wisdom an entity; it is a confident, assertive, vocal entity, sure of its position and importance. Wisdom "praises herself" (v. 1) in the midst of the heavenly host. This mythical element of

Homiletical Perspective

Today the Wisdom of Jesus Son of Sirach makes one of its rare appearances in the lectionary, as an alternative to Jeremiah 31:7–14. With the luminous prologue of John's Gospel also on the program, chances are slim that preachers will choose to focus on an apocryphal/deuterocanonical text; yet taken in concert with all of the other readings for the day, Sirach provides a pleasing alto line for the melody that unites them.

That theme is the praise of God, which emerges first in Sirach as Lady Wisdom's praise of herself. There is no false modesty in her prose. She is glorious, and she knows it. She also knows where both she and her glory come from. When the mouth of the Most High opened in the act of creation, she came out like a mist that covered the earth (v. 3).

This is beautifully tactile language that a preacher would be crazy to ignore. How does such a mist feel on the face? How does it smell, coming straight from the mouth of God? Seawater is one possibility; birth water is another. Here, as elsewhere, the evocative language of the biblical text challenges preachers to reach for language of their own that speaks to the body as well as to the mind.

While Wisdom says nothing here about being God's first work of art (as she does in Proverbs 8:22–30), the contrast between her misty genesis and

Sirach 24:1-12

Theological Perspective

Catholic theologian Elizabeth Johnson suggests that "Sophia is a female personification of God's own being in creative and saving involvement in the world. The chief reason for arriving at this interpretation is the functional equivalence between the deeds of Sophia and those of the biblical God." In keeping with Jewish monotheism, Wisdom represents "God's nearness to the world in such a way that divine transcendence is not compromised."[2] She, like God, is atemporal (created by God before time) and will endure, like God, for all time (v. 9). As a manifestation of God's power, Wisdom tells her followers in verses 22–23 that through her they will be saved from shame and sin, for she is Torah (v. 23).

What is at stake in this debate over Wisdom as woman in Wisdom literature like Sirach? For those concerned with the roles of women in society, remembering the works of women, often overlooked or underrepresented in Scripture, reminds readers and listeners alike that Miriam, Deborah, Esther, Mary, and Mary Magdalene, along with scores of others named and unnamed, have played important, often central, roles in promoting God's ongoing work in the world. Not only do women matter to God as agents of justice, liberation, and mercy, but God may manifest Godself in feminine form. If God chooses to send God's wisdom as female, then God comes near to us in the guise of a female.

This idea of the nature of God as containing a feminine aspect has implications for our understanding of the *imago Dei*. Though generally we are taught to understand that as human beings we are all created equally in the image of God, the history of Jewish and Christian thought has not always treated women as equal to men in their created state. Feminist theologians point out that women in their embodiment have been associated with "lesser" characteristics. For instance, whereas men have been associated with reason, making them more suited to leadership, women have been associated with passion and irrationality, making them in need of leadership. Women, beginning with Eve, have been associated with sinfulness and the power of seduction, to the point of being responsible for the fall of all humankind from the perfection of the Garden. Some scholars posit that this association of Eve, and from her all women, with sinfulness comes first in the book of Sirach, an association that does not occur in the Genesis account.[3]

Pastoral Perspective

Ephesians picks up the same themes of creation and redemption and applies them to the church. In the great hymn with which Ephesians begins, God has chosen God's faithful people in Christ, even before the world began. God redeems God's faithful people to live according to God's glory. The church is a microcosm of the cosmos—designed from before the beginning of time and destined in Christ for God's glory.

Almost certainly on this Second Sunday of Christmas the preacher will turn to John 1 as the central text for the sermon. However, in at least three ways Sirach can be combined with the texts from John and Ephesians to help shape our pastoral and ecclesial practice, perhaps especially in this Christmas season. For Sirach, the created world reflects God's Wisdom; for John, the world is made in the image of Christ; for Ephesians, the worship of the faithful on earth prefigures and represents the worship of the holy ones in heaven.

First, our worship on this Second Sunday of Christmas will partake in the worship of all creation. We will want to move beyond the cheery gratitude of a holiday season, to the blessed praise that the cosmos brings to God. Our music can capture something of that majesty. "Let All Mortal Flesh Keep Silence" and "Of the Father's Love Begotten" move us beyond the appropriate earthiness of "O Little Town of Bethlehem" and "Silent Night" to the equally appropriate grandeur of a universe joined in adoration.

Every Sunday our prayers acknowledge that God is our helper, but every Sunday—and perhaps especially this Sunday—we also remember that God is the Lord, the Lord, high and lifted up. If Christmas Eve services run the danger of nudging us toward theological coziness, Sirach (with John and Ephesians) recalls us to reverence and awe. Let our prayers reflect the faith that the baby we adored in the manger is not only a darling child but the Word and Wisdom that God used to map the universe, come to tent among, as God's glory tented in the tabernacle of old.

Second, we can rethink our church structures and organizations in the light of the theological insights provided by Sirach. Plenty of books tell us how ministry involves leadership, but not enough books suggest that in the church leadership is always profoundly pastoral, based in faith and moving toward obedience. Sirach, like John and Ephesians, suggests that the whole universe is structured according to a divine purpose. Whether we can see that purpose with unaided eye or not, the eye that sees the world in the light of Jesus Christ, incarnate Wisdom, can see in the

---

2. Elizabeth Johnson, *She Who Is: The Mystery of God in Feminist Theological Discourse* (New York: Crossroad, 1994), 91.
3. Alice Ogden Bellis, "Eve," in Carol Myers, Toni Craven, and Ross Kraemer, eds., *Women in Scripture* (Grand Rapids: Eerdmans, 2000), 82–83.

the heavenly host, the beings that surround and serve God, adds the security of the ancient to the poem. The poet, though writing in the second century BCE, reaches back to deep memories of a heaven filled with life. At a gathering of this heavenly host, Wisdom speaks up, praising herself for her influence and God's confidence in her.

After a brief introduction in verses 1–2, Wisdom begins her speech. Because the language of poetry is imprecise, the exact relationship between Wisdom and God is unclear. Wisdom proceeds from God, is an instrument of God for creation. By coming from the "mouth of the Most High" (v. 3), Wisdom identifies herself with both word and breath. Her relationship with the earth can be compared to a mist, which surrounds, pervades, and penetrates, providing nourishment and life. These mixed metaphors are powerful, but leave open the question of exactly how we should understand Wisdom, whether as a godlike creature or a hypostasis, or something else. Her influence has been comprehensive. She has encompassed time (v. 9), space (vv. 4–6a), and the human realm, including political divisions (v. 6b). From being a mist or a breath, Wisdom becomes a vagabond, seeking a place to dwell and perform her duties. At God's command, she chooses to dwell with Israel. These techniques present Wisdom as confident, pervasive, active, yet obedient to God.

Ben Sira, writing in the Second Temple period, was a man of impressive erudition. He wrote to encourage his Jewish readers to maintain integrity and piety in the face of creeping hellenization, the influence of Greek thought and philosophy. This poem shows that he does not disparage other nationalities or thought systems, but he considers the true source of wisdom to be the God revealed in the Scriptures of Israel. While acknowledging wisdom's influence on all people, he asserts that God chose Israel for a special relationship to wisdom (vv. 8–12). In that assertion, the poem ties together many strands of biblical thought. While maintaining the typical stance of the sage, that wisdom has a kind of universal quality, he nevertheless affirms Israel's special place in God's dealings with the world.

Later in the chapter, the author associates wisdom with both teaching and prophecy (vv. 32–33). He integrates the wisdom tradition into Israel's history and call to be a unique people, mediating God's presence to the world. Wisdom becomes a means for Israel to fulfill that calling. Because wisdom is universal (v. 6b), it serves as a common ground between Israel and other nations. That insight gives this poem a distinct

that of the mud creature Adam is striking. She does not even mention him, in fact. Perhaps this is because she was never earthbound the way human beings were. She shared God's perspective on things. When Wisdom looked at the world, she looked *down*; yet, for all the privilege of her position, something was missing.

Telling her own birth story, Wisdom says she lived in the sky for quite some time, enthroned in a pillar of cloud all by herself (v. 4). She went anywhere she wanted to go, from the highest heaven to the deepest abyss (v. 5). Oceans were no impediment for her; she traveled over waves as easily as she did over land. She held a universal passport, moving freely over every people and nation without being possessed by any of them (v. 6).

Wisdom is not bragging here, showing slides of her cosmic world tour. She logged all those miles because she was looking for something, she says. She was seeking a resting place on earth, a place to pitch her tent. As nice as it was to cover the earth like a mist, what Wisdom really wanted was a physical address.

So her Creator gave her not a suggestion but a command (v. 8)—that she make her dwelling in Jacob and receive her inheritance in Israel. Taking a moment to remember her genesis again (v. 9), Wisdom gave up the sky for the earth, accepting her God-given resting place in the beloved city of Jerusalem. She took root in a particular people, among whom she would grow tall as a cedar in Lebanon (v. 13).

The selection of this text for the Second Sunday of Christmas sets all kinds of harmonies in motion. There is first of all the obvious connection between the coming to earth of both God's Wisdom and God's Christ, sent to take root among the same honored people. Since in Matthew or Luke the baby Jesus does not have a lot to say about his own birth, the preacher may decide to borrow Lady Wisdom's narrative about her coming into being in order to say some touching things about incarnation.

With all the divine freedom in the world at her disposal, she longed for a resting place on earth. The mist envied the mud. The universal longed for the particular. Holding sway over every people and nation was not enough for Wisdom. She wanted to take root somewhere; she wanted to belong to someone.

When God granted her a "dwelling" in verse 8, the preacher has a natural connection to the Gospel reading for the day, where "the Word was made flesh, and dwelt among us" (John 1:14 KJV). A light touch remains important here, since pounding out such

Sirach 24:1-12

Theological Perspective

One result of the denigration of women's creation has been the determination by some sects of Judaism and some Christian denominations that women cannot be ordained as rabbis, priests, or clergy. They cannot represent God in those most obvious forms of leadership.

Thus considering the nature of God to include both masculine and feminine attributes suggests to some theologians that determining women to be lesser beings in their created state denigrates the very God in whose image we are all said to be made. Given that what we have in the book of Sirach is the groundwork for both negative and positive interpretations of females, it is up to the individual interpreter to decide how she or he will read 24:1–24.

Should we get "stuck" on questions of gender as we read this passage or as we do theology in general? In much of her work, theologian Sallie McFague reminds us that all language about God is metaphorical, that is, all language says something about what God is like, but language can never capture God. God is beyond human language, whether that language is traditional, as in "God the Father"; impersonal, as in Paul Tillich's "Ground of Being"; or feminized, as in Elizabeth Johnson's name for God, "She Who Is." None of these, nor any of the other multitude of names and signifiers for God, does justice to this greatest of mysteries. Thus "getting stuck" on any language for God gendered or not runs the risk of becoming idolatry, in which we mistake the metaphor for God Godself. In considering the language we choose for God, we should ask whether or not that language challenges us to think more broadly and deeply than we may have previously about the One who appears here as burning bush, there as whirlwind, and also through the voice of Wisdom who calls herself "she."

EMILY ASKEW

Pastoral Perspective

world itself the marks of God's providential purposes. For the faithful, according to the testimony of Sirach, John, and Ephesians, our own "wisdom," nourished in prayer, can actually catch glimpses of that divine wisdom toward which the whole creation moves.

What if we tried to reorganize our church structures, not according to the latest manuals on organizational theory, but according to prayerful consideration of the wise ways in which God seeks to shape the world? Paul tells the Corinthians that their worship and presumably their committees should be conducted in "decency and good order" (1 Cor. 14:40, my trans.). The order he has in mind is not the order by which corporations write their bylaws but the order by which God created the world at the beginning and creates it anew in Jesus Christ. Sirach says that Lady Wisdom took root in an honored people. By the mercy of Christ, God's wisdom can take root in our churches too, even in their structures and statutes.

Third, Sirach also provides a vision for the church's mission in our time, and any pastoral perspective requires attention to mission. Theological treatises sometimes suggest that we are supposed to choose between the priority of God as creator and the priority of God as redeemer. What Sirach reminds us is that what God sets out to redeem is the whole creation. Of course God's wisdom (like God's word) comes to comfort individual humans and to comfort humankind, but before the first one of our species breathed the very first human breath, God was moving the whole vast universe toward God's wise glory.

It may be appropriate to be wary of any theology that touts us humans as cocreators. God is too far beyond our ken for us to be cocreators any more than coredeemers. We have, however, discovered that we humans are pretty good as codestroyers. Fidelity to the God of Sirach, John, and Ephesians is fidelity to the God who created the universe for God's glory and not for our plaything. We are servants of that creative wisdom. As pastors we will bear witness to that.

DAVID L. BARTLETT

place in biblical thought. God offers instruction, prophecy, and wisdom to Israel, so that Israel can fulfill its special place in God's purpose for creation. That message was intended as an inspiration to the poem's first readers, and piques the interest of modern readers who seek to understand the role of the wisdom tradition in God's continuing work through the synagogue and the church. The Law and the Prophets are not that estranged from wisdom after all. The universal quest for wisdom can lead to the God who is revealed in the law and the prophets.

Several New Testament passages draw upon the ideas in this poem and Proverbs 8:22–31 for an interpretation of the Christ event. In these passages, wisdom is an instrument of creation. In this poem, wisdom stretches from the highest heaven to the abyss, a reference to the deepest part of creation. The reference to the "waves of the sea" indicates that wisdom reaches even the edges of the created world; no part is left uninfluenced by wisdom. The prologue to the Gospel of John (1:1–18) explicitly interprets the preexistent Christ (the Word) as an instrument in creation. Colossians 1:15–20 interprets the Christ event in similar terms, with Christ as a means of creation. Hebrews 1:2 makes a comparable interpretation. This poem in Sirach prepares the church for the idea of God using an instrument in the act of creation. The New Testament closely associates the preexistent Christ with the wisdom tradition of the Scriptures. The New Testament writers achieve a similar thing when they reach out to both Jewish and Gentile readers seeking an understanding of the Christ event. Christ is both the fulfillment of wisdom (for Jewish readers) and the creating, binding force of the universe (for Gentile readers). Christ then becomes a source of commonality among people, not a means of separation.

In the use of this passage in worship and proclamation, the preacher can affirm the special calling of God's people to mediate God's presence to the world. Two New Testament passages come to mind that develop (intentionally or not) the ideas in this magnificent poem. John 1:1–14 presents Christ as the means of creation that lived among us, similar to wisdom choosing Israel for her "tent." Ephesians 3:10 proclaims that God works through the church to make known to the universe the wisdom of God.

CHARLES L. AARON

parallels will not only give everyone a headache but also flatten glorious prose. Without putting Wisdom's words into God's mind or Jesus' mouth, the preacher may still be able to tell her story in a way that evokes rich reflection on what it means for heaven to come to earth.

With New Year's Day in view, another approach might be to stress the genesis theme apparent in the texts and context for the day. The readings from Sirach and John set up an especially lovely duet, in which it is not possible to speak of the genesis of Jesus without also speaking of the genesis of the world, the Word, and the Wisdom of God. This is a Sunday of divine origins, in which every new beginning begets another.

The reading from Ephesians supports the same theme, using words that offer aural links to both Sirach and John. God chooses the faithful "before the foundation of the world to be holy and blameless before him in love" (1:4).

The preacher who spends time humming each of these texts should be able to discover plenty of harmonies between them to lift the spirits of those in worship today. Genesis is not something that happened once, a long, long time ago. The Creator God goes on making all things new. Lady Wisdom still receives visitors to her tent. The Word who became flesh still comes to us in the flesh, giving all who welcome him ample reason for praise.

BARBARA BROWN TAYLOR

Wisdom of Solomon 10:15-21

¹⁵A holy people and blameless race
   wisdom delivered from a nation of oppressors.
¹⁶She entered the soul of a servant of the Lord,
   and withstood dread kings with wonders and signs.
¹⁷She gave to holy people the reward of their labors;
   she guided them along a marvelous way,
   and became a shelter to them by day,
   and a starry flame through the night.
¹⁸She brought them over the Red Sea,
   and led them through deep waters;
¹⁹but she drowned their enemies,
   and cast them up from the depth of the sea.
²⁰Therefore the righteous plundered the ungodly;
   they sang hymns, O Lord, to your holy name,
   and praised with one accord your defending hand;
²¹for wisdom opened the mouths of those who were mute,
   and made the tongues of infants speak clearly.

Theological Perspective

This seems like a strange lection for Protestants and even stranger as a reading for the Second Sunday of Christmas. Protestants have trouble even locating the book called the Wisdom of Solomon. (It is between the Additions to the Book of Esther and Sirach. Does that help?)

The primary theological interest of this book is the centrality and role of Woman Wisdom. In chapter 10 she appears as a partner of both God and humankind. It is difficult to discern whether she is goddess or superhuman. Arguing for goddess status are the ways in which she saved Adam after the fall—as well as Noah, Abraham, Lot, Jacob, Joseph—and in this passage Moses and the Israelites. In contrast to Sirach and Proverbs, this passage portrays her not as a past creation but as an eternal emanation from God. One might even understand Woman Wisdom as a dimension of YHWH.

She seems derivative from YHWH as well. To fill out the features of this complex being a bit, Wisdom is personified as a "woman," as one who has had a "course from the beginning of creation" (6:22); as having God as her origin and guide. Only if God sends her forth does one "obtain friendship with God" (7:14). Solomon desires to take her as his bride, and she is also described as God's throne companion. What is a theologian to make of all this?

Pastoral Perspective

When there is a Second Sunday after Christmas, it is inevitably the first Sunday in the new year. Coming at the end of a season of celebrative living, it might be accompanied by almost sincere resolutions to be less self-indulgent. The lectionary offers a rare opportunity to have two readings from the Apocrypha, each focusing on the Wisdom of God.

In both the Sirach lesson and the text from the Wisdom of Solomon, Wisdom is the agent of God's presence with Israel, especially in delivering Israel from slavery. "I dwelt in the highest heavens, and my throne was in a pillar of cloud," Wisdom says of herself, referring to the exodus (Sir. 24:4); and from Wisdom: "She brought them over the Red Sea, and led them through deep waters" (10:18).

In the Wisdom of Solomon, the book's namesake is a somewhat mystical figure. By attributing to her acts that in other places are attributed to the God of Sinai, Wisdom is identified as God. She is also identified as that agent *of* God that indwells the faithful. Referring to Moses, "She entered the soul of a servant of the Lord, and withstood dread kings with wonders and signs" (v. 16). For Christian preachers, Wisdom correlates directly with the Holy Spirit of the New Testament. The New Testament church discerned that the Holy Spirit is both God and *of* God. From the Apocrypha, the same seems to be true of Holy Wisdom.

Exegetical Perspective

This passage seeks to demonstrate the decisive importance of wisdom in the salvation history of Israel. The Jewish author of the Wisdom of Solomon composed his book in Greek late in the first century BCE in Alexandria, Egypt, the great center of Hellenistic culture. His goal was to strengthen the faith of the large Jewish community, which struggled to relate their religious beliefs, rooted in the Hebrew Bible, to the sophisticated philosophical heritage of the Greeks. The essential strategy of the book is to relate the Greek concept of wisdom (*sophia*), so important to the philosophers, to Hebrew wisdom (*hokmah*), which is fundamental to the thought of Proverbs, Ecclesiastes, Job, and such psalms as 73.

Hebrew wisdom sought to discern truth about life by means of critical reflection on human experience within the created world. In its conservative mode, as in the book of Proverbs, it collected and propounded practical behavioral guidelines deduced from the accumulated experience of the elders. Wisdom is the virtue that motivates one to heed those guidelines, and also names the virtue one acquires in the process. In its effort to convince the young reader that acquiring wisdom in fact aligns one with the basic fabric of reality, Proverbs provided the author of Wisdom of Solomon with his basic theological tool. In Proverbs 8:22–31, wisdom (which is feminine in Hebrew) is

Homiletical Perspective

The likelihood of most preachers preaching entirely on this text is small, although it is a poetic and provocative retelling of the exodus story. However, when used in a supporting role with the other lections, this reading can lend strength to the day's overarching theme: how the faithful respond with celebratory praise to God's providential salvation.

At least four different subthemes from this short lesson from the Wisdom of Solomon can be noted by the preacher.

First, as so often is the case, the cultural similarities between this ancient writing and our current day and age are striking. The writer was addressing Hellenistic Jews who were pious and loyal, well educated in the Greek and Hebrew languages and traditions, probably living in Egypt. Some had abandoned the faith of their foreparents and were attracted to the Greek culture. Others were faithful Jews who were perplexed in their time and needed encouragement. Perhaps still others were Gentiles, whom the writer wanted to introduce to Judaism's active God of history, who offers more than their mere imaginary idols.[1]

Preachers, whether heard in sanctuaries on Sunday mornings or over other media, often speak

---

1. Ernest G. Clarke, *The Wisdom of Solomon* (Cambridge: Cambridge University Press, 1973), 4–5.

Wisdom of Solomon 10:15-21

Theological Perspective

According to Sarah Tanzer in the *Women's Bible Commentary*, "Woman Wisdom receives a much more extended treatment in the Wisdom of Solomon than elsewhere."[1] In this tradition she has come forth from dwelling with God to associate with human beings. (One hears overtones of the incarnation in Jesus Christ, and some associations with Roman Catholic views of Mary.) She is present among all generations to those who seek her. Furthermore, she is associated with God's creative activity. (Are there overtones of the Spirit here, as was associated with creation in Jürgen Moltmann's *God in Creation*?)[2] She also teaches righteousness and offers deep counsel. Is Woman Wisdom part of the Trinity, a female dimension of the Trinity, a fourth member of the Godhead? She shares certain characteristics with Mary as well, since she is accessible to humans and can be looked to for wise counsel.

Perhaps the best theological resolution of the status of Woman Wisdom is that she represents elements in the Godhead that we have socially constructed as being feminine. Besides the textual evidence, this interpretation might be supported on the basis of the context in which the book was written. The author's audience was a group of Jewish people in Alexandria who were experiencing discrimination and at the same time wanted intellectual respectability by association with the dominant group's adherence to Stoic philosophy and the Hellenistic goddess Isis. The author intends to provide encouragement to those Jews undergoing suffering and oppression, and also to indicate some similarities to Stoic ideals and to the cult of Isis, who offered protection and counsel alongside her divine companion, Re, the sun god. Clearly the figure of YHWH differentiated Israelite religion from Egyptian, while the connection of Wisdom with Isis was a point of similarity. Furthermore, Woman Wisdom offered a special relationship to humankind (as did Isis). Is it too much to infer that the author was suggesting that God's providence will continue beyond that of Re and Isis?

In this chapter Woman Wisdom displaces YHWH as the one who protects, rescues, and sustains the righteous. It is *she* who offers salvation. Strongly associated with Moses and the exodus, she is presented as delivering the people from their terrible oppressors. She entered the soul of Moses, withstood the powerful kings, led the people through the wilderness, took them across the Red Sea, and

Pastoral Perspective

In our texts the depiction of Wisdom is not as feminine merely grammatically; she *is* female. For a congregation, speaking of a manifestation of God as female might be variously troubling or exciting. It is probably not a matter of indifference. In 1950, when Pope Pius XII declared the Assumption of Mary as dogma for Roman Catholics, the decidedly non-Catholic psychologist Carl Jung rejoiced that at last the feminine had been fully incorporated into the godhead.[1] Jung got the theology wrong—Mary is not God—but he was writing as a psychologist, and he startled his early readers. Jung could have found the same wisdom in the Pentateuch itself. From the opening chapter of Genesis, humanity cannot be complete without both male and female (Gen. 1:27). The implication is that God, in whose image humankind is made, is not complete without masculine and feminine. Our text from Wisdom carries that theme forward.

For many Christians, the idea of a feminine aspect to God is difficult to accept. For others, it is exactly the encouragement for which they hunger: the opportunity to be deeply engaged with biblical tradition while still embracing the fullness of human experience.

In both Wisdom and Sirach there is a lyrical beauty as "Wisdom praises herself, and tells of her glory in the midst of her people" (Sir. 24:1). We might wonder why the Wisdom of God was portrayed as female. How do we respond to such a depiction of God? A congregation that speaks comfortably of the Holy Spirit as "She" probably considers itself very avant-garde. The discomfort that church people can have about a feminine face to God is echoed in a similar unease about women clergy. Recently a consultant working with a pastor search committee spoke of the next hypothetical pastor as a "she." Parishioners immediately reacted, fearfully convinced that the bishop had already selected the candidate. There would have been no such reaction to a "he" reference.

A possible New Year's resolve: to listen with ears that are less selective, hearing beyond easy confirmation of that with which we are already comfortable. Perhaps the faithful can ask of the God who makes all things new that our own firmly grasped convictions might be refreshed by ancient feminine wisdom, just as Jesus' own understanding was deepened by a certain Syrophoenician woman (Matt.

1. *Women's Bible Commentary,* ed. Carol Newsom and Sharon Ringe (Louisville, KY: Westminster John Knox Press, 1998), 295.

2. Jürgen Moltmann, *God in Creation: A New Theology of Creation and the Spirit of God* (Minneapolis: Fortress Press, 1993).

1. Ann Belford Ulanov, *The Feminine in Jungian Psychology and in Christian Theology* (Evanston, IL: Northwestern University Press, 1971), 318f.

Exegetical Perspective

personified as a being that preexisted the world and was an intimate companion—and perhaps an instrument (cf. Prov. 3:19)—of YHWH at creation. If wisdom thus is not simply a name for a personal virtue, but also refers to an attribute or semipersonified agency of God, one could look for the operation of wisdom wherever the divine power seemed at work in Israel's history.

This is precisely what the writer of Wisdom does, especially beginning in chapter 10. Here he reviews the sacred history of the Hebrew Bible and identifies seven heroes, whose righteous behavior was pivotal to the progress of the story of salvation. It was wisdom (*Sophia*) that protected Adam (vv. 1–2), saved Noah (v. 4), sustained Abraham (v. 5), rescued Lot (v. 6–8), guided Jacob (vv. 9–12), and delivered Joseph to high office in Egypt office (v. 13–14). Then comes the climactic and lengthier description of the seventh hero, Moses, in verses 15–21, which is our lectionary text. Chapters 11–19 continue in a similar vein, demonstrating in great detail how *Sophia* was the key agent by which God led Israel through the exodus experience and in the desert wanderings.

The Pentateuch, probably in Greek translation, clearly is the author's source for his interpretative survey of Moses's life in verses 15–21. In the later chapters, the author is not reluctant to describe the spiritual failings of Israel in the desert, but in this brief synopsis he is content to label them "a holy people and blameless race" (v. 15). The term "blameless" is the adjective for Abraham in the Old Greek translation of Genesis 17:1. Verse 15 describes the deliverance from bondage in Egypt, and verse 16 refers to Moses's bold confrontation of Pharaoh and to the plagues. "Reward of their labors" in verse 17a must refer to the silver and gold objects that Israel took from the Egyptians when they fled (Exod. 12:35–36). "Marvelous" (v. 17b) refers to such miraculous events as the manna, quail, and water from the rock during the desert journey (Num. 11 and 20). In verse 17, *Sophia* itself is thought of as the pillar of cloud and fire that guided the Israelites in the desert (Exod. 13:21–22). The origin of the expression "starry flame" (v. 17d; literally, "stars of fire") for the pillar of fire is not known. When verse 19b says that wisdom "cast them up from the depth of the sea," it must be following the reference to "the Egyptians dead on the seashore" in Exodus 14:30. The Pentateuch narratives do not mention Israelites despoiling the corpses of the dead Egyptians. Verse 20a, "the righteous plundered the ungodly," may relate to a tradition deriving from the third-century-BCE Jewish writer Demetrius,

Homiletical Perspective

to such a variety of listeners. Naming the diversity they represent along the faith spectrum and claiming the relevance of God for them offer many preaching possibilities. Brian McLaren makes use of such different kinds of identities when he addresses his audience, "you may not be a Christian and wondering why anyone would want to be," or "you may not yet be a Christian, and you're thinking of becoming one," or "you may already be a Christian, struggling, questioning, and looking for reasons to stay in," or "you may have officially left the Christian community, but part of your heart is still there, and you wonder if you might someday return," or "you may be a Christian leader who has heard terms like *postmodern* and *missional*," or "you may be looking for dirt so you can write a hostile review," or "you may be new to the Christian way, and you're trying to learn the lay of the land."[2]

Preachers who identify and include all sorts of seekers, believers, and doubters stand a better chance of being heard. When they hear the preacher naming and normalizing their place along the faith trail, the listeners feel understood and accepted. This empathy with their situation can be a blessing for them, especially if they have felt harshly judged or even condemned by themselves or others in the past.

Second, this passage keeps the emphasis on God's ultimate mission for Christ. God in Moses brought liberation to the Israelites, and God in Christ brings liberation to us. The preacher can draw upon the philosophy of history that was begun within Wisdom literature and continues on into the first chapter of John, and the ability each passage has to bring reassurance and hope to people suffering from low morale or a shaky faith. The sermon could express the confidence we can have in God's saving power.

The writer uses concrete, well-known examples of how Wisdom has entered, enlivened, and guided the Israelites. A similar approach could be used effectively by the preacher; this is an opportunity to lay aside abstractions and speak about God's past, specific activity within the congregation or within the preacher's own life. How can we build confidence and trust in God if we lack anything worth testifying? Because Wisdom is characterized as a "lady," it would be appropriate to use a woman as an example of one who brings rescue and reward. We still live in a time when many congregations hear sermons with only men mentioned as worthy examples of faithfulness.

2. Brian D. McLaren, *A Generous Orthodoxy* (Grand Rapids: Zondervan, 2004), 19–21.

Wisdom of Solomon 10:15-21

Theological Perspective

despoiled their enemies. The implication is that she will continue to lead them.

Is this expansion of the role of Woman Wisdom a translation of the heritage, or is it a heretical interpretation, an acculturation or accommodation to a particular occasion? Perhaps her identification with YHWH will allow us to see Woman Wisdom as an expansion of just who God is. It is a way of seeing the Lord as existing beyond gender in all genders. Feminists have made a fair amount of theological capital of Sophia for reasons not dissimilar from our author's in writing to the Jews in Alexandria. I would argue that this expansion is entirely in keeping with the God and Father of our Lord Jesus Christ, born of Mary and clearly a feminist.

Finally, why include this reading in the middle of Christmastide? It seems a strange choice. The best I can make of it is the association of Jesus Christ the liberator with Moses, Wisdom, and the deliverance of the exodus. Out of Egypt God called his Son, just as Woman Wisdom led her slave people out of Egypt. The appeal to a woman as rescuer, intercessor, and counselor is very engaging. It is easy to see why the figure of Mary has been and continues to be an attractive one both to Roman Catholics and, belatedly, to Protestants.

Reinforcing this thesis is the place of Moses as the final of the seven righteous heroes mentioned in chapter 10, whom Sophia has providentially guided. Wisdom has saved those righteous ones, punished the unrighteous, and entered into God's saving history. Wisdom has elected special envoys or servants to do God's work. This way of working is less interventionist and seen more as the mediation of Wisdom. In some ways, we moderns connect with that mode of divine working more easily.

If Wisdom is associated with providence, protection, and covenant here, then she is related to the greatest of all acts of providence, even Jesus Christ. At Christmas we understand that the Divine has entered the world to dwell with human beings.

L. SHANNON JUNG

Pastoral Perspective

15:21–28). Rather than contenting ourselves with noble intentions about weight loss, perhaps we could resolve to analyze the way we think. What about our own thought patterns limits our ability to entertain new ideas, limits even our ability to recognize God outside of the preconceptions we have formed? How can these texts from Sirach and Wisdom nurture our own spiritual growth and our willingness to draw near to God through a richer array of images and metaphors?

Such a task is difficult. Although glass ceilings crack and shatter regularly in the worlds of commerce and politics, in the church the final barrier to acknowledging the feminine in God is still firmly in place, barely even chipped. Although there is ample precedent in Scripture for using feminine images for God, the church has held most steadily to masculine metaphors. It is as if the ceiling of the Sistine Chapel is a photograph of the Creator, replete with beard and all the other details of male anatomy.

While eagerly embracing new technology—learning how to program their Blackberries and iPods, applauding new treatments for old diseases—many adults have not seriously reconsidered their image of God since third-grade Sunday school. With this Wisdom text, the preacher has the opportunity to invite a congregation into a larger understanding of God, one that can push back the boundaries that we set around God.

The book of Wisdom was written between the end of the first century BCE and the beginning of the first century CE. It seems to have been composed in Egypt, probably in culturally sophisticated Alexandria.[2] The book encourages Jews to remain confident of God's presence even in a foreign and hostile environment. A twenty-first-century seeker, surrounded by a culture that gives no support to inward reflection and that often equates religious faith with a jingoistic patriotism, might need the same kind of encouragement. The Second Sunday after Christmas, the beginning of a new year, is a good and holy time to open our eyes to new understandings of ourselves and even of God.

MARTIN G. TOWNSEND

2. Michael Coogan, ed., *The New Oxford Annotated Bible, NRSV with the Apocrypha*, 3rd ed. (New York: Oxford University Press, 2001), 70 (Apocrypha).

Exegetical Perspective

who deduced that the Israelites must have stripped weapons from the dead Egyptian soldiers.[1] The allusion to singing hymns and praising in verse 20 clearly is based on the singing by Moses and the Israelites and Miriam in Exodus 15, but the specific description of doing so "with one accord," and the opening of the mouths of the mute and infants in verse 21 has no counterpart in the Exodus text. The writer here is making interpretative expansions, drawing on unrelated passages such as Isaiah 35:6. A similar interpretation can be found in the Palestinian Talmud and in *Targum Yerušalmi* to Exodus 15, but it is not known whether they drew on the Wisdom of Solomon or all are drawing from an earlier oral tradition. Philo also adds imaginative details about the singing in Exodus 15.[2]

This passage illustrates the conviction of the author of Wisdom of Solomon that what pagan Greek culture knew and valued as *Sophia* was in fact a form, albeit a very diluted one, of the wisdom of YHWH spoken of in the Hebrew Scriptures. It is evident here that wisdom has become virtually a synonym for the person of God. Our author's main hope was that this would strengthen his readers' orientation to the primacy of the Hebrew Scriptures and the theology found there, without forcing them to jettison altogether the idea of *Sophia*, which bore so many cultural attractions. He worked creatively within a tension experienced often by the religious community. On the one hand, only rigorous loyalty to the authority of the canonical tradition will sustain the identity of those called to faith in the God of the Bible. On the other hand, that same canonical tradition understands God to be the creator of the whole world and, via the instrumentality of such things as wisdom, the author of all good that develops within the world.

ROBERT J. OWENS

Homiletical Perspective

For instance, extolling the ministry of a certain woman within the community or one's own life would be meaningful. Like Wisdom, she should personify the gifts of determination, steadfastness, and compassion. There is no need for her to be Mother Teresa or Mary the mother of Jesus, two idealized female saints who so often are referred to in sermons. The preacher would do well to choose women who are within the reach of the listeners' present-day situations.

A third focus could be on praise as a faith practice throughout history. Today's lections abound with hymns. Praises to God's holy name occurred as soon as the Israelites crossed safely onto dry land, when the Israelites returned from bondage in Babylon, and continued on to Paul's singing a doxology to the Ephesians for the gospel salvation.

Despite the evidences of praise throughout the Scriptures, many churchgoers miss the important role of praise in either the liturgy or their own lives. Wisdom yearns to awaken our silenced voices as she "opened the mouths of those who were mute" (v. 21) to sing out, celebrating God's victory over all that would defeat us.

Ironically, it may be that Christmas carols are the best known, most sung of all church music, even though their theological messages are so often watered down and weak. In a church season when there is an inherent temptation to stay sentimentally stuck in Bethlehem, the preacher could choose to reflect upon how our worship music can, but ought not, become dumbed down. Today's readings challenge us to move from focusing on the infant in the manger to the deeper meaning of the incarnation and on toward Epiphany, when the church will celebrate the many ways in which Christ's true nature is revealed in his ministry. Any carols or hymns sung in this season need to be incarnational and true to Jesus. One suggestion of such a hymn might be "I Am For You," by John Bell and Graham Maule to the tune Incarnation.[3]

DEAN MCDONALD

---

1. David Winston, *The Wisdom of Solomon*, Anchor Bible 43 (Garden City, NY: Doubleday, 1979), 221–22. This is found also in the first-century Jewish historian Josephus, *Jewish Antiquities*, 2.16.6.
2. *On the Contemplative Life* 187; *On the Life of Moses* 1:180.

3. *Church Hymnary Full Music*, 4th ed. (Norwich, UK: Canterbury Press Norwich, 2006), 317.

Ephesians 1:3-14

³Blessed be the God and Father of our Lord Jesus Christ, who has blessed us in Christ with every spiritual blessing in the heavenly places, ⁴just as he chose us in Christ before the foundation of the world to be holy and blameless before him in love. ⁵He destined us for adoption as his children through Jesus Christ, according to the good pleasure of his will, ⁶to the praise of his glorious grace that he freely bestowed on us in the Beloved. ⁷In him we have redemption through his blood, the forgiveness of our trespasses, according to the riches of his grace ⁸that he lavished on us. With all wisdom and insight ⁹he has made known to us the mystery of his will, according to his good pleasure that he set forth in Christ, ¹⁰as a plan for the fullness of time, to gather up all things in him, things in heaven and things on earth. ¹¹In Christ we have also obtained an inheritance, having been destined according to the purpose of him who accomplishes all things according to his counsel and will, ¹²so that we, who were the first to set our hope on Christ, might live for the praise of his glory. ¹³In him you also, when you had heard the word of truth, the gospel of your salvation, and had believed in him, were marked with the seal of the promised Holy Spirit; ¹⁴this is the pledge of our inheritance toward redemption as God's own people, to the praise of his glory.

Theological Perspective

Called by God in Community. What does it mean to live in Jesus Christ? More exactly, what does it mean fully to participate in the life of God in Christ? For many, the days after the triumphal celebration of Christ's birth bring both excitement and apprehension. The birth of Jesus Christ affirms the ways in which God has entered into human history and now resides with believers in the power and presence of the Holy Spirit. Adoption, acceptance, redemption, forgiveness, wisdom, inheritance, grace, and love are all hallmarks of Christian living.

The overarching message in the Epistle to the Ephesians is that God in Christ has brought about a final consummation and unity of all creation in Christ. The nature of this unity, as the passage points out, is not grounded in human power and intellectual capacities. Its source is beyond human comprehension or abilities. It resides solely in the wisdom and life of God. It is God who brings about this reconciliation that occurs in creation, particularly between God and humanity. Through the wisdom and power of God, believers are now called to the chief end of love and to proclaim "the praise of his glory."[1] We as believers are able to have confidence in

1. Judith Gundry-Volf, in *The New Interpreter's Bible* (Nashville: Abingdon Press, 2002), 10:610.

Pastoral Perspective

There is something exciting about the Second Sunday after Christmas—in part because it doesn't happen every year, in part because it seems so countercultural. The secular trappings of the "holiday season" have faded away, the Christmas trees of many are already lying by the side of the road, extended family members have returned to their homes, and many have returned to work and school. Liturgically, we are still in the Twelve Days of Christmas—coming to the end of the season, sure, but still very much in the thick of it. The years when we *do* get to celebrate a Second Sunday after Christmas, we are given an opportunity to delve more deeply into the mystery of the incarnation, to ponder and to relish the vastness of the gift that is ours in Christ.

In these opening verses of Ephesians we are taken far from the narrative of the nativity, and beyond the cosmic comfort of the "God with us" aspects of the incarnation. In these verses it is as if the camera lens is backing up and lifting up, until now we are high above the earth, high above the galaxy even, and now we can see that in Christ we have been given a part in God's eternal plan, and we are swept up in a hymn of praise to the glory and the wonder of it all.

The language of the hymn is grand and exhilarating, and the punctuation underscores our elation.

Exegetical Perspective

A Christological Benediction (vv. 3–7). This letter begins with a typical Pauline greeting: "Paul, an apostle of Christ Jesus by the will of God, to the saints who are in Ephesus." Some scholars have concluded that this letter may have been written by a disciple of Paul and intended as an encyclical epistle. Perhaps it was a cover letter to be circulated with an early collection of Paul's letters. Ephesians does read like a "treasury" of Paul's familiar themes and phrases, and a few examples occur in this passage. The interpreter of this letter may wish to consider the authorship of this letter; this exegetical study assumes that Ephesians was written by one of Paul's disciples.

Ordinarily Paul's letters begin with a greeting followed by a prayer of thanksgiving for the recipients of the letter. The author of Ephesians eventually does offer such a prayer (vv. 15–23), but not until after several christological observations (vv. 3–14). After the greeting and before the prayer of thanksgiving, there is a traditional Jewish benediction with a christological twist. "Blessed be the God and Father of our Lord Jesus Christ, who has blessed us . . . in the heavenly places" (v. 3). As the benediction continues, the author has pushed Paul's notion of election in a temporal direction: God has "blessed us in Christ . . . just as he chose us in him before the foundation of the world" (vv. 3–4; see Rom. 8:29, 33; 9:5, 7; 11:28).

Homiletical Perspective

Nothing packs up and leaves town quicker than the Christmas spirit. On this Second Sunday after Christmas we begin to ask ourselves, Why? Why the tinsel and bells, why the presents and parties? There must be more. Yes, there is much more. God is beginning (or has begun) to make clear to us the divine purpose in the world, the plan of the ages and how we are a part of it. God has not left us alone to our own devices, nor are we left without meaning and direction for our lives. We are here for more than our own comfort and pleasure. We are a part of God's great enterprise of redemption, reconciliation, and the healing of God's broken world.

To this end Paul breaks out in an exultant doxology of praise of God, the Father of our Lord Jesus Christ, his beloved Son. He also notes that spiritual benefits are placed at the disposal of the church and these benefits exist in heavenly places. Christ and his people are one, and this causes him to praise God.

In preaching this text, the preacher has an opportunity to call the church (that now lives in Christ) to see its place in the scheme of things. We are chosen by God, redeemed by Christ, and sealed by the Holy Spirit. As the incarnation was the beginning on God's part, we now see that it includes us, the church, and our focus for ministry. This purpose is no longer hidden. It is to bring the entire universe—heaven and

Ephesians 1:3-14

Theological Perspective

living for Christ, not because of our earthly achievements, but because of the "mighty acts of God in Christ (1:19–2:7). The theme "in Christ" or "in Jesus Christ" appears regularly throughout the epistle, a reminder that what distinguished the work of Jesus Christ in the world was that Jesus was empowered by God. In fact, it was God at one with Jesus, fully divine as God incarnate, that gave Jesus the power to liberate the hearts, minds, and bodies of men and women throughout the generations.

To live in Jesus Christ also means to recognize that we do not walk alone. The Christian life is intelligible only within the context of Christian community, or what many would describe as the church. Whatever your ecclesiological position, this particular epistle makes clear that the church (those gathered as one in Jesus Christ) is indispensible in living responsibly and faithfully in Jesus Christ. What is the church? Indeed, all Christians must struggle with their theology of the church. However, when it comes to living out one's calling in Christ, the church takes on a particular meaning as the source of comfort, shared identity with the other, mutual sharing, and a means of understanding the nature of the Christian message in the world.

Christian living challenges many of the rugged individualistic assumptions of modern culture. It confronts the notion that we are independent, autonomous persons and that success depends on being able to live independently from others. To the contrary, the epistle maintains that it is through the church and Christian community that we ultimately recognize what it means to live in Jesus Christ. The idea of reconciliation, then, becomes a prominent theme throughout the letter—reconciliation with God and others. Hence, the church is indeed Christ's "body, the fullness of him who fills all in all" (1:23). The three-dimensional relationality of church/Christ/humanity is advanced as mystical and archetypal bridal connection. The love and profound sense of unity symbolized in a wedding offers a glimpse into the unity made possible between God and humanity through Jesus Christ.

God is now introduced to humanity as the God and Father of our Lord Jesus Christ. The prominence of "Father" as a metaphor for God in Scripture points to the significance of God's desire to relate to human beings in the most intimate way. The relationship of God to Jesus Christ serves as a preview of humanity's access to God the Father.

In the ancient world of first-century Palestine, the idea or belief in God was nothing new. Deities and

Pastoral Perspective

Like a child telling of an exciting adventure, Ephesians 1:3–14 can be written as one long sentence, each phrase as enthusiastic as the one before it. In Christ we are blessed with "*every* spiritual blessing" (v. 3). In Christ we have been chosen "before the foundation of the world" (v. 4). In Christ, we have a "destiny" that is born of God's "good pleasure" (v. 5). God's grace is "glorious," and it is "lavished" upon us (vv. 6, 8). Not with *some* wisdom and insight, but with *all* wisdom and insight, God has made known the mystery of God's will, and God has chosen to make it known to us in Christ Jesus.

This is exciting stuff, and we are a part of it! We have been chosen by God to be part of God's revelation. We have been chosen from before time to be part of gathering all things in heaven and on earth into Christ. What an honor, what a joy! These verses from Ephesians help us to step back from the stuff of the Christmas season here on earth and to view it all from a cosmic distance. God's coming among us in Christ and our coming to faith in Christ are part of a great plan. We are part of it, wherever we are, whatever we are doing. It is the destiny of those who believe.

Exciting as this is, though, it can feel harsh to those who do not believe, or to those who are uneasy about a relative few being an elite, predestined "elect." Indeed, the text can be used to justify a certain separation and exclusivity, but there is a clear expression of unity and universality in the text: that which has been given to the first *few* is meant for *all*. Those who already believe are blessed. They also are called to engage in a great ingathering of all things and of all people into the big tent of the household of God. Those who believe are those who are already able to see God's plan for all to be united with God through Christ. They also are those who are called to hold up a vision of unity, of oneness with God and with one another. This call goes with the territory of faith. Just how that happens is the work of other texts, other seasons. For this season, in this text, we simply revel in the glory and the grace that we have been given and that God intends for all.

Those who have faith have been made children of God, through adoption by God, in Christ. The presence of households of adoption among us can serve to remind us of the joy and wonder of this grace, this love, extended by God to us all. Out of unlikely and unforeseen circumstances comes a human household. Out of unlikely circumstances, foreseen only by God, comes the household of God.

Two phrases of the text stand out as a lens through which to see the rest of it: "the good

The followers of Christ were part of God's plan from the beginning.

Using a Pauline metaphor, our author understands that this community has been "destined" (*proorisas*, v. 5; see Rom. 8:29) for "adoption" (*huiothesia*, v. 5; see Rom. 8:15, 23; 9:4; Gal. 4:5). Here he has broadened a traditional Jewish understanding of this term (Rom. 9:4) to include both Jews and Gentiles.

In verse 7, our author makes a thematic shift. He describes what the community gains from its divine adoption: redemption, forgiveness, and grace—an interesting combination of Pauline ("redemption" [Rom. 3:24; 8:23; 1 Cor. 1:30]), non-Pauline ("forgiveness" [found mainly in Luke–Acts and Hebrews]), and ubiquitously Christian ("grace" [scattered throughout the New Testament]) terms. Our author does not dwell on these traditional Christian concepts, but simply notes them in passing. He seems in a hurry to get to his next important point.

A Mystery Revealed (vv. 8–12). In his letters to the churches at Corinth and Rome, Paul had teased his reader by using the term "mystery" (*mysterion*). The apostle declared that he was a steward of God's mysteries (1 Cor. 4:1), a mystery that God decreed before the ages (1 Cor. 2:7, NRSV "secret"), a mystery that has to do with Gentiles becoming part of God's chosen people (Rom. 11:25), a mystery that has been kept secret (*sesigēmenou*: fr. *sigaō*, "be silent")[1] and is now revealed (*apokalypsin*) (Rom. 16:25–26). While Paul offers hints about the mystery, he leaves it to his disciples (the authors of Ephesians and Colossians) to make this an "open secret." Unlike the gnostics, who guarded secret teachings and revealed them only to an inner circle of true believers, the author of Ephesians revels in revealing the content of this mystery—he uses the term "mystery" six times in this letter.

We must jump ahead into the body of Ephesians for a description of the mystery, and then come back to this passage to complete our understanding of the mystery. Our author clearly comprehends Paul's apocalyptic message: "it has now been revealed [*apekalyphthē*] . . . [that] Gentiles have become fellow heirs, the same body, partners in the promise in Christ Jesus through the gospel" (3:5–6, my trans.). Our lectionary passage pushes this notion to its limits. Not only are Jews and Gentiles embraced by God, but "when the times [*kairōn*, pl.] have come to an

earth—into unity in Christ. The promise is that people will respond to apostolic preaching and teaching. If the church sees its mission as any less than this, the church is not fulfilling its purpose in this world and not measuring up to the sacrifice of Jesus or moving on God's agenda.

This is why we were chosen before the foundation of the world. Here we confront the mystery of divine election, which is a wonder and mystery that calls us to praise. We are held and protected by God, not clutched by capricious fate. Christians have a moral authority to confirm their call and election. God's election is an expression of God's love. God's plan is to sum up all things in Christ. This means for each individual Christian there is no satisfaction or meaning for our lives unless we are doing what we were chosen by God to do. We have no meaning apart from this calling by God. It is imperative for the preacher to point this out clearly in sermons. The individual search for satisfaction is futile unless it results in being united with other Christians who are bringing God's unity into the world. God's plan is to sum up all things in Christ.

Our lives are not our own; to the extent that we seek to make them our own, we are out of step with God's eternal purpose, design, and calling. The Holy Spirit has sealed them and marked them as God's own. The preacher would do well to remind the congregation that, because of this, we do not use God to make our lives richer, healthier, happier, or more prosperous. Rather, we are used by God to heal the sickness, mend the brokenness, and reconcile the estranged. This is our vocation, our calling, even though we may have another way of making a living.

The preacher must lift the congregation to a larger purpose than their comfort. At the beginning of a new year and on the eve of the Epiphany season, this passage demands that we ask the question, how big is our God? Then let Paul answer it by responding that God is big enough to choose us, use us, and protect us.

This is a call for the people of God not to lose their way but to keep the main thing the main thing. This is also a reminder for the parish minister to be more than the private chaplain whose only purpose is to soothe the hurts of life. If this is all the pastor does, the church will never achieve God's purpose. The preacher must catch the vision of the larger purpose of God and show how the local congregation fits into it. This is the key to congregational renewal . . . not the style of worship, organization, or preaching . . . but an understanding of why they are together

---

1. On the theological importance of *sigē*, "silence," see Ignatius of Antioch (early second century), *To the Ephesians*, esp. chapters 15, 19.

Ephesians 1:3-14

Theological Perspective

talk of deities have existed since the dawn of human history. However, in this case the uniqueness of God the Father, according to the epistle, is the relationship God bears to Jesus Christ. That God revealed God's self in Jesus Christ as the God of love, grace, forgiveness, redemption, healing, justice, unity in God's self (monotheism), and thanksgiving is what set apart belief in the God of Jesus Christ from all others. God disclosed God's self in human history through Jesus Christ and has extended the invitation to others to participate in the life of God the Father as well.

Because of this, God meets us, even confronts us, in human history amid our daily lives. God moves and acts, but God also judges, and thus has the capacity to save and redeem.[2] As Blaise Pascal once observed, the God of Christianity is "a God of love and consolation, a God who fills the souls and hearts of his own, a God who makes them feel their inward wretchedness, and his infinite mercy, who unites himself to their inmost spirit, filling it with humanity and joy, with confidence and love, rendering them incapable of any end other than himself."[3]

In the end, perhaps the greatest expression of Christian belief is to sound "the praise of his glorious grace" (v. 6). There is something incredibly important about celebrating the ways in which Christ redeems our reality, creates new spaces of meaning, and establishes alternative paths toward hope, healing, and community. Understanding our lives as believers as members of a grand, historic, and holy community is essential to what it means to flourish and thrive in all of life. Affirming the ways in which human life is interconnected and interwoven into a tapestry of multiple differences and otherness provides a liberating view of God and what God is ultimately doing in the world. Second Corinthians 5:19–20 captures the essence of God's vision of interrelatedness when it says, "God was in Christ reconciling the world to God's self, not counting our trespasses but making us ambassadors of reconciliation" (my trans.).

JOHNNY B. HILL

Pastoral Perspective

pleasure of his will" (v. 5) and "the mystery of his will" (v. 9). The first phrase reminds us that everything that is, grew out of an expression of God's pleasure before all time. Everything that is to come when time is full, will reflect that pleasure once again. This is especially true of human beings. Human beings were created in God's image; it is for human beings that God became incarnate in Jesus.

The phrase "the mystery of his will" reminds us that much about the glory and the grace we have been given is beyond our understanding; it is part of God's mystery. It is a mystery how Christ's blood serves as means for our redemption. It is a mystery that Christ's sacrifice makes possible God's forgiveness once for all. It is a mystery that God "chose us in Christ before the foundation of the world" (v. 4). It is a mystery that we have been adopted by God in Christ, and now have been given an inheritance of redemption. We cannot understand it all.

Out of the good pleasure and the mystery of God's will, those who believe have been adopted and called. We have been called as God's children to participate in the great ingathering, to make known by word and example the forgiving, healing, and unifying love that is ours in Christ to all the world. This message is the gift of the Second Sunday of Christmas.

LISA G. FISCHBECK

---

2. Ibid., 614.
3. *The Thoughts of Blaise Pascal*, trans. M. Auguste Molinier (London: George Bell & Sons, 1890), 93.

end, God will gather up [*anakaphalaiōsasthai*][2] everything in Christ—all things in heaven and on the earth" (1:10, my trans.; also see 1 Cor. 15:24–28).

In verses 11–12 the author summarizes almost as a litany[3] what the community has gained by being "in Christ"—inheritance and a destiny, hope and a goal—to "live for the praise of his glory." This is a subtle reminder that while the end is at hand, God has not yet called time. We still have everyday lives to lead while anticipating the end.

The Down Payment (vv. 13–14). Our author reminds his readers that when they "heard the word of truth . . . [and] believed in him, [they] were marked with the seal of the promised Holy Spirit" (v. 13). He describes what this seal indicates. It is, first of all, a mark of ownership, but also the trademark that an artist might give to her creation—a potter's initials on the bottom of a bowl. In a mixing of metaphors, our author closes this passage with such disparate terms as "pledge," "inheritance," and "redemption." The author may have had "marked with the seal" (v. 13) in mind as he attempted to bring together two different ways of describing our life in Christ. "Redemption" indicates that we have been on loan, but God knows God's own marked property and, when the time comes, will claim us. "Pledge of our inheritance" suggests that we need not worry about the future. Those who have been adopted into the family of God have already received a down payment (a marked receipt) toward their full inheritance. They can be confident that they will receive the remainder of the inheritance when God calls time at the end of history. While Jews and Gentiles are the beneficiaries of the mystery of God's grace, this is not the ultimate goal of God's grace. The absolute end is God's glory (*doxa*, v. 14).

PAUL WALASKAY

and what they must do. This is why the church has been called out and sealed by the Holy Spirit for the task. John Wesley was right when he reminded his people that the world was his parish, and so it must be ours if we would live. However, if the parish is our world, we will die or, at best, slump into uselessness.

During the potato famine in Ireland, the government organized the unemployed into work details to build some much-needed roads. The workers did their work in a very unsatisfactory fashion and with little enthusiasm until the government supervisors drew them aside and showed them clearly how the roads would be used and the benefits to the villages along the route. They were to be a part of the process of economic survival for Ireland. After this, the work improved, because it now had meaning. No one wants to build roads to nowhere, not even a church.

Christ died to bring all the discordant elements in this universe into one: to heal the separations, to reconcile each of us to our neighbors and to our God. God's instrument of reconciliation was Jesus Christ. A sermon, or a series of sermons, on this text would renew the people of God, clarify their purpose, and refocus them for their mission. Think of it: there is no area of human society outside the scope of God's redemptive work, and no hostile force in heaven or hell that can frustrate God's eternal plan.

WILLIAM L. SELF

---

2. Paul uses this term in Rom. 13:9, though not in the theological sense of the author of Ephesians. Irenaeus develops the theme of recapitulation, *anakephalaiōsis*, into a comprehensive Christology (cf. *Against Heresies*, in *Ante-Nicene Fathers*, ed. Alexander Roberts and James Donaldson, 10 vols. (Buffalo: The Christian Literature Publishing Co., 1885–96), 3.18, 19; 5.14, 19, 21).

3. Scholars have seen in these verses hymnic features (Robert J. Karris, *A Symphony of New Testament Hymns* [Collegeville, MN: Liturgical Press, 1996]). The very earliest christological formulae may have been preserved in hymns to and about Christ (e.g., Phil. 2:5–11), and Ephesians is full of such christological material (1:20–23; 2:11–22; 4:7–16).

John 1:(1-9) 10-18

[1]In the beginning was the Word, and the Word was with God, and the Word was God. [2]He was in the beginning with God. [3]All things came into being through him, and without him not one thing came into being. What has come into being [4]in him was life, and the life was the light of all people. [5]The light shines in the darkness, and the darkness did not overcome it.

[6]There was a man sent from God, whose name was John. [7]He came as a witness to testify to the light, so that all might believe through him. [8]He himself was not the light, but he came to testify to the light. [9]The true light, which enlightens everyone, was coming into the world.

[10]He was in the world, and the world came into being through him; yet the world did not know him. [11]He came to what was his own, and his own people

Theological Perspective

Many people describe the Gospels as having only two birth narratives, those of Matthew and Luke. This Johannine text, however, presents a birth narrative unique for the ways in which it speaks in poetic language about God, creation, Word, light and darkness, and Jesus Christ. Unlike the Matthean and Lukan narratives, John reworks the categories of time, space, and matter to mean something quite different from the specific geographical and human realities of the other Gospel accounts. Preaching the Johannine birth narrative offers listeners a very different way to consider the doctrine of the incarnation.

Otherwise termed the prologue, these eighteen verses contain more than enough material to provide the preacher ample theological resources. Precisely because of the rich density of the linguistic, structural, and theological contents of these verses, the preacher will find it necessary to make several key sermonic decisions. The organizational key to preaching the theology of these verses is inextricably bound up in the structure of the text. Most sources agree that this is a form of hymn to Jesus Christ, with some verses interspersed that explain the role of John the Baptizer. While commentators disagree about the poem's precise structure, it offers materials that help the listener reflect on the existence, nature, works, and presence of "the Word." By following the

Pastoral Perspective

God Moved into the Neighborhood. The first eighteen verses of the book of John form the prologue and contain the themes of the entire Gospel: the divine Savior has come into the world and has been rejected by many, but to all who believe he has given the power to become children of God and the gift of eternal life. If the prologue is the summary statement of the entire Gospel, then one verse culminates and sums up the entire prologue: "And the Word became flesh and lived among us, and we have seen his glory, the glory as of a father's only son, full of grace and truth" (v. 14). Eugene Peterson, in his contemporary rendering of the Bible, *The Message*, has given us an alternative version of the text:

> The Word was made flesh and blood and moved into the neighborhood. We saw the glory with our own eyes, the one-of-a-kind glory, like Father, like Son, generous inside and out, true from start to finish.[1]

I love this rendering of this text because of the choice of the word "neighborhood." The Word was made flesh and blood and moved into the neighborhood. Neighborhood reminds me of the place where I grew up and the people with whom I grew up. I

1. Eugene H. Peterson, *The Message: The Bible in Contemporary Language* (Colorado Springs, CO: NavPress, 2002), 1916.

did not accept him. [12]But to all who received him, who believed in his name, he gave power to become children of God, [13]who were born, not of blood or of the will of the flesh or of the will of man, but of God.

[14]And the Word became flesh and lived among us, and we have seen his glory, the glory as of a father's only son, full of grace and truth. [15](John testified to him and cried out, "This was he of whom I said, 'He who comes after me ranks ahead of me because he was before me.'") [16]From his fullness we have all received, grace upon grace. [17]The law indeed was given through Moses; grace and truth came through Jesus Christ. [18]No one has ever seen God. It is God the only Son, who is close to the Father's heart, who has made him known.

Exegetical Perspective

The prologue to the Gospel of John is as daunting as it is profound. Familiar as it is, it defies our best efforts to interpret it, much less to preach it. John alone among the Gospels opens with a hymnic statement, and John alone interprets Jesus as the incarnation of the preexistent Logos. In context, the prologue is the initial exposition that renders intelligible the Gospel's account of Jesus' words and actions. As readers we know who Jesus is, while in scene after scene those around Jesus struggle to understand who he is.

Typically the prologue is divided into five stanzas: the Word and God (vv. 1–2), the Word and creation (vv. 3–5), the Word and John (vv. 6–8), the Word and the world (vv. 9–13), and the Word and the community (vv. 14–18). If the prologue is based on an ancient hymn, at least the references to John (vv. 6–8, 15) and possibly verses 12b, 13, and 17 were added later. The prologue can also be understood as a chiastic structure that turns on verse 12c: "he gave power to become children of God."

The Logos, like the divine Wisdom (Prov. 8:22–36), was the agent of creation. God's Word was later revealed at Sinai, and some speculated that the Torah had been preexistent with God. For other hymns to Wisdom, see Sirach 24 and Wisdom of Solomon 10. As the Logos, Jesus is the one in whom the creative power of God is still at work. Hence, he

Homiletical Perspective

In his painting "Holy Family," Rembrandt (1606–1669) portrays the nativity as if it were an event taking place in the seventeenth century. The attire and furnishings are what one would find in a typical Dutch home from Rembrandt's own day. Mary is seated with an opened, well-thumbed book, presumably the Scriptures, held open by her left hand. Her right hand, on the top of a rocking cradle, has pulled aside a covering to reveal a soundly sleeping Jesus. Mary's head is turned from the book to gaze upon the infant. Immediately behind her and in much fainter light is Joseph, bending over and planing a piece of wood. Above him we see in the upper left corner young cherubim hovering with outstretched wings.

Whether or not Rembrandt intended it, the painting is an icon of different ways to encounter and understand the word of God. On the one hand, there is the Bible, the book that Mary has been reading as Jesus sleeps and Joseph works in the background. The Word of God is to be found in the Scriptures. We read the words and find we are addressed by the Word of God. We read them again and again. That is why the book is well thumbed. Rembrandt pictures Mary as one who knows well the word of God and who ponders it in her heart.

She does not ponder the page alone. She also ponders the infant beside her, "the Word made

John 1:(1-9) 10-18

Theological Perspective

poem's structure, the preacher can enable listeners to grasp the powerful affirmations of these verses.

1. God and the Word (vv. 1, 2).[1] As with all parts of the hymn, the primary subject is the reality of "the Word." Each section contributes a perspective on the Word. Here, the first three words assert not only the Word's presence with God, but the Word as participant from the very beginning. What is meant by "the beginning" in verse 1? The hymn is not speaking of the earthly birth of Jesus, but ties the implied presence of Jesus Christ to God and as God from all eternity. This claim to the preexistence of Jesus Christ is breathtaking in its scope and dramatically widens the listeners' understanding of the more familiar Matthean and Lukan birth narratives.

2. God's Word in the Created Order (vv. 3–5). Several assertions are made here. First, everything that is created originates in this Word of life. Apart from the Word, nothing has an existence: life outside of God is a contradiction in terms! Furthermore, creation is not simply a matter of form, but is filled with the animating reality of *God's* life. This life is known by the particular characteristic of "light." The life of God displays itself obviously to all people. It cannot be "darkness," since that would contradict the nature of God's Word and remain unknown. These verses describe the operative quality of the Word in the world as that which creates life, offers the capacity to respond to and recognize God's Word, which is light and therefore salvation.

3. An Explanatory Aside (vv. 6–9). The hymnic flow of the first five verses is interrupted—or, more likely, interpreted more clearly—in these verses. Here the person of John the Baptizer is introduced as one who witnesses to the light. Verse 8 is emphatic in making sure the listeners know that John, despite his powers and work, is *not* the Christ, but is "a witness . . . to testify to the light." The preacher can note the crucial importance of human witness to God's relentless gift of the creative Word in the context of these verses in two ways. First, human beings, such as John, can recognize God's life; second, they have a role in proclaiming its presence. John's witness names the characteristic of God's life-giving presence as "true light," a theme that certainly continues into the Gospel itself.

Pastoral Perspective

remember the street corner where we played baseball that had four sewer covers; one sewer cover was first base, another second, another third, and the final one home. I ran around those bases thousands of times, dreaming that I was a professional baseball player. I remember the playground, where what seemed like millions of kids played basketball, Ping-Pong, pool, volleyball, dodgeball, and tons of games. I remember block parties, where all the neighbors would sit out on the front lawns with the streets blocked off, and all day we would just have food, games, and fun together. I remember the girl across the street. That's what I think of when I hear, "The Word was made flesh and moved into the neighborhood." The Word was made flesh and moved into my south-side neighborhood.

Such a thought is amazing because Jesus was the Word—the Logos. Logos ordinarily refers to the spoken word, with emphasis on meaning conveyed, and not just sound. The meaning conveyed is the Word, the expression of personality, authority, and action in communication—the Word.[2] God spoke the Word: "God said, 'Let there be light'; and there was light" (Gen. 1:3). The world was created through the Word of God. The psalmist attests: "By the word of the LORD the heavens were made, and all their host by the breath of [God's] mouth. [God] gathered the waters of the sea as in a bottle; [God] put the deeps in storehouses. . . . For [God] spoke, and it came to be; [God] commanded, and it stood firm" (Ps. 33:6, 7, 9). The Word of God, the expression of God, has creative power and called the universe into being. The Word is the source of all that is visible and antedates the totality of the material world. This Word, this cosmic Word, was made flesh and blood and moved into the neighborhood.

When Peterson says that the Word was made flesh and moved into the neighborhood, I hear that the Word moved into *my* neighborhood. The Word was made flesh and moved next door in my neighborhood. My neighborhood was not very affluent— lower-middle-class working people trying to pay the bills and raise their kids. There was not much money in my neighborhood, and it was not fit for the cosmic Word of God, but Jesus moved into my neighborhood anyway. The beauty of this text is that Jesus moves into every neighborhood: from barrio street corners to Gold Coast condos, from ghetto projects to suburban mansions, from the streets of

---

1. Raymond E. Brown, in *The Gospel according to John (i–xii)* (Garden City, NY: Doubleday & Co., 1966) lists a variety of structural approaches.

2. Frank E. Gaebelein, ed., *The Expositor's Bible Commentary*, Regency Reference Library (Grand Rapids: Zondervan, 1981), 9:28.

changes water to wine, walks on water, opens the eyes of a man born blind, and raises the dead. Because he was "with God" and "was God" (John 1:1), Jesus and the Father were one (John 10:30; cf. 14:28). In John, therefore, he would not pray, "Not my will, but thine."

The Logos is the one in whom there is life. In the Gospel of John, eternal life is distinct from the promise of resurrection, in that it characterizes the present experience of those in whom the risen Lord abides (11:25–57; 14:23). Eternal life is living in the fellowship of God: "that they may know you, the only true God, and Jesus Christ whom you have sent" (17:3). Consequently, those who believe have already crossed from death into life (5:24).

John (the Baptist) is a witness to Jesus. In contrast to the other Gospels, this Gospel says nothing about the Baptist's preaching on repentance. John proclaims Jesus as the light (1:6–8) and the one who came after him but was before him (1:15). John also bears witness to the coming of the Spirit upon Jesus (1:32) and declares that Jesus is the bridegroom, whereas he, John, is only the "friend of the bridegroom" (3:27–30). John did no signs, but everything he said about Jesus was true (10:40–41).

The Gospel of John affirms both that the true light enlightens every person (1:9) and that no one "comes to the Father" except through Jesus (14:6). The foundational irony of the Gospel is that the Logos came to his own people and they did not accept him. The whole structure of the prologue turns on verse 12. Jesus brought a new status for those who received him: "he gave authority to become children of God" (my trans.). Like Nicodemus, they would not be born of the will of the flesh; they would be born from above (3:3, 5). As children of God they drink living water and eat the bread of life. Through his death, Jesus would gather the children of God who had been scattered (11:52). They hear his voice and have life. They are known by their love for one another, and their vocation includes fishing (21:1–14), feeding the sheep (21:15–19), and bearing a true witness (21:20–25).

The mystery of the good news is that the Logos became flesh in Jesus and "pitched his tent" (1:14, NRSV "lived") among us. As children of God we can join the first to follow Jesus in saying, "we have seen his glory" (1:14). That glory was the mark of Jesus' true identity, but it was not immediately evident to that first generation (2:22; 12:16). The prologue declares not what the first disciples saw and heard, but what they later came to understand. Jesus' words

flesh," rather than the Word made paper and ink. The Word is a blood-warmed, breath-enlivened creature sleeping beside his mother.

When Mary returns to her reading, she will understand what she reads at a greater depth because she has encountered the Word through the Word made flesh. When she tends to the child, she will understand the child at a greater depth because she has encountered the Word through the words in the book. Back and forth between Word made flesh and Word through words: this is the dialectic suggested by Rembrandt's painting. It is a helpful image for preaching on the prologue to the Gospel of John (John 1:1–18) on the Second Sunday of Christmas. The prologue, as beautiful and profound as it is, can seem to some believers rather abstract and bookish after the celebration of the beloved nativity narratives of Matthew and Luke. The stories of angels and shepherds, of a couple in a barn with a newborn babe, of exotic travelers with extravagant gifts, go right to the heart. They awaken our capacity for wonder and delight.

Compared to the nativity stories, John's opening words, as magnificent as they are, have a more distant, reflective, intellectual ring to them. Instead of "a child wrapped in bands of cloth and lying in a manger" (Luke 2:12), John sets off echoes that go all the way back to creation: "In the beginning was the Word, and the Word was with God, and the Word was God" (John 1:1). If we had only the prologue to John and no nativity narratives, we would have no Christmas pageants, no Christmas carols, but what a loss it would be if we lacked John's splendid hymnlike poetry. What Matthew and Luke portray in homelier human terms, John gives us in grander theological declarations: "All things came into being through him, and without him not one thing came into being. . . . And the Word became flesh and lived among us, and we have seen his glory, the glory as of a father's only son, full of grace and truth" (John 1:3a and 14).

I can imagine a sermon that would begin with a description of Rembrandt's painting and that would develop the idea of the necessary dialogue between Mary's studying the Bible and studying the child, the Word made flesh. Like Mary, we come to understand the Word more and more fully as we oscillate between the book and the child, between the Word through words and the Word made flesh.

Since this is the Second Sunday in Christmas and New Year's Day is upon us, I can imagine a sermon that would build to a theological resolution for the

John 1:(1-9) 10-18

Theological Perspective

4. God's Light in the Human Community (vv. 10–13). There is a poignancy about this section. These verses, at the hymns' midpoint, honestly describe the world's responses to the coming of the true light. The sad truth is that the world "did not know him" and even "his own people" failed to recognize him. Here the preacher needs to consider how the "true light" can be either rejected or unrecognized. What compels such human responses to God's light-filled Word historically, personally, spiritually? Each of these dimensions can be explored in describing the rejection Jesus experienced.

Verse 12 describes how recognition unfolds: first, those who receive the Word affirm that through belief they receive the power of kinship and become "children of God." This is a dramatic description of the consequences of belief in Christ the Word of God. A new set of relationships is established, revolutionary in that it has nothing to do with kinship, human choice, or physical birth. God becomes the parent in response to those who believe. Belief in Jesus Christ serves as the catalyst for a new birth for each of us!

5. Presence and Witness (vv. 14, 15). Verse 15 reinforces verse 14. The preacher moves from the abstract language of praise to the pivotal verse, describing God in the flesh. God has come to our home (the Greek describes God as pitching a tent) in Jesus Christ. What do we witness to as a result? We understand God as human, among us as a parent and the center of all that is meaningful.

6. Benefits of the Presence of Life and Light (vv. 16–18). This final section offers the proclaimer the opportunity to enumerate the various aspects of God's grace toward believers. Believers are given grace (more than they can manage!), God's completion of the law in Jesus Christ (v. 17 reiterates v. 14's language), and the gift of vision. This vision allows us through Christ to see into the "Father's heart." To proclaim this text is to speak of the grand opening of a passionate love story. God comes intimately into creation from beyond time to offer in the flesh, and in words as well, the very gift of life!

SUSAN HEDAHL

Pastoral Perspective

South Central to the affluence of Palm Springs, from war-torn Africa to the extravagance of Dubai. The Word, Jesus, dwells with us all, in all of our neighborhoods.

When the Word moved in, he had a kind of glory that we all could see—a one-of-a-kind glory like God. Peterson says that "We saw the glory with our own eyes, the one-of-a-kind glory, like Father, like Son, generous inside and out, true from start to finish." God's glory in Jesus had two aspects:

—"Generous inside and out": Generous from the center of himself, not trying to impress anyone or curry political favors. Not generous for what he could get, but generous for what he could give. Jesus did not appear to be generous on the outside, but inside was another reality. There is no difference between inside and out. The Word did the right thing for the right reason because he was generous inside and out.

—"True from start to finish": True is the adjectival form of the word "truth." The Word is the truth and has integrity, honesty, and wholeness. Jesus lives in fidelity, good faith, honor, and sincerity. The Word has no break, impurity, or alloy. The Word is complete and undivided. The Word is true from beginning to end, from start to finish. The Word is a great neighbor.

The most beautiful part of this text, what impresses me the most about God, is God's love. Some people are impressed by the power of almighty God, that God could bring something out of nothing in creation. Others are impressed by the omniscience of God, the fact that God knows everything at the same time. I am most impressed with the love of God, because it is love that brings God to the neighborhood. Love and compassion bring God next door. It is this love that gives me great joy as I celebrate that the Word moved into my neighborhood and yours.

FRANK A. THOMAS

Exegetical Perspective

and signs revealed his true identity for those who would believe, but some loved the darkness instead (3:19–21). Jesus' glory was that of the unique Son of the Father. As the Son, Jesus was fully like the Father, full of grace and truth, which still distinguish those in whom his Spirit dwells. He carried to completion the work of Moses, who gave us the law, because "grace and truth came through Jesus" (1:17). Jesus' work as the "unique God" was to reveal the Father, which required not only his works and words but also his death and resurrection.

Interestingly, however, the death and resurrection of Jesus are not mentioned in the prologue. It is all about Jesus' identity, his incarnation of the Logos, and his mission to reveal the Father and empower those who believe in him as the children of God. Just as we sing our theology in hymns and gospel songs, so John gathered the key elements of his faith in this hymnic prologue.

It is worth pondering what it took to reveal God to humanity. It took creation—light and life. It took a human person—to the mystery of God Jesus gave a human face. It took the witness of another who could see Jesus' true identity. It took a sojourn of shared life—he "lived" among us—and the response of faith from those who perceived Jesus' true identity. It took a worshiping community to study Scripture, remember, and be led by the Spirit. It took the conferring of grace and truth. It resulted in a new status—a new relationship for those who could be called "children of God."

R. ALAN CULPEPPER

Homiletical Perspective

coming year: namely, to develop a richer, fuller faith by tending both to the Word through words and to the Word made flesh, the Christ who is with us in sacraments, with us in prayer, with us in our church, with us in our friends, with us in the stranger, and with us in creation, since "all things came into being through him, and without him not one thing came into being" (John 1:3).

George Herbert's life (1593–1633) overlapped with Rembrandt's (1606–1669). Although the poet and the painter may never have met or even known of each other's work, it is revealing to consider Rembrandt's painting in light of some lines from Herbert that resonate with John's prologue:

> We say amiss,
> This or that is:
> Thy word is all, if we could spell.[1]

How do we "spell" the Word? Drawing on the fullness of the Gospel witness, using both the nativity stories and John's prologue, we "spell" the word through stories and through eloquent theological declarations, through narrative and through hard thinking, through language and through the Word made flesh. We spell it in multiple ways.

Here in a carol that can be sung to a setting in short meter is yet another way to spell it:

> How do you spell the word?
> Where do you search and look—
> amidst the coos and cries you've heard
> or in a well-thumbed book?

> Hold back the swift reply,
> the pious, worn cliché
> that softens how the child will die
> when violence has its way.

> Instead, let all you do
> embody truth and grace,
> and you will spell the word anew
> in every time and place.[2]

THOMAS H. TROEGER

1. From George Herbert, "The Flower," in *English Poetry of the XVII Century*, selected and ed. Roberta Florence Brinkley (New York: W.W. Norton, 1936), 274.
2. Thomas H. Troeger, from a forthcoming collection of hymns and poems from Oxford University Press. Used by permission.

Isaiah 60:1-6

¹Arise, shine; for your light has come,
  and the glory of the LORD has risen upon you.
²For darkness shall cover the earth,
  and thick darkness the peoples;
 but the LORD will arise upon you,
  and his glory will appear over you.
³Nations shall come to your light,
  and kings to the brightness of your dawn.

⁴Lift up your eyes and look around;
  they all gather together, they come to you;

Theological Perspective

The call of the prophet Isaiah in this passage is spoken to encourage a dispirited people to see God's transformative light coming just over the horizon and to imagine that when that light breaks over Zion, the city will be radiant, filled with the glory of God. Metaphorically light is the power of God to break through the increasing despair of those who had returned from exile to a world that Second Isaiah promised would be verdant but that in reality was marked by poverty and famine. In this world, the author of Third Isaiah offers a vision of what will be—an apocalyptic vision in which abundance and honor will replace poverty and shame. Not only will all nations honor the restored Zion, but the light of God that the city reflects will attract the abundance of the natural world.

Hope for the future in this text not only comes through the final appearance of the divine light but begins with the prophet's encouraging vision. He invites this weary people to stand in the imagined future in which suffering will end and honor will be restored. By way of a faithful, theological imagination, the writer of Third Isaiah prepares his people to see God's light by envisioning it with them. His voice in this text prepares the way for God's light by helping his people reorient themselves toward a better future, a time when light will begin to appear over

Pastoral Perspective

One of the great gifts of Scripture is that it enables the church to stand within a biblical text and view the world through its lens. Through scriptural language and imagery, we can witness the difficult dance of divine promise and fulfillment between God and God's people from creation to the present day. This not only provides us with a history and an identity; it also creates space for hope amid our current struggles. Both individuals and communities who serve God experience the shadow of life's complexity and pain bearing down upon the light of the gospel. For the church, the joy of the experience of God's love can fade as it is buffeted both by the sins of the world and by discord and brokenness within communities of faith. Isaiah 60:1–7 casts an eschatological vision of the church that offers us the promise that one day all will be united in the glory of God.

The prophecies of Isaiah take various forms. In turn, they cajole and promise or threaten and condemn. In today's text, Isaiah simply calls for the people of God to arise and look at the glory of God drawing the world to Zion. This instruction is intimately connected to the completion of the work God has set before the Jews when they returned from exile. Though God commanded Israel to rebuild the temple upon returning home, this task foundered upon the shoals of political and social

your sons shall come from far away,
 and your daughters shall be carried on their nurses' arms.
⁵Then you shall see and be radiant;
 your heart shall thrill and rejoice,
because the abundance of the sea shall be brought to you,
 the wealth of the nations shall come to you.
⁶A multitude of camels shall cover you,
 the young camels of Midian and Ephah;
 all those from Sheba shall come.
They shall bring gold and frankincense,
 and shall proclaim the praise of the LORD.

Exegetical Perspective

The wise preacher will see more in this passage than simply background to the Matthew pericope for Epiphany. This text should not be shortchanged. Even the lectionary committee cuts the reading off in midthought. In its own right, the passage is a beautiful affirmation of God's favor and the significance of Israel's mission to the world.

These verses are part of a longer oracle of salvation that runs at least until the end of the chapter. All of chapters 60–62 are words of salvation to the weary people of Judah. Within the block of material assigned by scholars to Third Isaiah (chaps. 56–66), these words of salvation join oracles of judgment, confession, and intercession, among the diverse genres of this part of the book. Oracles of salvation are prophetic proclamations of God's favor, often in response to guilt or despair. Verses later in the oracle (see v. 10) acknowledge that the people have experienced God's wrath. That time is over, and God's favor has returned.

Because chapters 60–62 resemble the oracles of salvation in Second Isaiah (chaps. 40–55), scholars have debated whether these are misplaced oracles from the earlier prophet. Although they may have been written by Second Isaiah and placed here by an editor for theological reasons, they may also have been written by the earlier prophet's disciple, influenced by his

Homiletical Perspective

The feast of the Epiphany falls on the twelfth day after Christmas, closing one season of the church year and opening another. In countries where the Orthodox Church is strong (such as Ethiopia), Epiphany can be a bigger day on the calendar than Christmas—but since it often falls on a weekday, most U.S. Christians miss this principal feast day altogether. Preachers unfamiliar with the rich theological history of Epiphany and the local customs attached to its celebration around the world can look forward to doing some research on those subjects before settling down to the lections appointed for the day.

Anyone present in worship lately is bound to hear bells go off while listening to today's passage from Isaiah. "Arise, shine; for your light has come," the prophet announces in verse 1, "and the glory of the LORD has risen upon you." Here is an echo of Isaiah 9:2, read in some congregations during an Advent service of lessons and carols and in others on Christmas Day. Even those who miss that association may perk up at the mention of gold and frankincense in verse 6, a reference they will hear repeated in Matthew's story of the magi.

Christians trained to read Isaiah as a prophet of Jesus may assume that the "you" in today's passage is the child whom the magi have come to adore. This child has been the focus of attention for weeks now,

Isaiah 60:1-6

Theological Perspective

the horizon once more. By virtue of his prophetic vision, the way of hope is begun—a hope to be finally fulfilled by God. Without the prophet's preparation, the forlorn might not be able to live expectantly for God's new dawn.

We do not speak often enough about the power of theological imagination in the work of hope. Theological imagination is not frivolous fantasy. Rather, it is marked by the courage, the faith, and the wisdom to imagine and call forward the world God desires us to make—a world in which the light of God radiates through us as individuals and as a nation. The work of the prophet/preacher is not to paint impossible pictures for others, because these will surely fail. Rather, her task is to be the first voice to crack through the paralysis of despair, loneliness, selfishness, greed, and all other limiting conditions, to break open in us a place for God's light. She is the one to announce, "Arise and shine, for your light has come." In the case of the Epiphany, hope is prepared for by the word of the prophet calling his people to stand and face a different future. Theological imagination is a tool of the prophet, the preacher, and the teacher willing to address her people in their suffering and to help them open themselves to God's light.

We may also read the transformative light in this passage as a reminder of the deep bonds between Creator and creation. The light of the Epiphany shines as the hours of sunlight begin to increase and the dark winter days release us into the promise of spring's new life. Rays of hope for spiritual and physical renewal can be read together here. God's work of restoration is manifest in the spiritual return of Jerusalem and in the earthly abundance of vegetation, animals, and sea creatures.

We are made aware of the bond between Creator and creation as well in the offerings made to the restored Jerusalem, a Jerusalem now enlightened by God. The city has become a beacon to other nations who honor its radiance by offering up the bounties of the seas and the land, animals, minerals, and plants. After Jerusalem's transformation through God, the city is ready to receive these most precious gifts. The challenge for us in reading this passage comes when we ask ourselves how we use these gifts of creation. Have we been transformed to God, through God, such that we can respectfully accept the responsibilities assumed of us as recipients of both the abundance of creation and the honor of nations? How have we used the bounty of the earth? Do we squander those gifts selfishly by using more than our share, or by failing to act justly to the earth

Pastoral Perspective

strife. Nevertheless, Isaiah 60:1–7 casts an image of the world flocking toward Zion. This prophecy is not qualified. Its fulfillment is not dependent upon the faithfulness of God's people. Rather it is treated as a fait accompli. Thus, the text serves as a call to participate in the glory of God. It draws the Jews toward the completion of the new temple so that *they* may experience the rising of the glory of the Lord and share in God's glorification of God's house.

The promise of God in Isaiah 60:1–7 follows a declaration that God "will come to Zion as Redeemer, to those in Jacob who turn from transgression" (Isa. 59:20). It is a reassertion of the prophecy of Isaiah to the exiles in Babylon that God would turn the darkness of exile into the light of restoration and renewal in Zion. In the chapters preceding our text, the joy of the fulfillment of Isaiah's prophecy that the Jews would be freed from servitude by Cyrus of Persia was eventually replaced by confusion and doubt. The complex process of returning from Babylon and rebuilding their destroyed temple led to discord and fractures within the exilic community. Much of Isaiah's testimony of this period describes a deepening malaise of political strife, corruption, and economic uncertainty. The enthusiasm that engendered Sheshbazzar's initial attempt to rebuild the temple had long since faded, due to the continual failure to complete the task.

Rather than engaging in the rhetoric of retribution that is found elsewhere in Isaiah, in chapter 60, the prophet tacks toward a different kind of call to faithfulness. The prophet commands his people to behold the beauty of God's glory as it attracts all of the nations to Zion. This is not merely a spiritual vision; it is an image of the physical gathering of the world that is happening among them. One can imagine the power of this text for a people whose memories consisted of decades of exploitation and enslavement. Here Isaiah proclaims a reversal of all they have known. Rather than stealing the Jews' land, their possessions, and even their own bodies, the nations of the world will deliver the crown jewels of their wealth as offerings to God. The fulfillment of this prophecy is not dependent upon the obedience of God's people. It is a call to faithfulness, rooted not in threats or dire predictions of future suffering, but in the radiance and thrill of bearing witness to the unification of a broken world in the glorification of God's house. The completion of the temple is reframed as an opportunity to participate in redemption of all the nations.

Far too many corners of the kingdom have seen the enthusiasm of new ministries wane and

teacher's thought. In either case, they are words of encouragement to a dispirited people trying to rebuild the community under the difficult circumstances of return from the Babylonian exile. The initial joy of the return began to fade when the returning exiles faced obstacle after obstacle. They needed continued encouragement to maintain their hope and spirit.

The oracle begins with imperatives, instructing the people to arise and shine. The first imperative implies that the people have been prostrate, perhaps languishing in despair. The time for despair is over, as God is about to act. By beginning with imperatives, the oracle calls for the people to respond in faith even before God has acted. The exhortation to "lift up your eyes and look around" (v. 4a) is the call to see what is not yet true. The people should arise in expectation, trusting that God will fulfill the coming promises. The command to shine is even more subtle. The people will reflect the light God will give them. Because they cannot shine on their own, the second imperative is a call to open up to becoming God's instruments. Verses 1 and 2 repeat the promise that the people will experience the glory of the Lord. The term "glory" conveys God's greatness, importance, and seriousness. As it does here, it also carries the connotation of radiance. The glory of the Lord will provide light in the midst of the darkness that will envelop the nations.

The term "darkness" has a rich background. It can communicate sin or suffering. It connotes estrangement from God and alludes to the situation in creation before God began to act (Gen. 1:1–3). The nations that now seem to Judah to be basking in the light of military and economic success will be covered by thick darkness. Military success is no evidence that the light of God's favor shines upon them! When nations and kings come to Jerusalem, it will not be in defeat or under compulsion, but in joy and expectation. The nations shall join Jerusalem in offering praise to the Lord.

The prophet envisions the return of all of Judah's scattered exiles. Historically, of course, many Jews simply remained in their Diaspora locations. Foreign armies carried the defeated people in humiliation to exile. Now, foreigners will bring their offspring back, treating them as tenderly as a nurse carries an infant. Perhaps the prophet proclaims a kind of spiritual return, in which the exiles reclaim their faith and allegiance to Jerusalem and the temple.

The most audacious claim by the prophet is that the nations will come to Jerusalem. What a bold assertion that was to make during the ascendancy of

after all. In him "the glory of the LORD" has risen (v. 1). His light is the one to which all nations shall come (v. 3a). Already, kings have been drawn to the brightness of his dawn (v. 3b). Isaiah is clear that the "you" at the heart of his good news is not Jesus but Zion (59:20). This shift of focus—which is true to the text—provides the preacher with an interesting perspective on a passage that some Christians too easily claim for their own purposes.

One of the best ways to acquire an ear for this perspective is to read the passage in the *Jewish Study Bible*, a volume that belongs in every preacher's library. Those with bigger book allowances may decide to spring for *Etz Hayim*, a conservative Torah commentary, or *The Torah: A Modern Commentary*, produced by the Reform movement.[1] All three volumes use the Jewish Publication Society's Tanakh translation, which holds surprises for those who have gotten used to other English translations.

"Then you shall see and be radiant; your heart shall thrill and rejoice" (v. 5a NRSV) becomes, "As you behold, you will glow; Your heart will throb and thrill" (v. 5a JPS). "Herds of camels will cover your land, young camels of Midian and Ephah" (v. 6a NIV) becomes "Dust clouds of camels shall cover you, Dromedaries of Midian and Ephah" (v. 6a JPS). As every preacher (and prophet) knows, one of the best ways to enter listeners' minds is to woo their ears, and the JPS translation is truly lovely.

This is the first reason to consult a Jewish Study Bible. The second reason is the marginal notes, which provide fresh insights into a passage that was heard and loved long before Jesus was born. Chapters 60–62 portray Jerusalem as "a bereaved woman," the notes say. In them, the prophet surprises his own listeners' ears. Using the contemporary vocabulary of royalty, he applies it not to the house of David (as his listeners might expect) but to the city of Zion and Israel as a whole. In the first twenty-two verses of chapter 60 (from which today's passage comes), the "prophet does not look forward to the arrival of a human Messiah to liberate the Israelites or a human king to govern them. Rather, God will rule the nation directly in the future, and the whole nation will enjoy royal status."[2]

While Christians *do* celebrate the arrival of a human Messiah, this Jewish reading of the text offers

---

1. *The Jewish Study Bible*, ed. Adele Berlin and Marc Zvi Brettler (New York: Oxford University Press, 2004); *Etz Hayim* (New York: The Rabbinical Assembly, 2001); *The Torah: A Modern Commentary* (New York: The Union of American Hebrew Congregations, 1981).
2. *Jewish Study Bible*, 903.

Isaiah 60:1-6

Theological Perspective

itself, which produces the very elements the prophet tells are worthy as marks of honor? Has the light of God shone through us so clearly that we now behave as a global neighbor in ways worthy of God's glory?

The writer of Third Isaiah describes what comes to a people who wait for God and who are then filled with God's light. The power of God's light is *attractive* rather than *imposing*; the radiance that calls nations, sons, and daughters to us, the radiance that is honored by and honors creation, comes from waiting for God's glory to appear over us. It is God's light and not our own that is attracting. We must determine how we are using power. Are we attracting others by the God in us, or are we imposing ourselves on others (both other nations and other life forms)? As people and as a nation, are we behaving in ways that show us to be transparent to the divine light, or are we behaving toward creation itself and nations that look to us from within the mists of our human illusions of power?

God's transformative light appears in this passage in at least three ways: First, we are reminded of the place of the prophetic imagination in the work of hope, as the prophet's voice helps prepare the human heart for God's transformations. Second, we are reminded that power, to be truly of God, is attractive rather than imposing; God's light shining through us will be a beacon to all nations and will bring forward to good and sacred use the gifts of the earth. Finally, we remember that the darkness shall not last, neither as the dark days of winter nor as the dark days of the soul, for the light rises now just over the horizon.

EMILY ASKEW

Pastoral Perspective

eventually fade toward disillusionment. To varying degrees, all churches struggle to avoid having their labors become bogged down in the difficult realities of communal life. Far from escaping politics and discord, the church often seems to embody their most virulent forms. Darkness shall, indeed, cover the earth and thick darkness the peoples, but Isaiah 60:1–7 offers hope to the disenchanted. It is a call of hope to shake our churches from lethargy and disappointment to complete the task that God has set before them—whatever that may be.

Viewing Isaiah's prophecy through the lens of the Christian faith, we are reminded that the church's work continues in the knowledge of God's faithfulness, that in Jesus Christ our ministry is already fulfilled in the sight of God, though it is not yet complete. This liberates the church to serve as God's *partners* in the work of the kingdom. However humble the reality of our ministry may appear in comparison to our original vision, participation in the work of God casts us in the full radiance of God's light in the world. This frees us from becoming consumed by the imagined glory of each ministry by recasting our service to God as an opportunity to share the "brightness of [our] dawn" (v. 3) with the world. The church can do so in the faith that it does not labor in vain or spend its strength for nothing. There is no failure, no waste in the service of God. All shall be returned when the nations stream to Zion.

So, proclaim this good news to your church, with the faith and knowledge that the work you have done and the work you will do is already complete in the kingdom: "Arise, shine; for your light has come, and the glory of the LORD has risen upon you" (v. 1).

MATTHEW FLEMMING

Exegetical Perspective

the Persian Empire! The claim of the prophet should not be read as mere triumphalism, but as the promise that the chosen people will still fulfill their call to mediate God's presence to the rest of the world. The prophet promises not just that Judah's fortunes will be reversed, but that the chosen people still matter in God's plan to bless the whole world. By leaving out verse 7, the lectionary committee omits the promise that the rest of the world will participate in sacrifice to the Lord. The poem is not just about a transfer of wealth, but about reconciliation in worship.

The passage was chosen for Epiphany Sunday because of the promise that the nations shall bring gold and frankincense to Jerusalem, two of the three gifts brought by the magi to Jesus. Contemporary preachers should not see in this powerful text only a prediction of the events surrounding Jesus' birth. The early church looked back to texts such as these to interpret the Christ event. The coming of Christ is the manifestation of God's glory in the midst of the darkness of the world. The coming of Jesus is just as subtle and just as audacious as the claims of the prophet that the nations—who held Jerusalem's political fortunes in their hands—would one day recognize the significance of Israel's role to mediate God's presence.

The contemporary preacher can proclaim from the text that the church, currently marked by declining influence, is still an instrument to mediate God's presence and glory to a world shrouded in the darkness of war, violence, hatred, apathy, poverty, and despair. This poem calls the church and the synagogue to use our imagination to see what is not yet true and to act as though it already were true. In spite of the world's indifference to it, the church can arise and shine, acting under the assumption that God is still at work through both church and synagogue, offering light, healing, and reconciliation to the world.

CHARLES L. AARON

Homiletical Perspective

an angle for an Epiphany sermon—one that does not rely on supercessionism for its good news. For the prophet, God's glory is completed in the glorification of God's people. Their radiance is essential to any bright future of God's own imagining. If they hope to sit on the sidelines while someone else shines instead of them, then they have missed their central role in God's vision. They are not God, but God's presence will be seen over them (v. 2 JPS). They are not kings, but kings shall walk by their shining radiance (v. 3 JPS).

Preachers who decide to stay true to the prophet's theme may find there is no contradiction between proclaiming the epiphany of the Lord and the epiphany of the Lord's people. Jesus comes to bring God's own light into the world, not to keep it for himself. He comes to set other people on fire, not to burn like a torch all on his own. In the same way that Isaiah declares the rising of God's glory on all God's people, it is possible for the preacher to declare the shining of Christ's light in all Christ's kin.

If the preacher happens to be a universalist, like Isaiah, then there is no catch in this equation. People glow with God's light because God is present with them, not because of anything they have done to secure that presence for themselves. This may be a difficult stopping place for preachers accustomed to asking more of their congregations each week. What better time than the Epiphany of the Lord, after all, to ask a congregation to burn a little brighter?

To do that would be to do something different from what the prophet does (or the evangelist Matthew, for that matter). Today, in what is likely to be a midweek celebration, there is nothing more that anyone must do. Today Christ's kin get to behold his glow until they glow themselves. They get to pass the gold and frankincense around as if it belonged to the whole family. They get to rest in the glorious presence of God, whose bright dawn has broken not only upon Christ but also upon them.

BARBARA BROWN TAYLOR

Psalm 72:1-7, 10-14

[1]Give the king your justice, O God,
  and your righteousness to a king's son.
[2]May he judge your people with righteousness,
  and your poor with justice.
[3]May the mountains yield prosperity for the people,
  and the hills, in righteousness.
[4]May he defend the cause of the poor of the people,
  give deliverance to the needy,
  and crush the oppressor.

[5]May he live while the sun endures,
  and as long as the moon, throughout all generations.
[6]May he be like rain that falls on the mown grass,
  like showers that water the earth.

Theological Perspective

What makes this psalm so intriguing is its political impact, an impact seldom associated with Epiphany. As the culmination of the Christmas season, Epiphany is recognized as the time when God came to earth and appeared to humankind. The traditional Gospel reading is, appropriately, the visit of the magi.

There are any number of clues that this is a political psalm. The ascription "Of Solomon" (not printed above) triggers associations with wisdom, royal rule, and justice. The psalm begins as a prayer to God for the king, or as a description of the righteous king. In either case, the psalm describes the character of an ideal king; it sets the standard for what a king or governor should be.

For us, the psalm functions in something of the same way it did for Israel. It reawakens us to the belief that politics and economics are not only human products; they are theopolitical, God-given, and continually revealed. The Israelite understanding of kingship shifted away from seeing the king merely sociopolitically. Instead, the whole of life was understood theopolitically as the realm where God continued to be active. Psalm 72 asks YHWH to reveal God's divine law and prays that the king have the charisms to act righteously. That is a reawakening that we as citizens acknowledge in praying that God grant governing agents wisdom and courage.

Pastoral Perspective

The most obvious reason for Psalm 72 being read on the feast of the Epiphany is its reference to kings from Tarshish and Sheba and Seba giving tribute and bringing gifts to the new king. The echo of this psalm, the Gospel account of the visit of "wise men from the East [coming] to Jerusalem" to seek the new "king of the Jews" (Matt. 2:1–2), is the primary text of the day. Matthew tells the story that proclaims the universality of God's love; the psalm is a supplement to the Gospel story, that underlines an often-missed aspect of the newborn king.

Psalm 72 has long been associated with Solomon. With its reference to the king's righteous judgment and to the international honor in which the king is held, this may have been composed for an anniversary celebration for King Solomon.[1] For the preacher the heart of this text could be verse 4:

May he defend the cause of the poor of the people,
  give deliverance to the needy,
  and crush the oppressor.

In our own day politicans curry favor with the electorate by appealing to "the middle class," not to the poor and needy. Here a ruler is being praised for what he does for those from whom he can get little

1. J. Barton and J. Muddiman, eds., *The Oxford Bible Commentary* (New York: Oxford University Press, 2001), 387.

⁷In his days may righteousness flourish
   and peace abound, until the moon is no more.
. . . .
¹⁰May the kings of Tarshish and of the isles
   render him tribute,
   may the kings of Sheba and Seba
   bring gifts.
¹¹May all kings fall down before him,
   all nations give him service.

¹²For he delivers the needy when they call,
   the poor and those who have no helper.
¹³He has pity on the weak and the needy,
   and saves the lives of the needy.
¹⁴From oppression and violence he redeems their life;
   and precious is their blood in his sight.

Exegetical Perspective

This psalm probably originated in the Jerusalem temple in connection with a coronation liturgy for the Davidic king. The name "Solomon," son of David (in the superscription, not included above), was surely added later, prompted perhaps by the phrase "king's son" in verse 1b. Nevertheless, the presence of his name encourages one to read this psalm in terms of hopes that actually attached to the historical kings of Judah.

Although some voices in the Hebrew Bible express skepticism about the institution of kingship (e.g., 1 Sam. 8:4–18), the book of Psalms presents a high view of the Davidic king as nothing less than the unique delegate and agent of YHWH (see especially the so-called royal psalms: 2, 18, 20, 21, 45, 72, 101, 110, 132). Here the king is seen, not as a competitor to Israel's God, but as the chief instrument by which God's rule is executed on earth. The king bears ultimate responsibility for justice and civil order. The king's military prowess provides security against hostile foreign countries. Also understood as the embodiment of the whole community before God, the king's obedience to YHWH ensures the promised covenant blessings, so that, for example, needed rain falls and the fields and vineyards flourish.

Psalm 72 forms an extended prayer that the king will fulfill all of these ideals. The opening verse is

Homiletical Perspective

Although this reading is suitable for Epiphany because of its reference in verses 10–12 to gifts brought to Israel's king by foreign kings, preachers can seek a closer look at its deeper, more essential message. Perhaps in this liturgical cycle, Matthew's story of the magi can remain in the background, with the focus instead on this psalm.

Although considered a royal psalm for actual coronations or the commemoration of a crowning, the relevance of Psalm 72 for today is the "deliverance to the needy" (vv. 4, 12, and 13). The responsibility outlined for the Israelite king is, in fact, our shared responsibility with governmental leaders. The welfare of all people, according to God's purposes, that once rested on the king (Solomon most likely in this psalm), is now resting upon us and our current democratic system. The actions of the faithful and those in power alike are to mirror the justice of God. Any oppression of the poor and those at risk is to be overturned.

To put it in a more positive light, the psalm tells us—and history proves—that nations thrive when they show compassion for the poor and work on behalf of social equity. Peace, prosperity, and stable societies are possible only when the poor are defended and the oppressors—whether people or systems—are brought to justice.

Psalm 72:1-7, 10-14

Theological Perspective

Politically, this psalm puts believers in touch with their continuing responsibility and privilege of seeing politics and economics as integral with their faith.

Chief among the features of God's political agenda is the care for the poor and afflicted. The psalm could not be clearer about this. Indeed, there is a sense in this psalm that if the king (read: government) will see to it that the poor are treated well, then justice will be happening. Such treatment is the touchstone of whether YHWH has endowed the government with wisdom and righteousness. If justice characterizes the administration, then prosperity and peace will return.

Politics is not separated from ecology in the psalm's dynamics. We are attracted to the imagery of mountains bringing prosperity, and hills bringing righteousness (v. 3) and the ruler enduring as long as the sun and being like rain falling on mown grass (vv. 5–6). We may think such images merely aesthetically pleasing. There is more in these nature references, however. Indeed, justice and righteousness are conjoined to *shalom*, God's self-revelation in the whole of the natural order. The unity of the earth's flourishing is made manifest in human politics and in the working of natural dynamics. The working of nature and government both depend on following God's revelation.

I write at a time characterized by anything but such *shalom*. The poor are not well-treated; they lack health insurance, and food pantries are experiencing great demand; unemployment has risen; the economic picture—if it is distressing for the comfortable—is disastrous for the widow and orphan. I write at a time of war, when billions of dollars that might have been used for health care, education, and job training have gone into killing and aggression. I write at a time when climate change is no longer scientifically debatable theory but when island nations are threatened and the coastlines and species are being encroached upon. In short, there is neither justice, nor righteousness, nor peace, nor ecohealth. The poor are afflicted, and government can be seen more as the bringer of drought than of "showers that water the earth" (v. 6).

In vivid contrast, government that attends to God's law will see to it that the poor are not sold "for a pair of sandals" (Amos 8:6) and will challenge any human legislation that takes advantage of the powerless or voiceless, whether human or otherkind. The promise is that attentiveness to God's desires will bring peace and prosperity to all.

Pastoral Perspective

benefit. Administering justice and caring for the poor were the marks of a great king in ancient Israel.

Here is the thin end of a homiletical wedge. Contrast how modern leaders appeal, not to any idealism on the part of the electorate, but to the voters' own immediate self-interest. Cut taxes, limit immigration, rescue the institutions on which the acquisitive economy depends. Imagine a modern politician running on King Solomon's platform:

> For he delivers the needy when they call,
>   the poor and those who have no helper.
> He . . . saves the lives of the needy.
> From oppression and violence he redeems their life.
>   (vv. 12–14)

The pictorial image that defines the Epiphany for our culture dates to the Renaissance and has been popularized by Hallmark. Richly robed men and their retinues bow down before a perfectly serene Madonna and Child as angels, stripped of any terrifying aspect that knocked shepherds to their knees, hover above. Culture has robbed the story of its radical political implications. With Psalm 72, the lectionary editors have given the preacher a springboard from which to dive headfirst into the significance of Jesus' birth as humble, and how his life is, from the very first, an appeal for justice for all people and for generous care toward the poor.

The psalm begins with a prayer that God will give to the king God's own justice and God's own righteousness. In the parallelism of Hebrew poetry, justice is equated with righteousness.

> Give the king your justice, O God,
>   and your righteousness to a king's son.
> May he judge your people with righteousness,
>   and your poor with justice.

In the OT, righteousness, *tsedeqah*, is not a matter of according people their due and everyone being treated the same. Rather, righteousness is a matter of meeting the demands of a particular relationship, whether with God or a person. Within the community, righteousness consisted of keeping peace and fulfilling the needs of community life; it is a matter of living the covenant of mutual respect, honoring the aged, and of helping the poor.[2] Psalm 72 invites a sermon that reflects on how *tsedeqah* is both present and still needed in the world, locally and globally.

The text anticipates the Epiphany proclamation that in Jesus Christ, God has entered into a covenant

---

2. Elizabeth R. Achtemeier, "Righteousness in the Old Testament," *The New Interpreter's Dictionary of the Bible*, ed. G. A. Buttrick (Nashville: Abingdon Press, 1962), 4:80.

Exegetical Perspective

addressed to God as a direct request. Subsequent verses shift to the third-person jussive, "May he . . ." Following verse 1, they also should be read as essentially petitions, but their jussive form also suggests admonition: "O God, help our king to do X, because that is what he *should* do." Psalm 72 does not fit any standard literary pattern. There is considerable repetition throughout the text, but interpreters identify five stanzas: verses 1–4; 5–7; 8–11; 12–14; 15–17. The lectionary omits verses 8–9 in the third stanza and the entire final stanza.[1]

This omission increases the prominence of the theme of justice, which is the centerpiece of the expansive opening lines. The key terms in verse 1, "justice" and "righteousness," are emphasized by being artfully repeated in reversed order in verse 2. The Hebrew word translated "justice" relates concretely to a judge's decisions about civil and criminal cases or to a ruler's decisions about civic requirements. It can be used as a noun for an individual command (a "judgment"), but often, as here in verses 1–2, it refers to the general principle that is realized when such decisions are rendered properly. Three foundational ideas emerge in verses 1–2.

First, the only legitimate source for the community's justice is the will of God, probably to be understood primarily as revealed in Israel's covenant law tradition. No king is authorized to invent his own definition of justice, let alone to co-opt the judiciary or the governmental institutions in order to punish his political enemies or to curry favor with the wealthy and influential (compare the behavior of royalty in 1 Kgs. 21). The king's policies are to conform to the justice of YHWH, and he is to order the nation's judiciary by the same standard. This idea is illustrated by Deuteronomy's instruction to make a copy of the law for the king, who "shall read in it all the days of his life, so that he may learn to fear the LORD his God" (Deut. 17:18–20).

Second, the horizon of godliness in ancient Israel includes the people's whole life, economic and social activities as well as explicitly religious observances. Most disputes that required resolution by a judge or ruler would arise from ordinary daily activities: buying and selling, lending and repaying, hiring and firing, marrying and divorcing, inheriting and disinheriting, paying taxes. That such a high premium is placed on right decision making in such disputes

Homiletical Perspective

The sermon's application must not be limited to the nation in which it is preached. From the beginning of Matthew's Gospel and certainly in his Epiphany story, Jesus is recognized as the fulfillment of Israel's charge to be the "the light for the nations." It would be an error to overlook the universal intent of the day's lessons. In Matthew's lesson, Jesus is revealed to the foreigners from the East. In his letter to the Ephesians, Paul makes it clear that Jesus came for the Gentiles as well as the Jews. In our day, we must ask ourselves who are the "others" for whom Jesus came. The psalm prods us to see that the poor and outcasts, whether near at hand or far away, are the ones deserving of our attention and service.

All of the Epiphany texts point toward God's promised shalom for the world; however, the psalm most emphatically instructs us about our specific role as advocates in local, national, and international affairs. Like God, we are to reach beyond our church walls or geographic boundaries to show compassion to any in need.

Of course, many church members believe that working for justice is not a part of their calling and are quick to say that "politics and religion" should not be mixed. Psalm 72 illustrates that politics and religion are interwoven. The work of the king, or the Congress, and the citizens is to defend the cause of the poor. Let Archbishop Desmond Tutu be our inspiration: "I don't preach a social gospel; I preach the Gospel, period. The Gospel of our Lord Jesus Christ is concerned for the whole person. When people were hungry, Jesus didn't say, 'Now is that political or social?' He said, 'I feed you.' Because the good news to a hungry person is bread."[1]

In 2009 the World Alliance of Reformed Churches urged members to celebrate the 500th anniversary of John Calvin's birth by working for the unity of the church, by promoting social justice and respect for creation, and by addressing war and violence. These are fitting goals, since Calvin not only wrote about the call to social justice; he preached about it and labored so that the city of Geneva would itself be an example of it. "The city council organized ministries to care for the needs of all the people: the poor, the sick, the aged, those unable to work, the widows, orphaned and abandoned children, those suffering

---

1. As quoted in *God's Mission in the World: An Ecumenical Christian Study Guide on Global Poverty and the Millennium Development Goals*, published by the Episcopal Church Office of Government Relations and the Evangelical Lutheran Church in America, 2006.

---

1. Verses 18–19 and 20 are not part of Psalm 72. They were inserted after the end of Psalm 72 to mark the end of a major section within the book of Psalms.

Psalm 72:1-7, 10-14

Theological Perspective

The government will be acclaimed by many other rulers ("the kings of Tarshish," v. 10) and all nations; other wise people will bring him gifts (the magi?). Such fame or fortune for the governor, it may be inferred, is far less important than the condition of the needy. If the governor is YHWH's ruler, then the deliverance of those who have no helper will be the priority. "Precious is their blood in [the ruler's] sight" (v. 14). The standard being enunciated is that of YHWH's reign. The purpose of rulership is the fulfillment of God's will for the whole creation, a dominion synonymous with the care of the weak and voiceless.

For us the psalm may be most epiphanic when we are dismayed by the disparity between the actual operations of governance and the ideal of God's reign. Theologically, then, we may take Psalm 72 as an eschatological vision. When some resort to the use of the word "eschatological," the hope seems only a future one. However, there is always a system of governance in operation, even if it is one of warlords or tribal alliance or ego-centered greed. As inheritors of the Psalter, we have the task of working to bring the present political and economic system more in line with God's. Eschatology here puts pressure on Christians to bring even a little more justice and righteousness.

The placement of this psalm during Epiphany no doubt triggers visions of Jesus Christ as the eternal king. It is Jesus Christ alone who fulfills the terms of moral holiness and cosmic prosperity expressed here. Finally it is this fulfillment that will lead to peace among all peoples. The business of all kings bowing down and all nations serving the ideal governor (v. 11) has as its goal the reconciliation of all beings and the restoration of *shalom*.

It is important for us to remind all in governance that it is compassion, mercy, and justice that bring peace and prosperity. When power has justice as its goal, and the blood of all is precious to those in power, then will our nation and all nations be blessed. The epiphany of YHWH working for *shalom* will become evident again. May it be so!

L. SHANNON JUNG

Pastoral Perspective

of righteousness with all nations and peoples. No one is outside the covenant of God's steadfast love and continuing presence. No community is free of the obligation to respect, honor, and help those whom God has placed also in community. So the preacher could ask how a congregation hears this psalm as an invitation to deeper covenant relationships within the worshiping family and beyond. What are the responsibilities of baptismal faith? How do we live into the opportunities of the Epiphany season suggested by our psalm: secure justice for the poor, help those in need, and defeat their oppressors?

By January 6, people may be ready to turn away from the sometimes-forced jollity of Christmas and New Year's Eve and take on a more reflective mood. That readiness is the preacher's invitation to consider the experience of the past couple of weeks. As worshipers at midnight on Christmas, we are witnesses to a birth that has become a sign of hope for peace and justice. It is no accident that the liturgical calendar invites us to remember the death of Stephen, the first martyr, on the day after the nativity. And two days later we recall the Slaughter of the Innocents. Birth and death are intertwined; that is the wisdom of the season between nativity and Epiphany.

How has that wisdom taken shape in the world and in the worshipers' lives as the new year begins? Search out the evidence in the headlines for both life and death. How might people at prayer have caught a new glimpse of the world's need for a king who "delivers the needy when they call" and who "redeems their life . . . from oppression and violence" (vv. 12, 14). It is these realities that need the stable's flickering light shed on them.

The faithful in church at Epiphany have gone through all the liturgies of Christmas, both secular and sacred. Those liturgies have authentic power of their own that might not be noticed at the moment, emotions and music and words being all atumble amid excesses of the season. Sparks of light and grace have showered all around the congregation. Perhaps some ember of hope for a better and more loving world is there, waiting to be breathed into flame. Some turning aside from self-indulgence *is* possible as we pack away the tree ornaments and turn our less distracted attention to issues of justice, poverty, and oppression. Epiphany is the season for making Christ not simply celebrated in church, but known to the world.

> In his days may righteousness flourish
> and peace abound, until the moon is no more.
> (v. 7)

MARTIN G. TOWNSEND

Exegetical Perspective

shows that all aspects of Israel's life are important to the Creator who made it.

Third, the welfare of the poorest members of society provides the primary index of godly justice. Unlike the wealthy and high placed, the poor and helpless must rely on official guardians of justice to protect them, particularly if they are victimized by the powerful (vv. 4c and 14). They are the least able to compete economically and politically. Although the entire society benefits when governed justly, the treatment of the lowest social classes has special importance. The psalm returns to this theme again in verses 12–14. It uses five different Hebrew expressions to call attention to "the poor" (v. 2), "the needy" (v. 4), "those who have no helper" (v. 12), and "the weak" (v. 13).

The term "righteousness" is frequently paired with "justice" in the Hebrew Bible. The terms are synonymous, but "righteousness" points beyond the more rule-oriented justice of covenant law to the broader demand by God for active goodness textured by love and mercy. "Justice may be legal; righteousness is associated with a burning compassion for the oppressed."[2] Amos appeals to righteousness when he demands of his wealthy audience that they not force into debt bondage desperately poor persons who are legally in default on comparatively tiny loans no greater than the price of cheap sandals (Amos 2:6; 8:6).

When the psalm prays for the long life (vv. 5–7, 15–17, 19) and the broad dominion (vv. 8–9) of the king, this is not merely stock nationalistic political rhetoric. It reflects the covenant promise of stable, prosperous political life as divine reward for obedience (cf. Lev. 26; 2 Sam. 7:10–17). If the king's reign is long and uncontested, this will be because God grants it as a blessing, and the people can only hope that the "peace" (*shalom,* total well-being) experienced under the rule of such a just and righteous ruler will last forever (v. 5). Verses 3 and 6–7 hint at the fertility of the land, which was also one of the covenant promises. In verses 16–17, which the lectionary omits, such material prosperity as a corollary of godly kingship is made more explicit.

ROBERT J. OWENS

Homiletical Perspective

the plague, and refugees who had fled persecution in France and Northern Italy."[2]

Calvin would urge us—the elected and the electorate together—to pray the words of Psalm 72 and then to make them happen. Immigrants, children, the unemployed and underemployed, and the poor still need deliverance.

A sermon illustration of Christian advocacy might be Bread for the World (www.bread.org), a collective Christian voice urging our nation's decision makers to work to end hunger at home and abroad. Individual members and member churches study and pray about issues of poverty and hunger, and then they appeal to their congressional leaders to make effective changes to alleviate suffering. As a result of such advocacy efforts, legislation to address domestic and international poverty has helped countless people in need.

Recent surveys indicate that most Americans, and certainly most Christians, are concerned that so many children and adults in the United States and throughout the world go hungry. People polled understand that solving this huge problem will take more than charity; Christian activists can create just policies.

This Epiphany Day could begin a season when preachers lead their congregations into deeply pondering the revelation of Jesus as God's Son sent for the whole world's care and salvation, and especially for those in need. Will we merely sentimentalize his being born to a poor couple who become political refugees? Will we come to understand that by passionately responding to those in need with social justice, we worship God as the psalmist implores us to do? The prayer that is Psalm 72 humbles us, as the sight of the baby did the magi. It calls us to fall on our knees in praise and service (v. 11).

DEAN MCDONALD

---

2. Abraham Joshua Heschel, *The Prophets* (New York: Harper & Row, 1962), 201.

2. Anne Sanders, *Reformed Worship*, Issue #80, http://www.reformedworship .org/magazine/article.cfm?article_id=1

Ephesians 3:1-12

¹This is the reason that I Paul am a prisoner for Christ Jesus for the sake of you Gentiles—²for surely you have already heard of the commission of God's grace that was given me for you, ³and how the mystery was made known to me by revelation, as I wrote above in a few words, ⁴a reading of which will enable you to perceive my understanding of the mystery of Christ. ⁵In former generations this mystery was not made known to humankind, as it has now been revealed to his holy apostles and prophets by the Spirit: ⁶that is, the Gentiles have become fellow heirs, members of the same body, and sharers in the promise in Christ Jesus through the gospel.

⁷Of this gospel I have become a servant according to the gift of God's grace that was given me by the working of his power. ⁸Although I am the very least of all the saints, this grace was given to me to bring to the Gentiles the news of the boundless riches of Christ, ⁹and to make everyone see what is the plan of the mystery hidden for ages in God who created all things; ¹⁰so that through the church the wisdom of God in its rich variety might now be made known to the rulers and authorities in the heavenly places. ¹¹This was in accordance with the eternal purpose that he has carried out in Christ Jesus our Lord, ¹²in whom we have access to God in boldness and confidence through faith in him.

Theological Perspective

God's Grace and Our Stories. The mystery of Jesus as spoken of in this passage embodies the kind of transformative power to help heal, restore, and renew broken lives, communities, institutions, and even nations. This particular passage is a long prayer of the author's insight into the mystery of Christ. The church is presented as the cosmic organism for revealing and understanding God's divine will for humanity and all creation. The Epiphany of the Lord is made possible because of God's self-disclosure. God discloses or reveals God's self to human beings as an expression of God's inexhaustible love and mercy. The Epiphany speaks to an awakening, an enlightenment, and a revelation of the God revealed in the life of Jesus Christ. It is the kind of Epiphany that transforms lives and calls for new allegiances, goals, and directions.

Rather than as a prisoner of Caesar—which must have carried a great deal of street credibility, given the large-scale Roman persecutions of the day—Paul describes himself as a prisoner of Jesus Christ. The image of prisoner or of one in bonds to the gospel of Christ holds tremendous symbolism. It emphasizes the unbreakable chain or link between Paul and Jesus Christ. His identity as a follower of Christ would not be a passing fancy, nor would it involve light, moderate, and easy living. Paul is reflecting on the passionate

Pastoral Perspective

On the feast of the Epiphany we celebrate the arrival of the sages from afar to the manger in Bethlehem where the infant Jesus lies swaddled. He is surrounded by animals, watched over by his parents, and illumined by an amazing star. At its simplest level, Epiphany provides us the last scene of the Christmas story. It is a scene depicted in the Gospels, but its significance is given to us in the Epistles, as this text from the Letter to the Ephesians reveals.

Traditionally the feast of the Epiphany and the season that follows are a celebration of the manifestation of God in Christ Jesus. Epiphany is a season in which we hear story after story of God revealing God's presence and power in the actions and person of Jesus. In his baptism, his acts of healing, his transfiguration, Jesus provides a way for God to say, "This is my Son."

The wise men in the Epiphany story come "from afar," from the East. They are not Jews. Their arrival at the crib of the infant Jesus, the homage that they pay him, signifies that Jesus is the Christ, the one sent by God, not only for the Jews, but for all—Jew and Gentile alike. Paul, writing from prison to the church at Ephesus, describes and glories in this universal work of Christ. He exclaims with verve his own particular call to make Christ known to the Gentiles throughout the then-known world. He is

Exegetical Perspective

Ephesians and Epiphany (vv. 1–3a). In Christian tradition, Epiphany Sunday remembers the visit of astrologers from the East who had followed a star to the child Jesus in Bethlehem. What is often missed in our traditional Christmas pageants is the two-way recognition that occurs in this event. The wise men have come to see and venerate the "the king of the Jews" (Matt. 2:2). The Jewish Messiah is made visible (the literal meaning of *epiphaneia*) to them. To press this scene just a bit, at the same time the Jewish Messiah has been revealed to the magi, Jesus has recognized these Gentiles as children of God.

Much of the Letter to the Ephesians is an expansion on this theme—the revelation of Christ to the Gentiles. The author of the letter couches this revelation in terms of "mystery," which he had already mentioned in the opening paragraph of the letter (1:9; see last week's lectionary exegetical notes, pp. 183–87). Our author now returns to discuss in greater detail the content of this mystery. Structurally, this passage looks like a parenthetical insertion into the body of the letter between the repeated phrase *toutou charin* ("for this reason," 3:1 and 3:14). It is as if he began a thought, then remembered that he had more to say about the mystery. He reminds the reader that he had already written "a few words" (v. 3) about this topic (1:8–10). Now he returns to explore the theme more completely.

Homiletical Perspective

There comes a defining moment in the life of every preacher of the gospel when he or she is going to look in the mirror and ask the question *Who am I? Why do I do this difficult work?* The preacher is certainly more than the sum total of his or her possessions, the size of the congregation, and infinitely more than the word received from his or her critics.

It happens to most of us—when in the still of the night we are hanging on to the last rung of the ladder by our fingernails, our grip goes white with strain, and our next choice determines whether we live or die emotionally and spiritually. How we answer that question determines our ministry and shapes our message and mission. This searching is painful and difficult, but from this comes our authority to preach and minister to God's people. The answer to this shapes and informs everything we say and do from that point on. Frankly, some choose to stay in ministry, and some choose to leave. Either way, life is changed.

The opening verse of the third chapter of Ephesians, so often passed over by the preacher or Bible teacher, is the defining moment for Paul. Here is his authority. The chains that held him may have been placed on his body by the emperor's command, but they were part of God's purpose for him as the apostle to the Gentiles and a prisoner of Jesus Christ,

Ephesians 3:1-12

Theological Perspective

and courageous energy of the martyrs during his time and those to come in future generations.

Paul reminds believers of their calling, as prisoners of Jesus Christ, to be stewards of God's grace, to be constantly aware of its significance and treasures, and not to take it for granted. Grace is not a privilege extended to some. Neither is grace a resource that can be sold, exchanged, borrowed, traded, or earned as a commodity of sorts. It is freely given and derives from God's abundant love. The grace that comes from God, as a consequence of God's redemptive plan for humanity through Christ, must be cared for and cherished, not abused.

Here is one of the most intriguing dimensions of the Christian narrative. That grace—abundant love revealed to humans in history—demonstrates God's desire for human life. In the nihilistic culture of today, many people all across the globe are in search of meaning and purpose. Unrestrained violence, racial and ethnic conflicts, and the growing culture of intolerance all pose real challenges for embracing the mystery of grace. Grace makes sense only in light of the life of Jesus Christ, a life given over to others in love, peace, justice, and reconciliation. Because of the life and death of Jesus Christ, believers have a sense of what God's ultimate plan is for creation and insight into the nature of God and the will of God in the world, which ultimately makes grace a gift that is desperately needed.

Paul points to his own autobiography to support the mystery of God's grace at work. Paul recognizes that his life reflects someone actually least worthy of the calling that he represents. As he testifies in this passage, "Of this gospel I have become a servant according to the gift of God's grace that was given me by the working of [God's] power" (3:7). Often our personal biography offers compelling evidence of the grace of God at work in the world.

James McClendon, author of *Biography as Theology*, once observed that theology, and more generally the Christian narrative, is best understood as an exploration into autobiographical stories. By delving deeply into the narratives of individuals and communities (in history and the present), according to McClendon, we are able to gain a deeper understanding of the activity of God. McClendon also recognized that the key to engaging the essence of the Christian faith, including doctrine, is to take seriously the narratives of those who have encountered the faith in so many creative and mysterious ways.

That is exactly what Paul was doing in this passage. By elevating the inner workings of God's grace

Pastoral Perspective

clear that the call was given to him as a "gift of God's grace" (v. 7).

We do not often experience the gift of God's grace as a calling or commission, especially one that can lead to burdens or imprisonment. Rather, we are inclined to experience grace as a fortuitous moment, a blessing, or a transformation within our psyche or soul that makes life smoother, more heavenly. Paul helps us to see that a gift of grace is one that draws us closer to God and to God's desire for us—be that something simple or complex, something comfortable or rough.

The feast of the Epiphany, indeed the whole season that follows, can be seen as a time for commissioning those who, like Paul, are given the gift of grace to make Christ known to those who are far off, as well as those who are near. Not just the story of Christ crucified and risen, but all the "boundless riches of Christ"—his forgiveness, his healing, his compassion, his love, the big tent he raises. No one is outside the reach of Christ's saving embrace. No one is beyond his mercy. Epiphany is a day, a season, for sending people forth to carry the light of Christ out into the sinful, broken, and divided world. All who have been baptized into Christ's body share the high calling and have been given the grace to respond.

Paul clearly believed himself to be called to make those boundless riches known to the Gentile world—to those whom former generations could not see to include. For "in former generations this mystery was not made known to humankind" (v. 5). God, first revealed to the Jews, now in Christ is revealed to all. This text tells the story of Paul's call to preach to the Gentiles. It also challenges every generation who reads it to consider God's call to them in their own place and time, to consider who—in their community, their society, their world, their pew—is being left out of the abundance of God's grace.

This text also challenges those who read it to broaden and deepen their understanding of the church. It is through the church, Paul claims, that "the wisdom of God in its rich variety might now be made known" (v. 10). It is not any single church—not a single congregation, nor a single denomination, nor even a single branch of the faith—that reveals the wisdom of God in all its rich variety. It is the whole of the church throughout time and place, with Jesus Christ as the cornerstone, that makes it known. It is the whole of the church, knit together as one body, the body of Christ. It is the whole of the church, in Word and sacrament, in Scripture and

Exegetical Perspective

The author begins by reminding the reader that Paul had been a prisoner for Jesus Christ "for the sake of you Gentiles" (v. 1). He reminds his readers "of the commission [*oikonomian*] of God's grace that was given me for you, and how the mystery [*mysterion*] was made known to me by revelation [*apokalypsis*]" (vv. 2–3). This verse has echoes in Paul (Gal. 1:15–16) and in Paul's disciple, Luke (Acts 22:6–11; 26:12–18), and the author seems to presume that his readers are familiar with this aspect of the apostle's life. Paul has told his readers that he had received a divine revelation that ended with a prophetic call (*kalesas*) to take the gospel to the Gentiles (Gal. 1:15). When the author of Ephesians describes this experience, he uses the term *oikonomia* (v. 2: NRSV "commission," NIV "administration," RSV "stewardship"); Paul was a steward of God's grace. It is clear from the divine passive ("The mystery *was made known* [*egnōristhē*] to me") that God has authorized Paul's stewardship.

The Mystery Is Revealed (vv. 3b–6). The author begins this section with a confusing note. He reminds his reader that he has already written about the mystery (1:8–10). Simply reread these verses, he suggests, and you the reader will clearly know what Paul knows about "the mystery of Christ" (v. 4). If this were true, why continue the discussion? However, the author and reader know that much more must be said before "the mystery of Christ" is clear.

At long last this mystery has been revealed not only to Paul, but also to "his [to whom does "his" refer? God? Jesus?] holy apostles and prophets by the Spirit" (v. 5). One has the sense that the author is writing in the context of a post-Pauline church when such offices as apostle and prophet are well established and highly honored in the community (*tois hagiois apostolois,* "the holy apostles"). At last in verse 6 the mystery is made known to everyone (not just to the gnostic elite).

The Gentiles have become *fellow heirs,*
the same body,
partners in the promise in Christ Jesus through
    the gospel.

(my trans.)

Those three descriptors of the Gentiles are linked by assonance (the prefix *syn*), perhaps as a memory aid in a confessional formula.

A Personal Note about Paul (vv. 7–12). Our author reiterates the word "gospel" (v. 6) to remind the reader that Paul was a servant of the gospel "according to the

Homiletical Perspective

not of the Roman government. The chains were his authority.

Paul knew that we must bleed before we bless, and that we must bleed before we lead. His willingness to face the humiliation of bondage to fulfill his ministry, his single-minded focus on his mission, to the point that he was not willing to compromise himself in order to save himself when opposition arose, spoke louder than any word he ever wrote. In fact, this authenticated his written words. It has long been noted that his letters had the stench of prison and the smell of midnight oil as well as the stain of his blood and sweat. The preacher or teacher of this passage needs to read "Letter from the Birmingham City Jail" by Martin Luther King Jr. to see a modern version of bleeding as authority for blessing and leading.

Paul's imprisonment was for a purpose, not a penance. Paul considered hardship for the gospel a privilege. He was a prisoner, not of Nero but of Christ. Once this is established in the preacher's life and attitude, he or she is free to preach with great authority. There is nothing more compelling, more life changing, than a call. It is life's defining moment. This defining moment for Paul consisted of a mystery revealed, a message compelled, and a mission understood. This should also be true for us.

God has revealed a mystery to Paul, a truth hitherto hidden from human knowledge and understanding, but now disclosed by revelation to Paul. This is revealed truth of which Christ is the source and substance. Paul makes clear in verse 6 that the Gentiles are members of the same body and partakers of the gospel of Jesus Christ.

Jew and Gentile are fellow heirs of the same blessing, fellow members of the same body, and fellow partakers of the same promise. They share the same privileges in Jesus Christ. This is a message of Christian unity—racial, sexual, and gender. How can the modern church separate and wall off sections of the population when the goal of God in Christ is to unite all God's children? The mystery of Christ is the union of humankind through the union of all with Christ. Our churches need to adopt this message, and our world needs to hear that "In Christ there is no east or west, in him no south or north."[1]

This revealed mystery, now open to all, is the proclamation by Paul and for the modern church. This mystery was revealed so that it could be proclaimed (v. 7). This is a ministry entrusted to us

---

1. John Oxenham, "In Christ There Is No East or West," in *Lutheran Book of Worship* (Minneapolis: Augsburg Publishing House, 1978), #359.

Ephesians 3:1-12

Theological Perspective

at work in his own life, he helps his readers to understand more fully the wisdom of God's redemption in Christ. Storytelling has always played a central role in uncovering the nuances of God's activity in the world since the very beginning. Old Testament Scriptures support the significance of storytelling, from the Genesis narrative to the story of God's liberation of Israel in Exodus. In storytelling, because of the broad range of possibilities of interpretation, there is an opportunity to demonstrate both the personal and social dimensions of grace.

Although Paul's story was indeed a personal, existential experience, its meaning and message was far reaching. His personal story had communal significance. Too often we make our stories personal, as if they apply only to our individual lives. This view ignores how our lives continually intersect with the lives of others and the fact that our stories become shared stories and experiences through the constant process of social interactions and relationships.

Desmond Tutu, the former Anglican archbishop of Cape Town who chaired the Truth and Reconciliation Commission in South Africa after the collapse of the apartheid regime, constantly repeated that human beings are caught up in "delicate networks of interdependence."[1] That interdependence is evident in the way we steward both human life and the grace of God—always through relationships, with God in Christ and with those around us. Understanding grace as simply personal reduces grace to a matter of privilege and individual prestige. However, when our individual stories of grace and redemption are expressed in a way that bears witness to what God is doing in Christ for all of creation, there is a more urgent and determined cause for praise and celebration all year long.

JOHNNY B. HILL

Pastoral Perspective

tradition, in historic texts and voices from the pew, that makes known the wisdom of God, the mystery of Christ, the One for all, known to all. No one part of the body has this commission alone; no one branch, denomination, century, or millennium, has it all figured out. Indeed, just about every part of the body has allowed itself to be led wildly astray at one time or another, which is why we need the balance of the whole.

This "wisdom of God in its rich variety" (v. 10) is to be made known, not only to the Gentiles of our world and time, but also to "the rulers and authorities in the heavenly places" (v. 10), those beings and forces that are beyond the beyond, and those that are everywhere in between. Just as God is boundless, so is the call to God's people. The halls of government, the malls of shopping, the marriage bed, the studio, the classroom, and the board room—all of these are places and contexts for the wisdom of God revealed in Jesus to be made manifest.

God's people are not meagerly equipped. The whole of history and creation is behind this work. Paul's zeal is invigorating. Through faith in Christ, the people of the church are able to go forth with "boldness and confidence" (v. 12). This is not the same as going forth with arrogance and fierceness. Rather, assured of the call, assured of the light and the life that are ours in Christ, we receive the commission to make known that light and that life, that forgiveness, healing, and compassion to those who come our way.

LISA G. FISCHBECK

---

1. Desmond Mpilo Tutu, *No Future without Forgiveness* (New York: Doubleday, 1999). This particular quote is repeated throughout the book and is considered a well-known theme of Tutu's work in South Africa.

gift of God's grace" (v. 7). In verse 8 the author has "Paul" reflect on his status in the community. While Paul had referred to himself as "the least of the apostles" (1 Cor. 15:9, *elachistos tōn apostolōn*), the author of Ephesians ratchets downward Paul's self-denigration so that he is now "the very least of all the saints" (*tō elachistoterō pantōn hagiōn*, v. 8).

The author also explicates "the gift of God's grace" (v. 7). Paul was commissioned to bring to the Gentiles good news (*euangelisasthai*; not just "news" as in the NRSV, v. 8) that is "boundless," *anexichniaston*, which can be understood in a variety of ways—temporal, geographical, anthropological. The love of Christ has no boundaries.

Paul understood that it was his task "to make everyone see [lit. "bring to light," unlike the gnostics, who keep such secrets hidden from the masses] what is the plan [*oikonomia*] of the mystery hidden for ages in God who created all things" (v. 9). At long last, according to our author, the church (not just apostles, prophets, or gnostics) is to reveal "the multi-colored [literally] wisdom of God . . . to the rulers and authorities in the heavenly places" (v. 10, my trans.). The church not only conveys the divine mystery on earth, but it has a heavenly mission as well. This is a grand and comprehensive statement regarding the role of the church. This statement is striking in its boldness, especially as part of a letter intended for a community embedded in one of the great cities of the Roman Empire. To top it off, our author supplies a theological warrant for this conclusion. All of this is part of the "eternal purpose" that God has carried out in Jesus through whom "we have access" (*prosagōgēn*, v. 12, the solemn approach one assumes in coming before a king). This reveals yet a paradox for these early Christians. Approach to earthly rulers, and especially the emperor, would have been highly unlikely for them, but they are able to approach the ruler of all creation with "boldness and confidence" (v. 12). Mysteries never cease.

After Matthew's magi had the mystery of God revealed to them in that cradle in Bethlehem, they carried the mystery of the incarnation with them back "to their own country" (Matt. 2:12). The Messiah of the Jews was also their Messiah.

PAUL WALASKAY

today also. It was a gift of God's grace and God would give power to proclaim it. It is God's mission and ours.

The mystery of the Epiphany is the inclusion of Gentiles among God's people. Submission to God's gift of light carries the obligation to accept and proclaim the inclusion of outsiders within the mystery. This is symbolized by its link with the magi following the light to the infant's manger; thus the Christ child is for all people. The unification of all human beings in Christ must have specific attention by any who would preach on Epiphany Sunday from this text.

When the church catches this vision, its mission is defined, and all that is done is measured by this. This revealed truth is held in stewardship. It is given to be shared, not monopolized. We are to share good news as we would the cure for cancer. We share not only good news in Christ but also the fact that Christ enriches those who trust in him. The world needs to know, and the church needs to acknowledge, that the gospel is both truth from God and riches for humankind.

The preacher should be aware that the principalities and powers could be the politicoeconomic structures of our culture. God's purpose is to use the church to inform, redeem, and bring them into harmony with the love of God.

This is strong stuff for the church. It delivers the people from reducing the gospel message to a personal relationship with Jesus Christ. Therefore, there is something for believers and the church to do. The church is the primary part of God's plan. If God is going to do anything in the world, God will do it through the church. The preacher's task is to keep before the congregation the vision of God's new society as God's family, God's dwelling place, and God's instrument in the world. This moves us to authentic worship as well as caring fellowship and compassionate outreach. The church is God's instrument to turn the vision into reality.

WILLIAM L. SELF

Matthew 2:1-12

¹In the time of King Herod, after Jesus was born in Bethlehem of Judea, wise men from the East came to Jerusalem, ²asking, "Where is the child who has been born king of the Jews? For we observed his star at its rising, and have come to pay him homage." ³When King Herod heard this, he was frightened, and all Jerusalem with him; ⁴and calling together all the chief priests and scribes of the people, he inquired of them where the Messiah was to be born. ⁵They told him, "In Bethlehem of Judea; for so it has been written by the prophet:

⁶'And you, Bethlehem, in the land of Judah,
    are by no means least among the rulers of Judah;
  for from you shall come a ruler
    who is to shepherd my people Israel.'"

Theological Perspective

Since this text is for the festival of the Epiphany, the basic theological questions to which the preacher is to respond are: *What is revealed, and how are we to respond?*

The text presents a great deal of activity. Journeys are made, meetings are convened, prophetic history is brought into play, emotions range from the worshipful to the fearful. The stage is set for two final actions in the text: the worship of "the child" and the magi's flight from Herod and harm. At the center of the eye of this storm is the child: the still point around which the entire text's actions and reactions revolve. The child is the one unmovable, fixed point.

One rhetorical approach to a sermonic framework involves asserting: "It is not this! It is not this! It is not this! It *IS* THIS!" This approach may prove useful in developing this text sermonically for two reasons. In dealing adequately with the text's core theology, the preacher faces the challenge of not allowing two perennial points of fascination—the magi and the star—to obscure Epiphany's core theology.

There is an enormous amount of Christian folklore surrounding the magi. For many listeners, these text figures hold center stage. Indeed, parishioners may sport bumper stickers reading, "Wise men/women seek Him." Some of the more eloquent responses regarding the magi, which could serve as

Pastoral Perspective

Follow the Star. There is a tremendous amount of diversity of scholarly interpretation about this text. Most of it comes from a reluctance to accept Matthew's accounting of the supernatural details or the historicity of the events in the text. The debate and commentary are extensive, and I will not render critical interpretive judgments on much of it. My intent is to follow one critical image in the text and illumine its meaning, for pastoral purposes, of people in Jesus' time and our time. I want to draw the reader's attention to the star that is announced in verse 2.

The star is a symbol of our need for divine revelation to see the Messiah and King. Without divine revelation, we would miss the Messiah. Often the overt commercialism and consumerist orientation of Christmas threaten to blind us to the real meaning of the coming of the Messiah. Because we are almost blinded by the culture, the star is a sign, a wonder, a revelation, a guidepost, a traffic light, a tracking device, and a global positioning system (GPS) that brings us to the point and place of divine revelation about the Messiah. For the real meaning of Christmas, we must "follow the star."

Scholarship about the reality of the star is varied, and many explanations and arguments are offered. Some argue that a conjunction of the planets

⁷Then Herod secretly called for the wise men and learned from them the exact time when the star had appeared. ⁸Then he sent them to Bethlehem, saying, "Go and search diligently for the child; and when you have found him, bring me word so that I may also go and pay him homage." ⁹When they had heard the king, they set out; and there, ahead of them, went the star that they had seen at its rising, until it stopped over the place where the child was. ¹⁰When they saw that the star had stopped, they were overwhelmed with joy. ¹¹On entering the house, they saw the child with Mary his mother; and they knelt down and paid him homage. Then, opening their treasure chests, they offered him gifts of gold, frankincense, and myrrh. ¹²And having been warned in a dream not to return to Herod, they left for their own country by another road.

Exegetical Perspective

The feast of the Epiphany started in the Eastern church in honor of the baptism of Jesus. It was introduced in the West in the fourth century, where it came to be associated with the visit of the magi. Epiphany is actually January 6, and in some parts of the world, families exchange gifts on January 6 instead of on Christmas Day, because Epiphany celebrates the coming of the wise men and the gifts they brought. For a while, the Western church celebrated Christmas on December 25 and the Eastern church celebrated it on January 6. The Armenian church still observes January 6 as Christmas Day.

Matthew's account of Jesus' birth connects Jesus to Moses and the experience of Israel. God's revelation to Joseph in dreams guides Matthew's story, reminding us that the Old Testament Joseph was a dreamer. Pharaoh killed the Israelite children; Herod killed the children of Bethlehem. Moses led Israel out of Egypt, so Jesus was taken to Egypt and then to the promised land.

Balak, king of Moab, summoned "from the East" a seer named Balaam to put a curse on Moses. Balaam was a non-Israelite, a practitioner of magical arts, who might have been called a magus. He came with two of his servants, but instead of cursing Moses, he offered a blessing (Num. 24:7, 17) that was understood as a prophecy of the coming of King David.

Homiletical Perspective

Sometimes tradition is a great aid to biblical interpretation. It highlights and deepens our understanding of the Scriptures, bringing with it the wisdom of our ancestors in the faith. There are other times when tradition focuses on one aspect of the text to the exclusion of others. The story of the magi is a case in point. The tradition that raised me presented this as the story of "three kings" or "three wise men" or "three magi" who gave Christ three gifts. The nouns for the travelers were used interchangeably, but the adjective never varied: it was always three.

Matthew, however, does not specify that there were three magi. The number three is an inference from the gifts they offer him in verse 11: "gold, frankincense, and myrrh." Because tradition has concentrated on the three gifts given by three magi, it has missed something in the passage that is much more central to its interpretation: a word that occurs at the beginning, in the middle, and at the end of the story (vv. 2, 8, 11). The word, *proskyneō* in Greek, is translated by the NRSV as "pay him homage." The phrase is a leitmotif in the story, far more important than whether there were three magi bearing three gifts. Paying homage to Christ gives the story its purpose, its direction, and its culmination.

I can imagine a sermon entitled "The Fourth Gift of the Magi." The sermon would begin with the first

Matthew 2:1-12

Theological Perspective

potential illustrative material in the sermon, are the hymn "We Three Kings of Orient Are"; "The Journey of the Magi," by T. S. Eliot; and the folk opera by Gian Carlo Menotti, *Amahl and the Night Visitors*.

The star is mentioned four times in this text. It brings its own long history of textual interpretation. This ranges from historical information on the role of astrology among the professional ranks of the magi to contemporary debates as to whether the star was a comet, a supernova, or the result of planetary conjunction. However one might preach about the star, the preacher needs to keep central this sermonic question: What does the star finally reveal?

The theological question of Epiphany finds its answer in the Christology that Matthew is offering in this text. What theological features should be highlighted in the sermon? First, Matthew displays his ability to quote or echo Hebrew Scripture as a backdrop for preparing his listeners to understand that the child revealed is the Messiah. Texts quoted or alluded to in this pericope include Micah 5:2; 2 Samuel 5:2; Numbers 24:17; 1 Kings 10:1–10; Isaiah 60; Psalm 72; and the infancy story of Moses.

The most explicit quotation, by way of a combination of texts, is found in verse 6, which establishes Bethlehem as the geographical site of the Messiah's coming. Behind this also stands other scriptural works that point to Bethlehem as the point of origin for David and his lineage. Given the staggering amount of textual information and its rich history, the preacher will need to decide to what extent tracing the background will affect sermon construction.

Second, in conjunction with an exploration of the texts employed as prophetic and signifying fulfillment of the coming Messiah, the preacher may choose to look at the shifting geographical points of this text. What do these places of the promise mean? Those mentioned are the East, Jerusalem, Bethlehem of Judea, Bethlehem in the land of Judah, and the final, elusive "their own country." The Epiphany question can be asked again: What is revealed at and through these places?

The East is a vague, undefined term and signals to the listener the insertion of a foreign element in the narrative. On the borders and boundaries of Israel and its faith enter the foreigners, who are neither Jewish nor known. Who are these people? What are they doing here? Why are they asking questions? What are their intentions? Already Matthew has staged the entrance of the stranger and alien on the scene of this text. Is this good news or not?

Pastoral Perspective

occurred in that Jupiter and Saturn aligned in the zodiacal constellation of Pisces. The magi saw the alignment and moved to follow the star. Another suggests that a supernova occurred where a star violently exploded and gave off enormous amounts of light for a few weeks or a few months. The magi followed the light given off by this exploding star until the light flamed out. Someone suggested that Halley's comet, which passed by in 12 BCE, could have passed and the magi followed that moving comet, and that is what the text means by star. Matthew could have presented the star as a purely supernatural sign and symbol. Regardless, the meaning of the star is that it leads human beings to the divine revelation of the Messiah. Let us follow the star.

The Star Leads to Judea. Jesus was born in Bethlehem, and the star of Christ appeared in the East. The magi saw the star, and with the star as a tracking device they came to Jerusalem and asked Herod, "Where is the one born king of the Jews?" They had seen his star in the East and had come to worship. Herod was disturbed and called together his chief priests and teachers and asked them where the Christ was to be born. The reply is, "In Bethlehem of Judea." Herod called the magi in secretly, asked them the exact time the star appeared, and sent them to Bethlehem, telling them to search for the child and when they found him to send a report back to Herod, so that he might come and worship too.

The Star Leads to the Messiah. The second appearance of the star was after they finished with Herod and went on their way to the child. The star went ahead of them until it stopped over the place where the child was. The text says when they saw the star—where the star stopped—they were overjoyed. They were overjoyed with excitement and anticipation as the culmination of their journey. They would see the one born king of the Jews. In verse 11, on coming to the place, they saw the child with his mother Mary, and they bowed down and worshiped him. They worshiped, which means they humbled their hearts. Then they opened their treasures and presented him with gifts of gold, incense, and myrrh. The gifts were expensive, uncommon presents.

The Fading Star and Enflamed Hearts. In verse 12, the text says that they were warned in a dream not to report to Herod, and they returned to their country by another route. There is no suggestion that the star led them back to their country, and I want to suggest

Isaiah later penned similar words about one of David's descendants when he wrote those famous, lyrical words that enchanted Handel:

> The people that walked in darkness have seen a great light: they that dwell in the land of the shadow of death, upon them hath the light shined. . . . For unto us a child is born, unto us a son is given. (Isa. 9:2, 6 KJV).

Matthew saw in these words a far greater fulfillment in the birth of Jesus. At the birth of Jesus, magi—magicians, astrologers, or wise men—came from the East. We do not know if they came from Babylon, Persia, or Arabia. Later tradition would make them kings instead of magi: "We Three Kings of Orient Are." Again, study of the Scriptures probably played a role in calling the magi kings, because Psalm 72:10–11 says, "May the kings of Sheba and Seba bring gifts. May all kings fall down before him." Tradition would also name the magi Melchior, Caspar, and Balthasar, but Matthew does not say that there were three of them. The tradition that there were three magi probably arose from the three gifts that they brought: gold, frankincense, and myrrh. Gold was precious, worthy of a king; frankincense was incense worthy of a divinity; and myrrh was a spice used in burials. So the gifts were appropriate for one who was a king, a God, and a suffering redeemer. They could also symbolize our response: gold—virtue or good deeds, incense—worship or prayer, and myrrh—suffering and sacrifice.

Jesus was born in Bethlehem, fulfilling the hopes and expectations of a Messiah from the line of David. At his birth the magi from foreign lands brought gifts, recognizing that this child would be a deliverer for all nations. He would fulfill the covenant with Abraham (cf. Matt. 1:1), which promised that in him all the peoples of the earth would be blessed (Gen. 12:3).

Taking a fresh approach to this passage, the preacher might focus on the responses of the people, rather than the astronomical phenomenon of the star. Although less spectacular than the star, the devotion of the magi is more impressive. When they saw something they interpreted as a sign of the birth of a king, they journeyed to Jerusalem in search of this king-child. They were not Jews, they did not have the Scriptures, but they saw something that led them to search for a new king. One might draw contrasts between the two sets of wise men, the magi and the chief priests and scribes whom Herod called together;

appearance of the theme, as the magi announce the reason for their long journey: "[We] have come to pay him homage" (v. 2). Because "journey" is a primal metaphor for the life of faith, the sermon might explore how the magi's faith journey begins with the need to give themselves utterly and completely to the only one who is worthy of worship. This implication is clear in the Greek, since *proskyneō* was commonly used to describe the custom of prostrating oneself at the feet of a king. The physical posture dramatically expresses the idea of giving not just gifts, but our entire selves to Christ. It appears that the translators of the NRSV wanted to make plainer this dimension of the text because they changed the RSV version from "worship" to "pay him homage," a phrase that suggests the more graphic, somatic meaning of the Greek.

The next appearance of *proskyneō* develops the complex implications of the word. Herod tells the magi that he wants them to report to him when they have found the child, so that he too may "pay him homage" (v. 8). We know this is duplicity on the part of Herod. When he hears nothing back from the magi, he orders the slaughter of "all the children in and around Bethlehem who were two years old or under, according to the time that he had learned from the wise men" (v. 16).

However, Herod's claim that he wants to pay homage to the child is more than a ruse. It is a piece of irony that communicates the earthshaking character of Matthew's story. The irony is that Herod unknowingly states what in truth he needs to do. The despot who rules by violence and fear needs to prostrate himself before the power of compassion and justice, needs to give himself entirely to the grace that is incarnate in the child whom the magi are seeking.

Herod's duplicitous and ironic statement helps us to understand more profoundly why the magi's quest "frightened" the tyrant "and all Jerusalem with him" (v. 3). Herod and his consultants recognize the implications of the birth the minute they hear what has impelled the journey of the magi: if there is a new king who can inspire people to undertake a strenuous journey to an unknown location so they can pay him homage, then the magnitude of their effort suggests that the established powers are at risk of being challenged.

Herod might prefer to arrest the magi on the spot and have them executed for insurgency against the Roman Empire. Like most tyrants, he is too crafty for that. What good would killing the seekers do, when it is the one who is sought that needs to be

Matthew 2:1-12

Theological Perspective

Bethlehem, while within the religious borders of the faith, also struggles for recognition. The text says reassuringly "by no means least among the rulers." Herod urges the wise men to go down to Bethlehem on his behalf to see who is who and what is what. Why, from the seat of faith and power in Jerusalem, did not a delegation of the chief priests and scribes, who had met earlier, do this? The clue may lie in verse 7. After hearing the prophets quoted on Bethlehem, Herod calls the wise men again to him "secretly." Was Herod fearful that the Jewish religious leaders would indeed find what he could not bear to contemplate in terms of his own power and rule?

Finally, the text closes the way it started, with the wise men warned in a dream to go home "by another road." The christological points Matthew is placing before the listener are now clearer. First, Hebrew Scripture speaks from its wealth of combined times and traditions to point to this child as the Messiah. Second, the to-and-fro-ing of the characters from place to place emphasizes—topographically—that Scripture is indeed fulfilled in the role that the various places play in this text.

Finally, what is particularly crucial in this regard is that Matthew begins and ends this text with strangers, that is, with Gentiles. This fact provides the widest expression and basis of the theology of this passage. It means that Matthew's nascent Christology affirms the fact that the Messiah's coming is an arrival that has meaning for all people! The entry of the wise men into the sacred texts, places, and actions of the Jewish faith are for Matthew the sign that the Messiah has indeed arrived in the person of the child. God, in the child, has breached the boundaries of traditional faith, and the nations are now entering to witness this Messiah, and doing so with joy!

SUSAN HEDAHL

Pastoral Perspective

that the star faded. The significance of fading star is that in the first part of the journey, the magi needed a sign, a wonder, a revelation, a guidepost, a traffic light, a tracking device, and a GPS. They did not know where they were going and needed the external presence of the star. The star led them to the child, and when they saw the child, they no longer needed the star, because the function of the star was to bring them to the point of divine revelation.

Once you see the divine revelation, then you do not need the star, because the external power of the star goes internal. Once they saw the child, they had an enflamed heart and incensed memory. Their hearts were enflamed because of the divine revelation, and their memory was illumined because they never would forget what they saw. The magi left with an enflamed heart and an illumined memory. The star faded because it had completed its task, and the power of the revelation was now on the inside.

When we follow the star to the Christ child and behold the Messiah, and after we have been overjoyed, have bowed down, have humbled our hearts and worshiped, and have given gifts to the child, we leave the season with an enflamed heart and an illumined memory. Our hearts are enflamed because of the divine revelations: we have been visited by the Messiah, and our memories are illumined because we cannot forget what we have seen.

FRANK A. THOMAS

Exegetical Perspective

and two kings, Herod and Jesus, one who ruled by killing and the other who triumphed by dying.

Like many other Gospel stories, this one is actually the gospel in miniature that describes the coming of the Messiah and various responses: reception and rejection. The magi come to worship him, and Herod seeks to kill him. At the beginning of the Gospel the Gentile magi come to worship Jesus. At the end of the Gospel, the disciples are told, "Go therefore and make disciples of all nations" (28:19). The magi could not find the king they were looking for until they heard from those who knew the Scriptures, but those who knew the Scriptures did not recognize the sign that the Messiah had been born.

Here is a meeting of two worldviews: Jewish and Gentile, devout and pagan. The seekers could not find the Christ without the guidance of those who had the Scriptures, but why did only one group of wise men go to Bethlehem? Why did the chief priests and scribes, the religious leaders of the people, not go with the magi? Had they ceased to take the promises of the Scriptures seriously, or were they unwilling to journey with the foreign seekers?

The magi were looking for the Messiah, but the Jewish religious leaders did not join them in the search, and as a result they did not witness the child Jesus. A new era was dawning, but those who had the Scriptures missed it because they did not join with the magi in their quest.

Again, a new era is dawning. Are we willing to leave the security of the familiar to journey with seekers from other religious traditions? Come, let us go to Bethlehem, that we may worship the King.

R. ALAN CULPEPPER

Homiletical Perspective

wiped out? Caesar would be furious to hear a report that Herod botched the situation by acting in a peremptory fashion. Caesar has empowered him to do anything necessary to maintain Rome's absolute dominion. If that includes murder, so be it.

The magi continue on their way until they find the child, and then something very significant happens, something that our traditions, pageants, carols, and Epiphany celebrations may have hidden. The magi do not immediately present their gifts of gold, frankincense, and myrrh. The text says that the first thing they do upon entering the house and seeing Mary and the child is kneel down and pay him homage (v. 11). Only after this act of worship, only after giving themselves completely to Christ, do they present their material gifts.

The order of actions, homage first and gifts second, is significant. Gift giving can be a way of controlling others. If the first thing the magi do is present their gifts, then it might seem that they are in command of the situation. There they would stand with precious goods in their outstretched hands. They would appear like rulers presenting treasures to each other on a state occasion while meeting in the middle of a ceremonial room, each of them on their feet and facing the other, in order to indicate their parity with one another. That is not the case with the magi. They express their relationship to Christ by kneeling and homage to him. First, homage. First, worship. First, giving themselves utterly and completely to Christ. Then, offering their regal gifts. It turns out that the magi's fourth gift, paying homage to Christ, is in fact their first gift. What is ours?

THOMAS H. TROEGER

Isaiah 42:1-9

¹Here is my servant, whom I uphold,
  my chosen, in whom my soul delights;
 I have put my spirit upon him;
  he will bring forth justice to the nations.
²He will not cry or lift up his voice,
  or make it heard in the street;
³a bruised reed he will not break,
  and a dimly burning wick he will not quench;
  he will faithfully bring forth justice.
⁴He will not grow faint or be crushed
  until he has established justice in the earth;
  and the coastlands wait for his teaching.

⁵Thus says God, the LORD,
  who created the heavens and stretched them out,
  who spread out the earth and what comes from it,

Theological Perspective

The Christian relationship to the teachings of the Old Testament has been complex throughout church history. The New Testament church struggled with this dynamic when Peter and Paul disagreed over whether or not Gentiles should follow the Jewish law and be circumcised with their conversion to Christianity. The "Judaizer" controversy was settled with the first council of Jerusalem in about 50 CE with the decision that Gentile converts would not be circumcised, given that "a person is justified not by the works of the law but through faith in Jesus Christ" (Gal. 2:16).

Nevertheless, the matter resurfaced in the subsequent century with Marcion, who taught the disjunction between the two testaments; the God of the Old Testament was a God of wrath, and the God of the New Testament was a God of love. In an effort to define the Christian canon, Marcion advocated the complete elimination of the Old Testament from Christian Scripture, limited the Gospels to Luke and the epistles to Paul, and purged Paul's epistles of any Judaizing aspects. With that, the heresy of Marcionism was born. Centuries later, when the Protestant Reformation began in sixteenth-century Europe, the emphasis on "justification by grace through faith" renewed controversy over the place of the Old Testament law in the life of a believer, with

Pastoral Perspective

In the first of the Servant Songs that shine out of Isaiah, the prophet offers a portrait of the kind of leadership we should expect from one called by God: patient, nonviolent, merciful. God's chosen does not "execute justice" by force. Indeed, this is a portrait of tender care—for those who are vulnerable, for ideas still coming into fullness, for small efforts struggling to plant their roots. "A bruised reed he will not break," Isaiah says, "and a dimly burning wick he will not quench" (v. 3). True leadership protects what is weak until it is strong enough to stand, and keeps gentle hands cupped around a weak flame until it can burn on its own. In this way, Isaiah says, the Servant "will faithfully bring forth justice" (v. 3).

Isaiah's portrait of God's Servant provides a genuine—even startling—contrast to contemporary models of leadership that leave a legacy of preemptive wars, secret (and not-so-secret) prisons, and torture as a form of interrogation. Can you imagine a candidate for public office running on a platform of tenderly caring for the bruised reed and carefully tending the dimly burning wick? Some would call this model of leadership unrealistic, self-defeating from the start. Isaiah insists that this form of leadership is tougher than most. The Servant called by God to bring justice, Isaiah says, "will not grow faint or be crushed until he has established justice in the

who gives breath to the people upon it
　　and spirit to those who walk in it:
⁶I am the Lᴏʀᴅ, I have called you in righteousness,
　　I have taken you by the hand and kept you;
　　I have given you as a covenant to the people,
　　a light to the nations,
⁷　　to open the eyes that are blind,
　　to bring out the prisoners from the dungeon,
　　from the prison those who sit in darkness.
⁸I am the Lᴏʀᴅ, that is my name;
　　my glory I give to no other,
　　nor my praise to idols.
⁹See, the former things have come to pass,
　　and new things I now declare;
　　before they spring forth,
　　I tell you of them.

Exegetical Perspective

This passage appears in the portion of the book of Isaiah (chaps. 40–55 or 40–66) that has come to be called Second Isaiah. Throughout history, interpreters have recognized that these chapters talk about the Jewish exile to Babylonia that followed the fall of the city of Jerusalem to Babylon in 586 BCE.

In 1780, German scholar Johann Benjamin Koppe (1750–1791) suggested that these chapters were written during the exilic period. This view has now been accepted almost universally. Chapters 40–55 are assumed to have been composed in the period just prior to the capture of the city of Babylon by Cyrus of Persia in 539 (Isa. 41:2–3, 25; 44:28; 45:1–4).

Four poems in Second Isaiah have received special attention since the publication in 1892 of a German commentary on Isaiah by Bernard Duhm (1847–1928). These are the so-called Servant Songs/Poems: 42:1–9; 49:1–6; 50:4–11; and 52:13–53:12. (Opinions differ as to whether all of these verses or even more should be included.)

In these texts, a Servant of the Lord either is spoken about, is spoken to, or speaks on his own. (Already in Isa. 41:8–10, Israel as God's servant is addressed and promised God's presence, support, and strength.)

In the text for this Sunday, the Servant is introduced in the first four verses and then directly

Homiletical Perspective

The community was fractured. One part was living in exile along the banks of the Euphrates. Another part was scratching out a living in the homeland of Judah. The exiles were managing well, given the circumstances. Their Babylonian captors granted them freedom to do business, while the homeland community languished in the aftermath of devastation. Marauding armies, raiders, and vandals had plundered the land, leaving the residents little to work with. Whether on the Euphrates or in Judah, the feeling of spiritual dislocation was pervasive. All shared the shame of defeat by a foreign power with imperial designs, their pride carried off like a trophy for a conquering king.

What could be worse? Their God had (apparently) been surrounded and bested by Marduk, Nebo, and the rest of the Babylonian pantheon. Probing questions—difficult to ask—were gaining currency: how does our God stack up against these others who claim allegiance? What is the character of our God? Does God have the power to protect us or even care for us? If so, how do we know that our God is with us? When questions like these spring from human experience, inspiration does not lag far behind.

Enter the poet/prophet who penned Second Isaiah to stand with the people in the space where a center used to be. Here is the challenge that the

Isaiah 42:1-9

Theological Perspective

the result that Martin Luther was beset with antinomian critiques. All such examples from church history reflect the theological significance of determining the dynamic between the two testaments.

Today, the Old Testament lectionary reading from Isaiah generates a great deal of interpretive controversy, particularly as it relates to the New Testament. For contemporary biblical scholars, the single most discussed aspect of this text and the other Servant Songs is the question "Who is this servant of God?"[1] Much of the dispute has sought to determine whether the Servant represents a single person or a group, such as Israel. Some suggest that the poetic style of the passage requires that the servant be understood symbolically, representing different people from various times seeking to bring about justice. Others declare that the Servant's identity is intentionally unclear and that attention should be directed to the nature of the Servant's work rather than the Servant's identity.

Historically, however, the book of Isaiah eluded controversy within Christianity, to the point of even being heralded "The Fifth Gospel."[2] The prominence of Isaiah in the theological history of the church is attributed in large part to the widely held hermeneutic that the prophecies find their fulfillment in the work of Jesus Christ, a point that Jesus himself made, according to Luke (4:16–21). Due to this symbiotic relationship, the place of Isaiah within the Christian tradition has been significant and may continue to be theologically illuminating for believers today.

The reformer John Calvin, for example, identified the Servant of Isaiah 42 with Jesus Christ primarily due to the theological implications of the Servant's work. The biblical imagery of light and darkness, sight and blindness, and captivity and freedom within Scripture commonly represents both a physical and spiritual restoration. Indeed, this very task of being "a light to the nations" (v. 6) is directly equated with salvation in the subsequent Servant Song, Isaiah 49:6. The Servant may, therefore, be perceived as mediating God's promise of restoration to the nations.

Interpreting the Servant's role as one of mediation for God held significant meaning within the context of the Protestant Reformation. In rejection of the mediation of the priest, and in affirmation of

1. For example, see Joseph Blenkinsopp, *Isaiah 40–55*, Anchor Bible (New York: Doubleday, 2000); Paul Hanson, *Isaiah 40–66*, Interpretation series (Louisville, KY: John Knox Press, 1995); Claus Westermann, *Isaiah 40–66: A Commentary*, Old Testament Library (Philadelphia: Westminster Press, 1969).
2. John F. A. Sawyer, *The Fifth Gospel: Isaiah in the History of Christianity* (New York: Cambridge University Press, 1996).

Pastoral Perspective

earth" (v. 4). Over the quick satisfaction of "shock and awe," the Servant chooses patient, but never-ceasing, work for justice, work that takes root, work that steadily fans good ideas into flames.

A great deal of scholarly energy has gone into figuring out whom Isaiah intended by the enigmatic title, "the Servant." Some have theorized that Isaiah had a particular person in mind, a historical figure like Cyrus, the Persian king who allowed Israel to return from exile and rebuild the temple. Other readers have understood Isaiah to refer to Israel itself, an interpretation supported by the explicit reference to Israel in another Servant Song in Isaiah 49. The author of the Gospel of Matthew found in this passage a prophecy about the life and ministry of Jesus (Matt. 12:17–21).

Biblical scholar Paul Hanson finds in this passage not a reference to a historical figure or community but "a catalyst for reflection on the nature of the response demanded of those who have received a call from God."[1] Hanson's reading highlights the pastoral work to which this passage calls us: to help ourselves and those to whom we preach hear the claim this Servant Song makes on us as people who have been called by God to the work of reconciliation and justice.

Certainly the passage can bear this interpretation. It falls very nicely into two parts, the first of which describes the work of the Servant and the second of which reminds the people of their calling. What God asks of them is very clear: to be "a light to the nations, to open the eyes that are blind, to bring out the prisoners from the dungeon, from the prison those who sit in darkness" (vv. 6–7). "Here is my Servant," God says at the beginning of this passage (v. 1). Then, halfway through: "Here are you."

Jesus took the shape of his ministry from the images, symbols, hopes, and visions of Scripture. On the Sunday on which we remember his baptism and the beginning of his ministry, we should try to hear the words of Isaiah 42 as Jesus heard them. Jesus clearly felt addressed by the model of ministry evoked in passages like these. After all, when he came to the synagogue in Nazareth, he chose to read a very similar passage from Isaiah to articulate the vision of his own ministry:

> The Spirit of the Lord is upon me,
>   because he has anointed me
>   to bring good news to the poor.

1. Paul Hanson, *Isaiah 40–66*, Interpretation series (Louisville, KY: John Knox Press, 1995), 41.

Exegetical Perspective

addressed in the last five verses. Both sections are presented as the direct address of God.

In the presentation of the Servant (vv. 1–4), attention is given to the divine chosenness of the Servant (a theme closely associated with the Davidic monarchy; see Ps. 89:19), his endowment with the spirit (see Isa. 11:2), his unassuming character and gentleness (a surprisingly innovative aspect in comparison with, say, the call of the prophets), his mission of establishing justice, and his persistence.

The references to justice (vv. 1, 3, and 4) are not totally clear. The Hebrew term used is *mishpat*. In specific cases, this term can refer to an ordinance, a rule, a regulation, a law (see Exod. 21:1). In this case, it seems to refer to something like "the true way" (NJPS), "how things ought to be," or "justice" understood in very broad and general categories.

Justice can be understood not only in terms of what we call procedural justice (the proper and unbiased understanding and application of legal factors in courts and human relations), but also as distributive justice (the equitable distribution and utilization of resources and responsibilities in nonlegal contexts).

Read in context and in the light of chapters 40–41, this interest in justice would clearly recall Isaiah 40:27, where there is a major complaint that God does not look after his people's *mishpat*. The term is translated in this passage in various ways, such as "right" and "cause." It parallels "way." The people are complaining about God's indifference to their plight. (On divine forgetfulness, see Ps. 44, esp. vv. 23–26.)

In the latter part of verse 4, establishing justice in the earth is associated with the servant's teaching (actually *torah*: law). The connection of torah with Jerusalem and the Davidic monarchy is noted in Isaiah 2:2–4; 11:10. It seems clear from Isaiah 2:2–4 (paralleled in Mic. 4:1–3) that Jerusalem and the Davidic kings were assumed to be a channel of God's law and justice for the world.

The establishment of justice is to be carried out, not with violence or the use of overriding strength, but through humility, passivity, reserve, and endurance. This contrasts with what is depicted of the ideal king elsewhere (see Isa. 11:1–5; esp. v. 4).

Verses 6–7 contain divine speech addressed to the Servant. Verse 5 describes the Deity who speaks to and commissions the Servant. The imagery used to speak of God is drawn from the conception of God as creator. Outside of Genesis 1–3, there is more about creation and God as creator in Second Isaiah than in any other portion of the Bible (see especially Isaiah 40).

Homiletical Perspective

prophet faced: to restore a sense of a Center to a people demoralized by war, captivity, devastation, and exile and cut off from their sacred stories and traditions of faith. Their call to live as a family of faith within the family of nations was a distant echo. The covenant made with the wild, whispering God of Abraham and Sarah was now, it seemed, a broken promise.

This is how many read their relationship with God during the dark nights of spiritual crisis, whatever the time or place. The challenge of the one who would dare speak a word of hope during such a time is to join in an intimate struggle with the predicament the people share and to bring the resources of imagination, inspiration, and tradition to the realities of their existence. Hope springs from a sense that a Center is present, but is hidden perhaps by difficult circumstances. For this prophet, the Center is a conviction about God's character.

This prophet crafts his witness in a series of four Servant Songs (42:1–4; 49:1–6; 50:4–9; 52:13–53:12). The first of the four is the first part of a text appointed for this Sunday. What a curious choice the prophet makes for fashioning a word of hope! Given the severity of the situation, why not make a bold announcement, uttered noisily in the streets to catch the ear of the passerby? Why does the singer appear instead of the street preacher? Why is the poet assigned to bring the message in place of the herald? Perhaps the prophet knew something about the nature of a song.

Songs express the hopes and aspirations of social movements for renewal and liberation. It is difficult to think of such a movement that does not sing itself into transformation. The pulse and rhythms of a song in performance arise out of the spirit of the movement, but they also give it stability and inspiration. Is there any wonder why our own ancestors in Christian faith found in these Songs of the Servant coherence and clarity for their own movement? As the stories of their founder Jesus began to circulate throughout the world they knew, our ancestors used the imagery of these texts as a palette to draw the portrait of their own Risen One.

The preacher's task during the season of Epiphany is to create a fresh portrayal of the one the church knows as its Christ. Epiphany is traditionally the season of gift giving that follows the arrival of the Christ child at Christmas. Think of this first Servant Song as Isaiah's gift to the church. In the first stanza (vv. 1–4), God sings of the intimacy enjoyed between the Divine and the human one. "I have

Isaiah 42:1–9   **221**

Isaiah 42:1-9

Theological Perspective

the "priesthood of all believers" according to 1 Peter 2:9, reformers emphasized the role of Christ as the sole mediator necessary for salvation. Indeed, as seen in Calvin's *Institutes* (2.15), Christ holds a threefold office, which includes his role as *the* Priest on our behalf. Mediation is necessary because of the theological affirmation of total depravity, which stresses that sin so consumes humanity that no one is capable of bringing about his or her redemption. Thus Calvin comments in his Isaiah commentary on verse 7, "under these metaphors he declares what is the condition of men, till Christ shine upon them as their Redeemer; that is, they are most wretched, empty, and destitute of all blessings, and surrounded and overwhelmed by innumerable distresses, till they are delivered by Christ."[3]

The theological resonance found in this passage with the accounts of Christ in the New Testament is also notable in the historical interpretations of this passage. The Servant of Isaiah 42 is one who will dutifully carry out the task of establishing justice as called by God without shouting, breaking, fainting, or quenching until it is done. Calvin points out that this Servant reflects the character of Jesus Christ by pointing to the *kenōsis* or self-emptying of Christ affirmed in Philippians 2:7. One might also consider Christ's words according to Mark 10:45, which states, "the Son of Man came not to be served but to serve, and to give his life a ransom for many." In this way, the question of identity is raised by the very nature of the work of the Servant, which raises the question, can anyone else do the Servant's work? Can any other person or group besides God free humanity from its fallen condition, from its blindness, from its slavery to sin? In answering this question, Christian theology has often turned to an understanding of the atonement that affirms the doctrine of the two natures of the one person of Jesus Christ, as in Anselm's famous *Cur Deus Homo*.

Thus, by approaching this question from a theological perspective attuned to the soteriological implications of the passage, historical interpretations enable one to see that the identity of the Servant is inextricably linked to the work of the Servant. For Christians, then, this is found in the incomparable person and work of Jesus Christ.

JENNIFER POWELL MCNUTT

Pastoral Perspective

He has sent me to proclaim release to the captives
    and recovery of sight to the blind,
        to let the oppressed go free,
to proclaim the year of the Lord's favor.
                                    (Luke 4:18–19)

Jesus received these words as powerfully as it is possible to receive them and sought to mark every moment of his ministry with the vision they expressed. His ministry did take care with the bruised reed; he cupped his hands around the dimmest wicks until they began to shine. The practices that the prophet Isaiah called the people to cherish captured Jesus' imagination and ought to capture ours as well.

The vision of this Servant Song is sweeping in its scope, but specific in the practices it commends. It seems particularly concerned with the suffering of prisoners, because it twice repeats the call to release them: "to bring out the prisoners from the dungeon, from the prison those who sit in darkness" (v. 7). Sermons on this text should help us feel the claim these words make on us, and guide us into practices that will allow us to respond as intentionally as Jesus did.

"See, the former things have come to pass," says the Lord at the end of this passage, "and new things I now declare; before they spring forth, I tell you of them" (v. 9). When Jesus rises up, newly baptized, from the waters of the Jordan, he enters into a ministry saturated with the vision Isaiah bequeathed to him and to us, a vision of leadership guided by mercy and a hunger for justice. Jesus' whole life was a passionate response to God's call for this new way of living. It is the pastoral work of the preacher this day to help us hear this text as Jesus did, with our whole hearts, and to respond as he did, with our whole lives.

STEPHANIE A. PAULSELL

---

3. John Calvin, *Commentary on the Book of the Prophet Isaiah* (Grand Rapids: Baker Books, 1999), 3:295.

Exegetical Perspective

In the actual commissioning statements, there is a break with creation imagery and a self-declaration of the special God of Israel ("I am YHWH" v. 6; see Exod. 6:2). The reference to the Servant's being called clearly parallels texts related to the commissioning for a special purpose.

God declares that God has taken the Servant "by the hand" (v. 6b). This may be a play on the Mesopotamian ritual where the king, in the New Year festival, took the deity Bel by the hand and escorted his statue back to the sanctuary.

The expression "covenant to the people" (v. 6c) is of uncertain meaning, although covenant terminology might be expected in the context of personal-relationship terminology.

The Servant has a function to perform not just to his own people but to the nations of the world. Here that function is described as being "a light to the nations" (v. 6c). Note that in verse 1, this task is expressed in terms of "bring[ing] forth justice to the nations."

Several earlier biblical texts relate Israel in a special way to the nations. The most famous of these texts is found in the call of Abraham (Gen. 12:1–3), where it is said that "in you all the families of the earth shall be blessed." (This idea is probably dependent on the preaching of the prophet Isaiah, who proclaimed that Israel would be "a blessing in the midst of the earth," Isa. 19:24.)

The work of God through the Servant is described with two infinitives: "to open" and "to bring out" (v. 7). Paraphrased, the idea is: "You shall be a light to the nations so that I might open the eyes that are blind, and bring out the prisoners from the dungeon."

The commissioning ends with a divine acclamation of uniqueness (v. 8). This is a common theme in Second Isaiah, who was Israel's first pure monotheist.

The concluding verse affirms that YHWH is the only God who can declare things before they happen. Earlier, in 41:21–24, the idols are chided because they cannot announce events before they occur.

What is coming—the rise of Cyrus, the release from exile, and the return to the land—is being declared and is as certain to happen as the former things are now past.

(The possible identities of the Servant are explored in next Sunday's exegetical notes on pp. 243–47.)

JOHN H. HAYES

Homiletical Perspective

given him my Spirit" God says, which is a spirit of strength and purpose ("he will make sure that justice is done" v. 3b, my translations). It is the opportunity for the preacher to show how invested God is in the task of "bringing justice everywhere on earth" (v. 4).

In the second stanza (vv. 5–9) we are reminded of what a gift creation itself is. God is now speaking directly to the Servant, reminding those who would accept the call to serve that justice is the heartthrob of the created order, since "all who live on this earth" are intended to be in right relationship with God and with one another. It is to be sure a grand vision, out of the reach of human effort alone, but has God as its source. Still, God assures the Servant that the "source of life" (NRSV "gives breath," v. 5) will be standing close when the promise is enacted in human life.

If the church opens only that part of Israel's gift that defines its understanding of Jesus, then it misses its wider blessing. There is the portrait of the church's Christ here, but there is so much more. Why confine the reach of this Song to one individual or even one servant community? It is a portrait, but it is also a silhouette. Anyone who "brings light and (God's) promise of hope to the nations" (v. 6) stands in the place of the Servant; he or she will be blessed with the spirit, intimacy, and strength that is God's gift to the Servant.

This account of God's investment in creation, through the agency of a servant people, lies at the heart of the church's gift to the nations at Epiphany. Israel received from her prophet Isaiah what the church received from its Christ, and that is what the church testifies to the world—the revelation that the God who creates is a just God who restores sight to the blind, freedom to the captives, and grants strength to those who serve.

RICHARD F. WARD

Psalm 29

[1]Ascribe to the LORD, O heavenly beings,
  ascribe to the LORD glory and strength.
[2]Ascribe to the LORD the glory of his name;
  worship the LORD in holy splendor.

[3]The voice of the LORD is over the waters;
  the God of glory thunders,
  the LORD, over mighty waters.
[4]The voice of the LORD is powerful;
  the voice of the LORD is full of majesty.

[5]The voice of the LORD breaks the cedars;
  the LORD breaks the cedars of Lebanon.

Theological Perspective

This most ancient text of praise is thought by many scholars to be originally of Canaanite provenance, a homage to Baal as storm god. According to Old Testament scholar William Holladay, Psalm 29 is one of a handful of early psalms that is poised at the cross-cultural intersection of Ugaritic texts and early Hebrew poetry, a Canaanite hymn adapted for the worship of Israel's God.[1]

There is a tendency to privilege orality and aurality in our dealings with the Divine. The focus on Word and its proclamation inevitably leads interpreters and communities of faith to focus on speaking and the sense of hearing when engaging revelation. The relationship of the psalms to hymnody can reinforce this perception. Psalm 29 with its seven repetitive references to "the voice of the LORD" (vv. 3, 4, 5, 7, 8, 9) may appear consistent with such interpretations. The connection between theophany and the oral/aural may even be embedded in the rhythm of the poetic language that simulates the roll of the very thunder that its Hebrew wordplay suggests (*qol* signifies both voice and thunder). In his reflections on this psalm, the late Pope John Paul II suggests "one can say that the Psalmist thinks of thunder as a symbol of the

Pastoral Perspective

The pastor is not going to feel particularly drawn to the psalm on a Sunday such as Baptism of the Lord. This is a shame. This Psalter text provides a powerful overlay for the Gospel story (Matt. 3:13–17). Lest we forget, the psalm reminds us exactly who it was who called Jesus "Beloved": it is the God of heaven and earth, the one whose voice spoke everything into being. The same God who broke the cedars of Lebanon also ripped the skies open. The same God who shook the wilderness sent the Spirit as a winged courier to the Jordan.

The psalm enumerates God's work in general, but with a specific focus: God's voice, which has the power to create and agitate, comfort and destroy. Pastors are well acquainted with the ways that the right word at the right time can be life giving. We also know that while sticks and stones break bones, words also can profoundly hurt. A sermon on Psalm 29 might bypass the baptism of the Lord altogether by focusing on the power of God's voice, and our voices, to wound and to heal, to curse and to bless.

The psalmist entreats the heavenly beings to "talk back" to this God who speaks. "Ascribe to the Lord" attributes of power and might, the psalmist commands. Are the verses that follow a "transcription" of the heavenly beings' response? Are they the words of the psalmist, who cannot but provide some suggested

---

1. William L. Holladay, *The Psalms through Three Thousand Years: Prayerbook of a Cloud of Witnesses* (Minneapolis: Fortress Press, 1993), 19–23.

^{6}He makes Lebanon skip like a calf,
and Sirion like a young wild ox.

^{7}The voice of the LORD flashes forth flames of fire.
^{8}The voice of the LORD shakes the wilderness;
the LORD shakes the wilderness of Kadesh.

^{9}The voice of the LORD causes the oaks to whirl,
and strips the forest bare;
and in his temple all say, "Glory!"

^{10}The LORD sits enthroned over the flood;
the LORD sits enthroned as king forever.
^{11}May the LORD give strength to his people!
May the LORD bless his people with peace!

Exegetical Perspective

This psalm highlights God's power and glory. It comprises three sections. The introductory section, verses 1–2, functions as the call to praise. The psalm then turns to descriptive statement. In verses 3–10, the large middle portion, the psalmist depicts God's activity vis-à-vis nature, and in verse 11 the psalmist describes God's action toward people (in the final verse the Hebrew verbs are indicative rather than the conditional tense rendered by the NRSV). Psalm 29 utilizes a relatively small vocabulary. Words tend to be repeated over and over again, even more than is typical in the Psalms. This technique gives a sense of the poem weaving around and around itself, crescendoing with each cycle.

Psalm 29 can best be categorized as a hymn or a song of praise, yet it differs significantly from more typical examples of the hymn genre in the Psalter. Astute readers will observe that human beings—typically the ones who are called to praise—are completely absent from the psalm until the final verse, and even there are only recipients of action, not the subjects. The focus of the text is not the human world but the divine realm; human beings seem almost an afterthought. Instead, it is the "sons of God" or "sons of gods" (*bene elohim*, NRSV note) who are commanded to worship (v. 1) and who obediently do so (v. 10). This designation reflects the

Homiletical Perspective

In Zora Neale Hurston's novel *Their Eyes Were Watching God*, a hurricane hits Florida. Many local residents evacuate the area before the storm, but the main character, Janie, and her husband, Tea Cake, remain in their shack alongside Lake Okeechobee. Tea Cake forecasts "nothin' but uh lil blow," but the high winds come, the thunder bursts, and the lake's waters rise.[1] Janie and Tea Cake huddle closely in the shadow of death. Their thoughts turn to God. Hurston writes, "They sat in company with the others in other shanties, their eyes straining against crude walls and their souls asking if He meant to measure their puny might against His. They seemed to be staring at the dark, but their eyes were watching God."[2] The God of that storm—a storm reminiscent of the Okeechobee Hurricane of 1929—is portrayed as the chief actor; God brings the awesome winds and causes the lake to breach its dike.

The hurricane in Hurston's novel, like the stormy scene of Psalm 29, allows us to consider the relationship between God's reign and a storm's destructive rains. In the storm of today's psalm, God's might is revealed in thunder, lightning, and devastating winds. The powerful voice of God "breaks the

1. Zora Neale Hurston, *Their Eyes Were Watching God* (New York: Harper & Row, 1937), 148.
2. Ibid., 151.

Psalm 29

225

Psalm 29

Theological Perspective

divine voice, with its transcendent and unattainable mystery, that breaks into created reality in order to disturb and terrify it, but which in its innermost meaning is a word of peace and harmony."[2]

However this psalm also opens the receiving and/or worshiping community to a multisensual experience. The text invites a visceral response from those who attend its words and feel its rhythms. There is physicality to the poetry, a call to the imagination to feel the thunder. An encounter with the Word of God is not primarily an oral/aural experience; rather it rattles persons right down to their very core. To borrow the powerfully descriptive language of the psalm, theophanies break, flash, shake, whirl, and strip bare those who experience the manifestation of the Divine. The voice of God is a multimedia appeal to the senses—visual, tactile, and even auditory. No one is left out as the power of the storm is felt at a profound level. The pairing of this psalm in the lectionary with the baptism of Jesus invites reflection on what type of response is expected from those who bear witness to God's self-disclosure. The Word made flesh is a multimedia, polysensual theophany that addresses our humanity in all its dimensions—including the sensory and our imaginations—and it invites an embodied response.

Often interpreted as a psalm portraying the power, majesty, and glory of God, this is underscored by the scope of the storm. Spatial relations play a key role in communicating the breadth of divine reach, from the sea through the forests to the desert, from northern Lebanon to southern Kadesh. The late Carroll Stuhlmueller, an internationally renowned biblical scholar, notes the theological significance of the geographic reference to Kadesh. This naming of the wilderness by the Hebrew poet transforms the Ugaritic "awesome wilderness" into the specific location of Kadesh, the Sinai, site of God's revelation to the encamped Israelites in the time of Moses.[3] The particularity of this theophany, wrapped in poetry borrowed from their Canaanite neighbors, speaks anew to postexilic worshipers generations removed from that grounding divine revelation; yet another indication of the creative fluency that distinguishes the voice of God.

The sheer magnitude of the storm is evident by the destruction caused in its wake, and its

Pastoral Perspective

content for the celestial choirs? Either way, the body of the psalm is a series of declarative statements. This God creates, agitates, and presides over all that is.

The Psalm and Baptism. We often focus baptism services solely on water, and for good reason. We see the stuff, hear it poured, and depending on the exuberance of the pastor, might feel the droplets as they are flung toward the pews with the reminder, "Remember your baptism!" This text allows us to expand the images we bring into conversation with baptism. Though water is the physical element we use, baptism is a sacrament that touches and transforms all of life. Appropriately, all four of the classic elements are present here in the psalm:

Earth. "The LORD breaks the cedars . . . makes Lebanon skip like a calf, and Sirion like a young wild ox" (vv. 5b–6). The calf and oxen are creatures of the earth, lowly beings, beasts of burden; but here they become symbols of unbridled and unselfconscious joy. We hear echoes of Eden here, an image of God's delightful and delighted creation. How does this image from the psalm relate to baptism? In the incarnation, God in Christ takes on our own "earthiness." Jesus' baptism, his first public act of ministry, shows that he shares our humanity, submitting himself to the same rituals and practices that we ourselves undertake.

Fire. "The voice of the LORD flashes forth flames of fire" (v. 7). In this verse we feel the heat of the Spirit's flame. The same Spirit who descended at Jesus' baptism appears again and again in Jesus' ministry and that of the early church. The Spirit drives Jesus into the wilderness and presides over a sort of forty-day "refiner's fire" that prepares Jesus for all that will come (Mal. 3:2). After Jesus appears, and disappears, at Emmaus, the two at table with Jesus realize that their hearts had been "burning" as he broke open the Scriptures to them (Luke 24:32). Surely that fire is the Spirit, who comes as tongues of flame at Pentecost, when thousands are baptized into Christ's body.

Wind. "The voice of the LORD causes the oaks to whirl, and strips the forest bare" (v. 9). The image is of a devastating windstorm—the last gusts before winter, when every tree is scrubbed of its leaves. Even leaves that are not ready to float gently down can be ripped off their branch. The wind of the Spirit is often described in hushed and gentle tones, a breeze caressing the cheek, but here God's Spirit is

2. John Paul II, "General Audience," Wednesday, June 13, 2001, #1, http://www.vatican.va/holy_father/john_paul_ii/audiences/2001/documents/hf_jp-ii_aud_20010613_en.html

3. Carroll Stuhlmueller, *Psalms 1 (Psalms 1–72)* (Wilmington, DE: Michael Glazier, 1983), 168–74.

divine council seen elsewhere in the Hebrew Bible (e.g., Pss. 82; 89:7; 103:19–21; Isa. 6; 1 Kgs. 22:19). The setting of the heavenly court, rather than the human temple, emphasizes God's sovereignty and complete "otherness."

The psalm is highly theocentric. The primary subject is YHWH; the name YHWH is repeated eighteen times. This repetition may be intentionally polemical. Some scholars hypothesize that the psalm is either adapted from or modeled after a Canaanite hymn. If the former, the psalmist would have changed the divine references from the weather god Baal to YHWH, thus emphasizing that it is the Israelite god who is in complete control.

The phrase "the voice of YHWH" appears seven times. It causes the actions, produces all the effects. This psalm is especially *noisy* (the term *qol* can also mean "sound"), with the divine voice cracking, shaking, stripping, and thundering through creation. It is the voice that provides the connection with two of the other readings for this Sunday. In Matthew 3:13–17, after Jesus' baptism, we hear "a voice from heaven." In contrast to Psalm 29, however, this voice utters actual direct speech, accompanied by divine Spirit and dove, rather than the raw destructive force of the psalmic divine voice. The pairing of these Scriptures suggests that the majesty and power of the "voice of YHWH" lies behind the milder "This is my beloved Son, with whom I am well pleased." Isaiah 42:1–9 likewise is linked to Psalm 29 through the voice (also *qol*, in v. 2), here the voice of the Servant who will refrain from crying out. The cosmic activity in the latter part of the prophetic reading (vv. 5–9) is also echoed by the cosmic imagery of the psalm.

The psalm presents a theophany, an appearance or manifestation of God, here through the natural world. In the natural arena, three realms (water, forest, animal) are highlighted, and the psalm displays a patterned sequence among them. Bounded by water imagery at the beginning (v. 3) and end (v. 10), God's activity rotates through forest (vv. 5, 8, 9b) and animal life (vv. 6, 9a). Even the famous cedars of Lebanon, traditional pillars of strength and pride (Pss. 92:12; 104:16–17; Isa. 2:13), are no match for divine power. Through its depiction of the natural world as YHWH's playground, the psalm suggests that nature ultimately belongs to God. It is not an arena for human manipulation or domination.

Some commentators imagine that Psalm 29 depicts a thunderstorm, moving eastward across the Mediterranean, then southward through Palestine. The language and imagery of the text is sufficiently

cedars," "flashes forth flames of fire," "shakes the wilderness," and "causes the oaks to whirl" (vv. 5, 7–9). The psalmist not only experiences the majesty of God in this storm but envisions God "enthroned over the flood" (v. 10). In the opening verse, the psalmist issues a call to worship God, to praise God's "glory and strength" (v. 1).

For today's preacher, the image of God "enthroned over the flood" bears extra weight. In the wake of Hurricane Katrina and the annual news stories of communities decimated by high winds and water, the preacher will pause before ascribing to God the glory—and destruction—of a violent storm. The pastor who has assisted in the rebuilding efforts on the Gulf Coast will not underestimate what a storm can do to individual lives and whole communities. The pastor who serves in a community that knows firsthand the havoc of "mighty waters" will hear the psalmist's refrain of praise with a hitch of ambivalence. Likewise, the preacher who considers the heartache of these sisters and brothers will hold lightly the psalmist's claim that God *causes* such natural events.

The psalmist's image of God directing a powerful storm raises many questions for the preacher and her congregation. Does God truly intend to uproot trees and lives? Does God sit aloof on a heavenly perch as a river erases its bank and all in its path? These and similar questions persist, but the psalm leaves us with far more than the aftermath of a storm. Indeed, the psalmist does not witness the loss of human life in the storm's path but finds in the storm an expression of an awesome God; that is, the strength of God is *like* the storm's burst of thunder, flashes of fire, and flow of flood waters.

As we celebrate the baptism of Jesus on this First Sunday after the Epiphany, the psalmist invites us to glimpse anew this "glory and strength" of God. The psalmist's description of God's "holy splendor" revealed in thunder and lightning ushers us to the Jordan River. There the voice of God thunders and the heavens are "torn apart," as if by lightning (Mark 1:10). In that moment the glory of God is made manifest in the person of Jesus. Later, one will ask, "Can anything good come out of Nazareth?" (John 1:46). Others will hear Jesus' teachings and ask, "Is not this the carpenter, the son of Mary?" (Mark 6:3). And yet, the riverside theophany reveals God's relationship with Jesus, "my Son, the Beloved" (Mark 1:11). Like the psalm's storm that breaks, flashes, shakes, and whirls, the thunder and lightning of that baptismal scene signal God's life-giving power in Jesus of Nazareth.

Psalm 29

Theological Perspective

destabilizing effects, for example, the breaking of cedars as if they were twigs, and the shaking of mountains (Lebanon and Sirion) as if they were playful calves and young oxen. Some scholars have contrasted this theophany with the more subdued one in the Synoptic Gospels on the occasion of the baptism of Jesus by John the Baptizer (Matt. 3:16–17; Mark 1:11; Luke 3:21–22). Comparisons can certainly be made in terms of the destabilizing impact of the subsequent ministry of Jesus.

All imagery that attempts to articulate the mystery that is God is partial and limited. While the richness and versatility of these images may communicate across contexts, it is the responsibility of interpreters to be aware of their own contemporary contexts and the living communities they accompany in any given time. Storms and natural phenomena as poetic metaphors of God's glory may cause anxiety. Posttraumatic stress remains in an age that remembers the devastation caused by such events as the tsunami born of an earthquake in the Indian Ocean in 2004 and the 2005 Hurricane Katrina and its aftermath, especially along the coastal United States bordering the Gulf of Mexico. It is hard to reconcile the power of God with the destruction of the innocent. For some who have witnessed, survived, or experienced loss amid quakes and storms and floods, it may be difficult to ascribe glory to God amid the thunder.

This theological quandary finds some address in the psalm. The image of God in verse 10 as "enthroned over the flood" and "enthroned as king forever" recalls for the worshiping community the God of creation (Gen. 1), who with an utterance brings order to chaos. Ultimately God is in control, a God whose "word is bond," to borrow an expression made popular by contemporary rap artists; as several of their lyrics continue, "bond is life." The response of the faithful to such a God is, as verse 11 proposes, to pray for strength and to participate fully in the peace of the divine promise.

CARMEN NANKO-FERNÁNDEZ

Pastoral Perspective

powerful, stripping away everything superfluous, leaving us vulnerable and open to God's transformation. In baptism we experience a seismic shift.

Water. One of the very first images of the psalm is of water. "The voice of the LORD is over the waters; the God of glory thunders, the LORD, over mighty waters" (v. 3). This image is then recapitulated at the end: "The LORD sits enthroned over the flood" (v. 10).

Too often, powerful untamable water gets forgotten when it comes to baptism. Baptism can too easily become "the cute sacrament"—an adorable baby, a bowl of water, a sprinkling on the head. Too often our response to baptism is not "Glory!" in the temple but a heartwarming "Awww . . . " The God of Psalm 29 is not to be trifled with. Water is not just something in which to splash around. It gives life, but it also has the power to destroy. So when we are baptized in water, something life giving happens, and something is also put to death.

Many Christian traditions permit three methods of baptism, colloquially known as "sprinkle, dunk, and pour." The sprinkle and pour churches far outnumber the dunking churches in most denominations that permit all three. A sermon on Psalm 29 would go a long way to help parishioners confront the wildness of the sacrament of baptism.

A note of pastoral caution is in order about a God who is "enthroned over the flood." Catastrophic hurricanes, tsunamis, and floods can devastate not only land and property, but hope and faith as well. Did God not promise Noah, "Never again"? It is the age-old question of how to understand the providence of God in light of natural disaster. An effective and pastorally sensitive sermon highlighting God's power in the midst of the elements of nature will tread lightly in such matters. Do we understand God as "enthroned over the flood" because God is somehow presiding over it? Could it simply be that the greatness of God is beyond even the greatest feats that nature can concoct?

MARYANN MCKIBBEN DANA

Exegetical Perspective

vague that such an interpretation is by no means necessary. For homiletical purposes, however, presenting the text in terms of a thunderstorm may indeed provide an excellent entry point. Experiencing a thunderstorm is a universal experience; most congregants can easily envision the cracking trees, flashing fire (i.e., lightning), and stripped forests, and from that point they can be encouraged to ponder theologically a God who acts with such awe-inspiring power.

Three terms are key to interpretation. *Glory* (*kabod*) is a recurrent motif, repeated four times. *Strength* (*oz*) is, at its first mention, connected with glory (v. 1). In the psalm, all of God's activity is encapsulated as God's "glory," a summary term for God's majesty as demonstrated by means of God's various activities (vv. 3–8). Thus, divine glory and strength are revealed in divine acts of power and dominance, and recognition of these attributes is required on the part of observers. Strength is initially attributed to YHWH. Then—surprisingly—the psalmist presents God as giving this same strength (*oz*) to the people (v. 11). In one sense this connection is rather frightening, to think that the same type of "strength" YHWH displayed in all the stormy and destructive activity will now, even if in lesser magnitude, be placed in the hands of human beings.

The term *flood* (*mabbul*) (v. 10; cf. v. 3) highlights important intertextual connections with the primeval narratives in Genesis. The only other place in the Hebrew Bible where "flood" (*mabbul*) appears is in the flood story of Genesis 6–10. The original great flood was a destructive act, following the original creation (Gen. 1–3), which is echoed by the psalm's devastation of nature. In light of this demolition, it is highly significant that Psalm 29 ends with "peace" or "well-being" (*shalom*). Peace is the final word in the Hebrew text, a detail reflected by the NRSV. It leads us to imagine the calm that comes after a storm, the rainbow, and dove (cf. Matt. 3:16) that came after the flood. The God who blessed and made a covenant with the ancient family (Gen. 9) is the God who continues to bless the people with peace (v. 11).

LINDA DAY

Homiletical Perspective

In the final verse of Psalm 29, the psalmist offers the preacher a more explicit word of hope. The psalmist speaks a prayer charged with faithful expectation: "May the Lord give strength to his people! May the Lord bless his people with peace!" (v. 11). This verse calls the preacher to higher ground, from which she beholds God's capacity to grant great power to God's people. As the psalmist witnesses the uncontrollable strength of God in the thunder, lightning, and tree-bending wind, so the psalmist hopes that such strength finds the faithful in expressions of blessing and peace—the currency of God's reign. Thus, the psalmist's prayer may resonate with our own: God of power and might, grant us strength for today.

Portraits of such God-given strength abound. Neighbors welcome a newborn who will endure several major surgeries before his first birthday. The child's prognosis for a healthful life is unclear and unsettling, but his parents ascribe to God what strength they have to face each day. Walter, a lifelong resident of coastal Mississippi, remembers the winds and water that threatened his life and ravaged his home. Still, tending a bed of tulips outside his waterlogged home, he speaks of the unfathomable strength of God that keeps him from the clutch of despair. An elderly woman, in the final hours of this life, labors to draw breath after breath, but she finds strength beyond her own to squeeze the hand of her estranged daughter. These storm-weary lives, like many before them, point to the brilliant turn in today's psalm. As the psalmist witnesses the awesome power of God in the storm, the author finds—and calls us to find—the equal power of God's blessings.

The storm of Psalm 29 leaves an impressive mark on the Mediterranean landscape. The ground is strewn with snapped cedars and oaks. Amid the brokenness, the psalmist lifts his eyes to a God who reigns above the tumult and offers a prayer to a God whose strength is far greater than his own. With the company of the faithful, he sings: "Glory!"

ANDREW NAGY-BENSON

Acts 10:34-43

³⁴Then Peter began to speak to them: "I truly understand that God shows no partiality, ³⁵but in every nation anyone who fears him and does what is right is acceptable to him. ³⁶You know the message he sent to the people of Israel, preaching peace by Jesus Christ—he is Lord of all. ³⁷That message spread throughout Judea, beginning in Galilee after the baptism that John announced: ³⁸how God anointed Jesus of Nazareth with the Holy Spirit and with power; how he went about doing good and healing all who were oppressed by the devil, for God was with him. ³⁹We are witnesses to all that he did both in Judea and in Jerusalem. They put him to death by hanging him on a tree; ⁴⁰but God raised him on the third day and allowed him to appear, ⁴¹not to all the people but to us who were chosen by God as witnesses, and who ate and drank with him after he rose from the dead. ⁴²He commanded us to preach to the people and to testify that he is the one ordained by God as judge of the living and the dead. ⁴³All the prophets testify about him that everyone who believes in him receives forgiveness of sins through his name."

Theological Perspective

Each year in the lectionary cycle, the first New Testament reading for the First Sunday after Epiphany, celebrating the baptism of Jesus, is from Acts, followed for the next five to seven Sundays in Epiphany with sequential readings from 1 Corinthians. Since this is a traditional Sunday for baptism, Peter's brief credo of God's work in Christ given in his speech in Caesarea is an apt confession of faith to highlight what baptism is all about, both for those about to be baptized, parents and godparents in the case of infant baptism, and the congregation in general. What stands out theologically in Peter's speech is the impartiality of God. "God shows no partiality, but in every nation anyone who fears him and does what is right is acceptable to him" (vv. 34–35).

In other words, God's gift and call in Jesus is to all. The universalism of Christianity is not about universal salvation for all who do what is right. That question may be left for another time. The universalism of Christian faith is that all are called, without regard to language, culture, or tribe. Cultural rites and wrongs are not requirements of faith. None are thereby excluded from the call to accept and follow Christ. The question that remains then is that of Christ and culture: what is of Christ and what is of culture?

In matters of morals or manners, Christians have always struggled to discern what is of Christ, as Acts

Pastoral Perspective

"I truly understand that God shows no partiality" (v. 34). This is a good example of why texts should be read within their immediate narrative context. The setting of Peter's speech, of which this is the opening statement, is the story of two visions, one of Cornelius, the other of Peter. The visions issue in two conversions: Cornelius and his household are baptized, and Peter accepts that Gentiles as well as Jews are offered "the forgiveness of sins" through the name of Jesus. Peter's speech concludes with that conviction, and the entire story reaches its climax when the Spirit is given to the Gentile household. Seeing them "speaking in tongues and extolling God" (v. 46), Peter calls for them to be baptized. Clearly, God "shows no partiality." Having started his speech by announcing this, Peter explains that God's impartiality means that Jew and Gentile alike are acceptable if they fear God and "do right." The simplicity of this is deceptive, though; this general theological principle does not stand alone, but requires the narrative of Jesus' ministry that follows it. Peter's exposition of that ministry and its fulfillment ends up transforming what it means for God to "show no partiality."

The Old Testament insists that God's justice may not be bought. Nothing will persuade God to look the other way or reward evil and punish the good. God's justice is always reliably different from human

Exegetical Perspective

The pivotal event in Luke–Acts is the conversion of Cornelius, as the length of the story (10:1–11:18) and the place of the narrative within the structure of Acts indicate. Unlike Luke's other stories, this one involves a series of scenes (10:1–48) before the characters retell what the readers already know (cf. 11:1–18). Within this narrative framework, the encounter of Peter with Cornelius is crucial in Luke's attempt to explain how the "hope of Israel" (cf. 28:20) culminated in good news for all nations. Luke anticipated this event at the beginning of the story in the aged Simeon's reference to the prophetic hope (Isa. 49:6) that Israel would be a "light to the nations" (Luke 2:32); in Jesus' inclusion of God's care for foreigners in his inaugural speech (Luke 4:24–29); and in his mandate to be witnesses "to the ends of the earth" (Acts 1:8). Having witnessed in Jerusalem, Judea, and Samaria (1:8), Peter speaks to Gentiles in his final missionary sermon in Acts (10:34–43), preparing the way for Paul's mission to the nations.

Although Peter's sermon to this Gentile audience shares some features with previous sermons, the focus is noticeably different, as the inclusion in 10:34–35, 42–43 indicates. Peter's interpretation of events indicates the focus of the passage. In saying, "I truly understand that God shows no partiality" (v. 34), he alludes to the previous scenes and his own process of

Homiletical Perspective

As Luke tells the story of Peter and Cornelius, it is clear that it took a lot of pressure to get Peter to speak the words recorded in today's lectionary text. It all began when Cornelius had a vision. Then Peter had a vision. Then Cornelius sent emissaries to Peter to persuade him to make the journey to see him. Then the Spirit told Peter to "get up, go down, and go with them without hesitation" (10:20). Then Cornelius told Peter his vision. Finally, "Peter began to speak to them" (v. 34).

It behooves us to be sensitive to the issues with which Peter was struggling when he encountered Cornelius, because they are issues deeply rooted in the human experience. People isolate themselves from others. People find their identity within a group, and fear that they will lose that identity if they do not guard their separateness. People find it difficult to relate to and associate with those who are different from themselves. People have a sense that they will lose their status within their own group if they dare to reach out to those on the outside.

All of us share in such ideas and feelings, which are part of our fundamental perspective on who we are and how we should live. If the ways in which we deal with and relate to others are challenged, it is no simple matter to change our mind and to act in a different way. Prejudice runs deep within us. It is hard

Acts 10:34-43

Theological Perspective

recounts in telling of the Jerusalem council (15:1–35), as Paul differently recounts in Galatians (2:1–10), and as Paul explicitly addresses in the First Letter to the Corinthians. We continue to struggle, for example, over what constitutes sexual morality and immorality as a matter of act and intent, of what we do and why we do it. As for manners, rather than over purity laws governing what goes into our bodies, we struggle (or should struggle) over how we should conduct our lives in a consumerist society—for example, how we should use and limit the use of electronic media and how we can be connected without being consumed by consumerism.

Peter's brief confession of faith does not in itself tell us what to do and not to do. Rather, his brief confession points to the larger purpose and ends that should govern our lives. Life in Christ is a new life marked by the forgiveness of sins, by doing good and providing justice to those who are oppressed, and by proclaiming to others that God has done mighty acts for us in Christ and that Jesus is Lord of all. To enter into Christian faith is to be at peace, to be made whole, in entering into the work of God in Christ. The church later comes to say that we remember and share our faith in Word and sacrament, in preaching and in worship. Always, though, this is a new life in which we are no longer separated by sin and instead serve one another, especially those who are outsiders, the oppressed.

At the center of Peter's confession is Jesus' death on a tree, his resurrection, and his appearance to the apostles. Jesus reveals the cruciform character of life in God. New life is given as it is spent and given up for others. Without overly specifying or speculating, we say that these fundamental theological convictions are the bedrock of faith. Peter's speech is the appropriate word for marking what Christian baptism and what the subsequent life of faith are all about (which may then be developed in the following weeks in conversation with Paul's First Letter to the Corinthians).

As emphasized in this year's Gospel reading for this Sunday from Matthew (3:13–17) and in the readings from Acts for liturgical years B and C, baptism is not only an initiation into a new life but a matter of baptism in the Spirit (Matt. 3:16). In baptism by water we receive the gift and power of the Holy Spirit, just as Peter describes in Acts: "after the baptism that John announced . . . God anointed Jesus of Nazareth with the Holy Spirit and with power" (10:37–38). In baptism by water in the community of faith we experience the power of God at

Pastoral Perspective

justice, which is subject to corruption (2 Chr. 19:7). Corrupt judges show themselves by taking bribes, and God will judge them for it (Deut. 10:17). Personal interest must not drive the exercise of authority; where that occurs, a human society is undermined. Not accepting bribes is a minimum standard expected of those who wield power on behalf of others. Even a minimal standard, though, is not always easy to keep. Bribery comes in such alluring forms, including the particularly subtle coin of flattery. God may judge judges because God is beyond flattery or "graft."

Nevertheless, the impartial God who is scrupulously fair is also an ambiguous figure. In some imaginings, this impeccable judge is quite terrifying, given that we find ourselves where we can scarce "escape whipping." Could we bear our "just deserts"? Perhaps, though God's "impartiality" expresses itself not so much in judicial probity but in the readiness to bless, in a generosity that swerves to neither left nor right. This is the evenhanded goodness that sends rain and sun without respect of persons (Matt. 5:45). Even this, however, pales beside the impartiality that Peter reveals as he presents the basis for his conclusion that God shows no partiality—a grounding that appears only as Peter moves from his general claim into the specific, particular details of Jesus of Nazareth, whom "God anointed."

Peter's speech has a rapid, dramatic movement that reaches an initial climax in the details of Jesus' ministry and then accelerates through Jesus' death to the resurrection and the confession that Jesus is appointed "judge of the living and the dead." This narrative rush from one climax to another supports Peter's telling of Jesus' story as a story of divine excess, of God's power and reach exceeding expectation. It is true that all who do right are acceptable to God and also true that this applies to Jew and Gentile alike. However, in itself, such a conviction was not foreign to first-century Judaism. Some insisted that the righteous among the nations would also have "a portion in the world to come."[1]

According to Peter, however, this "doing right" and "acceptability" is preceded by Jesus proclaiming God's peace and by the largesse of freedom and healing without restraint. Not even the horror of Jesus' death curtails the progress of this triumph of blessing. Rather, God raises Jesus and establishes this mercy once and for all. The theme of judgment now

1. Charles H. Talbert, *Reading Acts: A Literary and Theological Commentary on the Acts of the Apostles* (Macon, GA: Smyth & Helwys, 2005), 97–98.

Exegetical Perspective

discovery. At the beginning of this narrative, he had not understood this truth, for he held to the strict distinction between clean and unclean foods (10:14). Like his peers, he interpreted this distinction as excluding association with Gentiles. He responded with confusion (10:17) to the divine announcement that God had cleansed the unclean (10:15) before the course of events finally led him to say, "I truly understand." Only because God intervened did Peter comprehend that no human being can be called unclean. Thus the story is about the conversion, not only of Cornelius, but of Peter as well.

That "God shows no partiality" is actually no new discovery, for this principle is rooted in Scripture. According to the law (Deut. 10:17), God "is not partial and takes no bribe" in executing justice for the orphan and the widow. Peter's new discovery is that God's impartiality extends to people "in every nation . . . who fear God and do what is right" (v. 35). Before his speech is interrupted by another divine intervention (10:44–48), Peter reinforces this emphasis on the universality of God's summons, concluding that "everyone who believes in him receives forgiveness of sins through his name" (v. 43). The salvation of Israel becomes universal salvation, because God's impartiality extends to the whole world. Just as Peter in previous speeches has challenged listeners within Israel to repent (2:38; 3:19), he now extends that summons to the people of every nationality. Peter's discovery indicates the universality of God's offer of salvation. God's blessings are not limited to those who belong to a particular nation or keep its specific laws, but to those who believe and do what is right. The door is now open for the inclusion into the people of God of those who had previously been excluded, as the following scene indicates (10:44–48).

As Peter's sermon indicates (vv. 36–41), the message of universal salvation is anchored in Israel's story and the good news that was first proclaimed to Israel (v. 36). Recalling that the prophetic hope for Israel to be a "light to the nations" (Isa. 49:6) would be accompanied by the good news of peace (Isa. 52:7), Peter announces that this good news has become a reality in the ministry of Jesus. This description may be an elaboration of the angelic announcement in Luke's birth narrative of "peace on earth" (Luke 2:14). Peter's final missionary speech does not, like the earlier speeches, focus only on the crucifixion and resurrection of Jesus (cf. 2:22–36; 3:12–26; 4:8–12; 5:29–32), but gives the outline of his public ministry as well, summarizing the Gospel of Luke (vv. 37–41). Like the authors of the other

Homiletical Perspective

to overestimate the importance to us of being part of our own group. The way in which we have always done things often seems to us to be the only right way, and any change would be a violation of the fundamental convictions that have shaped our lives.

On many different kinds of issues people group themselves together and separate themselves from others. It may be the food we eat. Several years ago a Vietnamese refugee was frequently in our home before she finally dared to tell us that when we grilled hamburgers the smell of cooking beef literally made her sick. I asked if she liked to eat pork. She replied that she did, but that she liked dog better. We separate ourselves by racial characteristics. Many years ago as the civil rights movement was just beginning, a young woman reported that the first time she saw a black man and a white woman holding hands, she got physically ill. We identify and separate on the basis of sexual orientation. We identify and separate on the basis of religious conviction and practice. We identify and separate on the basis of cultural mores.

We can empathize with Peter when he confronted a challenge to his deeply held convictions. As a good Jew, it was unlawful for him "to associate with or to visit a Gentile" (10:28). As a good Jew, it was unlawful for him to eat "anything that is profane or unclean" (10:14). It took visions and the power of the Spirit to move him to go to Cornelius, and it took the plea of Cornelius for Peter to speak "all that the Lord has commanded you to say" (10:33).

When Peter did speak, he offered a new perspective on his relationship with Gentiles and on the promise of God to them manifest in Jesus Christ. He began by asserting that he had now come to a true understanding. It was not just a true idea that he had now developed about other people and how he should treat them; it was a true understanding about God and God's relationship to persons. Repeatedly Peter asserted that no person is beyond the care and concern of God: "God shows no partiality." "In *every* nation, *anyone*" can be "acceptable to him." Jesus Christ "is Lord of *all*" (vv. 34–36). Jesus healed "*all* who were oppressed by the devil" (v. 38). The prophets testify that "*everyone* who believes in him receives forgiveness of sins through his name" (v. 43; italics in this paragraph added).

As Peter came to his new conviction about God's care for all, and his new conviction about how he should relate to those he had previously shunned, he continued to stress what God has done and is doing. God is willing to accept all who turn to him. God sent

Acts 10:34-43

Theological Perspective

work. Here again, specifying and speculating about the work of the Holy Spirit leads in many directions. The more fundamental point is that entering this new life is a matter of dying to the old and birth into the new, a matter of cross and resurrection. God's action in Christ is given to us as the Holy Spirit acting in our lives. The Trinitarian character of God as Father, Son, and Holy Spirit is at least implicit.

Baptism as baptism in the Spirit, moreover, means that our relationship to God has an ecstatic as well as ordered dimension. Entering the divine life is always the experience of something that is beyond ourselves, an experience that overwhelms and opens a new heaven and a new earth. While the character of the Christian life may be described as cruciform, as signed by cross and resurrection, Christian faith cannot be reduced to a philosophy—what Paul calls worldly wisdom in contrast to the wisdom of the cross, which appears as "foolishness to those who are perishing" (1 Cor. 1:17–18).

Such a theology of baptism requires preparation and commitment. It is why the early church required a catechumenate, an extended period of initiation into the life of faith, marked by the teaching of the Christian story, practices of prayer and worship, and the shaping of a way of life. It is why baptism happens at the conclusion of a catechumenal process. As a way of life, such is necessarily the case, especially in a culture that is shaped by individualism and consumerism.[1]

TIMOTHY F. SEDGWICK

Pastoral Perspective

returns in quite a new light. Jesus, once rejected and crucified, has become the judge; but instead of "just deserts," he offers the forgiveness of sins. God's impartiality is nothing short of reconciliation with enemies. Fairness and evenhanded goodness fall far short of this. God raises Jesus to offer forgiveness. Only the excessive goodness that reconciles with enemies reaches the meaning of God's impartiality.

"God shows no partiality." This raises another question that hovers around the entire speech. What about Israel? Is not God partial to Israel? The suggestion that God's care for Israel is like the partiality of a corrupt judge would horrify any Jew. Certainly, though, it is a favor, and Israel is an especially beloved child. This is a rich and tender favor, for which God gives a promised word and which God demonstrates in faithful constancy. On its own, of course, Peter's speech is not the source for an adequate theology of Israel. As Luke connects Jesus' ministry to the Jewish people, he tends here toward a somewhat instrumental account: the universal gospel comes by way of the Jews who are the means of Jesus' death and provide the first "witnesses" to God's salvation. That being said, as the speech concludes, Luke does find deeper roots in Israel for Peter's proclamation.

"All the prophets" testify (v. 43), not just to Jesus as "judge," but precisely to the unrestricted offer of forgiveness, to this fullness of divine impartiality. God's partiality to Israel is thus the embodiment and guarantee of the promise that, in Jesus, God will take the part of all, without restriction. The church is also implicated in the prophetic witness and in the role Luke gives to Israel. The church knows God's partiality, and so its mission proclaims God's impartiality. Christian communities treasure God's love, but they do not hoard it; they do not embrace mercy as a mark of their privilege, nor make Christ's hope a hope only for them. The church enjoys the blessing of God's presence in Jesus, but it enjoys it as a prophetic partiality, as taking our part in the great, excessive impartiality of the world's reconciliation.

ALAN GREGORY

---

1. On the origin and theology of baptism, see Aidan Kavanagh, *The Shape of Baptism* (New York: Pueblo, 1976).

Exegetical Perspective

Gospels, Luke demonstrates that the Christian message includes not only the cross and resurrection, but also the memory of the deeds in Judea and Galilee of the one who died and was raised. In Peter's claim that the one who began in the obscure region of Galilee is "Lord of all" (v. 36), Luke points to Peter's new insight and summarizes this two-volume work: the story that began within Israel is the message for the world.

Peter's speech is selective in recalling the ministry of Jesus. Consistent with Luke's earlier narrative, Peter indicates that the ministry of Jesus is the beginning of a new era "after the baptism of John" (v. 37; cf. Luke 3:21–24; 16:16). Just as Luke's narrative portrays the baptism of Jesus as the moment when the Holy Spirit empowered him for ministry (Luke 3:21–23), Peter indicates that "God anointed Jesus with the Holy Spirit and with power" (Acts 10:38) in the same way that he had commissioned David for service with anointing and the empowerment by the Spirit (cf. 1 Sam. 16:13). Jesus' baptism was the occasion for the empowerment for ministry and the prelude to the words inaugurating his ministry, "The Spirit of the Lord is upon me, because he has anointed me to bring good news to the poor" (Luke 4:18). Peter's summary of Jesus' ministry as "[going] about doing good and healing all who were oppressed by the devil" (Acts 10:38) recalls Luke's account of Jesus' many acts of healing in the Gospel and his response to the disciples' report of the success of their healing mission: "I watched Satan fall from heaven like a flash of lightning" (Luke 10:18).

The conclusion of the sermon turns to the role of those who have been faithful to Jesus' mandate, "You will be my witnesses" (Acts 1:8). Like witnesses in a courtroom, Peter and the other witnesses first observe the events before they report what they have seen. They have observed the death and resurrection of Jesus (Acts 10:39–40) and eaten with the resurrected Lord (Luke 24:30, 43), and now they testify that the one who once lived in Galilee is "Lord of all" (Acts 10:36), the universal "judge of the living and the dead" (10:42), and the founder of a community that knows no ethnic boundaries.

JAMES W. THOMPSON

Homiletical Perspective

the message of peace through Jesus Christ. God anointed Jesus with the Holy Spirit and with power. God continued to be with Jesus throughout his ministry. God raised Jesus after people had put him to death. God enabled Jesus to appear to those whom God had chosen as witnesses. God commanded those to whom Jesus appeared to preach to the people. God ordained Jesus to be judge of the living and the dead.

Peter's word to Cornelius resonates with other preaching of the early disciples as recorded in Acts and elsewhere. Peter's word focuses on the life, the work, the death, and the resurrection of Jesus. It offers the promises of peace and forgiveness and fulfillment of life to those who hear and respond to the one whom God sent as Lord. The word was not new for Peter, but the people to whom he offered the promises of God—Gentiles—were different from those to whom he had spoken before.

This story of the radical transformation of Peter's perspective and action informs the way in which we can be enabled to transcend the limitations of our relationship with others. Our prejudices are deeply ingrained. Our perspective on what is right and proper in how we deal with others has permeated our whole understanding of who we are. We *can* be opened to new understandings and new perspectives as we confront again and again the ways of God in Jesus Christ. It is a difficult matter indeed for us to break through the limitations of how we see and deal with others. Our only hope is to be open to the Spirit and to seek ever new understanding of the God who "shows no partiality."

HARRY B. ADAMS

Matthew 3:13-17

¹³Then Jesus came from Galilee to John at the Jordan, to be baptized by him. ¹⁴John would have prevented him, saying, "I need to be baptized by you, and do you come to me?" ¹⁵But Jesus answered him, "Let it be so now; for it is proper for us in this way to fulfill all righteousness." Then he consented. ¹⁶And when Jesus had been baptized, just as he came up from the water, suddenly the heavens were opened to him and he saw the Spirit of God descending like a dove and alighting on him. ¹⁷And a voice from heaven said, "This is my Son, the Beloved, with whom I am well pleased."

Theological Perspective

The celebration of the baptism of the Lord is traditionally a time to contemplate both Jesus' baptism and our own. To make sense of both these mysteries, it is also necessary to contemplate the incarnation itself. For Christians of the first centuries of the church, and for contemporary readers who embrace that tradition, neither Jesus' baptism nor our own makes sense if not considered in the light of the incarnation. Reflecting on how we are restored in the waters of baptism requires reflection on how God created, entered into, and radically transformed those waters. Pondering the reasons for Jesus' own baptism requires pondering what it means for the Son of God to have become a human. In short, to understand baptism, we must understand the reality, the physicality, of being human, and what it means to say that God saved us by becoming just like us.

Building on Scripture, the Apostles' and Nicene Creeds make clear that to be human is to be physical, to be tangible, to have senses, and to be sensed. We are not wispy souls trapped temporarily in a body that is foreign to who we really are. That is the claim of the gnostics, whether ancient or modern. Christians who subscribe to these creeds believe that our bodies are integral to who we are as human beings. We live out our existence within the possibilities and limitations of our bodies. When we look forward to the coming

Pastoral Perspective

Kyle was nowhere to be found, and I missed him. In the weeks following his baptism and confirmation on Pentecost Sunday, he was noticeably missing. Several other members of the confirmation class asked about him too, as did his confirmation mentor. Kyle and his family had come to the congregation when he was in the fifth grade. They attended sporadically, so I was more than a little surprised when I asked him and his parents if he was interested in joining the confirmation class and they responded positively. In this congregation, the confirmation class happened during the ninth-grade school year (as if God calls all ninth-graders simultaneously to be confirmed, just because they are in the ninth grade). Kyle and his parents came for the orientation meeting and agreed to the covenant to participate in two retreats, a mission activity, work with a mentor, and weekly classes for study and exploration. Kyle was serious in attending and missed a class or event rarely. He quickly became a significant part of the group and developed some wonderful friendships with other ninth-graders who had barely known him. Since Kyle had not yet been baptized, he was not only confirmed but also baptized on Pentecost Sunday. It was a marvelous celebration for all the confirmands, their families, and their mentors.

Exegetical Perspective

Matthew, like the other canonical Gospels, records an account of Jesus' baptism, which precedes and inaugurates his public ministry. After many years of literary silence, Jesus now comes onto the scene with a paradoxical blend of magnificence and humility.

The account begins with Jesus going out from Galilee to the Jordan River, a pilgrimage shared by others who were seeking (or inquisitive about) John's ministry of proclamation and baptism. Matthew chiefly characterizes John's ministry as a call to repentance for the forgiveness of sins (3:1–6). From this encounter of John and Jesus, two things become clear: (1) Jesus consciously identifies himself with the already active ministry and proclamation of John—chronologically speaking, it is not inaccurate to say that Jesus follows in line with John's ministry—and, (2) as a result, later on some seemingly take Jesus' baptism as being in direct response to John's message, thus connoting Jesus' need for forgiveness of sins. Matthew consciously aims to help navigate his readers through these issues.

Commentators often note Matthew's distinct apologetic emphasis. His retelling of some stories and events is intended not simply to act as a historical record, but also (and maybe more pointedly) to provide a response or defense to his audience concerning certain implications that others, and maybe

Homiletical Perspective

In many liturgical traditions, the First Sunday after the Epiphany, which commemorates the baptism of the Lord, is one of the Sundays normally set aside for baptisms. If a baptism is taking place in the service where you are preaching, it will strongly affect your homiletical situation. You may be preaching to a congregation whose primary attention on this Sunday is toward that liturgy of baptism; you may also be speaking to some who have attended only to witness the baptism. The possibility of communicating core truths about the faith to a new audience—as well as the opportunity of remembering core truths with longtime parishioners—makes this Sunday a preaching opportunity rich with promise and challenge.

New Testament scholar Raymond Brown has said that the Gospel of Matthew "has served as the foundational document of the Church," making this Matthean baptism story a normative text for our understanding of *Christian baptism*, but the text can be opened in many directions, depending on the interests and needs of your congregation.[1] This may be a good opportunity to explore the theological ramifications of the baptism your congregants witness on

1. Raymond E. Brown, *An Introduction to the New Testament*, Anchor Bible Reference Library (New York: Doubleday, 1997). 171.

Matthew 3:13-17

Theological Perspective

kingdom of God, we look forward to our bodies being resurrected and made new. Our hope is not to become a disembodied soul, for that would mean hoping to become something less than what we are—something less than what God created us to be. Instead, we hope for the renewal of all creation, including the renewal of our bodies. Our hope is to become fully and completely human.

Because we are both incorporeal and embodied, our salvation is worked out through both divine and physical elements. In the case of baptism, the physical element is water. Matthew echoes Genesis when he describes Jesus' baptism. Genesis records that, in the beginning, the Spirit hovered over the waters. The Word of God was present from the beginning and created the world. What the Word created was good. In Matthew, the Spirit of God once again hovers over the waters, and once again the Word of God speaks. Genesis describes God bringing order to chaos through his Word. Matthew describes God taming the chaos of our sins through his Word. Genesis describes the abundant possibilities of God's creative work. Matthew describes the renewal of those possibilities through God's entering into creation in order to redeem it. The parallels are stark, and they clearly link baptism to God's creative acts more generally.

Water is crucial to creation. It is not the author of life, but it is part of and necessary for life. Water is also part of and necessary for new life in Christ. Water gives witness to God's love for God's people. Blessed by the Word, water is the means by which we are buried and, at least vicariously, experience death. Water is also the means by which we are scrubbed clean of the sins that lead to darkness and death. Water washes us and regenerates us. In the water of baptism, we foreshadow our deaths and emerge victorious to new life.

Of course, water alone does not accomplish any of this. In his *Small Catechism*, Luther attributed the efficacy of baptism to the Word of God "in and with the water." While Luther wrote this to explain how our baptism is effective, he also offered a way to understand Jesus' own baptism. Not water alone, but the Word of God "in and with the water." What is Matthew describing other than Jesus of Nazareth, the Word of God made flesh, in and with the water of the Jordan? By entering this water, Jesus did not seek his own repentance, for he had nothing of which to repent. Instead, Jesus offered himself as the answer to John's call for all people to repent.

Thus, in his baptism, Jesus showed what it means for the Word of God to become incarnate, to take on

Pastoral Perspective

That is pretty much where it ended. That is when I knew we had done something wrong. When I checked in with Kyle and his folks, they all seemed a little surprised that I was calling and checking up on them. I distinctly remember his mother saying, "Oh, well, I guess I thought Kyle was all done. I mean, he was baptized and confirmed and everything. Isn't he done?" That is the problem. Despite our best intentions and despite all that we say and try to communicate, too many people seem to think that the baptism of the infant or the young adult or the adult is the culminating activity of faith, and then we are all "done." Matthew's description of Jesus' baptism tells us the opposite.

In Matthew's text, the baptism of Jesus is not the ending of his ministry. In Matthew's text, the baptism of Jesus is the *beginning* of his ministry. It is his launching. It is his commissioning to begin the public ministry for which he was created and to which he was called. To be sure, the baptism of Jesus named his identity, and this is crucial. Identity, however, is not a static thing. One's identity grows and deepens, as did Jesus' identity throughout his public ministry. His identity is as much about purpose as it is about personhood.

In days past, some Christian traditions called preparation for confirmation a "communicants class," because children were not allowed to partake of the Lord's Supper until they had taken this class. Eventually, many of these traditions realized the problem with this, since many of our children were already baptized and were therefore eligible to receive Communion. So the name changed. Many congregations now call it "confirmation" because it confirms the vows made on many children's behalf by their parents and the congregation at the child's infant baptism. This term too has its problems. It is misleading because it indicates for persons like Kyle and his parents that this is the end of the journey, rather than the beginning, as it was for Jesus. For this reason, more and more congregations are adopting the title "confirmation and commissioning" to indicate that this is not simply the end of a journey but an important marker that sends us out into a new form of ministry and a new way of being faithful. While this term is a mouthful, it conveys the important idea that all is not done and that your identity, named in your baptism, is not finished but still growing and developing.

Jesus was confirmed in his baptism, to be sure. He was named by his cousin John as the one who was to come. In his baptism, Jesus' identity was confirmed

they, have drawn. For example, Matthew's birth narrative, which notably lacks details about Jesus' actual birth (in variation from Luke), seeks to communicate primarily that Jesus is *not* conceived out of wedlock (1:18–25). Matthew is chiefly interested in communicating and defending the conception and virgin birth of Jesus, concepts which some of his Jewish readers may discount. Matthew's account of Jesus' baptism also reflects this type of apologetic emphasis. Of the four Gospels, only in Matthew do we see the conversation between John and Jesus concerning John's self-identified inadequacy to baptize him. Matthew seemingly anticipates that some of his readers will wonder about or even assume that Jesus had prebaptismal sin and thus needed John's baptism like the other pilgrims. John's penchant *not* to go through with this baptism (3:14), specifically on the basis of his own unworthiness and his identity as a preparatory figure in God's purposes, communicates to the reader that Jesus is not the typical baptismal candidate.

Jesus' response to John's protest also pushes in this direction. The imperative "let it be so" (v. 15)—more literally, "permit it"—affirms that John's reluctance to baptize Jesus is rightly placed. It should, however, be permitted "now" (*harti*, v. 15)—at this specific time—because it must be done under these circumstances and in this way "to fulfill all righteousness" (v. 15). Here "righteousness" is not used in a forensic manner (i.e., it is not indicating a "legal" standing or position before God), but as an aspect of discipleship. John is to baptize Jesus as an act of submission and obedience to God. In doing so, John not only participates in God's unfolding purpose for Jesus, but he also behaviorally testifies to the coming of God's kingdom.

As we see elsewhere in Matthew's Gospel, especially in the Sermon on the Mount (chaps. 5–7), the dawning of the kingdom of heaven calls for and is signaled by a higher kind of righteousness, one that "exceeds that of the scribes and Pharisees" (5:20). Therefore, instead of something that should arouse suspicion concerning Jesus' identity, Matthew's account of Jesus' baptism is presented as a righteous act of solidarity with those to whom and for whom he has come. The one who is now being baptized by human hands, amid a call to repentance, is also the one who will usher in God's kingdom and bring the good news of forgiveness to those same human hands.

The final events recounted by Matthew cap and reinforce the message noted above. The heavens opening up reflect an act of revelation and/or

this Sunday. What does the baptismal liturgy in your service suggest about your theology?

Chrysostom wrote that although John's baptism was intended for "repentance," Jesus clearly had no need to repent of his sins.[2] The Greek word *metanoia*, used in verse 11 to explain what is happening in John's baptism, suggests *transformation* and *turning* rather than simple repentance for sins, as the Greek is often translated. The baptism we read about in Matthew does suggest a transformation of some sort, perhaps even a rite of passage for Jesus. In more sacramental Christian traditions, the holy sacraments of the church are said to represent a passage or transformation for those who enter into them. In what ways does your tradition understand the transformation or turning that takes place in the sacrament of baptism? From what and to what is it a movement?

Baptism is an archetypal act, and water an archetypal symbol often associated with birth and rebirth, so relevant stories and cultural examples of this symbolism will be easy to find. The biblical story of God's people contains several notable stories of rebirth after passing through water, among them the parting of the waters for Moses as the children of Israel escaped Egypt, and the parallel version of the parting of the waters for Joshua when the people reached the promised land. In each case—and generally, when water is used as a symbol of rebirth—people enter the water as one thing (slaves or wanderers in these particular stories) and emerge as something entirely different.

The writer of Matthew employs the narrative structure found in the other Gospels: he places the baptism of Jesus at the very beginning of his ministry, a *preparation* for what will later follow. How do we understand baptism as preparatory to our lives in Christ? For what is God preparing each of the baptized? Further, for what is this communal act preparing the community? Theologian and ethicist Stanley Hauerwas writes that Christians are called to be a community "capable of forming people with virtues sufficient to witness to God's truth in the world."[3] How might your community be—or become—a community capable of forming people who will witness to God's truth? What does your tradition suggest those virtues might be? How are they previewed in the baptismal liturgy and/or baptismal vows your congregation witnesses? How might these virtues be

2. Manlio Simonetti, ed., *Matthew 1–13*, Ancient Christian Commentary on Scripture (Downers Grove, IL: InterVarsity Press, 2001), 51.
3. Stanley Hauerwas, *A Community of Character: Toward a Constructive Christian Social Ethic* (Notre Dame, IN: University of Notre Dame Press, 1982), 3.

Matthew 3:13-17

Theological Perspective

flesh. As a historical, tangible man, Jesus accomplished the salvific acts of the eternal, divine Son of God. In his baptism, Jesus restored water to its proper role and made even more poignant the necessity of water for life. The water of baptism is necessary for everlasting life.

Luther was not the first to make this point. When writing about baptism, Gregory of Nyssa explored how various elements of creation play a role in our journey toward union with God. Gregory took up how Jesus' baptism established an affinity between humanity and God. Theologians from Augustine to Bede looked at Jesus' baptism as a precursor to his crucifixion, sometimes describing the crucifixion as the ultimate baptism. Cyril of Alexandria embraced Paul's theme of Jesus as the new Adam, arguing that, in order to rescue humanity, it was necessary for Jesus to experience the fullness of what it means to be human.

These separate threads from the early church can be woven together to form a cord that firmly ties Jesus' baptism to contemporary incarnational theology. Jesus was not just a paradigm or generic representative of us all; he was also an individual who lived at a particular time and in a particular place. By becoming a particular person, the Son of God showed us not only how to be human beings, but also how to be particular men and women. Living as one before the fall, Jesus offered us a glimpse of what God intends for us, if only we can embrace those intentions. Born into a fallen world, Jesus sacrificed himself for others and took on their sin and pain. Thus, in the incarnate Son of God, in the man Jesus of Nazareth, we catch a glimpse of what it means to be fully human, and in baptism we are offered the possibility of embracing our humanity.

STEVEN D. DRIVER

Pastoral Perspective

through heaven's opening and the dove coming down to him and the voice from heaven naming him as God's Son, God's Beloved, the very one who holds God's pleasure; but this confirmation was not the culmination of his ministry. It was the beginning of the remarkable journey that was to lead him to the cross and beyond.

This step beyond baptism, beyond confirmation, is essential; sadly, the church does not call persons to it. That is why all too many young people experience their confirmation as a final act, and we end up confirming young people by the thousands to leave the church following their confirmation. Confirmation done right must be paired with commissioning, so that at every turn, as we help persons claim their identity as created in God's image and belonging to God forever, we remind them of their purpose in living out this identity through the ministries to which they have been called.

When I talked more with Kyle and his parents, I tried better to explain this and to help them understand why I was calling and how much we missed not only Kyle but the whole family's presence in our community. They were all remarkably understanding, and his folks were apologetic. "I guess we just missed this somehow," they said. "And I don't think we did a very good job of conveying this to you and to Kyle," I replied. I also explained that Kyle's relationship with his confirmation mentor is not over and that his mentor hopes to continue to be in contact with him in the months and years to come. Both Kyle's parents were impressed with this and expressed their appreciation. "Kyle's baptism and confirmation was not simply about his profession of faith," I further explained. "It is about his continuing to grow in his understanding of what God is calling him to do as he lives out his identity as a child of God."

The next Sunday, Kyle and his family came to church and were warmly greeted. They even seemed a little relieved at the realization that the journey was not over but was only beginning.

RODGER Y. NISHIOKA

provision by God (cf. Ezek. 1:1; Isa. 64:1; Acts 7:56; 10:11). Grammatically constructed as a "divine passive," God is the one who opens up the heavens and unequivocally endorses and unveils Jesus as God's Son. God then anoints Jesus with the Spirit, something akin to God's anointing of prophets in the Old Testament (e.g., Isa. 42:1), which is preparatory for Jesus' messianic work. As Hagner writes, "the one who is to baptize with the Spirit must himself experience the formal anointing of the Spirit."[1] One should not read Matthew as indicating that Jesus was devoid of God's Spirit prior to this time, for we read earlier that he is "from the Holy Spirit" (Matt. 1:20). Matthew indicates that the giving of the Spirit is a ceremonial anointing of Jesus for his earthly ministry (note that in 3:16 the Spirit, like a dove, alights *on* him and does not seize or infiltrate him).

The final words that boom from the heavens, "this is my Son, the Beloved, with whom I am well pleased" (3:17), have a variety of functions: (1) as further divine approval of the earthly Jesus and the ministry in which he is about to embark, (2) as an echo of or allusion to Psalm 2:7, which is a royal psalm appropriate for the coronation of a king, and (3) as a foreshadowing of what is to come later for Jesus. These words are again audible in Matthew's Gospel at the transfiguration, with the command to "Listen to him" (17:5), and are palpably absent in Jesus' godforsaken cry on the cross (27:46).

Evident at Jesus' baptism is an ironic tension that remains constant throughout his entire earthly ministry. Jesus' uniqueness is known in and shouted from the heavens—a higher authority, there is not!—but his own baptism and ministry are characterized by a consistent and conscious submission to those for whom he is bringing the gospel. It may well have been this type of paradox that led early Christians to sing the Christ hymn in Philippians (2:6–11) in celebration and worship of Jesus' utter humility, which God affirmed as the way of righteousness in the coming kingdom through exalting him.

TROY A. MILLER

understood from the succeeding chapters of the Gospel of Matthew, from which this witness to baptism is taken?

Harper Lee's *To Kill a Mockingbird* offers a potent vision of a community that has the potential to form those under its charge in one of two ways: into people of tolerance, love, and bravery, or into people of fear, bigotry, and greed. Scout Finch, who narrates the novel, and her brother Jem are formed by their father Atticus, their maid Calpurnia, their neighbors, and by others into people with great virtues—what we would probably call Christian virtues. This and other stories of community formation may help your congregation understand their role in shaping and supporting those who enter the family of God on this day.

If baptism is not to be celebrated alongside this preaching occasion, this lectionary passage contains other elements worth examining with your congregation. Matthew's baptism, unlike Mark's, features a public manifestation of the Spirit of God, as well as a direct announcement of Jesus as the Son of God to John the Baptizer and possibly to bystanders as well. This early manifestation of *the Trinity* present at the baptism parallels Matthew 28:19, where new followers of Jesus are to be baptized in the name of the Father, Son, and Spirit. Following Augustine's lead in seeing this text as an invitation to explore the Trinity, we could well use this day to do the same. We find few enough opportunities to preach on the Trinity—and often we duck those. This passage might constitute an opportunity to preach a teaching sermon on how your tradition understands the Trinity.

Finally, this scene contains a clear showing forth of God's power and beauty, what we might call a *theophany*. In the Hebrew tradition, God often appeared at significant natural locations: mountains, springs, rivers. How did God reveal God's self to God's people in the Scriptures? Do we sometimes have trouble recognizing how God might be moving in the world today? How might God appear—or be speaking—in your community today?

GREG GARRETT

1. Donald A. Hagner, *Matthew 1–13*, Word Biblical Commentary 33A (Dallas: Thomas Nelson, 1993), 57.

Isaiah 49:1-7

¹Listen to me, O coastlands,
   pay attention, you peoples from far away!
The LORD called me before I was born,
   while I was in my mother's womb he named me.
²He made my mouth like a sharp sword,
   in the shadow of his hand he hid me;
he made me a polished arrow,
   in his quiver he hid me away.
³And he said to me, "You are my servant,
   Israel, in whom I will be glorified."
⁴But I said, "I have labored in vain,
   I have spent my strength for nothing and vanity;
yet surely my cause is with the LORD,
   and my reward with my God."

⁵And now the LORD says,
   who formed me in the womb to be his servant,

Theological Perspective

American culture is fascinated with the notion of destiny and the idea that a person has the potential to go beyond one's station in life to reach the unattainable. The "American dream" of social mobility is alive and well, and it is manifest in the abundance of reality shows that promise instantaneous fame (or infamy) and a worldwide stage to exhibit one's talent. Such aspirations are further reflected in popular fiction stories of superheroes who suddenly overcome human physical limitations and discover supernatural powers. These cultural tendencies reflect a longing to be discovered, to be recognized as special, or to become something more. When we observe our current social patterns from a theological perspective, the deep-seated sense that humans are destined for greater things becomes apparent. In fact, this sense manifests itself in our society because we *are* destined for more than what we are. According to Scripture, we are called beyond our finitude, not only to a higher purpose as children of God, but to everlasting life through our Lord Jesus Christ.

Isaiah 49 illustrates this higher calling and the intimate care that God bestows upon the one whom God calls. Even before birth, God knew this unborn Servant, and God named, called, and equipped this one so that the tasks of restoration and salvation may be accomplished. As Christians, we most

Pastoral Perspective

In the first of Isaiah's Servant Songs (Isa. 42:1–9), it is God's voice we hear: "Here is my servant, whom I uphold, my chosen, in whom my soul delights" (Isa. 42:1). The first Servant Song celebrates the patient, nonviolent, merciful ministry of the Servant who "faithfully bring[s] forth justice" without breaking a "bruised reed" or quenching "a dimly burning wick" (Isa. 42:3). "The coastlands," God sings in the first of the Servant Songs, "wait for his teaching" (Isa. 42:4).

In the second Servant Song, we hear the Servant's own voice, singing toward those same coastlands, calling to "peoples from far away" (v. 1). To these strangers living far off, the Servant sings a song about the unfolding of a remarkable vocation.

Whose vocation is it? As with the first Servant Song, there is considerable scholarly debate about the identity of the Servant in this passage. The Servant quotes God as saying, "You are my servant, Israel, in whom I will be glorified" (v. 3), which seems straightforward enough. There is textual evidence, however, that the designation, Israel, was an addition to the original text. This has led some scholars to seek the identity of the Servant in individual historical figures rather in the community of God's people.

The pastoral impact of this text is not dependent, however, upon a definitive answer to the question of

to bring Jacob back to him,
    and that Israel might be gathered to him,
for I am honored in the sight of the Lord,
    and my God has become my strength—
⁶he says,
    "It is too light a thing that you should be my servant
    to raise up the tribes of Jacob
    and to restore the survivors of Israel;
I will give you as a light to the nations,
    that my salvation may reach to the end of the earth."

⁷Thus says the Lord,
    the Redeemer of Israel and his Holy One,
to one deeply despised, abhorred by the nations,
    the slave of rulers,
"Kings shall see and stand up,
    princes, and they shall prostrate themselves,
because of the Lord, who is faithful,
    the Holy One of Israel, who has chosen you."

Exegetical Perspective

This reading is the second of the so-called Servant Songs (the others are Isa. 42:1–9; 50:4–11; and 52:13–53:12). (The Song unit seems to end with verse 6. Verse 7 begins a new unit, extending at least through verse 12, that constitutes an announcement of salvation for Israel.) In this reading, the Servant is depicted as the speaker, addressing the coastlands and peoples far away.

In the second half of the first verse, the Servant declares that he was predestined, designated, or called by God before birth, when still in his mother's womb. The idea of being formed by God in a mother's womb occurs in a few Old Testament texts. Isaiah 44:1–2 speaks of the Servant and God's formation of the Servant in the womb: "Thus says the Lord who made you, who formed you in the womb, and will help you." Similar language is found elsewhere in the Bible. Psalm 139:13 contains the psalmist's affirmation that God oversaw even the person's formation, just as God oversaw every time and aspect of the person's existence: "For it was you who formed my inward parts; you knit me together in my mother's womb." The Servant in Isaiah 49:1–6 claims not only prenatal oversight but also prenatal commission. He was appointed before birth and named before he was born.

This type of high-flung rhetorical speech was probably originally at home in royal circles in which

Homiletical Perspective

There is a stage set in Isaiah 49:1–7—not for one moment in time but for all time. Someone standing in the wings is preparing to address a restless crowd. The identity of the one who is to speak is elusive, leaving the listener to wonder: is the speaker a person or a personification of a people? If the identity is not so clear, the speaker's mission certainly is. It is a sense of mission that flows from the depth of God.

On an earlier occasion (Isa. 42) the speaker listened quietly to the charge from God to "make sure that justice is done" (42:3b, my trans.). Now appointed as "a light to the nations" (v. 6), the Servant is preparing to speak on God's behalf as God's emissary. In 49:1–7 the moment has come; the Servant has found his voice. Here is one who will speak with authority on behalf of the one who created the heavens and the earth, the seas and all that dwell within.

All who dwell within are the intended audience for the address. Through the voice of the Servant, God will catch the ear of all the nations for all time and make a claim for their attention. We are in their company and will listen with all the rest. We will all be listening for different things, of course. Those who are representing the community that the poet/prophet serves are anxious for a word from the one who brought them out of Egypt and established

Isaiah 49:1-7

Theological Perspective

commonly understand this passage as anticipating the salvific work of Jesus Christ. Furthermore, this depiction of God's providential care in the choosing and equipping of an individual is a prevalent theme evident in other portions of Scripture as well, texts that echo the words of Isaiah. For example, Paul recounts the story of his calling in Galatians 1:15–16, "But when God, who had set me apart before I was born and called me through his grace, was pleased to reveal his Son to me . . . " Jeremiah 1:5 resonates with Isaiah's words as well: "Before I formed you in the womb I knew you, and before you were born I consecrated you; I appointed you a prophet to the nations." For this reason, John Calvin interpreted today's passage as relating to the work of Christ as the head of the church, as well as to the church and its ministers. In both cases then, God prepares particular individuals and equips them with gifts necessary to carry out God's plan.

The fact that some are called by God for particular tasks leads one to consider a theological matter that has been much contested within Christian history: does this mean that God also elected individuals to salvation? Although Calvin is most commonly identified with the doctrine of election or predestination, Augustine in the fifth century was the first to formulate this doctrine, as a result of his dispute with the views of Pelagius and his followers. Augustine maintained predestination in light of Ephesians 1:4–5, which states that God "chose us in Christ before the foundation of the world to be holy and blameless before him in love. He destined us for adoption as his children through Jesus Christ, according to the good pleasure of his will."

For both Augustine and Calvin, the affirmation of predestination stemmed from belief in the total depravity of humanity due to original sin and in the absolute sovereignty of God. By this doctrine, salvation is maintained as a gift resulting from God's mercy rather than from human achievement. During the medieval period, distinctions were made among scholastics like Thomas Aquinas and William of Ockham over whether or not election was carried out *ante praevisa merita* or *post praevisa merita*, meaning before or after God's foreknowledge of human merit. Due to the significant implications of this question, sixteenth-century reformers reaffirmed that God in no way elected individuals to salvation based upon their merit. This emphasis on the basis of God's election is, indeed, evident in Calvin's reflection on verse 7 in the following statement: "Isaiah therefore points out the secret will of God, from

Pastoral Perspective

the identity of the Servant. As biblical scholar Paul Hanson has put it, "the Servant is both faithful individual and obedient community."[1] The call of God that the Servant describes, while powerful, is not unique to any historical figure. The psalmist also sings of being known by God before birth (Ps. 139:13), and God tells the prophet Jeremiah, "Before you were born I consecrated you" (Jer. 1:5). God never ceases calling, the psalmist tells us; God "speaks and summons the earth from the rising of the sun to its setting" (Ps. 50:1). The call of God about which the Servant sings is a call that comes to the beloved people of Israel, to the earth itself, and to each of us, in the specificity of our own lives.

The Servant sings a song of God's call in four parts. The first part echoes stories of God's call like the ones described above. God called me from before I was born, the Servant sings. God hid me, polished me, tucked me away in his quiver. "You are my servant," God says, "in whom I will be glorified" (v. 3). The Servant has been prepared by God for nothing less than to bring the glory of God into view through the restoration of Israel. No wonder we are reading this text during Epiphany, when the glory of the Lord shines all around us.

The next movement of this song, however, describes the Servant's failure to live up to this calling, a story of wasted time and spinning wheels. "I have labored in vain," the Servant admits. All the strength God gave me, the Servant grieves, I spent "for nothing and vanity" (v. 4).

In spite of his failures, hope still lives in the heart of the Servant. Even though the Servant has worked without result and used God's gifts for vain purposes, he remembers God's call; God's high purposes still reach him. God called me "to bring Jacob back to him . . . that Israel might be gathered to him" (v. 5). The Servant knows who he is and with whom his loyalties lie. "Surely my cause is with the LORD," the Servant sings, "and my reward with my God" (v. 4).

It is the Servant's memory of the mighty work of reconciliation to which God has called him that opens a space in which the Servant can once again hear God's voice. When God speaks again, God not only renews the Servant's original calling but enlarges the scope of it, so that it encompasses not only the restoration of Israel but the salvation of every nation on earth. Rather than looking upon the Servant's failures and adjusting the call downwards

---

1. Paul Hanson, *Isaiah 40–66*, Interpretation series (Louisville, KY: Westminster John Knox Press, 1989), 128.

kings made extravagant claims about their right to rule. (For divine naming of children—by prophets—see 2 Sam. 12:25, where Nathan gives Bathsheba's second son the name of Jedidiah ["Beloved of the LORD"], and Isa. 7:14, where Isaiah names Ahaz's unborn son Immanuel.)

Two other texts, clearly not related to kingship or royal rule, claim a prebirth commission. The prophet Jeremiah claims that God told him (Jer. 1:5): "Before I formed you in the womb I knew you, and before you were born I consecrated you; I appointed you a prophet to the nations." As in Isaiah 49:1, the task of the called one is related to other nations.

Paul, in Galatians 1:15, says, "God . . . set me apart before I was born and called me through his grace." Paul is probably borrowing here from these Old Testament texts to affirm his special status in a situation where his authority was being challenged.

In verse 2, the Servant describes how God prepared him and concealed him for a time. He was prepared to speak with a mouth like a sharp sword. Here the focus of the Servant's task would appear to parallel that of a prophet. This contrasts with the first Song (42:1–4) which stresses the administrative royal function of the Servant.

In verse 3, the Servant is clearly addressed as "Israel." Some interpreters argue that the term "Israel" is a later gloss added to the text or a marginal note that got incorporated into the text, but elsewhere in Second Isaiah, Israel is referred to as "servant" (41:8–10; 44:1–2, 21).

Verse 4 contains a reflection by the Servant in the midst of a speech to the nations. "I said" here is best understood as "I thought." Here the Servant expresses his reserve, lack of success, or sense of inadequacy. This hesitancy is found in several Old Testament call narratives (see Exod. 3:11; Jer. 1:6).

The special task of the Servant depicted in verses 5–6 is described as bringing Jacob (greater Israel) back to God (v. 5) and raising up the tribes of Jacob and restoring the survivors of Israel (v. 6). This is how the NRSV understands the text.

The New Jewish Publication Society translation probably gives a more adequate translation of the Hebrew:

> And now the LORD has resolved—
> He who formed me in the womb to be His servant—
> To bring Jacob to Himself,
> That Israel may be restored to Him. . . .
> "It is too little that you should be My servant
> In that I raise up the tribes of Jacob
> And restore the survivors of Israel."

a covenant with them. Where is the promised presence of the one who brought them into being as a people?

They are facing a crisis on two fronts: on the one hand, their homeland has become a landscape of disaster, a wilderness of a different kind. It is not a wilderness where bushes burn with a Word from God, where manna falls, or where a rock yields up life-giving water. It is, rather, a landscape littered with the ruins of war. What is to keep them from being swept completely from the face of the earth the next time the eyes of empire notice their plight? They are looking for assurance that God has not abandoned them like a delinquent parent.

On the other hand, there is the predicament of those in exile on the banks of the Euphrates. To survive, they have to make accommodations with the surrounding culture. What is to happen to their distinctive ways of being in the world God created? The lure of assimilation is strong, and the foreign gods seem powerful. Has their God become mute, or simply powerless in the competition for their loyalty? The primary concern of the exiles is not survival; it is, rather, how they are to be in relation to others of different faiths, different mores, different understandings.

Those concerned with God's identity and character, the relationship between religions, or their own survival and preservation as an established community are not the only ones within the scope of the speaker's message. When the speaker takes the stage, the focus is broad: "*Everyone*, listen, even you foreign nations across the sea!" (v. 1, paraphrase). This speaker has a global perspective. God's message is not just for those in Judah or for those in exile on the banks of the Euphrates, but for everyone, even those who do not have the history with God that Israel has had. Why should they pay attention to what this deity has to say?

All take note: God's representative is speaking not from a place of weakness but with the tongue of a warrior. In the place of weapons, there are words "piercing like a sharp sword or a pointed arrow" (v. 2, my trans.). The aim? Salvation, not just for the "tribes of Jacob" and "the survivors of Israel" but salvation that will "reach to the end of the earth" (v. 6). Salvation includes but is not confined to Israel's concerns; those would be "too light a thing" for this Servant to take up. Salvation is nothing less than the establishment of what the poet sings of in Isaiah 42:1–4, an "order of compassionate justice that God has created and upon which the wholeness of the

Isaiah 49:1-7

Theological Perspective

which sanctification proceeds; that Israel might not think that he had been selected on account of his own merits."[1]

Likewise, Karl Barth affirms the significant place of the doctrine of election within theology, calling it "the sum of the Gospel."[2] However, for Barth, election does not refer primarily to the election of individuals. This is demonstrated in *Church Dogmatics* II/2, where Barth argues that Jesus Christ is both the electing God—the one who elects to be God *pro nobis*, "God for us"—and the elected human. In this way, God is both the subject and the object of election, and humanity is elected in Christ. Moreover, Barth advances a reinterpretation of Calvin's double predestination so that Christ himself is the elect as well as the reprobate: "there is only one Rejected, the Bearer of all man's [*sic*] sin and guilt and their ensuing punishment, and this One is Jesus Christ."[3] In this fashion, Barth asserts that election is indeed double—but the reference points for both aspects of election are found in Christ.

Critics of Barth's view argue that it lacks scriptural support, particularly when compared with the exegesis of passages like Ephesians 1:4. Meanwhile, critics of Calvin's view ask, if God could save some, why not save all? When faced with this conundrum, coupled with added responses to the question of election as seen in Arminianism, Isaiah 49 offers an important reminder. Verse 6 reveals that the Servant undertook the work of God in order that "salvation may reach to the end of the earth." Here Isaiah represents a shift from an exclusive to an inclusive restoration, in that the Servant comes to open the door of salvation for those to whom it has been closed. This illustrates that God has in store a greater destiny for humanity, more than could have ever been imagined, as the adopted children of God through the work of Jesus Christ. Let us, therefore, answer God's calling upon our lives with all our mind, heart, soul, and strength.

JENNIFER POWELL MCNUTT

Pastoral Perspective

to meet diminished expectations, God says to the Servant,

> It is too light a thing that you should be my servant
>   to raise up the tribes of Jacob
>   and to restore the survivors of Israel;
> I will give you as a light to the nations,
>   that my salvation may reach to the end of the earth.
>   (v. 6)

The vocation to which I first called you, God seems to say, is not everything I want from you. In the Servant's own return to God, a larger vocation is given: shine as a light to all the nations, so that there is nowhere my salvation does not reach. All of life is your business, God sings to the Servant—every nation, every person, every life.

Surely this is the song God sings to each of us: that all of our work, no matter how local, must have the good of the whole world as its aim. In our globalized world, in which a seemingly innocuous action—a purchase, say—in one place can contribute to suffering in another, this is no easy vocation. Embedded in this call to be a light to the nations is a call to know the world in which we hope to shine. Through study and encounter, through travel and prayer, through seeking to understand the results of our choices of what to buy, what to wear, what to eat, we return, like the Servant, to God and receive a deeper vocation, one that encompasses strangers far off, as well as dear ones close at hand.

In the season of Epiphany, may we see our lives and the life of the world in the light of the glory of God, in which all our aspirations are lifted up and returned to us in forms we never would have imagined.

STEPHANIE A. PAULSELL

---

1. John Calvin, *Commentary on the Book of the Prophet Isaiah* (Grand Rapids: Baker Books, 1999), 4:21.
2. Karl Barth, *Church Dogmatics*, ed. G. W. Bromiley and T. F. Torrance, II/2 (London and New York: T.&T. Clark, 2004), 10.
3. Ibid., 346.

Exegetical Perspective

In this translation, the main tasks are performed by God, working through the servant.

The Servant is assured that he will be "a light to the nations" ("a source of good fortune") so that "salvation may reach to the end of the earth" (v. 6). The restoration of Israel will have worldwide consequences.

Who was understood to be the Servant in these prophecies of this anonymous prophet? Numerous proposals have been made by interpreters over the years. It would seem to the present writer that the person assigned the role of the Suffering Servant was most likely the exiled King Jehoiachin and his fellow exiles carried to Babylon in 597 BCE. Jehoiachin's father Jehoiakim had rebelled against the Babylonians and broken the treaty of fidelity sworn in the name of YHWH (see Ezek. 17:17–21). Breaking of the treaty was thus a profaning of the name of God, a trespass upon the holy. This required a reparation/restitution/guilt offering (see Lev. 5:14–16). In Hebrew, this offering was called an *asham*, a term used of the Servant in Isaiah 53:10.

The rebellious King Jehoiakim died before Jerusalem was captured on March 16, 597 (2 Kgs. 24:1–7; the exact date is known from a Babylonian text). His eighteen-year-old son Jehoiachin succeeded him, but Jehoiachin and the royal family and many other citizens were carried into exile (2 Kgs. 24:8–17). The king and the exiles were the penalty/reparation offering (see Isa. 53:10) that was required to compensate for defiling the holy name of God. Their innocent suffering was suffering on behalf of others who had sinned against God in breaking the treaty with Babylon. Their task was to restore the people as a whole. Note that in 2 Kings 25:27–30, Jehoiachin is given special status, just as is predicted of the Servant in Isaiah 52:13–53:12.

However one interprets the identity of the Servant, the role of the Servant as one who suffers innocently on behalf of others has shaped theology and preaching through the generations.

JOHN H. HAYES

Homiletical Perspective

universe depends."[1] The gift of salvation is intended for all people, not just for a select few.

The Servant bears the weight and gravity of God's authority as Creator and Redeemer, and the Servant feels it. "I'm completely worn out; my time has been wasted" is the lamentation (v. 4, my trans.). Confidence in God's message and God's promises does not come easily to communities struggling to maintain their identity. Nor can the message take root unless it rings true with the reality of human experience. A saving message that resonates with the Servant's in this text admits to frailty as well as assurance of God's promise to honor those who pick up the Servant's mantle. The Servant finds strength not only in human effort but in relationship to God.

Then as now, a message like this is greeted with skepticism. How does rhetoric measure up to an arms race? How can a God whose people are held captive or victims of violence dare to promise the restoration of an order of justice? How can the community of faith we call the church bear the Servant's message when the secular culture that holds it captive considers its witness banal or a "waste of time" (v. 4)? These are questions that the church takes up during Epiphany.

If we look closely at the Servant's audience, we will see ourselves represented. We too are concerned about our survival as a community of faith; we wonder how to be in relationship with people of other nations and other faiths without losing our own distinctive witness. Epiphany is the season where the church finds its way again through confusion and uncertainty. Our mission is to become a "light to the nations" by becoming agents of God's order of compassionate justice.

RICHARD F. WARD

---

1. Paul D. Hanson, *Isaiah 40–66*, Interpretation series (Louisville, KY: John Knox Press, 1995), 129.

Psalm 40:1-11

¹I waited patiently for the LORD;
    he inclined to me and heard my cry.
²He drew me up from the desolate pit,
    out of the miry bog,
  and set my feet upon a rock,
    making my steps secure.
³He put a new song in my mouth,
    a song of praise to our God.
  Many will see and fear,
    and put their trust in the LORD.

⁴Happy are those who make
    the LORD their trust,
  who do not turn to the proud,
    to those who go astray after false gods.
⁵You have multiplied, O LORD my God,
    your wondrous deeds and your thoughts toward us;
    none can compare with you.
  Were I to proclaim and tell of them,
    they would be more than can be counted.

Theological Perspective

The lectionary presents the first half of this some-what enigmatic psalm, in its totality. The strong resemblance between Psalm 70 and Psalm 40:13–17 leads scholars to conclude that Psalm 40 results from the merger of two separate texts into one. This adds yet another level of complication, as the section featured in the lectionary appears to be a psalm of thanksgiving, while the remaining verses constitute a song of lament. This ordering of thanksgiving followed by lament suggests a reversal of fortunes that bewilders those who might expect a progression from supplication to gratitude for divine favor bestowed.

The psalm begins on a contested note with respect to matters of translation. Most English translations begin, "I waited patiently for the LORD" (v. 1). A closer reading of the text might make a reader wonder whether the tribulations of a person mired in a desolate pit really elicit a patient waiting for rescue. The Hebrew, more literally translated as "waited, I waited," or "waiting, I waited," seems to lack any indication of patience, especially in terms of "quiet resignation."[1] So much so that the Spanish Old Testament scholar Luis Alonso Schökel offers an alternative in *La Biblia de Nuestro Pueblo*, a translation prepared for

1. Robert Davidson, *The Vitality of Worship: A Commentary on the Book of Psalms* (Grand Rapids: Eerdmans, 1998), 133.

Pastoral Perspective

Preachers on the Second Sunday after the Epiphany might consider preaching sermons that bring the psalm and the Gospel into conversation with one another. In the Gospel, John the Baptist is engaged in the work of proclamation, pointing out to anyone who will listen, "Here is the Lamb of God!" (John 1:29). John himself is not the focus of his message; John is merely an instrument for proclaiming Jesus, who is the one who "ranks ahead" of John (John 1:30).

This ethos of humility even in the midst of proclamation permeates the psalm as well. The text recounts God's good work in the life of the psalmist—God puts a song in the psalmist's mouth—but God's deeds are many, beyond the psalmist's ability to enumerate (v. 5).

An imaginative preacher might also offer a meditation on the image of the rock that appears in the psalm and is suggested in the Gospel. The psalmist rejoices that after his period of great despair in a "miry bog" (v. 2), God sets the psalmist on a rock, a place of security and strength. In the Gospel of John, Jesus gives Simon a new name, Cephas/Peter, meaning "rock." It is the rock on which Christ will build his church. Could it be that the sturdy rock on which God sets our feet is not a geologic formation, but a body of people dedicated to the way of Jesus?

⁶Sacrifice and offering you do not desire,
   but you have given me an open ear.
 Burnt offering and sin offering
   you have not required.
⁷Then I said, "Here I am;
   in the scroll of the book it is written of me.
⁸I delight to do your will, O my God;
   your law is within my heart."

⁹I have told the glad news of deliverance
   in the great congregation;
 see, I have not restrained my lips,
   as you know, O LORD.
¹⁰I have not hidden your saving help within my heart,
   I have spoken of your faithfulness and your salvation;
 I have not concealed your steadfast love and your faithfulness
   from the great congregation.

¹¹Do not, O LORD, withhold
   your mercy from me;
 let your steadfast love and your faithfulness
   keep me safe forever.

Exegetical Perspective

Psalm 40 displays elements of two different genres: the first half is a thanksgiving song of an individual, and the latter half an individual lament. The compositional history of this psalm appears complicated. The text of verses 13–17 is found elsewhere in the Psalter, constituting the entirety of Psalm 70. It is highly likely that Psalm 40 was composed by linking two texts that originally existed independently of one another, although some scholars argue that the psalm is a unitary composition, the final portion of which was later taken to form an independent psalm. In light of these details, the lectionary breaking off of the psalm at v. 11 is not inappropriate, and indeed, recognizes the approximate place of disjunction in the whole of Psalm 40. This aspect of the psalm may serve well as an entry point to the Scripture reading. Congregations today also show flexibility in using hymns for worship, often not singing an entire hymn but just certain stanzas, a practice that—evidenced by composite psalms such as this one—seems also to have been common in ancient Israel's worship.

With regard to the structure, verses 1–3b serve as a recollection of the psalmist's distress and God's response of rescue. The remainder of the psalm can be seen as the psalmist's "new song," her "song of praise" (v. 3). In verses 3c–4 is a description of the

Homiletical Perspective

In the spring of 1985, U2's The Unforgettable Fire tour stopped in Hartford, Connecticut. Twenty years later the band's lead singer, Bono, would be nominated for the Nobel Peace Prize, students of divinity would read of his theology and experiment with an alternative service of Holy Communion set to the music of U2, and Bono would gain the audience of heads of state and wield his celebrity status to assist the poorest of the poor. On that mid-spring evening in the mid-eighties, one could already hear the singer's passion for peace and justice. This was rock 'n' roll with a conscience. This was music infused with a deep spirituality.

The final encore that evening was "40," a lyrical adaptation of today's Psalm 40. As the band left the stage one by one, the enthusiastic crowd continued the song's refrain: "I will sing, sing a new song." Even as the crowd poured out of the stadium, huge bands of fans carried the tune onto the city streets: "I will sing, sing a new song." I thought little of it at the time, but that refrain springs forth from the psalmist's claim, "He put a new song in my mouth, a song of praise to our God" (v. 3).

The central claim of this psalm is well worth our singing and preaching: God hears our cries and delivers us from times of trouble, so we will respond with a joyful noise, a song of praise. Traces of this

Psalm 40:1-11

Theological Perspective

the pilgrim peoples of América Latina (a term that includes the United States), where the verse reads: "Yo esperaba impacientemente al Señor" ("I waited impatiently for the LORD").

The text's commentary implies that it is the divine response to the supplicant's earlier cries and *impatient* waiting that fuels the hope of a new liberation in the presence of yet another tribulation (vv. 11–17).[2] The anxiety of the endangered petitioner finds voice in these later verses with pleas for God to "make haste" (v. 13) and to "not delay" (v. 17) in delivering the supplicant from imminent harm. Confidence in God's steadfast love and faithfulness to provide safety, as manifest by divine action in the earlier verses, serves as promise for salvation in time of trial.

The psalm does not conceal the tension experienced by the one in danger, nor does it suggest that delivery from harm is a onetime event. On the contrary, the move from trial to delivery to trial in many ways is more reflective of daily living, as is the impatience and fear of the one in trouble. The psalm in its totality conveys a pattern of attention from an accompanying God, who, when called upon, has an established record of deliverance. In some ways, the degree of danger is highlighted by the anxiety expressed in the impatient waiting of the afflicted, and the physical reality of the suffering is communicated by expressions like "desolate pit" and "miry bog" (v. 2).

The response of the one delivered by God is an embodied gratitude with a public dimension. As both the trouble and salvation are depicted in very physical terms, so too is the response to this divine action. Konrad Schaefer observes that the whole body participates, as is evident from the poet's mention of a variety of body parts: feet (v. 2), mouth (v. 3), heart (vv. 8, 10), lips (v. 9).[3] This embodied gratitude bears public witness to the action of God and invites others to put their "trust in the LORD" (v. 3). The news of one's deliverance is not a private revelation; rather, it is sung, proclaimed, told, and spoken of in the "great congregation" (v. 10). This testimony to the God who accompanies in times of trial is meant to be shared and lived in a public manner. Those who are delivered are themselves responsible to the greater community; God's action makes

Pastoral Perspective

These are just a couple of the ways that the Gospel text and the psalm might "read" each other. However, the psalm text also has plenty of gospel in it to stand alone as a focus for the sermon.

Authentic Evangelism. Like many psalms proclaiming God's deliverance, this text exemplifies and calls forth a spirit of authentic and heartfelt evangelism. The psalmist simply cannot help sharing what God has done; the good news bubbles forth in an exuberant combination of testimony *about* God and praise *to* God. The psalmist shifts from description of God to direct address in verse 5, which serves as a good reminder of what is at the heart of sharing the good news of God's love: we cannot share what we have not truly experienced. Faithful proclamation of the gospel flows from a genuine relationship with God and cannot be faked.

The psalmist is well aware that people are listening: "many will see and fear"—thanks in part to the song that the psalmist sings about God's good work (v. 3)—but the listeners are not the focus. They are not prey to be targeted with a heavy-handed message. The psalmist simply declares, "*here is what happened to me.*" Verses 9 and 10 provide the most complete record of the psalmist's evangelistic work: "I have told the glad news of deliverance in the great congregation. . . . I have spoken of your faithfulness and your salvation."

The psalmist's testimony moves effectively between poetic, evocative language (pit, bog, rock, song) and religious terminology (sacrifice, deliverance, salvation). As previously mentioned, the psalmist knows that there is always more to be said about God than the psalmist is capable of saying. This idea can be a comfort to reluctant evangelists in our congregations, who often feel stymied by pressure to get the words right and to adhere to some doctrinal correctness. As Karl Barth famously wrote in *The Word of God and the Word of Man*, "As ministers we ought to speak of God. We are human, however, and so cannot speak of God. We ought therefore to recognize both our obligation and our inability and by that very recognition give God the glory."[1]

What God Has Done. What exactly has God done to and for the psalmist? The placement of God is interesting in the opening verses. God has "inclined" to the psalmist's cries, suggesting upward movement.

2. "La súplica escuchada, como repuesta a la espera impaciente [2–4 o 2–6] se convierte en apoyo ante una nueva tribulacíon y la espera de una nueva liberacíon [12–18]," in *La Biblia de Nuestro Pueblo: Biblia del Peregrino América Latina*, trans. Luis Alonso Schökel (Maryknoll, NY: Orbis Books, 2008).

3. Konrad Schaefer, *Psalms*, in David W. Cotter, series editor, *Berit Olam: Studies in Hebrew Narrative and Poetry* (Collegeville, MN: Liturgical Press, 2001), 100.

1. Karl Barth, *The Word of God and the Word of Man*, trans. Douglas Horton (Gloucester, MA: Peter Smith, 1978), 186.

proper actions of righteous persons. The language shifts to direct address at verse 5. Following is a confession of God's action (vv. 5–6), a report of the psalmist's compliance (vv. 6–10), and an affirmation of the psalmist's confidence (v. 11; the Hebrew verbs are indicative, "you do not withhold," "you keep me safe"). This portion of the psalm ends on a note of complaint (v. 12), which can seem dissonant, but is actually a quite common type of conclusion (other examples are Pss. 12; 38; 39; 40; 44; 70; 88).

Language of abundance and calculation is especially prominent. The term "great" or "many" (Heb. *rab*) appears four times throughout these verses. It describes people—the many who will see (v. 3), the large congregation (vv. 9, 10)—and divine activity ("you have made many," v. 5). In addition, the sense of counting, represented with the Hebrew root *spr*, appears twice. God's innumerable deeds are "more than can be counted" (v. 5). In verse 7 is the psalmist's enigmatic reference to "the scroll of accounting" or "the scroll of the book" (scholars are not sure what this scroll might have been or how it might have functioned; perhaps a written account that worshipers would bring to the temple). These expressions reflect a progression. First, God does a great many things for the psalmist, and this abundance then yields a great many humans who recognize these wondrous deeds.

Psalm 40 depicts particular characteristics and activities of a faithful person. What God desires (v. 6) influences what the psalmist desires (v. 8; the verb *haphats* is used both places). The first aspect is proper *attitude*. Reminiscent of certain prophetic instructions (see, for instance, Isa. 1:12–17; Hos. 6:6; Amos 5:21–24), the psalmist views God as wanting an offering of one's very self. Not exterior cultic action but interior attitude is what is important; the poet stresses this with two somatic images, ears and stomach. The first description is enigmatic, to be rendered possibly as "you carved open ears for me" or "you inserted ears in me" (v. 6). The second image, in verse 8, is of God's instruction (torah) residing in the psalmist's inner being (*me'eh* means literally one's belly). Along with verse 4, these descriptions are reminiscent of the righteous person described at the very beginning of the Psalter, who meditates on YHWH's instruction (Ps. 1:1–3). Thus, having an attitude of attention and openness to learning is essential. Then when calamity strikes—as it always will—this inner fortitude will allow one to "wait patiently" (more literally, "I hoped urgently," with an infinitive absolute construction; v. 1).

tune echo through the ages, from Israel's deliverance in Exodus to the praise songs Paul sings in prison. Time and again in Scripture God hears the lament of God's people, swings low, and gives us reason to hope. Time and again in the pulpit, preachers aim to tell "the glad news of deliverance in the great congregation" (v. 9).

On this Sunday in Epiphany, a season when we consider the ways in which our God is made manifest in Jesus, preachers may heed the psalmist's call personally to witness to the God who draws us up "from the desolate pit" (v. 2). While a surplus of first-person narrative can distract from a sermon's aim to illuminate the Word, today's psalm invites the preacher to offer such testimony.

I recall a conversation with a woman who reentered the church after many years away. She spoke of her childhood congregation with deep affection, naming the people who taught her and modeled for her the ways of discipleship. Surprised by her obvious affinity for that church, I asked her why she left it. Her response is instructive. She said, "As I sat in the church week after week, I had the feeling that the preacher was keeping the best stuff to himself—that he knew the goodness of God but did not think to share it." Surely, there are good reasons to draw from the riches of others' experiences and to commend their "glad news of deliverance" to our congregations, but at the heart of today's psalm lies a personal accounting of the psalmist's faith. How, then, might the preacher account for her faith amid the trials of life?

That question, of course, is not the sole possession of the preacher. Each week, the sanctuary holds a living catalog of redemption songs. In this light, the preacher may consider sharing the joyful burden of public witness with the people she seeks to serve. Lillian Daniel, a United Church of Christ pastor, writes of such a venture in *Tell It Like It Is*. In the book she conveys the challenges and the spiritual growth born of her former congregation's attempt to honor the tradition of testimony—to express the "best stuff" of God. We can imagine a member of that congregation recognizing the psalmist's voice and sharing his own experience of lament and trust and God's deliverance. Likewise, we can imagine how such remembrance of God's graceful interventions might embolden others to hope that a "new song" of praise will again be on their lips.

By whatever means the message of Psalm 40 is conveyed, the messenger will do well to remember what verse 11 (and the remainder of the psalm) makes clear. Life's trials persist. The fluidity of verb

Psalm 40:1-11

Theological Perspective

evangelizers of those who experience liberation. This manifestation of divine fidelity belongs to all. This intention is underscored by the song put into the mouth of the saved and the proclamation expected of one within whose heart the law is inscribed.

Divine deliverance of this particular "poor and needy" one (v. 17) is also an act for the community. There is a subtle shift from the first person singular to the first person plural in verse 5: "You have multiplied, O LORD my God, your wondrous deeds and your thoughts toward us; none can compare with you. Were I to proclaim and tell of them, they would be more than can be counted." The indication is that this particular experience is only one of a consistent pattern of God's saving intervention in the history of this people.

The liturgical function of the Psalms across time demonstrates the ongoing communal responsibility to retell, proclaim, and sing in praise of the wondrous deeds, not of my God alone, but of "our God" (v. 3). The public recounting of those acts, too numerous to count, affirms the constant love and fidelity of this God and invites an affirmation of trust. Some scholars caution against the temptation to read into verse 6 a refutation of ritual sacrifice. Rather, God's faithful accompaniment calls the community to integrity of worship, where ritual action is consistent with the disposition of hearts informed by God.

The shift to the communal voice is most evident in the liturgical function of psalms. The new song is the hymn of the community, shaped by its relationship to the God who is deserving of praise. Thanksgiving and lament both belong to the community, a reminder that those who suffer remain in their midst. Lest the community be moved to a complacency of liberation completed, anxiety returns in verse 11 with a plea for God not to withhold mercy; and the psalm concludes in verse 17 much the same way as it began, with the supplicant impatiently waiting, begging God "do not delay."

CARMEN NANKO-FERNÁNDEZ

Pastoral Perspective

This is not a God who "condescends" from on high to those calling out for help. The psalmist proclaims the happiness of those who rely on God, rather than on the proud (v. 4). This juxtaposition suggests that God's own nature is not proud. This is the God of Psalm 139, who is already in the pit of Sheol by the time we arrive there. This is a God who is near enough to hear the cries of lament.

The words "deliverance" and "salvation" both make an appearance in the psalm, but it is the combination of "faithfulness and steadfast love" that shine as a refrain throughout the text, notably in the concluding line of our lection (v. 11). A sermon on Psalm 40 might need to unpack these words for the congregation. What about people who wait in vain to be delivered from the miry bog, who spend long painful years in the desolate pit? Is there any significance to God's faithfulness and steadfast love being lifted up more prominently than God's work of salvation? Perhaps God's faithfulness and love are the foundation from which everything else flows.

The psalm ends on a seemingly incongruous note when the psalmist prays that God in God's love will "keep me safe forever." A plea for safety has not made an appearance up to this point. It is perfectly understandable that one might long for safety after logging time in the pit and the bog, but is it reasonable to expect? Is this the abundant life that God promises?

A pastorally faithful sermon on these matters must acknowledge that many of us, in our heart of hearts, hope that God's favor will somehow immunize us from pain and vulnerability. The psalmist is perhaps no exception to this tendency. It is good news that we are free to offer all of our needs to God without censoring ourselves. The Psalms, in all their gritty variety, grant us that freedom. We also affirm that God does not protect us from all harm. God is present with us in the pit and has the power to draw us out, but a life of discipleship requires turning right back around and entering the pit once again, in the name of preaching good news to those still held captive within it.

MARYANN MCKIBBEN DANA

Exegetical Perspective

After the psalmist's deliverance, her actions are specifically external. The second aspect of faithful persons stressed by the psalm is their *witness*. Psalm 40 emphasizes that the proper response to God's activity is not only to ponder it in one's heart but also immediately to tell others. In verse 9 the verb (*basar*) used of the psalmist's action of witness often means particularly to announce good news. It is frequently found also in Second Isaiah, that great text that anticipates the restoration of Israel after exile (for instance, Isa. 40:9; 52:7). Salvation is therefore not primarily a private issue but ultimately a public, even evangelical, issue; personal rescue is not merely to benefit the individual but rather for public benefit, to lead others also to recognition of the divine deliverer. The individual vocally bears witness (vv. 9–10), the goal of which is for many others to trust YHWH, just as the psalmist does (v. 3b).

Verses 10–11 are remarkable for their concentration of terms describing YHWH's character. Six nouns are used in these two brief verses, two of which are repeated, which provides an overwhelming sense of God's essence. YHWH shows righteousness (*tsedaqah*, v. 10), faithfulness (*'emunah*, v. 10), salvation (*tishu'ah*, v. 10), kind loyalty (*hesed*, vv. 10, 11), truth (*'emet*, vv. 10, 11), and compassion (*rahamim*, v. 11). Because this theological attribution comes after God's active response, after the rescue of the psalmist, these terms should be understood not merely as static descriptors but instead as holistically suggesting divine activity.

The aspects of divine faithfulness and human witness and waiting intertwine the Psalms reading with the other Old Testament reading and the Gospel and Epistle readings for this Sunday. The Servant, as "a light to the nations" (Isa. 49:6), like the psalmist is an individual witnessing to the many, and John the Baptist serves as a witness to Jesus (John 1:29–36). Paul exhorts his addressees to wait for the revelation of the Christ (1 Cor. 1:7–8), just as the psalmist hopes and waits patiently for YHWH (v. 1). The character of God as "faithful" is emphasized by three of the readings (Ps. 40:11; Isa. 49:7; 1 Cor. 1:9).

LINDA DAY

Homiletical Perspective

tenses in verses 1 through 11, between past and present, underscores what the psalmist and congregants know well. Our present hope stands on the solid foundation of the past, saving acts of God. Therefore, as the psalmist offers praise for God's "mercy," "steadfast love," and "faithfulness," today's preacher keeps in heart and mind members of the church—and sisters and brothers beyond the church walls—who are still waiting for the Lord, who are still crying, who are still in the pit.

The whole of Psalm 40 may reflect the psalmist's attempt to stir in God a remembrance of holy protection and to petition God for more of the same, but this psalm is written—and read—not only to God. It is intended to stir in the psalmist himself, and in all who overhear his prayer, a remembrance of God's "wondrous deeds"—"more than can be counted" (v. 5). Crossing the border of the lectionary's selection, taking the psalm in its entirety, we hear a song of praise emerging from the shadowy places of uncertainty, where "evils" and "iniquities" loom large (v. 12). In the grip of trouble, the psalmist praises God both for being yesterday's sure footing and for being the promise of tomorrow's hope.

For psalmist, preacher, and congregant alike, our great hope is that we will sing a new song of God's deliverance. In the meantime, we join the chorus of faithful souls from every age who have spoken of God's steadfast love and faithfulness and have put their trust in God. Together we tell it like it is in the congregation; then we take our glad news to the streets.

ANDREW NAGY-BENSON

1 Corinthians 1:1-9

¹Paul, called to be an apostle of Christ Jesus by the will of God, and our brother Sosthenes,

²To the church of God that is in Corinth, to those who are sanctified in Christ Jesus, called to be saints, together with all those who in every place call on the name of our Lord Jesus Christ, both their Lord and ours:

³Grace to you and peace from God our Father and the Lord Jesus Christ.

⁴I give thanks to my God always for you because of the grace of God that has been given you in Christ Jesus, ⁵for in every way you have been enriched in him, in speech and knowledge of every kind—⁶just as the testimony of Christ has been strengthened among you—⁷so that you are not lacking in any spiritual gift as you wait for the revealing of our Lord Jesus Christ. ⁸He will also strengthen you to the end, so that you may be blameless on the day of our Lord Jesus Christ. ⁹God is faithful; by him you were called into the fellowship of his Son, Jesus Christ our Lord.

Theological Perspective

There is indeed conflict in the church at Corinth, and not about any single issue. Divisions threaten the church, and Paul seeks to call the church to its identity in Christ. Following the introductory verses appointed for this Sunday, the reader enters the tensions and divisions that divide the church and continue today to divide the church: matters of following different leaders with different claims, matters of morals, matters of right worship, and matters of right belief about the resurrection of the dead. Through these matters—and not above them—naming and addressing the conflicts that beset the community, Paul proclaims and explores (and so offers the preacher the opportunity in successive weeks to proclaim and explore) what it is to be a follower of Christ as lived through the saving mystery of the church.

Nineteenth-century Anglican theologian F. D. Maurice observed that here in such epistles are "the deepest writings of the New Testament. . . . [I]nstead of being digests of doctrine . . . [they explain] to those who had been admitted into the Church of Christ their own position, bringing out that side of it which had reference to the circumstances in which they were placed or to their most besetting sins, and showing what life was in consistency, what life at

Pastoral Perspective

Paul starts his letter to Corinth with the conventional Hellenistic beginning. First, he greets his audience, naming himself and "our brother Sosthenes," and also the church to which he is writing. He follows this with a thanksgiving to God for those who will read or hear the letter. This opening is conventional only in its form. As an introduction it is notably detailed and extended. Paul uses the literary device to register themes that he will take up in the body of the letter. More importantly, he provides a concentrated theology of the Christian community, a forceful and insistent description of the church as alive by God's gift.

This rhetorical strategy is pastorally significant. There is much to criticize in the Corinthian church, and Paul is about to roll up his sleeves and let them know it. First, though, he stops to tell the Corinthians the good news about themselves, the truth of who they are in the calling of God. They are the saints of God, made rich in Jesus Christ. All the criticism proceeds from this truth and no criticism undermines it. The Corinthians' identity as those "sanctified in Christ Jesus" does not depend on them or their efforts. Paul's rebuke to the church, however severe, does not threaten what God has done. This critique is merciful. It does not bind the Corinthians to their failures and divisions; it does not make their

Exegetical Perspective

Although 1 Corinthians 1:1–9 has the standard features of the salutation (vv. 1–3) and thanksgiving (vv. 4–9) of ancient letters, Paul reshapes these literary forms to address a tense situation in the Corinthian church. He has heard from Chloe's people about factions in the church (1:11), received reports of their acceptance of sexual immorality (5:1), and received a letter (7:1) informing him of the problems of communal life. Despite the eighteen months that Paul had spent teaching the Corinthians and forming a community composed of people from diverse backgrounds, even his own authority is in question. The competitiveness of Corinthian society has emerged in the disputes over such spiritual gifts as speech and knowledge (1:5–7; cf. 8:1, 7; 12:8). The Corinthian insistence on individual freedom (6:12; 10:23) has undermined Paul's attempt to build a cohesive moral community with clear boundaries separating it from Corinthian society.

Paul's skillful adaptation of the traditional epistolary introduction indicates his rhetorical sensitivity. According to the teachers of rhetoric, the introduction of a speech (*exordium*) should introduce the topic and make the audience favorably disposed. In the salutation in 1:1–3, Paul addresses the issues in this tense situation without alienating his audience.

Homiletical Perspective

A crucial dynamic in human relationships is the perception that people have of themselves and of others. If a person perceives herself as articulate and competent, she will interact with others in a way of which she would not be capable if she saw herself as fumbling and inept. If a person perceives others as informed and able, he will deal with them in ways that he would not if he saw them as incompetent and ill informed. Furthermore, the way people respond to him will be strongly influenced by the perception that he has of them. People sense how they are viewed by others and respond accordingly. If people discern that another has high regard for them, they often live up to that expectation. Conversely, if they discern that the other has a low opinion of them, their attitude and behavior often reflect that assessment.

As Paul begins his letter to the church at Corinth, he expresses both his perception of himself and his perception of the congregation to which he is writing. Both those perceptions make a strong impact on what Paul writes and how he deals with the people.

First, how does Paul see himself? He writes with confidence, clearly indicating that he has something to communicate that will be important to them. He writes with such confidence not simply because he thinks that he has some good ideas or because he

1 Corinthians 1:1-9

Theological Perspective

variance, with it."[1] They are in this sense "narratives of communal discernment."[2] They call the community together, now as then, to discern what faithful discipleship is all about in light of what stands at the heart of Christian faith itself.

As the lesson for the Second Sunday after Epiphany, the opening greeting (vv. 1–3) and thanksgiving (vv. 4–9) are Paul's declaration of faith and as such provide in cameo a theology of salvation as a theology of the church. Christian faith is a matter of calling, to be called by God, to be followers of Jesus Christ. While we are individually called, as God addresses each of us, we are not called individually into faith. To enter into faith, to be in union with Christ—in other words, to be sanctified, to be saints—is to be set aside together as a new people or new society made up of those in every place who call Jesus Lord. What is striking rhetorically and theologically is that the church as God's chosen people, God's new covenant, is defined not by Jewish ancestry but by discipleship. The peace of God, wholeness and reconciliation, is given, a gift that is a matter of grace, not of birth or status.

This theology of salvation as a theology of the church begins with the claim that life is given as a people. As an apology for Christian faith in the fifth century CE, at the time of the fall of the Roman Empire, Augustine begins *The City of God*, "The glorious city of God is my theme in this work."[3] As revealed and given in Christian faith, God calls us to enter into a city, a society, that begins within our earthly society but is distinct from and transcends the human city. As Augustine goes on to say, the city of God is moved by the love of God and neighbor while the human city is moved by self-interest. Paul has much to say about our motivation, but what must be said first is that God's call to us in Christ is to be a people, an alternative society, that reveals new life, a new way of being and living together.

Among contemporaries, this claim that life is given as a people is expressed by Desmond Tutu in the African word *ubuntu*, which connotes that a person is a person only through other persons. To be is to be "we" and not "I." The other is gift to us. Together in Christ gathered as the church, the community of faith lacks nothing that is needed as they

1. F. D. Maurice, *The Kingdom of Christ*, ed. Alec R. Vidler (1842; repr., London: SCM Press, 1958), 1:254.
2. See David Schlafer and Timothy F. Sedgwick, *Preaching What We Practice: Proclamation and Moral Discernment* (Harrisburg, PA: Morehouse, 2007), 124–47.
3. Augustine, *The City of God*, trans. Marcus Dods (New York: Modern Library, 1978), 3.

Pastoral Perspective

calling dependent on their reformation. It is not the sanctity but the failures that are untrue; they are false, not to an ideal that these Christians have yet to fulfill, but to a character with which they are already gifted. Godly, Christian critique is always an exhortation to receive what has already been given.

Paul is "called to be an apostle of Christ Jesus by the will of God." Undoubtedly, Paul is asserting his authority here, his right to address the Corinthians and expect to be heeded. The assertion is subtle, though. He establishes a parallel with the Corinthians themselves; they are also "called" and "sanctified in Christ Jesus." Paul possesses a God-given authority, but that authority differentiates him only within a common calling. Primary is the call of God that embraces both Paul and his audience. The apostolic authority is intelligible and properly exercised solely within that shared calling. Neither Paul nor the Corinthians can claim apostolicity or sanctity except as vocation, on the terms of God's call.

Significantly, Paul never uses the singular form of "saint" to refer to the individual Christian.[1] We are saints in our common vocation, a shared gift. A "holy people," in this sense, is one marked by God, determined for "the fellowship of his Son" (v. 9), both now and in the coming glory. Sanctity, therefore, does not refer, in the first place, to righteous behavior. That is not to say, of course, that holiness has nothing to do with goodness. Were that so, Paul would be wasting his notepaper. The relationship with God that makes a people holy is, in regard to active righteousness, like a force field within which objects are charged and changed.

The greeting concludes with the unity of the saints under their Lord. Unity and division are a constant theme in this epistle, and Paul will turn to the matter of divisive behavior in the next section. The greeting, then, establishes the theological reality that no human quarrel can destroy: all are called by one Lord and sanctified by that one Lord. Paul finishes by addressing the Corinthian community "together with all those who in every place" (v. 2) call on Christ. The unity of this fractious community exists within the larger unity of Christ's church. The local community is, therefore, an open unity, permeable to the whole body.

Paul now gives thanks for the Corinthians and, given the critique that is to follow, puts this conventional form to effective pastoral use. The Corinthians are graced, enriched, and strengthened by God. God

1. Hans Conzelmann, *1 Corinthians* (Philadelphia: Fortress Press, 1975), 23.

While both ancient and Pauline letters commonly begin by identifying the names of the author and recipients, Paul addresses the issues with additions to the traditional form. Although he does not claim apostolic authority in some letters (Phil. 1:1; 1 Thess. 1:1; Phlm. 1), here he gives his credentials, "called to be an apostle of Christ Jesus by the will of God" (1:1), and addresses the Corinthians' questions about his authority (1 Cor. 4:1–4, 14–21) and indicating that he has been called by God to be an apostle. Although the church in Corinth is composed of two or more house churches and divided into competing factions, he addresses the letter to "the church of God in Corinth" and "all who call on the name of the Lord in every place" (v. 2, my translations), reaffirming the corporate consciousness that he had first instilled in the community. He speaks neither to solitary individuals nor to factions, for "the church at Corinth" is the local manifestation of a universal church that meets "in every place."

The redundancy, "those who are being sanctified in Christ, called to be saints," echoes the Old Testament command to be holy as God is holy (Lev. 19:2) and subtly addresses the Corinthians' failure to be a holy people. It also anticipates the reminder that they have been washed, justified, and sanctified (6:11). Just as Paul has been "called" to be an apostle (1:1), they have been "called" to be a holy people. The reminder that God has created a holy community is an implicit statement of the seriousness of undermining what God has given. With the customary "grace to you and peace" (v. 3), echoing the liturgy of the church, Paul attempts to make the audience favorably disposed to his words as he addresses the whole church, including those who question his authority.

Inasmuch as the thanksgiving (vv. 4–9) permits the readers to overhear Paul's prayer, it serves a pastoral and didactic purpose, preparing the way for the message that follows and reaffirming their corporate identity. Despite the quarreling among the Corinthians, Paul expresses thanks for what God has done for the whole church. In the second-person plural, "for you" and "for the grace of God given to you," he anticipates his later insistence that God has distributed gifts of the Spirit to the whole church (12:4–11), not to factions within it.

The focus of the thanksgiving is on the activity of God among the Corinthians in a corporate narrative that involves past, present, and future. Paul speaks first in the past tense, referring to the beginning of the journey. The aorist passives "You have been enriched in him" and "the testimony of Christ has been

believes the Corinthians are obligated to pay attention to him. He perceives himself as one who has been "called to be an apostle of Christ Jesus by the will of God" (v. 1). Paul has been given a mission and a message as an apostle. All of this has come about because God has willed it. Because this is Paul's perception of himself, he writes with neither arrogance nor apology.

Second, how does Paul see the people of Corinth? They are "sanctified in Christ"; they are "called to be saints"; they are part of a broader community of those "who call on the name of our Lord Jesus Christ" (v. 2). Paul has no illusions about the Corinthians. He has heard about their quarrels and divisions. He says that they are "people of the flesh," "infants in Christ" (3:1). He has heard "that there is sexual immorality among you" (5:1). Nevertheless, Paul begins his letter by affirming his understanding of who they are and reminding them of who they are: They are of the people who have been set apart and sanctified in Christ; they are those called to be saints. When Paul admonishes them for their faults and failures, he does so because he is calling them to be who God has called them to be.

C. S. Lewis wrote *The Screwtape Letters*, letters from a devil named Screwtape to his nephew on earth named Wormwood. Wormwood is charged with keeping his patient in the clutches of the devil. In one of the letters, Screwtape rebukes Wormwood because his patient has become a Christian, but he tells Wormwood how to remedy the situation:

> One of our great allies at present is the Church itself. Do not misunderstand me. I do not mean the Church as we see her spread out through all time and space and rooted in eternity. . . .
>
> Fortunately it is quite invisible to these humans. All your patient sees is the half-finished, sham Gothic erection on the new building estate. When he goes inside, he sees the local grocer with rather an oily expression on his face bustling up to offer him one shiny little book containing a liturgy which neither of them understands. When he gets to his pew and looks round him he sees just that selection of his neighbours whom he has hitherto avoided. You want to lean pretty heavily on those neighbours. Make his mind flit to and fro between an expression like 'the body of Christ' and the actual faces in the next pew.[1]

Paul begins his letter to the church at Corinth with a clear theological perception of who these

1. C. S. Lewis, *The Screwtape Letters* (New York: Macmillan Co., 1943), 15–16.

1 Corinthians 1:1-9

Theological Perspective

wait upon God. It is in this sense that Paul gives thanks to God for the gift of each member of the church (vv. 4–9). While clearly a classical rhetorical strategy to appeal to his readers, thanksgiving is theologically grounded in the fact of *ubuntu*. Grace is given in Christ (v. 4) for the sake of being called together in community (*koinōnia*) (v. 9).

The task of discerning what this life is as the people of God remains. In the midst of differences and conflicts, the first word is thanksgiving. Redemption is given in and through creation, in our life together. The city of God and the human city are not separate realms. The city of God is known, revealed, in the human city, in the midst of our life together, amid our loves and passions, conflicts and divisions. In good Platonic fashion, the city of God is the form that grounds, directs, and transforms the human city. Life together is not given abstractly in terms of a picture of the heavenly city or in terms of a list of virtues and vices. As F. D. Maurice suggested, we discover and enter more deeply into Christian faith only as we address our specific situations, discern how to address our differences, and so claim and proclaim what is central to Christian faith.

These opening verses of 1 Corinthians are both a proclamation of Christian faith as a new way of life and an invitation to enter into the difficult but essential task of addressing the conflicts and differences that are part of being a people from every language, culture, and tribe.

TIMOTHY F. SEDGWICK

Pastoral Perspective

has made them witnesses to Christ. Thanksgiving must go before criticism. One may always give thanks for a fellow Christian. No matter how deep the division or how acrimonious the argument, other Christians never pass beyond thanksgiving: thanks that God has called them, thanks that their true lives are from grace to grace.

If "call" binds the greeting together, "gift" and "grace" unify the thanksgiving. Throughout this opening, Paul establishes the "eccentricity" of Christian life. Grace, strength, blamelessness, fellowship with Christ: all come from outside. The source of life is from without. The Corinthians *are* what they have *received*, and they have received much. There may be a note of irony in Paul's observation that they are rich "in speech and knowledge of every kind." Divisive speech, in tongues and otherwise, and prideful claims to knowledge are core problems in Corinth. A materially poor community for the most part, their claims to spiritual richness may, to some extent, be a compensating mechanism. Nevertheless, Paul does not dispute that, in truth, they are rich. They have, however, grasped God's gifts as possessions and markers of personal distinction. Paul insists that "speech and knowledge" are genuine gifts, and thereby he claims them back, for the sake of the Corinthians, who by false possession estrange themselves from what they truly have. Paul will finally spell out the manner of proper possession and use in his famous appeal to love as sole criterion.

Paul's thanksgiving closes by looking to the future: to the day of Christ's revealing. Another dimension of the underlying theme of giftedness is made explicit. Though the Corinthians do not lack, they have not yet concluded, they are still waiting. There is more, even for those who "are not lacking in any spiritual gift" (v. 7). On the day of the Lord, when not lacking will not be enough, they will yet receive fullness and be united with Christ. Once again, this is given, not earned. Blamelessness comes from God's strengthening. Though the critique of the Corinthians is just about to begin, we see them here in their end, brought to life by the faithfulness of God. All Christian critique must begin with thanksgiving and a glance to the future, to our fellowship in God's glory.

ALAN GREGORY

strengthened among you" (vv. 5, 6) point to the activity of God at the beginning of the journey. Undoubtedly Paul speaks ironically about the Corinthian situation, for he subtly addresses the problems that have created divisions within the church. "You have been enriched in him" anticipates Paul's sarcastic comments about the arrogance of some of the Corinthians: "Already you have become rich! Quite apart from us you have become kings!" (4:8). The expression of gratitude for the Corinthians' "speech and knowledge" anticipates the later correction of the congregations' emphasis on rhetorical power, gifts of tongues, and prophecy, and their claims to wisdom and knowledge (3:18; 8:1). Paul initiates the conversation, not by scolding the congregation, but by reaffirming that the gifts come from God.

The gift that God has given in the past remains a present reality, for Paul is also grateful that the Corinthians do not lack any spiritual gift (1:7), even though the spiritual gifts are the center of the conflict (12:4–31). However, their story is not complete, for they are still waiting for what God will do in the future. Paul responds to the arrogant claims of the Corinthians that they are "already rich" (4:8) with the assurance that God will "strengthen [them] to the end" (v. 8). Paul can express thanks because he is confident that the church that is now torn by division will ultimately be "blameless"—the unified and holy community that God has called them to be. Thus the whole community lives in the middle of a narrative between what God has done and what God will do.

Because "God is faithful" (v. 9), Paul is confident that the Corinthians will no longer act like infants (3:1–5), but will grow to maturity. What God has done in the past by calling the Corinthians into the fellowship of the Son assures the community of God's faithfulness in the future. Despite the childish behavior of those who have received God's grace, God has not abandoned them, but will bring them to maturity in a unified church. To be in fellowship (*koinōnia*) with Christ, as Paul explains later (10:16–17; 12:13) is to be in fellowship with others in a corporate journey in a community that includes rich and poor, Jew and Greek (12:13).

JAMES W. THOMPSON

people are: "those who are sanctified in Christ Jesus, called to be saints" (v. 2). The church can be called to be what God intends it to be only when we have a clear perception of who these people are and what grace has brought them to this place.

So Paul goes on to give thanks for the "grace of God that has been given you in Christ Jesus" (v. 4). In spite of all the failures of the people of Corinth, Paul can discern the gifts of God in this community. Using the metaphor of wealth, Paul declares that they have been "enriched" (v. 5). He asserts that they have received the capacity for speech and that they have been given knowledge. Furthermore, they are not lacking in any spiritual gift (v. 7).

As we look at the church in our own time, the weaknesses and failures are often all too evident. Paul can teach us to be grateful for the gifts that God has given to the church even with its frailties—gifts of understanding, gifts of caring, gifts of words that help and heal, gifts of faithfulness to Jesus Christ, gifts of shared community. The church is rich in blessings, not because of the accomplishments of the people within the fellowship, but because of the grace of God that has enriched and sustained the people.

One final perspective that Paul has on the church can be noted. Paul is quite aware that the church is not fulfilled in the present, but that the church waits for "the revealing of our Lord Jesus Christ" (v. 7). The church seeks to minister in this day and to be faithful in this day, but the church is a community that waits in hope for a future day. The church can live in hope because Jesus will be its strength to the end and because God is faithful.

HARRY B. ADAMS

John 1:29-42

²⁹The next day he saw Jesus coming toward him and declared, "Here is the Lamb of God who takes away the sin of the world! ³⁰This is he of whom I said, 'After me comes a man who ranks ahead of me because he was before me.' ³¹I myself did not know him; but I came baptizing with water for this reason, that he might be revealed to Israel." ³²And John testified, "I saw the Spirit descending from heaven like a dove, and it remained on him. ³³I myself did not know him, but the one who sent me to baptize with water said to me, 'He on whom you see the Spirit descend and remain is the one who baptizes with the Holy Spirit.' ³⁴And I myself have seen and have testified that this is the Son of God."

³⁵The next day John again was standing with two of his disciples, ³⁶and as he watched Jesus walk by, he exclaimed, "Look, here is the Lamb of God!" ³⁷The

Theological Perspective

In this passage from John's Gospel, we hear something of a retelling of two key moments in Jesus' life: his baptism and the call of the first disciples. Last week, on the First Sunday after the Epiphany, we heard of Matthew's account of the baptism. Next week, on the Third Sunday after the Epiphany, we will hear Matthew's account of the call of Peter, Andrew, and the brothers James and John, sons of Zebedee. Years B and C of the lectionary follow this same general pattern but rely on Mark and Luke instead of Matthew. John, however, always holds sway on this Second Sunday after the Epiphany. What is it that makes John important on this particular Sunday every year?

Context is everything, and the first thing to note is that this is the third Sunday of ten that find their orientation only in relation to the Epiphany of the Lord. This Sunday, like the two before it and the seven that follow it, is thus a Sunday in a string of Sundays on which the church celebrates the fact that God is manifest (epiphany) in the human being named Jesus of Nazareth (incarnation). With these theological terms in mind, the choice of John for this Sunday is not surprising, since his Gospel provides us with the most direct display of both the incarnation and the epiphany: "and the Word became flesh and lived among us, and we have seen his glory" (1:14).

Pastoral Perspective

Christ has no body now on earth but yours,
    no hands but yours,
    no feet but yours,
Yours are the eyes through which to look out
    Christ's compassion to the world;
Yours are the feet with which he is to go about doing
    good;
Yours are the hands with which he is to bless men
    now.

This poem is attributed to Teresa of Avila, a sixteenth-century Spanish mystic, composed by her in a letter sent to her nuns toward the end of her life, although the actual documentation is obscure. Nevertheless, it has taken on a popular presence in Christian spirituality and reflects a common understanding of what some call an incarnational theology—the idea that we are to be Jesus Christ to the world. At its foundation, incarnational theology reminds us all that God became incarnate—became flesh—in Jesus Christ to embody fully God's love for the world. Teresa of Avila takes this incarnational theology one step further and calls on us to incarnate Christ in our own selves and to love the world as Jesus did, even to the point of "always carrying in the body the death of Jesus, so that the life of Jesus may also be made visible in our bodies" as the apostle Paul writes to the church at Corinth (2 Cor. 4:10).

two disciples heard him say this, and they followed Jesus. ³⁸When Jesus turned and saw them following, he said to them, "What are you looking for?" They said to him, "Rabbi" (which translated means Teacher), "where are you staying?" ³⁹He said to them, "Come and see." They came and saw where he was staying, and they remained with him that day. It was about four o'clock in the afternoon. ⁴⁰One of the two who heard John speak and followed him was Andrew, Simon Peter's brother. ⁴¹He first found his brother Simon and said to him, "We have found the Messiah" (which is translated Anointed). ⁴²He brought Simon to Jesus, who looked at him and said, "You are Simon son of John. You are to be called Cephas" (which is translated Peter).

Exegetical Perspective

Do you remember the old Sesame Street game that had four squares and a jingle that went something like, "Which one of these is not like the other, which one just doesn't belong"? If you played that game with the four Gospels, John's Gospel would certainly be the one with the lights blinking around it at the end. John records no birth story but has two temple-cleansing stories. He records no parables and identifies Jesus' miracles as "signs." He quite often relates not simply *what* Jesus did or taught, but also *why* or *for what reason* he did such things. When compared to the other Gospels, John paints a more divine portrait of Jesus, seemingly not wanting his readers to forget or miss the fact that this earthly Jesus is God's Son who existed before all time.

Another distinctive feature of John, which is evident in the passage for this week, is the greater depth of insight concerning certain individuals in the various stories. Here, at the time of Jesus' baptism, we do not hear Jesus speak, as in Matthew, nor do we get the fuller set of details related in Mark or Luke. Instead, the evangelist records a first-person reflection by John the Baptist concerning Jesus' baptism. In the end, John the Baptist's words serve as a record of the event, but even more as a testimony concerning its significance. As when the evangelist signifies Jesus' miracles as "signs," here he signifies Jesus'

Homiletical Perspective

Following the baptism of Christ as recorded by Matthew, this Sunday we have the baptism of our Lord (as remembered in the Gospel of John) and the beginning of his ministry. As with the Matthean baptism, John is a witness to the voice from heaven (and to the Spirit descending on Jesus, unlike Matthew's account), and his witness to Jesus' lordship is in accordance with the high Christology of the Gospel of John. But this testimony is presented alongside human stories of encounter, discipleship, and relationship. The reading thus offers some interesting homiletical possibilities: baptism, the true identity of Jesus, witness, and evangelism all appear as themes in this week's lection.

Baptism. The baptism of Jesus in the Gospel of John is told about, rather than shown, evidence for the conclusion reached by New Testament scholar Sandra M. Schneiders that the readers of the Gospel of John were assumed to already know the "Jesus-story."[1] Thus John's interest in presenting the baptism is not to describe the actual baptism itself (which took place the day previous), but to focus on the signs that might lead others to belief in Jesus as

---

1. Sandra M. Schneiders, *Written So That You May Believe: Encountering Jesus in the Fourth Gospel* (New York: Herder & Herder, 2003), 38–39.

John 1:29-42

Theological Perspective

The second thing to note is that the celebration of the Epiphany has an interesting and complex history within the life of the church. As the West came to emphasize Christmas, eventually deciding on the date of December 25, the East emphasized Epiphany, which included a celebration not only of Jesus' birth but also of his baptism and other significant events like the miracle at the wedding in Cana. Eventually the West adopted the celebration of Epiphany on January 6 and used it to mark the end of Christmas, placing a special emphasis on the arrival of the magi in Bethlehem. The East eventually adopted December 25 as the date for celebrating Jesus' birth, which then placed the emphasis of Epiphany on Jesus' baptism.

What might all this shifting and sharing between East and West teach us about the theological importance of Epiphany? Take as a starting point the fact that in the West the Epiphany of the Lord marks the end of Christmas. In many churches, this end is performed symbolically but definitively by moving the magi and their gifts to the manger, after having held them back for the twelve days of Christmas. Children often ask about this delay: Why wait?

Of course, there is a practical response: the magi had to travel a long distance to Bethlehem, so it would be wrong to place them at the manger too soon after the birth. There is also the familiar theological response that the magi are Gentiles from "the East." Thus their arrival at the manger to pay homage to a baby born to be king of the Jews marks the moment when God is manifest to the world beyond Israel. God is the God of the whole world, but we do not know that until the magi show up. These practical and theological answers often suffice for inquiring children, but will they satisfy an especially inquisitive child—and are they theologically sufficient?

One might, for example, press the question and ask why, if God was incarnate already in Mary's womb (as John the Baptist, still in Elizabeth's womb, noticed), and was then born sputtering into the Judean air (as the shepherds noticed), do we have to wait to celebrate the Epiphany? Is not Christmas enough? Indeed, many an impatient child, seemingly quite clear about the amazing moment of God become human in the baby Jesus, is quite happy to speed up the arrival of the magi to acknowledge that God is manifest in the manger. So, again, why wait?

An answer to our impatience rests in the Eastern church's original celebration of the birth of Jesus, the baptism of Jesus, and certain of Jesus' miracles with

Pastoral Perspective

In this text in John, however, we come to see a different understanding of incarnational theology. Here, John the Baptist sees Jesus, God incarnate, coming and calls attention to Jesus, testifying to all within hearing distance that this is one who baptizes with the Holy Spirit. Later, when John is standing with two of his disciples, he sees Jesus walk by and tells his disciples that Jesus is the "Lamb of God!" (v. 36); John's disciples follow Jesus, and Jesus then begins to call his own disciples. Throughout these verses, John the Baptist plays an important role. He provides testimony as to who Jesus is and points the way so that others come to recognize Jesus Christ.

Several years ago, when the What Would Jesus Do? campaign was at its peak of popularity among young people, I had a conversation with a young high schooler. She had been given a WWJD bracelet; while she was wearing it, she was also troubled by it. After youth group one night, she shared that she was struggling with the concept of the bracelet. I tried to explain that the bracelet is supposed to be a tangible reminder that we are followers of Jesus and that we are to be guided by his actions in every facet of our lives. She assured me that she understood all that. Her problem was that she did not see how it was possible for us even to know what Jesus would actually do in any situation, let alone to do it faithfully. When I tried to explain that we have the Bible and the wider community of believers to help us, she explained in an exasperated tone, "Yeah, but don't you see? I am not Jesus! I am fully human, but I am not fully divine. I just don't think it's fair to even assume that I could imagine what Jesus would do because I am not God!" She had a point.

I teach at a seminary and love what I do. I feel tremendously privileged to journey with these students for these years as they study and reflect upon and engage in various expressions of ministry, even as they prepare for a further call to ministry. I enjoy that there is a clear starting point—the beginning of each school year in the late summer—and an ending point—the end of the academic year in the late spring. This kind of rhythm fits my soul. Here is the problem: graduation. The great majority of our students, when they finish their academic work, are conferred the Master of Divinity degree. Even on the best of days that is a rather audacious claim: Master of the Divine. Some of them, I can tell, actually believe it. They are the ones who make me the most nervous. If I had my way, as soon as they received that parchment with their name and the degree and the gold seal on it, I would like to be standing there

baptism as a testimony of his true identity, not just as the earthly Christ but also as the very Son of God (1:34; cf. 1:7; 15, 19).

After the prologue (1:1–18), the remainder of the first chapter is structured by a series of four days (1:19–51). The events of these four days can be summarized as follows:

—Day one: The priests, Levites, and also Pharisees come out (from Jerusalem) to question John about his identity (is he the Messiah? Elijah? a prophet?) and his baptizing activity (vv. 19–28).

—Day two: Jesus comes out to be baptized and receives the Spirit from heaven; John recognizes Jesus' superiority to himself and announces Jesus as "the Son of God" and "the Lamb of God" (vv. 29–34).

—Day three: John, standing with two of his disciples, sees Jesus and proclaims him again as "the Lamb of God." John's two disciples accept Jesus' call to follow him, and Simon also becomes a follower (vv. 35–42).

—Day four: Jesus goes with these new disciples to Galilee, recruits Philip and Nathanael, and teaches them that they will see and experience even "greater things" (vv. 43–51).

As a whole, the evangelist communicates several very important points about Jesus' identity at this early stage of the movement: (1) "Jerusalem" is cognizant of John's activity in the wilderness, and there is wonderment about his identity; (2) John is not the Messiah; (3) the Messiah will come later, and he will be the Son of God; and (4) when the Son of God comes, John's disciples are to follow John no more.

The verses for this week encompass the middle two days in the sequence. In the first of these two days, John the Baptist's testimony includes a declaration of Jesus as "the Lamb of God" (1:29). Though some contend that John recognized Jesus as such at first sight, it is clear from John's words that this was not the case; twice he says, "I myself did not know him" (vv. 31, 33). The image of a "lamb" often communicates a weak, vulnerable animal ready for sacrifice or slaughter. However, as it is used here and in some other Jewish writings, the lamb is powerful. The lamb reigns in the heavens and will bring about judgment on the wicked and secure salvation for the righteous.

It is in relation to this lamb that John recognizes his own inferiority or lower rank. Jesus "ranks ahead" (v. 30) of John because Jesus precedes him in time (i.e., Jesus preexisted, vv. 1–5), because Jesus baptizes with the Spirit and John only with water, and finally

the Son of God. Preaching the baptism from John's Gospel thus requires us to wrestle with different questions. Why doesn't John describe the actual baptism? How does this baptism compare to the description we find in Matthew (or the other Synoptic Gospels)? How do these signs from Jesus' baptism operate in the world of John's Gospel? What does it mean to say that Jesus baptizes with the Holy Spirit, rather than with water? How will your congregation's understanding of baptism shape their hearing of this reading?

The True Identity of Jesus. This lection contains several scenes of witness to the true nature of Jesus. John's Gospel, of course, has the highest Christology of the canonical Gospels, and we know from the prologue forward that Jesus is the Son of God, but this lection gives us both the startling assertion of Sonhood and the radical notion of the Lamb of God. A sermon might explore these tensions—or focus exclusively on the idea of the Lamb of God, depending on the location of your congregation. Jack Miles, who has explored the "lives" of God and Jesus as narratives, has written that the startling image of the Messiah as lamb radically rejects earlier biblical images of royal majesty, and that in choosing this metaphor, God (through Jesus) is choosing weakness and electing to play the role not of the All-Powerful Passover Deliverer but of the sacrificial Passover Lamb.[2]

The Catholic novelist Graham Greene wrote a number of stories that offer us examples of heroes and heroines who sacrifice themselves for others. These sacrificial characters in *Brighton Rock*, *The Power and the Glory*, and *The Heart of the Matter* may help in explaining the challenging concept of the Lamb of God for your congregation. Be alert for other literary and cultural examples of sacrifice, particularly sacrifice that is consciously chosen, as is the sacrifice of Jesus in the Fourth Gospel.

Witness. The Johannine focus on belief in the person of Christ, rather than in following a path or seeking the kingdom, may shape your preaching of this lesson. What is John the evangelist saying about Jesus (and about God) through his witness? Why is the true nature of Jesus revealed boldly in this Gospel when in other Gospels this nature is revealed gradually or even kept secret? How do we understand Jesus

---

2. Jack Miles, *Christ: A Crisis in the Life of God* (New York: Random House, 2001), 210 and passim.

John 1:29-42

Theological Perspective

a single festival on January 6: the Epiphany of the Lord. Theologically considered, this Eastern emphasis on a continuum of events that, taken together, add up to the Epiphany was an open acknowledgment of just how difficult a notion the incarnation is.

By holding together, on a single feast day, the birth, the baptism, and miracles like those at the wedding in Cana, the Eastern church was, in effect, building a liturgical case for the incarnation: not just a baby in a manger, but one who attracted the attention of the world; even more, one for whom the heavens opened up so that he might be claimed with the words from last week's reading, "This is my Son, the Beloved, with whom I am well pleased" (Matt. 3:17). More still, add in the wedding at Cana, where John says of the water that became wine, "Jesus did this, the first of his signs, in Cana of Galilee, and revealed his glory" (John 2:11). Epiphany. God manifest. God manifest as a human being. Incarnation.

This string of Sundays that we encounter in the lectionary as "after the Epiphany" serves to remind us that a baby in a manger is not enough to support our theological claims for the incarnation. We need more than Christmas, even if we wait patiently for the arrival of the magi. We need to see Jesus walk into the Jordan. We need to see the clouds part. We need to hear the booming voice name Jesus a beloved Son. We need to hear Jesus himself ask us, as he asks Peter and Andrew in this passage from John, "What are you looking for?" (John 1:38). We will be tempted to rush our reply, just as the children hurry the magi on their way to the manger. Before we answer, we need to be mindful that there are seven more Sundays "after the Epiphany," and six of them are devoted to the Sermon on the Mount. We would do well to wait to hear what Jesus has to say in the coming weeks before we answer his question and finish the celebration we started on Christmas.

DAVID TOOLE

Pastoral Perspective

to scribble something like "in process" or "by the grace of God" on the edge of their diploma.

While I fully understand what Teresa and the apostle Paul are saying to us, that we are to live lives that embody Christ, it is equally important that we not take on some messianic identity that says we are Christ to the world. A couple of years ago, a good friend and colleague here at the seminary, who was concerned about my schedule and commitments and hectic pace and looking tired, insisted on taking me out to lunch and said it was urgent. When we sat down at the table, I asked what was going on. She told me she had some good news for me. Perplexed, I asked her what the good news was. She smiled and said, "I want you to know the Messiah has come!" Now I was thoroughly confused, so she told me she had even better news for me: "You are not him!" The real danger in a distorted incarnational theology is that we come to believe that if we truly are Christ's body in the world, then if the world is going to be saved, we have to do it.

It may be better for us to ask, not so much WWJD? but rather WWJBD? What would John the Baptist do? Lately, I have been challenging myself and my students to be more like John the Baptist— to call attention to Jesus Christ and then to say to all who are within hearing distance, "Hey, look! See! God is alive. God is in our midst. The Holy Spirit is at work in us and through and for us and even in spite of us! Behold! The Lamb of God!"

RODGER Y. NISHIOKA

because in God's plans John is preparatory in function (see Isa. 40:3 in John 1:23). However, John's testimony is not diminished by this. Though "no one has ever seen God" (v. 18), just various manifestations of God, John *has* seen the Son of God. In line with the writing of Philo, the Jewish philosopher, hearing God takes second place to actually seeing God (when the person doesn't die!). John has seen God because God has allowed it, and now he voices the testimony—that Jesus is the Son of God—even before Jesus demonstrates it in his earthly ministry.

The events of the subsequent day (i.e., day three) communicate the relative positioning of John and Jesus already testified to by John. Jesus' superior rank and priority mean that any disciples of John, if they rightly digest his testimony, must move their allegiance to Jesus. John's exclamation in verse 36 is one that calls his disciples to detach from him. Then Jesus' question, "What are you looking for?" (1:38), serves as both an invitation and examination for those same disciples to follow him. As with all persons who would be followers of Jesus, it is not simply *if* they wish to follow, but *what* and *whom* are they looking for? These two disciples, one of whom is Andrew and one of whom is unnamed, not only followed but "remained" (v. 39) with Jesus that day.

It can be safely assumed that since it was already the tenth hour, or four o'clock in the afternoon, the disciples had ample time to converse with and learn from Jesus that day, and they might even have remained with him overnight. Though we are not privy to what was discussed during such time, we may well see in Simon's change of name to Cephas (i.e., Peter/rock) a sign of the transformation that was beginning in these disciples. May this transformation, this new identity formation, occur within the whole world through John's testimony (and ours) of Jesus as "the Lamb of God who takes away the sin of the world!" (v. 29).

TROY A. MILLER

in the Fourth Gospel? What does the Gospel of John suggest might follow belief?

Evangelism. The approach to evangelism of your congregation (and your tradition) will affect their understanding of this lection. Evangelism is clearly more of a challenge in some mainstream Christian traditions than in evangelical traditions, but this lection provides ample narrative material for a sermon on coming to Jesus—and on bringing others. The excitement of John the prophet, the simple command from Jesus to potential followers: "Come and see," and the first generation of followers bringing those they loved to meet the Messiah are all fuel for a sermon on evangelism. Although it may sometimes be uncomfortable telling others our story, the church is the church because of Jesus and who he is, and in this passage we get the entire shape of his story: baptism, the beginning of his ministry, the transformation of followers like Peter, and, implied in the descriptive term "Lamb of God," even his death and resurrection.

However we understand these events theologically, we can say, with Rowan Williams, archbishop of Canterbury, that we know forgiveness through the resurrection event, and that we "cannot be understood apart from Jesus," since we received our name and identity in the process of baptism, a beginning that reminds us of the end, the death, burial, and resurrection.[3] It is this story—our understanding of ourselves in the larger story of God through Jesus—that we can tell others. So a sermon on evangelism using this text might overcome your community's anxiety about evangelism—or its narrow focus on a salvation moment—to show how the first disciples invited others to experience how they might know hope, peace, and joy because of this Jesus and with the community that has formed around him.

Does your congregation remember stories in which people were invited to come and see? Have there been faithful witnesses in your community whose stories might enliven your sermon? This week's lection may offer an opportunity to retell the story of your own faith community, or important aspects of it, as a way of expressing how you might invite others to come and see today.

GREG GARRETT

---

3. Rowan Williams, *Resurrection: Interpreting the Easter Gospel* (Cleveland: Pilgrim Press, 2002), 55.

Isaiah 9:1-4

¹But there will be no gloom for those who were in anguish. In the former time he brought into contempt the land of Zebulun and the land of Naphtali, but in the latter time he will make glorious the way of the sea, the land beyond the Jordan, Galilee of the nations.

²The people who walked in darkness
    have seen a great light;
  those who lived in a land of deep darkness—
    on them light has shined.
³You have multiplied the nation,
    you have increased its joy;
  they rejoice before you
    as with joy at the harvest,
    as people exult when dividing plunder.
⁴For the yoke of their burden,
    and the bar across their shoulders,
    the rod of their oppressor,
    you have broken as on the day of Midian.

Theological Perspective

On January 20, 2009, the world watched with bated breath as the inauguration of the first African American president of the United States took place. On that day Martin Luther King Jr.'s dream of 1963 came to life in a remarkable and unique way. While former times had seen the anguish and oppression of a people wrongly discriminated against, on that day a new light shone forth, bringing joy and the hope of prosperity to the nation. Such a momentous turning point would not have been possible without the tireless leadership of King and those who followed in his footsteps. In fact, one development that was an immediate outworking of King's ministry and that contributed to this dramatic turn of events was the inauguration not of a newly elected president but of a newly emerging consciousness—black Theology. With the pioneering work of those such as Joseph R. Washington and the National Committee of Black Churchmen, a new hermeneutical perspective was brought to the table—one that had been heretofore marginalized and silenced with a violence that will never be forgotten. Theological emancipation brought with it the insight that, as James H. Cone wrote in his essay "Black Theology in American Religion," the true meaning of the

Pastoral Perspective

For Christians, the light of Isaiah's oracle breaks over us on the Third Sunday after the Epiphany, only a month after the shortest day of the year. Sunlight hours have begun to lengthen, the light remaining with us a little longer each day. The light Isaiah looks toward, however, is not light that grows gradually over time. The brightness of the light Isaiah proclaims shines on a people walking in darkness like a brilliant dawn suddenly breaking. This, surely, is the kind of light that illuminates every secret place, bringing a path obscured by shadows suddenly into view. It is the kind of light that gives direction and drives out fear.

Isaiah speaks his prophecy of light into a moment of tremendous fear for the people of Israel, a time of "distress and darkness, the gloom of anguish" (Isa. 8:22). Assyrian invaders have attacked the northern kingdom, shearing away portions of Israel to create Assyrian provinces. With its images of "the boots of the tramping warriors" and "garments rolled in blood" (Isa. 9:5), the oracle in Isaiah 9 reflects the oppressive military occupation under which Israel struggles to live. Isaiah speaks his word of light and hope into a time of desolation.

It is clear from the previous chapter that Isaiah experiences this desolation theologically as well as

Exegetical Perspective

Three points should be made about this lection initially. First, these four verses are part of a larger rhetorical unit which begins in 8:21 and extends through 9:7. Second, few verses in the book of Isaiah are so variously translated and interpreted as 8:21–9:1. If one compares several modern translations of these verses, the general reader cannot be certain of which translation to trust. (The NRSV is one of the poorest.) Third, the language in this text is extremely metaphorical and imprecise to modern readers. No doubt the allusions would have been clear to the prophet's audience.

The following exegesis is based on what can be reconstructed of the history of the time and the events to which the prophet alludes. The decades from about 760 to 730 BCE were extremely tumultuous and trying times in the Middle East, especially for Israel and Judah. Assyria, on whom Israel and Judah relied and with whom they were treaty partners, was greatly weakened. The Urartians had seriously hampered Assyrian trade, civil war tore at the fabric of Assyrian life, and plagues killed much of the population. While Assyria was weak, its allies— Israel and Judah—were also weak.

This period of Assyrian weakness provided an opportunity for states in the west to organize against

Homiletical Perspective

The preacher might be surprised at the appearance of this text so soon after Christmas. Resist the temptation to pass it by. Lend it a second hearing. The text can serve both as a spotlight and a window. Matthew uses the text to shine a spotlight on the beginning of Jesus' ministry and its meaning. The preacher can use this snippet of a text to open a window to the global themes of Isaiah's "gospel."

Remember: at Christmas, the hand lowered the taper to the wick and the Christ candle burst into flame, illumining our place in the story—"for a child has been born for *us,* a son given to *us*" (9:6a). That was our cue to join in singing with the chorus of angels in welcoming the Christ child into our family as we do for children at their baptism. Behold the "Wonderful Counselor" who now joins us on our journey toward God! Soon "the authority that rests on his shoulders, will grow continually" (vv. 6, 7) as this child takes on the role of the Servant described in the prophet's vision.

Now the occasion is different, and so are the parameters of this text. It is Epiphany, a season that gives the church time to reflect more carefully on the incarnation of the Word, the mystery that dawned at Christmas, and see it in action in the life of Jesus. The light from the candle at Christmas now fills the

Isaiah 9:1-4

Theological Perspective

gospel is "God's liberation of the oppressed from bondage."[1]

The truth of this statement is evident when we read the oracle of Isaiah 9, which declares a remarkable turning point in the history of Judah from oppression to liberation. This passage affirms that God hears the "anguish" of those who suffer and responds with deliverance: "For the yoke of their burden, and the bar across their shoulders, the rod of their oppressor, you have broken" (v. 4). For biblical scholars, the exegetical analysis of this passage raises important questions regarding historical particularity. Scholars debate over whether the passage refers to the postexilic or preexilic period; whether the passage points to the accession of Hezekiah or Josiah; and whether the rod broken was that of the Syro-Ephraimite coalition or of Assyria.

More important, however, is what we learn in verse 6—namely, that the burden of the oppressed is lifted by the birth of a new ruler, lending credence to the notion that this passage represents the accession of the foretold Immanuel child. This is no ordinary turn of events, but one without precedent. As Walter Brueggemann states,

> What we have is a glorious, celebrative affirmation that Yahweh, through a human Davidic king, will create a wondrous new possibility for Judah that is unqualified and unconditional. The theological point is Yahweh's capacity and resolve for a newness that is completely fresh and without extrapolation from anything that has gone before.[2]

Through this child, Isaiah 9 offers a message of deliverance from oppression for the people of God.

What type of "liberation" does God offer to humanity? Liberation represents a twofold reality within the Christian faith. On the one hand, through Christ, believers are spiritually liberated from the bonds of sin; the captive will is no longer bound by the sinful state of humanity, but is freed to respond to the good news of grace in obedience to God. On the other hand, as specified in Galatians 3:28, life in Christ includes liberation from the racial, social, and gender divisions of society. As specified in Galatians 2:19–20, believers have been crucified with Christ, and it is no longer they who live, but Christ who lives in them. That presence is transformative, turning believers into new creations who are called to carry out the work of the Lord on earth (Matt. 28).

1. James H. Cone, "Black Theology in American Religion," in *Journal of the American Academy of Religion* 53, no. 4 (Dec. 1985): 755–56.
2. Walter Brueggemann, *Isaiah 1–39*, Westminster Bible Companion (Louisville, KY: Westminster John Knox Press, 1998), 82.

Pastoral Perspective

politically. "I will wait for the LORD," Isaiah writes, "who is hiding his face from the house of Jacob, and I will hope in him" (Isa. 8:17). God's gaze may be turned away, but Isaiah waits and hopes.

As he waits in the darkness of cruelty and oppression, Isaiah imagines and proclaims that the light of God's face will again shine on the people of Israel. Do not be afraid, Isaiah seems to say. Do not give up. God's light will break through our gloom and anguish, scattering it. Isaiah sings a song of liberation into the darkness, a song of the God who lifts the burdensome yoke under which the people are trapped by raising up a ruler who will drive out the oppressors, unify Israel, and initiate a time of "endless peace for the throne of David and his kingdom" (Isa. 9:7).

It takes courage to preach hope in the midst of such desolation. Courage, or a dangerous naiveté. For preaching hope can be done badly, hurtfully. When people are living in "the gloom of anguish," a word of hope too easily spoken can leave that anguish unacknowledged, deepening the pain.

Isaiah does not speak carelessly, however. Nor does he speak as one who can afford to hope because he is exempt from the suffering he addresses. Isaiah speaks as part of the community, one of the people who walk in darkness. He speaks with authority, passion, and confidence that God is still present.

Many scholars believe the oracle in Isaiah 9 celebrates the ascension of Hezekiah to "the throne of David and his kingdom" (Isa. 9:7). Certainly Isaiah's words celebrate with joy the new king in whom so much hope is invested, but he celebrates the king in words that transcend the accomplishments of any particular leader, words that express the deepest longings of his community. Isaiah's oracle keeps before his listeners and his readers the vision of a day when the life of the world will be shaped by justice and righteousness and blessed by a peace that will never end.

No matter what political party is in power, no matter who our leaders are, there will always be a need for voices like Isaiah's that proclaim a vision of a world at peace. There will always be a need for prophetic voices to say clearly what is unacceptable: the rod of oppression, the exploitation of the poor, the rule of fear. There will always be a need for prophetic voices to stand outside of the halls of power and lift up a vision of what our world, and we, can become, to call us to new ways of living.

Isaiah reminds us of the importance of imagination in our pastoral work, the capacity to see beyond things as they are and to imagine things as they might be. He reminds us not to lower our sights, not

Assyria. Since Israel and Judah refused to join this anti-Assyrian coalition, they became the object of harassment. (The nations noted in Amos 1:2–2:3 were the local enemies of the two kingdoms.)

Israel and Judah were themselves torn by civil strife and warfare. When the long-reigning Israelite king Jeroboam II died in 747, his son Zechariah succeeded him but was put to death after six months by a certain Shallum, who was killed after a one-month rule (2 Kgs. 15:8–16). In addition to this, from about 750 BCE, Pekah, with the support of King Rezin in Damascus, had ruled over Israelite territory east of the River Jordan.

Verses 21–22 of Isaiah 8 describe the movement of the counterking Pekah against Samaria, the Israelite capital city, in the fall of 734 BCE (see 2 Kgs. 15:27, 37). Immediately upon taking Samaria, Pekah threw his support behind the Syro-Palestinian anti-Assyrian coalition headed by King Rezin of Damascus. Pekah was thereby breaking a longtime treaty of friendship between Israel/Judah and Assyria.

Verses 21–22 may thus be translated and understood as follows:

> He [Pekah] has passed over [the Jordan] into it [the land of Canaan], fierce and hungry. And when he becomes ravenous and works himself into a rage, then he will revolt against his king and his god. And he will turn to go upward [toward Samaria] and set his sights [to take] the land [of Israel]. Then surely [there will be] distress and darkness, gloom and oppression, and widespread calamity.

Pekah's takeover of the government in Samaria and his support of the anti-Assyrian movement would be calamitous to Israel. (Assyria fought for three years against the coalition, from 733 to 731 BCE, killing or subjugating all the leaders, Pekah included.)

The opening verse of today's lection (9:1, in the Heb.) may be translated and paraphrased:

> Surely there will be no gloom on her [Jerusalem] for whom there has been anguish, like the time the former one [King Hadianu of Damascus] treated contemptibly the land of Zebulun and the land of Naphtali and the latter one [King Rezin of Damascus] treated harshly the Way of the Sea, Beyond the Jordan, and Galilee of the Nations.

First of all, the adjectives "former" and "latter" are masculine. The noun "time" is feminine. Therefore these two adjectives do not modify "time" as assumed by the NRSV's "former time" and "latter time." Instead they refer to a previous and a present male ruler. Second, the verbs are past tense and must be

room, and Isaiah is one of its sources. The child of promise has now grown into adulthood and, according to Matthew, uses Isaiah as the text for the sermon that inaugurates his ministry. Gone are verses 5–7; included is verse 1, which gives him his focus— "those who were in anguish," who felt "in the former time" as if they were being held in contempt, not only by their oppressors but even by their God.

A look back to a particular time of darkness, when the northern territory of Israel was occupied by the Assyrians (733–732 BCE), helps Matthew's Jesus to fashion a word of hope for the present and for all time. The text speaks of the "latter time" (v. 1) when the northern territory—the "Galilee of the nations"— will be glorified, as signified in the ministry of Jesus. Isaiah offers the backdrop for Matthew's presentation of Jesus as the one who opens a new chapter in God's dealings with creation through God's people Israel, a chapter that will include the "Gentiles" or the "peoples from far away" (49:1).

For the church, Jesus is an agent of God's salvation and is invested with both the power and the authority to stand against the oppressions of imperial occupation, hunger, blindness, lameness, poverty, and even death. Jesus will give voice to those "held in contempt" through practices of exclusion and through his ministry will demonstrate signs of God's favor. In his name there will be a new community that celebrates and continues God's intrusion into history.

Matthew's choice of this text for Jesus' preaching offers some clues for how the preacher might employ it. Isaiah trains the eye and ear to look at world events. Through the window that the text provides, one can see and hear hidden and explicit purposes of God at work through human history. Isaiah takes a hard look at the "deep darkness" that is the experience of those languishing under the "boots of the tramping warriors" (v. 5) in his day. Matthew's Jesus follows that lead when he speaks to those in his own time who were squirming under the boot of Rome. The preacher can take a look around and see how imperial ambitions have displaced populations, exploited resources, and plundered the world's wealth. In the darkness of exile and exploitation, Isaiah sees God's light, a light that illumines God's character. It is a God who calls to accountability not only God's own people but all nations.

The judgment is not the capricious act of an eccentric deity; it has an eye on the benefit to the created order. God's judgment exposes the machinations and intentions of empire. It is aimed at salvation, an

Isaiah 9:1-4

Theological Perspective

All that resulted as a consequence of the fall of Adam was redeemed and overturned by the raising up of the second Adam. In Christ, then, the spiritual lives of believers have been redeemed, and the oppressions of this world have been overcome. This is the promise that was given by Christ in Matthew 11:28–30: "Come to me, all you that are weary and are carrying heavy burdens, and I will give you rest. Take my yoke upon you, and learn from me; for I am gentle and humble in heart, and you will find rest for your souls. For my yoke is easy, and my burden is light." The release of the captives is, indeed, the true meaning of the gospel.

In this Jesus Christ, the gentle-hearted and the one who suffered and died for all, those who have faced the oppression of the world have found comfort and deliverance. The work of womanist theologian Jacquelyn Grant illustrates this point in her description of Jesus as the "divine co-sufferer":

> For Christian black women in the past, Jesus was their central frame of reference. They identified with Jesus because they believed that Jesus identified with them. As Jesus was persecuted and made to suffer undeservedly, so were they. His suffering culminated in crucifixion. Their crucifixion included rape, and babies being sold. But Jesus' suffering was not the suffering of a mere human, for Jesus was understood to be God incarnate.[3]

This cosuffering God incarnate is a welcome response for those with questions of theodicy raised by the war, violence, and oppression of the last century. Since King, a new world order is emerging, one in which my mother—the Rev. Dr. Pamela Powell—could minister as an ordained white woman to a struggling black church community in Texas and become a transformative part of their lives, as is documented in the book *The Gospel in Black & White: Theological Resources for Racial Reconciliation*. Such remarkable achievements are not the work of human hands. Deliverance of the oppressed from bondage, the true meaning of the gospel, is the work of the Lord.

JENNIFER POWELL MCNUTT

Pastoral Perspective

to get comfortable with the status quo, not to be satisfied with anything less than the release of those held captive, the end of war making, and the lifting of the burden of oppression from all peoples everywhere. Long after the memory of Hezekiah's accomplishments, and his compromises, has faded into the past, Isaiah's vision of what is possible continues to inspire the fiercest hopes of human beings for the future. Even in a time of desolation, Isaiah is able to imagine and to describe a great light breaking, illuminating the path of those who walk in darkness, fear, and pain.

Where that path leads, as later passages in Isaiah proclaim, is outward: outward to the coastlands, outward to the ends of the great, wide world. Isaiah not only promises that God's people will be given a light to see by and a light to walk by; he promises that following that light will lead them ever more deeply into the life of the world. To those who have been waiting for God's light to break in upon their darkness, God says, "I will give you as a light to the nations, that my salvation may reach to the end of the earth" (Isa. 49:6).

During Epiphany, we remember the magi, who set off with their gifts on a journey into the unknown, their path illuminated by the light of a single star. Isaiah reminds us that God intends those upon whom God's light shines to be themselves a gift, "a light to the nations." Isaiah reminds us that we are called to share the light we can see and feel. We are also called, like Isaiah, to share the light that we can only yet imagine.

STEPHANIE A. PAULSELL

---

3. Jacquelyn Grant, *White Women's Christ and Black Women's Jesus: Feminist Christology and Womanist Response*, American Academy of Religion series, no. 64 (Atlanta: Scholars Press, 1989), 212.

Exegetical Perspective

taken as describing past action. The NRSV translates one verb in the past tense ("brought into contempt") and the other in the future tense ("will make glorious"). This of course is grammatical nonsense.

We now know that Assyrian forces under General Shamshi-ilu had attacked Damascus in 773 BCE. (An inscription reporting on this attack was discovered during the recent construction of a dam in Turkey.) No doubt the Assyrians attacked Damascus to stop the Syrians who had invaded the Israelite tribal areas of Zebulun and Naphtali. Most recently, Rezin and his sidekick Pekah had taken over the Way of the Sea (the highway from Damascus running across northern Israel and down the coast to Egypt), Trans-Jordan, and the land of Galilee.

Verses 2–4 describe the new status of Jerusalem (also Judah and the house of David). "Those who had walked in darkness" refers to the southerners who for decades had been submissive to Samaria and Israel. When King Ahaz of Judah, guided by Isaiah, refused to join the anti-Assyrian coalition, they had "seen the light" and declared their independence. Because they took this action, Rezin and Pekah invaded Judah to depose and kill the uncooperative house of David (see Isa. 7:1–9 and 2 Kgs. 15:29–16:20).

When King Amaziah of Judah had earlier sought to assert his independence from the Israelite king, he was attacked and defeated, and part of Jerusalem was torn down (2 Kgs. 14:1–14). After Ahaz declared the south's independence from the north (in 734 BCE), his name and that of Judah ("Jehoahaz of the land of Judah") make their first appearance in Assyrian inscriptions (in 733 BCE).

Verses 3–4 have the prophet praising God for supporting the independence movement and freeing these people from Israelite dominance. In these verses, the prophet addresses God directly as in prayer. Two consequences have been produced: God has multiplied (better "emboldened") the nation and increased its joy. Isaiah describes the celebration as comparable to the celebration at harvest time or when troops and their families divided up the loot taken from the enemy in battle. It was Judah's Fourth of July celebration!

Verse 4 implies that Israel's dominance over Judah (see 2 Kgs. 14:1–14) had often been oppressive and exercised with "yoke . . . bar . . . and rod." The rescue from oppression was like the time when the people were freed from the dominance of Midianites (see Judg. 7:19–25) by Gideon.

JOHN H. HAYES

Homiletical Perspective

initiative that breaks yokes of burden and the rods of oppression (v. 4). Oppression, as Isaiah reads human history, does not have the last word. Those who live in the land of the "deep darkness" of political, social, or religious oppression in any age are not living outside the sight of God; they will see God's light, and upon them it will shine.

The preacher's sermon can shine God's light on those times in our own experience when oppressions were lifted, including those times when we found ourselves as a people in the role of the oppressor. We see through the window of this text the overarching message of Isaiah. God's purpose is to turn the humiliation of the vulnerable into liberation and exultation, and it will not be thwarted, even by God's own people! At an appointed time, God's light shines on those human agents who are in service to God's purpose. With a faith rooted in the character of God, Isaiah forecasts new possibilities through human and divine effort, even when nations with imperial ambitions are wreaking havoc on the world stage. Through Jesus, says Matthew, a new possibility has emerged in the faith communities founded in his name. It is an inclusive vision that suits an emerging global view and that can thrive in religious pluralism.

Today the preacher may stand in the light of that vision and bring a congregation into its sphere. She stands in the trajectory of an eighth-century-BCE prophet who spoke to regal power and advised sovereign heads of state about the ways of God in the world. It is a place where Matthew has Jesus stand to speak Isaiah's gospel to a beleaguered people brought low by oppressions of many kinds. The good news is this: in the shadows of empire, God is at work in the world, bringing about salvation through the restoration of a compassionate order of justice. Open your eyes and see the light penetrating the darkness. Repent, and believe the good news!

RICHARD F. WARD

Psalm 27:1, 4-9

¹The LORD is my light and my salvation;
   whom shall I fear?
The LORD is the stronghold of my life;
   of whom shall I be afraid?

. . . .

⁴One thing I asked of the LORD,
   that will I seek after:
to live in the house of the LORD
   all the days of my life,
to behold the beauty of the LORD,
   and to inquire in his temple.

⁵For he will hide me in his shelter
   in the day of trouble;
he will conceal me under the cover of his tent;
   he will set me high on a rock.

Theological Perspective

When my nephew was a young child, escalators and stairs terrified him. His mother recalls his efforts to conquer his fears: standing at the top step with all the courage he could muster, he bolstered his resolve by repeating words of encouragement to himself over and over. With its opening mantra (v. 1) and its concluding verse (v. 14), Psalm 27 reminds me of my nephew's internal conversation to reassure himself and to inspire the confidence necessary to face the dreaded source of his insecurity. While several biblical scholars find a tone of confidence running through the psalm, certain elements in the text give more of an impression of one trying to build self-confidence, convincing oneself on the basis of prior experience that in this time of trouble God will deliver.

This psalm is thematically consistent with Psalm 40, which appears a week earlier in the lectionary readings for the Second Sunday after Epiphany. Like Psalm 40, this psalm combines trust in God with lament and concern in time of trial. Throughout both texts the anxiety of the petitioner is palpable, as affirmations of trust in divine deliverance are set side by side with plaintive cries begging God not to "withhold mercy" (40:11), and not to "forsake" the endangered servant (27:9).

Psalm 27 begins with a rhetorical question, "whom shall I fear?" (v. 1). The response to this

Pastoral Perspective

The New Revised Standard Version labels Psalm 27 a "triumphant song of confidence." It is paired on this day with a Gospel text detailing the beginning of Jesus' public ministry. "Repent, the kingdom is near," says Jesus, and later, "Follow me, and I will make you fish for people" (Matt. 4:17, 19).

Reading the psalm in light of this label and Gospel pairing, our ears will prick up with the positive language in the text: the Lord as light, salvation, and stronghold; the Lord as one who hides and protects the psalmist, who sets the psalmist on solid ground; the Lord as the one to whom the psalmist makes a bold song of joy and thanksgiving.

A thread of confident trust is woven throughout the psalm. The lectionary locates this psalm in the season of Epiphany, the season of God's "showing," of being manifest. It is an apt placement of Psalm 27 in the liturgical year: not in the expectation of Advent or the reflective wilderness of Lent, but in the "already" between them. God has been revealed, and whatever might have gone before and whatever is still to come, the psalmist has hope and assurance in God, who is at hand.

While the language is not overly effusive, the psalm does point to a relationship with God that is ever deepening in intimacy. At first, the psalmist is content to live in God's house, to "inquire in [God's]

⁶Now my head is lifted up
  above my enemies all around me,
and I will offer in his tent
  sacrifices with shouts of joy;
I will sing and make melody to the Lᴏʀᴅ.

⁷Hear, O Lᴏʀᴅ, when I cry aloud,
  be gracious to me and answer me!
⁸"Come," my heart says, "seek his face!"
  Your face, Lᴏʀᴅ, do I seek.
⁹ Do not hide your face from me.

Do not turn your servant away in anger,
  you who have been my help.
Do not cast me off, do not forsake me,
  O God of my salvation!

Exegetical Perspective

Psalm 27 features the faithful attitude and the needful prayer of an individual. With regard to form, this psalm is somewhat of a hybrid, though recurring vocabulary suggests that it was a unified composition. The first half of the psalm (vv. 1–6, along with v. 10) contains statements of trust and confidence. Some scholars hypothesize that the psalmist may have addressed them to an assembled congregation. At verse 7 the voice shifts from third person to second person, and the psalm is now addressed directly to God: "Hear, YHWH . . . to you my heart speaks" (as the Hebrew text reads; the NRSV reading alters the Hebrew vocalization). The second half of the psalm includes the psalmist's lament and petition for God's help in times of trouble, either current or anticipated. This dual nature of the psalm's contents reminds its hearers that even in times of solid faith and confident hope, the problems of life do not disappear. In the world, evil—here depicted in terms of violence, deceit, fear, anger—abounds. It is trust, however, that wins out: the psalmist's final word (vv. 13–14), like her initial word (v. 1), is one of confidence.

The psalm begins in an especially noteworthy manner. Unlike many psalms of an individual, verse 1 is not a petition or request but instead a descriptive, even bold, announcement about God. It includes two parallel statements of fact ("YHWH is my light and

Homiletical Perspective

We know what the author of Psalm 27 knows: troubles and trials abound. That things go badly is well established. That things *might* go badly is the wellspring of worry. From early morning to late evening, from the early years to the late evening of life, anxiety persists. A child worries about an upcoming move to a new school. A father fears the pending diagnosis of his adult son's illness. Pangs of anxiety seize a senior in the wake of her husband's death. The trouble we face today is compounded by the uncertainty of tomorrow.

In his book *The Joy of Worry*, the satirist Ellis Weiner offers an anecdote that may be recognizable to many in our congregations. He writes:

> A young woman of high-school age was out late one evening. . . . Her father fell into an untroubled slumber, but her mother sat up, fretting and brooding and imagining a variety of disasters that might have befallen their daughter. Finally the mother could stand it no longer. She looked down, punched her husband, and said, "Wake up. It's your turn to worry," at which point the man took over worrying and the woman went to sleep.[1]

Weiner makes light of the anxiety parents bear, but his humor holds a kernel of truth. We are spared

1. Ellis Weiner, *The Joy of Worry* (San Francisco: Chronicle Books, 2004), 107.

Psalm 27:1, 4-9

Theological Perspective

question (vv. 2–3, 12) is omitted from the lectionary. In some ways the psalm has been sanitized in the lectionary. The lectionary version insulates contemporary worshiping communities from the violence that threatens the petitioner. The evildoers, enemies, encamped armies, adversaries, and false witnesses are excised from the scene. Gone too is the vivid language that helps one to comprehend both the fear behind the pleas for God not to turn away (v. 9), and the concluding admonition to wait and "be strong, and let your heart take courage; wait for the LORD" (v. 14). This reference to waiting is also reminiscent of Psalm 40. Both psalms evoke an anxious waiting grounded in perceptible, even imminent threats of harm, yet confident in the hope of deliverance by a trustworthy God with a proven track record.

It is the type of faithful and hopeful waiting that for subsequent generations of Christian receivers of the Word characterizes that in-between time during which we live from day to day in hope. This sense of waiting is captured in a brief psalm that comes from the pen of New York Puerto Rican poet Jack Agüeros: "Lord, hurry up and give me patience!"[1] Like his ancient Hebrew poetic predecessors, Agüeros's contemporary psalms reflect on the challenges of our times and of his barrio. Like poets and psalmists who wrote before him, he neither shies away from nor sugarcoats the sometimes perilous conditions that give rise to psalms like his.

What has been said about Agüeros's psalms applies to his poetic antecedents as well, "There is a wry social satirist at work in these poems, for the questions he asks are pointed as much at the church, or the government, or the corporate culture, or us, as they are at the inscrutable Lord."[2] This insight also highlights the public function of psalms. Each worshiping community interacts with the texts within the context of their respective times and trials. The lectionary ensures that these cyclic encounters occur in conversation with other texts.

With this use in mind, the metaphoric language of the psalm deserves particular mention. In this case, the lectionary readings focus attention on light (Isa. 9:2, Ps. 27:1, Matt. 4:16). With light comes the defeat of chaos and the restoration of cosmic and social order; with light comes liberation from forces of oppression. Light makes it possible to discern the footprints of God's presence in our daily living and

Pastoral Perspective

temple" (v. 4). As the psalm progresses, however, it is God's own *self* that the psalmist seeks: "Your face, LORD, do I seek. Do not hide your face from me" (vv. 8–9). A sermon on Psalm 27 could explore the different ways of knowing and experiencing God and how this experience shifts with time. There are moments when we literally hunger and thirst for God, when merely residing in God's temple is not enough; we want to be face to face with God.

In this intimate relationship, however, we are led to risky places. There is an apparent conflict between the psalmist's request for concealment and safety and the psalmist's loud "shouts of joy." Would not the safe thing be to remain quiet? The psalmist is unable to do so, because of all that God has done. In another paradox, the psalmist seeks God's shelter, even in the midst of extolling the joy of God's setting the psalmist on a high rock (v. 5)—a visible, vulnerable place to be. Clearly the life of faith does not render us invisible, anonymous faces in the crowd. Instead, we assume some personal risk in following God.

Indeed, in the midst of the confident assurances, the psalmist's confident language is hard won. The psalmist has experienced real hardship and trusts in God in spite of, or perhaps because of, those difficulties. Some psalms of praise border on the cheeriness of a pep rally—"God is in his heaven; all is right with the world." It is a message that has a place in our liturgical toolbox, but such messages can also feel false when used to paper over the difficulties of faith. Church people can tell when unabashed praise is sincere, and when the messenger is trying too hard. Psalm 27 strikes an authentic balance between God's goodness and the gritty reality of our lives.

God has been present in some tough situations for the psalmist. There are hints throughout: the "day of trouble," the awareness of enemies lurking, the need for concealment in times of difficulty. If the psalmist were to come to the pastor for counseling, these hints would merit some gentle probing. Who are the enemies? What is at the root of that need to hide in God? To the question, "Of whom shall I be afraid?" (v. 1), we might say, "Good question. What do you think?"

It is our call as pastors-who-preach to bring those questions to our conversation with the text. What might the fears of the psalmist have been? More to the point, with what fears do our congregations struggle? How do we understand God as our refuge, a place to hide? When is it healthy to hide, and when is it antithetical to the purposes of God and God's reign on earth? A sermon on Psalm 27 might address one or more of these angles.

---

1. Jack Agüeros, "Psalm: For Patience," in *Lord Is This a Psalm?* (Brooklyn, NY: Hanging Loose Press, 2002), 23.
2. Martín Espada, "Jack Agüeros," *Boston Review* 18:5 (Oct./Nov. 1993), http://bostonreview.net/BR18.5/poets2.html

my salvation," "YHWH is the stronghold of my life"). Both of these are followed by rhetorical questions that also parallel ("whom shall I fear?" "of whom shall I be afraid?"). This opening verse summarizes the premise of the entire psalm. The remainder of the psalm serves as exposition, fleshing out the attributes of God and the attitude of the psalmist.

These two statements of fact in verse 1 characterize YHWH by means of three metaphorical terms: light, salvation, and stronghold. The third term is ambiguous. It may signify a fortress or stronghold (from the root 'zz) or a place of safety or refuge (from the root 'wz). In either case, the psalmist's assertion reflects a connotation of divine protection. Along with the imagery of God as "salvation," these depictions give a sense of strong and sure redemption, even assured military victory. The first metaphor, "light" (Hebrew 'or), is the most unique descriptor and especially significant for our purposes. There exists a biblical tradition that connects God with light, either imagining God directly as light (e.g., Isa. 2:5; 10:17; 60:1; Mic. 7:8–9; Ps. 43:3) or as one who brings light (e.g., Amos 5:18–20; Pss. 97:11; 112:4). The psalm's divine light imagery connects this text with two other readings for this Sunday. In Isaiah 9:1–4, which is quoted in Matthew 4:15–16, the prophet envisions the time of redemption in terms of dark and light imagery. The tradition also connects light with seeing God's *face*, the divine face for which the psalmist pleads to dispel the darkness (repeated thrice in vv. 8–9) and for which Isaiah hopes (8:16–22, immediately preceding the lectionary passage). The psalmist's description of YHWH as "my light" taps into this rich, visual heritage.

A time of darkness, however, is suggested by the psalmist's questions in verse 1; she infers that there is something that might be frightening, were she not so confident in God. Indeed, the remainder of the psalm suggests fearful situations. The psalmist speaks particularly of personal threats, asking "who" (*mi*) rather than "what" (*mah*). Then all the difficulties imagined are in terms of persons, not events or situations or the like: evildoers (*mere'im*; v. 2), adversaries (*tsarim*; vv. 2, 12), foes ('*oyebim*; vv. 2, 6), enemies (*shorerim*; v. 11), false witnesses (v. 12), an army waging war (v. 3), and parents who abandon (v. 10). A sense of interpersonal tensions, of persons at odds with others in the community, links this text to the Epistle lesson for this Sunday (1 Cor. 1:10–18). Both it and Psalm 27 attest to how challenging it can be for faith communities to keep disagreements from escalating into hostile situations.

from neither the difficulties of life nor the capacity to worry about what may be.

Today's psalm paints a fearful scene. The details of the psalmist's difficulties remain hidden, but the author expresses good reason to worry. The landscape of the psalm is populated with "evildoers" who aim to "devour my flesh" and "an army" that threatens the psalmist's life (vv. 2, 3). We hear in the psalmist's fourfold cry for help the seriousness of his straits (vv. 7–9). In the face of persecution the psalmist offers a song of praise and a bold statement of faith. He confidently declares that God "will hide me in his shelter in the day of trouble; he will conceal me under the cover of his tent; he will set me high on a rock" (v. 5). This expression of hope casts light on the tension between fear and faith.

In the light of this psalm, faith's opponent is not doubt. The psalmist does not question the presence or goodness of God. Rather, the psalmist helps us see that fear is the foe of faith. Great are the troubles and trials that loom over the psalmist, but his faith in God equips him with strength to endure "the day of trouble" (v. 5).

As preachers we find evidence of such faith-born strength in our congregations. Days after a baptism, the mother of a newly baptized infant visits her pastor. She tells him about the worries she bore during a complicated pregnancy. She speaks of the anxiety she felt during her daughter's earliest days. Then with wet eyes, she recounts the words she heard during the rite of baptism, how nothing could separate her daughter from God. She searches for words of adequate praise to describe her newfound confidence in God's care. The mother's trust echoes the psalmist's assurance that the goodness of God is greater than the sum of life's trials.

At a recent funeral service, a ten-year-old granddaughter of the departed stood in the chancel before family and friends. She sang Robert Lowry's "My Life Flows On in Endless Song":

> My life flows on in endless song; above earth's lamentation,
> I hear the sweet, though far-off hymn that hails a new creation.
> Through all the tumult and the strife, I hear the music ringing;
> It finds an echo in my soul—how can I keep from singing?

Life is difficult, especially in the midst of heartrending loss, but the gathering of mourners was strengthened that day. The young girl's courage to sing, like

Psalm 27:1, 4-9

Theological Perspective

dispels the darkness, whether this is represented metaphorically or concretely in the psalm. The vulnerability of the supplicant in Psalm 27 underscores the power of the metaphors employed for God. God as light, salvation, and stronghold in verse 1 make profound sense in relationship to the potential for harm described in verses 2, 3, and 12. The desire to remain in the secure presence of God is not unexpected from a beleaguered supplicant, nor is the joyful response that such protection would evoke.

While some scholars point to imagery of the temple, the house of the Lord, in verse 4, it is only in verses 7–9 that the psalmist shifts from the anxious introspection of the first part of the psalm to addressing God directly in prayer. Urged on by the heart, the psalmist seeks the face of God, the one who has been of help in the past. With confidence in this relationship, the psalmist finds sustaining hope in the fidelity of the saving God, which is beyond human comparison and even exceeds parental commitments (v. 10). From this God, the petitioner expects attention, heed, and response (v. 7) amid the dangers that threaten the integrity of daily living.

At the same time, dreading the very absence of this intimacy with the Divine, the supplicant begs not to be forsaken. As Augustine has noted in his commentary on the psalm, "What can be a greater sorrow than this for the one who loves and seeks the truth of your face?"[3] Brought to an awareness of God's presence through prayer, with confidence the psalmist ends by encouraging others, "Wait for the LORD; be strong, and let your heart take courage; wait for the LORD!" (v. 14).

CARMEN NANKO-FERNÁNDEZ

Pastoral Perspective

Just as the lectionary texts always invite consideration of what comes immediately before and after the selected pericope, we might also consider verses that have been removed from it. The excised verses 2 and 3 from the Psalm 27 text mention evildoers, adversaries, and foes: an army that has encamped against the psalmist. Perhaps it is more prudent pastorally to de-emphasize these verses. Doing so casts the psalm in a more individualistic light, with fewer political or even communal implications. The psalm thus serves as assurance that, whatever the personal trials and tribulations one might face, God is good to save and to protect.

Certainly the language of us vs. them, of enemies and war, is problematic and can be taken too literally as a means of justifying any manner of aggressively self-righteous behavior. However, the savvy pastor might address this head-on in the sermon. In fact, verse 4 offers a keen corrective. When the army encamps against the psalmist's people, the psalmist prays not for victory, not for a slaughter of the enemy, but to "live in the house of the LORD . . . to behold the beauty of the LORD, and to inquire in [God's] temple." With the threat of violence and defeat looming, the psalmist asks only for God.

Too many of our members have a caricaturized version of the Old Testament as the domain of an angry, vengeful God, and Christ's arrival in the New Testament as the welcome counternarrative. Ignoring verses 2 and 3 of Psalm 27, rather than alleviating the problem, actually serve to exacerbate it: in the psalm's entirety, we see God's gentle answer turning away wrath (Prov. 15:1), God (and the psalmist) fighting violence with a plea for salvation. For the psalmist, the worst-case scenario is not defeat, but alienation from God.

MARYANN MCKIBBEN DANA

---

3. Augustine, as cited in Pope John Paul II, General Audience (April 28, 2004) #5, http://www.vatican.va/holy_father/john_paul_ii/audiences/2004/documents/hf_jp-ii_aud_20040428_en.html

Exegetical Perspective

At this point, however, the lectionary selection does the psalm a disservice. All the statements that illustrate what difficulties individuals might face in their lives of faith are in those verses omitted from the reading. We are left with only the very general, sanitized language of a "day of trouble" (v. 5) and foes (v. 6), which downplays the hard situations that persons must overcome to reach the level of trust and confidence affirmed by the psalmist.

Verse 4 is the emotional heart of Psalm 27. The psalmist expresses strong yearnings and single-minded devotion (the assertion of "one thing" is not a common biblical expression). The psalmist's unified purpose includes three elements. First, the psalmist longs for the presence of God. The language of living in YHWH's house one's whole life long is reminiscent of the sentiment of Psalm 23, another psalm of trust. Second, the psalmist desires to know the pleasantness, the loveliness (*no'am*) of God, hinting at an aesthetic and sensual engagement. The third wish is for intellectual understanding, a request that resumes when she also requests to be taught (v. 11). This rare verb (*baqar*) means to investigate or to scrutinize, suggesting that the psalmist brings an inquisitive mind to this quest. All of these activities sum up what it means actively to seek God, to seek God's essence, God's face (see also v. 8).

This verse highlights the centrality of the temple, "the house of YHWH." The psalmist's search is not an isolated one, a private endeavor, but rather occurs within the context of worship and service. A faithful individual goes into the community of worship, does not retreat from it. A useful homiletical connection might be made here with the passage from Matthew. When reading it, we so easily focus on the actions of Jesus and the called disciples. If we shift our point of view to those persons who come to the synagogues to hear him (4:23), we find individuals who must be very much like this psalmist, yearning for divine presence, for spiritual understanding, and traveling to the temple to seek it.

LINDA DAY

Homiletical Perspective

the hymn itself, reflects the message of Psalm 27. Amid life's greatest challenges and in the dimly lit face of an unknowable future, we find voice to "sing and make melody to the LORD" because God can be trusted (v. 6).

To preach Psalm 27 is to remember not only a mother's glimpse of God's abiding presence or a girl's song of faith at a funeral service. To preach this psalm is also to keep in mind the members of the congregation who strain to hear the good news of that "far-off hymn" and this psalm. In today's pews sit faithful souls who do fear the incoming waves of tumult. Anxious questions choke statements of faith. Will my cancer return? What if I lose my job, my health insurance? Will my boy return home safely from the war?

As these and other questions collide with the psalmist's confidence, the preacher has an opportunity to proclaim the trustworthiness of God on behalf of those who are burdened with the uncertainties of life. The preacher amplifies the psalmist's faith to offer a fearful congregant the assurance that God is with us—yesterday, today, and tomorrow.

Years ago a beloved, longtime church member was wracked with worry about his son. Sunday after Sunday the man returned to the sanctuary. When the congregation sang its hymns, he stood without a hymnal. He listened to the familiar tunes, but he had lost his voice for singing. The congregation's alleluias felt far off.

One Sunday he rose during the time of congregational prayer. He offered a prayer of thanksgiving for the people in those pews. He thanked his fellow churchgoers for keeping the faith when he could not, for singing hymns when he could not, for seeing the goodness of God when his eyes were too cloudy to see it. To be sure, his concern for his son continued, but he had begun to recognize again the source of his strength. His words were his own, but they echoed an ancient faith: God *is* my light and my salvation. God *is* the stronghold of my life. I will sing to the Lord.

ANDREW NAGY-BENSON

1 Corinthians 1:10-18

¹⁰Now I appeal to you, brothers and sisters, by the name of our Lord Jesus Christ, that all of you be in agreement and that there be no divisions among you, but that you be united in the same mind and the same purpose. ¹¹For it has been reported to me by Chloe's people that there are quarrels among you, my brothers and sisters. ¹²What I mean is that each of you says, "I belong to Paul," or "I belong to Apollos," or "I belong to Cephas," or "I belong to Christ." ¹³Has Christ been divided? Was Paul crucified for you? Or were you baptized in the name of Paul? ¹⁴I thank God that I baptized none of you except Crispus and Gaius, ¹⁵so that no one can say that you were baptized in my name. ¹⁶(I did baptize also the household of Stephanas; beyond that, I do not know whether I baptized anyone else.) ¹⁷For Christ did not send me to baptize but to proclaim the gospel, and not with eloquent wisdom, so that the cross of Christ might not be emptied of its power.

¹⁸For the message about the cross is foolishness to those who are perishing, but to us who are being saved it is the power of God.

Theological Perspective

The divisions within the church at Corinth—some claim they belong to Paul, some to Apollos, some to Cephas (v. 12)—reflect the human city and offer, by way of contrast, a vision of the church as a new people who live as in the city of God. By looking at these divisions Paul helps his reader to discern the common mind or purpose that animates Christian faith and life as a life lived in relationship or communion with God as revealed by Jesus Christ.

The problem of division in society is a problem of elites, of those who have power and status because they know more. Division means hierarchy based on some natural scheme of qualities or talents. People are valued for what they know and what they can do because of superior knowledge and power—whether spiritual, commercial, cultural, scientific, or technical. Such elites may boast of their status, cultivate the dependence of others, and indulge in the honor and benefits that others give to them. Self-interest becomes the rule. Division, difference, and dependence result in dissension and resentment.

Paul's call for "no divisions among you" (v. 10) shows the purpose of God's work in Christ, reconciling the world and bringing peace. This is the gospel and is nothing other then Paul's theology of the cross. "Christ did not send me to baptize but to proclaim the gospel, and not with eloquent wisdom, so

Pastoral Perspective

Paul has greeted the church in Corinth and has completed a theologically pointed thanksgiving for God's work of grace among the Corinthians. That done, he turns swiftly, and with feeling, to exhort the Corinthians concerning the disunity and quarrels among them, a disputatiousness about which he has got wind from "Chloe's people" (v. 11). Paul "appeals" to his audience and warrants his exhortation as made "by the name of our Lord Jesus Christ" (v. 10). Crucially, for what follows, this is not simply Paul's particular desire; it comes from Jesus, who is not just *the* Lord but *our* common Lord. An alternative translation, "beseech" (NRSV "appeal"), suggests both the emotion and the intensity of what is far stronger than a recommendation, and yet not a command.

Christian unity cannot be commanded; it must proceed from our "discerning the body" (1 Cor. 11:29), acknowledging that Jesus has bound us to himself. That body is recognizable to others insofar as Christians are "united in the same mind and . . . purpose" (v. 10). Doctrinal orthodoxy is not the issue here, still less a uniformity of speech and behavior. Later in his letter Paul will affirm, in spite of all the spiritual cliques in Corinth, the diversity of gifts and ministries. His concern here is more general and perhaps best expressed from the outsider's

Exegetical Perspective

After expressing gratitude for what God has done among the Corinthians in the past and his hope for God's work among them in the future (vv. 8-9), Paul abruptly confronts them in verses 10–17 with his dismay over their present situation. In the exordium (vv. 1–9), Paul introduces the major topic of the letter in a way that should make the audience receptive, giving thanks for their enrichment in speech and knowledge (v. 5) and their possession of every spiritual gift (v. 7) in anticipation of the end when they will be "blameless" in God's sight (v. 8). The gap between Paul's vision for the church's future and the reality in the present becomes evident in 1:10–17 as Paul addresses the crisis that has evoked the writing of this letter.

In creating a community among people of such varied backgrounds, Paul has attempted what scarcely anyone had tried before. A church composed of rich and poor (see 1 Cor. 11:17–34), Jew and Greek (7:17–19), and slave and free (7:21–24) lacks the normal bonds of ethnicity and family that hold a community together. With such diversity, the factions mentioned in verses 11–12 were probably inevitable. These factions do not reflect different theologies, but the kind of quarreling that was commonplace in ancient communities. The strife (*eris* v. 11; NRSV "quarrels") and jealousy (*zēlos* 3:3) over leaders that were at the center of civic conflict in antiquity have

Homiletical Perspective

The church today faces some of the same difficulties and problems that the church faced when Paul wrote his letter to the Christians in Corinth. Specifically, Paul wrote of his concern that they be "in agreement," that "there be no divisions," that he had heard that "there are quarrels among you" (vv. 10–11).

Disagreements and divisions and quarrels are frequent in the church in our time. A bishop in one denomination was severely chastised by many within his own communion because he participated in an ecumenical prayer service at Yankee Stadium a few days after the events of 9/11. Many churches have had bitter struggles over the issue of gay and lesbian people assuming leadership positions in the church. Disagreement about the authority and interpretation of Scripture drives churches apart. It is obvious that whatever the admonitions Paul made to the church at Corinth about their divisions, they have not succeeded in bringing unity to the churches of succeeding generations.

That regrettable reality does not mean that Paul's words to the Corinthians have no relevance for contemporary churches as they seek to cope with conflict and disunity. Paul's reaction to what he had heard from Chloe's people can indeed give insight to the situation in which churches today find themselves.

1 Corinthians 1:10-18

Theological Perspective

that the cross of Christ might not be emptied of its power" (v. 17). It is wrong to identify Christian faith with ritual cleansing or healing, with a particular understanding of baptism, or with the beliefs and practices of a particular person or group. The gospel is given in the cross as self-sacrifice, giving oneself up in response to and care for the other, the cross as bearing the burdens of others—not as self-denial and resignation, but in joy and thanksgiving. To claim anything else empties the cross of Christ of its power.

As Friedrich Nietzsche claimed and feminist theologians have explored, a singular emphasis on the cross and on *agapē* as self-sacrificial love has led to self-abnegation or self-hatred, a servile will, and the loss of self. Nothing, however, could be farther from the new life, marked by reconciliation and peace, that is the promise of the gospel. Instead, Paul claims a theology of the cross that is life affirming. Foreshadowing much of contemporary theology on sacrifice, nineteenth-century Anglican F. D. Maurice wrote, "As self-will and disobedience are the obstacles to the communion of men [and women] with their Creator, so are they obstacles to communion with each other." At the same time, we "cannot confound the mortification of the evil nature with the destruction or weakening of a single faculty which God has bestowed. For those faculties are impaired and ruined by the dominion of the evil nature; they are strongest when it is most subdued"[1] and, we should add, when we are joined together. This is the "foolishness to those who are perishing, but to us who are being saved it is the power of God" (v. 18).

The development of a theology of the cross is persistent in the letters of Paul. It not only shapes our response to the needs of others but equally shapes how we should listen and not rush to judgment, how we may discern what to do, and in what spirit we may make decisions and undertake actions. As Paul addresses specific conflicts, his theology of the cross is developed practically in terms of how we are formed morally, ascetically (as a matter of a way of life), and in prayer and worship (doxologically and liturgically).

What is clear in this reading from the beginning of the First Letter to the Corinthians is that Christian faith is not a matter of learning expressed in sophisticated theology. The truth of Christian faith is more that of practical wisdom that is gained by living into the cruciform life revealed in Christ. In this

Pastoral Perspective

point of view: "so speak and act that no one will doubt you are brothers and sisters in Christ."

The Corinthian church is breaking out in "divisions" and "quarrels." The character of these disputes, and the pastoral lessons to be learned, depend rather on the nature of the "parties." Paul gives us very little to go on, and speculation as to various doctrinal schemes, Judaizing or gnostic, for instance, strains the evidence.[1] The Corinthian church is a diverse, lively community, seemingly with social tensions around matters of wealth and need, perhaps also concerning education (1 Cor. 14). There are strong feelings and a corresponding assertiveness and folk are being drawn into groups, possibly to gain a stronger sense of shared identity, of special belonging. Some are gravitating toward loyalty to certain Christian leaders.

The statements "I belong to Paul," "I belong to Cephas," and "I belong to Apollos," are most likely Paul's own constructions, not Corinthian slogans. Certain members are appealing to Paul, Peter, and Apollos in defense of their own views or practices, and the appeals are belligerent enough to be divisive. Links with the specific leader through baptism have reinforced the drift to party-mindedness. Possibly some Corinthians claimed a "mystical" relationship between baptizer and baptized, analogous to mystery cults. Whatever the claim, Paul robustly denies that special relationship. Baptism is in the name of Christ alone, because only Christ was crucified for us.

What about "I belong to Christ" (v. 12)? Did some Corinthians claim a distinctive unity with Christ? Again, attempts at reconstructing a Christ sect, perhaps Gnostic, have not proved persuasive. Alternatively, did some church members react to appeals to Paul's teaching or Apollos's example by reasserting against them an authentic "way of Christ"? This is more plausible and would be no less dangerous in Paul's view, since it makes Jesus just another contender, another position in the squabble. If you understand aright Christ's relationship to the church, though, "I belong to Christ," strung at the end of the list, appears as a reductio ad absurdum of the whole business. Belonging to Christ simply excludes belonging to anyone else; put more positively, it frees the Christian from the burden and the division that goes with belonging to anyone else.

Paul is an apostle, yes, but solely and entirely through Christ's calling; the Corinthians are indeed

---

1. F. D. Maurice, *The Kingdom of Christ*, ed. Alec R. Vidler (1842; repr. London: SCM Press, 1958), 2:68–69.

1. Raymond F. Collins, *First Corinthians* (Collegeville, MN: Liturgical Press, 1999), 72.

Third Sunday after the Epiphany

now shaped community life in Corinth.[1] Indeed, the claim "I am of . . ." is not unlike the boasts among the Sophists and their pupils.[2] The reference to whose who are attached to Paul, Cephas, Apollos, and Christ signifies neither the existence of four factions nor the role of Cephas or Apollos in encouraging this partisanship, for Paul later comments positively on both of them (9:5; 16:12).

Although we cannot reconstruct the nature of the conflict with certainty, we can ascertain that the emphasis on individual freedom at the expense of the community (6:12; 9:1; 10:23) and the disregard of the rich for the poor (11:17–34) lie beneath the many issues that confront the Corinthian church. At the heart of the problems at Corinth is the fact that members are "puffed up" against each other (4:6). Paul's argument against human wisdom (1:20–23; 2:6–8; 3:18–23) and denial that he uses "persuasive words of wisdom" (2:4, my trans.) suggest that the Corinthian factions were created by those who claimed that the rhetorical power of their teachers was a demonstration of their wisdom.

This conflict is the background for the appeal in 1:10, which is the thesis statement of the letter. In the challenge to be in agreement (literally, "say the same thing"), have no divisions, be together in "one mind" and "one opinion," Paul calls on the listeners to overcome the quarreling and jealousy that have undermined the community. Having established heterogeneous communities in other cities, Paul frequently instructs his readers in other letters to "be of one mind" (Rom. 12:16; Phil. 1:27; 2:2; 4:2). Just as the divisions at Corinth are not essentially theological, Paul's challenge does not call for uniformity of opinion. The phrase "to say the same thing" (*to auto legein*) is commonly used in Greek literature in the appeals of ancient orators to live in political or social unity (Dio Chrysostom, *Or.* 34.17; Aristotle, *Or.* 24.52). For Paul, diverse people have "one mind" and "one spirit" only through a common commitment to the Christian confession (1 Cor. 8:6; 15:3).

The description of the situation at Corinth in 1:11–17 is the history of the case, in which Paul recalls the foundations of the community's existence and the recent history reported by Chloe's people. The criticism of their conduct in verses 11–12 indicates that the Corinthians have become a collection of special-interest groups. The rhetorical questions

First, it can be noted that Paul is clearly distressed by the conflicts in the church at Corinth. He appeals to them "that all of you be in agreement" (v. 10). He appeals to them "that there be no divisions among you" (v. 10). He appeals to them "that you be united" (v. 10). It can happen that we become so accustomed to a divided church that we simply accept the situation. We have always known a divided church, and we are not shocked or dismayed because that is the way things are. Paul will not let the Corinthians or us be satisfied with the church in its divided condition. There may be no quick solution to the problem, but there can be no casual acceptance of it.

Second, Paul appeals to the Corinthians as "brothers and sisters." Twice in the beginning of his appeal to them Paul refers to them in this familial way. Whatever their problems and failures, they are part of his family. Paul is obviously deeply concerned about what is happening in the Corinthian church, and in the course of this letter to them he rebukes them sharply for some of their beliefs and practices, but he does so because he cares for them in the ways that family members care for each; he cares for them as brothers and sisters.

Divisions in religious communities can often engender bitter animosities. People rightly discern that the issues separating them from others are exceptionally significant, dealing with fundamental convictions about the meaning of life and the eternal destiny of persons. Strongly held views on such issues can lead people to reject those who have different views, to break fellowship with them, even to condemn them. Paul can help us to discern that even those who differ with us are brothers and sisters, and can help us deal with those who differ with us in a spirit of care and compassion and love.

Third, Paul identifies issues that cause divisions. Paul writes that he has heard from Chloe's people about quarrels, and then he goes on: "What I mean is that each of you says, 'I belong to Paul,' or 'I belong to Apollos,' or 'I belong to Cephas,' or 'I belong to Christ.'" In the first three instances, Paul is concerned that people in the church at Corinth are separated from each other because they give their allegiance to different people who have been leaders in the community. It may be that they are simply attracted by a powerful personality and want to find their identity in the relationship with him or her. It may be that they are gripped by the particular ideas that have been espoused by Paul or Apollos or Cephas and find the only expression of truth in what they have heard from him. It may be a combination of both, which leads to a power struggle.

1. L. L. Welborn, "On the Discord at Corinth: 1 Corinthians 1–4 and Ancient Politics," *Journal of Biblical Literature* 106 (1987): 1.
2. Margaret M. Mitchell, *Paul and the Rhetoric of Reconciliation* (Louisville, KY: Westminster John Knox Press, 1990), 90.

1 Corinthians 1:10-18

Theological Perspective

sense Paul contrasts "eloquent wisdom" with "the cross of Christ" (v. 17). Christian faith is not first of all a matter of right belief, a theory about how God saves humankind, the meaning of the resurrection of the dead in terms of bodily presence and temporal consciousness, or what is the ultimate fate of the universe. Theology as quasi-science—in terms of knowledge that describes or predicts the future—is not the saving knowledge that is the truth of Christian faith. This wisdom of the cross stands against worldly wisdom (*sophia* or *gnōsis*). Through and through, Christian faith is a way of life. Its truth is grounded in the truth of Christ as a life lived, as God incarnate.

Theologically, for the preacher the Epistle readings from 1 Corinthians offer the opportunity to focus on the nature of Christian faith as a way of life grounded in a theology of the cross. This leads to a theology of the church as a new covenant, a new people, a new society. More specifically still, Paul offers an exploration of conflict and division that through the cross we may discern how to listen and respond. Always these readings pose the question of baptism as initiation and formation into a way of life that stands in judgment of our daily lives in society and as the promise and invitation to new life. In our post-Christian age, this offers particular opportunities for proclamation and evangelism. Only as we see a way of life, only as the story of Christ is told as an invitation to new life, only as Christian faith is spiritual wisdom and not pseudoscience, will the power of the gospel be heard.

TIMOTHY F. SEDGWICK

Pastoral Perspective

sanctified, but solely and entirely by Christ. Paul, Peter, Apollos, the Corinthians all owe what they are, as well as what differentiates them as apostles, teachers, community members, to Christ. As Paul concludes, "all things are yours" (3:21), including Paul, Cephas, and Apollos, and much else, "but you are Christ's." To divide this belonging by pitching loyalties against each other is to contradict theological reality.

The situation Paul describes is not remote. The church is easily divided by "causes." "Social justice" is pitted against "biblical faithfulness," progressivisms against traditionalisms, and a stand on one issue divides the true hearted from the reprobate. Furthermore, any loyalty may be foisted onto Jesus as his special concern, thus bringing Christ down into the melee as one cause among others. This, however, can only ever tear the body. Jesus is not a cause, he is Lord and life-giver for all; our enterprises, even the godly and proper ones, cannot reflect but a fraction of the glorious good he has done and will do for his creation. Our theological and ethical disputes, our controversies over Christian practice, are hopelessly comprised as soon as we fail to recognize those with whom we contend as also "in Christ." All our initiatives, parties, groupings, causes are, as it were, "inside the brackets," Christ alone is outside, as "Lord of all."

Would it be better if Christians simply eschewed causes about which they felt strongly? Such a bloodless church would not reflect Christ any better than a contentious one. Paul, though, gives us a clue as to the manner of pursuing our passionate convictions. We are to hold and offer them, as those who possess their riches as if they had them not (7:29–31).

Having fretted over his accuracy as to the baptismal record, Paul reminds the Corinthians that his vocation is proclamation, not baptism. This serves as a bridge to the following treatment of the "foolishness of the cross." He contrasts a polished, practiced, and refined rhetoric with preaching the cross. Paul is no mean rhetorician, of course. Even his critique of rhetoric has great rhetorical force. What he does, though, is provide a basic criterion for Christian preaching: do not obscure the cross. Words that strike because of their cleverness, sermons crafted first as entertainment, will hide the cross. A screen of distracting attractions will cover its fierce judgment and its urgent summons to life and love.

ALAN GREGORY

Exegetical Perspective

in verse 13, all assuming a negative answer, indicate the absurdity of dividing into factions. "Is Christ divided?" anticipates the later argument that members are nothing more than the feet and hands in the one body of Christ composed of people from every background (12:12–13). "Was Paul crucified for you?" suggests the distortion of the confession "Christ died for our sins" (1 Cor. 15:3). Similarly, "Were you baptized into the name of Paul?" suggests that the Corinthians have substituted human leaders for Christ. What the Corinthians have missed, therefore, is an understanding of Jesus Christ, the foundation of their faith.

The reference to baptism in verse 13 provides the transition to Paul's memory of his role in the founding of the church in verses 14–17. Paul's own demeanor was the model of the values that became the basis for shaping a unified community (cf. Phil. 1:12–26; 3:2–21) and an alternative to the perspective of the Corinthian partisans in two respects. In the first place, the Corinthian factions are probably rooted in the members' claim of special status based on their identification with the one who baptized them. Paul is reticent to recall whom he baptized and insists that he baptized only the households of Crispus, Gaius, and Stephanas. In his claim that Christ did not send him to baptize but to preach, Paul is not denigrating baptism (see 1 Cor. 12:13), but indicating that he did not encourage the acrimony at Corinth by creating special bonds through baptism.

In the second place, in not preaching with "eloquent wisdom" (v. 17), Paul refused to participate in the Corinthians' competition over teachers with rhetorical ability, for the emphasis on human wisdom and rhetoric would "empty the cross of its power." While the extension of the passage in the lectionary to include 1:18 is rarely found in the commentaries, the lectionary appropriately reflects Paul's focus on the cross in verses 17–18. Paul conducted himself (v. 17) according to the basic conviction that "the message about the cross is foolishness to those who are perishing" but the "power of God" to those "who are being saved." The church will have one voice and one mind when it recognizes, as Paul did, that the cross, the world's symbol of foolishness, is God's power.

JAMES W. THOMPSON

Homiletical Perspective

Such division can still be found in the church, of course. Dynamic preachers may develop a cult following of people who are more moved by the power of rhetoric than by the claims of the gospel. People may give allegiance to the statement of the Christian faith articulated by a past or present theologian, and separate themselves from those who find truth in different articulations.

Paul is referring to those who give their allegiance to human leaders when he is talking about belonging to Paul or Cephas or Apollos, but what does he mean when he writes about those who say, "I belong to Christ"? Paul does not go on to explain what he means, but we do have examples of how claiming to belong to Christ can be divisive. People can articulate particular theological interpretations of who Jesus was and what Jesus did, and then claim that only those interpretations are right and any other interpretations are so deficient that they cannot be accepted.

Fourth, Paul seeks ways in which the divisions and the quarrels can be dealt with meaningfully and constructively. He reminds the people that the saving grace of God does not come through any human leader, but only through the gospel that manifests the saving love of God. Paul is clear that he did not bring the saving power of God: "Was Paul crucified for you?" (v. 13). Paul is clear that the expression of God's saving love is not in human wisdom, but in the cross of Christ, the awesome manifestation of the way and the power of God.

We can seek to deal with the tragedy of our divisions as we focus not on the power struggles or on the wisdom that we have accumulated, but on the sacrificial love of Jesus Christ, most fully expressed in his suffering death on the cross, which "to us who are being saved. . . . is the power of God" (v. 18).

HARRY B. ADAMS

Matthew 4:12-23

¹²Now when Jesus heard that John had been arrested, he withdrew to Galilee. ¹³He left Nazareth and made his home in Capernaum by the sea, in the territory of Zebulun and Naphtali, ¹⁴so that what had been spoken through the prophet Isaiah might be fulfilled:

¹⁵"Land of Zebulun, land of Naphtali,
　　on the road by the sea, across the Jordan, Galilee of the Gentiles—
¹⁶the people who sat in darkness
　　have seen a great light,
　and for those who sat in the region and shadow of death
　　light has dawned."

Theological Perspective

This Third Sunday after Epiphany is also the Third Sunday of Ordinary Time—that time during the year when the life of the church is neither aiming at nor celebrating the events of Christmas and Easter. Protestants tend to treat these Sundays after Epiphany as a "season" of Epiphany. Catholics think more about these weeks as the beginning of Ordinary Time. Thanks to this "common" lectionary, however, the readings should lead the divided church to think about the same things—and in fact it is helpful to think about Epiphany and Ordinary Time together.

Although the term "ordinary" is related to "ordinal" and meant to convey numbers and counting (thus the "Third" Sunday of Ordinary Time), our everyday sense of "ordinary" is in fact a helpful entry into thinking about Ordinary Time—and about this particular Sunday after Epiphany.

Ordinary time is "ordinary" in part because of what it *is not*: it is not Advent or Christmas or Lent or Easter. It is not, therefore, the time during which the church is engaged in preparations for, or celebrations of, the birth, death, and resurrection of Jesus. Ordinary Time is also ordinary because of what it *is*: it is the liturgical season that makes up most of our time—thirty-three or thirty-four weeks of every year, depending on the dates of Epiphany and Easter. It is the time during which we are called, like Peter

Pastoral Perspective

When I was growing up, there were several rules in our home. One rule was there was no television while eating dinner. This rule was broken every Sunday evening, however, because Dad wanted to watch Mutual of Omaha's "Wild Kingdom." Sponsored by the Mutual of Omaha insurance company, "Wild Kingdom" was a nature program, a precursor to today's Animal Planet channel. For my Presbyterian pastor father, each episode was a theological journey demonstrating to us all yet once again the wonders of God's creativity and imagination in the natural world. From the savannas of Kenya to the barrier reef in Australia to the jungles of Borneo, we ate dinner together and watched with fascination as the host introduced new creatures and opened the world to us.

One episode I remember fondly was about the elephant seals of Argentina. The show focused on a mother and her seal pup, who had just been born. Soon after birthing her baby, the mother, now famished, abandoned the pup on the shore so she could go feed in the rich waters off the coast. After feeding, she returned to a different part of the beach and began to call for her baby. Other mothers had done the same, and all had returned at a similar time; I remember thinking they would never find one another. The camera then followed the mother as

¹⁷From that time Jesus began to proclaim, "Repent, for the kingdom of heaven has come near."

¹⁸As he walked by the Sea of Galilee, he saw two brothers, Simon, who is called Peter, and Andrew his brother, casting a net into the sea—for they were fishermen. ¹⁹And he said to them, "Follow me, and I will make you fish for people." ²⁰Immediately they left their nets and followed him. ²¹As he went from there, he saw two other brothers, James son of Zebedee and his brother John, in the boat with their father Zebedee, mending their nets, and he called them. ²²Immediately they left the boat and their father, and followed him.

²³Jesus went throughout Galilee, teaching in their synagogues and proclaiming the good news of the kingdom and curing every disease and every sickness among the people.

Exegetical Perspective

The focal passages for the previous two weeks have been concerned with the interplay between John the Baptist and Jesus. Two weeks ago we saw John's baptism of Jesus in Matthew. Last week, John's Gospel provided John the Baptist's testimony concerning the baptism, as well as his version of the call of the disciples. The text for this week (Matt. 4:12–23) moves one step forward in this progression. After the inaugural events of Jesus' baptism (3:1–17) and temptations (4:1–11), Matthew records the launch of Jesus' public ministry. He relates several key aspects of the circumstances surrounding these beginnings, some of which are unique to his Gospel.

At the head of the passage, the reader sees that the onset of Jesus' proclamation comes directly on the heels of the interruption of John's public activity. In verse 12, Matthew indicates that John has been arrested. The reason for his arrest is not provided, but it is safe to assume that it is in connection with his proclamation and baptizing activity. The Greek term translated in the NRSV as "arrest" (4:12) is *paradidōmi*, which is commonly rendered elsewhere as "handed over" or "delivered up." In fact, Matthew consistently uses the term in Jesus' passion to denote not just his literal arrest but also his intentional advancement toward the cross (see 17:22; 20:18; 26:2). Matthew also uses the term in its participial

Homiletical Perspective

In Christian life, we are always beginning something, and such beginnings may be comforting, because they come with regularity and bring a sense of familiarity. However, outside the familiar rhythms of the liturgical calendar, beginnings often come bearing both hope and challenge. This week's Gospel offers homiletical opportunities to speak from incidents at the beginning of Jesus' ministry into new situations that may be arising in the lives of your congregation, many of them revolving around Jesus' call and our response to it.

After the arrest of John, Jesus begins to proclaim that *the kingdom of heaven* is drawing near, a message of good news. Many Christians have difficulty understanding the "kingdom of heaven" references in Matthew, and their misunderstandings may shape the way they respond to the call embodied within this lection. Jesus' references here and throughout Matthew, as Anglican bishop and Bible scholar N. T. Wright notes, are not teachings about how to go to heaven. They are not about "our escape from this world into another one, but to God's sovereign rule coming 'on earth as it is in heaven.'"[1] Your congregation may need to be reminded that the call of

1. N. T. Wright, *Surprised by Hope: Rethinking Heaven, the Resurrection, and the Mission of the Church* (New York: HarperOne, 2008), 18.

Matthew 4:12-23

Theological Perspective

and Andrew in this passage from Matthew, to follow Jesus, not because of the star that announced his birth, nor, yet, because of the excitement conjured by the promise of a trip to Jerusalem, but simply because he has said, "Follow me."

It is not a liturgical accident that today, "after" Epiphany (and Christmas) and before Lent and Easter, Jesus tells us to follow him, and that for the next six weeks we will be listening to him preach from the Mount. There is a sense in which we are being reminded in these weeks between Christmas and Easter that, for all their wonders, neither of these great celebrations is sufficient to sustain us in the hard work of following Jesus during the daily ordinariness of our lives.

What, then, does sustain us? A brief look at a liturgical calendar offers a hint. The liturgical year begins with Advent, which—when the calendar is depicted in circular fashion, with each season appearing as a slice of pie colored according to the liturgical season—appears at the top of the circle. The four weeks of Advent appear in purple and, as we move clockwise around the circle, are followed by a narrow slice of white for Christmas. Then these weeks of Epiphany appear as a significant slice of green, followed by a large section of Lenten purple, and an even larger section of the white of Easter. White turns briefly to red for Pentecost, just past the bottom of the circle, and then, as the calendar sweeps back up to the top of the circle, everything turns back to the green of Ordinary Time for the half year it takes to reach Advent once again.

When we take in this color-coded depiction of the liturgical year in a single glance, one thing stands out: these weeks of Epiphany, colored green because of their role as the first weeks of Ordinary Time, are cut off and stranded from the rest of Ordinary Time by large swaths of purple and white. Given the way in which this slice of green appears to interrupt the otherwise continuous run of purple and white from Advent through Easter, it is not surprising that Protestants extend the celebration of Epiphany into a season that connects Advent and Easter by bridging Christmas and Lent. This treatment of Epiphany embodies a theological instinct.

Theologically speaking, during these weeks "after" Epiphany, which also serve to jump-start Ordinary Time, we are called to deepen our reflection about the meaning of what we began to anticipate with Advent and then celebrated at Christmas: the incarnation of our Lord—God's becoming a human being. With its emphasis on the birth of the infant

Pastoral Perspective

she called to her pup and listened for the response. Following each other's voices and scents, soon the mother and pup were reunited. The host explained that, from the moment of birth, the sound and scent of the pup are imprinted in the mother's memory, and the sound and scent of the mother are imprinted in the pup's memory. This fascinated me especially when Dad turned to me and said, "You know, that's how it is with God. We are imprinted with a memory of God, and God is imprinted with a memory of us, and even if it takes a lifetime, we will find each other."

The text from Matthew's Gospel describes the beginning of Jesus' public ministry. Matthew describes Jesus walking by the Sea of Galilee and calling the first four of his disciples. All fishermen, he called them to follow him. Matthew says they immediately left what they were doing and followed Jesus. As readers, we are struck by this idea that immediately they left what they were doing. It is as if they were compelled to follow Jesus and to obey him, almost as if they had been waiting all their lives to hear this voice, to be issued this call, so that when it came, they dropped what they were doing.

Augustine opens the first book of his *Confessions* with the prayer and statement that "our hearts are restless until they rest in thee." Indeed, it would seem that even these four who were already in a worthy vocation had restless hearts—so restless that when they heard Jesus' call to them, they could do nothing else but leave everything behind and follow. Perhaps they were simply responding to what had already been imprinted on their souls from birth—the knowledge of the voice of God—so that when they heard the voice, all they could do was obey.

I wish the task of discernment was that easy. In one sense, it may be; but in another sense, it is so complicated. It is complicated because it seems that the voices—many of whom are claiming to be God's voice—are so numerous these days. This is why the last verse in today's reading is so important. The reading for the day does not end with disciples following Jesus. The reading ends by reminding us what Jesus sets about doing, as these four and others become his disciples. Jesus goes throughout Galilee, "teaching in synagogues and proclaiming the good news of the kingdom and curing every disease and every sickness among the people" (v. 23). To discern whether the voice we are hearing is truly the voice of God, we have to examine the person behind the voice, to see if the person is consistent with the God who is revealed to us in Scripture.

form as a description of Judas, as the one handing Jesus over (see 26:25, 46, 48; 27:3). In the end, Matthew clearly conveys that Jesus' ministry is going to advance independently from John's ministry. No continued contact between the two is recorded after Jesus' baptism, and, with John's arrest, any contact after this point is highly unlikely. John's arrest (or "handing over") soberly foreshadows to what end Jesus' earthly ministry will come. Thanks be to God, though, that Jesus still launches into the kingdom message and ministry to which God called him.

After John's arrest, Matthew uniquely records that Jesus moves residence from Nazareth to Capernaum, which is on the northwest coast of the Sea of Galilee. Matthew continues a consistent emphasis in the early chapters of his Gospel by noting that this move by Jesus fulfills prophecy (see Isa. 9:1–2 in Matt. 4:15–16). "The people who sat in darkness" (v. 16)— in the Isaiah passage—seems to refer to those who have been exiled by the Assyrians. They are the ones to whom God will bring the "light." Now, with Jesus' move, it is those in Capernaum, those in the surrounding areas, and, as the Gospel later spreads, even those in the whole world who are now going to receive the light, in the person of Jesus.

Matthew signals the beginning of what God is doing in and through Jesus (in v. 17) by declaring his kingdom message—"Repent, for the kingdom of heaven has come near"—which coincides with but also extends John's proclamation. In short, this is what Jesus has come for: to announce and usher in God's kingdom. Though it is not untrue to say that Jesus came to earth to die, it is more true to the Gospels to say that he came first to live. He came to announce, invite sinners into, proclaim the demands of, and in the end bring in God's kingdom. For this, he ultimately was killed. Though some of the very early Christian creeds jump directly from Jesus' birth to his death, the reason for which he lived must not be minimized. In fact, it can be rightly said that Jesus' death takes on its true significance only in connection with that which he lived for and proclaimed—God's kingdom.

Following Matthew's recounting of the "launch" of Jesus' public ministry, we see his account of the calling of disciples (vv. 18–22). The calling of the disciples is an episode that varies a good bit in each evangelist's description. Though they are not contradictory, the accounts vary in what led up to it, which disciples are mentioned, what order those disciples are called, and what they were doing when summoned. John provides the fullest account (1:35–51),

Jesus in this lection is not to future salvation, but to contemporary action, to fish for human beings.

This Third Sunday after Epiphany thus offers another opportunity to preach on *evangelism*. In last week's lesson from the Gospel of John, Jesus encouraged those who had questions to "come and see." In this lesson, he calls disciples directly, encouraging the fishermen to "follow me." How will your congregation understand the metaphor of fishing for human beings? Are there more contemporary or more creative comparisons that might help explain evangelism? Narratives with relevance to your congregation can help show how people have been called from their everyday lives into service and community.

In some parts of the country, stories from the civil rights era may be appropriate. Taylor Branch's magisterial three-volume social history of the period (*Parting the Waters, Pillar of Fire, At Canaan's Edge*) contains many stories of call and involvement that could be meaningful to your congregation. African American sharecroppers, college students, Northern priests and pastors—all felt themselves called to leave behind the lives they had known and devote themselves to the civil rights struggle. Local stories of community involvement might also create powerful ways your congregation could hear this story of disciples dropping what they had thought was important and joining something larger than themselves.

Joseph Campbell, who did groundbreaking work into the archetypal stories found in cultures around the world, spoke of *the beginning of something* as a Call to Adventure. In this opening moment in the ministry of Jesus, when he has begun to call others to join him, we can see the moment when things begin to change: "From that time Jesus began to proclaim, 'Repent, for the kingdom of heaven has come near'" (v. 17). Campbell said that such moments signify "that destiny has summoned the hero and transferred his spiritual center of gravity to a zone unknown."[2] All of us face such a moment in our lives (or many such moments) that challenges our center of gravity, that wants to shift it from a story of self to one that will mean something in a larger context.

What things in your community are struggling to be born? Is your community beginning a major program or project? Have spiritual seeds been planted in your community just waiting to sprout? Are there particular calls that individuals or the larger community might need to hear? As you shape your sermon,

2. Joseph Campbell, *The Hero with a Thousand Faces* (1949; reprint, Princeton, NJ: Princeton University Press, 1968), 58.

Matthew 4:12-23

Theological Perspective

Jesus, Christmas can sometimes obscure the true wonder of the incarnation, which is in fact not about Jesus but about God. More accurately, it is not about Jesus as a human being, but about Jesus as God manifest as a human being.

In its original festival of Epiphany, the Eastern church better embodied the theological stakes by celebrating the birth of Jesus, the baptism of Jesus, and certain of Jesus' miracles on a single feast day—thus accenting the theological fact that Jesus is God, and that this is what we celebrate as we aim now for Lent and Easter. When Protestants turn Epiphany into a liturgical season, they have recaptured the early insights of the Eastern church: we need to celebrate Epiphany to remind us that Jesus is God incarnate.

What are we to make of the no less important theological fact that these same weeks are the beginning of Ordinary Time? The Dominican theologian Herbert McCabe has wise counsel in this regard. Speaking of the meaning of the incarnation, McCabe notes that

> we do not simply examine Jesus historically to see what he was like; we *listen* to him, he established communication and friendship with us, and it is in this rapport with Jesus that we explore a different dimension of his existence. . . . It is in the contact with the person who is Jesus, in this personal communication between who he is and who [we are], that his divinity is revealed in his humanity.[1]

In this slice of Ordinary Time that is also an extended celebration of Epiphany, we are called, like Peter and Andrew, to follow Jesus and, in following him, to listen to him as he commands repentance and proclaims the good news of the kingdom. No bright stars. No earthquakes. Just a voice that strikes our ear amid the ordinariness of our lives and announces that God is among us.

DAVID TOOLE

Pastoral Perspective

Last year, as a speaker at a youth conference in California, I met a young man who was deeply distraught. I had preached that night on discerning God's call. One of the adult leaders from this young man's group brought him to me and asked if I would talk with him. I asked the adult leader to stay with us and asked the young man for his permission. He said that would be fine. The young man said that for some time he had been hearing God's call to him to end his life—that the world would be better off if he were dead. As he broke down sobbing, I held on to that young man and prayed with and for him. After several minutes, I whispered to him that while I believed he was hearing a voice that was telling him to end his life, it was not God's voice. The young man asked if I was sure. I told him I was certain.

Then he asked me how I knew for sure and I told him that in Psalm 139 he is described as fearfully and wonderfully made and that Jesus himself said in John 10:10 that he came that he might have life abundant. "God made you in God's own image," I told this young man. "God said you were wonderfully and fearfully made. God sent God's Son Jesus so that you might have life." I assured the young man that I believed he was hearing voices, but I told him again that the voices were not from God, because it did not fit God's nature to call him to take his own life.

It is our responsibility, in the midst of the many voices calling us, to know the person of God so well that we are able to discern what voices are consistent with the God who created us in God's own image, redeemed us through God's only Son, and sustains us by God's Spirit in and through the body of Christ.

RODGER Y. NISHIOKA

---

1. Herbert McCabe, "The Incarnation," in *God Matters* (London and New York: Continuum Press, 1987), 71.

Exegetical Perspective

recording that some disciples transferred allegiance from John the Baptist to Jesus, and he orders the response of the disciples as follows: Andrew and one other unnamed disciple, Simon, Philip, and Nathanael. Luke records a miraculous catch of fish as part of the call of disciples (5:1–11) and identifies the presence of Simon, James, and John. Mark, in a briefer account, simply notes Jesus passing along the Sea of Galilee prior to the calling and likewise notes Simon, James, and John (1:16–20).

Matthew's account, like Mark's, yields no preparatory details before the calling of Simon, Andrew, James, and John. This lack of detail, though, is not without its own significance. As commentator Douglas Hare notes, "the call story is here reduced to its barest essentials: Jesus summons with irresistible authority, and the men respond with radical obedience."[1] Matthew's portrayal of the obedience of these would-be followers is radical for at least three reasons. First, they "immediately" (vv. 20, 22) follow him, seemingly with no qualifications or questions asked. Second, they leave their profession, a likely lucrative business of fishing, to walk after Jesus. There are no suggestions as to how they will be provided for, and there is no promise of "upward mobility." Finally, though not explicitly stated, their response is radical due to the fact that they also will leave their families. This call, put rather baldly by Matthew, is given unapologetically as being what Jesus demands.

Jesus' call to radical obedience has not changed over these many years; the demands have not been reduced. Jesus waits not for persons to apply to him in hopes of learning under him, as many young Jewish males would have done for their rabbinic education. Instead, rabbi Jesus is the one who seeks out followers, learners, apprentices who do not have to qualify for such a relationship, save the willingness to lay down everything else. What a call! What a mission! What a Savior!

TROY A. MILLER

Homiletical Perspective

be alert to new things coming to light for your congregation. Also think practically: How might people recognize their own calls to adventure and respond to them faithfully?

Many stories begin with a Call to Adventure, so it should be easy to locate contemporary narratives in film or fiction (or a story from your own life) to use as an example. Here are two possibilities: in the movie *The Matrix*, Neo (Keanu Reeves) is sought out by Morpheus (Laurence Fishburne), a man who joins others in telling Neo that he is called to change the world; in the novel and film versions of *The Fellowship of the Ring*, Frodo Baggins is urged by the wizard Gandalf to leave behind his comfortable existence and set out on a quest. In both cases, the characters are confronted with a call that will change their lives completely.

As mentioned above, how we *respond* to the call is also a topic worthy of examination. Simon Peter and Andrew—and later, James and John—are said to have responded to this call straightaway. The Greek *eutheōs* indicates a direct response. These fishermen did not pause to think; they did not consult their families or their bank balances.

Jesus called, and they responded.

To what does Jesus call us? Too often perhaps, we answer that question in terms that do not require enough of us. Some Christians would say we are called to belief; others would say, to church membership; others would say, to service. Others would say it is all these things and more. Dietrich Bonhoeffer said that the call to "follow me" was a call "to absolute discipleship," and that only in surrendering ourselves to Jesus' command could we, paradoxically, know our greatest joy.[3] Do not be afraid to use Jesus' radical call—and the radical response of the first disciples—to call your own congregation to give all that they have for something worth infinitely more.

GREG GARRETT

---

1. Douglas R. A. Hare, *Matthew*, Interpretation series (Louisville, KY: Westminster John Knox Press, 1993), 30.

3. Dietrich Bonhoeffer, *The Cost of Discipleship* (1959; reprint, New York: Touchstone, 1995), 37–38.

Micah 6:1-8

¹Hear what the LORD says:
  Rise, plead your case before the mountains,
  and let the hills hear your voice.
²Hear, you mountains, the controversy of the LORD,
  and you enduring foundations of the earth;
  for the LORD has a controversy with his people,
  and he will contend with Israel.

³"O my people, what have I done to you?
  In what have I wearied you? Answer me!
⁴For I brought you up from the land of Egypt,
  and redeemed you from the house of slavery;
  and I sent before you Moses,
  Aaron, and Miriam.
⁵O my people, remember now what King Balak of Moab devised,
  what Balaam son of Beor answered him,

Theological Perspective

One timeless question that many people have pondered and asked time and again is "What is God's will?" In the eighth century BCE, the prophet Micah asked a similar question, and the response given remains at the heart of right relationship with God, with humankind, and with all other communities of life on the planet. In eight verses, the poet describes the experience of a long-suffering God who remains faithful to an unfaithful people for whom the prophet makes intercession. The passage consists of a series of speeches that implore rather than accuse, despite initial sentiments of justified divine frustration directed toward a people chosen by God (Deut. 7:7)—a people entrusted with Torah who now are guilty of transgression (see Mic. 1–3).

The setting for Micah 6:1–8 is a courtroom. In verses 1–2 the poet makes clear that God has a "controversy" with the people and intends to "contend" with them. One would expect an expression of righteous anger on the part of God as the case unfolds, but instead, words of heartfelt bewilderment and plea are proclaimed (vv. 3–5).

The relationship between Israel and God is an intimate one, communicated by the double vocative "O my people" (vv. 3, 5). In verses 3–5 the poet depicts God as a conciliatory deity who raises two poignant questions, as if God were at fault. The

Pastoral Perspective

If Judeo-Christian ethics had to be summarized on a bumper sticker, Micah 6:8 would fit the bill: "What does the LORD require of you but to do justice, and to love kindness, and to walk humbly with your God?" There may be no better summary of the neighborly ethic voiced by the prophets, codified in the commandments, and incarnated in Jesus of Nazareth. At a time when attention spans are shrinking, the church may well benefit from catchy, "purpose-driven" creeds that articulate the fullness of the faith in the length of time it takes for a cell phone to ring. However, there is a holy danger in voicing "justice, kindness, and obedience" too far afield from the socioeconomic realities that give this text meaning. In fact, Micah himself warns of this danger and the judgment that follows the community that becomes skilled at "talking the talk" but not "walking the walk."

The "talk" that Micah critiques in this eighth-century BCE is the exclusive attention paid to the cultic practices of religious faith, without the ethical obedience that faith in YHWH requires. "With what shall I come before the LORD, and bow myself before God on high?" (v. 6) The question is posed in the cultic arena that Micah deprecates. An escalating list of potential offerings is offered (vv. 6–7). Burnt offerings? Calves a year old? Thousands of rams? Ten thousands of rivers of oil? My firstborn? Micah's answer, of

and what happened from Shittim to Gilgal,
  that you may know the saving acts of the Lord."

⁶"With what shall I come before the Lord,
  and bow myself before God on high?
Shall I come before him with burnt offerings,
  with calves a year old?
⁷Will the Lord be pleased with thousands of rams,
  with ten thousands of rivers of oil?
Shall I give my firstborn for my transgression,
  the fruit of my body for the sin of my soul?"
⁸He has told you, O mortal, what is good;
  and what does the Lord require of you
  but to do justice, and to love kindness,
  and to walk humbly with your God?

Exegetical Perspective

The Lord's Case against Israel. This passage is a
covenant lawsuit (*rib*). The usual outline of this
prophetic genre includes (a) a summons; (b) a call
to witnesses or judges; (c) a list of benefits that the
plaintiff has conferred upon the defendant; and
(d) complaints against the defendant. Typically, a
lawsuit should culminate in a judgment and sentence, but this one concludes instead with the lyrical
passage that my beloved old Sunday school teacher
referred to without qualification as "the Golden Text
of the Old Testament."

The punctuation in the NRSV delineates the
minidrama that takes place in this covenant lawsuit.
The first and last to speak, in verses 1–2 and 8, is the
prophet, functioning as narrator. The injured plaintiff is YHWH, who speaks in verses 3–5. Israel, the
defendant, speaks in verses 6–7; and the judges—the
mountains, hills, and foundations of the earth—are
acknowledged in verses 1–2 as entities present at the
proceedings.

The Proceedings. Speaking for YHWH, the prophet
introduces the case in verses 1–2 by demanding that
the people defend their sinful behavior. He then
enjoins the mountains and hills to listen to the case.
In verses 3–5, YHWH recalls "the saving acts of the
Lord" (v. 5). The people of Israel have no gripe

Homiletical Perspective

Many who attend our churches grew up in a different world. The message from the Jewish prophet
Micah is an opportunity for preachers and parishioners to consider how Christians should respond to
the religious pluralism we now experience.

One morning in my eighth-grade social studies
class, the teacher said, "The world is about one-third
Christian, 20 percent Muslim, and 13 percent
Hindu." We thought it was the goofiest thing we had
ever heard. In my small town in Mississippi there
were four religions: Baptist, Methodist, Presbyterian,
and heathen—and in that order. Almost everyone we
knew went to church. The small number who were
not Christians kept it to themselves. The idea that
two-thirds of the people in the world are not Christians was hard for some of us to believe.

The statistics are not as hard to imagine as they
once were. The United States is increasingly home to
Muslim mosques, Hindu temples, Sikh communities,
and Buddhist retreat centers. Protestant Christians
are a minority in the United States.

Believing that Christians are in and everyone else
is out may be comforting for some, but it does not
make sense. The idea that God's grace is only for a
relative few insults God. Most American Christians
recognize that if we had been born in Indonesia, we
would probably be Muslims.

Micah 6:1-8

Theological Perspective

command, "Answer me," is a candid expression of divine frustration, followed by a picture of God's graciousness conveyed through the brief recounting of the exodus event (v. 4), and a plea for the people to remember the Balak-Balaam encounter (v. 5), which resulted in Balaam providing Israel with a great blessing on the eve before the people entered into the promised land (see Num. 22–24). The people seem to have forgotten their "story" and, in doing so, have forgotten their saving God. Thus the people have fallen out of "right" relationship with their God and consequently with one another because of a lack of mindfulness. They no longer seem to be centered on or in their God. Throughout Israel's history, God has always remembered the people and the covenant made with them (Gen. 8:1; 30:22; Exod. 2:24; 6:5), and the people have been exhorted time and again to remember their God and all God's wondrous ways and deeds (Deut. 8:18–20). Now God calls on the people to "remember" once again. This remembering will be their starting point back to "right relationship."

Verses 6–7 are a response to God's questions, plea, and demand for an answer. Here the poet features the prophet Micah in a humbled, self-reflective, penitential state, representing his people, who have yet to come before the Lord. Micah raises three soul-searching questions aimed at atonement. Each question reflects a willingness to offer some sort of sacrifice, culminating in the offer to sacrifice one's firstborn for the sake of one's sin.

The list of sacrifices reflects Israel's ancient theological tradition. Whole burnt offerings were the typical daily offering at the temple. These offerings maintained the relationship between the Israelites and God. The suggestion of sacrificing one's own firstborn, though, raises two theological questions: (1) was child sacrifice part of Israel's religious tradition, and (2) did Israel's God want child sacrifice as a sign of oblation?

Human sacrifice was forbidden in ancient Israel and Judah (see, e.g., Lev. 18:21; 20:2–5; Deut. 12:31; 18:10). In times of crisis, however, this type of sacrifice seems, on occasion, to have occurred, especially prior to the seventh century BCE. Human sacrifice did take place in the Canaanite religion, stemming from the god Molech and a human king who had a particular interest in this sort of sacrifice. Elsewhere in the OT, God expresses divine outrage at the practice of sacrificing the firstborn because they were "God's" children (Deut. 32:16–19; Ezek. 16:21). Hence, the reference to the sacrifice of the firstborn is more hyperbolic and metaphorical than actual.

Pastoral Perspective

course, is that none of these symbols of sacrifice pleases God when they are stripped from the context that gives them meaning. God desires more than empty words. God desires justice that is measured by how well the most vulnerable fare in the community, a loyal love (*hesed*) that is commensurate with the kind of loyal love that God has shown toward Israel, and a careful walking (*halaka*) in one's ethical life.

Micah's judgment is that the high religious claims of the urban elites of Jerusalem are not commensurate with the ethical obedience that YHWH requires. So offerings are made and cultic practices are followed, while "aggressive land practices" and "exploitative policies that generate wealth at the expense of the vulnerable" continue.[1] The fact that the faithful continue to "talk the talk" in worship while failing to "walk the walk" outside of it serves only to ignite YHWH's rage.

Examples abound in the church. Recently this text was voiced at the funeral of Senator Jesse Helms, a public official who ran racially charged campaigns, voted against civil rights, and rarely voiced poverty as a legitimate political concern. The funeral homily focused on the way Helms stood up for what he believed, even when it was unpopular. In another instance, an Internet video attempted to explicate the meaning of Micah 6:8 in a tribute to a fallen soldier. The video featured pictures of a young man in his military uniform and the expectations of church family in welcoming him home, expectations that turn to grief at the news of his death in Iraq. The reference to Micah arrives at the conclusion when the video brusquely asserts that the soldier "did justice, loved kindness, and walked humbly with God."

Of course, this young soldier may well have exhibited the kind of life that the prophet bespeaks. It may also be possible that Senator Helms's public service was more faithful to the prophetic vision than many have judged. In both cases, however, greater attention to the text is necessary to understand what Micah means by doing justice, loving kindness, and walking humbly with God. In the case of the funeral, justice, kindness, and obedience are defined in a way that is alien to the text—"he stood up for what he believed"—with no reference to the kind of obedience that God requires. In the case of the video, the creed is simply asserted as fact without concrete examples of obedience that are needed to give meaning to the creed—the very situation that Micah critiques!

---

1. Walter Brueggemann, *An Introduction to the Old Testament* (Louisville, KY: Westminster John Knox Press, 2003), 234.

coming against an unjust or uncaring God. This resume of the history of salvation opens in verses 3–4 with the exodus from Egypt, when the Lord "redeemed" the Hebrew slaves and provided them leaders from the memorable family of Moses. In verse 5, YHWH mentions two benefits conferred on Israel during the wilderness period. First, God recalls thwarting the plans of Balak, king of Moab, to curse Israel. The seer, Balaam, had been engaged to do the job, but instead he blessed Israel in four oracles. Although he was a foreigner, apparently his God was YHWH, and he was pledged to utter only the words of that Lord (Num. 22–24). God then recalls Joshua's miraculous crossing of the Jordan from Shittim (Josh. 2:1, 3:1) into the promised land at Gilgal (Josh. 4:19).

The defendant, Israel, personified as an individual, responds with a series of questions (vv. 6–7). These are cultic questions, even though the sacrificial cultus had not been mentioned before this. The practice of making burnt offerings and other kinds of sacrifices was well established long before the time of Micah's preaching (ca. 725–700 BCE). So the defendants' notion that YHWH expected the gift of life on the altar was not an unusual idea. Burnt offerings and calves a year old (v. 6) were routine sacrifices. What makes the ensuing defense unusual is the apparently ironical exaggeration by the people of their estimation of YHWH's expectation (v. 7). Thousands of rams? The ram is frequently mentioned as a prime sacrificial animal. In Numbers 7:12–88, the leaders of the tribes offer as many as twelve rams along with other animals at the dedication of the altar of the wilderness tabernacle. But thousands? Ten thousand rivers of oil? Do they really think that the Lord will be excessively pleased with such excess?

Finally, the people dare to suggest that YHWH might require the ultimate sacrifice, their firstborn children (v. 7b). Human sacrifice was not a routine practice in any ancient Near Eastern religion, though reports of occasional immolations can be found. Israel was no more prone than the other nations to make holocausts of human beings. The principle that the firstborn of any living species belonged to the Lord was well established (Exod. 13:1–2, 11–16; 22:29–30), and yet from the beginning provision was made for the "redemption" of the firstborn male child in a human family (Num. 18:16 fixes the redemption price at five shekels of silver).

Some scholars have taken the story of Abraham's near-sacrifice of his son, Isaac, on Mount Moriah (Gen. 22:1–19) to be the narrative repeal of the practice of human sacrifice in Israel. No evidence that

Surely God is at work everywhere; if so, then we should not dismiss the rest of the world as having nothing to say. God loves us all too much to play favorites. We make a mistake when we try to divide the world into those who attend Christian churches and those who will never have a chance at God's grace.

There is, of course, an opposite mistake. It is popular to say that religions are all about the same—as if we could combine the great traditions into one big mess of a melting pot. People who think that all religions teach the same truths have not listened. Christianity, Islam, Hinduism, Buddhism, Judaism, Confucianism, Scientology, materialism, astrology, and Pilates say very different things. When religious tolerance discourages the honest evaluation of beliefs and practices, it also discourages commitment. Tolerance by itself is apathy. To say that all religions are equal is to say that no religion makes any real difference.

How should we feel about being a minority in a world filled with different religions? Preparing to preach from Micah helps us recognize that we are not the first to ask the question. While religious pluralism may be a new experience for many Christians, it was the everyday experience of the Hebrews. The Israelites were surrounded by hundreds of gods and goddesses that belonged to their neighbors. They knew all about pluralism. Sometimes they responded by destroying their neighbors, and sometimes they bought some of their idols just to be safe.

Seven hundred years before Christ, Israel was in the middle of a revival. The temple was crowded. Giving was over budget for the first time in years, but Micah knew that something was wrong. Israel was arrogant and uncaring.

The prophet pictured God charging Israel with a crime and taking them to court (v. 1). God calls the mountains, the hills, and the foundations of the earth as witnesses for the prosecution. God's accusation is that they are selfish people. They have forgotten God's generosity. God loved Israel, brought them out of slavery, and gave them a home. God speaks in pleading tones, as a parent to a child who ignores the parent's love.

After they hear the accusation, the people, as usual, miss the point: "God, what more could you possibly want from us? Do you want more sacrifices, more expensive livestock? How about a thousand sheep? Just how religious can we be?" (vv. 6–7)

They are religious, but their idea of what religion means is far from God's hopes for them. They think that religion consists of worshiping "correctly" and staying away from those who do not.

Micah 6:1-8

Theological Perspective

Whether or not such a sacrifice would be pleasing to God and suffice for atonement comes clear in verse 8. What God requires is for one to do justice, love kindness, and walk humbly with God. The last is the most important one. Only when one walks humbly with God will one come to learn and understand how to do justice and love kindness.

Theologically, *justice* is identified with the nature of God (Isa. 30:18) and is an activity of God (Gen. 18:25; Ps. 9:4). Justice is a transformative virtue that seeks to establish or restore community, while aiming to balance personal good with the common good. Three types of justice include (1) commutative justice, which focuses on relationships between members of the community; (2) distributive justice, which functions to ensure the equitable distribution of goods, benefits, and burdens of a community; and (3) social justice, which affects the social order necessary for distributive justice. *To love kindness* involves both affection and ethical love of neighbor and fidelity to covenant and law. *To walk humbly with God* implies an attitude of reverence and openness, coupled with a sense of personal integrity, candor, and honesty. God's people are called to godliness and to live out the fullness of justice and love.

The early church fathers have interpreted Micah 6:1–8 in a variety of ways. Cyril emphasizes God's compassion. Tertullian states that God expects people to act with the same divine mercy and compassion that have been bestowed upon them. Both Theodore of Mopsuestia and Augustine note that the love of God, the love of neighbor, and the offering of self in loving service to one another are far superior to any other sacrifice or burnt offering.

In sum, the poet has proclaimed a prophetic message that attests to God's deep and abiding love, while providing God's people with a proscription for "God's will," "right relationship," and the full flourishing of the common good. Given the scientific fact that all of creation is part of one unified web of life, the practice of justice and love now needs to embrace both human and nonhuman life, and the humble walk with God is a walk of holy reverence and awe across the planet, with people being attuned to and learning from the divine Spirit that pulsates at the heart of all.

CAROL J. DEMPSEY

Pastoral Perspective

The ecclesiastical leaders who handle this dangerous text must remember that it emerges from God's deep disappointment in the people, who have failed to fashion the kind of just community envisioned by the God who liberates people from political and economic bondage. The people of God have been put on trial in this text. God has already outlined the specifics of the charge: the powerful "covet fields, and seize them; houses, and take them away" (2:2); they "tear the skin off my people" (3:2); they send violence on the poor (3:5); the political leaders take bribes, and the religious leaders sell out for money (3:11). By the time Micah poses his rhetorical question in verse 8, an indictment has already been handed down. Israel is on the defensive.

This kind of frontal assault on the people ought to evoke confession from the church. Often, like the Israelites whom Micah confronts, we remove cultic language from the context that gives it meaning. This text is a challenge to do justice as part of our worship experience, and to do worship with our acts of justice as part of the liturgy. We forget the "controversy" that the Lord has with the people prior to the chosen snippet of text and conveniently ignore the judgment that immediately follows it.

This temptation has never been greater for the North American church than it is today. Deep divisions in church and in the American landscape shape pastoral leaders who are reluctant to get specific about Christian ethical imperatives. So divided are many of our congregations and the communities where they reside that even well-intentioned appeals to dialogue on ethical issues are sometimes viewed negatively as violations of Christian unity.

There are, of course, plenty of places in the biblical canon where unity does weigh more heavily on the minds of pastoral leaders than issues of justice, *hesed*, and *halaka*. Micah is not one of those places. Before we handle this text, we must prepare ourselves to be handled by its prophetic vision, a vision that sees the ethical world not as a threat to unity but as the place where faith finds its legs.

ANDREW FOSTER CONNORS

Exegetical Perspective

such a practice ever existed has been offered, however. The Bible does note with disfavor rare incidents of the cultic offering of the lives of human beings. We are told that Hiel of Bethel rebuilt Jericho at the cost of two of his sons (1 Kgs. 16:34). The story of Jephthah, a father who sacrificed his daughter in order to fulfill a vow (Judg. 11:30–40), is told as a tragic aberration and not normal behavior. Finally, two Judean kings are condemned for making their sons "pass through the fire." King Ahaz participated in this ritual of the Canaanite god Molech that was practiced in the valley of Hinnom, near Jerusalem (2 Kgs. 16:3). So did his grandson, the bad king Manasseh (2 Kgs. 21:6). Through the prophet Jeremiah, the Lord acknowledges that the citizens of Judah and Jerusalem offered up their sons and daughters to Molech, "though I did not command them, nor did it enter my mind that they should do this abomination" (Jer. 32:35).

The "Golden Text" of the Old Testament. In verse 8, the prophet reenters the courtroom drama with a response to the exaggerated pleadings of the people. In other prophetic contexts we would hear a verdict and sentence (e.g., Mic. 6:16) following the unconvincing pleading of the people. Here, however, the narrator takes a surprising turn. The typical prophetic polemic against sacrifice (e.g., Isa. 1:10–20; Hos. 6:6; Amos 4:4–5, 5:21–24; see also next Sunday's text, Isa. 58:1–5) held that religious activity of this sort is of no avail unless the worshiper has sincere intentions. In this verse, however, the Lord, speaking through Micah, moves beyond polemic against Israelite cultic custom into positive moral teaching that has two dimensions. First, by using the vocative, "O mortal" (the NRSV's substitute for the Heb./KJV/RSV "O man"—a legitimate translation because in this case "man" is generic and genderless), the commandment that follows is presented as a universal rule, good for all people and all time. Second, the "good" is defined in lyrical terms that draw upon the great moral values of the Hebrew Bible and have major implications for life in community. Justice, kindness, and the humble walk carry the reader beyond the confines of personal piety into life-giving, reciprocal relationships with God and with God's other beloved children.

W. SIBLEY TOWNER

Homiletical Perspective

"What does God want?" the prophet asks. God wants us to do justice (v. 8)—to be a voice for oppressed persons, unprotected persons, widows, and foreigners, and to fight for the rights of handicapped persons, minorities, elderly persons, poor persons, and every person treated as less than God's child.

God wants us to love kindness. The Hebrew word *hesed* means God's loving-kindness. We respond to God's love by sharing it with others.

We are to walk humbly with God: listening for God's voice wherever God may be heard; listening to Jews, Muslims, and Buddhists; learning how other people make sense of their lives; thoughtfully examining what it means to live with faith.

We will be more faithful Christians, not if we can refute every idea that is not Christian, but if we can affirm the truth and keep searching. We should not agree with everything, but we should recognize that Christians have much to learn as well as much to offer. We should find ways to say, "I have something I want to share with you, and you have something I hope you will share with me."

Some people think that hearing other viewpoints will lead us to lose our faith, but that is not true for most of us. We become more mature Christians when we see that the great religions struggle with things that matter, that each expresses a real human experience, and that each deserves attention for the wisdom it offers the rest of humanity.

Could it be that whether we have the right answers is less important to God than whether we show compassion? Is that what Micah says?

Christians should cling to the conviction that what we believe comes closest to truth, hold to the story we have been given, test it, doubt it, try it again, believe it passionately, share it, and celebrate it.

In a world of countless religions, what should we do? We should do justice, love kindness, and walk humbly with God.

BRETT YOUNGER

Psalm 15

[1]O Lord, who may abide in your tent?
   Who may dwell on your holy hill?

[2]Those who walk blamelessly, and do what is right,
   and speak the truth from their heart;
[3]who do not slander with their tongue,
   and do no evil to their friends,
     nor take up a reproach against their neighbors;
[4]in whose eyes the wicked are despised,
   but who honor those who fear the Lord;
 who stand by their oath even to their hurt;
[5]who do not lend money at interest,
   and do not take a bribe against the innocent.

Those who do these things shall never be moved.

Theological Perspective

The psalmist asks the question, "Who shall dwell in the house of God, and who may live in the holy hill?" The psalm is part of a processional liturgy specifying the moral qualities required for admission to the temple. Both moral values and ways to worship are addressed. Is God's house our house? The psalm directs us to reimagine the environment of worship and to prepare our moral behavior; the psalm directs us to both physical and spiritual entities.

This psalm is a dialogue between a custodian of the house of God and those who have come to worship there. (The theme and the temple-ascending ritual are repeated in Psalm 24.) In the first verse begins an inquiry to the congregation who seek admission to the sanctuary. This antiphonal, sound-against-sound ritual, divided into two parts, demonstrates the tension between the two representations (priest and worshiper) in this worship procession.

Before getting to the next verses, we ask a question about physical building plans of God—whether tabernacle, house, tent, hill, or high mountain. In this multiple language of sacred space and church architecture, we are entertaining an idea of our mortal body as the living sacrifice of God (Rom. 12:1).

The space of worship may be different from church to church. Its architectural setting and tradition reflect the history, culture, and theology of each

Pastoral Perspective

In her insightful book *The Psalms for Today*,[1] Old Testament scholar Beth LaNeel Tanner does a lovely job of engaging the reader to experience the psalms as both praise and deeply felt prayer. She points to the Hebrew title of the psalms, *tehilim*, meaning, "songs of praise," and to the ancient title, *tepilith*, which means "prayers," indicating the purpose of our treasured inheritance. She goes on to point out the way in which, during the Protestant Reformation, the Psalms were sung as a part of public protest and so were also prayers for strength and God's presence.

The recovery of this tradition, just at this time in the North American "mainline" churches, is vital, I think, for a couple of reasons. First, it is well documented that we live in a post-Christian country. Certainly, any pastor trying to do ministry in the United States today has discovered that we do our ministry in a mission field. The culture no longer speaks the language of "church." Even in the so-called Bible Belt, coaches can demand Sunday morning practices from their athletes and parents will allow it. Fewer and fewer Americans can answer even the most basic questions about the Bible or Christian teaching,

---

1. Beth LaNeel Tanner, *The Psalms for Today* (Louisville, KY: Westminster John Knox Press, 2008), esp. 2–3.

Exegetical Perspective

Psalm 15 is usually classified as an entrance liturgy, a psalm that was performed at the temple gates prior to entering the holy confines.[1] It is often compared with Psalm 24, another entrance liturgy. Particularly striking are the parallels between Psalm 15:1 and Psalm 24:3, which pose the question of who may dwell in the sanctuary, and between Psalm 15:2–5b and Psalm 24:4–5, which answer the question. Whereas Psalm 24 concludes with the opening of the gates to allow the worshipers to enter, Psalm 15 ends with a statement that those who meet the qualifications shall never be moved (Ps. 15:5c).

Psalm 15 falls neatly into three sections. Verse 1 asks who may abide on God's holy hill, that is, Mount Zion, the location of the temple in Jerusalem. Verses 2–5b answer the question by stating the characteristics of those who are worthy to enter. This section is arranged in an alternating pattern of positive and negative characteristics. Verse 2 states what those who are worthy do. Verse 3 follows with a list of wicked things the worthy worshipers do not do. The psalm returns to a positive statement in verse 4, but then ends on a negative statement in verse 5ab. Being worthy to enter the temple complex is not merely a

1. J. Clinton McCann Jr., "Psalms," *New Interpreter's Bible* (Nashville: Abingdon Press, 1996), 4:732.

Homiletical Perspective

With such a simple structure—pose the question, answer the question, conclude—Psalm 15 reads more like a high school essay than a song of worship. Its plain sense is quite clear, and it is short enough that listeners can retain all of it in one hearing. We may well ask whether it is necessary to preach on such a passage, whether such a clear and direct word truly needs breaking open; but just as a simple meal can be the most satisfying, this simple text contains riches for God's people.

"Who may abide in your tent? Who may dwell on your holy hill?" (v. 1) The first thing we note is the particularity of the question. It does not ask how to "get right with God." It asks how to enter a specific place: the temple in Jerusalem. The question assumes that there is a physical location for God's presence, and that we can enter it by following the moral norms of verses 2–5a.

Of course, there is no physical temple in Jerusalem to enter now, but that does not mean we throw out the text or preach it as a set of disconnected moral laws. Instead, we might trust that God is still very much in the world, even physically present, and that we enter God's presence when we live by the norms established in the text. This approach is especially fitting in the season of Epiphany, when we celebrate the physical

Psalm 15

Theological Perspective

community. Twenty-first-century theology teaches us that we cannot predict or control God's presence. God is always, by way of a surprise, shaking us from the foundation. We live in this world of fast-changing space, and nothing is secured as permanent rock. However, the psalm's final verse assures us that the person who follows God's instruction will never be shaken, creating an archetype of the secured house of God where people dwell.

The holy temple and holy hill are vivid visual images of daily living for people who live in mountainous areas. This point of reference gives directional approach and a state of being that represent an unchanging form of security. In times of trouble, people take refuge in the high mountain, seeking hideouts and searching for food to sustain life. In the time when everything is fast moving and constantly changing, God stands firm and unshaken to the people who are seeking their entrance at the gate of the divine presence:

> To the high and kindly hills I lift my eyes; where is someone to rescue me in my plight? Truly from the dear Lord above help will come. God is the maker of heaven and earth: all is well. (Ps. 121)[1]

Who may dwell and who may live in God's presence? The question is answered in the following verses of the psalm, which portray the moral values of a righteous person. The answer parallels the themes of the Ten Commandments, especially the sixth through the tenth. Are you worthy to enter the gate? Have you practiced justice and compassion toward your neighbor and community? These verses teach that worship requires an authentic commitment to social and personal justice; and the one who does these things has permission to enter the house of God.

To the liturgical setting of space and architecture of God's dwelling, a personal commitment to justice and compassion is accented as part of the call-and-response ritual that marks the entrance into the temple: walk blamelessly; do righteously; speak the truth, speaking no slander, no wrong, no slur; fear God; keep oaths; lend money without interest; and take no bribe.

What a beautiful place to enter with such a zeal and compassion, preparing oneself in this lifetime to meet the requirements of God's righteousness! The beauty is in dwelling and living in the presence of God, drinking, eating, bathing, and playing together:

Pastoral Perspective

which means that even if we can get them into church, we need to teach them the basics.

The Psalms, at their best, do that. To pray (or to sing as prayer) the Psalms is to learn who God is. Take Psalm 15, which is our text for the week. It begins with the rhetorical questions: "O Lord, who may abide in your tent? Who may dwell on your holy hill?" (v. 1). The reference is, of course, to Mount Zion. Is this best understood literally, as a moral test used by the priests to determine who should be allowed into the temple?[2] Is it, rather, a longing for the kind of community the psalm ends up describing and for the kind of God who would be in the company of such people? In the verses that follow those two rhetorical questions, there is a description of just such a community and just such a God.

The winners are those who walk blamelessly and do what is right; those who speak the truth from their hearts. Then the language changes, as if the litany now comes from another voice, across the aisle in the temple. The language moves from describing what the blameless *do* to what the blameless *do not do*. The blameless do not slander their neighbors with their tongues and do no evil to their friends; nor "bear reproach for his kin" (NRSV, "take up a reproach against their neighbors").[3] The language then turns back to what the blameless will do (again, as if in litany, across the aisle): despise the wicked while honoring those who respect God, and keep their promises even if it costs them a loss of profit. Finally, one more change in voice: the faithful do not lend money at interest and do not take a bribe against the innocent. To these faithful comes this promise: those who do not do these things shall not be moved, or shall not stumble.

In the midst of the greed on Wall Street and the combination of greed and incompetence in Washington in the early years of the twenty-first century, even unchurched people can look at this list and know exactly what it is saying about whom God wishes to keep company with—not that God is not capable of forgiving. God's love is unconditional, but the psalmist makes clear to all of us that our God's nature and our God's command is that we be just, that we be fair, that no evil falls from our lips. God will work with those of us who fall short. Frankly,

---

1. *Come, Let Us Worship: The Korean-English Presbyterian Hymnal and Service Book* (Louisville, KY: Geneva Press, 2001), hymn #121, words written by Song-suk Im and paraphrased by James Minchin.

2. See, for example, Robert Alter, *The Book of Psalms: A Translation with Commentary* (New York: W. W. Norton and Co., 2007), 43.
3. Ibid. The translation is Alter's, his reproduction of what he describes as "the cryptic formulation of the Hebrew." He argues that its meaning might be that when one's family member behaves badly, one does not silence the reproach simply because it is family (44).

matter of refraining from evil; positive acts of righteousness are required as well. The third section of the psalm, verse 5c, summarizes the benefits of those who meet the qualifications of verses 2–5b. They will be allowed to enter the sanctuary; more importantly, they will never be shaken. Leading a worthy life bears fruits in ways far beyond just being allowed to dwell in God's tent.

The first verse asks the question, who may abide in God's tent and dwell on the holy hill? The vocabulary used is instructive. The verbs both for "to abide" (Heb. *gur*) and for "to dwell" (Heb. *shakan*) denote remaining in a place for a short period of time. In its nominal form, *gur* refers to non-Israelites who have come to live in Israel for a short period of time, that is, resident aliens (Exod. 12:19; 20:10; 22:21; Lev. 19:33–34; Deut. 24:17). In the same way, the Israelites can come to stay in God's temple, but only for a short period of time. The tent mentioned in this verse is the tabernacle, the residence of the ark of the covenant, which was brought by David to Jerusalem (2 Sam. 6:12–19). It was later installed in the temple by Solomon (1 Kgs. 8:1–11). The holy hill is a common way for the psalms to refer to Mount Zion, where the temple was located (Pss. 2:6; 3:4; 43:3; 78:54). The verb *shakan* is also related to the word for the tabernacle (Heb. *mishkan*). The tabernacle, where God comes to dwell with the people, is represented here as the place where the people can come to dwell with God.

Verses 2–5b record the qualifications of those who may enter the temple confines. Although the Hebrew text uses masculine participles throughout (e.g., v. 2, "He whose walk is blameless" [NIV]), the NRSV has used the plural to avoid noninclusive language (e.g., "Those who walk blamelessly"). This obscures the fact that the focus here is on each of the individuals who seek to enter the temple. Perhaps a better translation would be "The one who walks blamelessly," which preserves gender neutrality while remaining faithful to the Hebrew.

Verse 2 characterizes the one worthy to enter as someone who "walks blamelessly." The word translated "blamelessly" here is *tamim*, which carries the meaning of "completion, perfection." Although some might be tempted to see this as barring everyone from the temple, because Paul said no one is righteous (Rom. 3:10), OT authors viewed such a state as obtainable. Both Noah and Job, for instance, are described as being blameless (Gen. 6:9; Job 1:1), and numerous psalms speak of people who were blameless (Pss. 18:23; 37:18; 84:11; 101:6; 119:1). Those

incarnation of the one who promised to be with us to the end of the ages.

The norms established in verses 2–5a are challenging, but they are ripe for preaching. "Those who walk blamelessly" (v. 2) is one point of entry. Who among us does not carry some blame, some guilt that eats at us? The struggle to be set free from that blame, to be forgiven, is what brings us to worship. Does the congregation yearn for such freedom? Do they experience it in their worship? If not, what prevents it?

A sermon can ask what it means for someone to "speak the truth from their heart" (v. 2b). What makes truth from the heart different from other kinds of truth? Does the light of God's presence enlighten our hearts in a way that changes our understanding of truth?

The people in God's presence "do not slander with their tongue" (v. 3a), and this opens the door to a sermon on the sin of gossip, which too often plagues churches. How easy it is to slip from sharing news about a community to speculation and titillation! The text reminds us that gossip, even when it seems harmless, does evil to our friends. Far better to speak the truth from our own hearts and let others do the same.

Verse 4 offers challenging words: "in whose eyes the wicked are despised" (v. 4a). Those who hear the text will remember these words, and a sermon that ignores these words will be ignored as well. How can these words be reconciled with the Christian imperatives to pray for our enemies and love those who hate us? Perhaps we ought to despise wickedness rather than wicked people? A sermon might not be able to resolve this tension, but should at least acknowledge it.

Those in God's presence also "stand by their oath even to their hurt" (v. 4c). There is a hunger in the world today for this kind of integrity. In an age of disposable promises—political, spiritual, marital—the idea of honoring one's word above one's own immediate interest seems more like the stuff of fiction: George Washington and the cherry tree or *To Kill A Mockingbird*'s Atticus Finch. However, that is God's call, and there is a real-life example given in God's faithfulness to the promises of Scripture, even when keeping those promises led to the cross.

The moral focus of the text shifts in the first half of verse 5. Up to this point, the emphasis has been primarily on honesty and integrity in speech: truthfulness, honoring one's word, refraining from gossip. In verse 5 the emphasis is on financial integrity.

Psalm 15

Theological Perspective

a sacrament of unity. It involves physical edifices and what is in the heart of people who worship there. In the midst of the call-and-response antiphonal ritual, we recognize the tension between liturgical and personal requirements in preparing oneself to enter God's house.

The theology of the psalm asks the liturgical question and asks for personal devotional preparation. We see the tension: God's house in a temporary tent (reflecting the exodus wilderness period) vs. the secure foundation of a temple edifice on a high mountain (reflecting the royal power of Davidic kingdom). The emphasis is not on one or the other, but both. To worship God in an authentic manner, we are called to find the beauty in a form as well as in freedom, corporate as well as personal, and in truth as well as in spirit. The high liturgical art reflected in the responsorial exchanges between clergy and congregation stands alongside important requirements for personal devotion and for lifetime commitment to justice and righteousness. The tension that holds the opposing dynamic in the multidimensional element of worship is beautifully structured to narrate the role of each worshiper in this praise song.

In response to the Hebrew reading of this week's lectionary, Micah 6:1–8, the psalm corresponds with what to do beyond the ritual: doing justice and righteousness. "He has told you, O mortal, what is good; and what does the LORD require of you but to do justice, and to love kindness, and to walk humbly with your God?" (Mic. 6:8) Moral values are once again emphasized over the blind practices of hiding behind the edifice of institutional jargons. We are asked to live and dwell in God's house, not just be a captive of its building structure. To the question "Who may dwell?" we join the community of believers daring to answer, "We will live, doing God's justice for others!"

PAUL JUNGGAP HUH

Pastoral Perspective

God has not had much of a choice! God's own nature remains pure, high, and lifted up.

Indeed, there is a longing in these words. Even as the psalmist must know that no one could possibly live up to all of them, there is an aching for what could be, for what should be and is not. Oh, but the psalmist has imagined it! In that sense it does exist. God wants it, wills it, has made it a part of the promise of the commonwealth of God and in that sense has provided for it. In that sense, it does exist: "The kingdom is with you now!"

Learning this kind of hope is another powerful thing that we should be offering to a culture that has forgotten how words can beget worlds. Politicians and pulpiteers alike sometimes diminish the power of words by resorting to simple-minded slogans or vague repetition. We who live under the Bible remember that words *can* make all the difference: "God said, 'Let there be light'; and there was light" (Gen. 1:3). Genesis claims that the Word created our world and words make a powerful difference, for good or for ill. What the psalmist knows is the same thing the rapper and the jingle writer know: put an idea to rhythm, to song, and you will teach a people something that sticks with them. More importantly, add an inspiring, important idea to that rhythm and song, and now you have gone beyond the level of the advertiser and jingle writer. Now you have taught a people a life-changing idea that they will never forget.

BARBARA S. BLAISDELL

Exegetical Perspective

who wish to enter must also do what is righteous and speak the truth. All aspects of their behavior must be acceptable.

Verse 3 deals with how those who seek to enter the temple must treat their neighbors. Although the second two clauses in this verse are relatively clear, the first is not. The Hebrew contains the idiom "The one who does not step/walk on his tongue," which the NRSV renders "Who do not slander with their tongue." It is unclear whether "tripping over one's tongue" means something as specific as slander or encompasses a broader category of sins committed with the tongue (cf. Jas. 3:5–12).

Verse 4 returns to a positive statement of what the worthy entrants must do. It features a contrasting pair, as the righteous must both despise the wicked and honor those who fear the Lord, a contrast also found in Proverbs 10:27. The final clause of this verse paints the picture of those willing to do the right thing, even when it is not to their benefit. The righteous will keep their vows, even when doing so will cause them harm.

Verse 5ab brings to a close the description of the righteous, those worthy to enter the sanctuary, by mentioning two rules involving money. The first is a prohibition of taking interest, a proscription that is found throughout the Torah (Exod. 22:25; Lev. 25:36–37; Deut. 23:19–20). The second forbids the taking of a bribe against the innocent. Because bribes caused a perversion of justice, they were forbidden by the Mosaic law (Exod. 23:6–8; Deut. 16:19; 27:25).

The final clause in verse 5c brings the psalm to a close with a promise that extends far beyond mere entrance to the temple. It promises that "those who do these things shall never be moved." This is a constant concern in the psalms. Although the wicked think they will never be moved (Ps. 10:6) and look forward to seeing the righteous shaken (Pss. 13:4; 38:16), God will firmly establish those who keep their ways blameless (Pss. 16:8; 21:7; 55:22; 62:6; 112:6; 121:3). Those who are able to enter the temple will be as immovable as the holy city itself (Ps. 46:5; 125:1).

KEVIN A. WILSON

Homiletical Perspective

Those who wish to enter God's presence do not lend at interest or take bribes. Are we compliant if we refrain from these particular practices, or does the text ask more challenging questions about our faith and the way we use money? Do we obey if we purchase clothing manufactured under abusive conditions, or if the coffee we drink after church was bought at a price that keeps a farmer in poverty?

A sermon might address the idea of God's presence. The text does not tell us what God looks like, but it does tell us what God's presence looks like; it looks like a community, a holy company gathered around God. We imagine them, real people who "walk blamelessly, and do what is right, and speak the truth from their heart." They treat one another with the kindness, mercy, and integrity described in verses 2–5a. Such people are able to enter God's presence. In light of Jesus' promise that when we gather in his name he is in the midst of us, we might ask whether this community invokes the divine presence rather than simply entering it.

We might also ask what this psalm tells us about God. It is founded on the idea that God is present in the world, and that there is a place for us with God in the world. Where? How do we experience the holy? Those gathered on the holy hill are guests and are expected to behave accordingly. Are we doing it? If we believe that God becomes present when we gather in the name of Jesus, then we have an even greater responsibility to maintain God's presence. We become stewards, house sitters for the presence of God. How well are we taking care of it?

DREW BUNTING

1 Corinthians 1:18-31

[18]For the message about the cross is foolishness to those who are perishing, but to us who are being saved it is the power of God. [19]For it is written,

"I will destroy the wisdom of the wise,
and the discernment of the discerning I will thwart."

[20]Where is the one who is wise? Where is the scribe? Where is the debater of this age? Has not God made foolish the wisdom of the world? [21]For since, in the wisdom of God, the world did not know God through wisdom, God decided, through the foolishness of our proclamation, to save those who believe. [22]For Jews demand signs and Greeks desire wisdom, [23]but we proclaim Christ crucified, a stumbling block to Jews and foolishness to Gentiles, [24]but to those

Theological Perspective

How do human beings come to know God? How is fellowship possible between frail, finite human creatures and the Creator of the cosmos?

Dietrich Bonhoeffer's famous call for a "religionless Christianity" drew a distinction between religion, understood as human attempts to connect with the Divine, and Christianity, which he viewed as a response to God's decision to engage human beings.

The question is a basic one: Does authentic spirituality follow the pattern of Babel, with human beings constructing towers to heaven from the building blocks of their own spiritual wisdom or philosophical insight? Does true religion, rather, conform to the pattern of Sinai, where knowledge of God results from the sovereign, divine decision to come down from heaven and establish fellowship with humanity?

Paul in this passage stresses that fellowship with God is the product of God's decision to come to us. He bases this claim on God's act of reconciliation in the cross.

This unlikely means of salvation, in which the Son of God suffers and dies an ignominious death for the redemption of humankind, is not something that conventional spiritual wisdom or philosophical reflection could have anticipated. As a result, says Paul, the religious "experts" who were staking their claims on human wisdom have completely missed

Pastoral Perspective

A story is told about a wealthy early colonial Virginian who asked his Anglican rector if it was possible to find salvation outside of the Church of England. The rector wrestled with the question, because he knew it was within the realm of possibility that those who were not Anglican might go to heaven, but he did not want his socially elite parishioner to be socializing with Christian riffraff of all sorts. So after pondering the question deeply, the rector replied, "Sir, the possibility about which you inquire exists. But no gentleman would avail himself of it."[1] The social reality reflected in this story is not unique. The truth is that status consciousness afflicts most religious groups. Sociologists from Emile Durkheim to H. Richard Niebuhr have noticed how often religious affiliations are directly related to social and economic class.

Status consciousness appears to have been one of the many problems afflicting the church at Corinth, as we can surmise from Paul's letter to this church—a church he had founded. The ancient Greek city in which it was located had been destroyed by Rome in 146 BCE and rebuilt by Julius Caesar about a hundred years later as a colony for freed slaves and other poor folk. So in Paul's day Corinth was a city of

1. Walter Russell Mead, *God and Gold* (New York: Alred A. Knopf, 2007), 3.

who are the called, both Jews and Greeks, Christ the power of God and the wisdom of God. [25]For God's foolishness is wiser than human wisdom, and God's weakness is stronger than human strength.

[26]Consider your own call, brothers and sisters: not many of you were wise by human standards, not many were powerful, not many were of noble birth. [27]But God chose what is foolish in the world to shame the wise; God chose what is weak in the world to shame the strong; [28]God chose what is low and despised in the world, things that are not, to reduce to nothing things that are, [29]so that no one might boast in the presence of God. [30]He is the source of your life in Christ Jesus, who became for us wisdom from God, and righteousness and sanctification and redemption, [31]in order that, as it is written, "Let the one who boasts, boast in the Lord."

Exegetical Perspective

Though Romans may be Paul's greatest theological epistle, and Galatians his most impassioned, 1 Corinthians shows Paul as the well-rounded pastor, teacher, and rhetorician. This first chapter offers historical and theological insight, as well as providing a subtle pastoral model that remains useful. The letter is specific, trouble-shooting exigencies in the Corinthian church of which the apostle has been apprised by its members (Chloe's people, 1:11; a letter, 7:1; the visiting trio Stephanas, Fortunatus, and Achaicus, 16:17; the disillusioned Apollos, 16:12). It also plumbs theological and ethical depths, providing foundations for pastoral advice. Paul follows his usual epistolary template (address and greetings; prayer and/or thanksgiving; body; exhortation, closing salutations), but adapts this because of the "shopping list" nature of the epistle. Thus, he combines exhortation within the "body" of the letter, rather than separating these out, as is his usual practice. The sharply specific nature of this letter is signaled from the first chapter, which makes a strong appeal for unity. Chapter 1 includes the salutation (vv. 1–3), the initial prayer of thanksgiving (vv. 4–9), and the first foray into Paul's first combined topic, that of wisdom and unity in the church (vv. 10–31, a discourse concluding at 4:21).

The apostle begins by referring to his apostolic calling and office, while he also recognizes the

Homiletical Perspective

I serve a congregation named for Francis of Assisi, who among other things is credited with "inventing" the crèche. The Christmas pageants and live nativities with which most of us have become so familiar can also present us with a serious theological challenge. These celebrations and ruminations tend to want to carry us back in time—away from a world of cell phones and space travel to a world of shepherds and falling stars; to a place I sometimes call "Bible-land." (Bible-land is where people wear long flowing robes and talk with bad Elizabethan accents.) The carols we sing do not help matters much, because we are tempted to believe that all was "calm and bright" in that little town of Bethlehem as the little drummer boy played *pa rum pum pum pum*. This journey back to a more innocent time and place can combine with our own sense of nostalgia for what we remember as a more innocent time in our own childhoods.

I am really not as much of a Scrooge as this opening paragraph may suggest; I honestly do love Christmas! I have no doubt overstated and even caricatured the problem. I have done so to make a more serious theological point: the jagged pieces of the scriptural narrative—like the backdrop of Roman imperial power, and the slaughter of the innocents, or maybe the reality that most of our own childhoods were not quite so "innocent" as we may

1 Corinthians 1:18-31

Theological Perspective

the boat. They have failed to recognize God's redemption of the world!

This failure to recognize what God has done takes two forms, corresponding to the division of the human race into Jews and Gentiles. Gentiles (Greeks) desire *wisdom*: the religious insights they recognize as valid are those that are based on philosophical reason. Jews, for their part, being the heirs of a tradition that preserves the memory of dramatic divine interventions within history, demand *signs*—impressive displays of divine power that are obvious to all.

In both instances, the failure to recognize God's salvation of the world in Jesus is the product of prior expectations about what God's work must look like. Both Jewish and Greek unbelievers suffer a form of blindness caused by human religious preconceptions about what God *must* be like. As a result of their reliance on this accumulated stock of religious "wisdom," both groups fail to recognize what God actually *is* like. Neither group recognizes God's saving intervention into time and history in the cross of Jesus.

Paul apparently does not believe the blindness of these groups is an accident. He cites Isaiah 29:14 in support of the unsettling idea that God has *deliberately* humbled the pretensions of human beings who claim knowledge of the Divine on the basis of their own spiritual insight (v. 19). This humbling takes place as God chooses to save the world through *foolishness*— the proclamation of Christ's saving death on the cross.

What is the effect of God's pulling the rug out from under human religious ideas in this way? Paul is not simply developing an abstract theory about how human beings properly come to know God. He believes that the way God has acted carries profound implications for the life of the Christian community.

The first part of chapter 1 makes it clear that Paul was dealing with a church in Corinth that had divided itself into factions. These rival subcommunities had coalesced around favored teachers, resulting in arguments about which of the various "schools" possessed superior religious wisdom.

Remarkably, Paul refuses to take on the role of a referee in this situation. The apostle never considers the particular teachings that divide these groups from one another, nor is he interested in passing judgment on the differences in theology and practice that fuel the divisions. Instead, as we have seen, Paul proclaims his message about God's humbling of human religious pretension through the foolishness of the cross.

The effect of this strategy is to call dramatically into question the whole cult of the religious "expert,"

Pastoral Perspective

"upwardly mobile" folk. There was little "old money" in the town, but it was full of folk trying to "make it." These aspirations were reflected in the divisions and animosities of the church at Corinth, where members were prone to follow one leader or another in light of the social status that would then be conferred upon them.

Most of our churches reflect similar inclinations. For instance, if you were to ask a churchgoer, "Why are you a member of your particular congregation?" you might get the answer, "I am a member of this church because it cares for the poor and the outcast." Another might say, "I attend the church of the Reverend So and So, who is a great preacher." Still another might answer, "I attend the church that speaks truth to power," or "This church promises that faith will lead to prosperity and prosperity to social success." In other words, that which conveys status or pride is often given as a reason for attending a particular church.

Flannery O'Connor tells a wonderful story about a woman named Ruby Turpin—a woman obsessed with status consciousness. In the story, Ruby entered a doctor's waiting room, sizing up everyone there in the room as to their class. In fact, at night Ruby Turpin would occupy herself by naming classes of people. On the bottom were, in her worldview, poor blacks and white trash; above them were homeowners like her and her husband Claude; and on top were people with lots of money and much bigger homes. The complexity of her rankings used to "bear in" on her, because she knew that some of those people who had lots of money were actually very "common and ought to be below she and Claude." While Mrs. Turpin was reflecting out loud on these matters in the doctor's waiting room, there happened to be a college student sitting there reading a book entitled *Human Development*, who decided she had had just about as much of Ruby Turpin as she could stand. So she hurled the book across the room, hitting Mrs. Turpin just above the left eye, and then began to strangle her, saying, "Go back to hell where you came from, you old warthog!"

In many respects, Paul's words to the people of Corinth are no less jolting than a book on human development between the eyes, for he reminds them of the foolishness of the gospel of the crucified Christ. You see, crucifixion was more than state-sponsored execution; it was meant to demean and shame the victim. Indeed, it may have been embarrassing to the early Christians that their Lord had met his fate by crucifixion. However, New Testament

importance of the entire holy (*hagios*) and "called-out" (*ekklēsia*, my trans.) community, speaking of his "brother" Sosthenes, and the church local and cosmic. As with all Paul's letters, he greets his readers with grace (*Charis!*) and peace (*Eirēnē*, Greek equivalent of Hebrew *Shalom!*). It is perhaps significant that Paul has transformed the usual Hellenistic greeting, "Have joy!" (*Chairete!*) to the noun "Grace!" thus grammatically matching the Hebrew greeting. These salutations demonstrate the eclectic nature of the early Christian community. However, the composite greeting is redolent not simply of the church's social reality. It also functions as a prayerful blessing, recalling for them the gifts of grace and peace received by the sanctifying Spirit, from the Father, through the Lord Jesus Christ. (The Father and the Son are mentioned explicitly at vv. 3 and 9, foreshadowing Paul's binary restatement of the Shema [cf. Deut. 6:4] in 1 Corinthians 8:5–6. The Spirit's presence lurks behind the appeal to sanctification and calling; in 2 Corinthians 3:17–18, Paul will actually name the Spirit as Lord.)

Following the greeting, Paul offers thanks for the rich life of the Corinthian church and for the believers' acumen in both "word" and "knowledge"—themes upon which he intends to focus. As with the salutation, the thanksgiving is offered not merely for its own sake, but rhetorically previews the appeal and teaching that he will launch beginning at 1:10. *They* are rich in speech and knowledge, though *he* will exhibit apostolic poverty for their sake. They have begun to show forth gifts of the Spirit, though he reminds them that not all is yet revealed, and that even strength they possess comes from the one who has called them into "the fellowship [*koinōnia*] of his Son" (v. 9). Already in this prayer, Paul directs them toward the cross, anticipating his call to unity, his teaching on the use of spiritual gifts, and his reminder that knowledge and speech from God are distinct from the worldly standards of wisdom and powerful rhetoric.

Paul's "theology of the cross" comes more clearly into focus in his first appeal, at 1:10. The Corinthians' true corporate identity depends upon remembering that their baptism is into the death of the one "who was crucified for" them. Because of Christ's unifying name, divisions are a contradiction. However, Paul does not simply tackle the vice of "party spirit," as though their divisions were merely a matter of pride and petty "quarrels" (v. 11 NRSV). Rather, the "contentions" (*erides*, v. 11) among them must be somewhat substantive, and so each group has sought to authenticate itself by evoking a key

remember—all get lost along the way. We figure that sin and death can wait for Holy Week—this story is all about innocence and life.

That reading of the Christmas narrative is distorted, and that distortion can have drastic consequence for the opportunities that Epiphany offers to preachers and their congregations. Perhaps the core truth of this great liturgical season can be recaptured if we take a verbal clue from the way we proclaim the Paschal mystery ("Alleluia! Christ *is* risen!") and dare to use that same present-tense verb form in proclaiming the incarnation: Christ *is* born! (As the traditional French carol puts it, "*Il est né le divin enfant*" [he is born, the divine child].) Indeed, the scandalous claim of the incarnation is that the Word has become flesh to dwell among *us*—not only among people who lived long ago in Bible-land.

Is it not the preacher's task during this Epiphany season to proclaim this good news that insists that the Word is being made manifest in *this* time and place? To make that shift, it seems to me, requires that preachers be engaged in exploring and cultivating spiritual practices that allow twenty-first-century Christians to notice the ways that God is being made manifest today, in our very midst.

At first glance it may seem as if Paul did not get the liturgical memo that this is Epiphany season. More accurately, one may wonder why those who structured the Revised Common Lectionary are calling us away from these central themes of Epiphany to focus on a theology of the cross. The point is that it is all of a piece, as T. S. Eliot noted in "The Journey of the Magi," when he asked: "were we led all that way for birth or death?"[1] The answer, of course, is yes. So, as Paul invites us on this fourth Sunday of Epiphany to "survey the wondrous cross," the preacher might see this, not as a call away from Epiphany, but deeper into its great mystery: as an opportunity to discover (or rediscover), as Isaac Watts did before us, a love that is so amazing and so divine that it demands "our souls, our lives, our all."

In this letter to the first-century disciples in Corinth, Paul sets forth his ecclesiology, not as a systematic theologian, but as a pastor reflecting theologically in the midst of a particular congregation of real flesh-and-blood Christians who are polarized and factionalized. There is a great deal of quarrelling and bickering about who is right and who is wrong, and plenty of meetings after the meetings in the

---

1. T. S. Eliot, "The Journey of the Magi," in *Complete Poems and Plays, 1909–1950* (New York: Harcourt Brace & Co., 1952), 68.

1 Corinthians 1:18-31

Theological Perspective

which forms the rationale for preferring one school of faith over another. God's undermining of human religious wisdom means Christianity is not some ladder of spiritual achievement that truly enlightened experts could teach us to climb, no matter how sophisticated. Christian discipleship is not the product of some breakthrough in human insight, not a bold, new philosophy of life, nor even a set of time-tested principles for happy and fulfilled living.

Its heart and center is rather a bald historical claim about what God has done on a hill outside Jerusalem during the reign of Pontius Pilate. For that reason any attempt to divide the church into "schools" based on human wisdom has completely missed the point, and any boasting that takes place among Christians should focus, not on the achievements of human teachers, but on what God has accomplished.

A number of very promising avenues for exploration and reflection are contained in all this. Preachers and congregations might consider to what extent the factionalism evident in today's church, or even its division into denominations, is the product of human wisdom of the sort God has undercut in the cross. How does Paul's proclamation offer hope in the midst of the church's divisions? What strategies of reconciliation does it suggest?

Congregations might be invited to consider ways in which religious claims grounded in human wisdom or a desire for signs confront them today. What picture of God is presented by today's human wisdom, and what kind of faith community? How does the God proclaimed by Paul differ from such human-based pictures?

Another avenue of reflection might consider ways in which contemporary church life is affected by a "cult of the religious expert." Do contemporary believers feel intimidated around the Bible because they don't believe they are qualified to read it? What does Paul's proclamation have to say about the way we view the clergy, and how might it empower nonspecialists in religious practice and devotion?

Yet another possibility would be to invite hearers to reflect on how preconceived, human understandings of what God *must* be like may lead contemporary believers and churches to miss ways in which God actually *is* at work in their lives. What sorts of circumstances might require us to let go of our preconceptions, and what sorts of disciplines and practices could help us recognize the presence of God working in unexpected ways?

P. MARK ACHTEMEIER

Pastoral Perspective

scholar Robert Jewett, in his interpretation of Paul's letter to the Corinthians, argues that by enduring a shameful death, the crucified one "overcomes our shame by letting us experience the boundless love of God. . . . Christ takes the ultimate weight of shame to lift our heaviest and most secret burden, the feeling that no one loves and respect us."[2] In other words, facing into the foolishness of the gospel of the crucified Christ removes the burden of our shameful feelings about ourselves, enabling us to see the foolishness of our inclination to shame others.

So what happened to Ruby Turpin? Later that evening she went into the pasture beside her house and was talking to herself, puzzling with great intensity over the reason for the assault on her obvious goodness and respectability. She stood there gazing into the evening sky until there was only a purple streak cutting across the sky like an extension of highway. Then, in a revelatory moment, she saw it as a vast swinging bridge extending upward from the earth and on it a horde of souls was marching toward heaven. There were companies of white trash, clean for the first time in their lives, and bands of blacks in white robes, and battalions of lunatics shouting and clapping and leaping like frogs. "And bringing up the end of the procession was a tribe of people whom she recognized at once as those who, like herself and Claude, had always had a little of everything and the God-given wit to use it right. She leaned forward to observe them closer. They were marching behind the others with dignity, accountable as they had always been for good order and common sense and respectable behavior. They alone were on key. But she could tell by their shocked and altered faces that even their virtues were being burned away."[3]

So also, the message of the cross can remove our inclination to shame others and invite us into a new reality of boundless love. The cross may be "foolishness to those who are perishing, but to us who are being saved it is the power of God" (v. 18).

ROGER J. GENCH

2. Robert Jewett, *Saint Paul Returns to the Movies: Triumph over Shame* (Grand Rapids: Eerdmans, 1999), 44, 51.
3. Flannery O'Connor, *The Complete Stories* (New York: Farrar, Straus & Giroux, 1978), 508.

name—Paul, the apostle Peter, or the philosophical Apollos (who seems to have had enough of it all, 1 Cor. 16:12!). Instead of this "solution," Paul urges them to remember the gospel and their baptism, "to put themselves in order" (*katartizō*, v. 10) and to have "the same mind and the same thought." This is not a call to surface harmony, but to agreement in approach and in doctrine. Truth and love are not at odds, but must cohere, because at the center of the church's life is one who has died (v. 17), and who is himself word and wisdom.

What, however, is the gospel, the "word of the cross" (v. 18)? Its effect is to induce derision or scandal. Though it is a "word" (*logos*), it may well be considered by (Greek) philosophers not to partake in wisdom, and by (Jewish) recipients of God's past revelation as blasphemy. It has been passed over as neither exalted enough in wisdom nor powerful enough as a sign. However, declares Paul, it is the power and the wisdom of God, even if it is not received by some. Paul alludes to passages in Isaiah (Isa. 29:14; 33:18) that struggle with God's action and true wisdom. He also uses the classical strategy of the rhetorical question (v. 20), pointing out the paradox: what seems foolish and weak is utter wisdom and absolute strength. The Corinthian Christians, themselves of humble origin, validate God's course of action (v. 26), since Christ became weak that humans might become strong.

God has acted, but many have not discerned, in the life and cross of Jesus, God's visitation. At this word, at this sign, every mouth will be stopped, whether the self-important scribe (cf. Isa. 29:13) or the scoffing philosopher (cf. Isa. 29:20): "God chose what is weak in the world to shame the strong . . . the things that are not, to reduce to nothing the things that are" (vv. 27–28). The word of Christ is as valid in the realm of ontological discourse as in salvation history. For Christ Jesus is both the measure of being and the measure of action. He is "the source of [the] life" of the church (v. 30), whether of wisdom or holiness, justice or redemption. Paul closes by commending the humility of Jeremiah (Jer. 9:24) who learned by trials to "boast in the Lord" (v. 31).

EDITH M. HUMPHREY

church parking lot. It does not take a great deal of imagination for preachers in our day to imagine a congregation like this one. For these Christians (and for the church of every generation, including our own) Paul reframes the question. Rather than trying to "solve" the disputes with a technical fix, by entering into a process of mediation or conflict resolution, he sees these conflicts as an opportunity for the whole community, in spite of their very real differences, to encounter the living Christ in their midst again. One might put it this way: in the midst of their very real differences, "*il est né, le divin enfant.*"

Preaching this particular epistle in this particular season provides twenty-first-century Christians with an opportunity to explore and deepen our faith by rediscovering the mystical side of Paul. As Paul reflects on the death of Jesus in light of the Scriptures, he is not advocating for a particular doctrine of the atonement, and certainly not that the power of the cross is about how the death of Jesus satisfied the wrath of an angry father. The preacher who wishes to stay close to the text (rather than imposing his or her favorite atonement theories onto this text) does well to notice that Paul seems much more aligned with the Johannine perspective found in the Farewell Discourse. As Christians, we are commanded to love one another (John 13:34–35; 15:12), so that the love of God might be made manifest in the world. In the process of learning to be the church, the light continues to shine in the darkness. The power of God is revealed wherever the love of God becomes flesh. There we behold that "God's foolishness is wiser than human wisdom, and God's weakness is stronger than human strength" (1 Cor. 1:25).

RICHARD M. SIMPSON

Matthew 5:1-12

¹When Jesus saw the crowds, he went up the mountain; and after he sat down, his disciples came to him. ²Then he began to speak, and taught them, saying:

³"Blessed are the poor in spirit, for theirs is the kingdom of heaven.

⁴"Blessed are those who mourn, for they will be comforted.

⁵"Blessed are the meek, for they will inherit the earth.

⁶"Blessed are those who hunger and thirst for righteousness, for they will be filled.

⁷"Blessed are the merciful, for they will receive mercy.

⁸"Blessed are the pure in heart, for they will see God.

⁹"Blessed are the peacemakers, for they will be called children of God.

¹⁰"Blessed are those who are persecuted for righteousness' sake, for theirs is the kingdom of heaven.

¹¹"Blessed are you when people revile you and persecute you and utter all kinds of evil against you falsely on my account. ¹²Rejoice and be glad, for your reward is great in heaven, for in the same way they persecuted the prophets who were before you."

Theological Perspective

Dale C. Allison, in his book *The Sermon on the Mount: Inspiring the Moral Imagination*, discusses two broad historical trajectories in the interpretation of the Sermon of the Mount. The first trajectory, described as "the monastic interpretation," derives from medieval and later Catholicism. According to this interpretation, the hermeneutical key is 5:48 where Jesus commands, "Be perfect, therefore, as your heavenly Father is perfect." It follows then that there are two sorts of Christian believers: those who have a special religious calling (monks, nuns, ascetics) and ordinary Christians; the former are the ones who are able to fulfill the command to be perfect. The second trajectory, described as "the theory of the impossible ideal," is grounded in a Protestant hermeneutic associated with Lutheranism. According to this interpretation, the reality of sin makes it impossible for anyone to fulfill the commands of the Sermon, and the point of the Sermon is to teach "the necessity of grace."[1] Theological reflection on the Sermon along either of these trajectories tends to limit its message to insights into an eschatological future.

Two broad contemporary methods for interpreting the Gospel of Matthew—(1) social scientific and

Pastoral Perspective

The late writer Madeleine L'Engle wrote a book about Lent called *The Irrational Season*, in which she attempted to make sense of a church year that had fallen on hard times.[1] Given the context in which we now live, she might well have written a book with this suggested title: *The Irrational Teaching: Reflections on the Beatitudes.* Whenever we hear the Beatitudes, we are struck with their poetic beauty and, at the same time, overwhelmed by their perceived impracticality for the world in which we live. We admire the instruction, but we fear the implications of putting the words into actual practice. We live in a time when the blessings given are to those who succeed, often at the expense of others. To be poor in spirit, peaceful, merciful, and meek will get you nowhere in a culture grounded in competition and fear. Perhaps this is why most references to the Beatitudes imply that in giving this instruction, Jesus was literally turning the values of the world upside down. Who can survive in attempting to live into the spirit of the Beatitudes?

The answer resides not in their impracticality but in their *practicality*. We often approach them as an impossible challenge for ordinary living. Only the greatest of saints are up to the task. Therefore, we

---

1. Dale C. Allison, *The Sermon on the Mount: Inspiring the Moral Imagination* (New York: Crossroad, 1999), 2–4.

1. Madeleine L'Engle, *The Irrational Season* (New York: Seabury Press, 1977).

Exegetical Perspective

The Beatitudes are not entrance requirements for the kingdom but eschatological blessings. Although the later sections of the Sermon are full of ethical imperatives, the Beatitudes are in the indicative mode, not in the imperative. Jesus is not asking the crowd to become poor in spirit, or mourners, or persecuted for righteousness' sake; instead, he offers consolation to those who find themselves poor and in mourning and persecuted. Here we get to hear what Jesus' "proclaiming the good news of the kingdom" (Matt. 4:23) exactly amounts to.

This insight will help us to navigate three different ways to read the Sermon and the Beatitudes. The first is to see in "the mountain" of verse 1 an allusion to Mount Sinai: Jesus would then be the new *Moses*, and his preaching of the Sermon analogous to the giving of the Torah. On this reading, the phrase "to go up the mountain" is an allusion to Moses's ascent of Mount Sinai (Exod. 19:3, 12; 24:15, 18; 34:1–2, 4). This reading is supported by the observation that the sequence of events in the first chapters of Matthew mirrors the sequence in Exodus: both narratives tell the stories of slaughter of infants, the return of the hero, the passing through water, and a temptation in the wilderness, followed by the lawgiving on the mountain. Moreover, in the passages following, Jesus himself refers to the law and the prophets that he has

Homiletical Perspective

When I was serving as the minister of a local congregation and regularly making pastoral calls, I often saw the Beatitudes on the walls of the homes of our parishioners. There were beautiful aesthetic renderings, some that were almost garish, some that were stitched, and even one that was crocheted. Because they are so familiar and are such a staple of popular piety, preaching on the Beatitudes can be challenging. Along the way the preacher needs to deal with six important matters.

First, the preacher needs to help the congregation place the Beatitudes in the context of the apocalyptic realm of God (or realm of heaven). For Matthew, history is divided into two ages: the present evil era that God will soon end, and the coming realm when all things will take place according to God's purposes of love and justice. God will bring about the final transition from the old age to the new by means of the second coming of Jesus, an apocalypse that will interrupt history.

This context is the key for understanding the first word of each beatitude: "Blessed." To be blessed is not simply to be happy, but to know that one is included in the coming realm.

This notion was important to the Matthean congregation, because they faced both external and internal problems. Externally, they were in tension

Matthew 5:1-12

Theological Perspective

(2) literary—are prominent in the scholarly literature and provide a basis for interpreting specific texts such as the Sermon on the Mount. Among the aims of *social scientific* approaches are the reconstruction of the Matthean community (its religious ethnic identity and its relationship to Judaism) and the retrieval of a social memory (uncovering the social dynamics of the Matthean community's identity as related to the social construction of their history). When we rely upon such approaches to the Gospel of Matthew, the social context, the community's self-identification, and relations between groups serve as the point of departure for interpretation of specific texts, such as the Sermon on the Mount.

Literary approaches stress the importance of interpreting a specific text within its larger narrative context. One of the objectives of literary approaches is to ensure that specific texts are interpreted by contextualizing them. For example, we know who the Jesus of the Sermon on the Mount (chaps. 5–7) is because of what we read in chapters 1–4: his genealogy and conception (1:1–25),the fear of him by imperial and elitist powers (2:1–23), his identity as the judging and saving presence of God (3:1–4:16), and his mission to reveal and enact what the reign of God looks like among humans (4:17–25). When the Sermon is placed in this narrative context, it is interpreted as an envisioning of all that has been foretold as Jesus imagines and commissions an alternative community for his disciples and the crowds who follow him.[2] In the end, both social scientific and literary approaches render interpretation as a matter of contextualizing texts, and these approaches guide theological reflection upon the Sermon that invites us to consider to whom it is addressed, why its particular message, and how disciples of Jesus Christ are to be an alternative community in the present in light of the future reign of God.

Today's text, the opening of the Sermon on the Mount, is an excellent one for doing theological interpretation in tune with contemporary approaches. These first verses, referred to as the Beatitudes (God's blessings), can be placed in both a social and narrative context for discerning the mes-

2. See Anders Runesson, "Re-thinking Early Jewish-Christian Relations: Matthean Community History as Pharisaic Intragroup Conflict," *Journal of Biblical Literature* 127, no. 1 (2008): 95–132, and Samuel Bryskog, "A New Quest for the *Sitz im Leben*: Social Memory, the Jesus Tradition, and the Gospel of Matthew," *New Testament Studies* 52 (2006): 319–36, on social scientific approaches. See Warren Carter, "Powers and Identities: The Contexts of Matthew's Sermon on the Mount," in *Preaching the Sermon on the Mount: The World It Imagines*, ed. David Fleer and Dave Bland (St. Louis: Chalice Press, 2007), 10–14, on a narrative approach.

Pastoral Perspective

wait for the occasional figures like Martin Luther King, Dorothy Day, and Desmond Tutu to show us the way. In the meantime, the world does not get any better, and we remain unfulfilled in our pale expressions of Christian discipleship. The truth is that Jesus meant the Beatitudes to be for everyone. How can such a task be accomplished in our own time?

Living daily into the spirit of the Beatitudes involves looking at them as a collection of the whole, rather than looking at each one individually. Each is related to the others, and they build on one another. Those who are meek, meaning humble, are more likely to hunger and thirst for righteousness, because they remain open to continued knowledge of God. If we approach the Beatitudes this way, we see they invite us into a way of being in the world that leads to particular practices. There are three principles for living into the spirit of the Beatitudes: simplicity, hopefulness, and compassion. These three principles allow us to be in the world, while not being totally shaped by it. We offer an alternative to what the world seems to be pursuing.

Responding to Jesus' instruction, *simplicity* has little to do with lack of sophistication. It has to do with hearing the words of Jesus for what they are, not what we would prefer them to be. We might say that we are open to hearing this teaching for what it simply is, rather than layering it with our own prejudices and subjectivity. That would include the prejudice of already deciding that the task at hand is impossible. The philosopher Søren Kierkegaard made reference to the importance of hearing the Gospel in a "primitive way," stripped of all refinements that we so often bring to any difficult text, in order to avoid its meaning. To approach the Beatitudes simply is to hear the words clearly, without prejudice, and to know that the words are spoken directly to us. We do receive more courage than fear when we hear Jesus saying, "You are blessed in this life whenever you demonstrate humility, bring a peaceful presence, open your heart to others, and show mercy on those who cry for it." Hearing Jesus' words, simply spoken, is the first principle for living into the spirit of the Beatitudes.

There is little disagreement on the lack of *hopefulness* in our world. The distinguished theologian Jürgen Moltmann stated that the death knell of the church is when the overall attitude moves from anger to cynicism.[2] Cynicism differs from anger. Cynicism has decided to accept whatever is,

2. Jürgen Moltmann, *Theology and Joy* (London: SCM Press, 1973).

come "not to abolish but to fulfill" (v. 17). If this reading is correct, it should, nonetheless, not tempt us to read the Beatitudes as ethical imperative rather than eschatological blessings. If the Sermon is the new Torah, the set of Beatitudes, as its preamble, is analogous to the opening claim of the Ten Commandments: "I am the LORD your God, who brought you out of the land of Egypt, out of the house of slavery" (Exod. 20:2). As Moses's Torah is legitimized by the liberation from slavery, Jesus' commandments are the ethics of the promised land.

This leads us to consider a second perspective in which to place these texts: that of the prophet *Isaiah*. If the Beatitudes are imbedded in texts that refer back to Moses and the exodus, the Beatitudes themselves contain a multitude of indirect quotations of Isaiah 61, which itself in turn should be read with an keen eye to all the allusions to Second Isaiah (Isa. 40–55) and the texts concerning the jubilee (Lev. 25). We know about the importance of the Isaiah text in Jesus' ministry: Jesus refers to it in his answer to John the Baptist (Matt. 11:2–6) and in his sermon in the synagogue of Nazareth (Luke 4:14–22). The Beatitudes reflect this importance as well. The Isaiah text speaks of the proclamation of the good news to the poor (Isa. 61:1; Matt. 5:3); of the comforting of all those who mourn (Isa. 61:2; Matt. 5:4); and of the healing of the brokenhearted (Isa. 61:1; cf. Matt. 5:8). Moreover, the LXX translates the Hebrew *'anawîm* (Isa. 61:1) as *praeis*, meek (Matt. 5:5), who shall inherit the earth (*klēronomēsousin tēn gēn*). In addition, the notion of righteousness (Matt. 5:6, 10) resonates with the promises of Isaiah 61:3, 8, 11. The eschatological events promised to an oppressed, brokenhearted, exiled people who are mourning the ruins of their cities have come near. This, by the way, should call our attention to the particular political situation in which these words are spoken. The ethics of the Sermon is not a general ethics; the Beatitudes are not spoken in a vacuum. Jesus' Sermon is addressed to a particular people, Israel, which finds itself in a particular situation: returned from exile, but nonetheless still captive to the empire, oppressed by the soldier's boot, and suffering from robbery and wrongdoing.

Many of the latter ethical passages of the Sermon can be read as Jesus' intervention in a heated contemporary theological and political debate raging between the parties of his day—Zealots, Pharisees, Sadducees, and Essenes: What course should God's people choose under these circumstances? How should they relate to their enemies? How should the

with leaders of traditional Judaism regarding the degree to which the Matthean community was faithfully Jewish. Internally, some people were in tension with one another, and some were drifting away.

Through the Beatitudes, Matthew assures the community that while life may be difficult now, those who faithfully endure can look forward to the realm. When the Beatitudes say that the community is blessed, they do not mean that everyone is bubbly, but that in the midst of turmoil, the congregation can live with confidence because they know they are secure.

The preacher could explore tensions between today's congregation and the larger culture, as well as tensions within the community. How might the promises of the Beatitudes encourage the congregation to remain faithful?

Second, the preacher needs to encourage the congregation to hear the Beatitudes in the indicative mood rather than the imperative. The Beatitudes are not direct calls to action, to become poor in spirit, to mourn, to be meek, and so forth. Rather, the Beatitudes are promises. Indirectly, of course, the Beatitudes do imply that people who have responded positively to the coming of the realm will manifest the values and behaviors that are exemplified in the Beatitudes. However, the preacher who moves too quickly to call people to hunger and thirst for righteousness, to become merciful, and to be pure in heart, and so forth, runs the risk of drifting into legalism and works righteousness.

Third, the preacher needs to help the congregation understand the specific content of each beatitude from the perspective of the first century. People today tend to hear the Beatitudes in terms of casual twenty-first-century associations, but the ancient meanings typically have much more theological muscle. For example, today's naive reader is likely to hear "Blessed are those who mourn" in reference to the sadness that accompanies the death of loved ones. By contrast, Matthew has in mind the mourning of the faithful who recognize that the present condition of the world is far from God's purposes. They see idolatry, injustice, exploitation, and violence, and they mourn. This beatitude promises that "they will be comforted," that is, they will see the realm come. When working with this beatitude, then, the preacher could lead the congregation to name characteristics of life in the contemporary world for which mourning is an appropriate response. The harder preaching task is to help the community identify points at which the manifestations of the realm encourage (bring comfort to) the congregation.

Matthew 5:1-12

Theological Perspective

sage of the text. Jesus delivers the blessings to an audience of followers (his disciples and others) whose sociopolitical context is the Roman Empire and whose religious context is the elite Jewish establishment. What Jesus teaches in the Beatitudes critiques both contexts because of the groups upon whom these blessings are pronounced. Those who receive God's favor are not the privileged classes of the Roman Empire or the Jewish establishment. The Beatitudes are spoken to those groups whom God deems worthy, not by virtue of their own achievements or status in society, but because God chooses to be on the side of the weak, the forgotten, the despised, the justice seekers, the peace makers, and those persecuted because of their beliefs.

When Jesus teaches this message about whom God blesses in his social and religious context, the import of his teaching may be described thus: "The Jesusian political agenda is thus organized around the pursuit of righteousness by those who are able— at potential risk to their own lives—for the sake of a world in which the unvalued (including they themselves when they are persecuted) are at last fully valued as human beings."[3] The narrative context of 5:1–12 is that it follows 4:18–22 (Jesus' calling of his disciples) and 4:23–25 (Jesus' proclaiming his message and healing crowds who follow him). Within this context, these opening verses provide a commissioning that undergirds the necessary instructions (the rest of the Sermon) for Jesus' chosen disciples and others in the crowd who desire to follow Jesus. As Jesus pronounces God's blessings, he frames the call to discipleship in terms of both who they are to be (their character) and its consequences for their lives in the present sociopolitical and religious context, as well as in God's future.

Finally, the theological heart of the Beatitudes is a call to be disciples who live out the virtues of the blessings in pursuit of righteousness grounded in God's righteousness (God's steadfast love, goodness, justice, and mercy). God's blessings are our command, because God first loved us, giving us the blessing of Jesus Christ, our salvation.

MARCIA Y. RIGGS

Pastoral Perspective

regardless of the consequences. Cynicism offers little hope that things will get better. The mantra is "Do not worry about it. That is just the way things are. You will get used to it." The Beatitudes invite us to the opposite point of view, which is hopefulness. We place our hope on Christ, who offered hope to the hopeless. Thus we are able to approach the world with a spirit of hope, even when the outward signs indicate otherwise. When we are hopeful, we stand in the world sure of the possibility that the day will come when mercy, humility, peace, and love are the descriptions of what it means to live.

The third principle of Beatitude living is *compassion.* Compassion is not associated with either pity or sympathy. It goes deeper. To have pity on another person means that you feel sorry for them. Sympathy means that you understand what another person is experiencing, and so you offer some advice. The late Henri Nouwen offers an insightful description: compassion "grows with the inner recognition that your neighbor shares your humanity with you. This partnership cuts through all walls which might have kept you separate. Across all barriers of land and language, wealth and poverty, knowledge and ignorance, we are one, created from the same dust, subject to the same laws, destined for the same end."[3] We are distinct, but more importantly, we share that gift of being created in God's image; thus we belong to one another as family. Compassion requires not walking the same path with a companion, but walking in his or her shoes.

The pastor who wants to apply the Beatitudes to the life of the congregation will look for ways that through study, common prayer, and mutual service the congregation can grow as a blessed community.

Living into the spirit of the Beatitudes with a commitment to simplicity, hopefulness, and compassion is something that we can all do. In the process, we discover this is not irrational at all. It is the only truly rational approach to living.

CHARLES JAMES COOK

3. Tod Lindberg, "What the Beatitudes Teach," *Policy Review*, no. 144 (Aug. and Sept. 2007): 16.

3. Henri Nouwen, *With Open Hands* (New York: Ballantine, 1972), 86.

people of God preserve their identity? Jesus' answer is prefaced and shaped by a unique perspective, as expressed in the Beatitudes: the promises of God about God's reign are about to be fulfilled (cf. the exegesis of next Sunday's Gospel text, pp. 333–37).

However, in saying so, Jesus does more than just proclaim the coming of the kingdom of God; he also says that the coming of the kingdom is bound up with his own ministry. This leads to a third and final exegetical perspective on the Beatitudes: they should be read from a *christological perspective*, and this in a threefold sense. First, in taking up Isaiah 61 to characterize his ministry, Jesus casts himself in the role of the one who is speaking in the Isaiah text: "The spirit of the Lord GOD is upon me, because the LORD has anointed me; he has sent me to bring good news . . ." (Isa. 61:1). Matthew underscores this point in his narrative, wherein the mission of Christ is bound up with the guidance of the Spirit and the witness of God (1:18, 20; 3:16, 17; 4:1–11, 17, 23–25). However, second, Matthew casts Jesus not only in the role of the eschatological agent, but also as the one who embodies the characteristics mentioned in the beatitudes: he is the one who is meek (11:29, 21:5), who is merciful (9:27, 15:22, 20:30), and who is persecuted for righteousness' sake. Finally, while not explicit in the text, it is certainly in the spirit of the Gospel to see therefore also the eschatological future as bound up with the presence of Christ. The one who is meek and persecuted inherits the earth and receives the kingdom, because it is he who is "seated at the right hand of Power and coming on the clouds of heaven" (26:64).

The Sermon, therefore, becomes an eschatological declaration of God's reign and promise for God's people.

EDWIN CHR. VAN DRIEL

Fourth, the preacher needs to decide whether to preach on all of the beatitudes in one sermon, or whether to preach from a small group of representative beatitudes, perhaps even on a single beatitude. In the former case, the preacher has a wonderful opportunity to help the congregation toward a general vision of living faithfully toward the realm. Not long ago, a lay person told me that she gets "bits and pieces" of the Christian life from sermon to sermon but seldom gets "the big picture." Using the broad strokes of the Beatitudes, the sermon could offer such a vision.

Taking another tack, the preacher could note that the Beatitudes are not a comprehensive list of attitudes and behaviors of living toward the realm. The Beatitudes use the specific nine qualities as representative of many others. The preacher might create fresh beatitudes using issues and language from today.

As noted, the preacher could also focus on a limited group of beatitudes, perhaps even a single one. In this case the preacher would consider which beatitude(s) speak most importantly to the congregation's current context.

Fifth, while the Beatitudes do not directly suggest a detailed form or genre for the sermon, they do suggest a function and a tone. In grammatical terms, the Beatitudes are not imperatives (commands) but are indicative statements—descriptions of the way things are. The function of the Beatitudes in this regard is a model for the sermon. The preacher could lure people to the promise of the realm (in the manner of the Beatitudes) rather than exhorting or badgering them. Indeed, hearing the sermon could itself become an experience of blessing.

Sixth, the preacher needs to help the congregation recognize that the Beatitudes are Jewish in character. Christians sometimes see the Beatitudes (and the Sermon on the Mount) as an innovation in religious thought, even superseding Judaism. A bitter irony is that the church has used these realm-anticipating Beatitudes to justify the brutal treatment of Jewish people. In fact, the ideas in the Beatitudes and the Sermon on the Mount are Jewish in origin. The innovative element is not in their core theological content but in interpreting the ministry of Jesus as signaling that the realm and the apocalypse are at hand. A preacher could help the congregation discover how the values at the core of the Beatitudes are shared with the synagogue down the street.

RONALD J. ALLEN

Isaiah 58:1-9a (9b–12)

¹Shout out, do not hold back!
  Lift up your voice like a trumpet!
  Announce to my people their rebellion,
    to the house of Jacob their sins.
²Yet day after day they seek me
  and delight to know my ways,
  as if they were a nation that practiced righteousness
    and did not forsake the ordinance of their God;
  they ask of me righteous judgments,
    they delight to draw near to God.
³"Why do we fast, but you do not see?
  Why humble ourselves, but you do not notice?"
  Look, you serve your own interest on your fast day,
    and oppress all your workers.
⁴Look, you fast only to quarrel and to fight
  and to strike with a wicked fist.
  Such fasting as you do today
    will not make your voice heard on high.
⁵Is such the fast that I choose,
  a day to humble oneself?
  Is it to bow down the head like a bulrush,
    and to lie in sackcloth and ashes?
  Will you call this a fast,
    a day acceptable to the LORD?

⁶Is not this the fast that I choose:
  to loose the bonds of injustice,

Theological Perspective

With gusto and rhetorical skill, the poet Isaiah delivers a divine indictment against the people of Judah (vv. 1–5) and instructs them on the nature of true fasting (vv. 6–9a). The main character in the poem is God, who speaks through the prophet. Here the prophet anticipates Matthew 25:31–46, the judgment on the nations, but also draws on a rich and long tradition of prophetic proclamations against false worship (e.g., Amos 5:18–27), citing that worship without justice has no value in the eyes of God.

The people to whom this proclamation is addressed are outwardly religious despite their transgressions, namely, their lack of righteousness and their disregard for Torah (v. 2). A gap exists between their seeking God and God's ways and their actual way of life, which reveals the people's hypocrisy. This people seek God relentlessly, delight to know God's ways, ask for righteous judgments from God, and enjoy drawing near to God (v. 2). They fast; they humble themselves; yet God does not take notice (v. 3a). Not surprisingly, Judah's religious practices

Pastoral Perspective

Isaiah does not realize how good he has it. His people can hardly wait to get themselves out of bed and into worship. They "seek God" and "delight" to know God's ways. They "delight to draw near to God." There is nothing they would rather do than fast. Worship is not quite so attractive to YHWH's followers in my city, not even to a lot of members of my church. Church is not the first place that most people go when searching for delight. Coffee shops and book stores are open on Sunday mornings, the games start at noon, and while worship at our church is optional, kids' sports teams have mandatory practice. The few parishioners who decide to fast during Lent this year will not "delight" in skipping lunch.

No pastor, of course, needs to be told that many mainline North American churches are in crisis. We hear enough about it in the journals, from the seminaries, and in conversations with colleagues and friends. Budgets, membership, and attendance are all down across the board. There is a surprising consensus that the mainline church has to change or die.

to undo the thongs of the yoke,
        to let the oppressed go free,
        and to break every yoke?
    ⁷Is it not to share your bread with the hungry,
        and bring the homeless poor into your house;
    when you see the naked, to cover them,
        and not to hide yourself from your own kin?
    ⁸Then your light shall break forth like the dawn,
        and your healing shall spring up quickly;
    your vindicator shall go before you,
        the glory of the LORD shall be your rear guard.
    ⁹Then you shall call, and the LORD will answer;
        you shall cry for help, and he will say, Here I am.

    If you remove the yoke from among you,
        the pointing of the finger, the speaking of evil,
    ¹⁰if you offer your food to the hungry
        and satisfy the needs of the afflicted,
    then your light shall rise in the darkness
        and your gloom be like the noonday.
    ¹¹The LORD will guide you continually,
        and satisfy your needs in parched places,
        and make your bones strong;
    and you shall be like a watered garden,
        like a spring of water,
        whose waters never fail.
    ¹²Your ancient ruins shall be rebuilt;
        you shall raise up the foundations of many generations;
    you shall be called the repairer of the breach,
        the restorer of streets to live in.

Exegetical Perspective

The Situation. Today's OT text is part of the final section of the book of Isaiah, chapters 56–66, commonly known as Third Isaiah. The prophetic ministry of the original Isaiah of Jerusalem (ca. 738–701 BCE; chaps. 1–39) gave rise to an Isaiah tradition, perhaps preserved by a school of disciples (Isa. 8:16–17). Nearly a century and a half later (ca. 540 BCE; chaps. 40–55) Second Isaiah—an anonymous, passionate, lyrical poet of the exile—foresaw the liberation of Judah from Babylonian captivity and the glory of a restored land of promise. Not long after, yet another voice was added to the book of Isaiah. Now the setting is Jerusalem and Judea restored after 538 BCE (see Isa. 62:6–7). The temple, however, apparently remains in ruins: "Our holy and beautiful house, where our ancestors praised you, has been burned by fire, and all our pleasant places have become ruins" (64:11; see also 58:12; 61:4). Because Ezra 6:15 reliably dates the rededication of the temple at 515 BCE, we can guess that this anonymous Third Isaiah prophesied between 538 and 515.

Homiletical Perspective

Preachers who follow the lectionary are usually good at ambiguity. We know how to preach, "On the one hand . . . but on the other hand . . ." What throws some of us is a clear-cut text without any haziness. Isaiah 58 is a harsh, unequivocal call for religious people to worship in a way that leads them to care for the hurting.

Most cities in the United States have more churches than gas stations. Every Sunday morning we go to our worship services and say our prayers. In some churches, those prayers are written out. In some, they are not even thought out. We all sing. In some churches it is three hymns and the Gloria Patri. In others, it is a dozen choruses. In some, people genuflect. In others, they dance. In other churches, worshipers hardly move. Some churches try to make everything seem very today. Others make everything seem fifty years ago. Our churches are filled with good people. On Sunday morning at 11:00, when so many are in church, our cities seem like good places.

Isaiah 58:1-9a (9b–12)

Theological Perspective

and way of life are no different from those of their Canaanite ancestors whose religious practice was to pressure the gods into performing various functions. Ironically the only fast commanded by the law was the Day of Atonement (Lev. 23:26–32). Hence, some of God's people are overzealous, and unfortunately, their zeal is for their self-serving interests.

While they are engaging in pious rituals, they are oppressing their own workers and becoming embroiled in quarrels and fights (vv. 3b–4). This dichotomous situation is the root cause for the absence of a divine response to their "self-sacrifices." Furthermore, the people's fasting includes other pious yet empty acts, such as bowing down their heads and wearing sackcloth and ashes (v. 5). The theological point is clear: acts of religious piety as private acts of devotion are meaningless when they are divorced from acts of justice and righteousness.

In verses 6–7 the poet gives voice to God, who reveals the kind of fast that is most desirable. This kind of fast does not include the usual abstention from food and drink. Rather, the fast desired is outreach to those in need, which involves not only feeding the hungry, clothing the naked, and caring for one's own, but also addressing the attitudes and structures responsible for injustices. According to Torah, "hiding oneself from one's own kin" (v. 7b) means pretending that some people do not exist or that care will be given to the needy by someone else. Deuteronomy 22:1–4 gives a clear instruction that assistance is not to be withheld. Thus, true fasting involves dealing with those conditions, situations, and people that are ethically corrupting and corrupted, for the sake of the oppressed individual and for the common good. In the text, God does not reject the practice of fasting, but insists that the practice be transformative for the community.

In the ancient Near East, fasting was meant to influence a deity to act on behalf of the one fasting. Usually, a fast occurred to ease a drought, to abate a military invasion, to exorcise a demon, or to lessen the severity of a political or economic crisis. The act of lying in sackcloth and ashes was a sign of mourning, lament, and penitence. Here God's people have been given a new instruction on fasting that has as its end "right relationship." This type of fast, different from other kinds of fasts, brings with it four personal blessings: (1) new life; (2) healing; (3) security; and (4) a free-flowing relationship with God (vv. 8–9). As the one seeking God responds to the needs of another, so God will respond to the one who seeks.

Pastoral Perspective

There are "postliberal," "postmodern" or "post-Constantinian" Christians; "new monastic," or "new Reformation" Christians—anything to distinguish ourselves from what came before. Often this change is most concentrated in the worship life of the church. Churches experiment with "contemporary," "emergent," "charismatic," "praise," or even "postliturgical" styles. In identifying the mistakes of the past and avoiding those mistakes in the present, the hope is that the people of God can secure a new future.

Isaiah's people too are looking back to figure out what went wrong that led to their demise. They too have to rethink what it means to worship the God of Israel in a "post" world: posttemple, postexile, post-Davidic monarchy. Worship for them has become a proxy for all of the change that must occur if the covenant community is going to avoid the mistakes of the past and secure a new future.

Worship style and practice are not what pleases or offends God, according to Isaiah. Worship style and practice are not to blame for the exilic decline of the community. They are not the measuring sticks by which the people of God will be judged. They will not restore or preserve a relationship with God in and of themselves. This is a curious thing to say to a community reconstituting itself following a return from exile. It is a frustrating thing to say to a church trying to reinvent itself, beginning with the practice of worship. Worship is the most important thing we do together. It is the place that forms us into the people of God. It is the place where we inhale God's love and grace, so that we can be sent forth to exhale God's love and grace in a broken world in need of redemption.

The critique that God offers through the mouth of Isaiah is that the more Israel has become self-conscious about its improved worship life, the less it has remained open to God's vision for the community. Praise, prayer, and fasting are cherished not as gifts that nurture the covenantal relationship, but as techniques for drawing attention to its human participants. That is why the people spend so much time in worship, according to Isaiah. They fast so that God will see them. They humble themselves so that God will notice (v. 3). They fast to make their voices heard by God.

Isaiah is concerned that the obsession with right worship distracts the people from what really determines the future of the community—its effort to fulfill the ethical obligations of justice. In Isaiah's imagination, the rejection of the practice of justice is the cause of exile. The future of the community will

Exegetical Perspective

This Isaiah speaks in a voice more muted than that of the Isaiah of the exile. Our passage for today suggests that the people have reverted to some of their old forms of false worship. Elsewhere we hear that they are engaging in idolatry (57:13), perverting justice (59:4), and eating the flesh of swine (65:4). Yet this Isaiah can also sound themes of extraordinary hope and joy. Through him or her, God repeatedly promises that the "wealth of nations" will flow to restored Jerusalem (e.g., 60:5–7; 61:6; 66:12), as though Jerusalem and Judah will emerge at the center of a worldwide polity in which YHWH exercises universal hegemony and Israel, as God's people on earth, takes the leading role. Third Isaiah speaks of the ingathering of the exiles from Diaspora (60:4) and uses the audacious imagery of the Mighty One of Jacob giving leave to the elect people to "suck the milk of nations . . . suck the breasts of kings" (60:16). The vision of the peaceable kingdom articulated by earlier prophets is repeated in the futuristic vision in Isaiah 65:25. The vision of the restored Jerusalem in 60:1–22 is so exalted that the NT Apocalypse found in it language adequate to describe the new Jerusalem (Rev. 21:23–26).

Faithless Fasting (vv. 1–5). Obviously not all of these themes appear in today's pericope. In fact, this passage contains only these three elements: (a) a critique of ritual behavior (in this case, fasting) that substitutes outward form for inner commitment (the same outrage that animated last week's text, Mic. 6:1–8); (b) statements of the social gospel of Third Isaiah and, for that matter, of the rest of the prophets; and (c) promises of restoration, satisfaction, and happiness that flow from obedience to this prophetic torah. The prophet is charged to announce to the people how they have gone astray, thinking they are practicing righteousness when in fact their ritual fasting is hypocritical and self-serving. Through the prophet, to those who say, "Why do we fast, but you do not see?" the Lord replies, "You serve your own interest on your fast day" (v. 3). With three embarrassing rhetorical questions (v. 5), YHWH exposes the phoniness of sackcloth and ashes put on in self-interest. The answer to all three questions is no.

Faithful "Fasting" and Its Reward (vv. 6–9a). In this section, YHWH, speaking through the prophet, succinctly states the essential tenets of the social ethics of the prophets (vv. 6–7). This "prophetic torah" in no way conflicts with the Torah of Moses, but characterizes the righteous life as it would have been

Homiletical Perspective

Our hometowns, however, are not always good for everyone. Most cities try to hide the homeless. Prejudice makes every day more difficult for minorities. The working poor have it hard. The lack of public transportation makes keeping a job complicated. The mentally ill fall through the cracks. The distance between the haves and the have-nots keeps growing. We know which parts of town to avoid.

For all the progress that has been made, it is still hard for women to compete for some jobs. It is difficult to be old in a society that idealizes youth. It is not easy to be single in a culture that is designed for couples. It is hard to be gay when many are quick to ostracize. Some cities are not easy places to be a stranger. Newcomers may feel as though our hometowns are clubs that are not accepting any new members. An outsider might find it hard to make the connections between what happens on Sunday morning and the many in our cities who hurt all week long.

Is it possible that some come to church only to spend time with their friends? Are there people who yawn through worship? Do you know any teenagers who spend the service writing notes?

Most people in most churches know all *about* the Christian faith, but they get bored during worship. How can they do that? How can anyone go to sleep ten minutes after singing "Holy, Holy, Holy"? How can anyone not pay attention when Holy Scripture is being read? Lots of churchgoers know everything about worship except that it should change us. Cities in which so many go to church on Sunday ought to show the results of their worship in the quality of their lives from Monday through Saturday.

Part of the problem is that preachers give in to the temptation to share only what listeners want to hear. The worship of God easily becomes a reflection of the values of the culture. The church carefully selects the words that will attract crowds. Many look for congregations that offer comfort rather than challenge. Churches begin to value survival more than courage.

During Isaiah's time, the temple in Jerusalem was standing room only. No one missed a service. They sang psalms—old ones, new ones, all kinds of psalms. They said prayers and gave offerings.

What they did not do was let worship trouble their consciences. If they kept their distance from God, then they could also keep their distance from God's children. They did not want to make connections between their worship and their neighbors. They ignored the poor and everyone else they wanted to ignore.

Isaiah 58:1-9a (9b–12)

Theological Perspective

In sum, the community's responsiveness to one another has a direct effect on how God will respond to the community. Isaiah instructs his listeners that when they live out a life of love in accordance with Torah, God will answer them when they call (v. 9). Theologically, Isaiah's proclamation heralds a vision of worship that must exceed faithfulness to external practices and rituals. Isaiah redefines worship as a lived experience of being in "right relationship" with one another and with God, made manifest through ethical practice rooted in and flowing from divine love (see Deut. 6:1–8), which demands justice, righteousness, and compassion.

Many of the early church fathers' understanding of fasting was influenced by the poetry of Isaiah. For example, according to Ephrem, fasting should never be used to serve one's own end. For Cyril, drawing near to God was associated with living a life worthy of God, not just asking God to draw near in favor and providence. Cassian makes clear that fasting without good works is neither pleasing nor acceptable to God. Many of the ancient church fathers and members of religious orders fasted on a regular basis, but always the fast was connected to their life of prayer and good works. Fasting was a means of freeing one's self to receive the gifts of God, which were always intended for the common good.

For many communities of faith today, fasting is primarily a pious deed associated with various holy days and ritual celebrations. Fasting usually consists of the reduction of food to one full meal. For example, Roman Catholics are required to fast during Fridays in Lent and before receiving Eucharist. In Eastern Orthodoxy and Greek Catholicism, fasting is an important spiritual discipline and is performed during four "fasting seasons." The rules of fasting are extensive. In Protestant communities, fasting is encouraged as part of Lent and sometimes Advent. Observant Jews fast up to six days, with Yom Kippur being the only fast day ordained in the Torah. Tension exists between Isaiah's vision of fasting and contemporary fasting associated with piety and ritual. Isaiah's vision can inform the ritual of fasting, reminding the one fasting that the goal is not only personal holiness but also, and perhaps more importantly, the fullness of life for all creation as God envisioned.

CAROL J. DEMPSEY

Pastoral Perspective

be determined by its willingness to embrace justice and a new sense of community—the very ethic that forms the content of the people's worship. Isaiah's call to this new fasting becomes the cornerstone that joins worship and Christian discipleship.

One year during Holy Week, a few Christians from well-endowed congregations in a major metropolitan area spent a night with homeless friends on the street. They were looking for the suffering Christ in the lives of those who spend their days and nights suffering from hunger, disease, and rejection. It was a chilly night, and rain rolled in close to midnight. Looking for shelter, the handful of travelers felt fortunate to come upon a church holding an all-night prayer vigil. The leader of the group was a pastor of one of the most respected churches in the city. As she stepped through the outer doors of the church, a security guard stopped her. She explained that she and the rest of their group were Christians. They had no place to stay and were wet and miserable, and would like to rest and pray. Enticed by the lighted warmth of the sanctuary, she had forgotten that her wet, matted hair and disheveled clothing left her looking like just another homeless person from the street. The security guard was friendly, but explained in brutal honesty, "I was hired to keep homeless people like you out." As the dejected group made their way back into the misery of the night, they knew they had found their suffering Christ, locked out of the church.

Isaiah would not have been surprised. Just like the city church, his people had every intention of excelling in their worship of God. Their intentions may have been as pure as the intentions of those who held vigil all through the night in the name of their God. Even so, their worship was a fraud. True fasting—and, by extension, true worship—leads not simply to a reordering of the liturgy, but a reordering of the life of the community. Those who have share with those who need, those who are free loosen the bonds of those who are yoked with injustice, and those with shelter extend it to the homeless. What concerns God is not our reordering of worship, but how worship reorders us.

ANDREW FOSTER CONNORS

understood in Israel. It contrasts the fast of the foolish with the fast that YHWH demands, which is no fast at all, but consists instead of acts of justice, liberation, and care for the hungry, homeless, and naked. This is the ethic to which prophets early and late summoned the people Israel. In the very first chapter of Isaiah, the prophet of Jerusalem expresses concern for the orphan and the widow (two especially vulnerable groups of people, for whom the Torah of Moses made explicit provision; see Exod. 22:21–24). In Isaiah 1:12–17, the people are summoned to "cease to do evil; learn to do good" (vv. 16–17) after a polemic against insincere and manipulative worship—the exact sequence of the text before us. Examples can be multiplied. Amos, an eighth-century-BCE Israelite contemporary of Isaiah of Jerusalem, voices YHWH's rejection of cult and in diametrical opposition cries, "Let justice roll down like waters, and righteousness like an ever-flowing stream" (Amos 5:24). Another contemporary of Isaiah of Jerusalem, the prophet Micah, juxtaposes prophetic torah with hollow worship, as we saw in the lection for last Sunday (Mic. 6:1–8).

No one need have any doubt about how he or she should relate to the community. To those who do in fact reject empty form and turn with compassion to the helpless, God makes promises (vv. 8–9a). These culminate in a wonderful assurance of divine constancy: "Then you shall call, and the LORD will answer; you shall cry for help, and he will say, Here I am" (v. 9a).

"If . . . Then": The Conditionality of Promise (vv. 9b–12). The same sequence, prophetic torah followed by divine promise, structures the final segment of this text. It differs rhetorically from verses 6–9a only in its conditional structure. "If" fingers are not pointed (the obnoxious behavior of the scoundrel and the villain who seek to blame the innocent [Prov. 6:12–15]), and food is offered to the hungry and the afflicted are ministered unto, "then" the promise follows. You, the righteous, shall shine like a beacon in the darkness, "and your gloom [shall] be like the noonday" (v. 10). The promise concludes with lovely similes that liken the righteous people to a watered garden (v. 11), and "the repairer of the breach, the restorer of streets to live in" (v. 12). The references to ancient ruins being rebuilt and streets restored point to the tasks confronting the returned exiles; however, they can remain undaunted because "The LORD will . . . satisfy your needs" (v. 11).

W. SIBLEY TOWNER

God told Isaiah, "Go tell them what's what. Blow the trumpet. Shout it loud. Tell them what hypocrites they are" (v. 1).

Preachers who have wished that God would tell them exactly what to say need to look carefully at what Isaiah had to preach. The trumpet was often used to summon the Israelites to war. God tells Isaiah it will make a fine introduction to the sermon.

Isaiah's people appear to be very religious. They not only go to worship daily; they also fast frequently. The people complain that they have observed the fasts, but God has not answered their prayers. Isaiah has to point out that the wealthy are fasting on the holy days, but their employees still have to work (v. 3). God requires both worship and merciful attention to others.

Those who attend worship services usually do not appreciate having their insincerity pointed out, but Isaiah tells them that religious people can be the most quarrelsome (v. 4). The prophet sounds sarcastic (v. 5) when he calls them to the kind of worship that does more than anesthetize the conscience.

While the people believed fasting made them look good, God wants worshipers to fast as a means of sharing with others (vv. 6–7). Those listening to Isaiah must have been relieved when he began to list the benefits of genuine worship—light, healing, and protection (v. 8).

God will respond when the barrier of insincere worship has been removed. Evil can be set aside and replaced with kindness. God's people will share their food with the poor, understanding that not only do the hungry need our food, but also God's people need the hungry. It is in giving that our "gloom [will] be like the noonday" (v. 10).

How would your congregation respond to this call to worship? "We hope you are not planning to go through the motions in worship, singing the songs but never engaging your hearts, hearing the Scripture but not listening for God, or giving an offering but not giving yourselves, because if so, you are not doing God any favors. You do not get points for attendance. If you really worship God today, then you will share with the poor, listen to the lonely, and stop avoiding those in need."

The preacher who dares to preach as Isaiah preached will tell those who come to church that if they are not there to give themselves to God, then they should have stayed at home.

BRETT YOUNGER

Psalm 112:1-9 (10)

¹Praise the LORD!
  Happy are those who fear the LORD,
  who greatly delight in his commandments.
²Their descendants will be mighty in the land;
  the generation of the upright will be blessed.
³Wealth and riches are in their houses,
  and their righteousness endures forever.
⁴They rise in the darkness as a light for the upright;
  they are gracious, merciful, and righteous.
⁵It is well with those who deal generously and lend,
  who conduct their affairs with justice.

Theological Perspective

One main theological theme in this psalm is that all children of God are engaged in learning and teaching wisdom. The duty and delight of keeping the law is beautifully laid out in this perfect alphabetic acrostic psalm, which begins with a chorus of alleluia, "Praise the LORD!" Even though there is no single word indicating the teaching element in this psalm text, the form itself indicates that the psalm is favored by teachers of the law. They can use the psalm as a primary resource for their lesson plan to help students memorize the verses on the law. The role of educators in teaching ministry is not to force knowledge into the learners but to encourage them by passing on what it means to live this life as Christians.

The first letters of each line are the twenty-two letters of the Hebrew alphabet in order, two lines each for verses 1–8 and three lines for verses 9 and 10. This alphabet psalm may give fun and excitement to all ages as they memorize it. It is a learning tool for content and can be important throughout the learner's life.

The didactic function of this psalm matches the catechetical function of the Christian sacraments. Teaching the centrality of God's Word takes many different forms of liturgy and sacrament as well as personal devotion. The word "catechesis" means

Pastoral Perspective

Psalm 112 is one of nine psalms in the Hebrew Scripture to use acrostic, a marvelous aid to memory, as well as a delight to the ear. Acrostic is a device that begins successive lines of the psalm with successive letters of a word or other easily remembered group of letters such as the alphabet. I have occasionally attempted to approximate the acrostic of one of the nine psalms, at least partially, in a sermon, so as to give the English reader of the psalm some very crude sense of what the Hebrew poetry does far more elegantly. Such an attempt, using the first seven letters of the English alphabet to begin seven lines of the beginning verses of Psalm 112, is offered with many apologies to the great poets of Israel.

Alleluia!
Blessed are those who live in deep awe of YHWH.
Contentment and delight in God's commandments
  are theirs; and their
Descendants will be mighty in the land.
Each generation of the upright shall be blessed.
Fortune and abundance shall undergird their
  homes, and
Goodness and righteousness shall endure with them
  forever.[1]

1. Obviously, the desire to illustrate in English what the acrostic device does in the Hebrew overrides considerations of careful attention to exact translation. I hope I remain true to the general intent of the Hebrew. I make no pretense of maintaining the original quality of the poetry.

⁶For the righteous will never be moved;
   they will be remembered forever.
⁷They are not afraid of evil tidings;
   their hearts are firm, secure in the Lᴏʀᴅ.
⁸Their hearts are steady, they will not be afraid;
   in the end they will look in triumph on their foes.
⁹They have distributed freely, they have given to the poor;
   their righteousness endures forever;
   their horn is exalted in honor.
¹⁰The wicked see it and are angry;
   they gnash their teeth and melt away;
   the desire of the wicked comes to nothing.

Exegetical Perspective

Psalm 112 is a Wisdom psalm, a type of psalm closely connected with the wisdom tradition represented by Proverbs, Job, and Ecclesiastes. The Psalter includes a number of Wisdom psalms, such as Psalms 37, 49, 73, 127, and 128. Like other works of Wisdom literature, these psalms project a world in which those who obey God are happy, while those who disobey are miserable. Although Proverbs, Job, and Ecclesiastes tend to use the contrasting terms "wise" and "foolish," Wisdom psalms usually refer instead to the "righteous" and the "wicked."

Psalm 111 and Psalm 112 form a closely related pair. Both center on the theme of the happiness of those who follow God. Psalm 111 focuses on God's power and goodness in providing for those who follow the Lord. It gives a top-down perspective. Psalm 112, on the other hand, views the situation from the ground up, describing all the benefits and security that comes to those who fear the Lord.

These two psalms have an additional feature in common: both are acrostics. After the initial command, "Praise the Lᴏʀᴅ!" both are structured in such a way that each successive phrase begins with a different letter of the Hebrew alphabet in sequential order.[1]

1. Other examples of acrostic psalms are Pss. 9–10 (taken together), 25, 34, 111, 119, and 145.

Homiletical Perspective

Psalm 112 is an exhortation. It begins with the call to "Praise the Lᴏʀᴅ!" then gives the reason for doing so: those who fear the Lord are happy. The text assumes that the audience fears the Lord and keeps the commandments; therefore, they ought to praise God because of all the blessings described in verses 2–9.

A preacher can make the same assumptions. It is still the case that those who live faithfully are happy. They may not experience continuous pleasure, and they will face trials, but there are lasting joys to be found in a life of faith.

In making this claim, though, one should be cautious. Two of the blessings the psalm promises the faithful are problematic: that they "will be mighty in the land" (v. 2a) and that they will have "wealth and riches" (v. 3a). These claims call to mind the prosperity gospel that often enriches the preacher far more than the congregation. It is worthy of note that in this text the mighty in the land are also upright, just, and righteous; and that the wealthy and rich are generous and give freely. Blessings are given so that they can be shared.

In some contexts it might be necessary to address the idea of the fear of the Lord (v. 1). Preachers may be so familiar with Scripture that they forget how disturbing this idea is to a contemporary seeker. People do not come to churches to be told to be afraid.

Psalm 112:1-9 (10)

Theological Perspective

instruction by word of mouth, especially by questioning and answering. Though it may apply to any subject matter, it is commonly used for instruction in the elements of sacraments, especially in preparation for initiation into the Christian community. Cathechesis refers both to the act of instructing and the subject matter of the instruction—both method and content.

The instructional element of Wisdom literature is firmly grounded in the admonition to "fear the LORD." The word "fear" does not give adequate justice to the Hebrew term's breadth of meaning. The positive meaning of "fear" is respect for the one we know is in control of our total lives. This comprehension is woven into this acrostic song, which projects symbolic meanings of God as alpha and omega, the beginning and end, aleph and tau, and everything in between.

The content begins with "Alleluia!" followed by the trademark of Wisdom literature: "Happy are those who fear the LORD." The joy and delight are expressed in this duty, and we are asked to follow in action. The moral development process of contemporary psychology comes with many steps of educational methodology, according to each age group of the learners, and repeated practice of community enforcement. The teaching of the psalmist and the community is presented in a perfect form of a word game that portrays the perfect character of the one who fears the Lord.

Following the same pattern as Psalm 111, the psalm repeats and reinforces the prior teaching of God's greatness, singing what it means to be the person who stands in the happiness of the Lord, completely satisfied to be in the shining light, even in the world of darkness (v. 4).

In Isaiah 58:1–9a (9b–12), today's Hebrew Bible reading, Israel has strictly followed the law regarding fasting, but the Lord seems not pleased with the action. Why? "Because they pursue their own interests," according to the Lord. They call attention to their fasting while continuing to quarrel and fight and to oppress others. Do you think God approves of that? The lesson is that we are to give aid to the hungry, the homeless, the naked. When we liberate others, we will see God's favor shine like the dawning of the sun's light.

The light of Epiphany and Christmas is behind us in this Ordinary Time of the church year. We may even have forgotten the excitements of the liturgy that led us through the feast time of the holy days. Now, before we enter the time of fasting during Lent

Pastoral Perspective

Both the device of the acrostic and the poetry itself remind us that the Psalms are not simply to be read over quickly, but are to be committed to memory, so that the words form part of our own faith-based consciousness. In many ways pastoral ministry is dedicated to building communities that remember and live out such visions of the faithful and obedient life. Church education, music, mission outreach are ways of embodying what the heart learns to remember and cherish.

The reader who is familiar with the Wisdom literature of Scripture will recognize the list of virtues for the wise person, the attributes that make for the good life. I wonder just how anachronistic this list of virtues will sound to anyone in the congregation under thirty-five, who happens to be visiting, perhaps coerced there by parents while on a rare visit home. This list of what makes for happiness is so far from what he or she has been taught by Madison Avenue and Hollywood and the magazines of fashion industry. Our culture teaches that the light dawns in the darkness and shines upon those with the biggest toys. Those who will be remembered are the ones who made the most noise. Happiness is harder, but it has something to do with getting one's way as much as possible, so power is important. So, as a preacher called to translate these psalms into something that will make a difference in the lives of the people in my mission field, which is the contemporary American culture, how do I even begin?

I begin with what they know: that what they have been sold is a lie. They may not know how to articulate it. They may still be under the influence of the lie, still following its precepts and teachings (and are we not all, to some extent), but something in them is still restless and unfulfilled and hungry for something more. So you point out the lie. If self-care, for example, is the true way to happiness, how much self-care does it take? How many massages, how many aroma therapy candles? Do you need the $35 candles, or will the $10 candles do? How do you know? The only authority on the subject is the aroma therapy candle salesperson, of course, who is going to say, "You get what you pay for." So, of course, if you really care about yourself, you are going to buy the $35 candles. See the problem? Self-care is so self-referential that it has us going in circles.

Suppose the point of your life is not self-care. Suppose the whole point of your life and the true way to happiness is to live in awe of God and to obey God's commandments (which Rabbi Jesus simplified

Exegetical Perspective

It is possible that the acrostic format was used in order to aid memorization. The acrostic form is not immediately apparent in English translations, however, as it is difficult to reproduce accurately. In addition to the difficulty posed by the fact that the Hebrew alphabet has twenty-two letters while the English has twenty-six, finding English terms with the same meanings that begin with the correct letters is almost impossible. A rough translation, however, of a short section of Psalm 112 can capture some of the feel of the acrostic:

> ¹Anyone who fears the Lord is happy,
>   Because they delight in God's commandments.
> ²Children of theirs will be mighty in the land,
>   Descendants of the upright will be blessed.
>   (my trans.)

Although such a translation retains the feature of the acrostic, it sometimes obscures the meaning and flow of the original. For this reason, few translations attempt to reproduce the acrostic form in translation.

Although the initial letters in English do not reflect the acrostic, the overall acrostic structure is still visible in most English translations. The NRSV, for example, accurately divides the phrases according to the acrostic format. This gives the psalm twenty-two phrases, most of which are grouped into two-phrase verses.[2] The exceptions to this are verses 9–10. The fact that these two verses have three phrases apiece is not accidental; it plays a structural role in dividing the psalm. Verse 9 closes out the first part of the psalm, while verse 10 changes to a reflection on the fate of the unrighteous.

An additional structural feature of Psalm 112 is the near repetition of the phrases in verses 3b, 6b, and 9c. Both verses 3b and 9c read "their righteousness endures forever," while verse 6b says that "they will be remembered forever." This repeated statement of the enduring quality of the righteous divides the psalm into its three major sections: verses 1–3, verses 4–6, and verses 7–9. Verse 10 closes out the psalm with a negative reflection on the wicked.

Psalm 112 begins with the expression "Praise the LORD" (Heb. *halelu yah*), a feature that ties it together with Psalm 111. It then moves into the initial section, which extols those who fear the Lord and keep the commandments. The rewards it envisions include both material prosperity and numerous descendants. In Hebrew, the psalm speaks of the

2. The psalm has twenty-two phrases, because *sin* and *shin* are treated as one letter.

Homiletical Perspective

What, then, is the fear of the Lord? Is it terror? Is it awe, a recognition of one's own smallness in the face of the Divine? If it is the latter, the second half of the verse is easier to explain. The faithful delight in God's commandments because, awestruck in the face of God's immensity, they find in the commandments a rock of stability. Delight in the commandments, then, is a response of gratitude rather than of terror.

A preacher might use this text to address conflict in a congregation. If the community is in turmoil, the first verse can be turned around and put to the congregation as a question: if those who fear the Lord and keep the commandments are happy, and we are not happy, then do we truly fear the Lord and keep the commandments? If not, what keeps us from it? The descriptions of those who do fear the Lord repeatedly mention our treatment of one another. In what ways are we falling short?

The word "forever" appears three times in the text. Those who fear the Lord "will be remembered forever" (v. 6), and "their righteousness endures forever" (vv. 3, 9). There have been, however, countless millions of faithful people who are not remembered today. Is the text untrue? Are they remembered through the ramifications of their righteous actions?

Verses 7–8 speak a message especially needed today. The life of faith frees us from a life of fear. In the age of terrorism and nuclear weapons, cataclysmic violence is always a possibility. A sermon might examine how it is that, in the face of that threat, our hearts are "secure in the LORD" (v. 7b).

Does faith lead to military victory, as verse 8b implies? Believers might hesitate to make this claim. In the case of terrorism, though, perhaps steady hearts and freedom from fear are the true triumph. Without the weapon of fear, the desire of the wicked truly comes to nothing.

The psalm's rhetorical structure offers tools for preaching it. For example, the text begins with the claim that those who fear the Lord are happy, and it closes with the contrasting claim that the wicked are angry and come to nothing. Verse 10 is optional in the lectionary, and preachers may wish not to end on a negative note, but there is nothing new or wrong about ending an argument with a warning. Some circumstances call for such a warning and challenge, and ending a sermon with one can ensure that it will be remembered.

Verses 2–5 pair temporal and spiritual attributes to describe those who fear the Lord. Their descendants will be mighty/they will be blessed (v. 2). They will be wealthy/they will be righteous (v. 3). They

Psalm 112:1-9 (10)

Theological Perspective

(today's texts are not read in those years when the date of Easter is very early), let us not forget that God Immanuel is with us, even after the big star is no longer there to guide us. However, the light of the flame continues to shine upon us. The ritual required during the Ordinary Time is to reflect on one's behavior and heart, to examine their congruency with each other.

Are we truly walking the talk? Is the instruction truly accompanied by right actions and desires? In instrumental music making, musicians practice daily ascending and descending scale exercises. This helps them memorize the finger movements and coordination of the body for the key in which they will be playing. In a similar way, the psalm's alphabetical acrostic layout helps the reader to memorize not only the contents of God's blessing on those who fear the Lord and God's condemnation on those who do not; it also implants the perfect image of God's eternal power "unshaken" (v. 6) from generation to generation (v. 2).

The teaching is not limited in practicing learning exercises; right teaching prepares the learner to make beautiful music by doing justice and being righteous in playing the Lord's commandments with duty and delight. This psalm is a recapitulation of the introductory theme that the very first psalm in the Psalter presented:

> Happy are those
> who do not follow the advice of the wicked,
> or take the path that sinners tread,
> or sit in the seat of scoffers.
>
> (Ps. 1:1)

The theme laid out in this clear division between the righteous and wicked presents two contrasting images. Like the image of light that is shining because it is in the darkness, the acts of the righteous are displayed because of the acts of wicked ones. The objective of the psalmist is to encourage learners to make a rightful choice.

PAUL JUNGGAP HUH

Pastoral Perspective

this way: love God with all your heart, soul, mind, and strength; and love your neighbor as yourself). That will even fit on a bumper sticker: "Happiness— live in awe of God and love God and neighbor." OK, that is a long bumper sticker.

I would argue that to live in awe of God (what most translations call "the fear of God") is more appropriately communicated to today's young people as living under the wonder and trembling awesomeness of the creator of the Milky Way and the aurora borealis; the God who made the humpback whale and is furious at the possibility that humankind may cause its extinction! Happy are those who understand the awesomeness of the God who knows the name of every single child on this earth, and is fighting for health care for each one who does not have health care, and for peace for each one who must go to bed in a war zone, and is fighting for justice for each child who goes to bed hungry while others of us overconsume. That alone ought to make us tremble!

Tremble as we do, we are always, always offered the amazing grace of both the promise of God's unconditional love and the humbling chance to have a purpose, to make a difference, to be a part of something bigger than ourselves. That is the obeying-God's-commands part of the deal. It turns out to be better than it sounds. Obedience, a word our culture hates, turns out to mean having a chance to make a difference, to make the world a better place. I have met very few people so jaded that they did not want to jump on that bandwagon.

Psalm 112 is a poem celebrating the happiness of obeying God's commands or, in a language that even contemporary culture can hear, the happiness of those who get to make a difference under God.

BARBARA S. BLAISDELL

Exegetical Perspective

"happiness of the man" who does what it right, a phrase that echoes the opening of Psalm 1. While the Hebrew of the psalm uses masculine pronouns throughout, the NRSV translators have adopted plural pronouns in order to render the psalm using inclusive language.

In the second section of the psalm, verses 4–6, the focus shifts from the benefits that accrue to those who keep God's commandments to the characteristic actions of such people. They are said to rise at night to give light. The Hebrew verb "to rise" is the same verb that is used for the sun. Given the sun's absence at night, however, the righteous must take the place of the sun to illuminate the darkness. Righteous persons are said to be generous in their giving and fair in their business dealings. In contrast with verses 1–3, which focus on the blessings that come to the righteous, this section portrays the blessings that the righteous bestow on others.

Section three (vv. 7–9) combines elements of the first two sections. The psalm returns to the theme of the blessings of the righteous, whom it now pictures as living in security. Because they have done what is right, their hearts are calm, even if facing the advance of their enemies. No troubling reports can shake them, and their generosity is praised once more. The final verse of the section is a three-phrase verse, which carries further the idea that "their righteousness endures forever" by adding the phrase "their horn [i.e., strength] is exalted in honor" (v. 9).

The final section of the psalm changes the focus from the righteous to the wicked. The righteous have been granted everything they need and want (security, descendants, wealth, happiness), while "the desire of the wicked comes to nothing" (v. 10c). Unlike the righteous, who are generous in helping others, the wicked cannot even be happy when others prosper. When they see what has become of the righteous, they are angry and gnash their teeth. Their fate is the ultimate contrast to the righteous. Those who fear the Lord "will be remembered forever" (v. 6), while the unrighteous "melt away" (v. 10b). The phrase "melt away" also brings to mind the melting of the heart (i.e., cowardice; Deut. 20:8; Josh. 5:1; 2 Sam. 17:10), which contrasts with the steady and firm hearts of the righteous (vv. 7–8).

KEVIN A. WILSON

Homiletical Perspective

will be a light in the darkness/they will be merciful (v. 4). It will be well for them/they will be just (v. 5). Interestingly, the text does not specify which comes first, the physical action or the spiritual attribute. A sermon could seize on this ambiguity to preach about the relationship between faith and action. Do our actions earn us spiritual favor, or does God's spiritual favor guide us into right actions?

In verses 6–8 the text moves to a series of contrasts describing those who fear the Lord. They are not . . . ; they are . . . In a sermon, these contrasts could be restructured as questions: "Are they afraid of evil tidings?" "No!" the congregation responds, and the preacher continues, "No, their hearts are firm." The psalm is an exhortation, and involving the congregation in this way makes it an exhortation from within the community as well as from without.

Verse 9 concludes the argument in three parts. It names an additional attribute (giving to the poor), repeats verse 3b, and reaches its climax by proclaiming that those who fear the Lord are exalted in honor. Verse 10 parallels verse 9, also in three parts. Verse 10a (the wicked are angry) contrasts with verse 1a (those who fear the Lord are happy). Verse 10b (they melt away) contrasts with verse 9b (endures forever). And verse 10c, like verse 9c, makes a forceful conclusion in favor of righteousness. These contrasts point to the futility of evil and a sermon that highlights them can remind a congregation that wickedness, more than just a rebellion against God, is an embrace of nothingness.

DREW BUNTING

1 Corinthians 2:1-12 (13-16)

¹When I came to you, brothers and sisters, I did not come proclaiming the mystery of God to you in lofty words or wisdom. ²For I decided to know nothing among you except Jesus Christ, and him crucified. ³And I came to you in weakness and in fear and in much trembling. ⁴My speech and my proclamation were not with plausible words of wisdom, but with a demonstration of the Spirit and of power, ⁵so that your faith might rest not on human wisdom but on the power of God.

⁶Yet among the mature we do speak wisdom, though it is not a wisdom of this age or of the rulers of this age, who are doomed to perish. ⁷But we speak God's wisdom, secret and hidden, which God decreed before the ages for our glory. ⁸None of the rulers of this age understood this; for if they had, they would not have crucified the Lord of glory. ⁹But, as it is written,

"What no eye has seen, nor ear heard,
  nor the human heart conceived,
what God has prepared for those who love him"—

Theological Perspective

In chapter 1 Paul has questioned the value of conventional religious and philosophical wisdom as tools for gaining a proper understanding of God. The effect is to undermine elitist assumptions about favored teachers that have been dividing the Corinthian church.

There is a danger here. Could Paul's assault on human wisdom undermine the credibility of *all* religious teachers, himself included? If neither the religious wisdom of the Jews nor the philosophical reasoning of the Greeks leads to a reliable knowledge of God, how could any human teacher claim to lead people to God? It is this dilemma to which Paul turns in chapter 2.

He begins by reminding his hearers about the shape of his own ministry. Something significant did happen in Corinth. Paul's proclamation did draw people into authentic relationship with God. How did it happen, if human religious wisdom is inadequate to the task?

It did not come about, says Paul (vv. 1–5), through anything that even remotely resembled human wisdom, but rather through the unadorned proclamation of "Jesus Christ, and him crucified" (v. 2).

Paul even emphasizes his own lack of rhetorical ability (vv. 3–4). An implausible and off-putting

Pastoral Perspective

The *New York Times Magazine* recently carried an article that compared National Football League locker rooms and Major League Baseball locker rooms. According to the article, walking into a MLB locker room gives one an unwelcome feeling. Baseball locker rooms are like private sanctums where you feel like an intruder, and baseball players behave as if someone might walk up to them and ask an awkward question, or maybe tell them they are being demoted. If you walk into an NFL locker room, however, you sense no resentment, and no one tries to make you feel as if you do not belong. If you are noticed at all, it is with curiosity. Most of the players will be friendly and do their best to help you out.

Of course, there is a reason for this. In a baseball locker room a reporter may be the physical match of the player, but in a football locker room there is no question as to which bodies belong and which do not. The football locker room is where very, very, very large men prepare to play football. There is no question about the pecking order; everybody knows it and observes it, and it puts everyone at ease. When a reporter walks in, everyone is at ease, because the reporter's legs are not like tree trunks, and his pectorals are not like those

¹⁰these things God has revealed to us through the Spirit; for the Spirit searches everything, even the depths of God. ¹¹For what human being knows what is truly human except the human spirit that is within? So also no one comprehends what is truly God's except the Spirit of God. ¹²Now we have received not the spirit of the world, but the Spirit that is from God, so that we may understand the gifts bestowed on us by God. ¹³And we speak of these things in words not taught by human wisdom but taught by the Spirit, interpreting spiritual things to those who are spiritual.

¹⁴Those who are unspiritual do not receive the gifts of God's Spirit, for they are foolishness to them, and they are unable to understand them because they are spiritually discerned. ¹⁵Those who are spiritual discern all things, and they are themselves subject to no one else's scrutiny.

¹⁶"For who has known the mind of the Lord
    so as to instruct him?"
But we have the mind of Christ.

Exegetical Perspective

This chapter, because of its reference to Paul's situation, tantalizes us, as we seek to fill in the details that remain unstated. Is this depiction of an initial visit to Corinth (in weakness, fear, and trembling) connected with Paul's own recollection of challenges in the Athenian philosophical arena, related by Luke in Acts 17? Some have been tempted to see Paul's humility in Corinth as the fruit of chastening, following upon his relatively unsuccessful deployment of classical rhetorical strategies in Greece. However, the critique of empty rhetoric is itself a classical trope, and 1 Corinthians 2 is by no means devoid of rhetoric!

Paul both exploits rhetorical technique and declares its inadequacy to proclaim the "mystery of God" (v. 1), Christ crucified. His desire for the Corinthians is that they understand true wisdom and power, a revelation from God that is designed to lead them, with all the saints, to maturity and glory. So, in chapter 2, Paul expounds the phrase he has articulated in 1 Corinthians 1:30: "Christ Jesus, who became for us wisdom from God." Wisdom is, first and foremost, a *who*, rather than merely a body of knowledge or a human capacity. Just as the Fourth Gospel celebrates the Logos made flesh, here Paul (cf. Matt. 11 and Luke 11) pictures Jesus as God's own Wisdom (Gk. *sophia*), at last among us with

Homiletical Perspective

Richard Hays has argued, I think quite convincingly, that in the second chapter of 1 Corinthians Paul really is being *ironic*.[1] By this he means that Paul is saying one thing but means something altogether different. In fact it is quite possible Paul is being sarcastic, and sarcasm is a form of irony. Hays proposes that Paul is adopting some of the Corinthians' own religious vocabulary to beat them at their own game and in the process to prove how silly the game really is. So he uses their own vocabulary: words like "wisdom," "mature," "spiritual" in order to play his trump card. I know of a double-secret hidden wisdom, maturity, spirituality. Now is that not ironic?

If Hays is right, this poses an extraordinary challenge, both to the lector assigned on this day to read these words aloud and to the preacher who tackles this text. It is hard enough to read Paul with his long run-on sentences, and to read this text in a way that allows the irony to be shared may well be almost impossible. As most preachers have experienced firsthand, both humor and irony are difficult to convey inside of a church. Sometimes the Scripture

---

1. Richard B. Hays, *First Corinthians*, Interpretation series (Louisville, KY: John Knox Press, 1997). Hays acknowledges that irony is a dangerous rhetorical device, because if the reader misses the clues, then the potential for misunderstanding is great.

1 Corinthians 2:1-12 (13-16)

Theological Perspective

message was delivered to the Corinthians by an unimpressive speaker, yet this proclamation took root in their hearts and brought them to saving faith. How could this happen? The explanation, says Paul, is a miraculous working of the Holy Spirit. The conversion of the Corinthians is testimony not to the skill or wisdom of any human teacher, but to the power of God at work in them. Given the lack of human wisdom and rhetorical power that characterized Paul's proclamation, its acceptance by the Corinthians testifies to the divine power at work within it!

One would not want to use Paul's point to excuse poor preaching, but it does point to a truth that preachers know all too well: The person in the pulpit does not have power to create faith in the hearers. Preachers bear testimony to the best of their ability, but it is ultimately a work of the Holy Spirit to write God's truth upon people's hearts and bring them to faith.

This insight can lead us to view the church with new eyes. In the context of a consumer society, it is tempting to view the church as just another commercial enterprise trying to get people to choose its "product." Ultimately the people in the pews on Sunday morning are there not because of a sales job or the particular qualifications of any minister. They are part of the community because the Holy Spirit has been at work in their hearts, leading them to faith in Jesus.

This recognition can be especially significant in situations where there is tension or conflict within the church. Christians often relate to other church members on the basis of the assumption that our place in the Christian community is something we *earn*, both by acting correctly and believing correctly. In situations where the allegedly misguided opinions of one side in a church conflict are prominently displayed, the other side often questions their right to be in the community. Do people who are so misguided really deserve a place in the church's life?

The situation looks very different, however, if we recognize that it is *God's* decision that has sown the seeds of faith in people's hearts and drawn them into the church. If the Spirit has brought them in, then perhaps we cannot so quickly conclude as a result of our disagreements that their place in the church's life is questionable. It is telling that Paul's method of addressing the conflict among the Corinthians is not to undertake a detailed consideration of which faction's views were correct. Instead, Paul shifts the community's focus to the power of God that undergirds the faith of everyone in the church, regardless of which faction they represent.

Pastoral Perspective

of Hercules.[1] In other words, the peace that prevails in an NFL locker room is like the *Pax Romana*, the famous peace of the Roman Empire in the days of the apostle Paul.

The peace of Rome, of course, came with a price. It must have been like having an NFL linebacker in your house day and night, for the Roman Empire was a legionary empire. A legion was the basic army unit needed in residence to control any given area, and the threat of military action ensured submission and cooperation. The Roman Empire was very stratified. The emperor and members of the elite class were at the top, and everyone else was tiered downward in a way that kept the hierarchy in place. This social world existed in the city of Corinth, and Paul was mortified to find it also exhibited in the very church he founded. Some, in their quest for honor and power, were dividing up into groups based on the status of designated leaders. Paul found this unconscionable. So he wrote: "When I came to you . . . I decided to know nothing among you except Jesus Christ, and him crucified. And I came to you in weakness and in fear and in much trembling" (vv. 1–3). In other words, he did not come as a power broker. The elite in the Corinthian church did not like hearing these words, because people in power are allergic to talking about it in public.

A Ghanaian friend who was visiting us turned to me at the dinner table and asked, "When will America stop being the bully of the world?" The question was not meant to be confrontational. I had invited it by airing my own opinions about American foreign policy. Nonetheless, the question made me uncomfortable, for I found myself in the X-ray vision of an outsider. He was exposing for me how people in other parts of the world view the United States.

I had a painful moment of recognition. I realized that by the world's standards, I am the citizen of an elite and powerful nation, I live in an elite and powerful city, and I am the pastor of an elite and powerful church. I am, in other words, the kind of person Paul is addressing. So is every average American Christian. We have access to a representative governing authority that is very powerful. We have the right to vote, and a number of very powerful people are very interested in our vote. We have a right to express our faith in the public square. We have access to resources that by the world's standards are extraordinary. How we carry ourselves in our social

---

1. Michael Lewis, "The Changing Room," *New York Times Magazine* (February 3, 2008), 32–37.

transformative power—"we speak God's wisdom, secret and hidden, which God decreed before the ages for our glory" (v. 7). Lurking behind this passage are, aptly, allusions to the Wisdom books, including Wisdom 9:6, which links wisdom with maturity or being "perfect" (*teleios*); Wisdom 9:17, where God gives the spirit and wisdom so that seekers might know the mind of God; and Sirach 1:6–10, which combines the themes of revelation and loving God with God's gift of wisdom. Paul thus has a rich treasury of resources from which to draw, both from classical rhetoric and from Jewish traditional writings, as he expounds the Christ, who surpasses all knowledge and all prior revelation.

Though Paul does not dispute that there are many mysteries, here he calls upon the Corinthians to relish the great mystery revealed among them—greater than any other thing, unseen and unheard, prepared by God from eternity. The source of 1 Corinthians 2:9 is debated, but the verse appears to derive from Isaiah 64:3–4 (though it varies from both the Hebrew and the Septuagint version by its reference to those who "love God"; cf. Sir. 1:10, rather than to those who "await his mercy"). Paul does, however, retain the general theme of being astonished by God, and may well have in mind the entire chapter (Isa. 64), which begins with an invocation of God to "tear open the heavens" and appear. This has indeed happened, exclaims Paul, in Christ Jesus!

So momentous is the visitation of the Lord in Jesus Messiah that even the "rulers of this world" (political and cosmic) never expected it; but knowledge of God's plan is the gift now bestowed upon those who believe what God has done. Indeed, the very Spirit of God speaks to the revived human spirit, because those who belong to Christ have the Spirit within them and among them (vv. 10–12, cf. Rom. 8:14–27), so that deep speaks to deep. Those in Christ are already on the road to glory, learning what it means to be "spiritual" and being taught by God himself (v. 13).

All this Paul explains by means of reestablishing his credentials among the Corinthians, by careful reasoning, rhetorical questions, and colorful language. His approach is both measured and mature, as he seeks to guide his readers into both maturity and the deeper world of God's own Spirit. Neither human wisdom nor human works are sufficient to the tasks of the proclamation and the transmission of God's mystery, and so Paul leans upon his weakness in order to accentuate God's power. Verse 4 alludes to his apostolic performance of signs in the

reading for the day is hilarious, but the joke is missed because we are too distant from the world of the Bible to get the joke. We have been raised to think that the Bible is an eminently serious book. The young preacher who intends irony in her sermon may well be greeted at the door by a sincere and outraged critic. While the truths we gather to proclaim and consider are no doubt matters of life and death, we lose the "lightness" of the good news when we are excessively literal—or excessively systematic in our approaches to biblical texts. I think this is further complicated by Paul himself, who always seems to be in the middle of an argument with someone.

What if Hays really is on to something here? What if, in using the word "wisdom" to refer both to ways of knowing in the world and to the ways of God, he is in fact being ironic? Would it not be ironic if the subtle (but crucial) point Paul is making is that God's wisdom is *always* at odds with the wisdom of this world—and that we create congregations of insiders and outsiders, those with double-secret wisdom and those not yet initiated? The great temptation that the church faces in Corinth is a desire for security and a reliance on their own ingenuity and knowledge.

It goes without saying that these challenges continue to plague the church in our own day. Threatened with decline, we flock to the latest guru who can help us to "grow" our congregations, if only we cultivate seven habits of highly successful congregations or follow twelve simple steps or adopt a new mission statement. "Jesus is the answer," we say, but what is the question?

Politicians (and pastors) who reduce complex questions to simplistic solutions (by assuming with the dominant culture that every problem we face can be fixed with a technical solution) are rewarded. This gives us the illusion that we are in control, and in our clarity we feel less afraid, but only for a while. Paul's message for the church, in first-century Corinth and in our own time and place, is that the "double-secret-hidden-mature-spiritual wisdom of God" is the cross. Wow!

In her extraordinary book *Pillars of Flame: Power, Priesthood, and Spiritual Maturity,* Maggie Ross insists that "the heart of Christianity is the self-emptying, kenotic humility of God expressed in Jesus the Christ."[2] Setting forth a theological approach rooted in the Syrian tradition of the

---

2. Maggie Ross, *Pillars of Flame: Power, Priesthood, and Spiritual Maturity* (New York: Seabury Books/Church Publishing, 2007), xvi.

1 Corinthians 2:1-12 (13-16)

Theological Perspective

Paul's teaching on the divine origins of faith also speaks powerfully to the ways in which the Christian community approaches its evangelistic calling. How many believers shrink from sharing their faith because they feel unqualified or incapable of explaining it well? These would be serious objections, if faith were the product of persuasive arguments and sophisticated religious wisdom.

Paul teaches that faith and conversion are the result of God's power, which can and does work through quite simple and unimpressive human testimony. This can be a source of enormous encouragement for ordinary believers who seek to share with others their trust and confidence in God, even when the outward form of their testimonies is quite humble.

Paul develops this insight in an astonishing direction as he reflects on *how* the Holy Spirit imparts faith to people (vv. 10–16). The Spirit has access to the innermost thoughts of God, says Paul. Consequently, when that same Spirit is at work within us, the very thoughts of God are within us. Paul puts this in stunning terms: "We have the mind of Christ" (v. 16).

This suggests a very different understanding of the relationship of human beings to God than what we often encounter. Many conceive our connection to God as something fundamentally *external*: Christ presents us with teachings and an example that we then strive to faithfully imitate.

The picture Paul paints, however, is of a much more internalized connection that involves *participation* in Christ rather than just outward imitation. We have the mind of Christ! That suggests that faith is a sharing in Christ's own knowledge and love of the Father. It further suggests that the simple acts of generosity and caring in the life of any congregation—acts we might be tempted to pass over lightly as people simply choosing to be nice to each other—are in fact the appearance of Christ's own love bubbling up in the lives of people in whom his Spirit dwells. In the midst of temptations to see the church as something ordinary, this understanding of Christian faith can lead believers to a proper awe and wonder and thanksgiving for the reality of the Christian community.

P. MARK ACHTEMEIER

Pastoral Perspective

world makes a huge difference, because—whether we realize it or not—when outsiders visit us, it is akin to visiting an NFL locker room.

In 1 Corinthians, Paul was dismayed that this same state of affairs existed in his church, because it was meant to be a radical alternative to the stratifications of imperial Rome. When Paul wrote, "When I came to you . . . I decided to know nothing among you except Jesus Christ, and him crucified" (vv. 1, 2), he was referring to an alternative way of residing in the world. He was contending that the disciples of the crucified one ought to stand with the oppressed and work for justice, reconciliation, and restoration. For Paul, this was the Christian way of residing in the world. Rowan Williams puts it this way: Jesus did not come to be "a competitor for space in the world." Rather, in his life, death, and resurrection "the human map is being redrawn, the world turned upside down," and "the whole world of rivalry and defense" is put into question.[2]

What does this kind of redrawing, reorientation look like? During the civil rights movement, the Student Nonviolent Coordinating Committee provided at least one illustration in what John Lewis spoke of as the bodily dimension of their work—a different manner of moving and dwelling with others. He said, "We were meeting people on their own terms, not ours. If they were out in the field picking cotton, we would go out in that field and pick with them." Where and how they placed their bodies was critical for their work.[3] So also, for Christians, how we move and dwell with others makes all the difference in the world as we follow in the footsteps of our crucified and risen Lord.

ROGER J. GENCH

---

2. Rowan Williams, *Christ on Trial* (Grand Rapids: Eerdmans, 2000), 6, 52, 69.
3. Stanley Hauerwas and Romand Coles, *Christianity, Democracy, and the Radical Ordinary* (Eugene, OR: Cascade, 2008), 69.

midst of the Corinthians (cf. 2 Cor. 12:12). Even miracles must not supplant the glory of God. Later, in addressing this congregation, Paul will warn them against an inordinate dependence upon even mighty acts. Throughout this section, the corporate nature of the church is emphasized, by reference to the first-person-plural and second-person-plural pronouns.

What then does it mean to be among the "spiritual"? Paul probably is reacting to an esoteric use of the term, such as that of followers of Philo, who saw in Genesis 2:7 a contrast between the *pneumatikos* ("spiritual") and merely *psychikos* ("soul-ish") human, or the threefold gnostic distinction of individuals into *pneumatikos, psychikos,* and *sarkikos* ("fleshly"), attested a century later than Paul's day. To "mirror-read" on the basis of a one-sided conversation is risky, but Paul may well be adopting popular terms and infusing them with a Christ-centered meaning. In this chapter (and the next) he delicately and painfully distinguishes between the mature and infants in the Lord, prompted by the conflict and lack of focus among members of the Corinthian church.

In speaking of the "unspiritual," he refers to those who have not yet received the Spirit, made available through the "Lord of glory." The immature are those who have the Holy Spirit but must continue to be led, as the Spirit searches everything (v. 10) and further interprets spiritual things to them. To be spiritual and to be taught by the Spirit is the birthright of every saint in Christ Jesus. Such growth is also the character of the whole church together, which, we will soon hear (3:16–17), corporately is the temple of the Spirit. There is a role for mature human teachers, a role that Paul takes on as he instructs; ultimately, however, it is the Lord who teaches his own (cf. Jer. 31:34), because the Spirit dwells among all those who together have "the mind of Christ" (v. 16b). Paul displays both boldness and humility, balancing his calling as an apostle with his knowledge that the gift of the Holy Spirit is the prerogative not of a select few, but the entire church.

EDITH M. HUMPHREY

Christian faith and especially indebted to Ephrem (fourth century) and Isaac (seventh century), she argues that this ancient Semitic approach to the Christian faith

> offers a passionate and unified vision of the love of God incarnate in Christ, indwelling the creation through the Spirit, unifying and transfiguring the universe, a vision toward which we in the West have been slowly and painfully struggling as we stagger away from the debris of exhausted philosophical categories, the shattered scholastic synthesis, the collapse of the illusion of objectivity, the corpses of holocausts, and the moral bankruptcy of nuclear commitments.[3]

Such an approach, virtually lost to Western academic approaches to theology, challenges our conventional wisdom about power: individually, socially, and institutionally. If we emulate the world's understanding of power, Ross argues, we cease to be the church. We merely mimic the power politics to which we have grown so accustomed. In discovering and rediscovering the "self-emptying, *kenotic* humility of God," however, we not only find our voice as God's people, but we are empowered to become the kind of community that brings healing and new life to the world.

This has everything to do with the larger argument that Paul is having with the church in Corinth, a congregation composed of urbane and sophisticated people who are certain that knowledge will lead them to the truth, a truth that they can control and manage. It is in truth, however, a way of masking their fear. The mystery of God about which Paul speaks cannot be proclaimed in "lofty words or wisdom"—not because the gospel is irrational or anti-intellectual, but because it is revealed in weakness and vulnerability and the self-emptying love of God on the cross.

RICHARD M. SIMPSON

---

3. Ibid., ix.

Matthew 5:13-20

¹³"You are the salt of the earth; but if salt has lost its taste, how can its saltiness be restored? It is no longer good for anything, but is thrown out and trampled underfoot.

¹⁴"You are the light of the world. A city built on a hill cannot be hid. ¹⁵No one after lighting a lamp puts it under the bushel basket, but on the lampstand, and it gives light to all in the house. ¹⁶In the same way, let your light shine before others, so that they may see your good works and give glory to your Father in heaven.

¹⁷"Do not think that I have come to abolish the law or the prophets; I have come not to abolish but to fulfill. ¹⁸For truly I tell you, until heaven and earth pass away, not one letter, not one stroke of a letter, will pass from the law until all is accomplished. ¹⁹Therefore, whoever breaks one of the least of these commandments, and teaches others to do the same, will be called least in the kingdom of heaven; but whoever does them and teaches them will be called great in the kingdom of heaven. ²⁰For I tell you, unless your righteousness exceeds that of the scribes and Pharisees, you will never enter the kingdom of heaven."

Theological Perspective

This text expands what we learn about the call to discipleship in 5:1–12. In verses 13–14, Jesus uses two metaphors to describe and prescribe who his followers are and what they do for and in the world. The first metaphor, "You are the salt of the earth" (v. 13), suggests that Jesus gives them as his disciples a distinctive capacity to elicit goodness on the earth. Like salt, which is used to alter or enhance the tastes of food, the disciples' capacity to elicit goodness as they participate on the earth should be of profound consequence, in the ways that we find in 5:3–10. The danger for disciples is that they may lose that capacity by forgetting that they are to disorder the status quo by valuing those who are dispossessed, caring for those who suffer loss, seeking to do justice, showing mercy, having integrity, being peacemakers, and courageously standing for what they believe. Disciples who do not engage in such practices that humanize life on earth will be like salt that has lost its taste.

The second metaphor, "You are the light of the world," invites us to consider the role of disciples as a gathered community (vv. 14–16). Light enables us to see things and is a kind of energy that gives things color, helps vegetation to grow, provides solar power for electricity, and can be focused for specific uses, such as a laser. Like light, the disciples as a gathered community have the overarching purpose of being

Pastoral Perspective

There is a remarkable scene in the book of Revelation where Jesus is standing and knocking at the door of the church. It has long been used as an evangelistic illustration, focused on whether the members of the church will accept Jesus or reject him, by either opening the door or not. This interpretation seems to miss an important point. Prior to the scene at the door, the church of Laodicea is rebuked for being neither hot nor cold, but lukewarm (Rev. 3:16). This is certainly not a compliment, particularly in reference to living out God's mission in the world. It would be better for the church to be either hot or cold than to remain lukewarm. This is definitely a perspective that Jesus holds in the Sermon on the Mount.

After presenting the eight Beatitudes, Jesus begins his Sermon by making the analogy that his followers are to be like salt and light. These are interesting choices, and both have implications for the exercise of mission and pastoral ministry.

To say that we are to be the salt of the earth implies that we are to bring some "flavor" to our pastoral relationships with each other. Salt has an edge as well as a satisfying taste. It makes come alive what would otherwise seem tasteless and bland. In certain circumstances, salt can be used as a preservative, keeping food fresh for an extended period of

Exegetical Perspective

The Gospel reading for this Sunday consists of two introductory passages. The first, Matthew 5:13–16, is a transitional passage between the Beatitudes and the following ethical part of the sermon. This ethical part consists of three major sections, concerning Jesus and the Torah (5:17–48), Jesus and the cult (6:1–18), and Jesus and social issues (6:19–7:12). The second passage of this Sunday, Matthew 5:17–20, functions both as an introduction to the first of these sections and as a safeguard to an incorrect interpretation of 5:17–48, namely, that Jesus' teaching contradicts that of Moses.

To appreciate both passages, it will be helpful to be aware of the original context in which Jesus spoke. Without doubt, Matthew wants to apply Jesus' teaching to the first Christian community; but when Jesus gave sermons like the one known to us as the Sermon on the Mount, his immediate audience was Israel. Moreover, Jesus' sermon was not an expression of some general ethical rules, but an intervention in a heated debate concerning the political and religious course Israel was called to steer. The immediate context of this debate was the occupation of Israel's land by the Roman Empire; the wider context was the fact that Israel had been a part of Gentile empires since the Babylonian exile. Even while the people of Israel had physically returned to

Homiletical Perspective

The reading for today implies two fundamental questions of life: Who are we? What are we to do? These questions hang in the back closets of the minds of many individuals and congregations today.

The situation of Matthew's congregation is analogous to that of many congregations today. Matthew lived in a time of theological and social tension following the destruction of Jerusalem and the temple. The Jewish community was in conflict regarding the future of Judaism and what it meant to be Jewish.

The preacher could encourage the congregation to recognize that the established churches in North America face similar issues. Many values and practices from previous generations are being questioned and jettisoned. Congregations in the historic denominations are getting smaller, and the denominations are losing social power. What does it mean to be disciples of Jesus Christ in this setting? How are we to live?

The preacher can use Matthew 15:13–16 as a theological resource to respond to these questions. Matthew begins, "You are the salt of the earth" (v. 13a). In Judaism, salt was a symbol of covenant. Matthew believed that his community was living shortly before the apocalypse that would fully establish the realm of God. Covenantal community for Matthew thus includes eschatological community.

Matthew 5:13-20

Theological Perspective

the mirror that refracts God's light so that all peoples and nations can know of God's justice and mercy. As a gathered community the disciples are like light when they engage others in the world, enabling diversity (giving things color), nurturing a healthy, ecofriendly world (helping vegetation to grow), generating policies for ecojustice (providing solar power), and restoring or repairing whatever relationships that need such (focusing for specific purposes). These are the good works that will glorify God.

As verses 17–20 remind us, it is because of who Jesus is and how he understands his mission that his disciples individually and collectively are enabled to be salt and light. As Jesus declares to his newly commissioned disciples and followers that he has not come to abolish the law or the prophets, he claims his place in God's history of the liberation of and covenant with God's chosen people. By so doing, Jesus extends the mission of God's chosen people, but he does so without dismissing the tradition or breaking the covenant, thus fulfilling rather than abolishing the law and the prophets. In an important sense, Jesus himself is the hermeneutical key for interpreting the law and prophets in line with God's will for the present time and until the end of time. Thus Jesus admonishes his followers that breaking the commandments oneself or leading others to do so is an offense against divine eternal purposes.

Moreover, verse 20 places the entire text within the larger narrative context of all of the verses that precede it. Here Jesus enjoins his followers in these words: "For I tell you, unless your righteousness exceeds that of the scribes and Pharisees, you will never enter the kingdom of heaven" (cf. vv. 6, 10). What does "righteousness" mean in this verse, and how does its use relate to or further inform its use in verses 6 and 10? Given the fact that verse 20 concludes Jesus' proclamation that he has come not to abolish but to fulfill the law and the prophets, righteousness must refer to the way that Jesus interprets the law and lives by it. The righteousness of the scribes and Pharisees is concerned with observance of tradition, public displays of piety, and adherence to the letter of the law. The righteousness of Jesus flows from his relationship with God and, in turn, is the ground of Jesus' relationship with his followers.

Accordingly, Jesus' followers are both commanded and enabled by Jesus to surpass conventional and institutional practices of righteousness. Exceeding conventional righteousness means that Jesus' followers seek to live justly as an expression of their worship of God (cf. v. 14; v.10); they have been blessed

Pastoral Perspective

time. Salt is also used to stimulate thirst. We can begin to see how this image of salt might relate to the practice of ministry, but two analogies seem particularly important at this moment in time.

For at least the past thirty years, the pastoral ministry practiced by ordained and lay professionals has been greatly influenced by what is called the therapeutic movement. The popularity of psychological insights, addressing almost any human condition, contributes to this influence. One result is that pastoral ministry has become defined almost exclusively as supporting and affirming one another, regardless of the situation. Support and affirmation have their place, to be sure, but there are times when the most pastoral response needs to be confrontational. Jesus could both be affirming of the individual person and challenge the person's behavior. Jesus accepted the rich young man, but challenged him to give away his possessions. He accepted the woman caught in adultery, and then instructed her to sin no more.

We might say that the affirmation of the person upholds a person's dignity, regardless of circumstance, while the challenge invites behavioral change for the better. Both responses are required for effective pastoral ministry to occur. The challenge for change is the saltiness that keeps the moment alive in order to grow, spiritually and personally. There are two ends to the proverbial staff of the pastor: the hook that holds the person close to the flock (support), and the pointed end designed to prod and encourage (challenge). The second implication, and somewhat paradoxical, is that the saltiness of the challenge for change, over time, becomes the preservative that keeps one alive. What was once experienced as only bitter, becomes at least bittersweet. Challenge leads to change that leads to perseverance.

Jesus tells his followers that they are the light of the world and that this light should not be hidden but seen. We often interpret this to mean that we are not to hide our gifts and talents by placing them under the metaphorical bucket. One of the favored offertory sentences in the *Book of Common Prayer* is "Let your light shine before others so that they may see your good works and glorify your Father in heaven." There have been numerous occasions when we have used this approach to encourage someone to step forward, to relinquish his or her shyness, and to come out of hiding. However, there is another reason for light to shine. There is darkness in life—external and internal.

Jesus encourages his followers to bring light to a dark and broken world. The light is the light of the

the land of their ancestry, the exile could be said to have continued: land, city, and temple ruled by *goyim*; soldiers' boots marching through the country; and the prophetic promises of divine kingship never fully fulfilled.

In a culture where religion and politics were never separated, this led to an array of anxious questions: How can it be that God's holy city and temple are occupied territory? What does this say about God's relationship to us? What does God want us to do? How does God want us to respond? To these questions, each of the different factions of first-century Judaism had their own response, ranging from a realistic collaboration with the occupier (the Sadducees) to a widespread desire to take up the weapons and fight the empire (the Zealots). The latter option seems also to have been popular with the Pharisees. However, the Pharisaic party of Jesus' time was a divided house. While some opted for the sword, others opted for the ghetto; realizing that the small Jewish nation was no match for the vast military resources of the empire, the latter steered toward deeper private study and practice of Torah. If one could not obtain one's political independence, at least one could preserve one's cultural and religious identity as a people called and set apart by God; at least one could live in covenantal righteousness, until God would express God's righteousness in the eschatological coming of God's reign.[1]

To a people divided and confused by these anxious questions and explosive answers Jesus preached his sermon, a sermon that was "a challenge to Israel to *be* Israel."[2] On the one hand, Jesus rejected the agenda of the Zealots: enemies were not to be hated, but to be loved; not to be resisted, but to be prayed for (Matt. 5:43–44) and met with astonishing generosity (Matt. 5:41). On the other hand, the strategy of the Pharisees was unfruitful as well: unless one's righteousness exceeded that of the scribes and Pharisees, one would not enter the kingdom of heaven (Matt. 5:20). For the exegete and preacher of this text, it is important to understand and make clear the nature of Jesus' critique of the Pharisaic agenda.

The point is not that keeping Torah is in itself wrong—after all, "not one stroke of a letter will pass from the law until all is accomplished" (Matt. 5:18). The point was rather that the strategy of the Pharisees was based on an outdated interpretation of Israel's situation. The Pharisees worked on the

---

1. For this interpretation of the Pharisaic agenda, see: N. T. Wright, *The New Testament and the People of God* (London: SPCK, 1992), 185–95.
2. N. T. Wright, *Jesus and the Victory of God* (London: SPCK, 1996), 288.

The preacher can help the congregation imagine itself as such a community.

Matthew uses verse 13b—the salt losing its saltiness and being thrown out—in reference to the final judgment expected in connection with the apocalypse. If the Matthean community is not faithful, the community can expect to be condemned at the final judgment. Even if the preacher does not believe that an actual final judgment will take place, this part of the passage underlines an important point: Those who do not remain faithful can expect consequences in diminished quality of life.

This theme of covenant is reinforced in verses 5:14–16, where the Gospel writer adapts the expression "You are the light of the world" from Isaiah 42:6, where it describes the vocation of Israel. God called Israel to be a light to the nations (Gentiles). Israel is to model God's covenantal ways so that all people can be blessed (Isa. 42:1–6; Gen. 12:1–3). Similarly, the Matthean community was to be a light in the first century, and the church is to be such a light among human communities today. A preacher might reflect on whether the life of the congregation is actually a model or simply a mirror of old values and behaviors.

Verses 14b–15 emphasize that the purpose of light is to illumine. In those days, lamps were small, yet in a dark one-room house in Palestine, even a small lamp "gives light to all in the house" (v. 15). Figuratively speaking, the light of a struggling congregation or denomination, even if small and dim, can illumine someone's house.

In practical ways, how is the community to let its light shine? By doing good works (v. 16), that is, covenantal acts of love, mercy, and justice. Given the propensity of North American congregations for works righteousness, the preacher needs to be clear that these works do not earn a place in the realm of God, but are responses to the gift of the realm. For the sermon, the preacher could help the congregation identify good works that shine the beam of the realm.

Verses 17–20 specifies further what it means to be salt and light. Here the congregation may be surprised. How does a community live in anticipation of the realm? By following Torah (as interpreted by Matthew).

This passage is a powerful corrective to congregations who think that Jesus or the earliest communities of Jesus' followers rejected the law and Judaism. To be sure, Matthew critiques some interpreters of the law (e.g., the Pharisees), but he assumes that Jewish members of the community will be law-observant and that

Matthew 5:13-20

Theological Perspective

and are passionate about being participants in God's vision for the world (cf. vv. 3–9). If Jesus' followers lack this passion for justice and living into God's reordering of human life, then they, in effect, break the covenantal relationship that originates with God and is extended to humanity through Jesus. When the covenantal relationship is broken, their future life with God is no longer possible—"you will never enter the kingdom of heaven" (v. 20b).

In an important sense a kind of theology of discipleship emerges from 5:1–12 and 5:13–20. This theology of discipleship is taught by Jesus to those to whom he has extended a specific call (his disciples) and to those who because of what they see and hear of Jesus are persuaded to follow him (the crowds). A first tenet of this theology is that God's blessings and God's favor are the beginning of the call to be a follower of Jesus. A second tenet is that God's blessings are the root of our right relationship with God and other humans. A third and final tenet is that the righteousness of God fulfilled in the person and ministry of Jesus makes possible human righteousness.

Finally, human righteousness is about being the salt of the earth and the light of the world. As the salt of the earth, we are disciples of Jesus when we allow our characters to be formed by God's blessings. As the light of the world, we are followers of Jesus when accept the covenantal blessings as a call into relationships with despised groups because of what we believe—even if it means that we may be persecuted. As disciples of the Jesus who came not to abolish but to fulfill the law and the prophets, we seek to live righteously in ways consistent with the new interpretation of the law that Jesus provides.

MARCIA Y. RIGGS

Pastoral Perspective

gospel, and it draws all people to its warmth and radiance. This mission has been primary, from the very beginning, throughout every age. Archbishop William Temple is often quoted as saying, "The church is the only organization on earth that exists for those who are not its members." In order for the light to be seen, we must be willing to go where the darkness exists, to engage and walk through it, so that, in time, the light can overcome it. Annie Dillard writes, "You do not have to sit outside in the dark. If, however, you want to look at the stars, you will find that darkness is necessary."[1] We must go into those dark places, bearing the light of Christ. The light is not given for our own personal enjoyment.

Effective pastoral ministry also involves looking at the darkness within ourselves, to seek the dark night of the soul. Parker Palmer refers to this process as looking or reading our inner landscape.[2] While this is never easy, it is essential. We cannot bring the light of Christ to others if we are unaware of where that light needs to shine in our own hearts. Pastoral leadership requires looking at those dark places within, which will also help us understand external darkness. We need not fear this internal exploration.

Finally, when we are salt and light for others, we are more likely to fulfill the law as Jesus suggested: To love the Lord our God with all our heart, mind, and soul; and our neighbor as ourselves.

CHARLES JAMES COOK

---

1. Annie Dillard, *Teaching a Stone to Talk: Expeditions and Encounters* (New York: Harper Perennial, 1992), 43.
2. Parker Palmer, "Leading from Within: Reflections on Spirituality and Leadership," Meridian St. United Methodist Church, Indianapolis, March 23, 1990.

Exegetical Perspective

assumption that the fulfillment of God's eschatological promises lay still in the future; that God's reign had not yet begun; that the exile, as it were, continued. Therefore they chose the ghetto; they withdrew and protected their identity so that they might be found righteous by the time that God would do a new thing. Against this, Jesus was "proclaiming the good news of the kingdom" (Matt. 4:23)—God *was already doing a new thing.* Preserving one's identity was therefore not enough. One did not put a lamp "under the bushel basket, but on the lampstand, and it gives light to all in the house" (Matt. 5:15). Israel was called to be a holy nation, a nation of priests, and now that the kingdom of God had come near, this was the time that "the mountain of the LORD's house shall be established as the highest of the mountains" (Isa. 2:2) and that "out of Zion shall go forth instruction, and the word of the LORD from Jerusalem" (Isa. 2:3). That was the way Israel was to confront the empire!

Living like this was not to abolish the law or the prophets, but to fulfill it. In Matthew, "To fulfill" (*plēroō*) was an eschatological category (cf. 1:22; 2:15, 17, 23; 4:14; 8:17; 12:17; 13:35; 21:4; 26:54, 56). That Jesus rejected the agenda of the Pharisees does not mean he rejected the Torah; it means he read and practiced Torah from a different perspective. The Pharisees read Torah in the context of a world governed by sin; Torah protected an occupied Israel against losing its identity. Similarly, the Torah itself situated its ethic in the context of sin, and allowed certain practices because of human hardheartedness (Matt. 19:8). Jesus read Torah no longer in the context of sin, but in the context of the kingdom. Now that the reign of God was being inaugurated, the measure was no longer human pettiness, but the abundance of God's righteousness.

EDWIN CHR. VAN DRIEL

Homiletical Perspective

Gentile members will adopt core values of the law, even if they are not fully initiated in Judaism.

This attitude is stated forcefully in verse 17. In this Matthean context the reference to fulfillment has the realm in view. To fulfill the law and the prophets is to bring their purposes to complete expression in everyday community. That is how the community is to live while awaiting the apocalypse, to which Matthew makes direct reference in verse 18.

The preacher might ponder verse 19 with the congregation. Almost every Christian congregation in North America contains ministers and members who have not only broken some of the commandments but have actively taught others to do so, often in the context of claiming that Christianity has superseded Judaism.

Verse 20 presents the preacher with an important teaching opportunity, especially since the congregation is going to be in Matthew for the next eleven months. This sentence (which gave rise to the phrase "a higher righteousness") presumes conflict between Matthew's community and some traditional Pharisees. While the verse is partly intended to spur the Matthean community to be faithful to Torah, the verse is also an attack on the Pharisees and scribes. The preacher can alert the congregation to the fact that Matthew's negative references to the Pharisees do not reflect the historical Pharisees but are caricatures in the service of Matthew's polemic against them. If Matthew *really* wanted to embody the realm, Matthew would relate to the Pharisees according to Matthew 5:21–26.

The preacher needs to lead the congregation in thinking about what parts of the law (both in spirit and in concrete expression) are central to today's largely Gentile congregations. The preacher can also encourage the congregation toward respect for Judaism. Indeed, perhaps the congregation could propose joining with a nearby synagogue in carrying out the good works referred to in verses 15–16.

While Matthew 5:17–20 could easily figure into a sermon on identity and behavior, it could also suggest sermons that help the congregation think about Christian attitudes toward the law, the relationship of Judaism and Christianity, and prophecy and fulfillment.

RONALD J. ALLEN

Deuteronomy 30:15-20

¹⁵See, I have set before you today life and prosperity, death and adversity. ¹⁶If you obey the commandments of the LORD your God that I am commanding you today, by loving the LORD your God, walking in his ways, and observing his commandments, decrees, and ordinances, then you shall live and become numerous, and the LORD your God will bless you in the land that you are entering to possess. ¹⁷But if your heart turns away and you do not hear, but are led astray to bow down to other gods and serve them, ¹⁸I declare to you today that you shall perish; you shall not live long in the land that you are crossing the Jordan to enter and possess. ¹⁹I call heaven and earth to witness against you today that I have set before you life and death, blessings and curses. Choose life so that you and your descendants may live, ²⁰loving the LORD your God, obeying him, and holding fast to him; for that means life to you and length of days, so that you may live in the land that the LORD swore to give to your ancestors, to Abraham, to Isaac, and to Jacob.

Theological Perspective

Part of God's final words to Moses that he delivers to the Israelites, this passage is rich not only in thought but also in theological themes. The first part, verses 15–16, focuses on choice and promise. The second part, verses 17–18, presents the consequences if the wrong choice is made. The third part, verses 19–20, is an exhortation to choose life, a choice that will result in blessings.

The main theological theme in verses 15–16 is obedience. Having experienced the hardships of Egyptian bondage, having been set free from such bondage, having entered into covenant with God, having been entrusted with God's law, and having survived much of the challenging journey through the wilderness, the Israelites now stand on the plain as Moses prepares to die and the people prepare to enter the promised land. Delivering God's message, Moses now declares to them that they have two choices—either life and prosperity or death and adversity—and the choice rests with them. If the people make the correct choice, then Israel will have a long future. If not, then Israel's days are numbered. For Israel, life and prosperity meant that all human activity would be under the protection of the Divine. They would live securely on the land; their land would be fertile and prosperous; and they as a people would be fertile, blessed with many offspring and

Pastoral Perspective

We are a nation of choosers: paper or plastic? Small, medium, large, or super? Fries or chips? Organic or conventional? Having a choice has become a staple of the American dream. Political agendas of all flavors are sold on a platform of choice—everything from private school vouchers to health-care reform. More choice is always the preferred value.

The choice offered in Deuteronomy does not sit well with a people inundated by choices. Actually "offered" is too generous—Deuteronomy does not *offer* a choice so much as *require* that a particular choice be made: "If you obey the commandments of the LORD your God . . . then you shall live. . . . But if your heart turns away . . . you shall perish" (vv. 16–18).

Most church people do not like these kinds of pronouncements. God sounds too autocratic or in conflict with the free grace we have come to expect from Jesus. Theologians in my own Reformed tradition do not like these kinds of pronouncements either. As a pastor, I do not much care for them. Given the reckless pronouncements of televangelists who have applied this brand of conditional theology to everything from hurricanes to AIDS, it seems safer to steer clear of judgments altogether.

However, the choice and its consequences are clear: Choose covenant, receive life; reject covenant,

Exegetical Perspective

The Valedictory Address of Moses. Today's passage concludes Moses's farewell address to the people of Israel gathered in plenary session in the land of Moab (29:1–30:20). In this sermon he sums up all that has transpired in the lengthy "repetition of torah" (*mishneh torah*) or "second law-giving" (*deuteronomion*) that is the book of Deuteronomy. Our text is expressed in the unmistakable style of the Deuteronomists. It is hortatory. The familiar "if . . . then" syntax of conditional sentences is in place. Like much of the book of Deuteronomy, especially the homiletical framework thought to have been provided by its final editors, it is structured around the "two ways": faithfulness and blessing vs. disobedience and cursing. Retributional theology seems to reign supreme throughout the book. God rewards the faithful and punishes the unfaithful.

One of the chief issues in the study of the book of Deuteronomy is its genre. After the discovery by archaeologists of the texts of "suzerainty treaties" in the ancient Near East (one of the most famous of which is the about 1280 BCE treaty between Ramses II and the Hittite king Hattusilis, extant in both copies), many scholars came to believe that Deuteronomy too was a kind of treaty between the sovereign God and the subject, Israel, in that its structure bears close resemblance to the stereotyped

Homiletical Perspective

Preachers deal with life-and-death issues every Sunday, but it will be particularly obvious as we preach on Deuteronomy 30:15–20. Many in our congregations, both young and old, are dealing with questions of mortality.

The obituaries we read often sound much the same. They tell how old people were when they died, where they will be buried, where they worked, what groups they joined, and to whom they were related. It is not the most meaningful information. It would be more interesting if obituaries told the truth.

> "Bob Hickman grew up middle class, and was so proud that he had worked his way up to upper middle class."
> "Marsha Lawson was known as a big talker, but no one could remember her saying anything that mattered."
> "Harold Riley ignored his family, but liked to brag that he had seen every episode of *Seinfeld* twice."

Obituaries do not say when a life has been wasted or when it has been celebrated.

> "Louise Chaplin loved her children and everybody else's."
> "Annie Quinlin noticed things—the beauty of the rain, a touching song, a well-placed hug."

Deuteronomy 30:15-20

Theological Perspective

descendants. On the contrary, death would mean that all human activity would be devoid of the divine presence. The people would be forced to exist outside of the land, without security and peace. They stand at a crossroads.

Part of their choosing life means that they choose to be "obedient" to God and God's ways. At first thought, the choice for life seems freeing. When coupled with obedience, the choice seems to be somewhat constricting, but is it really? The Israelites are called to obey God's commandments. Immediately the Decalogue comes to mind, which is not merely a set of laws set down to achieve perfection or individual holiness (see Exod. 20:1–17). These laws are meant to preserve covenant and, above all, right relationship with God (Exod. 20:1–7) and with one another (Exod. 20:12–17), with the central proscription being to remember and keep holy the Sabbath day (Exod. 20:8–11). This day was meant to be a day of celebration, rest, recollection, and reflection whereby people were afforded the time to delight in God's creation, to take stock of their relationship with God and with one another, and ultimately to enjoy rest in God and with God.

The commandments of the Lord also call to mind Deuteronomy 6:1–9, a text that beckons the people to love the Lord their God with all their hearts, soul, and might—to circumcise the foreskins of their hearts to God (Deut. 10:16). Obeying God's commandments means that the people are to love God wholeheartedly; to walk in God's ways, which are ways of justice, righteousness, and loving-kindness like what they have already experienced; and to observe not only God's commandments but also all the decrees and ordinances that are part of the commandments.

The people are called to live Torah as a way of life. Their reward for their fidelity and integrity will be divine blessing. To be blessed by God is to be guaranteed safety, well-being, strength, prosperity, and progeny. Furthermore, the people themselves will become "a blessing" (cf. Gen. 12:2–3). God's commandments and ways are meant not as restriction but rather as prescriptions that lead to the fullness of life for all; in that sense, their end is not meant to constrict but to set free.

Obedience is not merely doing as one is told. Obedience means "to listen," which involves more than just hearing and following. Obedience is a discernment process that involves not only the mind and will but also, and most especially, the heart. In Deuteronomy 11:13; 13:4; 30:2, Moses calls on the

Pastoral Perspective

choose death. Choose covenant, gain land; reject covenant, lose land. Choose covenant, receive blessing; reject covenant, receive curse. Schooled in a society that shops around for a "wider selection," we resist any effort to have our choices curtailed. We resist having our choices cut, because it threatens the illusion of our autonomy—perhaps *the* central value of our culture. We cannot imagine God as a credible actor in the world in which we live, demanding obedience that must be chosen if we are to have a future. We hesitate to agree that divine sanctions operate against the rabid independence and unrestrained consumption that resist fidelity to YHWH and the social vision that YHWH enacts.

The truth, according to Deuteronomy, is that there will be hell to pay for the choices we make when those choices run counter to God's covenantal obligations. We know this is true in the lives of the people we counsel. Promises are violated in marriages. Destructive secrets erupt from the places where families hide them. Irresponsible financial decisions run their ultimate course. The predictable destruction that lies in the wake confirms that there are severe consequences for violating covenantal norms. We know this is true in the dynamics of congregational life. Conflicts arise in the absence of healthy leadership, words are exchanged, sides are taken, splits occur. It takes years for these congregations to leave the pain and isolation of congregational exile. Some never do. We know this is true in our world. As I write, the markets of the world economy are crumbling. While we do not yet know the details, we know enough to conclude that God's ethical demands for fairness in the marketplace have been violated in the name of basic greed. There will be hell to pay for the choices that we make.

Perhaps our resistance to this kind of counsel is not simply a concern about God's beneficence, but our wish to live as though God were not so attentive to the choices that we make. Perhaps we have been led further astray than we first imagined. Perhaps we have bowed down to the gods of choice more often than we have been willing to admit.

Of course, misfortune is not necessarily connected to God's judgment. Neither is every material blessing a byproduct of covenantal faithfulness. The book of Job attests to the danger of universalizing the Deuteronomic formula in every place, in every life, in every time. Bad things sometimes happen to good people. Good things sometimes happen to bad people. Yet, as Martin Luther King reminds us, the

pattern of these treaties. That pattern is as follows: (a) a suzerain reviews the history of his beneficence toward a vassal; (b) treaty stipulations are listed; (c) the code is witnessed by the gods and sanctioned with rewards and punishments; and (d) provision is made for the public reading and deposition of the agreement.

The Deuteronomists may indeed have drawn upon memories of this ancient treaty pattern. Their book opens with a historical memoir by Moses (1:1–4:43), followed by a torah of Moses (4:44–28:68) that includes a corpus of law (12:2–26:15) and curses and blessings as sanctions (chap. 28). At the end of the book are provisions for public promulgation and archiving (chap. 31). In spite of these evident similarities, however, in recent years scholarship has preferred to take the encompassing genre of the book to be a last will and testament, Moses's final gift to his people. Enclosed within that pedagogical and homiletical frame is a covenant text, the torah of Moses and the sanctions attached to it. This covenant functions as a sacral constitution for the ideal theocratic state.

Unlike a suzerainty treaty, which is imposed by a sovereign on a subjugated vassal, this covenant or political charter requires community assent. Deuteronomy's task is to win that assent through exhortation, the carrot and the stick, even the hard sell! Our passage for today, Deuteronomy 30:15–20, reveals the passion for national unity and common loyalty that animate this great evangelical document, the book of Deuteronomy.

The Conditions for Life and Death (vv. 15–18). This climactic final paragraph of Moses's farewell address opens with the theme of retributive justice, cast in the familiar conditional syntax favored by the Deuteronomists. There follow summations of deeds that are reckoned to be good or evil. The good deeds to which Israel is summoned are expressed in verbs: "obey . . . loving . . . walking in his ways . . . observing." These lead to the multiplication of life, long tenure in the land, and God's direct intervention to bless (v. 16). In contrast, idolatry—the only sin listed in verse 17, but a cardinal one for sure—inevitably leads to alienation from the land and death (v. 18).

Choose Life! (vv. 19–20). At the end we reach the segment of the passage that causes this lection to be well known and loved. First, Moses sets forth in a stark form the two ways: life and death, blessings and curses. In his comparable sermon in 4:25–31, Moses

"Tony Martin enjoyed his job, and every now and then, he spoke a word of grace to a coworker who would not otherwise have heard it."

If poets wrote obituaries, then we would be reminded that we can either choose or refuse life.

Moses has been dealing with questions of mortality. He knows he is about to die. The Israelites are at the Jordan River about to enter the promised land. Moses is reminiscing on the peaks and valleys. He wants to tell his people once more how to live a good life. Moses wants them to hear what he is saying and take it to heart.

Moses's farewell address seems to have lasted twenty-six chapters—significantly longer than most Sunday sermons. Moses reminds them of what they have been through: slavery in Egypt, crossing the Red Sea, receiving the commandments, and wandering in the wilderness. Then, on the edge of the promised land, Moses lays out the two ways between which Israel must decide: "I have set before you today life and prosperity, death and adversity" (30:15).

What does it mean to choose life and prosperity? According to Moses, it means to love God with heart, mind, and soul (6:4–9). In the first few hours of his sermon (along with some ideas that you will not want to preach), Moses says that the good life includes canceling the debts of the poor (15:1–11), pushing government to guard against excessive wealth (16:18–20), limiting punishment to protect human dignity (19:1–7), restricting those who can be drafted (20:1–8), offering hospitality to runaway slaves (23:15–16), paying employees fairly (24:14–15), and leaving part of the harvest for those who need it (24:19–22). When Moses looked back, he saw that life was best for the Israelites when they were trying to please God.

Moses finally comes to the conclusion of a powerful sermon: "Listen to what I have said today. I have laid it out for you, life and death, good and evil. Love God. Walk in God's ways. Keep the commandments so that you will live, truly live, passionately, joyfully, blessed by God. I warn you. If you have a change of heart, refuse to listen, and serve little gods, you will die. It is your choice, life or death, blessings or curses" (30:15–19, my paraphrase).

The choices are not usually labeled "life" and "death." Most of our decisions do not seem important, but life and death are before us every day. We choose death when we ignore God and choose anything inferior. Death is a slow process of giving ourselves to what does not matter. Modern life is impoverished

Deuteronomy 30:15-20

Theological Perspective

Israelites to listen "with all [their] heart." In the biblical tradition, the heart is the most important organ, one that is central to God's relationship with Israel. God set God's "heart" on Israel and chose Israel because Israel was the fewest of all peoples (Deut. 7:7). God's love for Israel is an affair of the heart, and God, in turn, wants such a relationship to be reciprocal. Covenant is supposed to be grounded in mutual, wedded love. Obedience, then, calls the Israelites "to listen" to God's word in their inner selves, at their core, and to live out that word, which, in turn, will result in life transformed truly into God's image, according to God's likeness, with God's ways made manifest through the people's daily life together.

Having had two choices placed before them, the people are now warned that if they turn their hearts away, and do not hear, and consequently turn to idolatry, then serious consequences will follow. The people can choose a life of blessing or a death sentence with its curses.

In the last section of our reading, Moses gives the people a specific directive with regard to the choice they face. He exhorts them to "choose life" (v. 19). Now the Israelites are faced with not only a choice between life and death, but also a decision as to whether they will listen to the wise directive given to them. The scenario has been laid out before them; God's will has been revealed. The people are left free to exercise their free will. In his interpretation of this passage, Basil calls for life and death, good and evil, to be balanced within ourselves. Caesarius of Arles notes that by God's grace, people have been left to choose the narrow way, the way of life. Finally, a life blessed or a life cursed is the choice confronting the Israelites and people today. History bears out, however, that many times the Israelites chose their own way and suffered the consequences of their own decisions. God, however, remains faithful to the people in a myriad of ways, despite their wrong choices. Choosing life, then, is a lifelong process, sometimes learned only in the midst of struggle.

CAROL J. DEMPSEY

Pastoral Perspective

moral arc of the universe does bend toward justice. Deuteronomy claims it bends that way by design.

Walter Brueggemann has examined God's relationship to four superpowers in the Old Testament. He concludes that the break that occurs in the power of empires is always credited to God's activity. "Where Yahweh is not obeyed, a decisive break occurs in every individual life and in the life of every community or state. No power can live defiantly in the face of Yahweh's sovereignty."[1] Our choices are not always what they seem.

The flip side of these ominous warnings is that God desires for the community to be blessed. God desires life, not death. God hopes that Israel will make the right choice, for faithfulness. The right choice means blessings for the entire community, not just for some. The right choice means a home not just for God's people but for resident aliens as well. The right choice means economic policies that leave enough for everyone. The right choice means an equitable distribution of resources. The right choice means life—this is what God desires for us.

Both warning and promise arise from this text. The difficult choice the pastor faces is determining when to offer which. It is impossible to universalize such an interpretive move, but cues can be taken from the way Israel has handled this covenant. In times of expanding power—economic, political, and otherwise—the prophets often warn Israel that covenant violations cannot be sustained. In times of exile, the promises of land for the landless, hope for the hopeless, and life for those who keep God's ways have been announced. Said differently, when people are hurting from the wounds of their own hands, we voice God's hope for restoration. God does offer a future beyond exile. When people are thriving, we voice God's demand for faithfulness as expressed by our relations with our neighbors.

God has chosen to draw us into this covenant. It is this choice that makes life possible.

ANDREW FOSTER CONNORS

---

1. Walter Brueggemann, *Theology of the Old Testament* (Minneapolis: Augsburg Fortress, 1997), 519.

Exegetical Perspective

calls heaven and earth to witness against Israel (4:26; see also 31:28). There the people perish because of their fatal choice of idolatry over worship of the true God. In this passage the cosmic witnesses are invoked not to testify to Israel's sin, but to vouch that YHWH has placed before them the choice between life and death. Then comes the great challenge: "Choose life!" The sense if not the form of the Hebrew verb for "choose" (*ubaharta)* is imperative. It points to an as yet unresolved decision. What do they do? At the end of the book of Joshua, in the context of a covenant ratification ceremony, the people publically commit themselves to rejecting idolatry. They say, "We also will serve the LORD, for he is our God" (Josh. 24:18). They seal the covenant with their choice and consequently are liable for their subsequent apostasies.

In Deuteronomy 30:19, we hear neither sooner or later of a collective choice. For the interpreter that means that the offer remains open ended. This feature of the summary conclusion of the book of Deuteronomy, a book always held to be the centerpiece of retributional theology in the OT, suggests that it is not offering a closed system after all. God's hands are not tied to mandatory prison and death sentences for transgressors. The choice of life always remains an option.

This open-endedness, flowing from the one who cares about the people's fate, in spite of their constant betrayal, actually underlies the entire book. Moses's sermon in 4:25–40 comes to the same point circuitously, but it makes the key affirmation: "Because the LORD your God is a merciful God, he will neither abandon you nor destroy you; he will not forget the covenant with your ancestors that he swore to them" (4:31). Other evidences that the Deuteronomists sought more to win loyalty and inculcate hope than to set forth a rigid scheme of reward and punishment can be found in such passages as 7:12–16; 11:8–25; 26:15; 30:1–10. The covenant code contained within the book and the sanctions attached to it provided Israel a way of understanding why bad things such as the Babylonian exile happened to them. It also left them room always to make a new start, to reaffirm their allegiance to God, to choose life.

Finally, by leaving this appeal of verse 19 open-ended, the Deuteronomist exhorts all generations. Think of it! The choice of life is an option always open to everyone.

W. SIBLEY TOWNER

Homiletical Perspective

with a lack of purpose. We rush to meet deadlines that are insignificant and bow before ideas that are not worthy.

Moses's sermon reminds us that one of the preacher's tasks is to enumerate the ways we choose life. Love God with all of our heart, mind, and soul. Give to the poor. Fight for justice. Care for the hurting. Treat others fairly. Share food with the hungry.

This text offers preachers an opportunity to suggest a myriad of sacred possibilities. Learn things you have told yourself you would never learn. Enjoy simple things. Play with children. Laugh often, long, and loud. Cry when it is time to cry. Be patient with your own imperfections as well as the imperfections of others. Celebrate sex with the one to whom you have given your life. Surround yourself with what you love—whether it is family, friends, pets, music, nature, or silence.

Walk around the block. Turn off the television. Get together with your friends. Invite a stranger to lunch or dinner. Clean out a drawer. Read a book of poetry. Quit doing what is not worth your time. Do something so someone else will not have to. Give money to a cause you care about. Stop arguing. Apologize to someone, even if it was mostly his fault. Forgive someone, even if she does not deserve it. Have patience. Stop having patience when it is time to tell the truth. Figure out what you hope for and live with that hope.

Worship with all your heart. Pray genuinely. Love your church. Believe that God loves you. Remember the stories of Jesus. See Christ in the people around you. Share God's love with someone who has forgotten it. Delight in God's good gifts. See that all of life is holy. Open your heart to the Spirit. Search for something deeper and better than your own comfort. Live in the joy beneath it all. Let God make your life wonderful.

Moses preached that we choose life in an amazing variety of ways. This text provides a wonderful chance for preachers to say to their congregations, "Today I set before you life and death, blessings and curses. Choose life."

BRETT YOUNGER

Psalm 119:1-8

[1]Happy are those whose way is blameless,
who walk in the law of the LORD.
[2]Happy are those who keep his decrees,
who seek him with their whole heart,
[3]who also do no wrong,
but walk in his ways.
[4]You have commanded your precepts
to be kept diligently.
[5]O that my ways may be steadfast
in keeping your statutes!
[6]Then I shall not be put to shame,
having my eyes fixed on all your commandments.
[7]I will praise you with an upright heart,
when I learn your righteous ordinances.
[8]I will observe your statutes;
do not utterly forsake me.

Theological Perspective

The central theology of this psalm is the Word of God. At least 173 of the 176 verses mention the Scriptures by some title or another. Synonyms for the Bible in the psalm include law, testimonies, ways, precepts, statutes, commandments, and word. All these can be found in the first eight verses of the psalm, which are assigned for today's reading.

This complex psalm, the longest in the Psalter, celebrates the place of Torah in the life of Israel in twenty-two stanzas, each with eight verses, one stanza for each letter of the Hebrew alphabet. In the biblical world, the number eight signifies another complete teaching, as reflected, for example, in the Beatitudes of Jesus' Sermon on the Mount.

Jewish prayers often include eight liturgical movements: three adorations, four intercessions, and one doxology. The Lord's Prayer is a perfect example, as explained in *Didache* (8.2). The number eight is often associated with teaching elements as a complete score of one's prayer petition and instruction.

This psalm is an extended alphabetic acrostic. In the Hebrew, all the verses in each stanza start with the same letter, and the letter gives its name to the stanza. The first eight verses are categorized under the first letter, *aleph*, and thereafter each of the twenty-two letters, in order, of the Hebrew alphabet introduces eight verse lines. In today's reading, each

Pastoral Perspective

Psalm 119 is the longest and most complex of the Psalms. It is an acrostic, referred to by scholars as a Long Acrostic because it has twenty-two stanzas, one for each letter of the Hebrew alphabet, in order; in each stanza, its letter is used to begin each of eight verses. This makes a total of 176 verses of poetry. Why such commitment to what had to make for far more difficult and sometimes awkward writing? These words were written using a memory device so that this teaching pastor might be able to send students forth with these words in their hearts, so that they would be able to take them out and recite them when they were most needed in times of crisis, especially in times of moral wavering, when the scrolls that held the law would not be close to hand.[1]

Verse 9 indicates that this psalm was written in the wisdom tradition, with youth in mind. Imagine with me then a pastor of literary bent, who has been worried about and praying for his or her youth group. In every era, it is difficult to be a young person. This is why the timeless gift of faith is so very important. We have a treasure of such life-giving power to offer our young people, if we could but find compelling words. This is the very thing the

1. I am indebted for many of these insights to Robert Alter's *The Book of Psalms: A Translation with Commentary* (New York: W. W. Norton and Co., 2007). 419.

Exegetical Perspective

Psalm 119 is an extended meditation on the law. Along with Psalm 1 and Psalm 19, it belongs to a genre known as Torah Psalms because of their focus on the law. The first verse of Psalm 119 summarizes the entire poem: "Happy are those whose way is blameless, who walk in the law [Heb. *torah*] of the LORD." In contrast to Christian traditions that view the law as a burden on the ancient Israelites (see Acts 15:10), Psalm 119 expresses the Israelites' joy at having the perfect guidance the Torah provides. The fact that Psalm 119 is the longest psalm—as well as the longest chapter in the entire Bible—testifies to the Israelites' conviction that the Torah was the greatest gift any nation had ever received (Deut. 4:5–8).

Psalm 119 is an acrostic psalm, a form of Hebrew poetry in which each verse, phrase, or group of verses begins with the successive letters of the Hebrew alphabet. Other examples of acrostic psalms are Psalms 9–10 (taken together), 25, 34, 111, 112, and 145. Psalm 119 is unique among these psalms, however. Instead of having each verse or phrase begin with a successive letter, this psalm divides its 176 verses into twenty-two groups of eight verses, all eight of which begin with the same letter. The verses assigned for this Sunday, for example, all begin with *'alef*, the first letter of the Hebrew alphabet. This arrangement was done not only to

Homiletical Perspective

Why preach on Psalm 119? It is long, repetitive, and baroque in its complexity. Scholars note its elaborate acrostic structure; it is divided into twenty-two sections of eight verses each, every verse within each section beginning with the same letter of the Hebrew alphabet, and the sections themselves arranged in alphabetical order.[1] With such a complex structure, it is easy to lose sight of the text of Psalm 119 in favor of its design. However, there is more to the text than meets the eye, and we deprive ourselves of the text's riches if our exegesis stops with its architecture.

Looking at the text itself, one might be tempted to think of the psalm as a drawn-out appeal to simple obedience of the Torah. But the psalm invites us into more than compliance with the law. Walter Brueggemann, writing about the role of the law in Psalm 119, says, "The torah becomes a point of entry for exploring the whole range of interactions with [YHWH]. . . . A life of full obedience is not a conclusion of faith. It is a beginning point and an access to a life filled with many-sided communion with God."[2]

The first eight verses of Psalm 119 support Brueggemann's interpretation. What looks at first like a series of commands is found on closer examination

1. Mitchell Dahood, *Psalms III, 101–150* (New York: Doubleday, 1968), 172.
2. Walter Brueggemann, *The Message of the Psalms* (Minneapolis: Augsburg Publishing House, 1984), 41.

Psalm 119:1-8

Theological Perspective

verse displays a different meaning of the word "Torah." The many names of the Bible are introduced in the following categories: law (v. 1), decrees or testimonies (v. 2), ways (v. 3), precepts (v. 4), statutes (v. 5), commandments (v. 6), judgments or ordinances (v. 7), and again, statutes (v. 8). What a wonderful way of introducing the Word of God to the students of Torah! Torah is best translated as "instruction" rather than "law." It is a gift from God inviting us to engage in holy play!

When one is playing a game, in order to enjoy the game fully, it is very important to know the rules of the game. The pleasure of improvisation and imagination depends on knowing the basic rules of the particular game and mastering them. Unless you know the rules, you will not be free to engage in the fullest sense and with total commitment. Therefore, it is necessary carefully to go over the basic rules of the game and to encourage the player to play with great freedom and to enjoy the process.

The psalm is evidently intended as a manual of pious thoughts, especially for instructing the young. Its peculiar artificial structure was probably adopted to aid the memory. However, it is intended to be used not in a monotonous, boring way, but in a joyful search for the clues and guidelines in the composition—as if one is playing a holy game with the Lord.

According to the psalm, happiness comes from people of integrity, who follow the instructions of God (v. 1). Happy and joyful are those who obey the laws and seek to obey with all their hearts (v. 2). The joy of well-being, of being alive, is expressed in these verses. In today's reading in the Hebrew Bible, Deuteronomy 30:15–20, God loves the people of Israel and desires well-being for them. The question is, will Israel love God as a child loves a parent? Every day, Israel must decide whether to remain faithful.

One of the most famous verses of the psalm is verse 105, "Your word is a lamp to my feet and a light to my path." The psalm's theme, the Word of God, points to that Word in many ways. Sometimes several verses in a row point to a common topic. At other times, the subtopics change with each verse. The psalm's beauty lies in the continuous reminder to the people to return to the Word of God and its power in our lives. There are also numerous key verses, all in this very first section, that establish important doctrines about God's Word.

While the law (v. 1) points to the instructional perspective, testimony (v. 2) points to the covenantal relationship with the Word. The covenant was renewed and witnessed at Sinai, Moab, and

Pastoral Perspective

psalmist is trying to accomplish. So this pastor uses the familiar alphabet in order to help young people be able to recall these passages of verse whenever a time of temptation comes. These words allow one to lean on *torah* the way a person with an injured leg leans on a crutch until the weakness passes.

Consider, for example, when the hormones are raging, and a youth is on a date; how difficult it is to think clearly about one's moral obligations. So the psalmist has written in "rap" for the youth group to memorize: "With my whole heart I cry; answer me, O LORD. I will keep your statutes. I cry to you; save me, that I may observe your decrees. I rise before dawn and cry for help; I put my hope in your words" (vv. 145–47). As one Harlem youth pastor has translated: "No fling, no bling, 'cause He is King." In the few seconds it takes for the mind to remember these words, the body has begun to come back under the mind's control. Indeed, all it takes is the decision of a youth to remember the psalm, and the help of the Lord has already come.

So if the decision to use the acrostic is a pedagogical one, there is another interesting literary choice made by the author. A reader cannot get far into Psalm 119 without being struck by the sheer number of synonyms used for the "Law of God" as well as the felicity of the words that surround and describe those synonyms. Verse 1 in the NRSV reads, "Happy are those whose way is blameless, who walk in the law of the LORD." "Happy" and "blameless" are the adjectives describing both "the way" and "the Law," in the Hebrew *torah*. Happy and wholehearted is the description in verse 2 of those "who keep [the Lord's] decrees" (*'edut*). "Diligently," "steadfast," "not put to shame," "having my eyes fixed," "with an upright heart": all these are used to describe how the supplicant shall rightly observe the Lord's statutes (*hoq*) and precepts (*piqqudim*), as translated in the NRSV in verses 3–5. This language builds to those lovely verses 103 and 105: "How sweet are your words ['*imrah*] to my taste, sweeter than honey to my mouth!" "Your word [*davar*] is a lamp to my feet and a light to my path."

Here the variety of language is both aesthetically pleasing and a wonderful rhetorical device. The variety of language used for *torah*, as well as the richness of the language used to characterize *torah*, conveys its significance in the life of the people. We refer to it as "the law" and "the way" and "the truth" and "the Word" as well as "the Lord's statutes" and "the Lord's precepts" and "the Lord's decrees and utterances," and we all know we are referring to roughly the same

exhibit the skill of the psalmist but also to aid in memorization.

Psalm 119 contains a number of Hebrew terms for laws and commandments. The word "law" (Heb. *torah*) occurs twenty-five times in the psalm. Other terms include "decrees" (Heb. *edah*; fourteen times), "precepts" (Heb. *piqqudhim*; twenty-one times), "statutes" (Heb. *hoq*; twenty-one times), "commandment" (Heb. *mitsvah*; twenty-two times), and "ordinance" (Heb. *mishpat*; twenty-three times). Although in the Priestly corpus each of these terms has a precise meaning that differentiates it from the other words in the list, it is unlikely that such precision is being used in Psalm 119. Instead, these terms are probably being used synonymously to refer to the law as a whole and/or to individual laws.

Two other important words in this psalm are the noun "way" (Heb. *derek*) and the verb "to walk" (Heb. *halak*). Together, they form a metaphor for what the law provides: a path for the righteous to follow. According to verse 1, those who "walk in the law of the LORD" are said to have a way that is blameless. The laws of the Torah mark the boundary of this path, enabling the righteous to remain on the road. So important is this metaphor to Jewish ethics that the related term "halakha" is used to refer to the laws of the Hebrew Scriptures and the rabbinic interpretations of those laws in the Talmud.

The first two verses of Psalm 119 introduce the psalm with the repeated phrase "Happy are those . . .", which opens each verse. This echoes the beginning of Psalm 1, the Torah Psalm that stands as an introduction to the entire Psalter. Here, those who are happy are the ones who have kept their way blameless by obedience to the law. They keep God's decrees and seek after God "with their whole heart" (v. 2). Unlike Western modes of thought, where the heart represents the seat of emotion, in the Israelite conception the heart was the locus of thought and intention. The heart was responsible not only for understanding the law but also for having the intent to obey it. To seek God with the whole heart meant complete obedience to the Torah. Verse 3 reinforces the connection between upright behavior and keeping to the ways of God, bringing the metaphor of walking the straight path to the foreground again.

Verses 4 and 5 build upon each other. In verse 4, the psalmist states that God has commanded the law to be kept diligently (lit. "to keep the precepts exceedingly"). Wanting to obey but aware of his own limitations, the poet prays in verse 5, "O that my ways may be steadfast," asking that his path might

to be deeply personal, a journal of conversion describing the process of spiritual growth: from hearing the law, to obedience, to a close relationship with and dependence upon God. Each step along the way offers insights for preachers.

The psalm begins with an assertion of faith. "Happy are those whose way is blameless, who walk in the law of the LORD." Those hearing these words for the first time today would probably notice two words: happy and blameless. We desire happiness, and we seek it in our faith. We wish to be free of blame, not only before God but before ourselves. Our desire for both drives the psalm.

Verse 2 explores what it means to walk in the way of the Lord. First, it requires obedience to God's decrees. Equally important, we are to seek God with our whole hearts. The letter of the law is not enough; true obedience begins with a deep longing for God.

That longing for God is quite different from the force of habit that sometimes motivates a life of faith. People may take on ministries in the church because no one else will do it, or because they are pressured by the clergy, not because they are called. True ministry grows from a passion to seek and know God, and a sermon that names this can begin a conversation that will lead to a healthier spiritual life.

In verse 3 the psalm further explores what it means to walk in the law of the Lord. We do not just obey the law; we "also do no wrong." We refrain, not just from what is explicitly prohibited, but also from the moral wrongs the law implies. One mother brought her child home from summer camp and discovered that he had hardly used any of his shampoo. When asked why, the child replied, "The first night our counselor said to make sure to use soap and shampoo in the shower, but after that he just said to use soap." It is this sort of narrow literalism that verse 3a warns against.

The first section of the psalm concludes with verse 3b. The text then shifts from the third person to the second. A narrator emerges and engages God, recognizing that the law is not an abstraction but something that applies to her personally. Does the congregation feel the same way? It is easy to know what the law demands of others, but not as easy to accept its demands on oneself. Are parishioners aware of their own need for conversion, or are they focused outward, more concerned with seeing a change in elected officials and public policy?

Verses 5–8 shift once again, this time to the first person. Having recognized that the law applies to her, the narrator hopes in verse 5 to uphold it. We

Psalm 119:1-8

Theological Perspective

Jerusalem, and continues here in our present community. Walking in the ways (v. 3) of the Word means understanding the habits, behaviors, customs, and traditions of the previous generations so that the next generation may be properly prepared for its role. We are fully keeping the precepts (v. 4) that are laid down by the Lord as commanded for the people. The statutes (v. 5) are concretely secured by making the path straight. If we regard the commandments (v. 6) with the highest respect, we will not be put to shame. God's judgments or ordinances (v. 7) are causes of thanksgiving from one's pure heart. Again, statutes (v. 8) will be kept as remembrance of God's sacraments.

We keep God's words when we submit and obey with hope and expectation of the fulfillment of promise. We dream our dreams in the promised Word of the Lord. The promised Word is Jesus Christ. God's words are spoken in many different forms of the Word—in prophecy and preaching of the Word, in the written Word of Scriptures, and in the visible Word in the sacraments. All these words point toward the light of Christ.

> There is no speech, nor are there words;
>   their voice is not heard;
> yet their voice goes out through all the earth,
>   and their words to the end of the world.
>   (Ps. 19:3–4)

The Word of God revealed in Jesus Christ is the fulfillment of the Word that the Torah illustrates in this didactical and instructional psalm we sing today. That is right! We sing the texts because reading alone does not fully bring our joyful emotion and our glad heart as we live in the Word. Our sound will join the choruses of angels in heaven and earth telling the glory of almighty God. Alleluia! Praise the Lord!

PAUL JUNGGAP HUH

Pastoral Perspective

body of work. We would not have half so many names for Torah or the Word if it were not for its sweeping importance in our lives.

If the significance of the variety of names for the Word of God got past you, then the adjectives the psalmist applies either to "the Word" or to the person willing to trust in "the Word" would be hard to ignore. The person who trusts in the Word is happy, blameless, upright, unashamed, honest, delighted, insightful, wise, open, loved, lifted up, hopeful, consoled. This is a splurge of joyful promise offered to young people willing to walk in the way. How is that "Way" described? It is righteous, wonderful, gracious, life-giving, good, bountiful, trustworthy, true, kind, my heart's joy! This is a believer who has gotten inside the Scriptures and has allowed them to get inside him.

Does she recognize that there are passages with moral difficulties? Of course. You cannot read any midrash and not know that rabbis are fully aware that Scripture is holy not on its own (that would be idolatry), but because it contains God's word. Any fallible human must wrestle with a passage, lest the evil of this world deliberately lead one to misunderstand. The notion that anyone can simply read Scripture alone and understand its "plain meaning" underestimates the dark corners of the human heart and the real evil that roams the world. That having been said, when read in the company of the Holy Spirit where two or three are gathered, Scripture can indeed be sweet to the palate, more than honey to the mouth, a light unto our paths and our hearts' joy!

BARBARA S. BLAISDELL

conform to the path of God. The psalmist expresses hope that he might be able to keep the commandments, a hope that serves as a prayer God would keep him on the right path.

In verses 6–8, the psalmist turns to the results of obeying the Torah. Having kept God's commandments, he will not be put to shame. In a society like ancient Israel, where honor was of utmost importance, to be put to shame was to lose social standing (cf. Ps. 25:1–3). The psalmist states here that only through following the law will honor be kept intact. In verse 7 he states that after he has learned the law, he will be able to worship God with an upright heart. As the processional hymn in Psalm 24 makes clear, only those who have "clean hands and pure hearts" may ascend to the temple mount (Ps. 24:3–4). The connection between ethical behavior and the worship of God is strong. Only with a heart that is obedient to the law can God be worshiped in a worthy manner.

The final verse in this first section completes the verses that begin with *'alef*. Verse 8 makes a declaration and a request. The psalmist declares his intention to keep (lit. "guard," the same verb used in vv. 4–5) God's statutes. God has commanded the law to be kept (v. 4); the psalmist prays that he might be able to keep it (v. 5) and now states his intent to follow the law (v. 8). He closes this section with the request that God not abandon him completely. Although the reading for this Sunday ends with verse 8, this psalm deserves to be read in its entirety. In doing so on a regular basis, we will be brought to the place where we can say, "Oh, how I love your law! It is my meditation all day long" (Ps. 119:97).

KEVIN A. WILSON

are often aware of the distance between our intentions and our actions, and we yearn for steadfastness of faith to close the gap. Simply by acknowledging that distance, a preacher can comfort the congregation with the knowledge that they are not alone.

In verse 6 the narrator describes the benefits of obedience. "I shall not be put to shame," he writes. Again the text can appeal to a deep psychological need in the congregation. Do we live in shame? Do we want to be set free from it? What keeps us from pursuing that freedom?

When freed from shame, the psalmist will respond with gratitude: "I will praise you with an upright heart" (v. 7). The culmination of obedience is freedom from shame and heartfelt praise. A preacher might ask what such praise looks like. Is the congregation truly prepared for unadulterated praise? Does it secretly enjoy lifeless worship, valuing empty predictability over an intruding Spirit?

In verse 8 the narrator nears the end of the journey. He understands the demands of the law (vv. 1–4), knows that they apply to him (v. 5), and anticipates the joy and gratitude that come with obeying them (vv. 6–7). At last in verse 8 he makes a commitment to follow the law.

Verse 8b adds an essential follow-up to that commitment. Having promised to obey God's law, the narrator immediately pleads, "Do not utterly forsake me." However well we understand the commandments and strive to follow them, we cannot succeed on our own. It is perhaps these final words that a congregation needs to hear most of all. They comfort us in our shortcomings and failures, and they humble us when we assume we can satisfy God's law without a double portion of grace. The obedience called for in verse 1 is only a beginning, and leads in verse 8 to a much richer closeness with and dependence on God.

DREW BUNTING

1 Corinthians 3:1-9

¹And so, brothers and sisters, I could not speak to you as spiritual people, but rather as people of the flesh, as infants in Christ. ²I fed you with milk, not solid food, for you were not ready for solid food. Even now you are still not ready, ³for you are still of the flesh. For as long as there is jealousy and quarreling among you, are you not of the flesh, and behaving according to human inclinations? ⁴For when one says, "I belong to Paul," and another, "I belong to Apollos," are you not merely human?

⁵What then is Apollos? What is Paul? Servants through whom you came to believe, as the Lord assigned to each. ⁶I planted, Apollos watered, but God gave the growth. ⁷So neither the one who plants nor the one who waters is anything, but only God who gives the growth. ⁸The one who plants and the one who waters have a common purpose, and each will receive wages according to the labor of each. ⁹For we are God's servants, working together; you are God's field, God's building.

Theological Perspective

Paul is working to counter factions in the Corinthian community that have formed around claims of superior wisdom attributed to various religious teachers. Paul's response to this situation has been to deny that human wisdom, however exalted, has any ability to attain reliable knowledge of God (chap. 1). Paul argues instead that it is the Holy Spirit that equips human beings to know God truly (chap. 2), rather than rhetorical-philosophical cleverness.

It is easy to see how Paul's teaching would effectively counter the impulse to split the church into factions around the claims of rival teachers, but there is a possibility that the cure might turn out to be worse than the disease.

One could conclude, on the basis of what Paul has said, that Christian faith is simply a matter of receiving personal inspiration directly from the Holy Spirit, without any need for human teachers at all. The church has had some unfortunate experiences over the centuries with allegedly "Spirit-led" individuals deceiving masses of people with destructive self-serving. In this section Paul makes clear that this is not the picture of the Christian community he has in mind.

In 2:6–13 Paul has made it clear that religious wisdom is not a set of religious or philosophical principles that human reason could deduce on its

Pastoral Perspective

Jean Vanier, the founder of L'Arche community, suggests that we all carry a deep wound of loneliness that is not easily overcome, and that this wound is so much a part of our human condition that we cannot escape it, try as we might. We want to belong in the worst way, so we join communities, but they always tend to disappoint us. He further claims that we have carried these wounds since childhood.[1] I think that Vanier is right.

These wounds were much in evidence in the church Paul founded in Corinth. The people of the church of Corinth, it seems, wanted desperately to belong. They must have had mainline Christian leanings, because they divided up into groups with buttons announcing, "I belong to Paul" or "I belong to Apollos" or some other charismatic leader. In Paul's view this rivalry betrayed a misunderstanding of the gospel. Paul came preaching Christ and him crucified, one who identified most deeply with our human woundedness, reconciling us to God—a God who alone can give a sense of who we are and whose we are as beloved people of God. In Paul's view, the Corinthians are acting like children, "as infants in Christ." The image of childhood here is striking,

---

1. Stanley Hauerwas and Romand Coles, *Christianity, Democracy, and the Radical Ordinary* (Eugene, OR: Cascade, 2008), 197.

Exegetical Perspective

Paul resumes the description of his visit to Corinth, begun at 2:1–5 but interrupted by his explanation of true wisdom, maturity, and the work of the Holy Spirit (2:6–16). He recalls the unformed nature of the Corinthian Christians' life, reminding them that at the beginning, they were influenced by this world ("fleshly," *sarkikos*; "walking according to humanity," *kata anthrōpon*), and that this state of affairs is still evident because of their contentious behavior. Here is clear evidence that Paul's understanding of "the flesh" and of the baser nature of humanity is not tied to a dualism that plays off the body against the spirit or soul. Paul's objection to the Corinthians' common life is not that it is materially oriented, or caught up with what we would call "the sins of the flesh"—though he will in fact deal firmly with sexual immorality at later points in the letter (5:1, 9; 6:9; 7:2; and so on).

Rather, here it is a combination of *spiritual* or *psychic* sins (arrogance, jealousy, quarreling) that leads Paul to mourn the "fleshly" nature of these Christians. Paul alludes, it would seem, to a basic lesson for God's people: the instructions of Psalm 1, which warns against walking in the way of sinners and scoffers, for this route leads to death, rather than to growth and to life. For Paul, the term "the flesh" indicates "fallen human nature" and is manifested in various aspects of the human person, just as the

Homiletical Perspective

Irenaeus of Lyons counseled believers "to take refuge in the Church, to drink milk at her breast, to be fed with the Scriptures of the Lord." He went on to say that the church has been "planted in the world as a paradise."[1] Six weeks after the feast of the Epiphany, with those three eastern sages all packed up and stored once again in their boxes, along with the shepherds and lowing cattle, I wonder how many pastors are feeling that way about the congregations they serve as they prepare to preach on the third chapter of 1 Corinthians. Even the procrastinators among us are at least beginning to think about Ash Wednesday and the Lenten journey that lies ahead. Wilderness, at least, we understand, but how many of us feel as if we live and work for a community that has "been planted in the world as a paradise"?

I suspect that Paul's experience of the church is much more familiar to us. Like him, we live in the midst of strident cultural divisions from which no denomination or congregation is immune. In fact, far too often our fights simply mirror the dominant culture. So we separate into our camps on the left and on the right, certain of our own moral superiority. That Corinthian context, where some claim to

1. *Against Heresies*, V, 20, 2 as quoted in Olivier Clement, *The Roots of Christian Mysticism: Texts from the Patristic Era with Commentary* (New York: New York City Press, 1995), 96.

1 Corinthians 3:1-9

Theological Perspective

own. Rather, there is an authentic wisdom that consists of insight into the eternal plan of God for human beings that has reached its culmination in Jesus. Grasping such wisdom depends on the work of the Holy Spirit, who helps human beings to recognize truthfully what God has done.

Furthermore, within this divinely given wisdom there still exists a less and a more, a progression from "milk" to "solid food." Presumably this means that the divine plan made accessible to human beings by the Spirit has its own kind of order, rationality, and fittingness about it that human beings can in fact ponder and, under the guidance of the Spirit, come to grasp more deeply.

The problem with the Corinthians is not their desire to grow in divine wisdom. The problem is that they have been seeking the wrong kind of wisdom from the wrong sources!

Genuine insight into the plans and purposes of God is given only through the guidance of the Holy Spirit. Therefore persons who are truly in touch with divine wisdom are recognized, not by their philosophical sophistication or impressive speeches, but by signs of the Spirit's presence with them.

What kinds of signs indicate the presence of the Holy Spirit? The Spirit, of course, is none other than the Spirit of Christ. Indeed, Paul has already described those in whom the Spirit dwells as having "the mind of Christ" (2:16). So in general terms, acting, thinking, and loving like Jesus are signs that a person is one in whom the Spirit is active, and thus one who is capable of properly understanding the gospel.

Paul fleshes out this teaching in more specific terms at various places in his writings. In 4:9–13 he contrasts the trials and sufferings of the apostles with the spiritual pride of the Corinthians. He clearly implies that it is the Spirit-inspired willingness to suffer for others, as Christ suffered for us, that marks the apostles as true bearers of the gospel. Similarly, in chapter 13 Paul teaches that the preeminent spiritual gift is the Christlike virtue of love.

Such examples could be multiplied, but Paul's meaning is clear: the presence of the Spirit in a person's life gives rise to Christlike dispositions and actions, and these are therefore the true indicators that someone is a genuinely spiritual person who is capable of rightly grasping the gospel. The strife and jealousy that pit rival factions against one another in the Corinthian community are diametrically opposed to genuine fruits of the Spirit (see Gal. 5:22!). Such un-Christlike behavior marks the

Pastoral Perspective

because if Vanier is right, it is in childhood that we learn to build walls of protection that can be dismantled only by acts of tenderness and care.

I remember vividly one of my own first experiences of real loneliness as a child. My parents had taken my brother and me to visit their best friends in Atlanta, Georgia. It was the first time I had ever been that far away from home. The son of my parents' friends took my brother and me to the local pool. When I arrived and got in the water, I was scared to death. The water was not the problem, for I could swim just fine; it was what the water represented. Suddenly I began to sob uncontrollably. The lifeguard could not console me. The son of my parents' friends could not console me. My brother, of course, thought I was being stupid! Upon hearing of my meltdown, my parents could not figure it out. They said, "At home, he swims like a fish!" The key, of course, was the words "at home." I was a long way from home and in unfamiliar territory. It was an experience of real loneliness. I wanted desperately to be with my parents, but also to be at home. Loneliness is a wound not easily healed.

Vanier tells a story about a severely disabled man named Daniel, whose parents did not want him; so he ended up in one institution after the other. Even after becoming a part of L'Arche, a community that specializes in helping people like Daniel, he would hide his anguish behind hallucinations. As Vanier puts it, "He felt guilty for existing, because nobody wanted him as he was." "What we must do," said Vanier, "is walk with [the wound] instead of fleeing from it. We cannot accept it until we discover that we are loved by God just as we are, and that the Holy Spirit, in a mysterious way, is living at the centre of the wound."

How do you walk with wounds that are so deep and so alienating? The answer Paul gives is Christ and him crucified, who not only identifies with our loneliness, but who also carries our wounds, in order to show us the God who loves us. It is in Christ alone that we can learn we belong. By learning to live in Christ we grow into the discovery that we are loved. The image Paul uses for growth is a horticultural one: "I planted, Apollos watered, but God gave the growth" (v. 6). I recently came upon another image that extends Paul's: the notion of "ecotone," meaning a special meeting ground between two different ecological communities, for example, a forest and a meadow. Ecologists tell us that there is an "edge effect" between these two ecological communities that is particularly fertile

Sixth Sunday after the Epiphany

Holy Spirit transforms the whole of the person: body, mind, soul, and spirit.

It is especially the lack of unity, and the cleaving to a particular human being as a "mascot" rather than to the Lord, that demonstrates how fallen humanity is still riddling the church ("I belong to Paul, . . . to Apollos," v. 4). Paul is following the logic of the prophet Isaiah, who reminded the Judahites that idol worshipers become like "their gods." Similarly, those who set themselves to follow a human being will never attain the glory promised by the Spirit of God, which Paul has celebrated in 2:7. It is, after all, the Spirit of glory who brings the church to maturity, so that its members also show forth the glory of Christ. In this knowledge, sober Christians will assess brothers and sisters (*adelphoi,* 3:1) who are in ministry (v. 5, *diakonoi*), such as Paul and Apollos, according to their real place in the household of faith. They are planters and waterers of a crop that belongs to God. Since seed, water, and growth come from God, it is a moot question whether the planter or the waterer is higher in significance.

Here we may perceive, lurking in Paul's picture, an awareness of the teaching of Jesus concerning the laborers in the vineyard (Matt. 20:1–16), all of whom are God's servants, and all of whom will receive the wage that the Lord has promised. Paul and Apollos have separate assigned (v. 5) responsibilities, and each carries his own burden (see also Gal. 6:5–6), yet they are "one" (v. 8), just as Paul prays that the Corinthians will be united as one body in the way that God intends. (Contemporary translations such as the NRSV obscure the emphasis of Paul's words, softening this blunt statement that they "are one" [*hen eisin*] to the phrase "have a common purpose." Paul, however, is speaking of a unity that goes far beyond mere function or goal!) Moreover, just as the Corinthians cannot claim that their identity is defined by one human leader or another, so neither can Paul or Apollos claim that Corinth is, in the end, "theirs." *We,* says Paul, are workers together with God (*synergoi*); *you* are God's field, God's own building (v. 9).

Agronomic and economic (i.e., "building the household," *oikos*) metaphors for God's people are quite common in Scripture, both in the Old Testament and in the parables of Jesus. We think of the many OT references to Israel as a vineyard or field that the Lord planted (Isa. 5:1–10; Jer. 12:10–13; Jer. 32 passim; Ezek. 17:1–24), and the promise of God to build a house for David, when David had thought to build a temple for the Lord (2 Sam. 7:1–29). In

belong to Cephas and some to Paul and some to Apollos, requires very little hermeneutical imagination on our part.

Not all that long ago we tended to identify ourselves with Luther or Cranmer or Calvin or Ignatius, certain that our own denominations had gotten it right. Today, in our post-Christendom, postmodern, postdenominational context these fault lines seem almost quaint. Now our hostility has truly turned inward, as we define ourselves over against each other, over the authority of Scripture, human sexuality, and what kind of music we consider "sacred." How can the preacher stand among God's people, who know these painful fault lines all too well, to proclaim good news that offers an alternative vision rooted in the life, death, and resurrection of Jesus and the missional experience of the early church? Is it possible to live into that "mystic sweet communion" without being either nostalgic for a past that never really existed or naive about a future that will be fully realized only at the eschaton? To pose this question another way, how do we face the realities that Paul addresses in this reading, while nevertheless imagining with Irenaeus that our vocation really is to be "in the world as a paradise"?

The Epiphany season perhaps provides us with a way forward, and yet too often this season feels like a series of disconnected weeks to mark the time between Christmas and Lent. We are invited to contemplate the vulnerability of the child laid in a manger at his birth, a child whose family fled to Egypt in the midst of a slaughter far too common to human history. Paul points us in this epistle to the vulnerable "king" executed by a government that has all the paperwork in order, a government that dares to claim that all it does is done in the name of international peace. Such is the folly of the world. Far too often, such is the folly that the church merely replicates as we duke it out over what it means to be in the world but not of it, what it means to preach good news in a particular cultural context, without letting that context dictate the contours of the faith.

Paul insists that not only is God made manifest in the world but that on the cross we most clearly see that Christ comes among us not among the powerful but among the weak. Too often in the church our leadership styles mimic the patterns of the world rather than the gospel. So some say that they belong to Cephas or to Apollos or to Paul. All belong to Christ. Paul tells the Corinthian Christians that they are God's servants, God's field, God's building (v. 9). He will go on to remind them that Christ is the sure

1 Corinthians 3:1-9

Theological Perspective

Corinthians as unspiritual people who are not yet equipped to understand authentic divine wisdom.

This is a startling teaching for modern Christians, because we, like the Corinthians, place high value on technical skill in our preachers and teachers. We look for knowledge of Hebrew and Greek, facility with exegetical technique, historical and theological expertise, and above all an engaging speaking style! As useful as such skills are, Paul insists that the primary qualification for knowing God and understanding the gospel rightly is to be a certain kind of Spirit-formed person, living a life that looks like Jesus.

Note the reversal here in customary ways of thinking: it suggests that, instead of reading the Bible in order to learn to be disciples, we must first become Christlike persons in order to be able to read and understand the Bible rightly! Paul shifts attention from the technical qualifications of would-be teachers, because he is convinced that *God* is the primary agent in forming Christian disciples: "I planted, Apollos watered, *but God gave the growth*" (v. 6).

There is much room for practical reflection on this surprising teaching. Today's churches are still bombarded with rival claims about which teachers are the most reliable and effective, and Paul offers practical criteria for judging such claims.

The passage also offers an invitation to reflect on the priorities of the church's ministry as it seeks to make new disciples and strengthen existing ones. Paul suggests that this process of formation is much less about imparting information, at least initially, and much more about drawing people into a particular way of life in community.

If the Spirit is the real agent in conversion, our primary approach to inquirers and those on the margins of the faith should be to draw them into ministries of Christlike love and mercy, to pray for God to give them the Holy Spirit, and to expose them to the sacraments and other means of grace that God uses to impart this gift. If Paul's teaching is correct, only after they and we have been drawn into a Spirit-formed way of life are any of us capable of processing the books and pamphlets and arguments that so often constitute our initial presentation to outsiders.

P. MARK ACHTEMEIER

Pastoral Perspective

and life giving. Indeed, they speak of the "pregnancy of edges."[2]

This notion of the "edge effect" is particularly apt for describing the experience of the community of the wounded who encounter the living God in Christ, in whom we are healed. Indeed, the sacrament of baptism is a powerfully fertile place where we encounter the edge effect. Baptism reminds us of the story of God's love that comes to us amid our woundedness to give us healing and life. Theologian John Burgess says that baptism addresses our temptation to succumb to identity crisis, wherein "we wonder who we really are" and "doubt that our lives are worth much. We see only limitations and dwell on our failures." In baptism we confront the fundamental sin of identity crisis, that "inevitable tendency to believe that we are something different from the self that God has called us to be."[3]

Martin Luther suggested that Christians should begin each day by remembering our baptism, for in baptism one participates in the dying and rising of Christ. The water used in baptism reminds us of the story of creation, the story of the flood, and the story of the exodus. So it is a symbol of both that which threatens and that which gives life. It also reminds us of dying and rising with Christ and sets us on a path of walking with our woundedness in order to find life therein. Baptism, in other words, is symbolic of the fertile place for life—the edge effect—when the community of the wounded encounters God in Christ, who heals our wounds.

ROGER J. GENCH

---

2. The insights in these last two paragraphs are found in Hauerwas and Coles, 197–98 and 14 respectively.
3. John Burgess, *After Baptism: Shaping the Christian Life* (Louisville, KY: Westminster John Knox Press, 2005), 6.

Exegetical Perspective

the NT, we see the continuation of these themes in Matthew 13:24, Acts 7:49, and elsewhere. Jeremiah's use of both themes is particularly pertinent to Paul, who frequently incorporates the ideas of nurturing and edification as part of the apostolic calling, especially throughout the Corinthian correspondence, but in other letters as well. He understands himself as a kind of Jeremiah to the wayward Corinthian church, with power to "build up," since he does not want to "tear down" (see 2 Cor. 10:8). First Corinthians 3:9 links the two metaphors of growing and building, as Paul leaves the trope of the field, which he has used in verses 6–8, and moves toward the idea of building.

Though Paul's argument leads quickly in a particular direction, since it has the practical intention of instructing the Corinthians to put things into balance and to "grow up," many theological implications emerge in a careful exegesis of the text. We have seen that this passage sheds light on the meaning of "flesh" and "spirit" and prevents us from attributing dualism to Paul or taking it on board as an authentic Christian view of reality. This insight is underscored by the earthy nature of Paul's rhetoric in the Corinthian letters, which ranges from breastfeeding to planting and watering to laboring in a household.

At issue here is also the interplay between God and the people of God, a commerce given the (controversial) term "synergy" by Paul: "we are God's coworkers" (*synergoi*, v. 9). (Some, e.g., NRSV, have interpreted the synergy as simply that of the apostles together, but the Greek is ambivalent enough to include the notion of working together with God.) Clearly, everything is of God; yet Paul is unwilling to dismiss human agency, even when considering the spiritual task of bringing God's people to maturity. He can say both that the human ministers (*diakonoi*, v. 5) are "not anything" and that he and Apollos are God's coworkers, each with separate responsibilities and anticipating the astonishing "wages" of grace.

EDITH M. HUMPHREY

Homiletical Perspective

foundation upon which they have been built (3:11), and eventually that they are nothing less than the body of Christ, members one of another (12:12). This high ecclesiology demands that we not lose sight of our noble calling, even in the midst of our day-to-day quarrels.

The late Henri Nouwen often spoke about his journey to L'Arche, a community of mentally handicapped people and their assistants, trying faithfully and simply to live the gospel together. Nouwen, assigned to work with Adam, a twenty-four-year-old epileptic man who could not speak or dress himself, spoke of his real fears. A university professor who was far more comfortable with matters of the head than of the heart, he was now assigned the task of bathing and dressing a grown man. Over time, fear gave way to something new:

> Somehow I started to realize that this poor, broken man was the place where God was speaking to me in a whole new way. Gradually I discovered real affection in myself and I thought that Adam and I belonged together and that it was so important. . . . I want you to understand a little better what happened between Adam and me. Maybe I can say it very simply. Adam taught me a lot about God's love in a very concrete way.[2]

A pastor does not need to go very far to find manifestations of the Christ in the midst of her week. We just need to remember to look beyond the petty squabbles to the depths where Christ's love abounds: the spouse who tenderly cares for his wife in the Alzheimer's unit of the hospital, the child playing Nintendo on an oncology floor, the mother raising four kids on her own. Then we need to help our congregations to look there as well.

RICHARD M. SIMPSON

---

2. Henri Nouwen, "Journey to L'Arche," program #3301, October 1, 1989, http://www.csec.org/csec/sermon/Nouwen_3301.htm.

Matthew 5:21-37

21"You have heard that it was said to those of ancient times, 'You shall not murder'; and 'whoever murders shall be liable to judgment.' 22But I say to you that if you are angry with a brother or sister, you will be liable to judgment; and if you insult a brother or sister, you will be liable to the council; and if you say, 'You fool,' you will be liable to the hell of fire. 23So when you are offering your gift at the altar, if you remember that your brother or sister has something against you, 24leave your gift there before the altar and go; first be reconciled to your brother or sister, and then come and offer your gift. 25Come to terms quickly with your accuser while you are on the way to court with him, or your accuser may hand you over to the judge, and the judge to the guard, and you will be thrown into prison. 26Truly I tell you, you will never get out until you have paid the last penny.

27"You have heard that it was said, 'You shall not commit adultery.' 28But I say to you that everyone who looks at a woman with lust has already committed adultery with her in his heart. 29If your right eye causes you to sin, tear it out

Theological Perspective

Jesus as fulfillment of the law and the prophets: this is the Jesus speaking in today's text, delivering new interpretation of the law for his disciples and followers. In these verses, Jesus addresses some of the more contentious issues of his day. The issues covered in these verses are anger (vv. 21–26), adultery (vv. 27–30), divorce (vv. 31–32), and the taking of oaths (vv. 33–37). If we place today's text in the immediate narrative context of the previous verses (5:13–20), this becomes evident: when disciples and followers act consistent with the new interpretation Jesus offers here, they will be demonstrating what Jesus means by a righteousness that "exceeds that of the scribes and Pharisees" (5:20).[1]

The verses on anger offer us an interpretation that enlarges the frame for understanding the prohibition against murder. Jesus enlarges the prohibition by pointing to ways in which the anger of revenge or punishment that can lead to murder is also evident in the course of living. When you judge and insult a brother or sister in the community, as well as when you are in a legal conflict (both ways in which anger surfaces), you have an opportunity to rectify these situations by seeking the other person out so as to

1. See Charles H. Talbert, *Reading the Sermon on the Mount: Character Formation and Ethical Decision-Making in Matthew 5–7* (Grand Rapids: Baker Academic, 2006), chaps. 3–4 on the structure and functions of the Sermon.

Pastoral Perspective

What are we to do when we find ourselves at odds with the teaching of Jesus, or at least in some disagreement with it, based on our own personal experience? This section of the Sermon on the Mount provides such an occasion.

Jesus makes it clear that if we are in conflict with one of our brothers or sisters, we are to go and seek restoration or reconciliation with that person *before* we bring our gift to the altar. This would imply that old scores need to be settled and wounds healed before we gather around the holy table to receive the sacrament. Such action, of course, would serve as the ideal, in that each one of us could kneel before the Lord with a clear conscience and lighter heart. However, we also know that there are just those moments when the ideal is not immediately possible. The process of reconciliation and forgiveness often takes time, and not a small amount of patience on the part of both parties. It would be an awkward situation, for all concerned, if folk refused to offer their gift—"ourselves, our souls and bodies"—because of some unresolved relationship, yet to be mended. We probably approach the altar with enough feeling of "unworthiness" to begin with, and so the reality of forgiveness must intercede. Forgiveness is the first step toward reconciliation. It is the knowledge that we have been forgiven,

and throw it away; it is better for you to lose one of your members than for your whole body to be thrown into hell. ³⁰And if your right hand causes you to sin, cut it off and throw it away; it is better for you to lose one of your members than for your whole body to go into hell.

³¹"It was also said, 'Whoever divorces his wife, let him give her a certificate of divorce.' ³²But I say to you that anyone who divorces his wife, except on the ground of unchastity, causes her to commit adultery; and whoever marries a divorced woman commits adultery.

³³"Again, you have heard that it was said to those of ancient times, 'You shall not swear falsely, but carry out the vows you have made to the Lord.' ³⁴But I say to you, Do not swear at all, either by heaven, for it is the throne of God, ³⁵or by the earth, for it is his footstool, or by Jerusalem, for it is the city of the great King. ³⁶And do not swear by your head, for you cannot make one hair white or black. ³⁷Let your word be 'Yes, Yes' or 'No, No'; anything more than this comes from the evil one."

Exegetical Perspective

From the perspective of the literary structure of the text, the distribution of the Gospel passages over this Sunday (Matt. 5:21–37) and next Sunday (Matt. 5:38–48) is somewhat unfortunate. Matthew 5:21–48, the first major section of the ethical exhortations of Jesus' sermon, is divided into two triads, verses 21–32 and verses 33–48. That Matthew intended such division is clear from several aspects of the texts. After the threefold "it was said" (vv. 21, 27, 31), verse 33, the opening line of the second set of triads, starts with "*Again*, you have heard that it was said." Further, in verses 21–32, each "it was said" is followed by *hoti*; in verses 33–48 this construction does not occur. The phrase "You have heard that it was said to the men of old" (NRSV "those of ancient times") appears only in 5:21 and 33, the opening lines of the two triads. Finally, each of the three sayings of 5:21–32 refers to an OT text that appears in Deuteronomy; each of the three sayings of 5:32–48 appeals to a text from Leviticus.

As the preceding introductory section of the Gospel (vv. 17–20) makes clear, this section of Jesus' sermon presents an ethic that does not contradict as much as it *transcends* Moses. Jesus exhorts Israel to live Torah in a new way; not as a law that protects against the danger of sin, but as a law that expresses the abundance of the eschatological

Homiletical Perspective

Christians sometimes refer to texts in this lection as antitheses, on the assumption that they contrast the legalism of the First Testament with the new, higher righteousness of Jesus. This attitude feeds anti-Judaism and anti-Semitism. The preacher must lead the congregation toward important theological corrections.

Matthew sees the Sermon on the Mount not as replacing the First Testament but rather as being in theological continuity with it. For Matthew, the new element in the Jewish story is Jesus as God's eschatological prophet whose ministry signals the end of the present age and the imminent apocalypse that will inaugurate the realm of God. The ministry of Jesus anticipates or partially realizes the realm.

The lections for today interpret several Jewish teachings from this eschatological perspective. Matthew does not discard these teachings but instead shows how the deep intention of these commandments becomes operative in the presence of the realm. These readings thus invite the congregation to live as if the realm is fully present.

The reading puts forward four themes: reconciliation (vv. 21–26), adultery (vv. 27–30), divorce (vv. 31–32), and swearing (vv. 33–37). The preacher needs to choose whether to deal with the entire reading or to focus on a limited number of passages.

Matthew 5:21-37

Theological Perspective

apologize (in the former case) or by making amends outside of the legal process (in the latter case). In both cases the objective is clear: to restore relationships through acts of reconciliation. Clearly Jesus is not rescinding the prohibition against murder, but he does place murder on a continuum of outcomes related to anger. Furthermore, Jesus is recognizing that humans do get angry; rather than prohibiting anger, he teaches that it can be transformed by living as a peacemaker (cf. 5:9), initiating acts that manifest the reign of God in our midst.[2]

The next verses are on adultery (vv. 27–30) and divorce (vv. 31–32). With regard to adultery, Jesus expands the meaning of the term so as that it encompasses both intent and action. It is not just the physical act but also the desire for it and the coveting of another man's wife that constitutes adultery. According to the feminist biblical scholar Amy-Jill Levine, this expansion has particular relevance for women: "By collapsing the distinction between thought and action, this extension of the law against adultery to include lust suggests that no one should be regarded as a sex object. The burden here is placed on the man: women are not seen as responsible for enticing men into sexual misadventures."[3] Thus, the references to tearing out an eye and cutting off a hand are hyperbole used by Jesus to emphasize the need for an integrity of the self in terms of the relationship between intent and action, between attitude and practice. Again, Jesus does not abolish the command not to commit adultery, but his inclusion of intention broadens its scope.

In the verses on divorce (vv. 31–32), Jesus also stands in line with tradition in asserting the permissibility of divorce, but he places limits on the grounds for such. In other words, Jesus' interpretation here realigns the question of divorce with God's original intent for the union of man and woman before the fall. The intent is that the union will be forever; even though Jewish law can allow a writ of divorce, the divorce is legal but not spiritually valid. Given God's original intent for marriage, Jesus' followers are to participate in marriage in ways that will preserve it; husbands, in particular, are not to betray their marriage vows by seeking a divorce and thus leaving their wives vulnerable to the charge of adultery. Importantly, in the patriarchal context of Jewish society, Jesus' shifting of the onus of responsibility

Pastoral Perspective

and therefore we forgive those with whom we are in conflict.

It has been said that for most churchgoers, what is really closest to the heart and soul is the experience of worship. That is where one experiences confession and forgiveness, reconnection with neighbors, and the renewal of life to make a difference in the world. Scratch a true believer and you will not find a love of doctrine as much as the love of liturgy. Doctrine comes later and often gives shape and meaning to the experience of faith. If that is the case, then we have to make good use of the power that worship can bring into people's lives—even the power of reconciliation with one another. There are pastoral implications for the whole community.

One of the persons who recovered this insight for the church was the late Anglican bishop John A. T. Robinson, who interestingly enough had a reputation for being a bit radical (or as radical as a Cambridge scholar can be!). The good bishop defined the practice of Holy Communion as simply "making holy that which is common."[1] In other words, we offer to God the totality of our lives—the darkness and the light—and it is blessed, made holy, and returned to us as the presence of the living Christ. We symbolize this in the gifts of bread and wine. Thus, it is Christ working in us and through us that eventually makes reconciliation possible. What we were unable to accomplish before is now a possibility. We do not have to do this all on our own. This understanding begins at our baptism, when each of us (or parents and grandparents for us) answers the baptismal promises with the phrase, "I will, *with God's help.*" To think that we can accomplish everything on our own, without Christ's presence, is to carry a burden we cannot successfully bear.

During the great historical period in England known as the Oxford Movement, there was a renewed interest in the worship life of the church. Those in leadership positions, especially clerics, saw in liturgical practice the catalyst for being empowered for the mission of Christ to the world. While these clergy sought splendor in worship, most of them had soup kitchens and pantries for the poor. There was a deep connection between worship and a starving world. That should tell us something. If we want to be equipped for the task ahead, liturgical practice is where it begins. We might say that the bread on the altar has a deep connection with the bread needed to satisfy the world's hunger. One of

---

2. Glen H. Stassen, "The Fourteen Triads of the Sermon on the Mount (Matthew 5:21–7:12)," *Journal of Biblical Literature* 122/2 (2003): 270–75.
3. Amy-Jill Levine, "Matthew," in *The Women's Bible Commentary* (Louisville, KY: Westminster John Knox Press, 1992), 255.

1. John A. T. Robinson, *Liturgy Coming to Life* (London: SCM, 1964), xii.

kingship of God (see the exegesis of last week's Gospel text, pp. 333–37).

The first concrete exhortation (vv. 21–26) concerns forgiveness. Torah forbids murder (Exod. 20:13; Deut. 5:17), but Jesus says that not just murder, but anger, makes one liable to judgment. It is interesting to see the commentators debate whether such judgment against anger is absolute or not. Supporting an absolute reading of Jesus' words, other Scripture passages are equally strong in their condemnation of anger (Eph. 4:31; Col. 3:8; cf. 1 Tim. 2:8; Jas. 1:20, but also Ps. 37:8; Prov. 14:29; Eccl. 7:9). Against it, some commentators point out that the Bible nonetheless records God's and Jesus' anger (Matt. 23:17; Mark 3:5); others even refer to the biological basis of anger that makes it inevitable (of course, if biological urges were the measure of ethics, the next passage of Jesus' sermon makes even less sense!). The concern of Jesus' saying, however, seems to be less the *having* of anger than what one *does* with it: does anger shape our relationships, or preclude reconciliation? In this respect, Jesus' own life is, of course, the embodiment of his teaching.

In addition, it is worth pondering the political context of Jesus' exhortation (again, see the exegesis of last week's Gospel). The conflicts described in these verses are usually interpreted as interpersonal (vv. 22–24) and economic (vv. 25–26). However, what if behind the notions of accuser, guard, and hell of fire looms the face of the Roman occupier, and the anger described is that of the always popular option of Zealot armed resistance? Jesus knows that such expression of anger will finally lead to the military's destructive "hell of fire" (v. 22) poured out over Jerusalem. What if Israel, instead, would overwhelm its accuser with generosity and reconciliation, letting its "light shine before others, so that they may see [its] good works and give glory to [the] Father in heaven" (v. 16)?

The second exhortation (vv. 27–30) underscores the fact that Jesus' point is aimed at not so much our biological functioning as how we organize our biological life: "Everyone looking upon a woman *in order* to lust after her" commits adultery (v. 28, my trans.). In this Jesus goes again beyond the letter of the Torah (Exod. 20:14; Deut. 5:18) and urges Israel to discipline not just its acts, but also its intentions from an eschatological perspective.

Torah makes allowance for divorce (Deut. 24:1–4), but Jesus characterizes this provision as made for the sake of human hard-heartedness (Matt. 19:8). This is in line with other passages both from

The four themes cohere around a common motif: dealing with broken relationships from the perspective of the realm. The preacher could raise the question, what is wrong with broken relationships? God intends for people to live in mutual support. Fractiousness denies such support. The sermon could point out that, according to Matthew, the partial presence of the realm makes it possible for people in the present to transcend brokenness and to live toward the mutuality of the realm.

The preacher could help the congregation identify fragmentation in their personal and communal worlds. How does the realm make it possible to move beyond brokenness toward mutual support? The preacher might use the four themes in the reading as examples from antiquity, and then consider cases from the world today. Where are relationships going awry? How does the realm make it possible for those relationships to become mutually supportive?

The preacher could also develop a sermon focused on one of the themes. In this case, the preacher would determine which theme correlates most adequately with the present situation.

Matthew 5:21–26 deals with an issue that is as immediate as the latest newscast: anger. Two assumptions behind this passage are striking. First, anger destroys relationship in a way akin to murder. Second, regardless of who caused the problem in the relationship, the person who becomes aware of the difficulty is responsible for taking steps toward reconciliation. The preacher could help the congregation name personal and communal situations in which anger distorts God's purposes in community, and the preacher can commend reconciliation. Matthew does not offer specific strategies for trying to achieve reconciliation. The preacher needs to avoid drifting into amateur psychology, but might point the congregation to some resources that could help the congregation envision practical steps toward reconciliation.

An alternate sermon, on Matthew 5:21–26, could focus on the importance of treating others with respect. We are not to insult others or call them fools. When we engage in such behavior, we lower the realm possibilities of the moment.

With respect to Matthew 5:27–30, the preacher needs to help the congregation understand the meaning of adultery in antiquity. Adultery destroys God's purpose for marriage to anticipate the mutuality of the realm. Matthew implies that looking lustfully at another person creates adultery in the heart, which undermines the mutuality of marriage. Of course, the preacher should resist a rigid interpretation. From a

Matthew 5:21-37

Theological Perspective

from women to men in verses 27–32 earmarks the radical quality of his interpretation of the law.

The final verses in this lection (vv. 33–37) are concerned with the taking of oaths. Two matters are at stake in these verses: (1) whether Jesus is opposed to oaths in general and (2) the way oaths can function. The aim of this interpretation is to establish truthfulness as a critical value, as found in verse 37a: "Let your word be 'Yes, Yes' or 'No, No.'" Insofar as the followers of Jesus are living out a higher righteousness that is evidenced by truthfulness, there is no need for oaths. This does not mean that oaths are never to be used, but that truth telling is its own validation.

Finally, these three sets of verses both demonstrate the way in which Jesus interprets the law and provide guidance for the disciples and followers about living out a righteousness that exceeds that of the scribes and Pharisees. As readers of the text, we are exposed to Jesus as one who insists on interpreting the law from what can be discerned of God's intent or will for humanity, thus expanding or reframing what has been the traditional normative interpretation. God's intent or will for humanity is the hermeneutical key. Jesus locates himself within the tradition, but he does not allow the tradition to be the last word. Indeed we are pushed to remember this: "In the beginning was the Word, and the Word was with God, and the Word was God" (John 1:1). Here, as in the previous two Sundays' lections, we are reminded in these Sundays after the Epiphany that Jesus reveals God—God's nature and intent for humankind. Our quest as disciples of Jesus today is to continue to listen for and to follow the Jesus who came, not to abolish the law and the prophets, but to fulfill them.

MARCIA Y. RIGGS

Pastoral Perspective

the members of this Oxford group said that the Holy Eucharist is the only truly democratic moment in life. When we are willing to come together to the altar, offer ourselves completely, and receive in return all that we need not just to survive, but to live, then we have experienced something remarkably different and essential. It is the ultimate leveler—where status and opinion fade away—for those in relationship and those who are yet to be in relationship, including those estranged from each other.

While we strive for Jesus' ideal, when things fall short of the mark, coming to the altar, offering one's gift, is not a bad place to start afresh. Jesus invited all sorts and conditions of folk to the table and that served as a unifying experience. It also served to encourage those at table to begin life again, committed to living faithfully and in harmony with each other.

Dorothy Day, the founder of the Catholic Worker movement, used to say to her fellow workers, particularly in difficult and stressful times: "If each of us could just remember that we are *all* created in the image of God, then we would naturally want to love more."[2] At the holy altar, standing shoulder to shoulder, hand in hand, we remember once again that in God's realm there are no outsiders. Every gift is accepted, each offering received.

From there the hard pastoral work begins, but what once seemed impossible is now possible. Then we hear Jesus' words anew—"*Now, go and be reconciled.*"

CHARLES JAMES COOK

---

2. Paul Elie, *The Life You Save May Be Your Own* (New York: Farrar, Straus & Giroux, 2003), 275.

the Torah (Deut. 24:4 and Lev. 21:7, which forbids priests to marry divorcees) and the prophets (Ezek. 44:22, Mal. 2:16 [in which God says: "I hate divorce"]). In the third exhortation (vv. 31–32) Jesus urges all of Israel to be a nation of priests.

The fourth exhortation (vv. 33–37) seems to go more directly against the regulations of the Old Testament. There, oaths are permitted in everyday speech, as long as they are truthful (Exod. 20:7; Lev. 19:12; Num. 30:3–15; Deut. 23:21–23). Commentators have therefore wondered, as in the case of the first exhortation, whether Jesus meant to be as absolute in his judgments against oaths as the text suggests. In this they are supported by the fact that the New Testament itself does not shy away from swearing while calling upon God as witness (Rom. 1:9; 2 Cor. 1:23; Gal. 1:20; Phil. 1:8; and Rev. 10:6). Moreover, throughout the Bible not only do human beings swear, but God swears as well (e.g., Gen. 22:16; Exod. 6:8; Isa. 45:23; Luke 1:73; Acts 2:30)!

However, it seems that what Jesus says about the Old Testament's permission of divorce is like what he says about oaths: they were permitted because of human hard-heartedness. One way of looking at it is to say that using an oath to commit oneself to the truth of certain statements suggests that the speaker really uses two kinds of illocutionary acts: some to which she is committed, others to which she is committed not so much. To signal the true commitment to her utterance, the speaker uses the oath. Jesus, however, expects full commitment to every utterance: let your yes be yes, and your no be no. Another way of looking at it is that even if one speaks the truth, the hearer may be unwilling to believe the speaker and therefore the speaker has to underscore her commitment in an oath. The latter situation is, of course, the result of the former: because hard-hearted people do not speak the truth, speech (including God's speech!) no longer automatically finds belief. Jesus, however, challenges his hearers to speak as ones who inherit the kingdom, where everything is true.

EDWIN CHR. VAN DRIEL

psychological point of view, it is impossible to control what pops into the mind. It is possible, however, to control the subjects on which one meditates.

The congregation should be relieved to learn that most scholars think that verses 29–30 are hyperbole. However, these admonitions underline the importance of dealing with impulses that could lead to the destruction of community.

Matthew 5:31–32 presents the preacher with another difficult pastoral challenge, since about half of today's marriages end in divorce. The sermon should discuss reasons and consequences of divorce in Jewish antiquity, and should explain the clause "except on the ground of unchastity." Moreover, the preacher needs to avoid turning this text into a legalism that denies people the new life of the realm. The text presumes that the marriage relationship can be shaped by the presence of the realm. It appears to me that the dynamics of some marriages are realm resistant and that the purposes of the realm may be better served by freeing the couple to live into other relationships.

The preacher might help the congregation compare Matthew with the earlier form of this saying in Mark 10:10–12, which simply forbids divorce. Matthew added the clause making unchastity an exception. Presumably Matthew made this addition because the community found the absolute prohibition to work against the experience of the realm. The preacher might interpret a more pastoral approach for today as extending Matthew's insight.

When turning to Matthew 5:33–37, the preacher would need to explain the concept of swearing from the viewpoint of antiquity. This topic could naturally lead the preacher to meditate on the importance of integrity in both private and public spheres. Those who would embody the realm will speak truthfully.

The readings for today give rise to a theological tension. The purpose of these passages is to promote supportive relationships, yet Matthew supposes that those who fail to live into the realm will be condemned and even thrown into hell, the epitome of negative relationship. Even if the preacher does not believe in an apocalyptic judgment and a fiery hell, the preacher could see intensification of fractiousness as a consequence of failure to rectify broken relationships. A preacher could further develop a sermon that offers critical theological reflection on the tension inherent in the notion of a God who seeks a realm of universal love and support but consigns people to hell. Such a sermon might more broadly reflect on whether the notion of hell is theologically appropriate.

RONALD J. ALLEN

Leviticus 19:1-2, 9-18

¹The LORD spoke to Moses, saying:
²Speak to all the congregation of the people of Israel and say to them: You shall be holy, for I the LORD your God am holy. . . .
⁹When you reap the harvest of your land, you shall not reap to the very edges of your field, or gather the gleanings of your harvest. ¹⁰You shall not strip your vineyard bare, or gather the fallen grapes of your vineyard; you shall leave them for the poor and the alien: I am the LORD your God.
¹¹You shall not steal; you shall not deal falsely; and you shall not lie to one another. ¹²And you shall not swear falsely by my name, profaning the name of your God: I am the LORD.
¹³You shall not defraud your neighbor; you shall not steal; and you shall not keep for yourself the wages of a laborer until morning. ¹⁴You shall not revile

Theological Perspective

Leviticus appears just this once in the entire Revised Common Lectionary cycle—and in most years, Lent begins before seven Sundays after Epiphany elapse. The omission is more than unfortunate; it eviscerates the heart of Israel's theology from the Christian preaching cycle. Leviticus records more words from the mouth of God than any other book of the Bible.

The question of Christianity's relation to Israel's law cannot be avoided when we open Leviticus. Christians have often met the difficult question by avoiding it, appealing with great relief to the apostolic decree of Acts 15 lifting the burden of adherence to the ceremonial law for Gentile Christians. Might it be that, in shrugging off the burden, we also lose sight of the blessing that Leviticus intends to lavish on God's people?

The Reformed tradition holds that there is but one divine covenant, that the church of God includes both the original covenant people of Israel and those later adopted into God's family through Jesus Christ. Thus, the provisions of God's covenant with Israel belong also to the Christian church. To be sure, they belong to the church as mediated through the apostolic witness, with its release from a burdened adherence to ceremonies centered on a system of dealing with sin that predates the sacrifice for sin offered in Jesus Christ; but they still tell us much about the

Pastoral Perspective

I remember the day I decided that I would never be a tither. I was sitting in the pews as an associate minister, listening to the senior minister preach. The senior minister, who was a tither, was telling us about it. He was explaining that being a tither meant that he had always given the biblically commended tithe, 10 percent of his income, to the church, then still more to other causes, and that God had blessed him for it. This was not hypocrisy. He really did it, and he believed that financial peace had come to him as a result.

But I could not stand to hear it. I was paying off massive student loans, full-time day care, and, to be honest, even though I lived in a lovely parsonage, I was seriously underpaid by the church. Newly married, my husband and I had discovered that we were no different from most other couples in that the major stress in our marriage was money.

I felt that my colleague, a widower whose children were grown and whose house was paid off, had absolutely no understanding of my situation. It seemed unimaginable to me that I could be a tither when I had so little to begin with.

My anxiety was intense around these issues, but there was no place in my vocational life that I could express it. I preached generosity and grace, while inside I felt worry and resentment.

the deaf or put a stumbling block before the blind; you shall fear your God: I am the Lord.

¹⁵You shall not render an unjust judgment; you shall not be partial to the poor or defer to the great: with justice you shall judge your neighbor. ¹⁶You shall not go around as a slanderer among your people, and you shall not profit by the blood of your neighbor: I am the Lord.

¹⁷You shall not hate in your heart anyone of your kin; you shall reprove your neighbor, or you will incur guilt yourself. ¹⁸You shall not take vengeance or bear a grudge against any of your people, but you shall love your neighbor as yourself: I am the Lord.

Exegetical Perspective

YHWH's command of holiness and love in Leviticus 19 resists any attempt to confine it to a time period. The mandate of holiness in verse 2 and the call for the love of the neighbor in verse 18b frame the concrete guidelines of life that God desires for the people of God for all times (vv. 3–18a).

The lectionary selection is found in the law section commonly known as the Holiness Code, which focuses on purity and holiness before God (Lev. 17–26). The physical location of the passage illustrates its central place, as well, for it forms the kernel of the book of Leviticus, which in turn is located at the core of the Torah. While the book of Leviticus comes after the book of Exodus and defines what it means to live as those redeemed by God from the bondage of Egypt, Leviticus 19 presents quintessential concerns that are to shape the daily life of the people of God.

The Old Testament lesson lists a series of laws designed to guide the people of Israel into holiness. Two sets of directives for *imitatio Dei* follow: positive precepts (vv. 3–9, 17b–18) and negative prohibitions (vv. 10–17a, 18a). They recall the Ten Commandments found elsewhere in the Hebrew Bible (Exod. 20; 34; Deut. 5, etc.). The Hebrew text of Leviticus 19 mixes singular and plural verbs for these commandments, underscoring the intricate role that individuals

Homiletical Perspective

If you have never preached from Leviticus—and most of us have never preached from Leviticus—this may be just the opportunity you were not looking for. Leviticus 19:1–2, 9–18 is an excellent companion to the Gospel reading for this day, Matthew 5:38–48. Both passages give practical instruction for living ethically as the people of God. Leviticus 19 is concerned with internal integrity and outward behavior in daily life: in the home and in the field; in our words to God and in our words to each other; in the neighborhood and in the courtroom; in how the condition of our hearts affects the conduct of relationships. The settings may be wide ranging, but the common concern is love of neighbor. All three Synoptic Gospels quote Leviticus 19:18, "you shall love your neighbor as yourself" (Matt. 22:39, Mark 12:31, Luke 10:27), where Jesus makes it clear that loving one's neighbor is integrally related to loving God.

Indeed, how we love God is evident in every action we take. Leviticus 19:2, "You shall be holy, for I the Lord your God am holy," is matched in Matthew 5:48, "Be perfect, therefore, as your heavenly Father is perfect." Our behavior toward others witnesses, for good or ill, to the very character and nature of the God we worship and serve. This connection between our holiness and God's holiness is so critical that every ethical couplet of verses in this reading ends

Leviticus 19:1-2, 9-18

Theological Perspective

nature of God, of God's way with us, and the shape of our appropriate response.

Even in Christian traditions that do not subscribe to the "one covenant" understanding, Israel's moral law (if not its full Holiness Code) is regarded as having continued force, especially as distilled in the Decalogue. The Decalogue has long functioned as a critical block of Christian catechesis, alongside the Lord's Prayer and the Apostles' Creed. The catechisms deal with the Decalogue almost always in its Exodus/Deuteronomy version. Today's text, taken together with the intervening verses that the lectionary omits, is Leviticus's account of the moral law. It covers all the points of the Decalogue, adding some significant interpretive commentary.

The Leviticus account of the moral law strikingly shapes the teaching of Jesus. When he takes the command against murder as a prohibition of anger toward a brother or sister (Matt. 5:21–22), he is following verse 17 of our text. Jesus' repeated summary of the law quotes verse 18 of our text: "You shall love your neighbor as yourself." Implications of the law for how we treat the poor, a point Jesus frequently stresses, are spelled out in verses 9 and 10.

The social ethic framed by this telling of the moral law extends our horizon of responsibility beyond the covenant people to the alien. Already in verse 10, provision for the needs of the foreigner is given as part of the divine mandate for God's people. In a lesser-known but especially striking saying some verses beyond the lectionary passage, God's insistence on the covenant people's social responsibility stretches as far as can be imagined: "You shall love the alien as yourself" (Lev. 19:34).

In the Leviticus telling of the moral law, the people's life with God and with one another is the practical expression of their holiness: "You shall be holy, for I the LORD your God am holy" (v. 2). While the mood of "you shall" is certainly imperative, it may also be taken as declarative. The Holy One says, "In company with me, you shall grow to be like me." As the psalmist reminds us, we become like what we worship (Ps. 115:8). This correspondence of God's people to God's self goes beyond the *imago Dei* present in every human being. It is a likeness to the *otherness* of God, a way of being distinguished from the rest of humanity. Even as God fills all things, yet is wholly other, so God's people are very much part of humanity, yet set apart. This passage depicts a way of life that is pointedly *different* from the ways of the world.

Still, God's people sometimes want to be like the rest of the world: "Appoint for us, then, a king

Pastoral Perspective

I have since learned that this is not an uncommon state of affairs for clergy. So imagine how confusing we are to laypeople when we preach about such matters, particularly when they hear a passage like this, one of the iconic images for tithing and sharing as a way of life.

"When you reap the harvest of your land, you shall not reap to the very edges of your field, or gather the gleanings of your harvest. You shall not strip your vineyard bare, or gather the fallen grapes of your vineyard; you shall leave them for the poor and the alien: I am the LORD your God" (vv. 9–10). They can probably sense that often clergy are as fearful around money issues as they are, perhaps even more so if we are outearned by our congregations. We, and they, are not entirely sure we will have enough to eat if we leave a major portion behind for poor and alien persons. Maybe we ourselves are poor and alien. Providing for those in need is a lofty goal, central to Old Testament thought, and worth exploring.

When it comes to inner conflicts around money, most of us are shaped by our families. We are either repeating bad habits we learned when we were young, or trying deliberately to unlearn them. Biblical passages about possessions are the gateway to peace—a peace that few people have when it comes to how they feel about what they have and do not have. We can certainly use these passages to encourage fund-raising, but perhaps more importantly, we can use them as a jumping-off point to have, in a spiritual setting, an honest conversation about money.

When it came to money, in my family you were not supposed tell the truth. I remember my parents fighting late into the night, always about money—in particular, my mother's spending. What fell into the category of "her" spending was just about everything, from groceries to car payments to my school supplies and clothes. Because of this, my father was basically unaware of what anything cost, yet every now and then he would see a bill or a receipt and become irate.

To avoid such scenes, I was taught never to tell my father what anything cost. If I had a new coat, I learned in my early childhood to say, "I've had it for years." When I needed movie money, he would give me enough for a ticket ten years ago, and my mother would surreptitiously slip the difference into my pocket on the way out. "Why can't we tell Daddy what the movie really costs?" I asked. "Why can't we tell him I needed a new outfit for the dance?"

"Shhh . . . it will only upset him."

must play as moral agents whose action affects the well-being of the entire community.[1]

The omitted portion, verses 3–8, contains commandments of respecting parents ("mother and father" are listed in a reversed order, which according to a rabbinic tradition points to the equality of mother and father), observing Sabbath, and keeping away from idols (vv. 3–4). It also includes cultic details on the manner of offering "a sacrifice of well-being" (v. 5) that ensure it is acceptable before God. The minor nature of the rules of consumption of the banned food is juxtaposed with the hefty punishment of being "cut off from the people," the worst form of punishment for the people whose meaning of life is predicated upon being part of the people of God. The law code explains why the offense is taken so seriously: "they have profaned what is holy *to YHWH*" (v. 8, emphasis added).

The portion included in the lectionary passage (vv. 9–18) weaves rituals and ethical demands. Strategically positioned between verses 2–8 (whose focus is cultic) and verses 11–18 (whose focus is ethical), verses 9–10 creates a meeting point of the two categories. First, verse 9 begins with the law of gleaning under which one should not reap the field clean. The Masoretic Text and other ancient versions (cf. LXX and Vulg.) speak against thorough harvesting that leaves the field bare. Luther and the KJV suggest that the law demands that the corners should remain untouched. The RSV and the NRSV envision the kind of harvesting that leaves out the sides of the field. The same philosophy is applied to the vineyard, which in antiquity represents lucrative areas of agriculture (v. 10a). The law of gleanings is based on the desire of YHWH, who cares for the poor and the alien (v. 10b).

The ensuing verses continue to describe the proper ways for the people of God to relate to one another, enumerating requirements expected of the people who are called to be holy. The relationship is designated as "neighbor" (vv. 13, 15, 17) and is expected to be characterized by integrity and truthfulness. While each command is clear in content, the passage arranges them in a suggestive way. For example, the law of gleaning is immediately followed by the law against stealing, implying that the gleanings belong not to the landowners but to the poor and the alien. Unbiased altruism is further underscored by the rabbinic tradition that prohibits the owner

---

1. See Erhard S. Gerstenberger, *Leviticus: A Commentary*, Old Testament Library (Louisville, KY: Westminster John Knox Press, 1993), 262–63.

with the same refrain: "I am the LORD (your God)." Verses 11–12 are but one example: "You shall not steal; you shall not deal falsely; and you shall not lie to one another. And you shall not swear falsely by my name . . . I am the LORD." Think of those old cartoons where an angel appears on one shoulder of a character caught in an ethical dilemma and a red-suited devil lands on the other shoulder. The good conscience encourages right behavior while the bad conscience encourages self-indulgence that causes harm. With every action, God (who is more than mere conscience) says in our ear, "I am the Lord your God." Whenever we open our mouth, open our door, extend our hand in gestures kind or rude, our neighbor catches at least a glimpse of "the Lord our God."

The whole subject of holiness can make us uncomfortable. It is fine for God to be holy. Everyone knows that God is holy, but we have a pretty good sense that most of us are not holy—or holy enough. We are never holy enough. In fact, our discomfort on the matter has become a commonly understood expression of disdain, "holier than thou." Except for those in Holiness church traditions, most of us think true holiness is reserved for a few exceptional people of faith, like Mother Teresa or the pope or the Dalai Lama. Holy people live far removed from us and do with their lives things we cannot, or likely will not, do with ours. As appropriately modest as this may be, it is also a way of letting ourselves off the holiness hook. That is not biblical.

When we preach on Leviticus (as when we preach on Matthew), we remember that we are all on the hook for being holy. God says to Moses, "Speak to *all the congregation of the people of Israel* and say to them: You shall be holy, for I the LORD your God am holy" (19:2). Everyone, the whole congregation, is called to be holy. Being holy is what any person created in God's image is called to be . . . or, better put, to *do*.

In Leviticus (and in Matthew), holiness is not characterized by an ethereal state of being, but by how one acts in everyday places and relationships. Our sermon can remind people what everyday holiness looks like from a biblical perspective. You are holy when, harvesting your crop, you choose to leave some of the grain you drop and more uncut at the edges of your property, so that Ruth, or someone like her, does not go to bed hungry. Holiness is not always about making grand sacrifices to God or speaking pious prayers. Holiness is not stealing what belongs to someone else or telling a lie, even a lie that seems harmless. Holiness is being a good employer, paying someone on time for work done.

Leviticus 19:1-2, 9-18

Theological Perspective

to govern us, like other nations" (1 Sam. 8:5). The work of being holy is exactly that: *work*, swimming against the tide of prevailing human ways. It is always a work in progress through the process of sanctification. The Westminster Catechism describes sanctification in a startling way, "Improving our baptism."[1] It is very much our work to do, just as the fulfillment of the mandates and prohibitions of the moral law are the people's work. When we look in the mirror collectively and individually,[2] we see how far short we fall of the holiness toward which we are destined, and we could all too easily give up, but for hearing again and again God's covenant promise: "You *shall* be like me."

The focus in this process of becoming like the Holy One must be on the Holy One, rather than on the mirror. This is brought home with insistent force as we hear each command punctuated by the repeating refrain, "I am the LORD your God." Keeping the Holy One in view is the key to our becoming holy.

God's claim on these people is a done deal; they are already "the elect." The law is given, not as their gateway to salvation, but as salvation's way of life. To be sure, the law is beneficial for *all* humanity; but it is *this* people's special vocation to embody this way of life over and against all other peoples, as a public witness to the beauty and blessing of God. The law is God's "treasure map" to the blessedness for which God has claimed us, and in which the Holy One ever lives.

SHELDON W. SORGE

Pastoral Perspective

I remember as a little girl delighting in my brand-new blue coat, but being afraid to wear it out the door past my father. From an early age, material things elicited in me both inordinate delight and misplaced shame, perhaps because we did not tell the truth.

It is interesting that this passage from so many thousands of years ago, and from such a different culture, still makes the connection between generosity and truth telling. The passage on sharing a portion of what you have with the poor and the alien is followed by a call to honesty. "You shall not steal; you shall not deal falsely; and you shall not lie to one another" (v. 11).

The reading today has a word for me, and families like mine. It has a word for the church. It is a call to tell the truth and to take money out of the shadows. The rest of this passage is full of business-ethics advice that has stood the test of time. Do not commit fraud, do not lie, do not judge unfairly, and do not slander. Be decent with one another in your financial dealings, and do not forget the poor. Most important, be generous, and love your neighbor as yourself.

I went on to become a tither. It was an action I could not imagine taking until I did it. With it came a spiritual peace that has shifted me away from the bad habits of my family and into the strange habits of the Old Testament. I am not a biblical literalist, but I share this as one who has decided to tell the truth about my money.

LILLIAN DANIEL

1. The Larger Catechism, Q. 167, 7.277, in *The Book of Confessions* (Louisville, KY: Presbyterian Church (U.S.A.) Office of the General Assembly, 1999), 223.
2. Note that the commands in our passage alternate between the singular and plural "you," something lost in contemporary translations.

Exegetical Perspective

from choosing which poor person he should grant the privilege of gleaning.[2]

Verse 13 extends the neighborly fidelity to the laborers, from whom the wage should not be kept until the next day. They also are the neighbor whose well-being is ensured by God, and the violation of this law constitutes outright stealing. God's demand for justice for the neighbor protects the deaf and the blind, as well (v. 14). Legal proceedings must be based solely on the demands of justice, and justice should not be bent in the name of leniency or under the influence of the powerful (v. 15). One should not slander the neighbor. Nor should one seek to profit at the expense of the neighbor. Verse 17a prohibits one from willfully ("in your heart") hating one's own kin. The latter half of the verse demands one to be in a covenantal relationship with the kinsfolk. If they err, one must counsel them accordingly, for failure to do so will incur guilt for both the offender and those who neglect to correct the neighbor.

Throughout the passage, YHWH's words underscore the theological basis of these ethical demands, emphasizing that a breach of them constitutes a sin. Obvious social concerns are relegated to the background; the people of God are to heed the law because it is given by YHWH (vv. 10b, 12b). Verse 18 concludes the passage by prohibiting practices that would poison the community with enmity. It promotes the posture that will establish a community of neighborly love that Rabbi Akiba called "a central principle in the Torah."[3] The verse is often cited in the NT (Matt. 19:19; 22:39; Mark 12:31, 33; Luke 10:27; Rom. 13:9; Gal. 5:14; Jas. 2:8). In Leviticus 19:18, the love command is undergirded by God's identity as YHWH, who mandates holiness among the people of God on the basis of God's own holiness (cf. v. 2).

JIN HEE HAN

Homiletical Perspective

Some consider holiness doing notable, selflessly noble deeds. In Leviticus, holiness is at least not making life more difficult for someone with a disability or standing idly by when a neighbor is in trouble. You are holy when you do not gossip or slander or hold a grudge. You are holy when you are fair to everyone equally, without being influenced by either pity or greed. Holiness means you do not say, "Oh, God!" unless you really mean you want God's attention.

Holiness is not reserved for God alone or for the hermit in his cave or Hildegard of Bingen in one of her visions. In preaching, you might think of instances where your own church acts out holiness. We are all called to be holy in our life together in the neighborhood.

"Holiness in the Hood" was a three-day event held at Love Fellowship Christian Church in the summer of 2008. Everyone in the community was welcome to come together in "love and unity" for a basketball tournament in the church parking lot; to listen to rap music on the church steps; and to enjoy hamburgers and hot dogs in the side yard. Several hundred people enjoyed free snow cones, popcorn, and games of musical chairs. Assistant Pastor Vanessa Jones said, "We have the basketball without anger as a way of tending to the body, soul and spirit." Another pastor said they hoped to form a bridge between the church and the community: "Events like this show people we can have a good relationship with Christ regardless of race. We can make our cities better places to live in." A fifteen-year-old named Maria said events like "Holiness in the Hood" "get you ready for Jesus."[1] That scene makes a good gospel companion to Leviticus 19 too.

KIMBERLY L. CLAYTON

---

2. *Sifra Qed.* 2.5; Roger Brooks, "Support for the Poor: Leviticus 19:5–10," in *Sifra: The Rabbinic Commentary on Leviticus: An American Translation*, Brown Judaic Studies 102 (Atlanta: Scholars Press, 1985), 150.

3. Baruch A. Levine, *The JPS Torah Commentary: Leviticus* (Philadelphia: Jewish Publication Society, 5749/1989), 130.

1. "'Holiness in the Hood' draws youth to neighborhood church celebration," by Ron Ingram, staff writer, *Herald&Review.com*, Decatur IL, July 20, 2008, http://www.herald-review.com/news/local/article_0cef0d2f-b0a3-54a0-ab56-4f00076faa2d.html?mode=story.

Psalm 119:33-40

33Teach me, O Lᴏʀᴅ, the way of your statutes,
and I will observe it to the end.
34Give me understanding, that I may keep your law
and observe it with my whole heart.
35Lead me in the path of your commandments,
for I delight in it.
36Turn my heart to your decrees,
and not to selfish gain.
37Turn my eyes from looking at vanities;
give me life in your ways.
38Confirm to your servant your promise,
which is for those who fear you.
39Turn away the disgrace that I dread,
for your ordinances are good.
40See, I have longed for your precepts;
in your righteousness give me life.

Theological Perspective

Its construction in the form of an acrostic must have had some impact on its content, but the exceptional length of this psalm prevents its being used in its entirety in nearly all worship settings that also include preaching. Therefore, this essay focuses intently on the pericope included in this Sunday's lectionary with little attention to its context in the complete psalm. Within these eight verses there is substance enough for productive theological reflection.

The desire of the psalmist to understand—not simply to memorize and recall—the law of God points us toward the question of how we are to employ Scripture as source and norm for theological reflection. Though theologian Sarah Lancaster entitled her book *Women and the Authority of Scripture* in order to reflect its attention to the particular struggles that feminists have with the canon, the volume is useful for all ministers. It is a brilliant work that examines how Scripture has been regarded since the time of the Reformation. As she maintains, for Christians, the proper question has never been *whether* the Scripture is authoritative, but rather *how* it is to be viewed as authoritative for us.[1]

---

1. Sarah Heaner Lancaster, *Women and the Authority of Scripture: A Narrative Approach* (Harrisburg, PA: Trinity, 2002).

Pastoral Perspective

Word association, whether as a technique in psychoanalysis or as a game for fun, is a quick way to find out what someone really thinks about something. Before the mental filters set in and do their job, the quick response just puts it all out there. Very often what is really meant gets spoken before what one should have said is uttered.

For me at least, the word "righteousness" conjures up associations that are not particularly hopeful, helpful, or healthy. On first blush, "righteousness" evokes images of self-importance, self-righteousness, arrogance, rigidity, and on and on and on. I suspect I am not alone in that.

Jesus once told a story "to some who trusted in themselves that they were righteous and regarded others with contempt" (Luke 18:9). While it is commonly referred to as the parable of the Pharisee and the Publican, or the Pharisee and the Tax Collector, it is really a parable about false righteousness born of self-interest and true righteousness born of humility that gives way to God. "God, I thank you that I am not like other people: thieves, rogues, adulterers, or even like this tax collector. I fast twice a week; I give a tenth of all my income" (Luke 18:11–12). That prayer of the Pharisee is more an admiration of himself than adoration of God. That, I suspect, is one of the associations

Exegetical Perspective

Psalm 119 is a masterful prayer by a sage who desires to follow God through Torah obedience. This longest psalm in the Bible constitutes an elaborate acrostic. Each stanza of Psalm 119 contains eight lines beginning with the same Hebrew letter, and each successive stanza uses the next letter in the Hebrew *'alef-bet* (alphabet), totaling twenty-two stanzas. Further, the psalmist repeats at least six of an eight theme-word set ("statute," "law," "commandment," "decree," "promise," "ordinance," "precept," "word") in each lettered stanza, producing an extended, highly organized reflection on Torah, or teaching.

This literary feat alone would be worthy of awe; it is also marvelous poetry. This psalm about "teaching" also serves to teach, in the style and content of Wisdom psalms. Its meticulous structure makes the reassuring point that one can effectively follow YHWH through Torah piety. A stanza for each letter of the alphabet signifies the completeness of this Torah meditation—from A to Z—in Hebrew, from *'alef* to *tav*.

Despite its redundancy, Psalm 119 also includes remarkable diversity. The *'alef* or A section (vv. 1–8) begins with beatitudes ("happy are those who . . .") to commend Torah obedience, while the *samek* or S section (vv. 113–20) praises Torah by condemning those who neglect or reject it. Our pericope (vv. 33–40) corresponds to the letter *he* or H and

Homiletical Perspective

The 176 verses of Psalm 119 flow out in carefully ordered sequence, and the psalmist fleshes out the case for the abundant life found in God's law, using every letter of the Hebrew alphabet as its bones. Verses 33–40 represent the fifth of twenty-two sections of this lengthy acrostic, those verses beginning with the letter *he*. The content of Psalm 119 fits the form, providing comprehensive instruction for a life lived in keeping with God's law. The implicit message of the psalm is that following the Torah leads to a life characterized by security, contentment, and peace.

Despite the thorough treatment of Torah found in Psalm 119, the psalmist affirms the need for God's people to continue the pursuit of Torah knowledge, beginning verse 33 with the plea, "Teach me, O LORD, the way of your statutes." The psalmist speaks with longing and sincerity, seeking not only to know God's law, but also to understand it, that God's law may fill the whole heart. In verse 34, the psalmist acknowledges that God's gift is not only the law, but also the wisdom to understand it. Contemporary listeners who find themselves living and ministering in the midst of controversies rooted in differing approaches to Scripture may benefit from an exploration of the psalmist's humble posture seeking wisdom and guidance. Since the law encompasses every aspect of human life, the prayer for understanding extends to all areas of life.

Psalm 119:33-40

Theological Perspective

Poetry has a capacity for revealing the deepest of meanings, and this poetic prayer illuminates its author's conviction that the kind of authority the law of God should wield over his or her life is far more complex than that imposed by a set of rules that can be taken at face value or read in stark black and white. The Torah has never been understood as simply or even primarily a listing of laws that must be followed. Torah is instead a rich tapestry woven largely of stories that call for interpretation and reinterpretation at each encounter.

The kind of law that prescribes how many steps it is permissible to walk on the Sabbath is clearly not what intrigues the writer of these verses. Counting steps requires little or no understanding—such a law can be met with simple obedience. Appropriately, the psalmist is longing for much more than a list of things to do or to avoid doing. The writer makes reference to the "path" of the commandments, thereby portraying the acceptance of divine instruction as an ongoing journey. The reference to the "way" that she or he hopes to follow "to the end" also enriches the metaphor for a lifelong engagement with God's law.

While we trust and believe that a revelation from God and about God lies at the heart of our religion, all religions are necessarily human constructs. As such, they are the products of mixed—sometimes overlapping, sometimes complementary, sometimes contradictory—motives on the part of those who shape them. The maintenance of a coherent society that can protect and support those who live within it was (and usually still is) seen as good, and that is one of the goals religion has been well suited to meet. It was the law—or in a larger sense, the Torah—that bound the psalmist's community together. This psalm's mention of "disgrace that I dread" and the suggestion that disgrace accompanies the failure to recognize God's ordinances as "good" offer the preacher a moment to question whether the community's ostracizing (disgracing) one who offends its social mores should always and automatically be read as a sign that the marginalized one has truly displeased God.

The pericope thereby provides a chance for deeper reflection on the current Christian practice of the preacher's congregation, in order to help distinguish between those practices that allow genuine response to the ethical demands of the gospel and those customs that the community chooses to maintain largely for the sake of tradition. The use of red paraments on Pentecost Sunday, for instance, is a very useful teaching tool, but abandoning the practice would not mean a congregation had abandoned the basic mandates of

Pastoral Perspective

that are sometimes conjured up when we hear the word "righteousness."

That may be precisely where the words of Psalm 119:33–40 are enormously helpful, hopeful, and healthy. Here the praying poet pleads with God—not to show that he is above anybody, not in a manner of arrogance, not admiring himself in a mirror, but with incredible humility and wisdom—beseeching God for the life that only God can give.

Listen to the prayer being prayed in the poetry that is now Psalm 119:33–40: "Teach me, O LORD, the way of your statutes. . . . Give me understanding. . . . Lead me in the path of your commandments. . . . Turn my heart to your decrees. . . . Confirm to your servant your promise. . . . Turn away the disgrace that I dread." This is not polite discourse; this is passionate pleading that ends with a final testimony and declaration of faith: "See, I have longed for your precepts; in your righteousness give me life" (v. 40).

Righteousness here is not something humans create, control, or possess. It is not a possession at all. There is no place for any arrogance, pride, or haughtiness here. No, the psalmist prays, the psalmist pleads, the psalmist begs, not for his own righteousness—that would be self-righteousness—but for the righteousness of God. That righteousness is the ultimate source of true life, real life, life as God gives and intends for all God's human children. "See, I have longed for your precepts; in your righteousness give me life" (v. 40).

I am not a film critic, but I have the utmost respect for Steven Spielberg. He can make films genuinely entertain. He can also dare to go where we are afraid. He can speak of subjects of which we dare not speak, and, in so doing, speak a word of freedom. Putting Alice Walker's *The Color Purple* on the screen is a classic example. He can tell stories that need to be told again and again. He has shown the courage to face the murkiness and grayness of human life lived in the midst of much death and darkness and uncertainty. *Munich* is an example of that. *Munich* begins with the killing of Israeli athletes at the 1972 Munich Olympics by agents of the Palestine Liberation Organization. The film retells the secret story of how agents of the Israeli government were dispatched to execute those who participated in and planned the killings. They were given strict orders to kill only those who killed the Israeli athletes, no one else.

Early in the mission, they performed their tasks in a spirit of rightness, and even justice, but after a while the habit of killing began to get to them.

constitutes a prayer for right action in regard to Torah. Here the theme words are all possessives (e.g., "*your* law," v. 34), indicating God. These are no ordinary tenets for daily living. They are nothing less than characteristics of the Divine manifested for the sake of human guidance.

Throughout Psalm 119, the psalmist earnestly prays for righteousness in the ways of Torah and follows a pattern exemplified by verses 33–40. The poet aspires to follow in the Lord's ways by highlighting a particular trait in each consecutive verse: "your statutes," "your law," "your commandments," "your decrees," "your ways," "your promise," "your ordinances," "your precepts." This stanza includes seven of Psalm 119's eight theme words, excluding "word," but adding "ways" (v. 37). The psalmist longs for these aspects of the divine Torah one by one, poetically expressing the same sentiment with different words for eight verses.

We can get a better idea of the psalmist's intent by examining the theme words as they appear elsewhere in the Old Testament. "Your statute" or "ordinance" (*koq*, v. 33) refers to occasions (Passover, Exod. 12:24), customs (lamenting Jephthah's daughter, Judg. 11:39), or even limitations set by God (Job 38:10; Ps. 148:6). In Deuteronomy 6:1, "statute" introduces the shema, the central tenet of Judaism (6:4). Exodus 24:12 describes both "your law" (*torah*, v. 34) and "your commandments" (*mitsvot*, v. 35), which Moses will receive written on stone tablets. Deuteronomy 28:1 and 11:13 detail the rewards of obeying YHWH's "commandments." Later in Exodus, Moses receives these "tablets of covenant" (*'edot*, 31:18; 32:15; 34:29), "decrees" in Psalm 119:36. "Your promise" (*'imrah*, v. 38) also means "word," both in reference to divine statutes and theological guidance. YHWH's "ordinances" (*mishpat*, v. 39) comes from the same root as "justice." The prophets discuss this in terms of human behavior (Mic. 6:8; Isa. 1:17) while the wisdom writings reflect on divine justice (Job 8:3; Eccl. 3:16; 11:9). Here it indicates YHWH's judgments as analogous with the other seven terms. The term "precepts" (*piqqud*, v. 40) appears only in the Psalms (e.g., Pss. 19:9; 103:18), describing how properly to follow and obey YHWH. Finally, while "ways" (*derek*, v. 37) is not technically a theme word in Psalm 119, its frequent use here and throughout the OT provides a metaphor of the right road for pursuing YHWH.[1]

1. For a longer discussion of *derek*, "way" as a powerful metaphor in the Psalms, see William P. Brown, *Seeing the Psalms: Theology of Metaphor* (Louisville, KY: Westminster John Knox Press, 2002), 31–53.

The psalmist acknowledges that life according to God's law, while entirely dependent upon God, requires participation and reorientation on the part of the faithful. The psalmist prays, "Turn my heart to your decrees, and not to selfish gain" (v. 36). God provides the law and the understanding, but the psalmist has to follow the law and act with understanding. Turning toward God often means turning away from something else. The speaker cries, "Turn my eyes from looking at vanities," also translated as "worthless things" (v. 37).

The preacher might explore the biblical concept of repentance, the turning away from sin and toward God that is the mark of a grateful and contrite heart. Turning away from "worthless things" opens the way for renewed relationship with God. The psalmist admits to being occupied by things that have no value. The ways that we spend our time, our resources, and our energy show us the things that we value. Are those things really worth our attention? Are they worth our very selves? The psalmist calls us to examine our priorities, to ask ourselves what God holds dear, and to discern what it means to place God's will at the very center of our lives.

God's law provides everything necessary for the flourishing of God's people, but it does not subsume our need for love and mercy. The psalmist affirms that God's ordinances are good, but also implores God to "turn away the disgrace that I dread" (v. 39). The law helps the faithful to avoid disgrace, but in our sinfulness we will still find ourselves in need of God's grace and forgiveness. Scripture may provide a framework for living according to God's purposes, but even the best-intentioned adherents cannot perfectly follow divine ordinances. The law sets the boundaries for the flourishing of God's people, but these boundaries are permeable; they can be transgressed, and the story of God's people would indicate that we do it again and again. We will find ourselves needing to seek forgiveness and to reorient ourselves toward the one who holds heaven and earth.

According to Psalm 119, a Torah-centered life means living with the assurance that we belong to a good and loving God, a God who has gifted us with life and sustains life by continuously communicating divine will through the Torah. The psalmist's prayer is predicated on trust in the one who lies at the other end of the conversation, and the speaker fully expects a response to this prayer. The anticipated response will come in the form of the continuing revelation of the law, and through the spirit of understanding for which the psalmist prays. A treatment of the psalm as

Psalm 119:33-40

Theological Perspective

our faith. While honoring the community and its traditions is not necessarily bad, neither is it necessarily good. Some practices may have been originally instituted due to a misinterpretation of the revelation that underlies the Scripture, and others that were once appropriate may no longer be. Observing the psalmist's deep longing for a richer and more profound understanding of the law may help twenty-first-century congregations appreciate the need for critical reflection on how well their Christian walk responds to the call of God for them today.

Constant acquisition of greater understanding is a fundamental part of holy living. The reminder of the need to turn our eyes from "vanities" points to the Christian struggle to grasp what "sin" really is. Is the crux of the human problem a simple matter of *a failure to obey* God's laws, or is the nature of sin more complex? Verse 36, where "selfish gain" is posed over against turning the heart to God's decrees, can invite us to view sin more broadly as *a failure to love*. Primarily, though, this psalm acknowledges that *a failure to understand* is one of the chief impediments to living life in God's way.[2]

The quest for wisdom must have been foremost in the author's mind as these verses were composed. The writer twice implores the Deity, "Give me life" (vv. 37, 40). The Christian understanding of the Holy Spirit as "the breath of life" lets us consider this as a plea for divine presence and for the ability to live continuously within it. If one function of the law is to mediate the presence that caused Moses's face to shine after his descent from the mountain, then there is ample cause for wishing to observe that law with one's "whole heart" (v. 34).

"Life abundant" results not from rigid attendance to regulations, but from the constant, lifelong movement along the path of the commandments for which the psalmist expresses such ardent yearning. Seeking to understand the self-revelation of God within the Law—and the Prophets and the Writings and the gospel—brings us closer to the Holy One whose breath gives us life.

ELLEN J. BLUE

Pastoral Perspective

Agents of those they were killing set up a covert counteroffensive. At one point the counteroffensive took the form of a female agent sent to seduce and kill one of the Israelis. She did.

Now they faced a dilemma. They had strict orders to kill only those who had killed those innocent athletes. Now one of their own had been killed. Contrary to their specific orders, they moved to kill the woman who killed one of their brothers.

Now the mission morphed. The weeds of the killing field began to spread. The habit of killing was becoming a way of life. The habit of death was consuming even their lives. And one of the Israeli agents began to sense it.

So he confronted his leader and pleaded with him to stop the killing. This is an excerpt from the dialogue in the film.

Character A: "We're Jews, Everett. Jews don't do wrong because our enemies do wrong."

Character B: "We can't afford to be that decent any more."

Character A: "I don't know if we ever really were that decent. Suffering thousands of years of hatred doesn't make you decent. But we're supposed to be righteous. That's a beautiful thing. That's Jewish. That's what I knew. That's what I was taught. And now I'm losing it. If I lose that, I lose everything. That's my soul."

That is true righteousness! It is what God breathed into Adam. Soul! Life! Life that is human life reflecting the divine life of God. "See, I have longed for your precepts; in your righteousness give me life" (v. 40).

As we reflect on the pastoral implications of the psalm, we will want to think about the ways in which our worship, our educational programs, and our pastoral care help our people see that kind of righteousness. We will ask how we can grow them in the righteousness that gives life.

MICHAEL B. CURRY

---

2. Charles M. Wood and Ellen Blue, *Attentive to God: Thinking Theologically in Ministry* (Nashville: Abingdon Press, 2008), 120.

Exegetical Perspective

Ultimately, these eight words work together to bring the psalmist to Torah obedience.

Psalm 119:33–40 illustrates that "Torah" is not simply the Hebrew word for law. Given many Protestants' biases against law, that is an unfortunate translation choice to use in Christian settings. "Torah" firstly refers to the core portion of the Hebrew Bible, the Pentateuch (Gen., Exod., Lev., Num., Deut.). These five books contain not only legal codes, but also the defining sacred narratives of the faith community. The Pentateuch was canonized first, marking it as the earliest unifying text for Judeo-Christian tradition. Indeed, reverence and reading of the Torah still comprise the foundation of Jewish worship and religious observance.

Furthermore, "Torah" more broadly refers to teaching—though not just any teaching. Torah is *divine* teaching; the very teaching of YHWH. Some voices in Jewish tradition have understood Torah as preexistent or even prerequisite to creation. The physical Torah may be viewed as a tangible sign "pointing toward a transcendence that cannot be apprehended."[2] The intricate structure of Psalm 119 effectively illustrates such transcendence, as does the psalmist's prayer to follow Torah "with my whole heart" (v. 34). The Hebrew meaning of "heart" covers mind, body, soul, spirit, conscience, will; we could also translate it "with my whole being." Christians may better understand Torah as analogous to the profound meanings *they* intend with the phrase "the word of God," which may refer to Christ (John 1:1–5), the Scriptures, or the ongoing revelation of God's will.

Because the theme words in Psalm 119:33–40 appear with such regularity throughout the whole psalm, this snippet serves as a fitting sample of the whole. Since all 176 verses would be cumbersome for worship, this is a helpful starting point for a sermon on this magnificent psalm, and in turn an opportunity to invite parishioners to read the whole psalm. Here we have a short meditation on select theme words about following YHWH, within a long meditation on the same words, all teaching about following YHWH. The words harmonize in a chorus of Torah obedience. The cumulative effect becomes like a prayerfully repeated chant with varying descants. Perhaps it is like a verbal mandala, made up of variations on a theme, arranged with great artistry and intention, directing us on the path of the Divine.

LISA M. WOLFE

2. For instance, see Benjamin D. Sommer, "Revelation at Sinai in the Hebrew Bible and Jewish Theology," *Journal of Religion* 79 (1999): 448.

Homiletical Perspective

conversation with God might yield an interesting homiletical approach. The psalmist seeks God's response through faithful study and understanding of Torah. Where do we, the present-day hearers, look for God's answers to our prayers?

Torah for the psalmist is the ongoing revelation of God's life-giving promise. The last line of the psalm, translated in the NRSV as "in your righteousness give me life" (v. 40), captures only part the original Hebrew *hayah*, which carries the meaning of giving and sustaining life, as well as revival and restoration, captured well by the KJV translation, "quicken me in thy righteousness." For the psalmist, God's law has the power to initiate and restore life.

The psalmist most likely speaks from a position of privilege. A worldview that upholds the Torah as a basis for prosperity and shalom may find resonance in a community that is flourishing, prospering, and enjoying peace within its borders, but such a perspective might not sit well with someone whose life appears to be spinning out of control.[1] What happens when a person leads a faithful and God-centered life and encounters hardship after hardship? How does the faith expressed in Psalm 119 account for a person who is disgraced, not because of his or her own sinfulness, but because of systemic injustice perpetuated by the transgressions of others? As we seek to discern God's ways in the midst of complicated and troublesome situations, we would do well to echo the psalmist's prayer for understanding, seeking God's gift of abundant life not only for ourselves and those who are close to us, but for the whole world.

APRIL BERENDS

1. In his chapter on "Psalms of Orientation" in *The Message of the Psalms* ([Minneapolis: Augsburg, 1984], 25–27), Walter Brueggemann provides a helpful discussion on the topic of economic and social disparity as factors that pose serious challenges to a religious perspective articulated by royalty in times of prosperity.

1 Corinthians 3:10-11, 16-23

¹⁰According to the grace of God given to me, like a skilled master builder I laid a foundation, and someone else is building on it. Each builder must choose with care how to build on it. ¹¹For no one can lay any foundation other than the one that has been laid; that foundation is Jesus Christ. . . .

¹⁶Do you not know that you are God's temple and that God's Spirit dwells in you? ¹⁷If anyone destroys God's temple, God will destroy that person. For God's temple is holy, and you are that temple.

¹⁸Do not deceive yourselves. If you think that you are wise in this age, you should become fools so that you may become wise. ¹⁹For the wisdom of this world is foolishness with God. For it is written,

"He catches the wise in their craftiness,"
²⁰and again,
"The Lord knows the thoughts of the wise,
    that they are futile."

²¹So let no one boast about human leaders. For all things are yours, ²²whether Paul or Apollos or Cephas or the world or life or death or the present or the future—all belong to you, ²³and you belong to Christ, and Christ belongs to God.

Theological Perspective

While questions about christological issues may have dominated the theological debates of the early church, discussions about the nature and understanding of the local communities of faith, ecclesiology, also began to take place early on in the life of the Christian movement. As believers in various cities began to form those early Christian communities, it is understandable that they asked questions such as, How were these Christian assemblies different from the Jewish and Gentile ones that already existed in their cities? What was the defining characteristic, the sine qua non, of the new Christian congregations? How were these new Christian groups to be related to each other? Could churches that included many different types of people from different backgrounds work harmoniously toward the common goal of bringing in the kingdom of God?

Paul may not provide a comprehensive answer to all of the questions one could raise about the nature of the church, but he does contribute to the ecclesiological conversation in this passage from 1 Corinthians. Corinth might have been the best location for a conversation on these issues. It was certainly one of the most diverse cities in Greece, because of its importance as a major commercial and governmental center. Consequently, people from across the empire lived and worked in Corinth. Further, the Christian

Pastoral Perspective

Paul's words to the people in the church at Corinth are written for people of faith who, Paul insists, are distracted and mired down by misdirected priorities. Amid quarrels over who belongs to which church leader, Paul reminds early Christians in Corinth to remain unified, to remember that they have only one true leader—Jesus Christ—and that they must take care to build up the church that still is new and fragile.

While Paul was writing, of course, to the people of the first-century church, division and misdirected priorities are not unfamiliar to contemporary Christians. Election cycles pit liberals against conservatives. Crises over energy supplies pit environmentalists against business people. Contemporary mainline North American churches face seemingly intractable divisions over ordination standards and the role of denominational governance. Entire congregations are now becoming more and more polarized from each other, as church membership increasingly self-selects into "progressive" and "conservative" churches. It is easy to get mired down in quarrels over who is right, who is the most faithful, who is best suited to be a leader in the church.

Paul has something different to say: a timeless reminder to the church to place God at the center of everything they do together. To make his point, Paul uses the metaphor of a skilled master builder: "Each

Exegetical Perspective

"The church is not a building, . . . the church is a people." So goes the familiar hymn calling Christians into community with Jesus' followers around the world.[1] This song would sound strange to the early Christians. In today's reading, the community of believers *is* a building, a sacred place belonging to God, founded on the good news of Jesus Christ (v. 11). The early Christians did not have specific buildings associated with their communities. In fact, the word "church" (Gk. *ekklēsia*, see 1 Cor. 1:2) referred to a gathering of people, not to any kind of structure. As with the hymn, however, Paul's architectural imagery serves to draw the Corinthians' attention to the nature of their community.

Paul introduces the idea of the community as a building in verse 9, at the end of a section discussing the relationships among the Corinthians and various apostles. Paul has been concerned about the congregation's unity (1:10). Cliques have formed around certain leaders, including himself and Apollos (1:12; 3:4). He sees this sort of competition among groups as childish (3:1), because both he and Apollos are doing God's work. Paul uses two metaphors to make this point: the community is a field that God is

Homiletical Perspective

Our Epistle texts for today and next week have special interest for us preachers, and that is good. We also have to ask if they have interest for our people, and we will do that. First, though, consider these words from scholar Duane Litfin:

> How did Paul conceive of his preaching . . . ? Only one passage in Paul's extant epistles was written specifically to address [such a] question. That is, despite the fact that preaching was one of the Apostle's most persistent topics, there remains only one section in Paul's epistles in which we discover anything like a reasoned exploration of *how* he operated as a preacher and *why*. This section is 1 Corinthians 1–4.[1]

Much of Paul's explanation of his preaching comes in other parts of 1 Corinthians 1–4, especially 1:18–31, which we encountered in the Fourth Sunday after the Epiphany. Our text is primarily a reprise of Paul's assaults on Corinthian wisdom and divisions in the church, which indicates these matters were important to him. How did he approach them? Metaphorically. I remember someone saying that metaphor is an inadequate approach to interpretation, but it is the best way we have.

1. Richard K. Avery and Donald S. March, "We Are the Church," in *The United Methodist Hymnal* (Nashville, TN: United Methodist Publishing House, 1989), 558.

1. Duane Litfin, *St. Paul's Theology of Proclamation* (New York: Cambridge University Press, 1994), 2.

1 Corinthians 3:10-11, 16-23

Theological Perspective

community in this city was splintered into at least four different groups centered on different leaders. Each group asserted its status as the true and correct representation of the church of Jesus Christ. Thus, the Christian community in Corinth desperately needed to reflect on what it meant to be "the church."

In addressing the ecclesiological concerns found in Corinth, Paul makes three theological assertions about the nature of the church. The first is an obvious and basic one. He reminds the Corinthian believers that the foundation of the church is Jesus Christ. This statement emphasizes that the church, in all its manifestations, is built upon the foundation of the activity of God in human history. The church is not merely another human association. Because there is a divine element in the church, it should transcend the realm of human institutions. This divine element transforms the newly created communities of faith into the new people of God.

This understanding reverberates throughout the writings of the early church, as early church leaders such as Justin Martyr, Irenaeus, Clement of Rome, and the Shepherd of Hermas affirm this reality. Within early Christian writings, the church, regardless of the background of its members, is said to be one body and united in one soul; further, the members of the church are deemed to be formed together in a unity of understanding and faith. Paul also writes of this essential foundational truth of the church based on God's activity, as he describes believers being of "one Lord, one faith, one baptism" (Eph. 4:5).

The difficulty here, though, is in understanding exactly what this assertion meant for the early church and means for our churches now. Should there be greater uniformity in polity and practice among Christian churches because of it? Should the message and activities of every church be the same?

Every Christian church, from the most liberal to the most conservative, makes the claim that it is based on the foundation of Jesus Christ, and many condemn and exclude those who disagree with their own particular theological interpretations. Do the differences in theological approaches by these differing churches constitute changing the foundation, or is it only a difference in the "stuff" constructed on the foundation? (See 1 Cor. 3:12–15.)

A second theological assertion, made by Paul in verse 16, is that the church as a whole, meaning all the believers in all the groups of Christians, is the temple of God on earth, that is, God's dwelling place, and that the Holy Spirit resides in the entire

Pastoral Perspective

builder must choose with care how to build on it" (v. 10). Other translations use the phrasing "But each one should be careful how he builds"(NIV), indicating words of caution about how the church is constructed.[1] Paul is urging that each person involved in creating, running, or sustaining a congregation be intentional with the process of being church. In the process of constructing a building, once a solid foundation is poured, each person adds her own expertise. Carpenters frame out the house, an electrician adds the wiring, plumbers add the plumbing, and so on, until the building is completed. If even one person contributes poor work, the building will not function well when it is complete.

In the process of creating and sustaining a congregation, Paul reminds us to take the same care. Paul is urging intentionality, with a deep awareness that we build on the foundation of Jesus Christ. A foundation gives the footprint to the building. Paul asks the church to consider the question, What kind of footprint did Jesus leave for us to build upon? Paul's metaphor implores the church to carry that footprint through to every aspect of its life together. Is our congregation being intentional in showing God's love and justice as revealed in Jesus Christ in every way it can? Are we living God's love and justice in our worship life together? Are we demonstrating it in the way we govern our congregation? In the way we govern our denomination? Are we living God's love and justice in the way we include our youngest children and our oldest adults in the life of the congregation? In the way we welcome the stranger?

In this passage, Paul is speaking out of a desire to repair the division within the Corinthian church. Does division and disagreement over leadership build upon the foundation that Jesus laid for the church? Paul argues that it does not. Paul urges the church to take care: "Each builder must choose with care how to build on [the foundation]" (v. 10) that is Jesus Christ. Paul issues a call to be intentional in all aspects of the life of the church.

The lection for today omits one important aspect of building upon the true foundation that is Jesus Christ: testing by fire (v. 13). For Paul, all who built will be judged by fire. The ultimate test for our ministerial work is the test of fire, the test of endurance in times of difficulty and challenge. The test has nothing to do with growth, status, orthodoxy; these are contingent and contextual factors in the life of

---

1. Richard B. Hays, *First Corinthians*, Interpretation series (Louisville, KY: John Knox Press, 1997), 54.

cultivating (3:6–9) and a building that houses God's spirit (3:16–17).

Paul describes himself as a "wise architect" (v. 10, Gk. *sophos architektōn*), a master builder who oversees the project and directs the workers. Paul is confident that his own work has laid a good foundation, but warns any other builders to pay attention to what they are building. In the verses omitted for this week's lectionary, Paul depicts God as a rather surprising building inspector who will test the strength of a building by lighting it on fire! If the building is made of strong stuff, it will survive the fire. Although Paul has said that he and Apollos are simply God's servants (v. 5)—and thus presumably equal (v. 7)—his building metaphor suggests that he is not so sure about what is going on in Corinth, and he warns the community to pay attention to the fruits of the labors of their leaders.

The word "you" throughout verse 16 is in the plural; Paul thus equates the whole community, not individuals, with a temple (see also 2 Cor. 6:16), just as the whole community is famously the body of Christ in 1 Corinthians 12:12–31. In Paul's time, the Greek word for temple, *naos*, referred to a dwelling place for a god, either a statue of a Greek or Roman god or the spirit/presence of the God of Israel. In the Jewish Scriptures, the central building of the temple in Jerusalem was called the *bet YHWH*, or house of the LORD (see 1 Kgs. 7:12, 40, 45, 51).

Christians might be tempted to interpret Paul's imagery as a more personal and more Christian spiritual idea than the "Jewish idea" that God lives in the temple in Jerusalem, but this would not be true. The idea of a community as a temple is an old Jewish idea, as can be seen in the *Community Rule* from Qumran, in which the community is similarly a field and a temple: "an eternal planting, a temple for Israel, and—mystery!—a Holy of Holies for Aaron; true witnesses to justice, chosen by God's will to atone for the land" (1QS 8.5–6).[2] Here a Jewish community metaphorically serves all the functions of the Jerusalem temple.

What is important is that the community is a sacred place that belongs definitively to God and not to any particular leader. He calls the community to be self-reflective and to evaluate what they and their leaders are building together—not whether they need to renovate the Sunday school rooms or repaint the sanctuary, but whether their factions reflect the

2. Translation from *The Dead Sea Scrolls: A New Translation*, trans., with commentary by Michael Wise, Martin Abegg Jr., and Edward Cook (Rev. ed., San Francisco: HarperSanFrancisco, 2005), 129.

When I was a child, I used to wonder at the cornerstone of our old church. It said (KJV of course): "For other foundation can no man lay than that is laid, which is Jesus Christ" (v. 11). Not understanding metaphor, I was frightened by the inscription, afraid that we had squashed Jesus under the building. Later, in junior high school, my English teacher told me again and again not to mix my metaphors. Both of these experiences come into play with our text for the day.

Paul, wiser than he let on, must have skipped the eighth grade, because in this section he loved mixing metaphors. He portrayed himself as mother, nurse, farmer, master architect, servant, slave, father, and athlete. The plethora of images, surely used to help people understand his points, may have instead been confusing. One sometimes gets the sense with Paul that he thought faster than he could write (or dictate) and that the metaphors and images simply piled onto one another.

The main thing Paul wanted the Corinthians to understand about his preaching was the difference between Corinthian wisdom and his wisdom. Paul wrote his letter "at a time when it was not possible [in Corinth] to be considered wise without being eloquent." Moreover, he was writing to "citizens of a city in which, as everyone knows, rhetoric stood in the highest estimation."[2] Corinthian wisdom was grounded in human intellect and rhetoric, while Paul's wisdom was grounded in the cross. The cross was not primary to the wise ones; it was everything to Paul. Where do we preachers stand on this matter today? See my comments about scapegoating in the commentary on the Ninth Sunday after the Epiphany (pp. 423–27). Many people see the crucifixion as a kind of "suicide by cop." I do not see it that way, but I do stand amazed and overwhelmed, as someone now lost to me said, at how God could take the worst thing we ever did and turn it into the best thing God ever did. The danger with our love of our own rhetoric is that we will use our own skills to downplay the scandal of the cross, our smooth persuasiveness to evade the roughness of God's grace.

The question that remains to us as we are trying to get up a sermon is how people would hear a sermon of dueling wisdoms: human wisdom and fancy rhetoric opposed to the wisdom of the cross. There is some danger here. The Corinthian church was beset by an elitism that ran the risk of excluding others. On the other hand, a strand of anti-intellectualism has

2. Ibid., 244, 245.

1 Corinthians 3:10‑11, 16‑23

Theological Perspective

church. Again this appears to be a basic theological point, affirmed in a variety of theological reflections ranging from Martin Luther, who declares in his Large Catechism that the Holy Spirit resides in Christendom and is the one who brings individuals to faith and also causes the community to become strong in the faith and better equipped to do the work of God, to the Barmen Declaration, which sees the church as a gathering of the faithful where Jesus Christ, through the work of the Holy Spirit, acts.

The tension we may feel here is with the seeming emphasis on the corporate nature of Christian activity and identity. Many Western Christians are very familiar with stressing the individual nature of the Christian faith, that each person must come to faith in God and become stronger in faith and better able to do the work of God, because the Holy Spirit resides in that believer. As we deal with this passage, how do we balance the individualistic approach with a more corporate one? How is our understanding of the nature of the Christian life and walk changed if we give more credence to one or the other?

One last theological point to highlight is made in verses 21–23. Paul seems to indicate that the human leadership in the church and even all things in human existence, including life and death, are under the sovereignty of the church. This can lead to a kind of church triumphalism in which the church as a whole and, by extension, the individual believer, are seen as the "lord and master" of all of life. This is not Paul's point, though. The church is sovereign only as it remains under the sovereignty of Christ. The church can rejoice that it no longer must be subservient to the powers of the world, but must be cautious not to assert that its power over all things is its own.

As the early church struggled to understand the nature of the new faith communities it was creating, the contemporary church must continue the struggle. This passage may well help us in our search for this truth.

W. MICHAEL CHITTUM

Pastoral Perspective

congregation. The integrity and witness of the people of God throughout time is the true test of fire.

Another aspect of this passage is interesting in the questions it raises for the contemporary church. Paul writes, "Do you not know that you are God's temple and that God's Spirit dwells in you?" (v. 16). The you Paul mentions is not a singular, private you. Paul intends to say that God dwells in the figurative temple that is the community of believers. Here Paul is referring not to an individual but to the entire Christian church in Corinth. To suggest that God dwells among the gathered community was radical in first-century Corinth, because previously God was understood to dwell in the temple in Jerusalem. Paul extends the understanding of God's dwelling place in the temple to assert a new idea: Yes, God dwells in the temple, but the temple is not a building, it is a community. Community is what we are called to build, knowing that the Holy Spirit dwells in the people of God.

To think of God's dwelling place among the Christian community is radical today too, but it is radical for a different reason. People can have individual experiences of God, but God is not a private God. At a time when individualized spirituality is prevalent and churchgoers struggle to fit worship into the other demands of children's sports games, homework, housework, jobs, and family time, some are tempted to stop going to worship altogether. Paul's assertion that God dwells among the community of believers when it gathers together can serve as a reminder that worship within the context of a church community is essential for encountering God. For a church divided, whether in first-century Corinth or contemporary mainline North America, the suggestion that God dwells among the gathered community lends a powerful reminder that God desires the wholeness and unity of God's people.

KATE FOSTER CONNORS

wisdom of God or the foolishness of "this age" (v. 18). Paul is concerned that the community is mistaking their own (and certain leaders') wisdom for God's wisdom (see 1:17–2:16). In verses 18–20, Paul repeats his earlier reversal: the wisdom of this world is foolishness with God (see 1:20). This reversal is based on Paul's interpretation of the cross as a scandal (1:18, 23). How could God honor and redeem the life of someone condemned to death as a criminal of the Roman state? That sounds foolish, by human standards of who deserves to be honored.

In the same way, God has brought the Corinthians together as God's sacred place, even though the world considers them lowly and uneducated (1:27). In verses 19–20, Paul quotes Jewish Scripture to remind the community that God reverses expectations and exposes what we might think is wise as scheming or pointless (Job 5:12–13 and Ps. 94:11; see also 1:19). Paul encourages them not to boast in any person (v. 21) since their leaders—indeed everything!—belongs to them (v. 22). Because the community is God's temple, built on the foundation of Christ, the community belongs to God (see 6:19), not to any leader.

In this passage, Paul suggests that the community should take a good look at itself and see if they need a "building committee" that looks at whether they are building together according to God's measures. Presumably this kind of evaluation should be applied even to Paul himself, since no leader owns the community. We have to imagine how the Corinthians heard Paul's teaching, whether they had God-inspired ideas of their own about how to live in God's spirit, or thought that Apollos did. In our own communities, it is not so easy to discern among competing leaders or ideas. The challenge of this passage is not exclusively to valorize Paul's voice, but to heed his call to be a community that *all together* takes a good look at what kind of place it is making, and whether God and the "fools" of the world are at home there.

MELANIE JOHNSON-DEBAUFRE

long run through the fabric of American life. Tex Sample's "hard-living people" often disparage pointy-headed professors, and vice versa. We also face the possibility of fading churches in which everyone is alike. Preachers who run the gamut from tent revivalists to steeple pastors may have little to do with, or little respect for, the others. This can lead such preachers to building short-lived churches that look like themselves.

Here we see that Paul was right. The only possible common ground is Christ crucified. When we gather at the cross, we have the opportunity to see it and to see Jesus from a variety of perspectives. Respecting those perspectives of our neighbors might help us to realize what Paul was preaching, that it is not Paul or Apollos or Cephas or any of us who try to speak a good word for Jesus Christ, it is not the world or life or death or the present or the future—all of these belong to all of us, and we belong to Christ, and Christ belongs to God.

One useful way to describe this suggestion is to borrow a word from the ancient church by way of George Cladis. "John of Damascus, writing in the seventh century C.E., described the relationship between the three persons of the Trinity as 'perichoresis,' which is a kind of circle dance in which the persons move around the circle in a way that implies intimacy, equality, unity yet distinction, and love."[3] This text could be a wonderful opportunity to invite a variety of people to come together to share their understanding of the cross. The preacher might then look at the cross from the perspectives of different cultures in the congregation. Even if the preacher ends up sharing her or his preference for a particular view, others will feel that their perspectives have been taken seriously and not ignored. The danger of dissension is not eliminated by this approach, but it is lessened.

JOSEPH R. JETER

3. George Cladis, cited in Joseph Jeter and Ronald Allen, *One Gospel, Many Ears* (St. Louis: Chalice, 2002), 121.

Matthew 5:38-48

38"You have heard that it was said, 'An eye for an eye and a tooth for a tooth.' 39But I say to you, Do not resist an evildoer. But if anyone strikes you on the right cheek, turn the other also; 40and if anyone wants to sue you and take your coat, give your cloak as well; 41and if anyone forces you to go one mile, go also the second mile. 42Give to everyone who begs from you, and do not refuse anyone who wants to borrow from you.

43"You have heard that it was said, 'You shall love your neighbor and hate your enemy.' 44But I say to you, Love your enemies and pray for those who persecute you, 45so that you may be children of your Father in heaven; for he makes his sun rise on the evil and on the good, and sends rain on the righteous and on the unrighteous. 46For if you love those who love you, what reward do you have? Do not even the tax collectors do the same? 47And if you greet only your brothers and sisters, what more are you doing than others? Do not even the Gentiles do the same? 48Be perfect, therefore, as your heavenly Father is perfect."

Theological Perspective

The phrases of the Sermon on the Mount are so familiar and beautiful we can almost forget how demanding they are. "Turn the other cheek." "Go the second mile." "Love your enemies." "Be perfect, as your heavenly Father is perfect." How lovely, how close to home, how . . . impossible. Love your *enemies*? Respond to the fist by opening yourself up to more fists? Pray for your *persecutors*? As if that's not enough, *be perfect*. The final command is given as an afterthought:" "Oh yes, and besides all that, be flawless." Right.

It is no wonder Christians have developed elaborate strategies for avoiding these commands, impossible and offensive as they are. Some historians tell us that Jesus' admonition to turn the other cheek is buried in historical *obscurata*: it was an offensive gesture to Jews in the ancient world to be slapped with the back of the right hand. Turning the other cheek makes it impossible to be so slapped again. Suddenly the command seems historically distant and irrelevant to us. If you bind the hands of the text that way, sit back and listen for the congregation to exhale: "Whew, I was hoping Jesus didn't mean it." How can we rub the edges off the command to lend to everyone who asks? To love enemies? To be perfect? Here is how Christians have done it: These are spiritual admonitions, directed at our souls, not at the

Pastoral Perspective

Jesus often says things that make us chafe; he challenges the disciples to do things that seem contrary to human nature.

In this section of the Sermon on the Mount, Jesus tells the disciples to turn the other cheek, forgo revenge, give more than the required in a lawsuit, go the extra mile, give to all who beg, lend without limits, love the enemy, pray for persecutors, and greet the stranger. Jesus highlights the surprises that characterize life in God's realm; he challenges the disciples to do the opposite of what seems normal and reasonable.

In a world that is "all about me," Jesus offers an alternative we find difficult to imagine and embody. Today who can be perfect? It is easier to be mean, hold grudges, ignore those in need. If I give to everyone who begs, I will have nothing left for myself. If I turn the other cheek, I will get slapped again. If I get sued, I am hiring the best lawyer I can afford to find a loophole in my favor. If I love my enemies, I will be more persecuted or even killed. If I am too nice, I will be seen as weak, a pushover, a doormat.

We might not say these things out loud, but some may harbor these sentiments. For others, these feelings are justified—African Americans still suffering the vestiges of slavery and race discrimination, Japanese nationals and Japanese Americans who live

Exegetical Perspective

Stumbling into the kitchen after a long day of work, I put down my groceries and pressed the voice-mail button. It was my (then) ten-year-old daughter Erin. "Dad, I'm the lector at church Sunday, and I have that passage where Jesus says, 'Turn the other cheek.' You know that passage, right? Do the other Gospels have that same passage? Is it different in the other Gospels? Could you let me know, because . . . no offense, Dad, but I think Jesus is wrong."

Erin's objection summarizes how the church has interpreted this passage. The history of interpretation reveals something we would rather not say out loud: we are suspicious that Jesus is wrong. So we explain away his words in various ways.

—Jesus was setting forth a set of values to which his disciples should aspire. They are impossible but that's the point. By striving toward them, we live better than we would otherwise.

—Jesus' words throughout the Sermon on the Mount reveal the impossibility of human righteousness, preparing us for the advent of grace.

—Jesus was speaking to his disciples as individuals. In our modern world, with its complex relationships, global economics, and violent military threats, his advice simply does not hold.

—Jesus offers pragmatic advice to empower oppressed people. When you cannot force people

Homiletical Perspective

Good preaching comes down to good listening: alert, discerning attention to a local culture, and only then a response to it and through it. In this sense, a preacher is first of all a kind of ethnographer, a participant-listener finely tuned in to the conventional wisdoms of a particular time and place. At the same time, she likewise listens locally for the Word of God in Christ and the Holy Spirit resounding through Scripture, ecclesial life, and the wider symphony of creation. Only after all of this listening, then, does she ascend the pulpit and offer something for other listeners to hear. "So faith comes from what is heard," writes Paul (Rom. 10:17). As Jesus puts it repeatedly in the Sermon on the Mount: "You have heard that it was said. . . . But I say to you . . . "

From a homiletical perspective, then, a first thing to be drawn from Matthew 5:38–48 is the basic idea that Jesus does not preach from nowhere. Rather, he starts from somewhere quite familiar and concrete. He starts from what his listeners have heard said. In this sense, he meets them exactly where they are. He listens with them, articulates well-known conventional wisdom, and then alongside it places that bold little word "but."

In other words, Jesus names what is widely taken for granted, and then speaks against it. Thus he does not preach in what we might call a continuous or

Matthew 5:38-48

Theological Perspective

outward manifestations of our bodies, which may have to hoard stuff, bomb our enemies, and settle for being spiritual slackers.

The Sermon on the Mount is Jesus at his ornery best: offering "advice" that makes no sense divorced from the nature of the one giving it. In fact, the wisdom proffered here is not at all new, despite the formulation, "You have heard it said . . . but I say to you." In terms of *content*, Jesus offers here nothing he did not learn at Mary's knee. It is in terms of the *speaker* that these words take on radical resonance. Our constant temptation to boil down the hard particulars of Jesus into a mushy, vaguely deistic faith, suitable for a Hallmark card, is here put to rout. Jesus, in all his Jewish, biblical, demanding particularity, will have none of it.

"The Lord who accompanies us on our journey offers his own cheek to slaps and his shoulders to whips, to the increase of his glory," one ancient Christian teacher said.[1] We are called here to love as God loves. This cannot be done out of our own resources. So this is no admonition to try harder—if it were, it would indeed be recipe for despair. It is a plan of action rooted in the promise to be made "children of your Father in heaven" (v. 45). The Sermon here and elsewhere is a portrait of the very heart of God, one who loves the unlovable, comes among us in Christ, suffers our worst, and rises to forgive us. Turn the cheek, give the cloak, go another mile, lend, love the enemy—because that is how God loves. If you want to follow this God, fleshed in Jesus, you will be adopted into a life in which you find yourself loving this way before you know what you are doing.

One thing this text expressly is *not* is an admonition doomed to failure—a word of judgment meant to drive us into the arms of grace. It will seem that way if it is taken as isolated moral admonition for straining heroes to accomplish through their lonely determination, like marathon runners. If, however, this is a blueprint for the life of the church, a constitution for a new society, then we have a chance.

A friend grew up with missionary parents in a favela in Brazil. Asked how her family could live among the poorest of the world's poor without danger of being robbed, she said, "Simple. You can't own anything anyone would want to steal." Lend to anyone who asks, give to all who want to borrow. Then you can live among God's poor and receive the

1. Hilary of Poitier, *On Matthew* 4.25, quoted in the *Ancient Christian Commentary on Scripture*, ed. Manlio Simonetti (Downers Grove, IL: InterVarsity, 2001), 118.

Pastoral Perspective

with the tattooed numbers of the internment from World War II; survivors of the Holocaust; Hispanic Americans who are discriminated against with "English Only" requirements; women who make less money than men doing the same job; gay, lesbian, bisexual, and transgendered persons who are denied the right to marry; and those around the globe who suffer at the hands of oppressors. Jesus' call to forgive and be reconciled rings hollow and seems resigned to evil.

Jesus does state what the payoff will be: to inherit the reign of God. What do we get for loving, forgiving, being kind and gracious, and offering generosity? Some of us are too suspicious of the outcome and may resist living the values of God's realm. We are more intent on making sure no one has a chance to abuse or tyrannize us again. Some of us are so stubborn we would rather be right than be in relationship with others.

Then we frequently focus on the whole perfection piece—another can of worms that makes us feel either uncomfortable or overwhelmed. Some of us spend a lifetime seeking perfection and are frustrated when we fall short. Others shrug our shoulders and declare, "I'm only human," as a way to justify the failure we are unable to overcome on our own.

This text carries two challenges. First, Jesus teaches about life in God's realm. God's community is filled with people who think of others first. Every decision and action is carried out for the common good. Each person is sister or brother to the other and acts out of love. The capacity for this kind of love is due to the empowering love given by God, who is love. We are able to be gracious, forgiving, hospitable, and generous because we are children of the God who showers us with abundant grace, mercy, love, and protection. Those who know God's love now can love their enemies; those who experience God's forgiveness now can forgive those who persecute them; those who claim God's gift of generosity can now give back to those who have little or nothing. We are able to do these things because in Jesus we live in the days of God's reign.

Second, Jesus lets his listeners know that he himself embodies these values. He moves us from "you have heard that it was said" to "but I say to you." We no longer have to rely solely on the written word to understand God and God's will for creation. We simply have to look at and listen to Jesus. Jesus shifts the authority from what was *to himself*—God's word made flesh and dwelling in our midst. Because of Jesus, God's realm is already present and moving

to treat you justly, you can expose the injustice of the situation. When striking back will only get you hurt, confront the aggressor without retaliating. When your debts are out of control, show how your poverty leaves you without protection from the elements. When your occupier demands your labor, put him in an impossible situation by going beyond conventional expectations.

Though clever and insightful, all of these interpretations suffer from the same problem. Matthew's Gospel as a whole, and the Sermon on the Mount in particular, repeatedly insist that Jesus means exactly what he says. In Matthew's Gospel, to follow Jesus means to do what he says.

Within this pericope, one consideration rules out "explaining away" Jesus' difficult sayings. Jesus provides a theological rationale for the teaching. This rationale works at several levels.

Major point: Disciples are to love their neighbors and their enemies just as they love themselves.
Rationale: In this way disciples imitate God (or are "children of God"), as God blesses the righteous and the unrighteous without distinction.
Subordinate rationale: Imitation of God distinguishes disciples from others. Their behavior *should* be different.
Telos: Imitation of God is not merely an obligation; it provides the very goal of discipleship. "Be perfect, therefore, as your heavenly Father is perfect" (v. 48).

This telos of the pericope provides the goal for an entire section of the Sermon on the Mount, the famous antitheses ("You have heard that it was said . . . , but I say to you . . ."; 5:21–48). All of these challenging sayings point in the same direction, perfect imitation of the ways of God.

Beyond the pericope and the antitheses, there is the context of the Sermon on the Mount. The Sermon's setting evokes Moses's journey up Mount Sinai to receive the Torah. In Matthew, Jesus delivers his address from a mountain, and it revolves around the law. Matthew 5:17–20 provides the thesis for the Sermon. The thesis insists upon righteous conduct, including Torah observance, that exceeds even that of the scribes and Pharisees. With 5:17–20 as a determining principle, Jesus' sayings about the houses built on rock and sand (7:21–27) conclude the Sermon on the Mount. These sayings emphasize doing what Jesus says. "Not everyone who says to me, 'Lord, Lord,' will enter the kingdom of heaven, but only the one who does the will of my Father in heaven," Jesus warns (7:21). Meanwhile, the

conjunctive style, with each idea following constructively upon the last. Rather, he preaches here—and throughout the Sermon on the Mount—in an adversative style, naming supposedly sound advice and then contrasting it against his own. In this passage, the two pieces of alleged wisdom come from the legal world of Scripture and scriptural commentary. Like any good rabbi, Jesus is a consummate exegete. As such, he interprets the law within its proper horizon and according to its proper use, a task that at times involves criticism even, especially of particular features and interpretations of the sacred text itself.

The first piece of conventional wisdom Jesus treats here is the so-called *lex talionis* ("law of retaliation") found in Exodus 21, Leviticus 24, and Deuteronomy 19. In apparent contrast with this principle, Jesus paints a portrait of active nonretaliation, a stance so far from resistance to opponents (v. 39, "Do not resist an evildoer") that at first it seems to border on collaborating with them, offering them another cheek, another coat, another mile. Upon closer inspection, this stance is actually rooted in a profound resistance, an unexpected refusal to play the opponent's adversarial game. By voluntarily going a second mile, for example, the first mile is likewise refigured from something "forced" into something chosen; so what might superficially seem to be docility is actually, at a deeper level, a form of nonadversarial defiance. Mohandas Gandhi thought very highly of the Sermon on the Mount, in particular this passage—so much so, he wrote, that it influenced his nonviolent strategy against the British colonial occupation in India.

In one sense, Jesus critiques the *lex talionis*, advocating active nonretaliation against any brute policy of "an eye for an eye." In another sense, however, he thereby recapitulates the inner logic of the *lex talionis* on a deeper level: if "an eye for an eye" means that the proper restitution for a wrongful act is its mirror image or reversal (as in, "if you take an eye, then you will lose an eye"), Jesus effectively adopts this very principle, but argues that the true reversal of an opponent's opposition is not yet another act of opposition. Rather, the true reversal is an act of nonopposition, a creative response that works toward extinguishing not the opponent, but rather opposition itself.

Put another way, Jesus recommends a kind of moral jujitsu, a way of discipleship that ostensibly does not resist an aggressor, but in so doing actually does resist the underlying paradigm of hostility and contempt involved in striking a cheek, suing for a

Matthew 5:38-48

Theological Perspective

blessing of possessing nothing. For Jesus, God incarnate, possesses nothing, except our hearts.

Another potential mistake in interpreting this passage is to minimize its difficulty, for example, by romanticizing one's enemies or downplaying the difficulty of nonretaliation. The Bible was written by and for people under savage persecution. Scripture holds up well when read by powerless people under the thumb of an empire as mighty as Rome's. We think our "enemy" is the parishioner badgering us with critical e-mails. Think instead of a soldier with the power of life or death over you commandeering your labor, and your offering to do twice what he asks. For another modern parallel, think of the insurance companies asking ever more of our income to insure ever fewer of us. This text would say, they want how much? Give them more. God makes us enemies into divine friends, makes orphans into daughters and sons (v. 45) in God's incarnation and crucifixion. God gives to us extravagantly, even nonsensically. How can we do otherwise?

A hallmark of John Wesley's Methodist revival and the variety of Holiness movements he spurred (Nazarene, Holiness, Assemblies of God) was the great seriousness with which they took Jesus' command in 5:48 to be perfect. Why would Jesus command such a thing if it were impossible? Sure enough, saints often experienced full sanctification on death's door. Why not a day earlier? Or a year? Perfection does not mean always choosing the right fork at the dinner table, nor does it mean attaining to such divine attributes as omniscience. It means loving as God loves, with every breath God gives us. Impossible? Too much? "God well knew how ready our unbelief would be to cry out, This is impossible! And therefore stakes upon it all the power, truth, and faithfulness of God, to whom all things are possible."[2]

JASON BYASSEE

Pastoral Perspective

toward its fulfillment. Within us already are the marks of those fully embraced by God and empowered by God's will. Jesus calls us to maturity that results in more Godlike behaviors and motivations.

With the words of this text, Jesus seeks neither to set impossible goals nor to shame people who cannot reach perfection. Instead, he sets forth God's vision of God's world, where love, genuine and unconditional, reigns. The reign of God is inaugurated in the person of Jesus, and we, Jesus' followers, are empowered by Jesus' witness to live the reign of God's values.

Today we are caught in the tension between human nature and being children of God. To be perfect is not to add pressure to already overwhelmed lives; instead, it is to assure us that we are not alone in the world and that God continues to work in and through us. Perfection is less about getting things right and more about loving as God loves, and Jesus is God's concrete example of that love.

We are amazed by people's capacity to do things that defy our natural instincts: the survivor of a violent crime who is able to forgive her tormenter; black South Africans who work with their former oppressors to rebuild their country; the Mother Teresas of the world who give selfless service to outcasts; those who live modestly so they can contribute to the well-being of the less fortunate; and those who make a choice to commit random acts of kindness. We are surrounded by examples of unselfish love and caring; we need only look for them. God's realm is already active and moving toward fulfillment.

In his Sermon on the Mount, Jesus lets us eavesdrop on his instructions to the disciples. We too are encouraged to live as sisters and brothers in God's realm. "Be perfect" is not an indictment; it is a promise that carries the possibility that we may love the world as God has loved us—fully, richly, abundantly, and completely.

BARBARA J. ESSEX

---

2. John Wesley, *Explanatory Notes upon the New Testament*, 11th ed. (London: Mason, 1831), 1:31.

Exegetical Perspective

wise person "hears these words . . . and acts on them" (7:24).

Finally, there is the larger context of Matthew's whole story. At the Gospel's end, the risen Jesus sends his disciples on mission, charged with making disciples of all "nations." Their message? "Teaching them to obey everything that I have commanded you" (28:20). From the argumentation of the pericope itself, to the larger structure of the Sermon on the Mount, to the very ending of the Gospel, Matthew insists upon obedience to Jesus' teaching.

The pericope begins with five specific cases (vv. 38–42) before it moves on to principles. The first three cases envision disciples as victims of oppression; the final two portray disciples who possess the ability to perform works of compassion. In all five instances, love governs the disciples' response, at the expense of individual rights and prerogatives.

In vv. 38–42 Jesus calls his disciples to forfeit their rights in the presence of evil. The law empowers victims to seek restitution that fits the crime (Exod. 21:24; Lev. 24:20; Deut. 19:21). On the other hand, multiple scriptural passages voice the determination not to retaliate against a wrongdoer (Lev. 19:18; Prov. 20:22; 24:29), while other Jewish and pagan sources testify to the same sentiment.[1]

In the same way Jesus' instructions to give one's coat and to go the second mile go beyond asserting one's "rights." The law forbids creditors to take a person's outer garment (Exod. 22:26–27; Deut. 24:12–13). "Going the second mile" does not violate Roman legal principle, but it effectively demonstrates going above and beyond the requirement. Likewise, one is never obligated either to give or to lend, yet Jesus' disciples will do either upon request. In the face of need, they forfeit their right to private property.

Unfortunately, we Christians have traditionally exercised ourselves over the five cases rather than the theological rationale Jesus provides. Matthew's Jesus means what he says, and his teachings rightfully weigh heavily in discussions of Christian ethics. Nevertheless, the structure of Matthew 5:38–48 subordinates the five cases to a larger point about discipleship. Loving their neighbors, even their enemies, disciples sacrifice their own personal rights in order to demonstrate their imitation of God. How ought contemporary disciples to appropriate the five cases? How to enact love of our neighbors, regardless of their behavior, that is the question of the day.

GREG CAREY

Homiletical Perspective

coat, or forcing someone to walk a mile in the first place. Again, the nonviolent resistance movements associated with such figures as Gandhi and Martin Luther King Jr.—as well as, in a different way, recent interpretations of this passage by Walter Wink, among others—are in various respects consonant with this basic subversive pattern. In the end, Jesus' instruction "Do not resist an evildoer" points toward a deeper, more radical resistance: namely, noncooperation in the underlying paradigm of hate and brutality involved in evildoing. In fact, we may say that for Jesus, true resistance to evil entails active, creative nonresistance to the evildoer.

All this is summed up in verse 44: "Love your enemies and pray for those who persecute you." In the face of the most extreme opponents ("enemies") and acts of opposition ("persecution"), Jesus advises defiance—but not defiance directed against the enemies themselves, since this simply perpetuates and intensifies the relationship's adversarial character, but rather a deeper defiance directed against the vicious, endless cycle of enemy making. Do not fight fire with fire, Jesus says; rather, fight fire with water, and thereby refuse to take part in the incendiary, all-too-familiar work of injury and domination.

This is a compact, challenging teaching, and one of its chief hazards in a homiletical setting is that it can so easily be misunderstood as somehow recommending mere passive acquiescence in the face of violence and harm. In every congregation, to greater or lesser degrees, there are listeners who are suffering such harm, have done so, or soon will; any suggestion that Jesus is advising us simply to accept our wounds and embrace our assailants should be clearly rejected. On the contrary, the centerpiece of this teaching is noncooperation with harm in all its forms. While this does entail loving and praying for perpetrators, by that very same token, it also entails whenever possible discontinuing arrangements that allow or enable perpetrators to wreak havoc. After all, to do otherwise is in fact to disobey not only the instruction, "Love your enemies"—since the havoc perpetrators wreak is always self-inflicted—but also Jesus' signature command to love God and to love your neighbor "as yourself."

MATTHEW MYER BOULTON

---

1. W. D. Davies and Dale C. Allison Jr., *Matthew*, International Critical Commentary (Edinburgh: T.&T. Clark, 1988), 1:540–41.

Isaiah 49:8-16a

⁸Thus says the LORD:
In a time of favor I have answered you,
  on a day of salvation I have helped you;
I have kept you and given you
  as a covenant to the people,
to establish the land,
  to apportion the desolate heritages;
⁹saying to the prisoners, "Come out,"
  to those who are in darkness, "Show yourselves."
They shall feed along the ways,
  on all the bare heights shall be their pasture;
¹⁰they shall not hunger or thirst,
  neither scorching wind nor sun shall strike them down,
for he who has pity on them will lead them,
  and by springs of water will guide them.
¹¹And I will turn all my mountains into a road,
  and my highways shall be raised up.

Theological Perspective

In this grammatically complex passage—it variously addresses God's chosen one, the oppressed, the powerful, the world, the cosmos, and Zion—the theme of vocation unfolds in multiple ways. First, the passage is messianic, describing the person, message, and impact of the "Holy One of Israel's . . . chosen [one]" (v. 7). Then it addresses the vocation of Zion, God's chosen people, especially when they doubt their vocation. Moreover, the passage carries forward the theme, established earlier in the chapter, of God's call to all nations.

The anointed one addressed at the passage's outset is Isaiah's Suffering Servant, "one deeply despised, abhorred by the nations, the slave of rulers" (v. 7). Christianity sees in Isaiah's Suffering Servant a foreshadowing of Messiah Jesus. Certainly this Servant's mandate to proclaim the Lord's favor and release to captives portends the message and mission of Jesus (Luke 4:18–19).

This is not, however, just about Jesus' personal ministry. It addresses all ministry in his name, serving as a vocational guide for all who proclaim his gospel. Before conducting the appointed ministry, the minister is first ministered to. God begins by meeting the Servant's own personal needs—"I have answered you, . . . I have helped you; . . . I have kept you" (v. 8). Flush with a personal encounter with

Pastoral Perspective

There is a prison in the town where I live that is situated in one building in a large complex of county buildings. From the outside, it looks just like the courthouse building, or the building where you go to get shots to travel to another country, or the building where you pay your traffic tickets; but it is very different. You cannot just walk in and out of it. You know about it if you have ever had cause to be inside it, as a prisoner, correctional employee, or a visitor. If you have not ever been inside, you would never know what it was. The prisoners in our community are invisible, right in the center of things, but covered in darkness.

It is to strange situations like this that Isaiah says, "Thus says the LORD: In a time of favor I have answered you, on a day of salvation I have helped you; I have kept you and given you as a covenant to the people, to establish the land, to apportion the desolate heritages; saying to the prisoners, 'Come out,' to those who are in darkness, 'Show yourselves'" (vv. 8–9a).

Come out and show yourselves. That is not something we are always willing to do as communities. We want to show ourselves—to an extent. We want to show the good parts of ourselves.

We are proud of our parks when they are clean and well kept; but we would just as soon not have

¹²Lo, these shall come from far away,
  and lo, these from the north and from the west,
  and these from the land of Syene.

¹³Sing for joy, O heavens, and exult, O earth;
  break forth, O mountains, into singing!
For the Lᴏʀᴅ has comforted his people,
  and will have compassion on his suffering ones.

¹⁴But Zion said, "The Lᴏʀᴅ has forsaken me,
  my Lord has forgotten me."
¹⁵Can a woman forget her nursing child,
  or show no compassion for the child of her womb?
Even these may forget,
  yet I will not forget you.
¹⁶See, I have inscribed you on the palms of my hands.

Exegetical Perspective

The passage is found in the portion of the book of Isaiah (Isa. 40–55) dated to the late exilic period. About two hundred years after Isaiah of Jerusalem, the prophet of Isaiah 40–55, commonly known as Second Isaiah, built a new message based on the earlier prophet's tradition. He ministers to a new generation living in exile and exhorts them with an uplifting message of comfort, hope, and return. According to Second Isaiah, God is about to liberate the people of Israel from bondage and lead them home to the land of Canaan. The harbinger of hope is charged to spur the people out of the lethargy of exile. This week's OT lesson showcases the pith and passion of the exilic prophet's message and ministry.

At the outset of the lectionary selection, the prophet introduces the word of YHWH, who lays out the plan of deliverance. YHWH addresses a second-person-singular recipient, but the speech blooms into a discourse for a wider audience. On the one hand, one may well read the verses as God's response to the prophet's prayer of lament. On the other hand, it is God's good news directed to the people of God.

God's offer of salvation, presented in the first person, paints a favorable time when a prayer has been answered and God's help attested (v. 8a). God's design of protection, election, and settlement of

Homiletical Perspective

God's Partner in Newness. Without getting ponderously lost in an attempt to identify the Servant (Israel? Cyrus? the Messiah-anticipated?), a sermon might begin with the Servant's role as God's partner in newness. Israel in exile has fallen into despair and perhaps into resigned acquiescence to Babylon's ways and gods. God speaks into reality a decisive new exodus for Israel, once again enslaved and unable to move out.

Israel cannot see beyond the present boundaries of Babylon, yet God speaks as if they are already home. God gives concrete tasks to the Servant: establish the land and apportion it equitably; command those imprisoned to "come out" (an exodus verb), and those in darkness to "show yourselves." God empowers people who are not as helpless, hopeless, and abandoned as they presume. The Servant, given as a "covenant," is a partner with God, making the new future real. Israel is enabled to enter freedom's light; empowered to leave behind the false gods of an alien empire for God's intended future.

Questions for the preacher to consider include, What powerful "empires" and false gods invite us to acquiesce to ways that are not God's ways? The enticements are so powerful, our exile so long, that we may forget who we are. Complacency or despair makes us unable to see how life can be otherwise.

Isaiah 49:8-16a

Theological Perspective

God's redemptive work, the minister is equipped to go public with God's good news. This is the pattern of the ministry of Jesus, who announces the good news to others only after being rescued by God from the clutches of temptation and being ministered to by divine messengers (Matt. 4:1–17). Those who would minister in Christ's name must first tend to their own souls, availing themselves of God's help before offering it to others.

Ministry in Christ's name discloses to God's people a vocation that both comforts the afflicted and afflicts the comfortable, "saying to the prisoners 'Come out,' and to those who are in darkness, 'Show yourselves'" (v. 9). The latter phrase refers not to healing the blind, but to exposing the untruthful, especially those in places of power. This vocation of exposure predictably gets Jesus in trouble, and those who ministry faithfully in his name can expect no less. The earlier commission does this also: releasing prisoners overturns the judgments—and thus subverts the authorities—of the social order that has shackled them. Freeing wrongdoers is a sign that this ministry is all about God's gratuitous favor, rather than about people getting their just deserts.

Our text details the impact of this proclamation: hunger and thirst are satisfied, nature's elements are no longer enemies, and God's guiding hand leads the people to places of abundance. Only a bold eschatological vision of God's full and final reign can rightly inform and sustain ministry in Christ's name, but the immediate experience of God's people may be quite otherwise. After hearing the resounding call to rejoice in God's sure victory, Zion says, "The LORD has forsaken me, my Lord has forgotten me" (v. 14). Announcing good news of great joy does not always elicit a welcome response.

God's response to Zion's accusation is consummate tender mercy: "Can a woman forget her nursing child, or show no compassion for the child of her womb? Even these may forget, yet I will not forget you. See, I have inscribed you on the palms of my hands" (v. 15–16). This inscription is no mere writing, but an *engraving*,[1] a sure sign that God *cannot* disown Zion. Ownership of Zion is carved into God's *hands*, the part of one's body one contemplates more than any other. This image is a potent reminder that the covenant God makes with the chosen people is no external, bilateral contract, but a divine promise woven into the very fabric of God's being. Despite her history of disobedience and exile,

---

1. Hebrew *haqaq*, "to cut."

Pastoral Perspective

people see the drug dealing that goes on at night or the prostitution that takes place in the bushes. We are proud of our schools when the team wins the championship or the national merit scholars are announced; but we prefer not to have attention directed toward the special-needs program that got cut in the state budget or the ethics scandal that led to the firing of the principal.

To all this, God says, "Come out and show yourselves." We are the ones God has claimed as a covenant people. God has claimed us, as broken as we are, and wants us now to claim each other.

When I was visiting a prisoner at the local jail, upon entering I realized that nobody knew where I was. As I walked down the long hall to the visitor's booth and was locked in myself, I realized that I was at the mercy of the guards. They had spoken crossly to me and had chastised me for forgetting to leave my bag behind. When they barked at me through the speaker in the tinted glass, I was frightened. I did not want them to be angry with me. I waited for a long time for the person I was visiting to arrive. Without a bag, I had nothing to do. There was nothing to read, no calendar to check—just me, locked up and waiting, with no time line. Suddenly I realized the obvious. I was getting the smallest possible taste of prison life. I felt trapped in darkness, hidden away where no one could see me. The seventy-two-year-old woman I was visiting told me that that was what she felt every minute of every day: invisible, bored, trapped, and out of the sight of the world.

God is saying to the prisoners, "Come out," to those who are in darkness, "Show yourselves." Sometimes the people who are in darkness cannot come out. They are locked in. Then the responsibility falls upon the rest of us, the other members of the social body, to show these people to the world that has made them invisible. We cannot let them be forgotten.

This passage reflects that note of despair: "But Zion said, 'The LORD has forsaken me, my Lord has forgotten me'" (v. 14). That is how prisoners feel. It is how sick people feel, and grieving people feel, and anxiety-ridden people feel. We all have had that moment when, in the midst of our suffering, we worry that we have been forgotten. Often we have been forgotten. People grow weary of suffering people. They cannot take hurting people all the time, and sometimes they pull away and even forget—but God does not forget us.

"Can a woman forget her nursing child, or show no compassion for the child of her womb?" (v. 15a). The question that is posed has two answers. The first

Israel is about to be repeated (v. 8b). The first part of verse 9 continues to describe the mighty acts of God, who calls out the prisoners from their shackles and brings them from darkness to light. God will guide them through the wilderness once more. God will provide for them (v. 9b).

The NRSV captures the certainty of the prospect of God's guidance by translating verse 9b in the future tense (cf. LXX). The NRSV demonstrates that such hope is based on God's past deliverance (vv. 8–9). However, the KJV has already started using the future tense in verse 8b (cf. Masoretic Text). Translators of the KJV were apparently caught up with the prophet who cranes forward to the future charged with hope.

In the midst of these upbeat notes, the prophet takes note of a number of challenges represented by hunger, thirst, and threatening elements of nature (v. 10). The mountains make disheartening obstacles. There are no highways in sight that would lead them to their homeland (v. 11). Unflinching from the catalog of hardships, the prophet proclaims that God will move the mountains. God will prepare the path of their return. This reference to a road recalls 40:3, but what had been announced there as YHWH's road is now opened up as the people's path to freedom.[1] The captives are expected to come from a distance and from all directions (v. 12). The south is represented by the faraway land of Syene, modern Aswan. The east is not named, for it is from there that the prophet's immediate audience will start their journey to Zion.

Verse 13a resumes the imperative mood (see v. 9a). The prophet calls upon the heavens and earth to participate in jubilation over God's redeeming work. The call of comfort recalls 40:1. The charge of comfort that was pronounced in chapter 40 is now fulfilled. Isaiah 49:13 calls for a hymnic response from everyone, including creation. Mountains, the former obstacles (see v. 11), are now members of the choir praising God. The latter half of verse 13 reiterates the basis of praise. Praise is commanded, for the compassionate God has comforted the people who had suffered much.

There is a significant shift in verse 14. It is anticlimactic: it disrupts the strain of praise. However, in the present form of the text, God takes time to encourage those who may be harboring a shade of doubt and could not join the celebration of salvation. The scene contains a lament by a female figure of Zion/Jerusalem who pleads the case of "marital

1. John Goldingay and David Payne, *A Critical and Exegetical Commentary on Isaiah 40–55*, International Critical Commentary (London: T. & T. Clark, 2006), 2:176.

The divine imperative startles—"Come out! Show yourselves!" (v. 9)—moving us toward exodus, a new future. What "present circumstance" makes it hard for us (individually/corporately) to see new possibilities? How does God empower us to be partners in newness? God intends to bring all exiles home (north, west, and from the land of Syene/south). Where do we see exodus and newness taking place?

People on the way to freedom worry and complain as they leave the certainties of empire. God again provides shepherding. This time the way is clear, with abundant pastures, water, and protection. God comforts us in our anxiety and coaxes us toward freedom. We recall Psalm 23, John 10:11 (Jesus, the good shepherd), and Luke 15 (the shepherd who searches for and finds the lost sheep). We are not alone. A member of a church I served was a shepherd. One night after a late meeting ended, Anthony arrived at his farm. The sheep wandered nervously, bleating that unknown danger might be near. He walked toward the flock, calling, "It's me. You are safe." Recognizing his voice, the sheep quieted with confidence, as if replying, "Ah, it is you, you who cares for us and helps us out of trouble. Though it is very dark, we are not afraid."

No wonder that what follows verses 8–12 is an exuberant, cosmic hymn of praise (v. 13). Heavens, earth, and mountains sing a doxology for God's comfort and compassion, a climactic choral crescendo!

But Zion Said . . . The sermon, like the text, is not over. While the doxology for God's "comfort" and "compassion" still echoes from the choir loft, from the pews a countervoice breaks in: "The LORD has forsaken me, my Lord has forgotten me" (v. 14).

Israel still finds it hard to sing the Lord's song in a strange land. Comfort, compassion? No, forsaken, forgotten. The whole book of Lamentations is contained in this flat voice of grief.

We too speak this countervoice to doxology. The sermon may dispute our complaint. As one preacher says:

> Is it ever enough? What would a grand and powerful gesture by God be if we did not respond with a whine? The mountains get it, the children of God not so much. It is not easy for us to let go of suffering. Even when all of creation is recognizing God's comforting power, we are still left behind in an earlier time. . . . Free to come into the light . . . the people of God are too busy decrying how God has forsaken and forgotten them to recognize how

Isaiah 49:8-16a

Theological Perspective

Israel is assured that God has never forsaken her. God *could not* forsake her. Moreover, the mother's hand is the means of her children's sustenance and guidance; the children's names are engraved precisely there, assuring God's unrelenting providence for precisely *these* children.

Finally, our passage develops further a theme stated earlier in the chapter: messianic ministry and people are called by God to be "a light to the nations, that my salvation may reach to the end of the earth" (v. 6). When the good news is proclaimed, the Lord says, "I will turn all my mountains into a road, and my highways shall be raised up" (v. 11). To what end is this monumental highways project undertaken? That peoples "shall come from far away . . . from the north and from the west" (v. 12).

This image of nations streaming to God's holy mountain from the corners of the compass is appropriated by Jesus twice in the Gospels. In the first instance, Jesus is amazed at the faith of the centurion who asks Jesus, "Only speak the word, and my servant will be healed" (Matt. 8:8). Jesus exclaims, "Truly I tell you, in no one in Israel have I found such faith. I tell you, many will come from east and west and will eat with Abraham and Isaac and Jacob in the kingdom of heaven" (Matt. 8:10–11). In the other case, Jesus is responding to the question, "Lord, will only a few be saved?" (Luke 13:23). After unsettling those all too complacent over their status as God's chosen people, Jesus flings wide the doors of salvation to the whole world: "People will come from east and west, from north and south, and will eat in the kingdom of God" (Luke 13:29). These texts, harking back to Isaiah 49, have been adopted liturgically by the Christian church as the invitation to the Table of the Lord, an invitation extending to the whole world. This is the essence of the vocation of Messiah Jesus, and the community he calls forth: Proclaim the good news that God's bounty and peace are more than enough for all the nations. Our world may yet groan in the night, but God's promised deliverance and peace are coming as surely as the dawn.

SHELDON W. SORGE

Pastoral Perspective

would be, "Of course not. No mother would abandon her own child." When we reflect on real life, we know that is not really true. Some mothers do not show compassion for their children. Isaiah must know what we are thinking, because he adds these words from the Lord: "Even these may forget, yet I will not forget you" (v. 15b).

God is better than human beings. God can hang in there with suffering people. God will not get weary of your tears or your loneliness or your complaining. As for the prisoner, her plight will not be forgotten either.

Isaiah tells us that God has given us enormous responsibility. "I have kept you and given you as a covenant to the people, to establish the land, to apportion the desolate heritages" (v. 8b). We do not always handle this responsibility well. When it comes to our attempts to apportion the desolate heritages, we tend to apportion them to the other side of town, moving them away to the outer reaches, where it is hard to visit them. Sometimes prisoners are even moved across the country, or they are kept close by in town, in an invisible building that we are not supposed to notice. God knows where they are. God is keeping track of every jail cell, and every tear that is shed there.

"See, I have inscribed you on the palms of my hands; your walls are continually before me" (v. 16). It is as if God is willing to go to prison too. There is nowhere we could end up that God would not follow us, no matter how dark.

LILLIAN DANIEL

desertion" by her husband, YHWH.[2] In a juridical proceeding the abandoned wife Zion gets a day in court, thanks to the advocate, who is also named YHWH. In a figurative speech that strains itself (the mediator and the defendant are the same person!), reconciliation takes place, thanks to YHWH.[3]

The lamenters have their own reason for despair. They recall the past history of abandonment that seems to suggest divine forgetfulness. The paralyzing terror of history deprives them of a capacity to hope. The prophet halts his triumphant song to minister to them. This concern for flanking doubters is significant. Second Isaiah, known for the lofty drumbeats of marching to Jerusalem, turns to care for those who are bound by the disabling past. God's salvation is also for those whose vision of hope was impaired by the disappointments of the past and present.

God swiftly dismantles the basis of such deep-seated doubt. First, a rhetorical question introduces the metaphor of a woman who, though very unlikely, may blunder and forget her infant child (v. 15a). Verse 15b underscores the absolute nature of God's care by pointing out that God is not subject to such human frailty. According to the prophet, God is closer than parents to a child. Verse 16a offers an object lesson with the palms of God's hands that display the eternal reminder inscribed for divine remembrance—a striking image whose anthropomorphism has troubled translators (e.g., Targum).

The lectionary passage stops in the middle of verse 16. The latter half of the verse makes it clear that the pericipe has left out the unclear portion of the passage ("your walls are continually before me"). With the omission of the ambiguous part, the passage seeks to bring home the certainty of God's care with the graceful ending of "God's hands" that will bring the day of salvation to fruition.

JIN HEE HAN

keenly they are remembered and how gloriously they have been freed. Perhaps we do not need so much to pray for God's intercession in the midst of our broken-ness as to pray for the discernment to recognize how God is already interceding for us.[1]

The sermon, on the other hand, may legitimize the grief, acknowledging exile's pain, genuine loss, and experience of abandonment. Either way, there is another word to be spoken.

Inscribed on the Palms of God's Hands . . . God is cosmic, yet deeply personal. God's relationship to us is described in the most intimate, basic terms . . . a mother breast-feeding her infant. As intensely as Israel feels forgotten, God feels intensely connected. Women who have breast-fed know the ache of this life-giving nourishment; how milk spills at the softest cry. God's intensity more than matches Israel's, as their word "forgotten" (v. 14) is overturned not once, but three times (v. 15).

We are not forgotten. We are inscribed on the palms of God's hands. Every day in Washington, D.C., people visit the Vietnam Memorial, searching for a name etched into the wall bearing so many names. They trace their fingers over the letters, touching something deeper than name alone. Not forgotten. Remembered. Inscribed. Still, not all names are there, for even our best memorials are limited. Not so the palms of God: every name is written, everyone is included. What joy to find your own name and names of those you love on God's outstretched palm!

Might tattoos be an apt metaphor for God's inscribed hands? Indeed, people who get tattoos often want to indicate membership in a group, a way of life; or to make permanent note of an event or a person. However, an ink is being developed today that makes tattoo removal easier and less painful.[2] Our loyalties, our loves change. Not so with God. The covenant holds. We are inscribed on the palms of God's outstretched hands, hands that guide us toward freedom and welcome us home.

KIMBERLY L. CLAYTON

2. Joseph Blenkinsopp, *Isaiah 56–66: A New Translation with Introduction and Commentary*, Anchor Bible 19B (New York: Doubleday, 2003), 310.
3. Klaus Baltzer, *Deutero-Isaiah: A Commentary on Isaiah 40–55*, Hermeneia (Minneapolis: Fortress Press, 2001), 322.

1. From an unpublished paper on this text by the Rev. Doug King, senior associate pastor, Brick Presbyterian Church, New York City, presented to the Moveable Feast group in 2008.
2. King connects the images of the Vietnam Memoiral and "tattoo removal" in the paper cited.

Psalm 131

¹O Lord, my heart is not lifted up,
  my eyes are not raised too high;
 I do not occupy myself with things
  too great and too marvelous for me.
²But I have calmed and quieted my soul,
  like a weaned child with its mother;
  my soul is like the weaned child that is with me.

³O Israel, hope in the Lord
  from this time on and forevermore.

Theological Perspective

Important changes in the fields of theology and biblical studies over the past half century are reflected in the commentaries on this psalm. Most of the recent analysts have accepted what seems obvious once spoken—that the author is a woman or is, at least, quoting a woman. They tend to be occupied by questions about whether the Hebrew alludes to a still nursing infant or perhaps one being carried in a sling.

Some earlier writers engaged in convoluted reasoning to put the psalm's language into the mouth of a man. Despite the fact that verse 2 is the portion most indicative of gender, it is the first verse that has produced the widest gap in interpretation related to the speaker's sex. A woman, especially one engaging in some sort of liturgical observance (as the term "song of ascents" implies), might well have been wise to disclaim "stepping out of her place" before she spoke any further. From a woman, "My eyes are not raised too high, I do not occupy myself with things too great and too marvelous for me" may be an apology—not in the sense of Christian apologetics, but in the sense of an actual apology for intruding into male space in a time and place where that religious behavior was not universally accepted.

In the mouth of a man, the words have an altered connotation; they are easy to read as a warning that questioning the Deity is an unwise occupation.

Pastoral Perspective

The Wire was an HBO series from 2002 to 2008 that received critical acclaim and some popular recognition. Set in the center city of Baltimore, Maryland, *The Wire* depicted police, drug dealers, street youth, everyday real people struggling to live amid the politics, economics, corruption, and true courage that is life in the real world.

Part of the story focused on narcotics detectives battling in the war on drugs. Part focused on the street level and even cartel-level dealers. *The Wire* was a streetwise, earthy, gritty telling of stories.

The unique thing about the show is that it did not demonize the bad guys or canonize the good guys. As the old folk used to say when I was a boy, "there's some good in the worst of us and some bad in the best of us." And that is what you got in the stories told in *The Wire*. And that is why it was true to life.

But *The Wire* had the air of lived reality for an even deeper reason. There are time when the demarcation between that which is good and that which is evil is clear and incontrovertible. More often than not, however, the difference is not so much between obvious good and obvious evil as between what seems good or best and what seems less than the best, but maybe better than the worst. To say it

Exegetical Perspective

This concise psalm describes the spiritual stance of a worshiper through vivid physical descriptions. Eyes, heart, and mother's embrace all work together to express the psalmist's humble relationship to YHWH. The psalmist's imagery of the soul as a young child with its mother in verse 2 may suggest female authorship. The psalmist—whether male or female—employs imagery of distinctly maternal nurturance.

Psalms 120–134 all carry the superscription or heading "Song of Ascents," though not all mention David, as Psalm 131 does. Despite their common titles, the content in the Psalms of Ascent varies. In Psalm 131 an individual expresses trust and confidence in YHWH, though the final verse suggests a community setting. Others in the collection arise from a collective voice (Ps. 124), and describe perspectives such as lament (Ps. 130) and praise (Ps. 122).

The reference to "ascent" in this group of psalms may indicate the worshipers' actual journey up Mount Zion to honor YHWH at festival times. Similarly, this may have represented the return to Jerusalem from exile. In contrast, "ascent" could refer to the heightening poetic structure found in many of these psalms, or even a now-unknown musical setting. While we do not know for sure the origin or use of the collection, these psalms prompt us to speculate about the prayers pilgrims might sing

Homiletical Perspective

The gentle words of Psalm 131 create a powerful image for relationship with God. The psalmist describes this relationship as that of a child with its mother, the first human bond that a child knows. God provides comfort and satisfaction, and the speaker is like a quiet child.

Many of our earliest memories revolve around the bond of trust established in the first eighteen months of life. The child begins to understand her name and to articulate first words, shaping sounds for the names of her parents, for basic needs and wants. The child takes teetering steps, relying on the hands of his parents to provide support for tottering little legs. Learning to walk creates a newfound sense of independence; yet, if a toddler falls when a parent is within reaching distance, and the parent does not catch the child, tears often ensue. The preacher might engage in a playful recounting of some examples of memorable moments in parent/child relationships, painting a picture that has the potential to be both humorous and poignant. At the same time, the preacher should be sensitive to the fact that perhaps not all listeners recall memories of contentedness or trust.

The psalmist's description of the child as weaned indicates a certain distance between the mother and child. The first verse of Psalm 131 communicates the ways that the speaker is not like God, the effects of

Psalm 131

Theological Perspective

Hence, the psalm is portrayed in places such as the NRSV version of *The New Oxford Annotated Bible* as an "act of humble submission to God's will."[1] Instead of discouragement for questioning, verse 1 can be proclaimed as acknowledgment that there are aspects of God's intentions and activity that we do not and will not ever comprehend, no matter how much or how well we study theology. Although it is natural and even desirable that we ask questions about God, even *after* prolonged, serious engagement with the questions there will still be answers we do not know. Not even the most intelligent or most spiritual or most theologically gifted of us will completely understand the Deity, or ourselves, in this lifetime.

Among those individuals with extraordinary theological gifts was Charles Wesley, the eighteenth-century Methodist poet. The hymn "Come, O Thou Traveler Unknown" uses only four of his fourteen stanzas on "wrestling Jacob" (Gen. 32:22–32). Jacob has questions—most notably, "who are you?"—and clearly Wesley does too. As he works through his own struggle to name the divine Being and to determine what this Being is like, he develops an affirmation that Jacob does not reach, at least according to the scriptural narrative. Charles Wesley concludes that God's nature and indeed God's very name are "Love."[2]

The psalmist's comparison of her soul to a deeply cared-for child in the presence of a loving parent brings to mind an occasion when my own daughter was visiting the room where she would soon begin prekindergarten. Despite the teacher's urgings to explore the surroundings, my daughter found my lap the best spot from which to view the classroom. After a bit, though, she slipped down and moved away to study an aquarium, while I continued to converse with the teacher. Then she returned to my lap, where I welcomed her. In time, she ventured out again to see what the shelves on another side of the room might hold. This pattern continued until she had seen every corner of the classroom.

God offers, the psalm assures us, the same kind of refuge, and thus provides the freedom to leave its confines and accomplish the work that is necessary for intellectual and spiritual growth. My use of the term "leave its confines" is not to imply that one can

---

1. Bruce M. Metzger and Roland E. Murphy, eds., *The New Oxford Annotated Bible (New Revised Standard Version)* (New York: Oxford University Press, 1991), 788.
2. Charles Wesley, "Come, O Thou Traveler Unknown," *The United Methodist Hymnal* (Nashville: United Methodist Publishing House, 1989), 386.

Pastoral Perspective

another way, much of life is more gray than black and white.

To add to that, there is simply much in life that never gets resolved. Some questions simply do not get answered. On HBO's *The Wire* sometimes justice was done, sometimes wrongs were righted. More often than not, the outcome was murky, unclear, ambiguous.

It might seem that the murkiness of our culture, as depicted in *The Wire,* is in sharp contrast to the clarity of the biblical world, but both the New and the Old Testaments sometimes make room for ambiguity too.

A conversation between Jesus and some of his disciples really helps here. In the Acts of the Apostles, after the resurrection and before the ascension and Pentecost, Jesus has one final conversation with his followers. As though they sense something imminent, they question him. "Lord, is this the time when you will restore the kingdom to Israel?" (Acts 1:6). Is the kingdom about to come? Is God's reign about to commence? Is justice finally going to "roll down like waters, and righteousness like an ever-flowing stream," as Amos said (Amos 5:24)? Are the poor going to stop getting poorer? Are the rich going to stop getting richer? Are bad things going to stop happening to good people? Is the cure for the diseases that harm and threaten us around the corner? Is the day of war soon to be past? Is poverty soon to be history? Are all of our hopes and dreams and the unfulfilled longings of our ancestors soon to be realized and fulfilled? "Lord, is this the time when you will restore the kingdom?"

Paradoxically Jesus answers by saying that it is not for them, or us, to know all the answers. "It is not for you to know the times or periods that the Father has set by his own authority. But you will receive power when the Holy Spirit has come upon you; and you will be my witnesses in Jerusalem, in all Judea and Samaria, and to the ends of the earth" (Acts 1:7–8).

The disciple's task is not to know all the answers or to assure with idolatrous certainties, but to live by a radical faith that waits on the Spirit, that works in the Spirit's power, and that therefore makes a witness in the world to the liberating and life-giving love of God that has been disclosed in the teachings and the life of Jesus of Nazareth.

Said another way, our task here on earth is not to give easy answers or quick fixes, but to follow on the way. Jesus never said, "I'll give you all the answers." He did say, however, "I am the way, and the truth, and the life" (John 14:6).

while journeying and when they arrive at their destination—whether Jerusalem, Rome, Iona, or even a metaphorical location.

The reference to David in the superscription of Psalm 131 does not necessarily date the psalm to his time. Like so much literature of the Hebrew Bible, such attributions more likely honored and invoked a famous figure than indicated authorship or date. The date of the psalm is uncertain.

The opening emphasis on the word "ascents" could have been meant to exalt YHWH during a pilgrimage up to the temple or upon arriving there. In contrast, the psalmist three times undermines any exaltation of herself in verse 1. Neither her heart nor eyes are lifted high, nor do the trappings of her life suggest anything but humility. Rather, all exaltation belongs to YHWH.

In verse 2 the psalmist clarifies that she had not been speaking of *external* oppression or degradation in verse 1, though such experiences would not be foreign to a woman in that time and place. Instead, she has smoothed and quieted her*self*, or her *soul* (Heb. *nefesh*). She illustrates this with a fitting scenario: a mother holding her weaned or nursing child (v. 2). We can almost feel the child snuggling into that calming embrace. The psalmist has so stilled her spirit before YHWH.

Though we cannot definitively conclude that a woman wrote this psalm, the maternal imagery of verse 2, along with the stereotypically female demeanor described in verse 1, have led some scholars to that very proposal. The Hebrew of verse 2 is problematic, prompting debate among translators. The NRSV and some other translations suggest that in this metaphor the psalmist identifies as both the child and the mother on whom the child rests. These proposals give us good reason to consider at least partial female authorship.[1]

In addition, the child in verse 2 could be nursing rather than weaned,[2] which would strengthen the argument that this was a mother's prayer. Either way, the psalmist paints a vivid picture of tender intimacy. Some scholars view the Psalms of Ascent as a collection of laypersons' prayers, brought to the temple and later edited into their more communal settings.[3]

the fundamental gap between mother and child. The distance is heightened when the child becomes haughty, forgetting that his knowledge is less complete than that of the mother.

The psalmist begins by placing his own ego in check. This gives us cause to believe that at one point the speaker held the mistaken notion that he could manage his own situation without God's help. The preacher might explore the circumstances that would lead one to pray such a prayer: a troubled economy, a divided family, a friendship unraveling, or a rift in the denomination or congregation.

The second verse speaks of the closeness of relationship shared by the mother and child, the calm and contentment that result from a relationship in which the child accepts and leans into complete dependence on the mother. In taking the role of the child, the psalmist turns to God to provide for his or her needs; the child's satisfaction derives from the mother's care. The speaker is aware of separation from God, but the bonds of relationship still hold, inspiring joy and hope. As the prophet says, "Can a woman forget her nursing child, or show no compassion for the child of her womb?" (Isa. 49:15). Here the preacher might focus on the ways that God calls us into loving reunion.

The relationship that the speaker shares with God is elemental, aware of its source. The speaker understands that God's ways are "too great and too marvelous" to comprehend. So the psalm reiterates the theme of humility and trust found in other readings for the Eighth Sunday after the Epiphany, including 1 Corinthians 4:5, where Paul speaks of God "who will bring to light the things now hidden in darkness and will disclose the purposes of the heart," and the Gospel text from the Sermon on the Mount where Jesus bids his listeners to "consider the lilies" (Matt. 6:28).

Another potentially fruitful homiletical approach would be to explore the feminine imagery for God found in Psalm 131. The language of God liberating the prisoners, portrayed as a nursing mother who shows compassion, found in the accompanying lection of Isaiah 49:8–16, lends support to such an exploration.

As a song of ascents, Psalm 131 may have been used as a song of pilgrimage. The imagery is concerned with safety, a haven to which one can return. Used in preparation for worship, Psalm 131 provides a helpful means of putting our relationship with God into perspective. The first words of the psalm help to focus the attention, to put aside those things with which we should not be concerning ourselves,

1. Melody D. Knowles, "Critical Notes: A Woman at Prayer: A Critical Note on Psalm 131:2b," *Journal of Biblical Literature* 125, no. 2 (2006): 385–89.

2. C. J. Labuschagne, "Short Notes: The Metaphor of the So-Called 'Weaned Child' in Psalm cxxxi," *Vetus Testamentum* 57 (2007): 114–23. The age of weaning was two to five years old, or even later (Ibid., 117). Also see 2 Macc. 7:27.

3. Klaus Seybold and Sigmund Mowinckel; see Leslie C. Allen, *Psalms 101–150*, Word Biblical Commentary 21 (Revised, Nashville: Thomas Nelson, 2002), 196.

Psalm 131

Theological Perspective

truly leave God's presence, but rather to emphasize that growth is the primary task of a child (and an adult) and that spiritual growth always involves risk taking of one sort or another.

Theologian Charles M. Wood uses this psalm in its entirety as the final paragraph of *The Question of Providence*, a consideration of the problematic nature of traditional teaching on providence, the doctrine concerned with the way that God acts in the world. Wood argues for a rethinking of the traditional view, which insisted that all that happens does so because it is the will of God. In a move toward constructing a more helpful way to think about providence, he proposes a more thoroughly Trinitarian understanding. Granting equal legitimacy to the three persons of the Godhead will, in his view, allow us to assemble a fuller picture of God's nature. He reminds us that for Christians, the Creator is not any more representative of God than the Christ is. The abandonment of power is as fully an expression of God's nature as is the exercise of power. Wood also calls for expanded awareness of the third person's activity, that is, the Holy Spirit's cooperative work with us. Following H. Richard Niebuhr, Wood maintains that "All creation is 'being lived' or 'being being-ed'; its life is a kind of participation in the divine life." While the world is most decidedly one that we humans have helped to create, it is also still God's world, one where God is continually working toward what is beautiful and good.[3]

The last sentence of our psalm—an admonition to the people to "hope in the LORD from this time on and forevermore"—becomes the last sentence in Wood's book, reflecting his profound appreciation for the role of hope in the Christian's life. It is, he maintains, precisely the Christian hope that frees Christians from having to be optimists. The Christian need not conjure up belief that things are, or will be, "all right." Knowing that God's nature and name are, as Charles Wesley believed, Love, gives us sufficient grounding for hope.

ELLEN J. BLUE

Pastoral Perspective

This was the insight of the one who prayed the prayer that is now Psalm 131:

> O LORD, my heart is not lifted up,
>   my eyes are not raised too high;
> I do not occupy myself with things
>   too great and too marvelous for me.
> But I have calmed and quieted my soul,
>   like a weaned child with its mother;
>   my soul is like the weaned child that is with me.
> O Israel, hope in the LORD
>   from this time on and forevermore.

These are not the words of false modesty, humiliating humility, but a mature and accurate assessment of the life of humanity. There are some things I know and some things I do not. There are some answers I have and some that I do not. In the end, what I have is hope, and that hope is a light and power for the way.

The old words of Charles Tindley's hymn may well say it best:

> We are often tossed and driven on the restless sea
>   of time,
> Somber skies and howling tempest oft succeed a
>   bright sunshine;
> In that land of perfect day, when the mists have
>   rolled away,
> We will understand it better by and by.
> By and by when the morning comes,
> When the saints of God are gathered home,
> We will tell the story how we've overcome,
> For we'll understand it better by and by.[1]

When we compare the gritty reality of cultural works like *The Wire* with the prayer of the psalm, we realize that part of our pastoral task is to help our people pray faithfully, humbly, trustingly. They and we try to deepen a devotional life that is utterly honest about the ambiguity of the world and utterly confident in the goodness of God.

MICHAEL B. CURRY

3. Charles M. Wood, *The Question of Providence* (Louisville, KY: Westminster John Knox Press, 2008), 116, 110.

1. Charles A. Tindley, "We'll Understand It Better By and By," in *African Amerian Heritage Hymnal* (Chicago: GIA Publications, 2001), #418.

Exegetical Perspective

Psalm 131 may have been one such prayer, offered by a mother whose soothed child reminded her of her own approach to the Divine.

In verse 3, the psalmist finally articulates the purpose for her meekness. She implores her audience—Israel—to wait for YHWH forever. Perhaps this sense of waiting requires the maternal soul-stilling described in verse 2, paired with the humble approach of verse 1. This final verse may have integrated the woman's prayer of verses 1–2 into the collection.

Reflection on the central metaphor of Psalm 131 (v. 2) implies several remarkable points. Not only does it indicate that the psalmist may have been female; it draws attention to both women and children. The psalmist compares a devout worshiper to a child, although children were often ignored and oppressed in the ancient world. Furthermore, the poetic transition from verse 2 to verse 3 lifts up the act of mothering as comparable to the work of the Divine. As with any metaphor, caution is due that the reverse imagery does not hold: The passage does not belittle men, women without children, or children without mothers. While verses 1–2 depict a stereotypically feminine submissive approach to God—perhaps an example of *internalized* oppression—this illustrates only one of many approaches to the Divine. The Psalter as a whole, filled with complaining laments, gives no reason to advocate only this stance for women or anyone else.

In preaching on this passage, it could be helpful to invoke other biblical imagery that highlights both a mother and child's role in relation to God. Passages that similarly describe God in motherly—or at least parental—terms include Numbers 11:11–12; Deuteronomy 1:30–31; 32:10–18; Job 38:8–11, 29; Isaiah 42:14; 46:3–4; 49:14–16; 66:7–9, 12–13; Hosea 11:1–4. Matthew 23:37//Luke 13:34 places Jesus in a maternal metaphor, and Matthew 18:1–5//Mark 9:33–37//Luke 9:46–48 emphasizes a child's approach to God. Reference to some of these passages might helpfully remind a congregation that the Bible presents more diverse metaphors for God than the "Father" that is so singularly pervasive in contemporary Christianity. Furthermore, Psalm 131 brings to light the voices and experiences of mother and child as acceptable prayer offerings to God and as welcome contributions to the community's prayer book.

LISA M. WOLFE

Homiletical Perspective

and to find a space in which we can worship as humble, trusting recipients of God's abundant grace.

For the psalmist, preparation for worship involves recalling a relationship that has always existed, one that provides life, health, and *shalom*. This relationship is where we are most at home, where we can let our ambitions fall away and allow God to draw us in, to know the smell of the dirt behind our ears. Nestling more deeply into this relationship, we bury our faces in God's familiar presence, and let God hold us close.

Considering Psalm 131 as a song of preparation for entering God's presence, the preacher might invite the congregation to consider its own preparations for worship, perhaps even using Psalm 131 as a call to worship for Sunday mornings. How do we lift up our hearts, while making sure that our hearts are not lifted up with pride? How do we as congregations help to provide worship experiences that invite participants into deep and trusting relationship with God, where their souls can be calm and quieted?

Psalm 131 is attributed to David. We do not often hear such words of humility coming from people who hold power in political or religious spheres. What would it mean for a leader to take these words to heart? As we look to our own spheres of influence, would our own lives be different if each day we reminded ourselves that we are tiny children, entirely dependent on God's mercy and grace?

The gentle text of Psalm 131 provides an image of God that is calming and hopeful. While such words of comfort may not be the message that a congregation needs to hear Sunday after Sunday, they can offer a welcome respite, especially when nestled between sermons on texts that are more challenging and confrontational in nature.

APRIL BERENDS

1 Corinthians 4:1-5

¹Think of us in this way, as servants of Christ and stewards of God's mysteries. ²Moreover, it is required of stewards that they be found trustworthy. ³But with me it is a very small thing that I should be judged by you or by any human court. I do not even judge myself. ⁴I am not aware of anything against myself, but I am not thereby acquitted. It is the Lord who judges me. ⁵Therefore do not pronounce judgment before the time, before the Lord comes, who will bring to light the things now hidden in darkness and will disclose the purposes of the heart. Then each one will receive commendation from God.

Theological Perspective

In this reading, Paul considers more narrowly the issues of church leadership and the relationship between leaders and members of the church; thus, he turns more to pastoral theology. This was, no doubt, a direct response to the conflicted state of the Corinthian church. As we well know, groups within the church had fractured any sense of church unity by elevating specific church leaders to a position of adulation that concerned Paul. Hence, in last week's reading, he underscored the point that the foundation of the whole church was Jesus Christ, and everyone else, including him, built on that foundation.

As we think of church leadership, we are generally concerned only about the qualifications for church leadership. Such lists of qualifications are found, for example, in the Pastoral Epistles. In 1 Timothy 3 and Titus 1, the list of virtues for both bishops and deacons emphasizes the need for the leader to have a good reputation in the community and to manifest a moderate lifestyle. This advice is echoed in Chrysostom's *Treatise Concerning the Christian Priesthood*, in the essay *The Book of Pastoral Rule* written by Gregory the Great, and in the writings of Gregory of Nazianzus.

The point Paul raises, however, is the issue of how church leaders should function within the context of serving the church. He begins by making a

Pastoral Perspective

This passage is not an "old standard" of the Bible. It is anything but a feel-good, familiar text. It is not one of the familiar stories children are taught in Sunday school. There are no pageants written about the first few verses of Paul's letter to the Corinthians. This is not a passage that would make it onto a banner, or a cornerstone, or even a bulletin cover. No one wants to hear about judgment,. No one wants to walk into church and see a banner (or hear a preacher) shaking a finger at them for being judgmental. No one wants to hear about judgment, because judgment is uncomfortable, whether it is a judgment about us or a judgment about others. Judgment implies a pronouncement of opinion about a person or persons. Whether the judgment comes from our own mouths or is pronounced by another, it often is hurtful. "Judgment" is the kind of word that conjures up childhood memories of a parent's admonishing words: "If you cannot say anything nice, do not say anything at all." This text certainly would not make it onto any Bible passage popularity list.

Nevertheless, Paul's words on judgment are words that demand a hearing. People make judgments about other people, organizations, and leaders; the church and the people in it are no exception. While this text may broach an uncomfortable topic, it contains an important word for the church.

Exegetical Perspective

In today's reading, Paul is in the middle of making an extended case to the community in Corinth that they should not be divided by cliques or competitiveness (chaps. 1–4). Paul intertwines two images to further his argument: the community as God's household, and the future coming of God to judge humanity. Both have deep roots in the ancient world, and each raises a challenge for how contemporary people might hear anew God's word for today.

In 1 Corinthians 3:21, Paul urges the Corinthians not to boast in human leaders. Apparently some of the disagreements in the community have crystallized around a kind of leader-based factionalism. According to Paul, some people in the community are busy with jealousies and quarreling (3:3). He sums the problem up as a kind of competitive cheerleading (1:12; 3:4). One could add some extra emphasis to the community slogans to get a sense of the tension and conflict Paul hears in them: "*I* belong to *Paul*. Oh, yeah? Well, *I* belong to *Apollos*." Many scholars have suggested that Paul is dealing with a challenge to his own authority as the primary leader because some prefer the teaching of other apostles, particularly Apollos. This raises the question of how communities deal with theological diversity or differences in leadership styles. Paul

Homiletical Perspective

A common theme runs through all of the texts for this Sunday: "Don't worry." Each has its own perspective on that imperative. Our text deals with judgment of church leaders. In the chapters and verses prior to 4:1–5, Paul has been speaking about the content and method of his preaching and the dissention that has arisen in the church over that. Here he speaks about the various leaders—most likely Apollos, Cephas, and himself—and the cliques (can we say cults?) that have grown up around them.

Paul is blunt in his assessment. He has changed his description of the leaders from that of builders to that of servants and stewards. The one attribute of the leaders that Paul brings forth as necessary is trustworthiness. We cannot argue with that. Paul goes on to say that he really does not care if he is judged by the church or a court; in fact, he does not judge himself. He claims that he is not aware of any personal wrongdoing, which is unusual, given his intense persecution of the church early on (Acts 7:58–8:3 and 9:1–2). (We can guess that he regards that persecution as part of the life he has left behind. In the light of his encounter with the risen Christ, he is now a new creation, and should be judged according to his new loyalties, not his old.) Paul insists that he will be judged by God and tells the church to back off from judging him or the other leaders until

1 Corinthians 4:1-5

Theological Perspective

theological evaluation about the nature of church leadership as he describes Apollos and himself as not worthy of adulation but as "servants of Christ and stewards of God's mysteries" (v. 1). The minister, as subordinate to Jesus Christ, stands ready to render service to the cause of Christ by effectively proclaiming the gospel message.

The Corinthian church had elevated Paul, Apollos, and Cephas to positions akin to that of celebrities today. Paul makes the theological assertion that he and Apollos, as church leaders, were not the headliners of the show, but only the assistants who stood in the wings. They served, as presumably all ministers should, at the pleasure of Christ and functioned as overseers of the message of the gospel.

The second issue raised by Paul is whether the church should stand in judgment of the ministry performed by the church leadership. As one who had been harshly judged by the Corinthians because he was not as polished an orator as Apollos, Paul made certain that the Corinthian church understood that he was accountable only to God, who would evaluate his ministry, because only God was qualified to do so. While in other parts of the letter Paul calls on the congregation to be discerning (as in 5:12, 6:2, and 14:24), he makes the point here that only God had the proper perspective to see how effective a person's ministry actually was in the life of a church and only God could properly balance judgment and grace in the process.

These two theological points—the understanding of the nature of church leadership and what role a church should have in evaluating the ministry—raise many questions for the church in every age. How should we understand and apply these points to our churches?

Consider the first point Paul makes. Ministers in Christian churches have been seen in various roles at different times in the life of the church. The minister is valued for her pulpit skills or sought after because he is seen as a great revival preacher. Other churches seek ministers who are renowned for their piety or spiritual disciplines. Sometimes, ministers function more as church builder, counselor, or teacher. More frequently in larger congregations, the minister is valued on operational skills, similar to those of a CEO, of a spiritual enterprise. We still see ministers who assume the persona of celebrity leading a vast throng. Even among churches who advertise for "servant leaders" to be the minister at their church, there can still be a sense of wanting something more than the servant and overseer that Paul describes.

Pastoral Perspective

The good news in Paul's admonishment about judgment comes when he points to God: "It is the Lord who judges me" (v. 4b). God—not pastors or church members, not parents or children, not teachers or friends or colleagues—is the one who judges. All other judgments are of human design and do not hold the same authority. This is comforting news, for judgments are plentiful in churches and families, in friendships and workplaces. It is a loving and just God, the God of Israel, Creator of all that is good, who holds the authority to judge the integrity of our lives.

People make judgments. It happens all the time, about issues of great importance and issues that are inconsequential. If readers of this passage identify with the Corinthian people, they may hear a word of reproach in Paul's discussion about judgment. However, Paul's assertion about God is important: God is the judge. When we find ourselves in the place of passing judgment, we can remember that it is not our job. God judges right from wrong, good decision from bad decision; it is not our responsibility. This reminder can bring relief to those who identify with the Corinthian Christians to whom Paul is writing. It is only God's job to be concerned about the righteousness of our actions. The benefit is twofold: one, if God is the judge, then we do the best we can in our actions and decisions, for what we do and decide is for the glory of God; second, we do not have to make those judgments about ourselves or about other people.

On the other hand, people also find themselves in the position of being judged by others. Sometimes Christians are called to take unpopular stands, sometimes in daily life and sometimes when serving as a public witness for Jesus' call to feed the hungry, clothe the naked, or take care of the widow and the orphan. Paul's reminder that God is the judge, not other people, can serve to reassure those who face ostracism or negative judgments because of their choices or actions.

To the churchgoer who writes an unpopular letter to the local newspaper advocating for justice, and faces a firestorm of angry letters afterward: "It is the Lord who judges me." To the teenager who is ostracized and bullied at school for being "different": "It is the Lord who judges me." To the elderly couple who choose to stay in their own home rather than move into a retirement home: "It is the Lord who judges me."

To be sure, Paul is not handing Christians a free license to act without consequence. Nor is he advocating that we use God's authority to ignore others' feedback or opinions about our choices and actions.

emphasizes the equality of everyone before God and their accountability to God's final judgment.

Paul says that he and Apollos are "servants of Christ and stewards of God's mysteries." Both of the leaders that the community might place on a pedestal are now put *under* the supervision of a higher power, as servants and stewards are under the authority of the master of a household. The Greek word for "servant," *hypēretēs*, can refer to various people who carry out responsibilities under the direction of someone else (see Matt. 5:25 and Luke 4:20). Paul is stressing that he and Apollos do their work in the community not as *top* authorities but as *subordinates* to Christ. This idea is repeated in the phrase "stewards of God's mysteries."[1] The word "steward" translates the Greek *oikonomos*, which means a house manager, who was often a slave set in a position of authority over the financial affairs of a house (see Luke 12:42). In this imagery, neither Paul nor Apollos can claim (or be given) lofty status, since each is accountable to God, who is above them both.

Paul now turns to the issue of evaluation. He affirms that "it is required of stewards that they be found trustworthy" (4:2), but he does not say who does this assessment. Perhaps Paul feels unduly judged by the community as he says, "It is a very small thing that I should be judged [or examined] by you [plural]" (v. 3). Indeed, Paul places his own accountability outside of normal time when he says "or by any human court" (v. 3), which in Greek literally means "or by a human day." Paul does not mind being examined or judged *now* by other people because, for him, the definitive and final evaluation is God's. Paul does not even judge himself because, although he does not know of anything that might be held against him, even his self-examination would not exonerate him.

Paul places himself under God's judgment, and thus neither submits to the scrutiny of others nor claims the power to justify himself. He says, rather, "It is the Lord who judges [or examines] me" (v. 4). The word "Lord" here has a double meaning, because for Paul, Christ is Lord, but the *kyrios*, which is the Greek word for "lord," is also the master of the household. Thus Paul concludes the portrait of himself (and Apollos) as middle management in the household of God, empowered to do God's work, but accountable only to the master of the household. Are today's

1. "God's mysteries" for Paul refers to the hidden wisdom of God not always discernible to humans, communicated through the message of the gospel and through the power of the Spirit speaking in God's prophets and apostles (see Rom. 11:25; 16:25; 1 Cor. 2:7; 13:2; 14:2; and 15:51).

"the Lord comes" (v. 5). Then he and others "will receive commendation from God" (v. 5). It is most likely that Paul's concern is that the various splinter groups have already chosen one leader for commendation and all the rest for condemnation.[1]

This text raises serious problems for the churches of our time. On the one hand, there are some television evangelists who insist that the enormous amounts of money they have amassed "belong to God," so the "churches and courts" should leave them alone. There are sects whose leaders are abusive, especially to women and children, but claim they are acting in the name of God and exempt from civil law. What should "churches and courts" do? On the other hand, there are many, many good pastors out there who are being clobbered by toxic congregations who seem to rejoice in the breaking of ministers. There are also ministers out there who seem to take pleasure in bringing down other ministers.

Years ago I was writing about an important quartet of nineteenth-century American preachers. One woman said she remembered one of them and told me that when he was old and sick and confined to bed, he had himself carried to the church once a year on church election day so that he might vote against the current pastor. Paul, I do worry. Too much commendation can corrupt a leader, and unloving condemnation can break one. Even within the context of the community of faith, proper judgment, proper discernment, can have its place.

There is a tension here between Paul's saying that he and all (ministerial) servants must be found trustworthy and then his suggesting that it is not the people who must judge him, but God. Such a combination verges toward oxymoron. Of course, God is the final judge of our actions, but we will surely be judged by people: our application to seminary, our tests in seminary, our examination by an ordaining board or committee, our consideration by a pulpit committee, our vote up or down by a congregation, our supervision by a pastoral relations committee, and so forth. *Vox populi vox Dei*. The voice of the people is the voice of God. Paul knows that his ministry will rise or fall depending upon his trustworthiness. So will ours. We are wise to set that before our people at the beginning of our ministry in a congregation. We must pledge before God and people that, whatever weaknesses we have, we will serve them in a trustworthy manner. Then we must do it.

1. See William Baird, *The Corinthian Church—A Biblical Approach to Urban Culture* (Nashville: Abingdon Press, 1964), 54.

1 Corinthians 4:1-5

Theological Perspective

So, what would it mean if a minister saw himself as the servant or saw herself as the administrator of God's message? Would a church value that ministry, or would it seek someone else who functions in other ways? Would a church respect the minister, or would it try to dominate? What can we say about a congregation who seeks the celebrity minister and not the servant?

The second point Paul seems to make could be just as troubling for the life of the church. Many understand Jesus' teaching in the Sermon on the Mount (Matt. 7:1–5) to mean that no one should be able to judge anyone else. Did Paul actually mean that no one in any church can evaluate the effectiveness of how a minister leads the congregation or the appropriateness of the minister's preaching? Is Paul advocating allowing a minister carte blanche to do whatever the minister decides to do, without any intervention? If so, what do we say about the congregations that are deemed "clergy killers" because of their history of evaluating and, then, sacking ministers over any pretext? Where is the balance to be found between these two extremes? Can it be found within our congregations?

It is tempting, perhaps, for us to dismiss this passage as not as worthy of consideration in our churches as other readings may be. How could anything be more important for churches to consider, as they seek to do the work of the kingdom of God, than the points raised here by Paul? The apostle admonishes those who are called to church ministry to consider their role and their place in the ministry of the local congregations. He admonishes the congregations served by these ministers to function as a people who trust in the work of God and who are reliant on the leadership of God. Implicit in these verses is the promise that, as both ministers and congregations are faithful in this, God's kingdom will be well served.

W. MICHAEL CHITTUM

Pastoral Perspective

Rather, Paul issues a reminder that in making choices about how to live our lives, God is the only judge. In being accountable to God, Christians are held to a higher standard than the human judges that surround them.

Paul knows something about judgment: He is the object of it in Corinth. Paul is writing to the church there, where disagreement and division over leadership, and judgment about Paul and the other apostles, are undermining the unity of the Christian community. Many in the Corinthian church have begun to dismiss the authority of Paul and his cohorts. Here Paul employs the image of servant, or steward, to reassert his authority with the Corinthian Christians. Using servant language, he paints a picture of the relationship between master ("Lord") and the one serving the master, to remind Corinthian Christians of his position of authority (and that of the other apostles) as a leader in the church (vv. 1–2).

In Paul's day, being appointed a steward was a high honor, meaning that a person was trusted enough to manage the affairs of the master's estate. He thus is writing to deflect the (apparently negative) judgment of the Corinthian Christians by reminding them of his authority and trustworthiness as God's servant and as a steward of God's message. Describing himself using servant language, Paul aligns himself with God and reminds the Corinthian church that God is the one who does the judging. The church can learn from both messages: we can be God's servant, and in so doing, we can give up the need to judge, because that is God's job. Conversely, when we find ourselves the object of judgment, we can remember that human judgment does not hold authority.

KATE FOSTER CONNORS

Exegetical Perspective

church leaders accountable only to God? How do we reconcile the need for community responsibility and ownership with Paul's ancient imagery of the church as a hierarchical household of God?

Paul speaks directly to the community: "Therefore do not pronounce judgment before the time, before the Lord comes" (v. 5). The coming of Christ and the time of God's judgment of humanity are described in true apocalyptic (or revelatory) imagery—it is a time of the *revealing* of hidden things and people's true motives. At that time, says Paul, each person will receive God's approval, presumably according to the measure of his or her work (as in 3:12–15). The conclusion of Paul's example of himself and Apollos as equally accountable to God comes in verse 6 when he says that he has made this comparison "so that none of you will be puffed up in favor of one against another."

The idea that all people are equal before God has long been an important part of the Christian tradition—although not unique to it—that disrupts and rejects human hierarchies of injustice and privilege. The notion that we should not judge each other—as we are all equally liable to judgment—is echoed in the teaching of Jesus in the Sermon on the Mount (Matt. 7:1–5). These same values animate Paul's teaching in today's passage. However, his use of the ancient imagery of a hierarchical household also introduces a kind of inequality between community members and their leaders, and his belief that the day of God's judgment is coming soon can place the accountability of leaders outside of the community and in some future moment. Today's religious communities have seen the consequences of power centralized in the pastor, and leaders who place themselves beyond the evaluation and collaboration of the community. Thus Paul's messages of the equality and accountability should be applied to all people in the context of democratic structures that empower the priesthood of all believers, invite conversation among diverse viewpoints, and ensure oversight and accountability in the community today and not only in the future.

MELANIE JOHNSON-DEBAUFRE

Homiletical Perspective

There is a magnificent sermon by William Willimon in *Preaching to Strangers*, which he co-authored with Stanley Hauerwas. The sermon, "Be Imitators of Me," is based on Philippians 3:17: "Brothers and sisters, join in imitating me." Willimon describes how we would like to avoid saying this call to imitation, because we do not want the responsibility; but he finally yields to the judgment of God, Paul, and a church member who was following Christ better than he was.

"Go ahead," he said. "Imitate me. Demand that my miserable little life be a worthy example. Do me a favor. Don't let me off the discipleship hook. Insist that I teach by the way I walk rather than merely by the book. Insist that there be a congruency between what I practice and what I profess. Imitate me."[2]

Paul had a dream that people would be kind and respectful of preachers and not overly critical. So do I. I fear that it may be a pipe dream. Bottom line: we have to earn it. I can imagine a sermon where the pastor takes on the question of the mutual responsibility for ministry shared by clergy and congregation alike. It will work best if this sermon is not preached out of a defensive need to preserve the preacher's authority, but out of a deep concern for the shared life of the body of Christ. If one rejoices, all rejoice together!

JOSEPH R. JETER

---

2. William Willimon, "Be Imitators of Me," in Willimon and Hauerwas, *Preaching to Strangers* (Louisville, KY: Westminster John Knox Press, 1992), 49–50.

Matthew 6:24-34

24"No one can serve two masters; for a slave will either hate the one and love the other, or be devoted to the one and despise the other. You cannot serve God and wealth.

25"Therefore I tell you, do not worry about your life, what you will eat or what you will drink, or about your body, what you will wear. Is not life more than food, and the body more than clothing? 26Look at the birds of the air; they neither sow nor reap nor gather into barns, and yet your heavenly Father feeds them. Are you not of more value than they? 27And can any of you by worrying add a single hour to your span of life? 28And why do you worry about clothing? Consider the lilies of the field, how they grow; they neither toil nor spin, 29yet I tell you, even Solomon in all his glory was not clothed like one of these. 30But if God so clothes the grass of the field, which is alive today and tomorrow is thrown into the oven, will he not much more clothe you—you of little faith? 31Therefore do not worry, saying, 'What will we eat?' or 'What will we drink?' or 'What will we wear?' 32For it is the Gentiles who strive for all these things; and indeed your heavenly Father knows that you need all these things. 33But strive first for the kingdom of God and his righteousness, and all these things will be given to you as well.

34"So do not worry about tomorrow, for tomorrow will bring worries of its own. Today's trouble is enough for today."

Theological Perspective

Church camp kids of a certain age will remember sitting around campfires and intoning this melodious chorus: "Seek ye first the kingdom of God, and his righteousness, and all these things shall be added unto you, allelu, alleluia." That verse taken in isolation can be badly misread: trust God, ask for what you want, and you will get it. The prosperity gospel especially promises millions of stadium attenders and TV viewers around the world that sufficient trust will bring desired reward.

Jesus unsettles such easy calculus. Do not be anxious about what we eat, drink, or wear? Does Jesus not know that our entire industry of mood-altering drugs is premised on people's *inability* to avoid anxiety? Does he not realize that Western economies depend on massive spending on commodities people do not need? More gently now, are not some things *worth* being anxious about? Providing for one's family, the future viability and peace of the nations, the sustainability of economic and agricultural practices?

In a word, no.

This is a command from Jesus: "Do not worry about your life." The bucolic images of the birds and the flowers and the grass stand in contrast to the breathtaking nature of the command given. Fear nothing. It is said that this is the most oft-repeated command in the Bible. When angels appear to

Pastoral Perspective

Some years ago, singer Bobby McFerrin encouraged us to adopt a simple philosophy: "Don't worry, be happy."[1] We gave no mind to tomorrow and did whatever made us feel good. We continue to be a nation that seeks instant gratification. Advertisers feed our hunger for shiny things that we do not need. Lifestyles of the rich and famous beam into our living rooms, and credit cards make it possible for us to enjoy the finer things in life. We are told that more is better and biggest is best. Consumer-focused gurus spout the popular motto: the one with the most toys wins! No one thinks to ask the question: wins what? We "deserve" the best and we buy now and pay later in order to indulge ourselves. If we can sign our names on a dotted line, we can have anything we want; all the creditors tell us so.

In our minds, we know that money cannot buy us love or happiness, but many have a good time trying. Something has happened—our house of cards has come crashing down and many have been left drowning in debt. Keeping up with the Joneses has given way to just barely scraping by. In the United States a tidal wave of bad choices and decisions has resulted in massive government bailouts of financial

---

1. Bobby McFerrin's a cappella cover, "Don't Worry, Be Happy," won the 1989 Grammy Awards for Song of the Year, Record of the Year, and Best Male Pop Vocal Performance and is available from EMI Special Products.

Exegetical Perspective

The Sermon on the Mount includes many challenging teachings. Anger renders one vulnerable to judgment. A lustful eye ought to be plucked out. Love your enemy, and pray for those who persecute you. Many serious Christians have found these expectations so daunting that we have developed one rationalization after another to make sense of them.

Matthew 6:24–34 apparently offers a word of comfort, yet its instruction proves just as challenging. The passage concludes with the notorious instruction, "Do not worry about tomorrow." Taken directly, this *pro*scription can lead to serious side effects. What leads to anxiety more than forbidding it? Telling people not to be anxious is like telling them not to think of an elephant. Maybe elephants have not crossed their minds in weeks, but the suggestion itself provokes elephant on the brain. So it is with the command not to be anxious. For centuries, many Christians have felt anxious about their anxiety. Some preachers turn anxiety into a sin, or at least into a moral failure.

Perhaps we should breathe deeply, take a step back, and look at the big picture. Consideration of Jesus' literary audience in the Sermon, combined with attention to the structure of Matthew 6:24–34, may not end our anxiety, but may deepen our appreciation of Jesus' words.

Homiletical Perspective

Christian preachers very often speak of "faith"; indeed, "faith" may be one of the most common words heard from Christian pulpits today. Less common, however, are sermons devoted to clarifying the various dimensions of what faith looks and feels like in Christian life. Matthew 6:24–34 is a discourse on this subject. In the midst of the Sermon on the Mount, Jesus clarifies faith by clarifying what it is not.

In brief, it is not "worry about your life." The New Testament Gospels brim with examples of how "faith" is fundamentally a matter of trusting God, leaning on God—not so much believing that God exists as believing that God actually is an intimate, caring parent and a trustworthy deliverer, and moreover, that this care and deliverance is for me, for you, for us, for all. God feeds and clothes the world's creatures, Jesus insists, even the birds of the air and the grass of the field are fed and clothed by the divine hand; if God cares for them, then surely God cares for us as well. In this way, the preacher paints a portrait of ubiquitous divine nurture: the whole of creation, from wing to petal, is continually under God's delicate, loving care.

When it comes to our own basic well-being, however, there is an apparent competitor for our trust in this regard, another means of material provision that Jesus sums up under the Greek term *mamōnas*

Matthew 6:24-34

Theological Perspective

announce the incarnation, they tell Mary, Joseph, and the shepherds, "Fear not." When the disciples behold the level of Jesus' grandeur, he has to follow up very quickly with an admonition against fear. When Jesus is taken from them, whether in his death or his ascension, he comforts the little flock against fear. The order not to fear is perhaps not only the most reiterated in Scripture, but also the least obeyed. "Do not worry," our text says, "that's what Gentiles do" (v. 32).

We listening *are* Gentiles, for the most part. It is as profoundly unnatural that we would be listening to Israel's Messiah gathering Israel's scattered sheep around a new Torah as it is that we twenty-first-century Westerners should not worry. The former happened. Why not the latter? Karl Barth said, "In the New Testament the object of fear is primarily Jesus Himself—Jesus in the glory of his miracles and his resurrection."[1] The only way to crowd out our fear of loss of face, status, capital, home, family, or self is to replace them with the fear of Jesus.

"Who then is this, that even the wind and the sea obey him?" (Mark 4:41), the disciples asked after a miracle. Similarly we might ask of this text, Who is this, that he commands us not to serve money? Think now not of relatively well-off middle-class Westerners of the sort that attend many of our churches, but of believers in desperately poor places in Latin America, Africa, or that part of town you do not often venture to. For them, money in amounts we might deem trivial could mean the difference between a child's life and death. How can they not pine anxiously for it? Solomon in his glory may not have matched the lilies of the field, but that is cold comfort to a mother who lacks food or clothes for her children.

The items of longing Jesus points to—food, drink, clothing—are precisely those that will determine our place in the judgment. "I was hungry and you gave me food, I was thirsty and you gave me something to drink . . . I was naked and you gave me clothing" (Matt. 25:35–36). Jesus cares so passionately about the poor he identifies himself more closely with them than he ever does with the church, the sacraments, the Bible, or whatever else we Christians tend to equate with Jesus. So when the poor in our community or around the world cry out to God for mercy, the answer to their prayer ought to be *us*. Only if we crowd out our own worries for food, drink, and clothing with the fear of Jesus, can we begin to be the answer to their prayer.

1. Karl Barth, *Church Dogmatics*, II/2, trans. G. W. Bromiley et al. (Edinburgh: T. & T. Clark, 1957), 598.

Pastoral Perspective

institutions that ripple out to almost every industry in the nation. The collapse of the U.S. economy has had a dire impact on lives around the globe. Lives have been crushed, destroyed, and forever altered because we did not worry, we were happy.

Jesus echoes the words of Bobby McFerrin this week—well, sort of. Jesus states plainly that we cannot serve two bosses—especially bosses who require 100 percent allegiance and obedience. This week, the lectionary presents us with two familiar texts. The first, Matthew 6:24, is often used during stewardship drives with the intention of getting people to make a commitment to God and dispense with their obsession with materialism. The second, Matthew 6:25–34, intends to move people away from worries over necessities toward reliance on God.

Jesus taps into human nature—the desire for control and comfort. We want to believe that we are in control of our lives and that we make choices and decisions from a place of objectivity and rationality. When things get out of control, we feel overwhelmed and frustrated. These feelings lead to behaviors that are unhealthy and destructive—manipulation, self-medication, greed, possessiveness, and depression, among others.

Jesus, as usual, offers an alternative. If we are committed solely to obtaining wealth, we will worry: Will we get what we seek? How can we keep what we have? When is enough, enough? These are the questions when we are concerned with material things and fret over them.

Does choosing God, then, guarantee abundance and prosperity? It might. Does Jesus mean for all of us to be rich? Who really knows? Does Jesus think there is greater virtue in being poor? Not likely. Jesus offers a choice: wealth or God. If we choose wealth as our priority, we can expect great highs and devastating lows. If we choose God, in good times and bad we have no reason to worry. The point is that God will provide for our needs. Jesus is not preaching a prosperity gospel here; nor is he preaching a life of passivity, waiting for God's blessings to shower down.

Rather, he is inviting people into God's realm, where priorities are clear. The focus in God's realm is not how many toys people have, but where their hearts are. Our participation in God's realm is not about things with their built-in obsolescence, but instead is about God and God's vision for all of creation. In God's community, people look out for each other and share what they have; people take what they need and leave some for others. In God's community, people think about their neighbors, even

Exegetical Perspective

The Sermon on the Mount provides conflicting clues as to its audience. The Sermon's beginning suggests that Jesus calls his disciples on the mountain to get some distance from the crowds (5:1). Yet its ending implies a much broader audience; once Jesus finishes, the crowds stand astonished by the authority of his teaching.

Perhaps we might look beyond the question concerning whether the Sermon addresses insiders (the disciples) or outsiders (the crowds). Instead, whether they be disciples or interested auditors, we find signs that the Sermon speaks to *potential* insiders who find themselves on the underside of life. Some interpreters have long noticed that the Beatitudes, the blessings that constitute the Sermon's introduction (5:3–12), fall into three blocks. The second block (5:7–10) blesses people who live the ways of God—people who show mercy, cultivate pure hearts, make peace, and experience persecution for righteousness. Following upon the theme of persecution, the third block (5:11–12) speaks direction to the audience ("Blessed are *you*") when they undergo persecution.

The second and third blocks of the Beatitudes call for particular behaviors that demonstrate righteousness, but the first block of blessings (5:3–6) does not. Instead, it names people who are vulnerable. Who wants to be poor in spirit, to mourn, to be humble, to hunger and thirst for justice? In modern Western Christianity, we easily forget that humility points not only to a spiritual virtue but to a social status. Likewise, we often find justice elusive, but few of us keep in touch with those who almost never taste it, the world's majority who genuinely hunger and thirst for justice. In other words, the Sermon envisions vulnerable people who might just find someone striking them in public, might experience powerful persons calling for immediate payment of their debts, and might be familiar with the requirement to carry another person's gear. The Sermon begins by *blessing* them in the face of their vulnerability and *inviting* them to take on the life that Jesus sets forth.

As for structure, most commentators divide 6:24 ("No one can serve two masters. . . .") from the rest of the passage. That is somewhat of a mistake: the following verse begins with the Greek construction *dia touto* ("for this reason"). In other words, disciples are not to worry about material things *because* such concerns undermine their loyalty to God.

Having clarified the issue of loyalty, Jesus moves on to develop the argument. Verses 25 and 34 repeat the same thesis, "Do not worry." The material between these verses articulates why it makes sense

Homiletical Perspective

("mammon," "wealth"). As the ensuing verses make clear (note the "therefore" of v. 25), what Jesus has in mind is not great sums of money, or even mere money at all, but rather a money-centered approach to life's basic needs: a strictly material, commoditized, marketplace-driven outlook and practical path. Indeed, an astonishing proportion of our lives and work come down to precisely this sort of mammon-centered striving after commodities, so much so that a naive observer might be forgiven for concluding that many of us—"rich" as well as "poor"—are caught up in a sort of indentured servitude. "In God we trust," many Christians might insist, but as long as our striving is finally oriented toward the marketplace, mammon is the true coin of the realm (a preacher might provocatively begin by lifting up a dollar bill and reading its "In God We Trust" slogan).

We cannot, Jesus contends, have it both ways. That is, we cannot at the same time (1) trust ultimately in our own economic striving as the bedrock foundation of our basic well-being and (2) trust ultimately in God as that bedrock foundation. There can be only one ultimate foundation, only one ultimate trust. So we must continually, mindfully choose which of these we take to be the true bedrock of our lives, our own economic self-care or God's care for us. Our choice will determine the ground on which we stand. Jesus puts it this way: "No one can serve two masters" (v. 24).

This does not mean, of course, that Christians should cease all economic effort. If our ultimate trust is properly directed toward God's care for us, there is no reason to rule out the idea that God will graciously provide us a job and a salary. However, something else is ruled out, namely, "worry about your life." If we truly are under God's loving, personal care, if God truly does and will provide, then though we may and should work and "strive," in the end our own efforts are not the source of our well-being. In truth, God is taking care of that, no matter what circumstances may come and go. Look at the birds. Consider the lilies. They do not worry, and neither should you.

Were we to take this seriously, Jesus continues, we would not only live lives free from unnecessary anxiety; we would also be freed to live lives devoted to the most meaningful things imaginable. That is, as Jesus puts it, we would be freed to live lives seeking after "the kingdom of God," that new reign of mercy and justice dawning even now, the startling proximity of which Jesus proclaims at the outset of his public ministry (6:33; 4:17). What might we call this sort

Matthew 6:24-34

Theological Perspective

The command here cannot be one not to be worried for its own sake. The wealthy person without a care in the world for the poor with all her needs provided by others is, in a sense, unworried. The person without means who has given up is, in another sense, without worry—think of the drunk whom Augustine and Alypius spied in *Confessions* who made the two upstart professionals reconsider their lives. They wanted to work hard enough to be powerful enough to be without worry, and here this man had found their goal in a bottle. If the goal of faith is the erasure of worry, chemical substance is a much easier, more reliable means to that end.

However, what if the admonition here is the replacement of one master with another? The declaration that wealth is not Lord and that Jesus is? The result of that proclamation would undoubtedly be less worry, for money is a cruel master. "To have mammon for your master is already worse than any later punishment and enough retribution before the punishment for anyone trapped in it," John Chrysostom said.[2] Sin is its own punishment. Surely one who jettisoned that cruel master and took on Jesus' light load would be the better for it. The goal, however, is not psychological improvement. It is not lessening anxiety for its own sake. It is recognition of who governs the cosmos. It is awareness that the one chattering on about lilies and birds and grass actually created those with his own hand that would one day be pierced to renew them. It is an alignment of oneself with the community of those working to hasten the day when all creation rightly sings its Creator's praise.

That is a mouthful for one campfire song. It is nothing less than the full gospel in a nutshell. Do not worry or fear anything in this life. Fear only its Maker, who dies to take away all fear.

JASON BYASSEE

Pastoral Perspective

as they think about themselves. This is where the miracle of God's care for God's people is discovered.

"Don't worry, be happy" can sound shallow, frivolous, and unrealistic. Jesus tells us that the life of faith is not without its issues, concerns, and challenges. There are setbacks, delays, detours, failures, frustrations as well as joys, triumphs, victories, and accomplishments. Jesus condones neither wanton greed nor personal irresponsibility. The point is that when we are about God's business and operating out of God's vision for us, we have no room or need for worry. All is in God's hands, and we are assured that we can handle whatever happens, because God is in control and God's faithful people belong to each other.

Few of us are exempt from worry and anxiety. Most live with chronic anxiety, and we are scared of everything—losing our homes, losing our jobs, not having enough for retirement; caring for our children until they reach adulthood; avoiding danger and terror attacks. Those who have little, fret over having adequate shelter, food, and water; finding a decent job; taking care of their families; having enough money to survive. All of us—rich and poor, privileged and exploited—have legitimate reasons to fret and worry, even though we know such actions do not change the realities we face.

Jesus understands this; his call to worry-free living is not based on unrealistic views of the world. His words are for those who understand that God will not leave us without resources or support. We can face life with all its uncertainties and contingencies with the assurance that we are not alone—that God hears, sees, and cares about us and our situations. "Don't worry, be happy," because God is in control.

BARBARA J. ESSEX

2. Chrysostom, quoted in the *Ancient Christian Commentary on Scripture, New Testament*, vol. 1a, ed. Manlio Simonetti (Downers Grove, IL: InterVarsity, 2001), 143.

not to worry. First, Jesus calls his audience to attend to the birds of the air and the lilies of the field. The familiar argument from the lesser to the greater demonstrates that if God provides for lowly birds and mindless flowers, does not God care much more for God's people? To these illustrations Jesus adds three further considerations. (1) His disciples must not conform to the ways of Gentiles, who constantly worry over material things. (2) Moreover, God already knows what Jesus' followers need; if they attend first to God's reign and to God's righteousness, God will look out for their daily needs. (3) Finally, disciples cannot control their future; each day brings its own evil, regardless of their anxious planning.

If we take this passage as a straightforward logical argument that disciples ought not to worry about their daily needs, perhaps it fails to convince. Anyone can look around the world and see that many people who pursue God's ways do not receive "all these things" (v. 33). If Jesus means that people who follow his way will have all their needs met, history has proven him wrong.

Attention to the Sermon's audience, along with the structure of this passage, offers another path. Throughout the Sermon on the Mount, Jesus means exactly what he says when he tells people how to act or what to believe. In other cases, such as the Beatitudes (5:3–12), Jesus encourages them to imagine the world differently, to see it from a God's-eye perspective, and to value the things Jesus values. For potential disciples vulnerable to exploitation by others, Jesus conjures a world in which God's care is sufficient. He requires their loyalty to God, not to wealth, because God cares for them. Will they perceive God and the world the way Jesus does?

The literary audience, vulnerable potential disciples, is critical for our interpretation of this passage. Most preachers who read this resource serve congregations who are not especially vulnerable. Precisely because we seek mammon so devotedly, others find themselves liable to deprivation. Jesus' teaching poses an especially pointed challenge for contemporary disciples in mainline churches. If we want to join Jesus' audience, we must see the world differently, as one in which God looks out for the least.

GREG CAREY

of liberty, this sort of life? Call it a life of "faith," free from "worry about your life," and free to help usher in the dawning reign of heaven.

To the extent that we ultimately rely on our own resources, and not on God's graceful care, we will be plagued by worry, and Jesus will call us too "you of little faith" (v. 30). To the extent that we ultimately rely on God for our basic well-being, we may therefore be freed for a life of "faith." This message pertains to rich and poor, privileged and disinherited alike, for the amount of mammon involved is not at issue. Rather, at issue is the orientation of our ultimate trust, and therefore the goal and character of our striving.

This passage will be especially challenging for listeners struggling to make sense of experiences virtually impossible to interpret in terms of divine providential care. Experiences of personal violation (sexual assault, for example), an untimely death of a loved one, chronic or recurring suffering, widespread hunger and malnutrition, the deterioration of the environment—such events can seem to be devastating rebukes to the portrait Jesus paints here of a God who lovingly attends to all basic, bodily needs. Indeed, it is a great and difficult tension within Christianity that Jesus can both preach lyrical passages like this one and also cry from the cross, "My God, my God, why have you forsaken me?" (Matt. 27:46). There can be no easy answers here, and clearly naming such tensions can be a sensitive and credible homiletic strategy. Even the apparent contradiction just mentioned may point to an important liturgical resource in Christian life: traditions of lamentation (see, e.g., Ps. 22:1). Indeed, we might say that lament is the way Christians faithfully wrestle with apparent God-forsakenness. In other words, pushed to its outer limits, faith can also take the form of an anguished cry: "Why?" "How long?" and "Rise!"

MATTHEW MYER BOULTON

Deuteronomy 11:18-21, 26-28

[18]You shall put these words of mine in your heart and soul, and you shall bind them as a sign on your hand, and fix them as an emblem on your forehead. [19]Teach them to your children, talking about them when you are at home and when you are away, when you lie down and when you rise. [20]Write them on the doorposts of your house and on your gates, [21]so that your days and the days of your children may be multiplied in the land that the LORD swore to your ancestors to give them, as long as the heavens are above the earth. . . .

[26]See, I am setting before you today a blessing and a curse: [27]the blessing, if you obey the commandments of the LORD your God that I am commanding you today; [28]and the curse, if you do not obey the commandments of the LORD your God, but turn from the way that I am commanding you today, to follow other gods that you have not known.

Theological Perspective

Squirreled away into the remotest corner of the lectionary, this text comes around only when Easter is as late as possible, Christmas falls on a Monday, and the congregation chooses not to celebrate the feast of the Transfiguration. Yet the text is a central biblical guidepost for daily discipleship.

Just as Isaiah assures us of God's persevering love by saying that our names are engraved on God's hand (Isa. 49:16), so this text urges us to bind God's law on our hands.[1] Our hands are the parts of our body most frequently and fully visible to us. When we write the claims of this law on our hands, we constantly remind ourselves: We belong to God.

It is not enough to have God's law where *we* can see it; it is also to be displayed where *others* can see it—not on a T-shirt, but on our forehead. In our social environment, where religion is considered a private affair and public displays of loyalty to God unseemly, Deuteronomy's counsel strikes us as rather bizarre. Lest we are tempted to hide away while wearing our forehead markings, the text pushes us to write God's claims upon us on our doorposts and gates. The text makes public profession of faith incumbent on God's people—but not for the sake of

1. See my commentary on Isa. 49:8–16, pp. 386–90.

Pastoral Perspective

One Sunday in Advent, the children of the church were gathered after worship to rehearse for the annual Christmas pageant. We had the toddlers dressed as lambs, with woolly ears and caps. The angels wandered aimlessly, wings drooping as they awaited their turn to enter the stage. The stars of the show, Mary and Joseph, were being arranged at the front to make the classic tableau with a plastic baby doll that had played Jesus for decades. Suddenly a little shepherd shouted out, "Wait a second, wait a second. Do you mean to tell me we are going to do exactly the same story we did last year?"

In this Old Testament passage, we are told that these stories matter. Not only should we rehearse them over and over again; we should take them into our bodies: "You shall put these words of mine in your heart and soul, and you shall bind them as a sign on your hand, and fix them as an emblem on your forehead" (v. 18).

Furthermore, it is not enough that we understand them ourselves. We need to pass the wisdom down, one generation to the next. "Teach them to your children, talking about them when you are at home and when you are away, when you lie down and when you rise" (v. 19).

Exegetical Perspective

It is commonly believed that the book of Deuteronomy is based on ancient law. Many scholars point to seventh-century Judah under the reign of King Josiah as the historical context in which the Deuteronomic law made an enormous impact on the life of the people. In the current form of the text, the people are about to enter the land and are being instructed to put these words in the center of their life. The law is to ensure a life guided by God's commandments so that the present and next generations may always remain faithful to God.

The first part of the lectionary passage facilitates the proper means of remembrance. It seeks to be comprehensive. It goes through a list of all aspects of human life. It begins with the inward parts of human existence ("heart and soul"), recalling Deuteronomy 6:5, which mentions "heart, soul, and might." It touches upon the place one can readily see ("on your hand"; cf. "on your hands" in the Samaritan Pentateuch and the Syriac version), as well as the place others can also see ("on your forehead," v. 18). The notion of having the words of God on one's heart and soul recalls the ancient Near Eastern treaty documents in which vassals are mandated to remember the pact of loyalty by putting the suzerain's demand on their heart and

Homiletical Perspective

The text from Deuteronomy can provide much material for sermons that help us think about the way in which our faith has implications for the perspectives and passions we bring to our daily lives.

This text focuses attention on the primary content of our daily thoughts and conversations. Consider what occupies us. Mostly what we talk about by the doorposts of our homes or at the gates of our communities, mostly what we think about when we lie down and when we rise, mostly what we talk about to our children when we are at home or away . . . are the following:
—The price of gas and groceries and the status of our pension funds, the roof/gutter/porch that needs repair, the cost of insurance and taxes and neighborhood home values
—Tension at work and bills that are due, the call you forgot to return, the same tired argument at home that never gets resolved, and homework/band/softball practice/dental appointments to be juggled
—Please pick up your room. Have you done your homework? Did you brush and floss? Stop fighting with your brother/sister/the dog. Can we all agree on a place to eat? Did you put on sunscreen? Put on your coat, it is cold.

Deuteronomy 11:18-21, 26-28

Theological Perspective

informing or converting outsiders. We profess the faith publicly for our *own* sakes, so that the faith may flourish in us. We know and love the story of God's claims on us in direct proportion to how well we tell that story—both among ourselves and before others.

This combination of personal and public testimony is the heart of catechesis, of transmitting the faith from generation to generation. Our text is to be taken literally—this work is to be done at home, among household members. Results will never be fully the same when household responsibilities are deferred to the church. This daily home-work of catechesis clarifies and vivifies the life of faith for elder and youngster alike.

The benefits of keeping alive this ongoing conversation about God's ways with us are direct and very much this-worldly: "[S]o that your days and the days of your children may be multiplied in the land that the LORD swore to your ancestors to give them, as long as the heavens are above the earth" (v. 21). This echoes the promise in the Decalogue associated with honoring parents; taken together, these texts contend that rich mutual relations between parents and children bear the reward of longer and more blessed lives.

The lectionary skips over the paragraph promising conquest of other nations to those who follow God's commands. While Israel's conquest narratives certainly raise many thorny issues, it is noteworthy that the benefits of living according to God's law are traced out in terms of blessings to be enjoyed directly in this life. Obversely, failure to live this way portends misery.

Adherence to the law affords access to blessedness, not a pathway to salvation. This people already belongs to God; their status as God's chosen ones is not in jeopardy. The question is whether they will *enjoy* the blessings that accrue to those who keep God's law.

The Reformed tradition—particularly John Calvin's interpretation in his *Institutes*—speaks of three uses of the law: (1) to reveal God's standards of holiness (and thus our own sinfulness); (2) to restrain human society from ruinous behavior; and (3) to show God's people the way of blessed living.[2] This text relates to the third use of the law. Embracing God's law is depicted as the path to true and abiding blessing. While we could never choose whether we belong to God, we certainly are able to

---

2. The classic account of this understanding of God's law is by John Calvin, *Institutes of the Christian Religion*, trans. Ford Lewis Battles, 2.7.6–13, in Library of Christian Classics, vol. 20, ed. John T. McNeill (Philadelphia: Westminster Press, 1960), 354–65.

Pastoral Perspective

This text allows the preacher to remind the congregation of their crucial role as transmitters of the faith. This is a powerful word for church members who teach Sunday school, a reminder that their ministry is critical and desired by God. We do not all have children, but we can all be teachers of children. Sometimes the parent has the least likely shot at getting the message through, and it is another adult whom God can best use to shape a young mind.

Adults who volunteer to teach in the life of the church often tell me, as if they are confessing, that they are learning as much as the kids. Really, they are doing what the Deuteronomist suggests. As they wear the word on their foreheads as teachers, emblematically, they are also writing those words on their own hearts and souls.

It is a word of correction to congregations that suffer from a certain biblical illiteracy. Many members of the churches I have served are on the one hand well educated, but when it comes to Scripture, they are aware they do not know enough. They can be tempted to shrug and throw up their hands, regretting that they did not get the training when they were young. In this text, God appears to have no statute of limitations on biblical knowledge. We are expected to take the words and commandments seriously.

"Write them on the doorposts of your house and on your gates, so that your days and the days of your children may be multiplied in the land that the LORD swore to your ancestors to give them, as long as the heavens are above the earth" (vv. 20–21). Spiritual formation does take place in the home. On our very doorposts, we have a chance to learn the words that God has laid before us. So attach them with magnets to the refrigerator, decorate your bulletin board with the Bible study schedule from the church, and bring the Word home with you, in whatever creative way you can imagine.

If you did not get enough Sunday school as a child, try teaching it today. God can work with whatever we put out there to shape us in the Word. What the Deuteronomist says here is countercultural. The author does not say, "Learn the word; it will improve your life." The author does not set it out as one option among many. No, the Deuteronomist is bold enough to say, "You shall put these words of mine in your heart and soul, and you shall bind them as a sign on your hand, and fix them as an emblem on your forehead" (v. 18). "You shall" is not the same as saying "You may want to." Are we bold enough in our churches to say, "You shall," instead of "Why not

keeping away "an evil [that is, seditious] word" from their heart.[1]

The methodical exercises of reminding oneself and others are further extended to the active transmission of the lessons (v. 19). Teaching continues wherever they may find themselves—at home or away. The latter half of verse 19 lists two more aspects of daily activities, sleeping and rising, reiterating that a Torah lesson is for every moment of life. The order, lying down followed by rising, may be intentional, for it may suggest that learning does not take a break during the night (cf. Ps. 119:55). Writings on the doorposts and gates not only display teachings that guide the life lived inside the walls; they also provide precepts for guests and passersby (v. 20).

The verse immediately following offers tangible benefits of these commandments. The resulting clause states that the diligent activities of reminding and recalling of Torah will ensure the longevity and well-being of those who obey this law and of their children. The place where they will enjoy God's blessings is designated as "the land that YHWH swore to your ancestors to give them" (v. 21). This description of the land ascribes a significant role to human participants in the covenant. God's promise is as solid as the heavens and the earth, while it is their faithfulness that would make it come true.

The lectionary selection leaves out verses 22–25. A glance at these verses invites one to suspect that the thorny content may have caused their omission, for the promise includes driving out other nations to make room for the faithful children of God. After all, the land that they are about to enter is not an empty space (v. 23). These nations are described as "larger and mightier," which means that the people of Israel stand little chance of overcoming them. Their covenantal fidelity alone will ensure their victory (v. 24a). The place they will receive is circumscribed as "from the wilderness to the Lebanon and from the River, the river Euphrates, to the Western Sea"—the entire Fertile Crescent of the Near East (v. 24b). Their victory is assured through the intervention of God who will strike the enemies with "fear and dread" (v. 25). The omission of these verses may lead the worshiping community to focus on the demands of God's law in the rest of the passage, while sidestepping the difficult theological problem of the gift of the land that would entail the expulsion of others from their home.

The horizon at home can become pretty limited.

This passage seeks to expand and raise our sights. We can learn something valuable, faithful, from our Jewish heritage that might change the content and tone of our conversations. The primary claim that Jewish people were and are to keep in their hearts, talk about with their children, recite at home or away, when lying down at night and getting up in the morning, is the Shema: "Hear, O Israel: The LORD is our God, the LORD alone. You shall love the LORD your God with all your heart, and with all your soul, and with all your might" (Deut. 6:4–5).

If this were our first, our last, our every thought, imagine what could happen to the conversations in our homes and community, to the anxieties and responsibilities that disrupt our rest, to the mundane topics that take over our relationship with those we live with and love. If everything said and done among us began in this fact—that the Lord is our God, the Lord alone, whom we love first and fully—it would change the scope of our concern, the field of our vision, the quality of our relationships.

If . . . but it is hard to keep this greatest commandment before us all the time and in every place. We forget, become distracted, are drawn to idols that promise us things we desire other than God. God and the people of Israel themselves knew this human tendency very well. This passage is likely not a description, but a prescription. These verses were meant to help them in their weakness, to give them prompts—tangible reminders—of this commandment. The Shema was inscribed and placed in a small container, a mezuzah, that was affixed to the doorposts of home. Going out and coming in, the commandment was there and visible. Some people went further—binding the words on forehead and hand, too. Every thought . . . every grasp . . . connected to the command to love God. The responsibility for passing on to children this sacred way of life (the only way to life) is constant and comprehensive. The occasional grace said over a meal is not enough, nor is weekly worship.

For many Christians, such a strong connection between worship in the church and worship practices in daily life pales in comparison. If our tradition publishes a *Book of Common Worship*, it is mostly intended for the pastor's study or the pew racks of the sanctuary, not for the tables by our sofas or beds. An exception is the book *Catholic Household Blessings and Prayers*, produced by the National Conference of Catholic Bishops of the United States Catholic Conference. This book offers prayers and

---

1. Moshe Weinfeld, *Deuteronomy 1–11: A New Translation and Commentary,* Anchor Bible 5 (New York: Doubleday, 1991), 340.

Deuteronomy 11:18-21, 26-28

Theological Perspective

choose whether to live in a way that yields blessing. Blessing follows obedience to the law, while disobedience yields misery.

It is tempting to soften texts of cursing, such that God's hand is directly at work when it comes to blessing, while the alternative is simply an absence of divine intervention on our behalf. In that account, God lets us reap the natural consequences of what we sow when we violate God's law. However, "curse" involves divine agency, not mere passivity, but this curse is a matter not of divine rejection but of discipline. It is intended to lead to repentance. This pattern is vividly displayed in Israel's postexodus history, as chronicled in the book of the Judges. When the chosen people follow God's law, all goes well. When they follow the gods of their neighbors, the Lord moves their enemies to ravage them, but the Lord never abandons them. Their depredations are not merely punishment, but discipline designed to set them back on the path of blessing.

Attention to spiritual practices has flourished in recent years, to the benefit of many. This text commends a daily practice that goes beyond most contemporary accounts of spiritual disciplines, which typically advocate private practices. This text's practice goes beyond such accounts in two important ways: it is publicly visible, and it involves a household engaging certain practices together.

Jesus decries public displays of personal piety when they are undertaken merely to impress others; his antidote is to go entirely private with piety.[3] For most U.S. Christians today, the course correction would move in the opposite direction, because our piety is so private as to be frequently nonexistent. A reminder to live in a way that publicly marks us as people who belong to God is very much in order.

Finally, the importance of daily holy conversation about the faith with family or friends cannot be overstated. It is a spiritual practice that cultivates adherence to and love for God's law, for master and novice, elder and youngster alike. Personal spiritual practices are important, but by themselves insufficient to sustain the life of abundant blessing that loving obedience to God's law yields.

SHELDON W. SORGE

Pastoral Perspective

try this?" For this Old Testament author, the stakes are higher than mere self-improvement.

The passage goes on to point out a fork in the road: "See, I am setting before you today a blessing and a curse" (v. 26). Now this is the opposite of appealing and dynamic large-church programming. Much has been written about how to attract people to church, from powerhouse youth groups, to money-management seminars, to seminars on how to reduce the amount of stuff in your house. Nowhere in such literature do they suggest you announce to people, "See, I am setting before you today a blessing and a curse." Who would want to hear such a thing from God? Perhaps we could just leave out the part about the curse and stop with the blessing.

But no, the author will not let us off the hook, saying, "The blessing, if you obey the commandments of the LORD your God that I am commanding you today; and the curse, if you do not obey the commandments of the LORD your God, but turn from the way that I am commanding you today, to follow other gods that you have not known" (vv. 27–28). In other words, the other gods out there can actually do you harm. You could be cursed by worshiping yourself, or your wealth, or someone else's. Listen up, the Deuteronomist announces. These words actually matter. You need to know them, and know them by heart.

Readers of commentaries do not need convincing on this point, but many church members do. The tone of this passage is shocking in its intensity, but the answer to the angry little shepherd's question is clear. Yes, we will be doing the exact same story we did last year. We need to write it on our hearts and souls.

LILLIAN DANIEL

---

3. Matt. 6:1–18.

Exegetical Perspective

The last three verses formulate God's challenge, based on the promise of blessing. These verses, along with the rest of the chapter, form "a suitable conclusion to the first part of Moses' discourse,"[2] concluding chapters 5–11 and anticipating curses (chap. 27) and blessings (chap. 28). There are two possible consequences of the commandments. In English Bibles, verses 27–28 share the same wording: the "if" clause is followed by the result that comes from obedience or disobedience, hinting at the crossroad where the believing community finds itself. However, the Hebrew syntax in these verses shows a light variation that suggests that God desires the people to obey and enjoy blessings. The path to blessing is straightforward, requiring the observance of the commandments of YHWH. It leaves little room for adulterating the covenantal demand for faithfulness. The sheer length of the mention of disobedience (v. 28), which is twice as long as the section on the blessing for obedience, suggests that infidelity is a palpable threat that can undo the exodus and guidance into the land of Canaan (v. 28).

This last verse alludes to a form of apostasy in which the people turn away from YHWH's way and follow other gods. These contenders for the people's loyalty are described as "gods that you have not known" (v. 28). The expression deplores the insensible path of unfaithfulness in which the people would choose gods while abandoning the one true God, whose goodness is attested in the past experience of Israel (cf. Hos. 6:3; 13:4, et al.). At the same time, it recognizes the attraction of the unknown that could leave them ruined.

The lectionary passage succinctly spells out the importance of constant reminders that would be necessary to keep the people of God faithful. It highlights the important role that the home and the community play for good spiritual health. It states in no uncertain terms the outcome of blessings that follow obedience, as well as the devastation that would result from disobedience and betrayal.

JIN HEE HAN

Homiletical Perspective

blessings for use in daily life. There are prayers upon waking, washing and dressing, going out from home each day, and coming home each night. There are prayers for welcoming guests into one's home and a prayer for a child who is leaving for school. There is a blessing on the anniversary of a baptism and a blessing when setting up a manger scene at home. It is a remarkable book, intended for dog-eared wear and tear. Without such tangible helps as the mezuzah or prayer book, many feel at a loss about how to teach their children the faith outside of Sunday school and worship. Lacking tangible daily practices and reminders, we become distracted and influenced by so much else in our environment.

William Willimon, in a book on baptism, tells this story:

> Back in high school, every Friday and Saturday night, as I was leaving home to go on a date, I remember my mother bidding me farewell at the front door with these weighty words, "Don't forget who you are."
>
> You know what she meant. She did not mean that I was in danger of forgetting my name and my street address. She meant that, alone on a date, in the midst of some party, in the presence of some strangers, I might forget who I was. I might lose sight of the values with which I had been raised, answer to some alien name, engage in some unaccustomed behavior.
>
> "Don't forget who you are," was her maternal benediction as I left home.[1]

What are the ways we, the baptized children of God, "remember who we are" at home, at work, at school, in the car, in the neighborhood? The passage ends with talk of blessing and cursing. For Israel, God's blessing (and curse) was tied to covenantal faithfulness and specifically to the land. For us, the meaning may best be understood in this way: Every day, as we go out the door, we decide in a hundred little ways whether God alone is Lord and whether we will love God with all our heart, mind, and strength. If we remember who we are, there is blessing and life and a future.

KIMBERLY L. CLAYTON

---

2. S. R. Driver, *A Critical and Exegetical Commentary on Deuteronomy*, International Critical Commentary (3rd ed., Edinburgh: T. & T. Clark, 1951), 132.

1. William H. Willimon, *Remember Who You Are: Baptism, a Model for Christian Life* (Nashville: Upper Room, 1980), 105.

Psalm 31:1-5, 19-24

¹In you, O LORD, I seek refuge;
  do not let me ever be put to shame;
  in your righteousness deliver me.
²Incline your ear to me;
  rescue me speedily.
  Be a rock of refuge for me,
  a strong fortress to save me.

³You are indeed my rock and my fortress;
  for your name's sake lead me and guide me,
⁴take me out of the net that is hidden for me,
  for you are my refuge.
⁵Into your hand I commit my spirit;
  you have redeemed me, O LORD, faithful God.
. . . .
¹⁹O how abundant is your goodness
  that you have laid up for those who fear you,
  and accomplished for those who take refuge in you,
  in the sight of everyone!

Theological Perspective

Coupled with this psalm's images of God as fortress and rock of refuge, verse 23 could be wrongly proclaimed as a promise that God takes care of "good people" and never lets harm befall them. Unfortunately, this idea suffers from a basic incongruence with the lived experience of humanity, whether in Bible times or today. Verse 23 could also be taken as a restatement of Proverbs 16:18–19's warning, "Pride goes before destruction, and a haughty spirit before a fall" and its caution to be "of a lowly spirit among the poor" rather than with the haughty. Yet even this idea needs careful theological reflection.

Christian theology has traditionally identified pride as the common root of other sins. Valerie Saiving's classic 1960 essay "The Human Situation: A Feminine View" argued that ideas about the nature of sin were developed from a male perspective. For women, it is often not pride that underlies other sins; in fact, it is precisely the lack of sufficient pride, self-esteem, or self-worth that causes many of women's spiritual problems.[1] Today theological training does (or should) make careful distinctions between Christian love that is legitimately linked to a degree of self-denial, and the

1. Valerie Saiving Goldstein, "The Human Situation: A Feminine View," *Journal of Religion* 40, no. 2 (April 1960): 100–112.

Pastoral Perspective

It may seem rather self-evident to say it, but it is probably worth saying nonetheless. Faith is the key to the life of faith. Faith is the key to following the way of Jesus. Faith is the key to living life in the Spirit, with the integrity and the vitality of Jesus. After all, Jesus said, "If you have faith the size of a mustard seed, you will say to this mountain, 'Move from here to there,' and it will move; and nothing will be impossible for you" (Matt. 17:20).

James Russell Lowell (1819–91) was a man of deep principle and profound conviction. He was a leader in the movement to abolish chattel slavery in America. He had been a leading voice speaking in defense of the Indians and their right to lands and freedom. He had been a leading voice in opposition to the U.S. war with Mexico (1846–48). In the midst of this struggle, when many were on the verge of giving up the effort to end the war, Lowell wrote these words as part of a long poem to encourage and strengthen for the long struggle.

Truth forever on the scaffold,
Wrong forever on the throne,—
Yet that scaffold sways the future,
  and behind the dim unknown

20In the shelter of your presence you hide them
   from human plots;
you hold them safe under your shelter
   from contentious tongues.

21Blessed be the LORD,
   for he has wondrously shown his steadfast love to me
   when I was beset as a city under siege.
22I had said in my alarm,
   "I am driven far from your sight."
But you heard my supplications
   when I cried out to you for help.

23Love the LORD, all you his saints.
   The LORD preserves the faithful,
   but abundantly repays the one who acts haughtily.
24Be strong, and let your heart take courage,
   all you who wait for the LORD.

Exegetical Perspective

In Psalm 31, the psalmist sings the praises of YHWH, the ultimate guardian. The English vocabulary (NRSV) of Psalm 31 includes words such as "deliver" (vv. 1, 8, 15), "save" (v. 2), "take courage" (v. 24), "refuge" (vv. 1, 2, 4, 19), "rock" (vv. 2, 3) "fortress" (vv. 2, 3), and "shelter" (v. 20 twice). Through this language and imagery, the psalmist paints YHWH as a force and location of sanctuary, and gives thanks for a powerful deity of protection.

The superscription (prior to v. 1) addresses Psalm 31 "to the leader" or "music-director" and titles the song "A Psalm of David." This attribution, like others throughout the Psalms and in the Wisdom literature (Prov. 1:1; Eccl. 1:1; Song 1:1) does not indicate authorship or date so much as a tradition of association with this famous figure. In the case of Psalm 31, the reference to King David fits because the rock and fortress language (v. 3) for YHWH is attributed to David elsewhere (2 Sam. 22:2; Pss. 18:2; 71:3). Nonetheless, the timeless content of Psalm 31 does not allow for any certainty of date.

Much of Psalm 31:1–5, 19–24 illustrates divine care through metaphors of protective architecture. Though Martin Luther wrote "A Mighty Fortress" based on Psalm 46 and not Psalm 31, our Psalter reading relies on similar themes. Psalm 31 identifies

Homiletical Perspective

In the well-worn verses of Psalm 31 appointed for the Ninth Sunday after the Epiphany, the psalmist pleads with God, asking God to be a "rock of refuge." At the same time, the psalmist praises God's steadfast love. The psalm addresses one of the primary predicaments of people of faith: living in hope amid despair. It is at the same time a psalm of lamentation and a psalm of praise.

The rocky places portrayed in Scripture are often the places where God breaks in. The history of God's dealings with the people of Israel is punctuated by close encounters with God that take place on mountaintops (Gen. 22; Exod. 24, 34; 1 Kgs. 19). This phenomenon continues in the New Testament (Matt. 17:1–8//Mark 9:2–8//Luke 9:28–36). The psalmist's choice of metaphors makes good sense, given God's history of making fearsome appearances in the mountainous border regions between heaven and earth.

The psalmist—and perhaps the people of Israel— seems to be living in a border zone, at once seeking shelter and offering praise for God's steadfast love. While the refugees continue to look over their shoulder and cry out for assistance, they rejoice in the safe haven they have found in God. The psalmist communicates a sense of breathless desperation and then tumbles into relief and rejoicing.

Psalm 31:1-5, 19-24

Theological Perspective

self-loathing that troubles Christians who believe that any positive self-regard displeases God.

It may seem contradictory that the psalmist who is so concerned with the avoidance of shame cautions us that being haughty is not God-pleasing behavior. Pondering that idea and considering the loaded topic of shame—a word used repeatedly in the Psalms—are vital theological steps with regard to this pericope.

As Christians, we value the act of repentance, the turning away from sin. A recognition of guilt and sorrow for having done something wrong may open the heart to what John Wesley, Methodism's founder, termed "convicting grace," thus leading to a life-changing encounter with God. However, the appropriateness of feeling guilt from time to time is clouded by the common phrase "You should be ashamed of yourself." In many instances, shame may be a misnomer; the speaker may mean, "You should feel guilty about an action that you chose," while the hearer receives, "You are a bad person." Shame tends to result from things one is *not* responsible for and cannot change; it suggests something profoundly wrong with the individual—something that often cannot even be named.

A sermon could help congregants differentiate between feeling guilt and feeling shame. Scriptural examples of persons in shame-producing circumstances include the characters of Hagar and Ishmael as Abraham sends them into the desert (Gen. 21:9–16) and the New Testament's woman with the flow of blood who has been ritually unclean and untouchable for twelve years (Mark 5:25–34). Modern examples might include having an addicted parent or spouse or even a child with a birth defect (recall the disciples' question to Jesus in John 9 about whose sin caused the man to be born blind, and recognize that some churches are still teaching that sickness/disability occurs because we are out of proper relationship with God).

The church has historical complicity in dispensing shame. A few early (late eighteenth- and early nineteenth-century) instruction manuals for Sunday schools recommended the use of a separate area for isolating troublesome students, not in the current sense of a time-out, but rather in the sense of humiliating a child by making her/him sit in the corner while wearing a dunce cap. While today's religious educators would certainly not approve, many adults did receive important behavioral lessons as children by means of shaming, at home if not in church. When children are shamed, the lessons can penetrate so deeply that later critical theological reflection on certain actions (or nonactions) becomes almost impossible.

Pastoral Perspective

Standeth God within the shadow,
keeping watch above his own.[1]

In an incredible insight, Lowell realized that it is God's job, if you will, to keep watch. It is our job to keep the faith. Faith is the key to face hard times. Faith is the key to an endurance that runs the long-distance race. Faith is the key to living the life of God, following in the way of Jesus. Faith is the key to living a life that makes a difference and that matters.

This is a truth the psalmist grasped. "You are indeed my rock and my fortress; for your name's sake lead me and guide me, take me out of the net that is hidden for me, for you are my refuge. Into your hand I commit my spirit; you have redeemed me, O LORD, faithful God" (vv. 3–5). Faith is the key.

During my undergraduate years I took an economics course called "Money and Banking." I cannot say that I remember a great deal from the course, but a few things stand out in my mind. I well remember the prediction in the textbook that we would soon move to a cashless society. This was in the mid 1970s, and that idea seemed a bit far-fetched, but possible. Today in 2009 I rarely carry cash in my pocket, choosing usually to use my debit card. So much for the far-fetched.

At some point in the course the instructor told us that the national and international economic system of money, banking, markets, and commerce depends in the final analysis on trust and confidence in the systems that support it. The words "trust" and "confidence" are not the language of clinical economics. That is language of faith—but those were the words he used. While I did not disbelieve what he said, it did seem a bit of an exaggeration. Even the example of the great crash of 1929 and the Great Depression seemed somewhat remote.

In late 2008 and 2009 we saw the actually possibility of economic collapse. The faith language of that economics professor does not seem that far-fetched. Titanic firms on Wall Street fell down low. Invincible giants like General Motors and Chrysler became feeble shadows of their former selves. The actions of governments worldwide to stabilize and reverse the situation amounted to steps designed to restore confidence, trust, faith, and eventually health. Faith is the key.

Faith is the key to life and to the life of faith itself. In a letter from a Nazi prison, written less than a

---

1. James Russell Lowell, from "The Present Crisis," excerpts of which form the hymn "Once to Every Man and Nation."

Exegetical Perspective

YHWH twice as "fortress" (*metsudah*, vv. 2, 3) and twice as "refuge" (*ma'oz*, vv. 3, 5). On a literal level, we find "fortress" in 1 Samuel 22:1–5; 24:22, where David's "fortress" may have been the cave of Adullam when he was hiding from King Saul. We also see this pairing of "rock" and "fortress" in Job 39:28, where the eagle makes its home "in the fastness of the rocky crag." Indeed, the Hebrew word *sela'* for "rock" in these instances means "crag" or "cliff," suggesting a secure and remote hiding place. Such a protective scene provides a powerful description of YHWH.

This particular imagery calls to mind cave 4 of Dead Sea Scrolls fame, in which ancient believers hid their library of precious documents for safekeeping. Constructed high in a cliff, this cave preserved hundreds of scrolls for more than 2,000 years. Cave 4 and the ancient mountaintop stronghold Masada offer vivid illustrations of the psalmist's words.[1]

The word "refuge" (*ma'oz*, Ps. 31:3, 5) appears often in biblical poetry to praise YHWH as a protector from trouble and threats (Pss. 27:1; 37:39; 52:7; Isa. 25:4; Jer. 16:19). Indeed, those who seek help elsewhere are deemed unfaithful (Ps. 37:39; 52:9; Isa. 17:10). In concrete terms, "refuge" indicates architecture as a defensive shield; those locations from which troops and kings fight their enemies (Isa. 23:11, 14; Dan. 11:7, 10, 19). Ezekiel 24:25 conversely envisages the coming destruction of the people's "stronghold," which may have been the Jerusalem temple. Perhaps that was a comparable scenario to the psalmist's imagery in 31:21.

Psalm 31 may sound familiar to Christians because of verse 5a, which the writer of Luke places on the lips of the dying Jesus (Luke 23:46). Not only does "Into your hand I commit my spirit" sound familiar to anyone who has attended Holy Week services, but the second half of the verse contains a word precious to Christians, "redeemed." The Hebrew here, *padah*, has to do with saving, rescuing, or setting free. While these meanings certainly relate to the word "redeem," it is important to dissociate the psalm from the specific Christian understanding of salvation, lest it seem relevant only to Jesus' death. To early audiences of Psalm 31, *padah* likely recalled YHWH's saving work in the exodus (*padah* appears in Deut. 7:8, 13:5) and perhaps the return from exile (Isa. 35:10, Jer. 31:11 also use *padah*).

This lectionary excerpt from Psalm 31 effectively emphasizes the theme of divine protection, but it

---

1. The name Masada is related to the Hebrew word for "fortress" (*metsudah*; see above).

Homiletical Perspective

Psalm 31 demonstrates some of the cathartic properties of worship. In lamenting the challenges, the psalmist is reminded of God's goodness and faithfulness. In seeking God amid the dangers and threats pressing in upon the people, the psalmist's attentions turn toward the one who provides safety, assurance, and hope. The psalmist's prayer beckons us to do the same, to name the things from which we are running, the conflicts and challenges that threaten to undo us, and to turn to God. The psalmist affirms that God's shelter provides an effective barricade against human plots, protection against the slinging of hurtful words.

The psalmist implies that God's shelter is permanent, a constant, loving presence that remains steadfast despite destructive human efforts. The question for listeners, then, becomes how to abide in this shelter of grace. Taking up residence under God's protection should elicit some sort of response on the part of the refugee. How will our lives be different as a result of the safe haven that God has provided?

The psalmist's prayer provides a model. Alarmed, the speaker fears that he is driven from God's sight, but God has heard the psalmist's cry and draws the speaker back into relationship. Residence in the shelter of God's love is dependent on God's initiative and on human response to God's call. The psalmist calls the people to a life of faithfulness, shunning arrogance and haughtiness, encouraging them to "wait for the LORD," to be ready to embrace God's saving reach.

Psalm 31 provides the preacher with a platform for discussing mission and evangelism. In verse 21 the psalmist articulates his own doxology, citing God's wondrous and "steadfast love" in rescuing him from a perilous situation. This personal song of praise becomes an invitation to corporate praise, as the psalmist bids the people to join in prayerful response. In doing so, the psalmist acts as a witness, recounting his own experience of God's loving action as a means of inspiring others to offer praise. The speaker articulates what God has done, how God has responded to the speaker's own distress, how God has protected, sheltered, and shown loving care.

The preacher might encourage listeners to consider how they might share their own experience of God's presence in their lives in order to elicit praise from others. In an age in which many mainline Christians are reticent to engage in acts of evangelism, many find it challenging to articulate the basics of their faith. The preacher might engage in a discussion about the things in our lives that cause us to flee

Psalm 31:1-5, 19-24

Theological Perspective

This psalm is a reminder that God offers healing, even for shame, even when we feel that we have been "driven far from [God's] sight" (v. 22a). A reminder that God hears our supplications and that God's grace is sufficient for our deepest emotional distress is appropriate as we consider the psalmist's exhortation, "Be strong, and let your heart take courage, all you who wait for the LORD" (v. 24).

Further, leaving the theological work on this reading at the level of the individual is inadequate. In certain psalms, pronouns like "I" and "me" stand for "the people of Israel." This psalm is considered liturgical in nature, which gives support to a corporate reading of it. The phrase "beset as a city under siege" may bring the preacher's attention to corporate experience, especially the kinds from which the people might pray for relief. Wildfires, earthquakes, tornados, flooding, and other disasters that affect whole communities may be seen as "acts of God," and certain religious leaders are quick to deem them divine punishment for wickedness on the part of those affected by them.

As images of New Orleans lying flooded for weeks, due to levee breaks after Hurricane Katrina, were broadcast in 2005, many people blamed the residents who died or who were awaiting rescue for not leaving ahead of the storm. Grinding poverty and lack of transportation were not sufficiently taken into account in such assessments. The reputation of the city's French Quarter was decried by televangelists who called the flood "God's judgment," even though the French Quarter was one of the few areas that did not flood! The 2008 floods in the heartland of the United States triggered a resurgence of shame/blame for New Orleanians, who were unjustly accused of not working for their own recovery as hard as mid-Americans. Many thousands of Christians, from almost every denomination, have traveled to Louisiana to assist in recovery, but there is still awareness among New Orleanians that there are Christians, including some very vocal ones, who believe that the city's destruction and slow recovery are punishment for its sinfulness. Because of the intrinsic interconnectedness of God and all of God's creatures (and creation), proclamation anywhere that calls such beliefs into question will inevitably play a helpful role in the city's eventual healing and also strengthen the hearers' ability to judge the responses of various Christians to future disasters.

Such proclamation may open the listeners to hear verse 5 with new insight and conviction: "Into your hand I commit my spirit; you have redeemed me, O LORD, faithful God."

ELLEN J. BLUE

Pastoral Perspective

year before he was martyred, Dietrich Bonhoeffer spoke of such faith, not as escape but as true engagement with where God has gone in the world, and of obedience, not as blindness but as radical commitment to the teachings of Jesus, the way of the gospel.

> I discovered later, and I'm still discovering up to this moment, that it is only by living completely in this world that one learns to have faith. One must completely abandon any attempt to make something of oneself, whether it be a saint, or a converted sinner, or a churchman (a so-called priestly type!), a righteous person or an unrighteous one, a sick person or a healthy one. By this-worldliness I mean living unreservedly in life's duties, problems, successes and failures, experiences and perplexities. In so doing we throw ourselves completely into the arms of God, taking seriously, not our own sufferings, but those of God in the world—watching with Christ in Gethsemane. That, I think, is faith; that is *metanoia*; and that is how one becomes human and a Christian (cf. Jer. 45!). How can success make us arrogant, or failure lead us astray, when we share in God's sufferings through a life of this kind?[2]

Such radical obedience is not the outgrowth of mindless conformity but of a passionate commitment to God born of a relationship of radical trust in the God of Jesus. Only such faith risks self-interest and preservation for the cause of a better world more resembling the dream of God than the reality of a human nightmare.

That may explain why Luke's Gospel hears the words of Psalm 31 prayed by Jesus just before he died: "Then Jesus, crying with a loud voice, said, 'Father, into your hands I commend my spirit.' Having said this, he breathed his last" (Luke 23:46).

As the psalm shaped Jesus' faith in Luke's Gospel, we seek ways to help our people learn, sing, pray, memorize psalms. Our pastoral work consists in so grounding the faithful in the psalms that the words and the hopes of Scripture are their words and hopes as well.

MICHAEL B. CURRY

---

2. Letter to Eberhard Bethge, July 21, 1944, in Dietrich Bonhoeffer, *Letters and Papers from Prison* (New York: Touchstone, 1997), 369–70.

mainly does so through praise and thanksgiving. This selective reading omits most of the psalmist's description of what *requires* such a fortress-like hiding place. The lectionary selection hints at the psalmist's struggles (vv. 4a, 20, 21b–22a). In the excluded portion, the psalmist fully laments a life of exclusion, torment, sadness, and physical and spiritual pain (vv. 9–13). In another section that the lectionary passes over, the psalmist calls on YHWH for vengeance against his or her enemies (vv. 17b–18). In total, this is a psalm of lament. Reading the selected verses only, it appears as a psalm of thanksgiving.

The skipped portions of the Psalter reading (vv. 6–18) greatly inform the meaning of the appointed verses 1–5 and 19–24, heightening the thanksgiving and praise. The missing verses would also teach congregants that their own complaints and angry desires for punishment of their enemies rightfully belong in their conversations with God, for the psalmist's words invite people of all time even into these protests and calls for revenge. Laments are the most common psalm genre, and they serve a crucial purpose in the life of faith, reminding us that vacillating between praise, plea, complaint, and gratitude is deeply human—and even faithful. If such prayers of emotional sincerity seem shocking, it may be because we frequently avoid the complaints and imprecations sung by our ancestors in faith.

Psalm 31 closes with its thematic emphasis on YHWH as protector, with verses 19–24 primarily devoted to praise and thanksgiving, even adding imperatives to praise. One thing the psalmist extols is YHWH's "steadfast love" (*hesed*), in verse 21. In verse 23 the psalmist continues this emphasis, calling on all YHWH's "godly ones" (*hasidim*, from the same root as *hesed*) to join the praise. Here the ones who would best follow YHWH are identified by their embodiment of this key divine attribute. The translation of this as "saints" could mislead some into focusing on those who *died* in service to God. Instead, the passage commends those who *live* in the shelter of YHWH, their refuge, rock, and fortress.

LISA M. WOLFE

to God, and ask listeners how God has provided them with refuge. At this point, it would also be helpful to provide the congregation with ideas on how their own experiences of God's transforming love might help to encourage and inspire others.

The issues of evangelism and mission raised by Psalm 31 apply to congregations as well as to individuals. How can we as a church, as congregations, as individuals, proclaim God's goodness in the midst of hardship? Following the attacks on the World Trade Center in 2001, churches flung wide their doors. Many people who did not regularly engage in corporate worship returned to houses of prayer. Churches helped to provide a place of refuge, a place of encounter with God. The overwhelming number of people who flocked to houses of worship following the September 11 attacks may provide some helpful insight into ways that we as faith communities can minister in times of crisis, even when those crises do not take place on a national scale. Are our doors open? Do people know how to find us? Do we communicate a safe, nonthreatening presence? Do we offer guidance and counsel, while at the same time providing time and space for those who need to spend time waiting for the Lord? Do we take the opportunity to affirm God's steadfast love even in times of trial? Do we encourage one another to offer praise?

As the season of Epiphany draws to a close, the themes of the lectionary texts begin to move toward Lent, inevitably leading to the cross. The preacher might employ this selection from Psalm 31 as an invitation to consider the arrival of Lent, encouraging listeners to consider again our relationship to the God of life, our own need for deliverance, and how we dwell as God's people in the borderland of Christ's reign. This invitation might extend to individuals and to the entire community, calling the congregation to a time of discernment, a time for naming the challenges pressing in upon us, the things that prevent us from enjoying God's shelter, and a time for renewing our hope in the God who is our refuge and our strength.

APRIL BERENDS

Romans 1:16-17; 3:22b–28 (29-31)

^{1:16}For I am not ashamed of the gospel; it is the power of God for salvation to everyone who has faith, to the Jew first and also to the Greek. ¹⁷For in it the righteousness of God is revealed through faith for faith; as it is written, "The one who is righteous will live by faith." . . .

^{3:22b}For there is no distinction, ²³since all have sinned and fall short of the glory of God; ²⁴they are now justified by his grace as a gift, through the redemption that is in Christ Jesus, ²⁵whom God put forward as a sacrifice of atonement by his blood, effective through faith. He did this to show his righteousness, because in his divine forbearance he had passed over the sins previously committed; ²⁶it was to prove at the present time that he himself is righteous and that he justifies the one who has faith in Jesus.

²⁷Then what becomes of boasting? It is excluded. By what law? By that of works? No, but by the law of faith. ²⁸For we hold that a person is justified by faith apart from works prescribed by the law. ²⁹Or is God the God of Jews only? Is he not the God of Gentiles also? Yes, of Gentiles also, ³⁰since God is one; and he will justify the circumcised on the ground of faith and the uncircumcised through that same faith. ³¹Do we then overthrow the law by this faith? By no means! On the contrary, we uphold the law.

Theological Perspective

The book of Romans is universally recognized as Paul's crowning achievement and his most complex theological treatise. This selection contains what is generally seen as the summary statement for the book, 1:16–17, with the passage from Romans 3 being a further development of the central point.

Theologically speaking, Paul raises an over-whelming number of issues in this passage; any one of which would be worthy of consideration in the church, but none of which he fully explains. Reading this passage, it would be legitimate for the contemporary church to ask questions like these: What precisely does Paul mean by such terms as gospel, salvation, faith, grace, redemption, sacrifice of atonement, and justified by faith? Can we define these terms in such a way that the person in the pew can understand them and use them in conversations and reflections about her faith and not have the terms become merely "talking points" of the faith? What is salvation? From what are we saved, and for what are we saved? Who can be saved? How are they saved? Is there a formula to obtain salvation that all people must follow precisely? What is the nature of human beings that makes us need salvation? Is salvation to be understood as a past event, a present activity, or a future promise, or some combination of all three time frames?

Pastoral Perspective

Paul's letter to the Roman Christians of the early church contains some of the church's most treasured theological writings, and this passage in particular contains important assertions for the development of Christian theology. Theology, however, is not readily discussed in many congregations. How can we approach this text and help make it accessible for those who do not find Paul's language or concepts easy to decipher, easy to understand? We can begin by thinking about how the text itself is presented in the context of worship.

Rather than presenting Paul's theology in the kind of monotone reading that breeds glazed expressions and fidgeting children, we might be creative with our reading, so that our presentation of the text conveys some of its real import. For instance, we can ask people who know other languages and/or are from different cultures to read 1:16–17. We can also ask the congregation to exclaim: "This is the gospel of salvation to everyone who has faith!"after every reading. If we can do that, those hearing Paul's words might be able to listen through the theological language and connect with the life-giving message Paul is handing to the church.

In this text, Paul affirms the universality of God's power of salvation and love. Paul insists that "it is the power of God for salvation to everyone who has

Exegetical Perspective

These reflections on today's reading build on a new strand in Pauline scholarship called the New Perspective on Paul. After the Holocaust, Christian theologians and biblical scholars began to see how Paul's words are often used to justify a view of Jews and Judaism as rejected by God in favor of Christians and Christianity. They revisited Paul's thought with a thorough, historical study of ancient Judaism, and considered how Paul fits into his world as a Jewish thinker. The result has been a fresh interpretation of Paul's message that resists Christian anti-Judaism and does not make Paul sound so much like Martin Luther critiquing sixteenth-century Catholicism.[1]

The New Perspective takes Paul seriously when he says he is talking *to* Gentiles *about* Gentiles (Rom. 1:1–6). He is a Jew sent to bring the Gentiles, literally "the nations" (*ethnē*), into obedience to the God of Israel. We often think "Jew" and "Gentile" indicate religious difference, but they are also ethnic identities; the words *Ioudaios* and *Hellēn* in Romans 1:16 refer to someone who identifies with Judean or Greek culture and traditions, respectively. Paul sees himself as sent by God to cross ethnic and cultural borders. Paul is usually against boasting (1 Cor.

1. See the work of Krister Stendahl, E. P. Sanders, and James Dunn. For an introduction, see John Gager's accessible book *Reinventing Paul* (New York: Oxford University Press, 2000).

Homiletical Perspective

In this text we find one of the most well-known verses in Scripture, 3:23: "All have sinned and fall short of the glory of God." We might therefore think this text should have a prime spot in the lectionary. That is not the case.

One might also wonder why this text is placed here. Our Ninth Sunday after Epiphany exists only with a very late Easter. Only one Ninth Sunday will exist in the next twenty years (in 2011). The lectionary writers do give Paul and us a second chance, perhaps, by relisting this text if there is an extra Sunday after Trinity Sunday. Why then is there such a low regard for this chopped-up text?

If we plan not to preach from this text, even if an out-of-the-way Sunday should open up, we might want to reconsider. There remains good cause for engaging Paul's words that might lead to a sermon on a Sunday when the lectionary texts just do not set our hearts aflutter. Why has this text been given a seat in the fourth balcony? Is it because no one (including preachers?) likes to be reminded that he or she is a sinner? Is it because Paul's answer is that redemption comes through the "sacrifice of atonement" by the blood of Christ?

I confess that I am more uncomfortable with the scapegoating atonement of Jesus than I am with the old news that I am a sinner. I know that. I try. I fail. I

Romans 1:16-17; 3:22b–28 (29-31)

Theological Perspective

Paul wrote that a person is justified by faith apart from works; how then can we reconcile this view with other biblical passages and some of the writings of the early church leaders that suggest our actions, such as living a virtuous life, doing the will of God, and keeping God's commandments, also play a role in our salvation and our future eternal rewards? How do we understand the nature of what Christ did in obtaining forgiveness for the sins, referred to as atonement, of all people in every age? Was it sacrifice or example or something else? The humbling truth is that the church has asked these questions in every era of church history, and no one has articulated a completely satisfactory and conclusive answer to any of them.

Rather than being bogged down by all of these, we will focus on the crux of the passage. A central theological question in this passage is how we understand the phrase "the righteousness [the justification] of God" in 1:17. This issue has been discussed from Origen, who in the third century CE wrote one of the earliest commentaries on the book of Romans, through Martin Luther in the sixteenth century CE, to writers of today.

That the idea of righteousness is a significant biblical theme is not debatable. It is found throughout Scripture, from the time of the covenant between Abram and God in Genesis 15 to a description of the rider on the white horse in Revelation 19. In the Christian Scriptures, the term is used more frequently in the Pauline literature than in the rest of the writings, and there are more references to righteousness in the book of Romans than in the other letters. In the biblical texts, righteousness is often linked in some way to the concept of salvation.

In this particular passage, the debate generally revolves around whether "the righteousness of God" refers to an attribute of God, to something that God does, or to a gift that God will give to humanity. Famous voices involved in this debate throughout the centuries have included Augustine and Pelagius, Luther and the Council of Trent, and, more recently, John Macarthur and E. P. Sanders.

N. T. Wright provides an analysis of the possibilities of meaning for the phrase in his book *What Saint Paul Really Said*.[1] The dominant understanding of "the righteousness of God," particularly since the

---

1. N. T. Wright, *What Saint Paul Really Said: Was Paul of Tarsus the Real Founder of Christianity?* (Grand Rapids: Eerdmans, 1997), 96–103. Wright actually devotes a significant portion of the book (chaps. 6 and 7) to a consideration of justification. For more on this perspective, one can consult www.thepaulpage.com.

Pastoral Perspective

faith, to the Jew first and also to the Greek" (1:16b). The gospel, Paul asserts, is for all people everywhere who have faith in the God who brought forth Jesus. This is good news for everyone, for it means that God claims all people—Jewish, Greek, Roman, African American, Asian, Caucasian, Latino or Latina, poor, wealthy, able-bodied, disabled, female, male, liberal, conservative—God claims *all people* who profess a faith in God. This is an important message for the contemporary church, for the diversity of God's children is manifest both within the congregation and in the world around it. In a world divided by difference, Paul offers words that erase human-made distinctions between people: God's love is for *all people* who believe in God.

The text implicitly recognizes the complex reality of the ancient Christian church, a body of both Jews and Gentiles. From its beginning the church is given a diverse reality. Diversity is not a new configuration for the Christian religion. Nevertheless, the reminder is extremely important: our salvation—for Jews and Gentiles, and for people of all groups—comes through the power of the gospel.

Moreover, this lection also provides an insight into one of the mission challenges of the twenty-first century: the encounter and dialogue with people of other faiths. Paul's discussion about the relationship between the Jews and the emerging Christian community provides a ministerial bearing for the encounter with people of other faiths. If salvation is through God's power of the gospel and love, are we as Christians challenged to see and discover our experience of salvation in people of other faiths? Is there something to be discussed when we see people of other faiths embodying God's power of the gospel and love?

Paul's compelling argument for unity in God's power and love raises questions about the contemporary church's success at living out the broad reach of God's love: How willing is our congregation to embrace difference and welcome all people into the community of God's people? This question is not easily answered, for it reaches into all areas of a church's life together. Are the church's facilities accessible to people with disabilities? Does the music in worship draw from a diverse background of styles? Do church members know how to extend a warm welcome to all people who visit the church?

Later in today's reading, Paul claims that "a person is justified by faith apart from works prescribed by the law" (3:28). There is nothing anyone can do, short of putting one's faith in God, to earn God's grace. This is comforting news about a gracious

Exegetical Perspective

1:18–25), but in 1:16 he memorably declares that he is not ashamed of the gospel. He is confident that just when we think that *those* people cannot possibly be included in God's grace and mercy, the gospel displays "the power of God to save [or rescue] *everyone* who has faith [or trusts] in God, the Jew first and also the Greek" (1:16, my trans.). In Romans, Paul expresses this border-crossing theology by first explaining God's inclusion of the Gentiles in the promises to Abraham (chaps. 1–8) and then warning his Gentile audience not to think that the Jews are now outside the borders (chaps. 9–11). Thus Paul proclaims a God who takes the side of both Jews and Gentiles *as* Jews and Gentiles.

Verse 17 shows how important this border crossing is to Paul's theology. Paul says that *God's* righteousness is on display in the gospel. Why would Paul say this? Can God be *unrighteous*? Things may become clearer if we translate the Greek word for righteousness (*dikaiosynē*) into Spanish instead of English. In the *Santa Biblia*, God's *justicia*, that is, God's *justice*, is revealed in the gospel. What is at stake for Paul is not whether people are saved by faith or works, but whether God is a *just* God (see 2:9–11; 3:22b, 25; 9:14). This is a question of theodicy. Does God abandon whole cultures to sin and suffering with no opportunity for forgiveness? For Paul, God's justice is visible in the mission to the Gentiles, because God is inviting Gentiles to be in relationship with God, just as God gives that opportunity to Jews through the covenant with Abraham. Paul sees the redemption or freeing of the Gentiles being accomplished through the death of Jesus (3:24–25). Because God's Messiah ascended the cross instead of a throne, God made time for Gentile repentance (see the word "now" in 3:21, 24) and passed over previous Gentile sin (for Paul this is the age-old worship of idols and what he perceives as its consequences, see 1:18–32). In Paul's theology, Gentiles can now be judged righteous at the final judgment based on their faithfulness to God, which should resemble self-giving faithfulness of Jesus (3:26).[2]

In 3:27 Paul now rejects any boasting. Jews cannot claim that *they* have the covenant of Abraham and the law of Moses, but that *Gentiles* are sinners beyond the covenant (2:12). For Jews know that they themselves are saved by God's gracious election and Abraham's faithfulness (4:11). So the Gentiles are freed

2. Following the New Perspective on Paul, we should consider translating "faith in Christ" as "faith of Christ" (see NRSV notes at 3:22, 26). Paul may mean that it is *Jesus'* faithfulness to God, exemplified in his obedience unto the cross, which made it possible for the Gentiles to be judged righteous by God.

Homiletical Perspective

offered the following prayer some time ago and stand by it: "Forgive us, Jesus, for blithely dumping our sins on you. But we are not strong enough, and we earnestly ask your help that we might recognize our sinfulness and repent. Grant us God's mercy and God's help, that we might rise above our sins and come closer to what God wants us to be."

Is it because the language surrounding 3:23 is quite dense, laden with talk of righteousness, justification, redemption, atonement, and forbearance? I would guess that a very small percentage of contemporary church people know the theological meaning of all these words. The preacher may feel that this is a "teachable moment," but I suspect that a sermon given over to definitions of all these terms will most likely be forgotten before the service is over. Of course, Paul knew the meanings. We do not see as well as he (even if he saw through a glass darkly [1 Cor. 13:12 KJV]), but we might begin with two tiny words that will help people to see important things.

Consider again verse 23, where Paul says plainly, "All have sinned and fall short of the glory of God." What did he mean by the "glory of God," an inherent attribute of God, or something that humans give to God? Both are true, but the preposition is crucial. It could have been that people in their sin had failed to give glory *to* God, that is, to give praise and thanksgiving to the Holy One, but God does not need praise to be glorious in Godself. I have heard it said that prayer is the stuff God uses to change the world.[1] Similarly, we might say that the praise and glory given to God is the stuff God uses to beautify the world and those who live in it.

Paul, however, speaks of the glory *of* God, that shining radiance beyond our grasp and understanding. The Greek word for that radiance translates as *epiphany.* Here we are in these latter days on (perhaps) the Last Sunday of Epiphany. Way back in the days of the early church, Clement of Alexandria said that God is not simply the creator of beauty but that God is beautiful—indeed, beauty itself. Our untimely unbeautifulness, our sin, is a slap in God's beautiful face. Preachers can use this text like an ugly cudgel to hammer sinners into line, or they can graciously share with listeners the good news of a beautiful God, a beautiful world, and encourage us to find the beauty in people, even those whose beauty has been defaced by abuse and poverty. Give glory to God that God may use it to save the world. Rejoice

1. Theologian Marjorie Suchocki, in a panel discussion at Texas Christian University, Feb. 5, 1986.

Romans 1:16-17; 3:22b–28 (29-31)

Theological Perspective

time of Luther, has been a status of righteousness that humans have, either given to them or imputed to them, as they stand before God. Wright argues that this is incorrect. Rather, the "righteousness of God" should be understood as referring to God's own righteousness.

The phrase must then be seen against the backdrop of covenant as understood within Judaism, of its use in a legal setting, and of its eschatological import. In the Jewish Scriptures, especially in Isaiah and many psalms, the phrase refers to God's faithfulness in the covenant promises God has made, showing how God can be trusted by those in relationship to God. There is, though, that additional dimension from the legal system to understanding the phrase. Here, God is the judge hearing a plea from Israel to be delivered from the pagans who oppress her. Israel asks God to be faithful to the covenant promises that had already been made with her and to vindicate her in her distress. Finally, this faithfulness in covenant relationship will be seen in the future vindication of the people, when God is revealed to be the true Lord of the world who actively shows divine covenant faithfulness in actions taken on behalf of the people.

It is through the righteousness of God, then, that all of humanity is able to be declared justified with God. God's own righteousness means that those who are alienated from God because of sin, which is everyone, are now able to be in relationship with God. It means that those sins are forgiven and that person is deemed to be a true member of the covenant community, whether he or she is Jew or Gentile. Our understanding of "the righteousness of God," then, determines our understanding of the work of God within human life.

W. MICHAEL CHITTUM

Pastoral Perspective

God! What matters is our loyalty to a God who desires nothing more ardently than to be in relationship with us. Faith requires choosing to listen for God over the clamoring voices of the gods of our own making: the gods of the market, the gods of ambition and success, the gods of self-denial and self-hatred, the gods of self-sacrifice. We do not have to get it right, we have to want to be in relationship with God. Paul wants us to understand and know that when we can listen for God's voice, when we can turn ourselves so that we try to align our lives with God's will for us, we are living faithfully. We do not have to do anything to earn or justify God's grace for ourselves. We cannot earn more grace by being more faithful or doing more good works. We serve God because we are grateful to be loved and claimed as God's own. As Paul writes, God's grace is a gift (3:24). Our lives lived in service to God are the way we respond in thanks to God's gift of grace.

The power of this passage lies in Paul's assurance that God so desires to be in relationship with us, that there is nothing we can do to escape the grasp of God's love. He writes, "For I am not ashamed of the gospel; it is the power of God for salvation to everyone who has faith" (1:16). Later he writes, "For there is no distinction, since all have sinned and fall short of the glory of God; they are now justified by his grace as a gift" (3:22–24). For a broken people (and we all have brokenness), Paul's assurance of God's faithfulness to us is like a letter from an old friend that we can pull out when we need to be reminded that we are loved.

KATE FOSTER CONNORS

from slavery to sin by God's gift of Jesus Christ.[3] However, Paul is also very clear that Gentiles cannot boast that *they* now have the covenant and *Jews* are rejected or have to change (11:25–36). Although 3:28–30 stresses that God is the God of the Gentiles and not only of the Jews, the point is reversed when Paul asks, "Has God rejected his people?" He answers resoundingly: "By no means!" (11:1).

In the New Perspective on Paul, the Luther-influenced depiction of Judaism as a legalistic works-righteousness religion is replaced by a more historical view. Jews widely held that they received their covenant by God's grace and Abraham's trust in God. Jews respond to God's covenant with Torah obedience. Paul disagreed with others in the Gentile mission about whether the *Gentiles* had to be circumcised or keep kosher to receive God's gracious rescue from judgment. Christians might update this discussion by asking ourselves, how much do people have to become like us in order to receive God's grace? Is God the God of the Christians only? By imagining the debate that might ensue in our own communities, we can get a feel for the theological discussions going on in the mission to the Gentiles.

Christians usually equate themselves with the Gentiles. If we allow Paul's theological vision to speak about the people that *he* knew, then we might question our own confidence, and look for places where God's surprising grace is leading today across our own supposedly uncrossable borders to new possibilities of inclusion and reconciliation.

MELANIE JOHNSON-DEBAUFRE

in the shining glory of a beneficent God and a beautiful Savior.

If one should follow this track in a sermon, it might be appropriate to follow the sermon with a congregational hymn found in most hymnbooks, "Fairest Lord Jesus," originally titled "Beautiful Savior." And, if appropriate, the congregation might continue to sing the seldom-sung fourth and fifth stanzas as a benediction:

> All fairest beauty, heavenly and earthly,
> Wondrously, Jesus, is found in thee;
> None can be nearer, fairer or dearer,
> Than thou, my Savior, art to me.

> Beautiful Savior! Lord of all the nations,
> Son of God and [Prince of Peace];
> Glory and honor, praise, adoration,
> Now and forever more be thine.[2]

A second homiletical approach to the text looks carefully at v. 26: "[God] is righteous and . . . justifies the one who has faith in Jesus." Simply put: "To get right with God, have faith in Jesus." A number of translations and commentaries suggest that Paul does not mean "have faith *in* Jesus" but rather "have [the] faith *of* Jesus."[3] That is a big difference. The faith *of* Jesus is considerably more demanding than faith *in* Jesus. Sinners have hope in Jesus, but would not claim to have perfect faith. We hope to reach *of* but we are so glad to be *in* the community of faith that loves and trusts in Jesus.

JOSEPH R. JETER

---

3. The Greek word traditionally translated "sacrifice of atonement," *hilastērion,* is rare and difficult. It likely refers to a place in the Holy of Holies where God's grace resides, which is not normally a place of sacrifice. Several scholars suggest that Paul does not have a strong atonement theology. Given that this is one of the only Pauline passages where such an idea *might* appear (and that is debatable), a sermon about atonement should not be based on this word.

2. From the last two stanzas of "Fairest Lord Jesus," which for some reason are rarely sung except by Lutherans. The text was written by German Jesuits as "Schönster Herr Jesu" in the seventeenth century, published in the *Münster Gesangbuch,* 1677, and translated from German to English by Joseph A. Seiss, 1873.

3. N. T. Wright goes further to suggest that *pistis* in the text should be translated *faithfulness,* not *faith* (N. T. Wright, "Romans," in *The New Interpreter's Bible* 10 [Nashville, TN: Abingdon Press, 2002], 470).

Matthew 7:21-29

[21]"Not everyone who says to me, 'Lord, Lord,' will enter the kingdom of heaven, but only the one who does the will of my Father in heaven. [22]On that day many will say to me, 'Lord, Lord, did we not prophesy in your name, and cast out demons in your name, and do many deeds of power in your name?' [23]Then I will declare to them, 'I never knew you; go away from me, you evildoers.'

[24]"Everyone then who hears these words of mine and acts on them will be like a wise man who built his house on rock. [25]The rain fell, the floods came, and the winds blew and beat on that house, but it did not fall, because it had been founded on rock. [26]And everyone who hears these words of mine and does not act on them will be like a foolish man who built his house on sand. [27]The rain fell, and the floods came, and the winds blew and beat against that house, and it fell—and great was its fall!"

[28]Now when Jesus had finished saying these things, the crowds were astounded at his teaching, [29]for he taught them as one having authority, and not as their scribes.

Theological Perspective

"One may be orthodox in every point, and may not only espouse right opinions, but zealously defend them against all opposers; that one may think justly concerning the incarnation of our Lord, concerning the ever blessed Trinity, and every other doctrine contained in the oracles of God. That one may assent to all the creeds that called the Apostles', the Nicene, and the Athanasian and yet 'tis possible that one may have no religion at all. . . . That one may be almost as orthodox as the devil . . . and may all the while be as great a stranger as the devil to the religion of the heart."[1]

John Wesley's words serve as a commentary on this frightening conclusion to Jesus' Sermon on the Mount: "Not everyone who says to me, 'Lord, Lord,' will enter the kingdom of heaven, but only the one who does the will of my Father in heaven" (v. 21). These are not, mind you, the words of some fulminating big-tent evangelist, but those of Jesus himself. The accused have a ready defense, including an undisputed record of prophecy, casting out demons, and deeds of power. The Judge's dismissal of this weight of evidence is what really strikes fear. "I never knew you" (v. 23): if

1. John Wesley, in *The Works of John Wesley*, in *The Oxford Edition of the Works of John Wesley* (Oxford: Clarendon Press, 1975), 220–21, quoted in *The Quotable Mr. Wesley*, compiled and ed. W. Stephen Gunter (Atlanta: Candler School of Theology, 1999), altered a bit for reasons of gender inclusivity.

Pastoral Perspective

This week's text closes the Sermon on the Mount. Jesus has been addressing the disciples while a crowd has been eavesdropping. Jesus ends his teaching with words that send a message—only those who hear *and* do his words are acceptable disciples.

Hearing and doing are hallmarks of Matthew's understanding of discipleship. For Matthew, one does not rightly hear if one does not also do. For him, head, heart, will, and hands are integrated into a life that trusts God and serves humanity.

These days, it is difficult to think about more things to do. We are overwhelmed by schedules that do not allow ample time for rest, renewal, play, reflection, and connecting with others. The Sermon on the Mount seems to add more layers to our already overcrowded "to do" lists.

Verses 21–22 imply that those who do not follow the list of commands listed earlier in the Sermon will not be allowed into God's realm. Pretty words, empty confessions, and empty gestures are not keys into heaven, but who can actually do all the things required by Jesus' teaching? How can any human pass the test and enter into God's glorious community? Who is worthy to sit at God's great banquet table?

Let us remember that the teachings in the Sermon are directed at disciples—persons who have already committed themselves to God and God's

Exegetical Perspective

Matthew stands out among the Gospels by emphasizing the significance of doing what Jesus says. Matthew 7:21–29 insists that mere confession of Jesus means nothing apart from doing as Jesus teaches. The passage places an emphatic period on the Sermon on the Mount, the Gospel's introductory synopsis of Jesus' teaching regarding "greater righteousness" (5:20). Jesus' teachings, demanding as they are, offer the path to life.

The church has always struggled with the Sermon, because its rigorous expectations exceed our moral capacity—or at least our determination. Oliver Wendell Holmes is supposed to have said, "Most people are willing to take the Sermon on the Mount as a flag to sail under, but few will use it as a rudder by which to steer." Given Jesus' precondition that persons resolve their differences prior to worship, his counsel to pluck out one's lustful eye, and his admonishment to turn the other cheek, one understands why people might claim great things for the Sermon without attending to its particulars. In a consumerist society like our own, Jesus' exhortation to seek the realm of God without anxiety for our material needs (6:24–34) seems just plain naive. Whatever our reservations, Matthew 7:21–29 insists that, apart from faithful obedience, simple confession of Jesus' name opens the path for disaster. Security resides only in doing what Jesus says.

Homiletical Perspective

These words conclude the Sermon on the Mount, and from a homiletical point of view, they provide a glimpse into what Jesus thought about the purposes of preaching in the first place. Many teachers of Christian proclamation have emphasized that preaching is not about getting something *said* so much as getting something *heard*, but here Jesus makes quite clear that for him, preaching is not so much about getting something heard as getting something *done*.

For Jesus, a "true hearing" of his teaching involves not merely the ability to parrot it but also, and indispensably, the ability to embody it in life, and so to "[do] the will of my Father in heaven" (v. 21). Even such apparently salutary—and, please note, paradigmatically Christian—acts as calling on Jesus as "Lord" or performing "deeds of power" in Jesus' name are in themselves inadequate, Jesus insists, and in fact constitute a form of evildoing (v. 23), unless they take place in the context of doing the will of my Father in heaven. Thus Christians might hold impeccably orthodox beliefs; or say and sing, "Lord, Lord," with an exquisite liturgical correctness; or perform dazzling "deeds of power" as evidence of obedience and righteousness; but none of this matters a whit, Jesus contends, unless God's will be done. Apart from this key condition, Christians may earnestly

Matthew 7:21-29

Theological Perspective

you sit with those words a while, and feel the weight of their rejection, it might be enough to make you go forward at the most hyperventilated of altar calls. It is well to remember at scriptural moments like this that the preacher's job is not to explain away Scripture's difficulties, to rub its rough places smooth, or to make Jesus nicer than he is. It is to offer it up unvarnished. Naturally we must do so in light of the whole of Scripture: it is Peter who later swears never to have known Jesus, and Jesus who knew this was coming, predicted it, and forgave his fallen friend. That may be a topic for another sermon.

Matthew takes a bit more time to describe the storm that washes over the wise and foolish persons' houses than does his fellow evangelist Luke (see Luke 6:47–49).[2] "The rain fell, and the floods came, and the winds blew and beat against that house" (v. 27). Discipleship is no easy road, as anyone trying to live by the words of the Sermon can attest. It is certainly no way to decrease one's anxiety, blood pressure, or lack of self-esteem. Those who claim to love enemies will gain more of them. Those who refuse to be as anxious as the market demands will be a scandal to others. A storm is coming for all, those who live Jesus' words and those who do not—best to build on a solid foundation.

To build a life on enemy love, nonretaliation, and the return of good for evil will feel like a life lived in a hurricane. The house will shake, whirl, creak, and threaten to give. Those who have been through severe storms can attest to the feeling of utter powerlessness when the mightiest of our buildings can be tossed around by unfathomable wind and rain. In the life of faith, however, the center will hold, for the universe is created, maintained, and redeemed by the one who gives this Sermon. However uncertain the foundation feels—and such storms often result in bodily death—the house so built will stand. That house is the church. This is no promise of individual safety or flourishing, tempted as we are to turn these passages into promises for me instead of for us. The church is Noah's ark, tossed around helplessly, yet dry and safe, and smelly and rancorous. The only thing that makes it bearable inside, as it is often said, is the storm outside.

The final words should catch in the throat of any evangelist, preacher, or Christian leader, fulminating or not: "The crowds were astounded at his teaching, for he taught them as one having authority, and not

Pastoral Perspective

coming realm. They have already made changes in their behavior toward God, each other, and the community. They have seen glimpses of the expected life in God's realm, and they know what they must do to be good residents of that community. The Sermon is a text for the Christian community.

Jesus uses the image of two builders to make his point. Jesus, a carpenter, understands the construction business. No one builds a house in bad weather—too much heat or too much cold impede construction. Construction happens on good weather days; and good builders know that foul weather happens. The question then is, will the house be able to withstand bad weather?

The foundation must be solid. If the foundation is deep and on solid ground, the house will stand whatever comes. If the foundation is shallow or built on shifting ground, there is no way for the house to remain standing. New houses look pretty. Home inspections may uncover minor issues that are easily fixed, but the test of a house's strength comes only during bad weather. Although the roof looks fine, there is no way of knowing how sound it is until the rains come. Although the basement is cozy and spacious, there is no way of knowing how sealed it is until the floods flow. Although the windows look great, there is no way of knowing how strong they are until the winds blow. The strength of the house does not appear until the storms come.

Such is the life of the true disciple and of the community of faith. It is easy to learn the right words and to engage in rituals and rites, but the strength and character of the disciple is truly tested when the storms come. Those who build their faith on regular prayer, are community minded, and care about the environment are the disciples whose foundation is solid. Jesus calls us to a life of being and doing; words and deeds are interwoven. The life of the disciple—trust and service—springs from understanding that life is a gift from God and that God sustains that life.

Although the closing words to Matthew 7 sound stern, Jesus makes a point that resonates with Matthew's understanding of discipleship: the invitation to participate in God's realm requires committed service. This service is not another thing to do; it is a response to God who shows us how to live through the life, ministry, death, and resurrection of Jesus.

Matthew tells us that the crowd is astounded at Jesus' teaching, because he teaches with authority unlike any they have witnessed. We too are astounded. Jesus walks the walk and talks the talk—he *is* what he

---

2. I owe this observation to Daniel Harrington, *The Gospel according to Matthew*, vol. 1 of *Sacra Pagina* (Collegeville, MN: Liturgical Press, 1991), 109.

This prudential concern stands out within the Gospel. Matthew often seems focused not on this-worldly consequences but on the final judgment. Judgment imagery—weeping and gnashing of teeth—ordinarily expresses Matthew's sense of urgency. Moreover, Jesus' most formidable teachings do not come with this-worldly prudential explanations. "It is better for you to lose one of your members than for your whole body to go into hell" (5:30) hardly resembles sage self-help advice. In contrast, the imagery of two houses, one built on rock and one on sand, expresses urgency in the here and now.

The saying concerning the two houses blends diverse images to make its point. In this metaphorical world, building a house is like building a life. The two builders correspond to people, their houses to the lives they construct.

For all we know, the houses are identical. Both undergo the same troubles: rain, floods, and wind. Matthew sometimes uses winds and water as metaphors for the trials of life, particularly persecution. Interpreters have long noted how Matthew transforms the wind and waves of Jesus' two boat miracles (8:23–27; 14:22–33) into metaphors for the struggles of the church as it follows Jesus. All who follow Jesus should expect rains, floods, and winds. Jesus has already blessed them for their endurance toward the Sermon's beginning (5:10–12).

Only two things distinguish the houses: the builders and the foundations. One builder is wise, while the other is foolish. The wise builder constructs upon rock, the foolish one upon sand. The key in this system of images is the foundation. Jesus' teachings provide the "one foundation" for living through life's storms. Whether persons obey Jesus' teachings determines how well they endure the trials that accompany discipleship.

Implicitly at least, the passage seems an echo of Psalm 1. There, as in much of Israel's Wisdom literature, two ways of living are distinguished one from another. The person who follows the Torah will be like a stream planted by a stream of water (Ps. 1:3). The person who does not follow the Torah will be like chaff driven by the wind (Ps. 1:4). Like our passage, the psalm makes the distinction between obedience and disobedience. In each case, the consequences of the choice between obedience and disobedience are evident in this world. The tree flourishes or not; the house stands strong in the storm or is blown away. Again Matthew makes clear that, for Christian people, the teachings of Jesus

protest that we have been orthodox, reverent, prophetic, effective—but Jesus promises a simple, devastating response: "I never knew you" (v. 23).

According to this passage, "knowing" Jesus means listening to him—that is, both "hearing" his words and "acting" upon them—and so living out God's will. In other words, a particular life of action is how Jesus is actually and concretely "known," interpreted, encountered, companioned, followed: not merely by thinking or talking in any particular way, but by acting and living in a particular way—including thinking and talking, of course, but also innumerable other modes of life as well.

Exactly which "particular way" are we to live? Jesus does not specify or summarize this way of life here, and I take the omission to be advised. He certainly does not say, "Only the one who calls me 'Lord' will enter the kingdom of heaven," or, "Only the one who loves God and neighbor will enter it," or, "Only the one who prays," or, "Only the one who forgives," and so on. Instead, he says: "Only the one who does the will of my Father in heaven," and then glosses this criterion as "everyone who hears these words of mine and acts on them" (v. 24). Thus we are thrown back onto the sermon itself, and so back into the basic task of listening afresh to Jesus with an ear toward acting on his words here and now.

Indeed, we may go so far as to say that there is no "particular way" definable apart from Jesus, who is himself, Christians confess, the Way. In any given situation or circumstance, then, Christian discipleship is not a matter of attending to a specific ethical formula, but rather of attending to a specific, living person, Jesus Christ. This attention, precisely because it is directed toward another person, must be continually refreshed and renewed. Put briefly, a life of discipleship is a life of discernment, a way of ongoing listening for the risen Christ's own voice.

Accordingly, the Christian church—the Way is likely one of the earliest names of the movement following Jesus (Acts 9:2)—is a community of discernment, listening together for Jesus and the Holy Spirit. Thus preaching on and through Matthew 7:21–29 can be an opportunity to reflect on the character and mission of the Christian church as an ongoing community of hearing and acting upon what Jesus calls "these words of mine." This ecclesiological point is pertinent not only to Christian preaching, of course, but it is certainly pertinent there. So another possible direction for interpreting this passage is to preach on the act of preaching itself, that is, to clarify some proper purposes of

Matthew 7:21-29

Theological Perspective

as their scribes" (vv. 28–29). It is well to remember this, especially in preaching passages like this that can bring out the thundering preacher hidden in any pulpit mouse. Christians have a miserable history of reading the "their" as a reference to the Jews. What if "their" means "our," and Jesus' authority is here contrasted with the authority of anyone who claims to stand and interpret the places where Scripture intersects with lives? Any fear instigated by this passage, from "I never knew you" (v. 23) to the crowd's astonishment (v. 29) to the promised storm (v. 25), should as ever be directed to those claiming the closest proximity to God's house and not those farthest from it.

It would be dishonest, however, not to acknowledge that we who are charged to stand and say, "Thus saith the Lord," have a great deal of authority. It is a derivative authority, one that points away from oneself and toward an Other, yet it is inescapably ours. Authority, or in Sam Wells's words, power, "is not wrong or bad or inherently corrupt; it is given for a purpose—to reflect the truth, to set people free—and only becomes sinister when it is not used for the purpose for which it has been given."[3] Such power or authority encourages all listeners to build on rock, to trust not in our own achievements (even if we have done deeds of power or cast out the odd demon or two), and to point to the authority who clothes the lilies and loves his enemies all the way to the cross.

JASON BYASSEE

Pastoral Perspective

preaches and teaches. Through examples of surprising reversals and the unexpected, Jesus teaches that the life of the disciple includes prayer, repentance, reconciliation, generosity, justice, and hospitality. Hard work? Only if we try to make it on our own. Jesus shows us how disciples live—keeping God in the center and doing all things because we love one another. This makes for a sure foundation.

Being Christian is a deliberate choice and ought to shape what we do in the world. We do not render service for a reward in return; we do not help others so that we can have our fifteen minutes of fame. We serve others because we are grateful to God who loves, cares for, and watches over us. We are reminded that life is not just about us. It is about God and what God is up to in the world and in us; it is about what God is calling us to be and to do for the sake of God's realm.

Life in God's realm is a great equalizer. All persons are invited to participate and there is room for all, regardless of race, color, ethnicity, sexuality, ability, nationality. All disciples, ancient and contemporary, have the same expectation: integrated head and heart focused on God the Creator.

Words and deeds are important. They have the power to help or hurt. In Matthew 7, words and deeds go hand in hand. For the disciple, words and deeds are part of a whole that points to God's actions and our response of gratitude to God who creates and nurtures us. We are challenged by Jesus, who sets the standard, holds us accountable for life in the community, and provides a foretaste of life in God's realm. We are called to a life that is sustained by God's presence, power, and protection—in good weather, bad weather, and forevermore.

BARBARA J. ESSEX

---

3. Sam Wells, *Power and Passion: Six Characters in Search of Resurrection* (Grand Rapids: Zondervan, 2007), 48.

become a new Torah, and obedience to Jesus is the mark of the new righteousness of God's realm.

Such prudential advice serves as a remarkably fitting conclusion to the Sermon. The Sermon begins by inviting potential disciples into its audience. Though Matthew 5:1 suggests that only disciples hear Jesus' teaching, the Beatitudes bless all who find themselves beaten down by life (5:3–6) yet seek to live the way of Jesus (5:7–12). At the Sermon's conclusion, these potential disciples wonder at Jesus' authoritative teaching. To these potential disciples Jesus offers a highly rigorous path as the only secure foundation for endurance.

Wise preachers consider how things work in the real world before spouting theological maxims, and this passage calls for just such reflection. Is it true that life works out for people who follow Jesus' way? Of course not, nor is that the point of our passage. Our passage does not teach that following Jesus will keep one safe and healthy. Its promise is more narrow—and more realistic. Jesus' teachings provide a secure foundation for faithful endurance. Confession of Jesus' name, even accompanied by wondrous deeds, cannot sustain disciples in the long haul. Only tenacious adherence to the way of Jesus can do that.

Many interpreters separate verses 21–23 from verses 24–29. The logic behind this decision is that the preceding passage, verses 15–20, warns against false prophets. Eventually, Jesus instructs, their fruits bear out their true nature. In that light, verses 21–23 are not a warning to potential disciples that they had better step up their obedience but a conclusion to Jesus' admonition to discern true from false leaders.

The overall structure of Matthew 7:13–29 is difficult to assess, but there are good reasons to read verses 21–23 read along with verses 24–25. All the teachings of the Sermon address potential disciples and their conduct. Then 7:13–14 warns that the gate to life is narrow. Thus, the entire section of Matthew 7:13–29 concerns the "narrow" path to life. While it seems likely that verses 21–23 participate in the teaching concerning false prophets, its truth applies to Matthew's overall message as well. Obedience to the teachings of Jesus marks the test of true discipleship, whether that of would-be prophets or of ordinary disciples.

GREG CAREY

Christian preaching (including both the speaker and the community of listeners), emphasizing its basic relation to Christian mission and Christian life. A third and related theme is to interpret this passage as a critique of religiosity, in particular of Christian religiosity, that is, a meditation on the permanent temptation in Christian life to call Jesus "Lord, Lord" without obeying him, and so to hear his words without actually acting them out.

At stake here is the question of Christian obedience (from the Latin ob, "to," and audire, "listen"); so yet another possible homiletical direction is to explore the shape and character of this obedience. Intriguingly, Jesus' brief parable in this passage suggests that his instructions are less like heteronomous commands imposed upon us from the outside, and more like wisdom teachings that help clarify how the world inside us and around us is actually structured, appearances notwithstanding. That is, the parable of the wise and foolish house builders suggests that we should obey Jesus not merely because of his authority over us ("Lord, Lord!"), but also and decisively because he provides crucial guidance about how humanity actually flourishes and how the world actually works.

The wind and rain will come, Jesus warns, and both hearing and acting upon his words is akin to building a house on solid ground, a house able to withstand adversity precisely because it is "founded on rock." On the other hand, hearing his words without acting on them will be disastrous, not because Jesus punishes those who disobey, but because his words convey practical wisdom, sound advice for being human. Indeed, if Christian preaching is not so much about getting something heard as getting something *done*, then at the end of the day, the work Jesus means to get done—the very work in which he enlists his listeners to take part—is the work of making possible a safe, strong, flourishing human community: a community "founded on rock," and thus well prepared to face the inevitable wind and rain. For Jesus, this is what preaching is for.

MATTHEW MYER BOULTON

Exodus 24:12-18

[12]The LORD said to Moses, "Come up to me on the mountain, and wait there; and I will give you the tablets of stone, with the law and the commandment, which I have written for their instruction." [13]So Moses set out with his assistant Joshua, and Moses went up into the mountain of God. [14]To the elders he had said, "Wait here for us, until we come to you again; for Aaron and Hur are with you; whoever has a dispute may go to them."

[15]Then Moses went up on the mountain, and the cloud covered the mountain. [16]The glory of the LORD settled on Mount Sinai, and the cloud covered it for six days; on the seventh day he called to Moses out of the cloud. [17]Now the appearance of the glory of the LORD was like a devouring fire on the top of the mountain in the sight of the people of Israel. [18]Moses entered the cloud, and went up on the mountain. Moses was on the mountain for forty days and forty nights.

Theological Perspective

Within the book of Exodus, this passage marks a transition from narratives concerning the law (20:1–23:19) to those concerning worship (25:1–31:17). Consequently, at first reading, seams appear where these respective narratives seem stitched together: In the first part of the passage, God tells Moses to ascend the mountain to receive the tablets of stone on which is written the "law and the commandment" (24:12). At the same time, the ascent itself (24:15, 18) foreshadows the future liturgical movements of the priests on high holy days in the tabernacle, the architecture of which God later reveals to Moses during their summit meeting (25:9).

Commentators have often attributed these seams to the literary sources from which the passage is composed, but the clear purpose of this passage is to integrate the "ethical ear" and the "contemplative eye" in Exodus.[1] That is to say, there is in this passage an emphasis on hearing God's voice, and in Exodus this audio metaphor is connected to obedience. Hence, the passage begins with God speaking to Moses and his companions, inviting them to ascend the mountain in Sinai in order to receive even more

Pastoral Perspective

During the season of Epiphany the church probes more deeply the "good news of great joy" (Luke 2:10) that has come to all the world in the birth of Jesus. He is the light that "shines in the darkness" (John 1:5). To his light the nations are drawn, and in his light the people who dwell in "thick darkness" (Exod. 20:21) come and see the light of the grace and truth of the triune God.

The Old Testament lesson for the final Sunday after the Epiphany magnifies the image of light with additional images of the revelation of God—mountain, cloud, fire, and glory. Those images, which recur throughout Scripture, come to their "high point" in the Gospel lesson for the day (Matt. 17:1–9), the transfiguration of Jesus on the mountaintop.

As we reflect pastorally on Moses's encounter with the glory of God on Sinai, we must first respect the deep mystery of the story and not move too quickly to analogies of our own "mountaintop experiences." The revelation of God on Sinai is not offered as a model for religious experiences of the glory of God in general. It speaks of a decisive revelation of God to Moses that in time leads to the unique revelation of the glory of God in the "beloved Son" to whom alone we are commanded to "listen" (Matt. 17:5).

1. Samuel Terrien, *The Elusive Presence: Towards a New Biblical Theology* (San Francisco: Harper & Row, 1978), 134–36. Here I follow Walter Brueggemann, "Exodus," in *New Interpreter's Bible* (Nashville: Abingdon Press, 1994), 1:882–83.

Exegetical Perspective

Poised between the legal material known as the book of the covenant in chapters 20–23 and the section on the tabernacle in chapters 25–31 is the account of Moses ascending Mount Sinai in Exodus 24. This transitional chapter has three units, verses 1–8, 9–11, and 12–18. Most scholars attribute this passage to the Priestly and Elohist traditions. The presence of more than one tradition and the subsequent editing result in a narrative that appears to jump around. For example, Moses ascends the mountain several times with no reference to coming down, which makes it difficult to follow the narrative action. Although the narrative is not smooth, there is a clear goal in this passage, namely, the encounter between Moses and God on Mount Sinai, where Moses receives the law, torah or teachings of God.

Although chapter 24 easily divides into the three aforementioned sections, the chapter can also be seen as having two sections: verses 12–18 repeat a basic pattern established in verses 1–11. The repetition highlights the gradual and upward movement of Moses toward the presence of God on the mountain. The composite text has God commanding Moses to ascend the mountain in verse 1 and again in verse 12. The first time God calls Moses to come up and worship. The second time, Moses is called to receive the law that will be used to instruct the

Homiletical Perspective

The transfiguration falls on the Last Sunday after Epiphany, just before Ash Wednesday. Exodus and Matthew are very useful transitional texts as the people of God embark into the unknown with a God they barely know. Moses's meeting with God on Mount Sinai is essential to the people of Israel as they face a forty-year journey though the wilderness to the promised land. Likewise, the transfiguration in Matthew is essential to the disciples as they head into the terrifying time of the passion. Both texts are critical to us as we face into our own forty-day observance of Lent. Like Jesus, we set out into a spiritual wilderness to face temptations, to overcome our worst fears, to die to ourselves in order to gain faith that God is, indeed, present, loving, and wonderfully protective of our welfare.

The transfigurations of Moses and Jesus are meant to fuel the faith of their respective witnesses for the long and frequently frightening journeys ahead. In Exodus, God's purpose on Mount Sinai is to let the people know beyond all doubt that God will communicate with them through Moses. "God said to Moses, 'I am going to come to you in a dense cloud, in order that the people may hear when I speak with you and so trust you ever after'" (19:9). An echo of Exodus can be heard in the Gospel of Matthew when God speaks from the cloud: "This is

Exodus 24:12-18

Theological Perspective

specific commandments "for their instruction" (v. 12). The ascent itself is an act of obedience, one called for by the word of God. Later, however, the metaphor shifts from audio to visual. Moses ascends the summit alone and beholds "the appearance of the glory of the LORD," which "was like a devouring fire on top of the mountain in the sight of the people of Israel" (v. 17). In this way, the ascent, which begins as an ethical act of obedience, is transformed into a contemplative attempt to look into realms beyond human knowing.

Despite these seams, the passage has its own integrity. Running through it is a continuity embodied most straightforwardly in the figure of Moses, who makes the ascent by following his body's senses: he "hears" God's word and "sees" God's glory; but there is also a larger sense of embodiment evident. Just as we rely on both hearing and sight to negotiate our physical environment, so should we follow God's commands and prayerfully search for God in order successfully to negotiate our spiritual environment. Moses is, in other words, an exemplar of how to live a life that is prayerfully obedient and obediently prayerful.

In his *Life of Moses*, Gregory of Nyssa (ca. 335–ca. 395) offered a similar interpretation. "Religious virtue," he argued, "is divided into two parts, into that which pertains to the divine and that which pertains to right conduct." In this way, "purity of life is a part of religion." Gregory drew inspiration from the Platonic philosophical tradition, and thus he held that moral transformation moves from the contemplative to the ethical. He argued that Moses "learns at first the things which must be known about God" and then "is taught the other side of virtue, learning by what pursuits the virtuous life is perfected." Further, Gregory viewed the moral and spiritual life through an ascetic lens and accordingly interpreted the events in Moses's life in similar terms. He likened Moses's ascent on the mountain to the soul's attempt to ascend the chain of being and transcend the limits of the attachments of the body through contemplation. Indeed, for Gregory, the ultimate ground of Moses's progress up the mountain was an unending process of conversion in which "he continually climbed to the step above and never ceased to rise higher, because he always found a step higher than the one he had attained." This is so, because searching after the "vision of God" means that one is "never to be satisfied in the desire to see" the infinite goodness of God. Indeed, whatever glimpse of God we can have

Pastoral Perspective

One way by which we can enter the story pastorally without losing its distinctiveness is by noting its context in Exodus. The story rises dramatically above the chapters that precede and follow it. After the giving of the Decalogue to Moses on Mount Sinai (Exod. 20), amid thunder and lightning and a cloud of "thick darkness," we find a long, detailed application of the law to the ongoing issues of life in the community of faith. There are laws regarding worship, the treatment of slaves, acts of violence, property and its restoration, as well as laws regarding social and religious customs, festivals, and ceremonies. The dominant concern in these chapters is the right ordering of the life of the covenant community in accord with the revealed law of God.

Then, following the story of Moses's encounter with the glory of God on Sinai, we find another series of equally long and detailed chapters regarding the construction of the tabernacle, its architecture, decorations, offerings, and rules for the priests who conduct worship in the tabernacle. The modern reader is tempted to skip over these chapters that seem to have little relevance to us today.

However, the effect of reading Exodus 24 in its wider context can be dramatic. The theophany in Exodus 24 rises like a mountain peak above the flatlands of meticulous attention to the details of the moral life of the covenant community and the ordering of its worship. Suddenly we are startled by the mystical in the midst of the mundane—the awesome amid the ordinary, the breathtaking amid the boring. That is about as good a description of pastoral ministry as I know.

Pastoral ministry is conducted amid the ordinary lives of ordinary (if not ornery) people. Much of a minister's time is occupied with maintaining at least some semblance of order in the congregation's life and worship. Sermons are written between discussions of what color to paint the men's room and what kind of bread to use for Communion.

Yet, in the midst of the relentless routines of ministry "sometimes a light surprises,"[1] and we find ourselves startled by parables of the transforming glory of God—an elusive glory that cannot be programmed or administered, only received with awe and wonder. In such times we may catch glimpses of a glory that can break forth when we least expect it, with power to transform an otherwise quite ordinary event into an epiphany.

1. "Sometimes a Light Surprises," William Cowper, 1779.

people. The variation in the pattern suggests a link between the keeping of the torah and worship. Our reading begins with the second command, in verse 12.

Come Up to Me . . . The verb in verse 12 to "come up," *'alah*, appears four times in our passage (vv. 12, 13, 15, and 18). Each time the action is associated with Moses. The repetition of the verb suggests Moses's ascension was progressive. It also serves to highlight the fact that Moses, and Moses alone, is called to go all the way up the mountain for the encounter with God. The elders stay behind (v. 14), and Joshua accompanies Moses for part of the journey (v. 13). Moses's journey to the place of encounter embodies the process of sanctification, or being set apart. In order to receive the law, Moses must be set apart. Moses's ascent and descent of the mountain emphasizes his role as an intermediary. He ascends the mountain to receive the teaching that then must be delivered to the people.

. . . On the Mountain . . . The geographic location of the passage is significant for our exegesis. In the ancient Near East, the mountain is considered a pillar of the earth, holding the sky in place. With its head reaching toward the heavens, the mountain or high place is the bridge between earth, the realm of humans, and the heavens, the realm of the gods. As such, a mountain is the place for a divine encounter. Sinai is the place where Moses initially encountered God (Exod. 3) and the place God promised Moses he would return with God's people. Thus the presence of the people at the base of Mount Sinai is fulfillment of a divine promise. The fulfillment of the promise, however, is not an end, but a necessary stop on the journey to the land of promise. The consecration and legislation at Sinai are one of the ways that Israel embarks on her journey to become the people of God. In that sense, Moses's move up the mountain is symbolic of Israel's journey to encounter and be formed into the people of God. Present in this passage is the reference to the cloud, God's physical manifestation on the top of the mountain. This same cloud that led the entire people out of Egypt to this place is now at the top of the mountain. God's presence is consistent.

. . . And Wait . . . Along with the command to "come up" (v. 12) is the command to "wait" (v. 14). Moses's ascent of Mount Sinai occurs in stages. In verse 12 he is commanded to go up and wait. In verse 13 Moses goes up with Joshua after instructing the

my Son, the Beloved; with him I am well pleased; listen to him!" (Matt. 17:5).

For Moses it has been a "transfiguring" as opposed to a transforming moment. His physical appearance actually changes—a sure stamp of his proximity to God. When Moses descends from the mountain, the skin of his face is shining. Aaron and all the people of Israel immediately recognize this as proof that Moses has been in the presence of the Lord. They are struck with holy fear and know that, through Moses, they have found favor in the sight of God. From then on, the people may trust that the Lord is in their midst, protecting them against their enemies, nurturing and sustaining them with water and food, holding them back from dangerous territory.

The preacher might note that Moses does not "need" the mountaintop experience with God in order to bolster his own confidence and faith. Moses, after all, has been in continuing conversation with God since the moment of his call. The mountaintop exchanges with God are meant for the people of Israel, God's firstborn son (Exod. 4:22). So God pulls out all the stops: thunder and lightning, trumpets blaring, fire blazing, and thick clouds billowing. God's loving communication with the people of Israel assures them that "I AM WHO I AM" (Exod. 3:14) is with them.

Similarly, the preacher also might point out that, like Moses, Jesus does not "need" his encounter with God on the mountain (Matt. 17:1–9) to bolster his spiritual confidence or to enter into conversation with God. Nevertheless, God pulls out all the stops: the dazzling white robes of Jesus, his face shining like the sun, the appearance of Moses and Elijah. As in Exodus 24, the transfiguration of Jesus is meant entirely for the immediate benefit of Peter, James, and John, so that they may at least *begin* to understand the seamless relationship of Jesus to God the Father and the unlimited power behind it.

Along with the striking similarities of these two texts, there are significant differences. In Exodus, God's location is obviously separate from and external to Moses; God is located in the tabernacle. The stunning revelation in Matthew, of course, is the incarnation; God's location is in and with Jesus: "This is my Son, the Beloved; with him I am well pleased; listen to him!" (Matt. 17:5). While the purpose and mission of God may not have changed from the time of the exodus to the time of Jesus, the presence of God in Jesus is the epiphany of all epiphanies. God is no longer hidden in a cloud but mediated in the person of Jesus Christ. Now we see God face to face.

Exodus 24:12-18

Theological Perspective

in this life does not satisfy, but only increases the "desire to see more."[2]

As with other patristic commentators, in *Life of Moses* Gregory preferred to treat the Exodus narrative as grist for spiritual allegorizing rather than as a text with its own distinctive composition and message. Nonetheless, elements in Moses's life depicted in Exodus resonate with Gregory's theological vision of the contemplative search for union. Among other events, God calls Moses through the burning bush (3:2), during which Moses first hears God's word and glimpses his glory. Dramatic as the burning bush is, this moment of revelation represents the beginning of an unending search for God. Exodus ends with Moses's "work" finished (40:33) but the search for God incomplete. That this search continues for us is the result not of our striving but of God's grace.

Most of all, Gregory's interpretation of Moses's encounter with God on the mountain recounted in this passage rightly identified it as an iconic moment—as a moment in which Israel's new covenantal relation with God is embodied in Moses's meeting with God on the summit. This moment does not represent the final breaking away from human limitations and sin, as the rest of the narrative in Exodus makes clear, but it does represent a new moment of God's accessibility to Moses, and by extension to Israel and the rest of humanity, as a result of the covenant (24:1–11). The revelation of God on the mountain is truly a transfiguration, a moment in which the appearance of things is changed and transformed. Despite the themes of ethics and contemplation operating in the passage, the real moment that shines forth is not anything that Moses or Israel does, but what God out of mercy chooses to do as a result of the covenant with Israel. As an exemplar, Moses does not represent so much one who has mastered all virtue, as Gregory would have it, but one who walks with open ears and eyes, trusting in God's infinite grace.

WILLIAM JOSEPH DANAHER JR.

Pastoral Perspective

Consider two examples of how it has happened in this pastor's ministry. On the day of Edith's death, the sky was that low slate gray that usually means snow or freezing rain. The next day the temperature hovered in the low 30s. All day there was a light drizzle that froze on everything in sight. On that Monday and Tuesday the whole world appeared gray and depressing.

Then it happened! On the day of the funeral, shortly before the service, the sun came out with such brilliance that it was almost blinding. As we drove to the graveside, the road in the cemetery was lined with dogwoods whose branches met over the middle of the road. That day every limb was covered with ice and sparkled in the sunlight like a million tiny prisms, each reflecting a brilliant rainbow of colors. It was as if the whole world had been transformed into a crystal palace. Even the weeds and broom straw along the highway were covered with ice and sparkled like creation's most precious jewelry. It was an unforgettable scene. For a brief moment a world of dull, lifeless gray was transformed into what to eyes of faith could be seen as a brilliant foretaste of the new creation, a glimpse of a far greater transfiguration yet to come.

Consider another example. Toward the end of a committal service for a woman who had taken her own life, her husband poured a portion of his wife's ashes into the soil of the memorial garden, and their daughter poured the rest. As she was pouring the ashes, suddenly she exclaimed, "Look!" A butterfly had lit on a flower nearby. Throughout the rest of the service, it gracefully opened and closed its wings, as if offering its own silent benediction. When the service ended, the butterfly was gone. Was it a mere coincidence—a natural occurrence? Perhaps—and yet, even to one as hesitant as I am to make too much theologically of such experiences, for those of us gathered in that garden, burdened by a terrible weight of sorrow, amid the thick darkness of our grief, it was a minor epiphany indeed, a gracious parable of the final transfiguration, when all things will be made new, and the living God will wipe away every tear from our eyes (Rev. 21:4).

ALLEN C. MCSWEEN JR.

---

2. Gregory of Nyssa, *The Life of Moses*, trans. A. J. Malherbe and E. Ferguson (New York: Paulist Press, 1978), II.166, 96; II.227, 114; II.239, 116.

Exegetical Perspective

elders to wait. In the account of Moses's ascent, the text tells us the cloud, the glory of the LORD, descends on the mountain for six days (v. 16). It is not until the seventh day that God calls to Moses out of the cloud. Again, Moses moves and then awaits the word of God. With the seventh day begins another period of waiting. Moses is on the mountain for forty days, and for that time the children of Israel wait. The passage makes use of symbolic numbers. The six days of waiting followed by the seventh day when God calls evoke the six days of creation followed by the seventh day that God hallows, the Sabbath. Moses is on the mountain forty days. Forty years is a generation, and the forty days can suggest that the time Moses spends on the mountain represents the start of a new generation or era in the life of Israel.

. . . And I Will Give You Tablets of Stone. This greatly anticipated moment of Moses's receiving the tablets from God has been a long time coming. Our passage emphasizes Moses's ascent, who accompanies him on parts of the journey, and the physical manifestation of God on the mountain. Attention is given to God's manifestation both in the cloud and in the fire in verses 15, 16, and 17. This is more than a simple handoff—this is an encounter, an epiphany. It is no surprise that with the encounter there is torah/ teaching. As the geographic location suggests, God and humans do not regularly occupy the same realm. The chasm must be bridged. One way to do this is with the intermediary. Moses's role as the intermediary is altered with the gift of the torah. Now the keeping of the law is the foundation, the means by which Israel can enter into a relationship of encounter with God.

JUDY FENTRESS-WILLIAMS

Homiletical Perspective

What, the preacher might ask, is our human response? The people of Israel in Exodus respond with more disorientation and confusion than understanding. They rightfully and reasonably respond with holy fear. In their intense anxiety, they are woefully impatient. Unable to last the forty days while Moses is on top of the mountain with God, they start constructing the golden calf. Even Aaron caves in. The miracles that God performed to get the people out of Egypt seem to have been forgotten, and the larger picture of the vision and mission for and by the people of God is trumped by their fear.

The disciples also become impatient. They are confused, anxious, and, ironically, want exactly what they already have: the presence of God among them. Fear again trumps faith. Peter, who so frequently plays the role of our own weaknesses, will soon forget the miracles, the healings, and even the transfiguration, on the night of Jesus' arrest. Peter does as Aaron and the people of ancient Israel do: he turns his back to God.

Finally, these two texts prompt the preacher to raise a number of questions as the congregation embarks on its Lenten journey. When facing a wilderness without markers that is fraught with potential danger, are we tempted to let fear overwhelm our faith? Do we panic and begin to worship other, more instantly gratifying gods? With the abundant and gracious inbreaking of God into our lives, is our faith strengthened? Will we toss faith off when the crisis passes, because it has ceased to be of immediate use to us? Do we forget not only the witness of God's love, power, and favor, but also the cloud of witnesses throughout salvation history and in our own life?

If we would guard our epiphanies with our lives, as we guard our own children, then our faith might be strengthened step by step along the way of our pilgrimage, until we find ourselves headed toward the promised land that is the kingdom of God.

ERICA BROWN WOOD

Psalm 2

¹Why do the nations conspire,
  and the peoples plot in vain?
²The kings of the earth set themselves,
  and the rulers take counsel together,
  against the LORD and his anointed, saying,
³"Let us burst their bonds asunder,
  and cast their cords from us."

⁴He who sits in the heavens laughs;
  the LORD has them in derision.
⁵Then he will speak to them in his wrath,
  and terrify them in his fury, saying,
⁶"I have set my king on Zion, my holy hill."

⁷I will tell of the decree of the LORD:

Theological Perspective

This royal psalm celebrating the authority of YHWH and YHWH's anointed one, the Davidic king of Israel, naturally attracted considerable attention among early Christian interpreters. The announcement of verse 7, "You are my son," is obviously significant as a hermeneutical clue regarding divine speech throughout the Christian (or New) Testament. Indeed, from a Christian theological perspective, the psalm is particularly interesting for its Trinitarian hues and potential.

The political powers of this world are portrayed here as aligning themselves against the God of Israel and God's king, whom God places securely "on Zion, my holy hill" (v. 6). But their resistance is futile—so futile, in fact, that God "who sits in the heavens laughs" (v. 4). It is noteworthy that while YHWH "sits in the heavens" bemused by the rebellion of puny humans (v. 4), the anointed one "sits" authoritatively on the earth; this anointed figure, the king, need only ask of God to receive these recalcitrant nations as his "heritage, and the ends of the earth [his] possession" (v. 8). Jesus' great commission, we might say, is our charge to make it so. It is hardly surprising that the church traditionally has read this psalm with a blatantly christological lens.

This, however, does not imply that such a reading is easily accomplished. Of course, the direct address,

Pastoral Perspective

Psalm 2 is widely understood to be a royal psalm that most likely was composed for a royal coronation in Jerusalem. It refers to earthly kings (vv. 1–3) and includes words of consecration (vv. 7–9) and instruction (vv. 10–11). Since the days of the early church, Christians have understood the reference to the "anointed one" (v. 2) and to the Lord's son (v. 7) as foretelling Jesus Christ as the Messiah who is divinely enthroned after his resurrection.[1]

With this ancient context in mind, Psalm 2 has much to offer as we consider rulers and their use of power in our contemporary world. Verses 1–3 attest to the tendency of those in positions of authority to abuse their power. Throughout history and now, we see examples of this. Sometimes these abuses are atrocities, such as genocide committed under the regime of a dictator. Other times, as we see more often in the United States, the abuses are more subtle—the politician who takes a lavish trip on the taxpayers' dime, for example.

Even if we are not monarchs or elected officials, Psalm 2 includes warnings for us as well. All of us have power of some sort, and inherent in us is that same human tendency to crave power. The famous

1. Carroll Stuhlmueller, "Psalms," in *Harper Collins Bible Commentary*, ed. James L. Mays with the Society of Biblical Literature (San Francisco: Harper Collins, 2000), 396–97.

He said to me, "You are my son;
today I have begotten you.
⁸Ask of me, and I will make the nations your heritage,
and the ends of the earth your possession.
⁹You shall break them with a rod of iron,
and dash them in pieces like a potter's vessel."

¹⁰Now therefore, O kings, be wise;
be warned, O rulers of the earth.
¹¹Serve the LORD with fear,
with trembling ¹²kiss his feet,
or he will be angry, and you will perish in the way;
for his wrath is quickly kindled.

Happy are all who take refuge in him.

Exegetical Perspective

This messianic poem is one of ancient Israel's royal psalms, an eclectic collection of psalms concerning the Davidic king (including Pss. 18, 20, 21, 45, 72, 89, 101, 110, and 132). Scholars speculate that Psalm 2 was used as an ancient Israelite coronation liturgy, although there is no direct evidence for such enthronement rites in Jerusalem. This royal psalm celebrates the secure dominion of the Israelite king enthroned in Zion and his intimate relationship with the Lord enthroned in heaven.

Lacking a title or header, the psalm consists of four strophes with good poetic form and rhetorical structure. There is no formal identification of the multiple voices (foreign rulers, God, and the Davidic king) within the text, and it is possible that the entire psalm was originally spoken by the king in a cultic setting. The first strophe (vv. 1–3) depicts the futile plotting of the world's rulers against the rule of the Lord and his earthly representative, the king of Israel. The second section (vv. 4–6) describes God's derisive contempt for their impotent rebellion. The third stanza (vv. 7–9) rehearses the installation of the king in his own voice, recounting his coronation and divine promises of earthly sovereignty. The final strophe (vv. 10–12) exhorts the foreign kings to submit to divine authority, lest they be consumed by God's blazing

Homiletical Perspective

This psalm, like several others, predicts the anointing of God's chosen king. It may be just another in a series of kings, or it may be the promised Messiah. Certainly, Christians have historically read this text through a messianic lens (see Acts 13:33 and Heb. 1:5). As a result, this psalm offers a host of homiletical possibilities.[1]

On the surface, it features a warning to the rulers of the earth, who have placed themselves in opposition to God and God's people (vv. 1–3). The psalm takes on additional meaning, however, when considered in the context of the readings for Transfiguration Sunday. On this day we remember the experience of Moses on Mount Sinai, as recorded in Exodus, and the mountaintop anointing of Jesus, as recorded in the Synoptic Gospels.

The more obvious parallel is between Psalm 2 and the Gospel story of the transfiguration. Both describe God's anointing of a chosen one. The psalmist identifies the king as anointed (v. 2), and goes on to quote God as declaring, "You are my son; today I have begotten you" (v. 7). The story of the transfiguration echoes these words, as God's voice breaks through the clouds and similarly names Jesus

1. C. S. Rodd, "Psalms," in *The Oxford Bible Commentary*, ed. John Barton and John Muddiman (Oxford: Oxford University Press, 2001), 367.

Psalm 2

Theological Perspective

"You are my son," is picked up in the Synoptic Gospels' testimony about Jesus' baptism by John in the Jordan, but none of those testimonies extends the quotation any further, to include this psalm's "today I have begotten you." This did not discourage early proponents of an adoptionist Christology from making that very connection, that it was at Jesus' baptism that he was "begotten" by God, made to be God's own Son. Indeed, from the point of view of the development of Christology, part of the problem is the juxtaposition of "today" and "begotten." On the one hand, early theologians came to favor the imagery that the Son was and is "begotten" by the Father, against the Arian teaching that the Son was created by God; "begotten and not made" is the anti-Arian language of Nicaea. On the other hand, "today" implies the category of creaturely time, not at all conducive to the church's strong insistence upon the true deity of the Son. "Today I have begotten you" (v. 7b) plays havoc with these doctrinal rules.

Interestingly, in a christological reading of Psalm 2 we should note that the anointed one, the son, is actually the one who speaks beginning at verse 7: "I will tell of the decree of the LORD: He said to me, 'You are my son . . .'" It is YHWH who speaks the begetting decree, but it is the begotten one who quotes YHWH. Indeed, we may add another layer. In Acts 4, a prayer offered by a group of Christian disciples begins, "Sovereign Lord, who made the heaven and the earth, the sea, and everything in them, it is you who said by the Holy Spirit through our ancestor David, your servant: 'Why did the Gentiles rage?'" (vv. 24–25).

The text begins to drop these Trinitarian hints. In this psalm that God the Holy Spirit utters, God the Father announces "I have set my king on Zion, my holy hill" and God the Son responds "I will tell of the decree of the LORD" (vv. 6, 7). Similarly, perhaps, the Gospels gesture toward a Trinitarian logic of divine activity in Jesus' baptismal experience, during which he hears the divine decree, "You are my Son, the Beloved; with you I am well pleased" (Mark 1:11).

Of course it is not only in his baptism that Jesus hears this divine announcement. In the Synoptics' story of Jesus' transfiguration, Psalm 2 is reiterated. This time, however, the address is directed not toward the Anointed One but instead toward his inner circle of disciples: "This is my Son, the Beloved; listen to him!" (Mark 9:7). The decree is reverberating beyond Jesus to call these disciples to a reverence much like what Psalm 2 prescribes: "Serve the LORD with fear, with trembling kiss his feet"

Pastoral Perspective

Stanford prison experiment illustrates this. In 1971, a Stanford psychologist and his team of researchers wanted to learn more about the psychological effects of being a prison guard or a prisoner. They had students live in a mock prison. After just a few days, some of the "guards" became sadistic, and many of the "prisoners" began to show signs of depression and extreme stress after being subjected to brutal treatment. The results were so disconcerting that the psychologist was concerned about the well-being of those involved and consequently terminated the study early. Since then, the experiment has been an archetype for how quickly our desire for power can corrupt the humanity for which we were made.

Psalm 2 reminds us of this danger. Like the ancient kings of Jerusalem, we are accountable for how we use the power we are given. In response to the behavior of the earthly kings and rulers who set themselves against the Lord, verse 5 says, "Then he will speak to them in his wrath, and terrify them in his fury." Abuses of power are abuses not only against those without power, but also against our God, who desires justice and mercy.

How are we called to use and understand our power? The psalm offers instruction for this: "Now therefore, O kings, be wise; be warned, O rulers of the earth. Serve the LORD with fear, with trembling" (vv. 10–11). Leading or holding power of any kind must be understood as serving God. Too often, people profess a humble faith and attend church on Sunday, while failing to live out that faith in their use of power Monday through Friday. Our faith must determine how we use our power; the two are inseparable. In fact, is this not the case for all aspects of our lives? The journey of discipleship asks that we devote all that we do to serving God.

Again, according to the psalm we are called to serve with fear and trembling. The psalmist says that if we do not, the Lord will be angry (v. 12). However, we know that our God is merciful and forgiving, for we have received the good news of Jesus Christ. Our fear and trembling should be rooted not in fear of a punitive God, but rather in a sense of awe at the utter power of God.

It is not a coincidence that Psalm 2 is the appointed psalm for Transfiguration Sunday. There are, of course, many biblical accounts of God's power, but the story of the transfiguration in Matthew 17:1–9 is one of the most profound. Certainly witnessing the dramatic change in Jesus and the appearance of Moses and Elijah and hearing the booming voice of God through a cloud on the

anger. The psalm closes with a beatitude for those who take refuge in YHWH.

The poem opens with a rhetorical question, taunting the nations for their foolish and impotent conspiracies against the power and authority of the Israelite God and his king (cf. Ps. 83, a less bemused depiction of conspiracies against Israel). As a coronation psalm, the text affirms the consolidation of the new king's power in the face of rebellious vassals. Verse 2 identifies both "the LORD and his anointed" as those against whom the nations illegitimately rebel. The "anointed" or messiah (*mashiach*) is a royal title in ancient Israel (see Ps. 18:50; 1 Sam. 12:3; 24:6; 26:9; 2 Sam. 1:14; 23:1), although in later Jewish and Christian tradition (e.g., Acts 4:25–26) it signifies an eschatological savior.

The psalm's second strophe (vv. 4–6) provides a harsh and theologically challenging image of a contemptuous and wrathful God. God's derisive laughter at human vanity (v. 4) is also found in Psalms 37:13 and 59:8 (cf. Job 9:23). Verse 5 portrays the terrifying fury of a God on the verge of breaking out against humanity in wrathful destruction. This harsh rhetoric is meant to support the imperial aims of the Israelite king, who rules from Zion as God's surrogate. The NRSV does not adequately reflect the emphasis in God's declaration in verse 6, "I myself established my king" (my trans.), in response to challenges to divine sovereignty.

The psalm's most remarkable line (v. 7) quotes a divine oracle to the king: "I will tell of the decree of the LORD: He said to me, 'You are my son; today I [myself] have begotten you.'" The text employs the common verb for giving birth or fathering children (*yld*) and again emphasizes God's direct involvement with the (redundant) first-person pronoun. Although ancient Near Eastern ideas of divine kingship sometimes depict a physical relationship between the gods and the king, ancient Israelite royal ideology's use of the metaphor is better described as adoption.[1] It is likely that this line was part of an ancient cultic rite in which the Davidic king was formally adopted by God to act as "son" or representative (see also 2 Sam. 7:14 and Ps. 89:26–27). The NT quotes Psalm 2:7 as testimony to Jesus as the Son of God, in Acts 13:33; Hebrews 1:5; 5:5 (see also Acts 4:25–26). God identifies Jesus as "my Son" at his baptism and transfiguration (Mark 1:11; 9:7; and parallels).

the beloved son (Matt. 17:5). A preacher might choose to highlight the coincidence between the two texts, focusing on the history and evolution of the messianic tradition.

Psalm 2 envisions God's chosen king as a powerful military leader, ready to conquer the nations of the earth with the aid of God's wrathful fury (vv. 5–6, 8–9). This is one image of the expected Messiah; indeed, it is the dominant image recorded in Hebrew Scripture. With a few notable exceptions, this is also the vision of leadership most commonly embraced by the Israelite kings and proclaimed by the prophets. This is the Messiah for whom they longed.

Jesus would not conform to this expectation, however. He would not become the type of Messiah that Israel anticipated. In a sense, Psalm 2 paints a picture of the path not chosen. Again and again, Jesus rejects the mantle of a powerful, militaristic Messiah. We see this most notably in the familiar Gospel story of the temptation of Jesus, a temptation that this psalm almost foreshadows. Consider verses 8–9 of the psalm, in which God promises to grant the king possession over the ends of the earth and power over the nations. Place those verses alongside the dramatic scene from Luke's Gospel, where the devil shows Jesus the kingdoms of the world and suggests that they could all be his (Luke 4:5–7). You can almost see the devil's sinister smile as he makes his appeal. Ironically, the psalm mirrors that image, only it is God's laughter that we hear, mocking the feeble rulers of the nations (v. 4).

The Gospels tell us that Jesus rebukes the devil. Jesus has come to reveal a different kingdom, one defined not by power and might, but by humility and servanthood. Likewise, in the Gospel story of the transfiguration, Jesus signals that his mission is not about earthly glory. He does not stay long on that blessed mountaintop, basking in radiance. Instead, he leads the disciples back down the mountain, because he knows that his throne is not of this world, and that his true glory will be revealed on the cross.

Jesus does indeed become a king on a holy hill (Ps. 2:6), but it is the hill of Golgotha, not Zion. That day, he is clothed in shame, not in splendor. That day, we hear not God, laughing in derision (v. 4), but rather the crowds, mocking Jesus. That day, all messianic expectations are overturned, as the anointed one is crucified.

This contrast—between the expected Messiah foreshadowed by Psalm 2 and the unexpected Messiah that Jesus becomes—is fruitful material for a sermon. This reversal of human expectations is a key

---

1. On the ancient Near Eastern idea of "divine kingship" and the Israelite king's title "son of God," see conveniently Hans-Joachim Kraus, *Psalms 1–59: A Commentary*, trans. Hilton C. Oswald (Minneapolis: Augsburg, 1988), 130–32.

Psalm 2

Theological Perspective

(2:11–12). We should note that older translations, including the KJV and the NIV, translate the infamously ambiguous Hebrew here "kiss the Son." The church, early and often, has read this as a warning to the nations to render appropriate worship and honor to Jesus Christ, God's Son, as Lord over all earthly rulers and their peoples. In the Gospels, when God speaks, it is to announce Jesus as the beloved Son to whom honor and obedience are due (cf. Phil. 2:9–11).

At both Jesus' baptism and his transfiguration, the divine declaration of Psalm 2 provided the early disciples with the validation of scriptural precedent. And there is yet another moment in Jesus' history that benefits from the echoes of the second psalm. In Acts 13 Paul preaches in the synagogue in Antioch of Pisidia that "God raised him from the dead. . . . We bring you the good news that what God promised to our ancestors he has fulfilled for us, their children, by raising Jesus; as also it is written in the second psalm, 'You are my Son; today I have begotten you'" (13:30, 32–33). Even more explicitly than with Jesus' baptism or transfiguration, the New Testament associates this royal coronation hymn with God's raising of Jesus from death.

The point is not so much that there is a particular moment, a "today," in which God has begotten Jesus the beloved Son. Instead, the announcement "You are my Son" is the fundamental and paradigmatic divine speech for all of the Christian Testament. As the early Christian movement reflected on these moments in Jesus' history when that speech reverberated, the conviction eventually emerged that no one moment—in time or in eternity—can be isolated as the moment of the Father's begetting of the Son. Instead, their relation is characterized as an eternal begetting, a timeless generation, a perduring love.

MICHAEL E. LODAHL

Pastoral Perspective

mountaintop evoke fear and trembling in Peter, James, and John (Matt. 7:6)! This no doubt left them more than convinced of God's power.

Furthermore, Jesus' response to this extraordinary event serves as a model for how we should use our own power. He gently tells his disciples not to be afraid and leads them down the mountain to continue his ministry. Through his life and in his death, Jesus channels his power not for his own glory, but in service and obedience to God. He perfects the kind of ruling that Psalm 2 admonishes the rulers of the earth to embody.

The story of the transfiguration illustrates the message of Psalm 2. Whatever earthly power we may have ultimately is nothing compared to the power of God. Our human sense of being in control is an illusion, as the disciples learned that day on the mountain. This is not a loss. Rather, the knowledge that it is God—not we—who is in control comes as a huge relief. This relinquishing of power is the joy of the life of faith. While we are called to serve with fear and trembling and awe at the mighty power of God, we do so with the peace that comes with knowing everything rests in the hands of our loving, liberating, and life-giving God. As the psalm concludes, "Happy are all who take refuge in him" (v. 12).

ANDREA WIGODSKY

Exegetical Perspective

Universal dominion over the "ends of the earth" (v. 8) is formulaic and hyperbolic rhetoric (cf. Ps. 110). The royal psalm Psalm 72:8–9 has similar language: "May he have dominion from sea to sea, and from the [Euphrates] River to the ends of the earth. May his foes bow down before him, and his enemies lick the dust." Verse 9, which nicely contrasts the ruler's iron scepter with brittle pottery, is quoted in Revelation 2:27 (cf. Rev. 12:5 and 19:15).

The final strophe exhorts the rulers of the earth to "be wise" and submit to divine sovereignty. The meaning of verses 11b–12a is unclear. There are three main tendencies in modern translation. The first is to take the word *bar* in verse 12 as an Aramaic loanword and translate verses 11–12 as "Serve the LORD with fear and rejoice with trembling. Kiss the Son lest he be angry . . ." (NIV). The capitalization of "Son" (as in the KJV) seems christological. The Aramaic *bar*, "son," is attested three times in the Hebrew Bible (all in Prov. 31:2), although Psalm 2 uses the Hebrew *ben* for "son" in its declaration in verse 7.

A second approach (since at least Jerome) retains the Masoretic Text and understands *bar* as a Hebrew word for "pure," here meaning "purely" or "sincerely." The NJPS thus translates verses 11b–12a "tremble with fright, pay homage in good faith," noting that the Hebrew is uncertain.

The NRSV follows a modern reordering of the consonantal text (*wbr'dh nhqw brglyw*) to read "with trembling kiss his feet." Kissing the feet of the sovereign is a well-known act of submission in ancient Near Eastern sources, but the phrase is not otherwise attested in the Hebrew Bible, which instead refers to "licking the dust" before a king (Ps. 72:9; Isa. 49:23; Mic. 7:17). Whichever translation is preferred, the text explains that failure to show proper deference to God (or God's Son) will result in divine anger. Rulers who fail to "serve" (*'abad*) God will "perish" (*'abad*) in their way.

The psalm concludes with a beatitude (cf. Ps. 1:1) on those who take refuge in the Lord.

NEAL H. WALLS

Homiletical Perspective

element of the scriptural narrative, but it remains counterintuitive. It was hard for people of Jesus' day to understand, and it is hard for us today. We spend so much time and energy striving for success, for esteem, for power and control; that is how we define our earthly kingdoms. In contrast, Jesus' life and mission are defined by a relinquishing of power and a sacrificial journey toward death. We confess and somehow believe that God acted in him to overcome death with life. In his journey toward the cross, Jesus, the unexpected Messiah, reveals a kingdom more eternal and more powerful than any the world has known.

Among twentieth-century Christian writers, Mennonite theologian John Howard Yoder stands out in his analysis of this unexpected kingdom and its lessons for us. In *The Politics of Jesus* Yoder demonstrates how Jesus defies the traditional expectations of the Messiah and forges a different kind of kingdom, the kingdom of God. This kingdom does not depend on military might or economic prowess, but rather is made known through concern for the poor, justice for the oppressed, love for friends and enemies alike.[2] In this kingdom, Jesus introduces a new social ethic, rooted not in a quest for power and control, but in a commitment to servanthood and sacrifice.[3] It is truly an upside-down kingdom, where the last shall be first, and where suffering and death lie unavoidably on the path toward joy and lasting life.

A preacher may want to explore further the discussion of this new kingdom and this new social ethic, considering the implications for Christians today. Which type of Messiah do we follow and worship? To which kind of kingdom do we give our allegiance? How can we lessen our thirst for power and prestige, and become better servants of God?

JOHN D. ROHRS

---

2. John Howard Yoder, *The Politics of Jesus* (2nd ed., Grand Rapids: Eerdmans, 1994), 32.
3. Ibid., 38–39.

2 Peter 1:16-21

¹⁶For we did not follow cleverly devised myths when we made known to you the power and coming of our Lord Jesus Christ, but we had been eyewitnesses of his majesty. ¹⁷For he received honor and glory from God the Father when that voice was conveyed to him by the Majestic Glory, saying, "This is my Son, my Beloved, with whom I am well pleased." ¹⁸We ourselves heard this voice come from heaven, while we were with him on the holy mountain.

¹⁹So we have the prophetic message more fully confirmed. You will do well to be attentive to this as to a lamp shining in a dark place, until the day dawns and the morning star rises in your hearts. ²⁰First of all you must understand this, that no prophecy of scripture is a matter of one's own interpretation, ²¹because no prophecy ever came by human will, but men and women moved by the Holy Spirit spoke from God.

Theological Perspective

The Sunday of the Transfiguration is one of the major Trinitarian observances of the church year. Second Peter focuses on Christ's future return in glory, of which the transfiguration is a kind of foretaste.

History and Theology. Peter first defends the historical nature of the manifestation of Jesus' glory. Christ's "power and [future] coming [*parousia*]" is not a fabricated story or myth, since Peter, James, and John witnessed Christ's divine glory with their own eyes at the transfiguration (1:16; see 1:3). It is crucial for Christians to remember that Christ is deeply historical: he lived a human life and died a human death within the embodied and social parameters of this world, most specifically within the promises of God's covenant with Israel.

As many theologians have noted, if Jesus did not live a real human life, body and soul, then Christians are without hope for the salvation of their historical and bodily existence (the error of Docetism: see 1 John 4:1–3; 2 John 7). Similarly, it is a mistake to hold that Christ can be understood only in nonhistorical terms, whether as a mythic figure or the "Christ of faith," as distinct from the "Jesus of history." The Christian hope of God's final deliverance of creation depends entirely on Christ's manifestation of God's glory in the fragile and chaotic realm of human history.

Pastoral Perspective

Most have been in gatherings where someone asked the question: "Where were you when such and such happened?" For decades to come, many of us will hold fast to vivid memories of where we were and what we doing early in the morning of September 11, 2001. Sometimes, however, these defining memories do not function to bind people together, but rather demarcate generational differences and define different perspectives on history, if not on life itself.

Each January and April many of us remember, if not relive, the death of Martin Luther King Jr. This writer can remember where he was when he learned of the assassination of President Kennedy and later, his brother Robert Kennedy. I remember these events most poignantly when I am trying to convey the feeling and impact of them to someone who was not alive then. In turn, it has taken me many years to understand the impact of the Depression upon the lives and perspective of my parents, affecting their attitudes toward work and money, thrift and property. "You do not buy anything until you can pay for it with cash or a check!"

We all have experiences that anchor our lives, shape our values, and define our commitments. We find it frustrating when our narration of these experiences does not seem to influence the behavior of others, as if our stories could have the same impact

Exegetical Perspective

A rock concert? A sound and light show? Fourth of July fireworks? Those images come to mind when the Bible speaks about God appearing on Mount Sinai (Exod. 19:16–19) or the dazzling appearance of Jesus on the mountain of the transfiguration (Matt. 17:1–8). One always has to "come down" from such moments of religious ecstasy. The Israelites spend forty years in the wilderness, more complaining than in awe of the One who liberated them from slavery. The disciples will face the harshness of the passion that will expose their "little faith." To what extent can the memory of events in which the curtain of reality is pulled back to glimpse the glory of God inform our faith? That is the question which this final Sunday after the Epiphany, Transfiguration Sunday, poses.

Its vocabulary, sources (Jude), and engagement with Epicurean philosophy indicate that 2 Peter was not by Peter himself but by a teacher in the Petrine tradition. Disputes over understanding Paul's letters (3:15–16) suggest a crisis early in the second century CE. The author presents this letter as a final testimony of Peter, "servant and apostle of Jesus Christ" (1:1, 13–15). Its purpose is to provide a sure compass for authentic Christian faith amid the conflicting voices and false teaching that surround readers. Similar "last testaments" are associated with Paul in the farewell address to the Ephesian elders (Acts

Homiletical Perspective

The passage presents us with such a thicket of thorny questions about truth and myth, the authority of Scripture, and the second coming that many preachers have preferred to hike around it rather than try to pick their way through. For the intrepid soul, however, there are a number of themes that will preach.

First, 2 Peter adds an additional layer to the interpretations of the transfiguration that appear in the Gospels. Here the transfiguration does not reveal Jesus' secret identity or prefigure his resurrection, but affirms—perhaps even commissions—him as the divine agent of eschatological judgment. Jesus holds the future. If you are preaching in a congregation that is accustomed to hearing about end-time theology, the passage can contribute to a broad form of reassurance that the preexistent Jesus (John 1:1) is not only with us to the end of the age (Matt. 28:20), but also reaches out from the horizon of time with the arms of grace—accountability, yes, but grace nonetheless.

Even in congregations where the second coming is understood in a more metaphorical or process-oriented way, such as "Jesus is always coming to us," the passage can help us to expand our view of Jesus' transfiguration and its impact across time. The witness of Jesus' luminous life is an essential way that God continues to reframe our present-day activities

2 Peter 1:16-21

Theological Perspective

At the same time, Peter proclaims that Jesus reveals the *divine* glory—even if only partially, since creatures can never fully behold the face of God (Exod. 33:20). In the transfiguration Jesus shows his true identity as God's divine Son, an identity that derives from and points beyond this world. To behold the glory of God in Jesus Christ requires, above all, the kind of understanding that we call faith, which is made possible only through Christ's death and resurrection and the coming of the Holy Spirit. In faith, Christians see that the human being Jesus is not merely human. Christ can never be limited by the canons of human knowledge—particularly if we consider how little we understand about ourselves and the world in which we live! To know Christ as God's Son is ultimately a theological act, based on God's revelation in human history.

Christ the Coming One. The glory of Christ revealed in the transfiguration is much more than Jesus' divine status per se, as if this were a static thing. It is divine nature of the One who is to return and save the world at the end time. Peter specifically defends the message of Christ's future return against some who dispute its reality (see esp. 2 Peter 3). The Christian faith is not simply faith in Christ who lived, died, and rose for us at one time, but faith in that same Christ *who is still to come*, as foretold by the prophets. This means that far from having completed our moral and spiritual growth, Christians are constantly being transformed into Christ's future glory (see 2 Cor. 3:18). The divine nature and glory is always future driven, as it were, and the vision of God is a vision of God's future for us in Christ. In this sense, our faith is inherently unfinished (see 1 Cor. 13:12–13), yet at the same time boldly expectant, as we "wait for new heavens and a new earth, where righteousness is at home" (2 Pet. 3:13).

The Glory of the Trinity. When Christ reveals his majesty on the mountain and God the Father proclaims him as his beloved Son, we are shown the deepest truth of who Jesus is. Lifting the veil of his self-emptying just a bit, Jesus reveals that he has been given the divine nature of God the Father himself, who is the "Majestic Glory" (2 Pet. 1:17; see Deut. 33:26 LXX). Peter's witness to Christ's glory from God the Father is similar to that of John: "We beheld his glory, the glory as of the only begotten [*monogenēs*] of the Father" (John 1:14 KJV). Christ's self-revelation in the transfiguration, which can be perceived only through the Holy Spirit (1 Cor. 2:11;

Pastoral Perspective

as the experiences themselves. The writer of 2 Peter relates the event of the transfiguration as an experience that anchors his life and specifically frames his understanding of the "prophetic message" (v. 19).

This personal reference lies at the center of the writer's concern for the well-being and spiritual growth of his readers. It is grounded in an understanding of the role of memory in the development of the personality going forward, but also in the legacy of a person looking backward. Many people, in anticipation of their death, in addition to leaving a will that legally disposes of their remaining assets, leave another document—a "living legacy," if you will—that speaks to the values, experiences, and commitments that have animated and guided their lives. Second Peter is meant to be such a document and to function as such a legacy: "that after my departure you may be able at any time to recall these things" (1:15b). It is worth reading through the epistle and noting all the occasions when the author uses a word that means "remember" or "do not forget." Memory, the practice of remembering, is in the service of persevering, of persisting, of growing in constancy.

More than simply remembering, humans make plans, give promises, and take vows as ways of investing themselves in the future—and more importantly, as a way of creating a life of relationships. The mystery two people enter into when they marry is ritualized in a ceremony that is more than the exchange of vows. To accept and trust a promise is to enter into a covenant with time.

Likewise, the Christian life is a matter of "choosing to be chosen" and so entering into a covenant with eternity. The epistle writer urges readers to "confirm your call and election" (1:10), a covenant enacted in the forgiveness that is the gospel of Christ's ministry. To live in the faith that we are forgiven is to live in anticipation of "new heavens and a new earth" (3:13). The author of 2 Peter knows that, given the circumstances of life and the various temptations within a world at odds with God's purposes, the life of faith requires memory and hope, persistence and perseverance, if it is to manifest a constancy that achieves the level of character. "Faith" needs to be more than assent or acquiescence; it needs to actualize itself as—well, as all of the behaviors that are enumerated in 1:5–7. These behaviors are what faith will look like. Paradoxically, they are also what faith evokes, the faith that accepts the "call and election" as the gift of divine promise. If there were not a paradoxical relationship between faith and these other behaviors,

20:17–37) and 2 Timothy. The memory of an apostle's teaching and example is necessary for all the generations of Christians to come, "so that after my departure you may be able at any time to recall these things" (1:15).

Second Peter also answers specific challenges to Christian belief that Jesus would come in glory to exercise God's just judgment (as in 1 Thess. 1:9b–10). Therefore this selection has the form of a defense for that belief against arguments directed at believers that are described in 2 Peter 3:3–4: "scoffers will come . . . saying, 'Where is the promise of his coming? . . . All things continue as they were from the beginning of creation.'" That objection, coupled with the statement that the opponents promise freedom but are entangled by their passions (2:19) and that they deny the stories of God's creation through the word that sustains the world until the day of judgment (3:5–7), suggests that the opponents appealed to Epicurean slogans.

Epicureans taught that the world originated in the random movements of atoms in the empty space. They denied any possibility of life after death. They also rejected both religious and philosophical accounts of the world that understood its order to be based on a divine (or rational) intelligence. Therefore they claimed to free humans from ideas of divine providence, fate, and myths of divine punishment. Consequently people should arrange their lives to have as much pleasure and as little pain as possible.

Today's passage, which opens the reply to this attack, mentions two slanders against Christian beliefs. First, opponents argued that it is ridiculous for Christians to claim Jesus as the future judge of all humanity (1:16–18); second, they charged that in a world without any ordering divine intelligence, prophecy is meaningless (1:19–21). Second Peter does not refute these points by turning to one of the other philosophical schools, such as Platonism or Stoicism, that disagreed with the Epicurean views. Instead, it adopts the style of legal rhetoric, as though Christian teachers had been brought to trial for deceiving people with their teaching.

Consequently, the first item in the argument for the truth of Christian faith is the eyewitness testimony of the apostle Peter (1:16–18). Although the Gospels make a narrative connection between the story of Jesus' transfiguration (Matt. 17:1–7) and predictions of his suffering death that link it with resurrection, 2 Peter uses the story as evidence for Jesus' future coming as judge. Against the view that stories about the gods were "myths" spun out of

in light of God's priorities—like "a lamp shining in a dark place" (v. 19). What is more, God's resilient, persistent love is always coming to us. We can trust that it resides in our future—before we even know what tragedies and errors await—as much as in our present or our past. By the account of 2 Peter, we can glimpse that in the transfiguration.

Next, some congregations may be able to handle the possibility that this passage is deeply ironic. That is, the writer of 2 Peter is slamming "cleverly devised myths" (v. 16) in favor of eyewitness testimony, even as the pseudonymous writer himself is most likely using the Gospel stories to *imagine* how Peter might have written about Jesus' transfiguration. There is a certain dry humor in that, if you can tease it out. In a postmodern era when more and more voices suggest that one person's truth is another person's cleverly devised myth, the irony seems worth exploring. What happens when the distinction between myth and confirming testimony begins to break down? Can we speak openly today about Christian mythmaking, or about the interpretive lens of *any* eyewitness, and still affirm the value of a tradition that bases many of its claims upon its stories about apostolic witnesses?

The epistle writer's methods challenge us to think carefully about how we ourselves will hand on the transfiguration story to new generations. What does it mean to be a witness? What does the crucial shift from inheriting the tradition to becoming witnesses ourselves look like in our context, for our congregation? What would we be willing to claim as the truth of the transfiguration?

Related to this is another thorny issue of authority: the epistle's contrast between "one's own interpretation" of Scripture and interpretation that is divinely inspired. The complexity of such things as an author's social location or the historical conditions when a text was produced can make us nostalgic for a simpler time. Remember when an epistle writer could dismiss challenges to his view of Scripture by saying that he and those who shared his view were "moved by the Spirit"? If it is not that clear-cut nowadays, then how do we remain open to the inspiration of the Spirit without exercising a form of denial about our own interpretive lenses? How do we acknowledge our interpretive lenses without surrendering our openness to the Spirit? How, for example, do we speak with integrity and sensitivity about texts of the living Jewish faith, texts that for the epistle writer spoke prophetically of Christ?

This issue may seem like nothing more than a burdensome problem, but it provides us with one of

2 Peter 1:16-21

Theological Perspective

12:3), is thus a revelation of the eternal life of the Trinity given from the Father to the Son and the Holy Spirit, a revelation that remains focused on Christ and rooted in the biblical covenants.

The Confirmation of Scripture. The transfiguration of Christ, finally, shows that the Scriptures are "extremely reliable," having been written by people who were "moved by the Holy Spirit" to speak from God about Christ (1:19, 21). Here again we have a Trinitarian framework. Just as Moses and Elijah (the Law and the Prophets) accompanied Jesus at the transfiguration, so the light of Christ shines especially through the Scriptures of the Old Testament (1:19), as well as the apostolic writings of the New Testament (3:16). Perceiving the full meaning of Scripture, then, goes together with faith in Christ (see also 2 Cor. 3; Rom. 15:8). Scripture cannot be understood in merely human ways, either as a purely human creation (as the NIV; see 1:21; Jer. 23:16) or as subject to just any private interpretation divorced from the larger mind of the church (the RSV and NRSV; see 2:1; 3:16). Peter's point is extremely practical: It is in the Scriptures above all that we find the light of Christ to illuminate the darkness of our lives every day. As the Venerable Bede comments on this passage, "In the night of this world, so full of dark temptations, where there is hardly anyone who does not sin, what would become of us if we did not have the lamp of the prophetic word?"[1]

On this great Trinitarian feast, 2 Peter urges us to look for the illumination of God's future glory, as revealed to the disciples at the transfiguration of Christ and mediated to us today by the Holy Spirit through Holy Scriptures. In this way the Holy Trinity will transform us more and more fully into the divine glory (see 2 Cor. 3:18) until Christ, the Daystar, rises fully in our hearts (1:19; see Luke 1:78; Rev. 2:28).

CHRISTOPHER A. BEELEY

Pastoral Perspective

they would constitute a rather daunting, even boring list of shoulds and oughts.

William Sloane Coffin used to sermonize powerfully on the question, Who tells you who you are? Good question! Our behavior testifies to our sense of self, which is too often a construct of actions and words that say everything from "I will never amount to much" to "I am better than anyone else." The author of 2 Peter wants his readers to remember who they are and what they are called to be. Maybe that is why he tells a story about the manifestation of Christ's identity in the transfiguration, and not in the resurrection. It is a story about the author's knowing who he is, how he is blessed, and what he is called to do . . . in spite of what lies ahead.

I have two sons. I have shared with them what it was like to witness their births. I knew immediately how different they were. I have told them how they looked and behaved, how hopeful I was for them, how pleased I was to be their father—and how afraid I was for myself, not knowing how to be the father they needed and deserved. That was my experience. More importantly I have also had to say over the years, with words and deeds, that they were very "promising" and that I believed in their promise. It was their task and adventure to discern where that promise might take them.

The pastoral life of the church involves the reminding and remembering of the "call and election" that claim us and tells us who we are. It reminds us how promising our lives really are in light of those "precious and very great promises" (1:4). It does not reduce life to the cultivation of a privatized character. It echoes the heavenly "This is my beloved child," confessing and anticipating the promise of a new heaven and new earth.

DWIGHT M. LUNDGREN

---

1. Bede, *On 2 Peter* in *Patrologia Latina, Patrologiae Cursus Completus. Series Latina,* ed. J. P. Migne (Paris: 1844–64), 93.73.

Exegetical Perspective

human hopes and fears, the witness testifies that he and the others heard God's own voice proclaim Jesus the beloved Son. Of course, this argument would not convince an Epicurean, but it would remind the Christian readers that their faith is based on actual events and persons, not on mythical stories that followers attached to Jesus.

The second item in the charge concerns the possibility and reliability of prophecy in Scripture. (Epicureans attacked all forms of prophecy: venerable religious books, astrology, oracles, dream visions, and the like.) Second Peter employs biblical examples of divine judgment to prove that God does in fact punish the wicked (2:4–16) and refers to the words of the "holy prophets and the commandment of the Lord . . . spoken through your apostles" (3:2). Insistence upon reliable prophetic words probably refers to specific prophecies about divine judgment. The accusation appears to be that people can make prophecy say whatever they want—as sometimes happened when the oracle at Delphi was applied to politics, for example. Second Peter insists that prophetic words inspired by the Holy Spirit are not that sort of prophecy; they reflect God's purposes, not human cleverness.

All later Christians have is memory of the apostles' testimony and the prophetic words at the core of their faith. How can they secure a faith that hopes in God's just judgment? Second Peter 1:19b has a somewhat cryptic suggestion: "be attentive . . . as to a lamp shining in a dark place, until . . . the morning star rises in your hearts." Attention to the prophetic word of God will transform the heart, but not easily. Ancient oil lamps gave very little light, so the breaking of dawn was a much more significant fact of life than it is for many of us who in winter get up and head to work well before dawn. The regular cycle of moon, stars at night, and sun by day was also an argument for what we call "intelligent design," God's loving ordering of creation. So 2 Peter does have a way of attentive living and hearing God's word that transfigures . . . and it is not at all the "boom and bust" cycle of religious ecstasy followed by a letdown!

PHEME PERKINS

Homiletical Perspective

the few, direct opportunities (outside of 2 Tim. 3:16) to help congregations explore and claim both their own voices *and* the good news of the Spirit's work in our midst. A good place to start might be Calvin's *Institutes of the Christian Religion*: "We have no great certainty of the word itself, until it be confirmed by the testimony of the Spirit. For God has so knit together the certainty of the word and the Spirit, that our minds are duly imbued with reverence for the word when the Spirit shining upon it enables us there to behold the face of God."[1] Here the text, the Spirit, and the reader's mind are all knit together.

Finally, there is an important theme about accountability, control, and grace. Many churches today are woefully unable to provide a community of accountability for believers in their walk of faith. That being said, the epistle writer seems to be calling his readers back to the apostolic doctrine of the second coming mostly so as to scare them into being good. In some ways I am reminded of Jorge, the old monk in Umberto Eco's *The Name of the Rose*, who was driven to acts of murder in his desire to conceal a lost manuscript by Aristotle. He thought the book would cause people to lose their fear of God, and thus fall into disobedience, for, he said, "Law is imposed by fear, whose true name is fear of God."[2] The epistle writer's somewhat strident desire to reestablish in his readers a fear of God's judgment (see chap. 2) begs the question of whether such scare tactics actually result in lives that are formed in the shape of God's lavish grace. Certainly, we are not meant to use our freedom in Christ as a pretext for evil (1 Pet. 2:16); at the same time, lives of grateful and gracious service do not proceed easily from fear. They proceed most naturally and fruitfully from hearts overflowing with gratitude for God's steadfast love.

CHRISTOPHER GRUNDY

1. John Calvin, *The Institutes of the Christian Religion* (Edinburgh: Calvin Translation Society, 1895), 113.
2. Umberto Eco, *The Name of the Rose* (New York: Harcourt Brace Jovanovich, 1983), 475.

Matthew 17:1-9

¹Six days later, Jesus took with him Peter and James and his brother John and led them up a high mountain, by themselves. ²And he was transfigured before them, and his face shone like the sun, and his clothes became dazzling white. ³Suddenly there appeared to them Moses and Elijah, talking with him. ⁴Then Peter said to Jesus, "Lord, it is good for us to be here; if you wish, I will make three dwellings here, one for you, one for Moses, and one for Elijah." ⁵While he was still speaking, suddenly a bright cloud overshadowed them, and from the cloud a voice said, "This is my Son, the Beloved; with him I am well pleased; listen to him!" ⁶When the disciples heard this, they fell to the ground and were overcome by fear. ⁷But Jesus came and touched them, saying, "Get up and do not be afraid." ⁸And when they looked up, they saw no one except Jesus himself alone.

⁹As they were coming down the mountain, Jesus ordered them, "Tell no one about the vision until after the Son of Man has been raised from the dead."

Theological Perspective

The account of Jesus' transfiguration (*metamorphō-sis*) seems strange to the mind of all who have been conditioned by Western modernity to pay exceptional court to the great god Fact—and accordingly to suspect any account of reality that ventures out into the netherworld of trans-*anything*! With the dubious exception of those whose biblicism permits and even demands of them an extraordinary credulity where *the Bible* is concerned, none of us escapes the insistence of our science-bound culture that sacred texts too should conform so far as possible to "normal," empirically demonstrable truth claims. Whether we admit it or not, even those of us who think ourselves especially open to mystery feel uneasy in the presence of texts like this.

To be sure, at one level of perception, the experience of transfiguration is not *entirely* beyond the ken of most sensitive people. Who has not known moments of surprised illumination when, through some outwardly ordinary act, episode, or fragment of conversation, someone we thought we knew fairly well is suddenly revealed in a completely new light? Often in retrospect one is moved to consider the life of someone no longer living—a parent or grandparent, a friend or mentor—and to realize how inadequately, even perhaps how wrongly, one has grasped the real character of that one, or how one has missed

Pastoral Perspective

The wise way to prepare for joy or sorrow in this life is to take the road of the Stoics of antiquity. Cut yourself off from emotion. Keep everyone and everything at a distance. Build a fortress around your soul. Do not risk the price of wonder or of heartache.

Moving into Lent, the inevitability of the cross weighs heavily upon people in the pews and the pulpit. It weighs on that ever-faithful seventy-five-year-old woman who attends every week but boycotts Palm Sunday, refusing to chant, "Crucify him, Crucify him!" It weighs on the church school teacher who asks if there is a way to teach the miracles through Lent, because the cross seems too horrific, too difficult.

There is nothing we can do to change the fate of our Lord. We know the story only too well, and we remember the story as we endure the stories of loss in our own mundane lives: the suffering friends, the child who is ill, the career that has fallen apart, the relationship that seems beyond the point of healing. The question before us is this: will we be ruled by stoicism, or will we risk the price of weeping and suffering, celebration and surprise when life somehow is redeemed?

Peter, James, and John accompany Jesus up the mountain after hearing the news of Jerusalem and Jesus' imminent death. It is only human that in their

Exegetical Perspective

The account of the transfiguration continues Matthew's thematic emphasis on Jesus' divine sonship. Jesus is the Messiah, son of David and son of Abraham (1:1),[1] the heir of God's promises to them both (cf. Gen. 12:1–3; 2 Sam. 7:8–16; Deut. 18:15; etc.), who is conceived through the Holy Spirit (1:18), and whose birth moves inhabitants of heaven (1:20) and earth (2:1, 16). He is God's own Son, foretold by the prophets (2:15; 3:1–12; 5:17) and proclaimed from heaven (3:17), who teaches with God's own authority (7:21–29), whose restorative power transcends all other powers—disease (8:1–4), paralysis (8:5–13), sickness (8:14–15), demons (8:16–17, 28–34), nature's assaults (8:23–27)—and whose divine sonship is recognized by his disciples (14:33) and confessed (16:16). Now at this point in Matthew's Gospel, with the cross and the meaning of sonship coming into sharper relief (16:21–24), the transfiguration confirms Jesus' identity as the glorious Son of God Messiah. For the disciples who are present, it is also a sign of new life that awaits Jesus the Faithful One beyond the cross and signals new life for Jesus' followers as well.

1. On the significance of Jesus' dual sonship and the unusual genealogy in Matt. 1:1–17, see Robert A. Bryant, *The Gospel of Matthew: God with Us* (Pittsburgh: Kerygma, 2006), 16–19. For a thorough analysis of Matthew's Christology, see Jack Dean Kingsbury, *Matthew: Structure, Christology, Kingdom* (Minneapolis: Fortress, 1975).

Homiletical Perspective

The challenge and promise of preaching the transfiguration are abundantly demonstrated by the ways the three Synoptic Gospels preach the narrative given them by the tradition. Although it is probably impossible to trace the trajectory of the tradition, this singular story of Christ's glory—both hidden and revealed—almost certainly preceded the written Gospels.

When Mark preaches the transfiguration, it is as part and parcel of the "messianic secret"—probably better understood as a "messianic mystery"—when the glory of the risen Christ reaches back to enfold the historical Jesus. Although Peter's stammering (Mark 9:6) provides grist for homiletical humor, this story is not about the cloddishness of the disciples but the overwhelming magnificence of the glorious vision.

Throughout his Gospel, Luke highlights prayer (Luke 5:16; 6:12; 11:1; 18:1; 22:45–46). When Luke preaches the received tradition, he tells it as a story about what happened when Jesus "went up on the mountain to pray. And while he was praying" (Luke 9:28–29), the transfiguration occurs. Later in the Garden of Gethsemane the opposite of prayer is sleeping (Luke 22:45–46), and when Luke preaches the transfiguration, he explains: "Now Peter and his companions were weighed down with sleep; but since they

Matthew 17:1-9

Theological Perspective

the depths of meaning that he or she held for one's own life.

There may indeed be some hint of this common human experience in the account of Jesus' *metamorphōsis*: the earliest Christians, left with such enormous questions about the nature and vocation of the One in whom their nascent faith is centered, find themselves in a mood of disturbing-yet-fascinated recall. They remember conversations, encounters, and events that puzzled them at the time, but which now, in the light of all that has happened, they perceive with eyes of faith. The ordinary, in remembrance, takes on extraordinary significance. Epiphanies are rarely confined to the moments of their alleged occurrence; indeed, their character as extraordinary experiences of illumination may always, or usually, require significant lapses of time for contemplation.

Thus, reflection upon experiences that are at least potentially common to all of us can mitigate to some extent the feeling of strangeness in relation to this text. However, while such consideration may help us to understand the text, what is at stake here is something beyond ordinary human experience. Here, as at many other points in the scriptural testimony to the life of Jesus, we are being asked to confront the *great* question that the New Testament puts to us— the question that Dietrich Bonhoeffer famously stated: "Who is Jesus Christ for us today?"—the question that Jesus himself put to his disciples, "Who do *you* say that I am?" (Matt. 16:15).

In the long and sometimes acrimonious debate between those who cling to "the Jesus of history" and those who accentuate, rather, "the Christ of faith," I have always identified with Christians who could not embrace either side exclusively, and have felt that the historical Jesus and the Jesus Christ of Christian experience must be held together. Precisely this, I believe, is what the account of Jesus' transfiguration would have us affirm.

The transfiguration does not intend to transport the faithful into a transhistorical realm, where the Jesus known to fishermen, tax collectors, and prostitutes suddenly appears in ghostly mien, lit up from the inside, and having discourse with famous figures long since dead! Rather, it intends to confess that these untutored, down-to-earth men and women who left everything and followed him, hardly knowing why—that these same persons, later, knew that they had been drawn to him because, for all his obvious humanity, something radiated from him that spoke of ineffable and eternal truth. Some of

Pastoral Perspective

minds they play out the next few days and weeks. They begin to look for alternatives, desperate for a second opinion, a way to stop time. They want to build a safe sanctuary away from the world, to be content in the moment, saving Jesus and themselves from the heartache to come. They cannot, nor can we.

We glimpse that moment in a hospital room as we sit with two people who have just heard the worst news of their lives and watch the patient reach out to assure the companion, the healthy one, that all will be well. We glimpse that moment when the evening news reflects nothing but chaos, and then there is one story of a person's graceful act of healing a broken world by caring for another person the world would rather forget. These are the moments when people begin to understand that where there is suffering, there is Holy Ground.[1] These are the moments when we realize God is present in suffering and sacrifice, just as God is present in the promise and potential of our lives.

This moment of transfiguration is just such a moment. On one hand, the transfiguration affirms Jesus' divinity; on the other, it begins to give the disciples eyes to see God's light in the chaos to come: death, loss, fear and resurrection, the work of the early church. The challenge to the disciples is to live in a world without Jesus' bodily presence. The transfiguration anticipates this challenge, inviting us to live in "the light of the knowledge of the glory of God in the face of Jesus Christ" (2 Cor. 4:6). As that light shines in our hearts, the incarnate God is made real in the every day.

C. S. Lewis writes a final word from Aslan in *The Silver Chair*: "Here on the mountain I have spoken to you clearly. I will not often do so down in Narnia. Here on the mountain, the air is clear and your mind is clear; as you drop down into Narnia, the air will thicken. Take great care that it does not confuse your mind. And the signs which you have learned here will not look at all as you expect them to look, when you meet them there. That is why it is so important to know them by heart and pay no attention to appearance. Remember the signs and believe the signs. Nothing else matters."[2]

God prepares people in the transcendent encounters of our lives to endure the world below, the world of the cross, the world that has the ability to break us and yet is never beyond God's redemption. These encounters happen on mountaintops with a blinding

---

1. Robert Runcie, "Zeebrugge Ferry Disaster Sermon," in *Tongues of Angels, Tongues of Men* (New York: Doubleday, 1998), 740.
2. C. S. Lewis, *The Silver Chair* (New York: HarperCollins, 1981), 25–26.

A Glimpse of Glory (vv. 1–5). According to Matthew, the transfiguration occurs six days after Peter's public profession of Jesus' divine sonship in Caesarea Philippi (16:16; see also Mark 9:2–10 and cf. Luke 9:28–36). Peter calls Jesus the "Christ, the Son of the living God" (16:16), and Jesus begins showing the disciples the path of suffering servanthood that lies ahead for God's Messiah and all who "come after" him (16:21–25). Apocalyptic images permeate and conclude his teaching demonstration (16:17, 19, 27–28; cf. Dan. 7–12; Rev. 1:7; 22:12). Jesus now takes three of his closest disciples (4:18–22; 26:37)—Peter, James, and John—up a high mountain, such as Mount Tabor or Mount Hermon, for a revelatory encounter, a transfiguration that confirms Jesus' messianic identity and destination.

There are inescapable parallels with Moses's transfiguration on Mount Sinai (cf. Exod. 24:16–17; 34:29) and the Spirit cloud's presence with Israel in the wilderness and in the giving of the Law (Exod. 16:10; 19:9; 24:15–16; etc.). Certainly Matthew believes that Jesus is the great prophet and teacher of Israel foretold by Moses (Deut. 18:15; Matt. 5–7; 17:5; 28:18). Elijah also encountered God on a mountain (1 Kgs. 19:9–18) and was the anticipated herald of the Messiah (Mal. 4:5). The pairing here in Matthew of Moses and Elijah, the Law and the Prophets, as at the end of Malachi's prophecy (Mal. 4:4–5), highlights the early church's apocalyptic hope for the Day of the Lord and the age of faithfulness (cf. 1 Thess. 5:1–11).

The transformation of Jesus' form (*metemorphōthē*, 17:2) reveals Jesus' divine sonship. According to Matthew, Jesus' whole body—not just his face—exudes a glory as bright as the sun that radiates even through his clothing (cf. Mark 9:3; Exod. 34:35). The brightness of his appearance reflects his righteousness and the nearness of the kingdom of heaven (13:43). Moreover, the voice from heaven at Jesus' baptism (3:17) here confirms again Jesus' divine identity and righteous character but now adds a command to obey him (17:5; 7:21–25; 28:19–20). Nothing less than Jesus' identity and Israel's apocalyptic hope of resurrection glory is unveiled in this moment, for in the resurrection the righteous ones will shine like the sun (cf. Dan. 12:3; 2 Esd. 7:97; *1 Enoch* 104:2–3; 2 Cor. 3:16–18; Rev. 1:16). The disciples' "vision" on the mountain is a confirmation of Jesus' identity and a preview of the glorious form of life that will characterize life in the kingdom of heaven.

Focusing on Jesus (vv. 6–8). Jesus' altered appearance does not drive the disciples away (17:4; cf. Exod.

had stayed awake, they saw his glory" (Luke 9:32). In Luke's sermon, the transfiguration's glory is perceptible only to those who know how to pray.

When Matthew preaches the transfiguration, he addresses a congregation for whom Moses is a compelling interpretative template. Matthew's sermon is Moses-shaped and the mount of the transfiguration echoes Sinai. Just as Moses is born under Pharaoh's death sentence, so Jesus is threatened by Herod; just as Moses receives the law on Mount Sinai, Jesus teaches the "Sermon on the Mount" (Matt. 5–7). Moses interprets the commandments of God in Deuteronomy, and Jesus interprets the commandments, "You have heard that it was said" (Matt. 5:21, 27, 33, 38, 43, etc.). The transfiguration tradition comes already thick with Mosaic themes (three companions [Exod. 24:1, 9]; the mountain [Exod. 24:16]; the cloud on the mount [Exod. 24:15]; "six days" [Exod. 24:16]), but when Matthew preaches the transfiguration, he intensifies the Moses theme in order to preach Christ.

Matthew adds description of a "bright cloud" (v. 5), evoking memory of the cloud that accompanied the ark and tabernacle, and tells how Jesus' face "shone like the sun" (v. 2), as Moses's face shone following his encounter with God (Exod. 34:29–30). The genius of Matthew's preaching, however, centers on the way in verse 6 he echoes the terror and dismay of the Israelites who hear the voice of God (Exod. 20:18) and cry out, "You speak to us, and we will listen; but do not let God speak to us, or we will die" (Exod. 20:19). The glorious presence and commanding voice of the Holy One of Israel threaten to overwhelm those who encounter them, but to the disciples overwhelmed by the presence and voice of God, Jesus reaches out his hand, touches them, and reassures them: "Do not be afraid" (v. 7).

Does anything banish our fears more perfectly than a simple, human touch? For John Calvin, this was the great genius of God. God, who made the heavens and the earth and all that is in them; God, whose greatness is so vast that not even the heavens above the heavens can contain it; God, whose we are, is so magnificent that God is willing to come among us to reach out, touch us, and still our fears. For the Gospel of Matthew, Jesus is God-with-us. Remember the angel's promise at the very beginning of the story? "'They shall name him Emmanuel,' which means 'God is with us'" (1:23). Jesus' hand on the shoulder of the disciples, therefore, is nothing less than God's own touch. Anything more would be too much. God is so vast, however, so magnificent, so

Matthew 17:1-9

Theological Perspective

them remembered now, when he had left them, one incident in particular when this radiance seemed to manifest itself almost . . . visibly.

We cannot know what that occasion was *really* like, or even *that* it happened—in terms of its "facticity." Certainly we are not required to turn the *biblical* account of it *into Fact*. For what is significant in the account is not its "special effects," but what it affirms about the early church's foundational belief about Jesus: namely, that he was not just another exceptional human being, prophet, or great teacher and example for all, but the decisive representation of the Divine, the source and judge of life. As one of the three disciples who is said to have been with Jesus on that remembered occasion stated the matter bluntly: "You are the Christ, the Son of the living God" (Matt. 16:16).

Until the church is able, in whatever language, imagery, and act, to engage in such a "leap of faith," it will lack the confidence to take up its real mission in the world. No attachment to "the Jesus of history" can, by itself, dispel the skepticism that asks, "Why Jesus? Why not Socrates? Gandhi? Buddha?"

Let the "conservatives" who boast of their high christologies beware: it was the same Peter with his exuberant confession of Christ who, in the next breath, proposed an agenda for faith that earned him Jesus' harshest recorded rejection: "Get behind me, *Satan!*" (Matt. 16:22–23). It was the same three disciples who felt they had been specially elected to witness Christ's *metamorphōsis*, and so proposed that edifices be erected to commemorate the occasion, who had to be reminded that it was *Jesus' way* and not theirs to which they must be conformed: "listen to *him*" (17:5)—namely, to the one who has already assured them that true discipleship means taking up the cross, not building churches (16:24–26).

While the church today, as always, is challenged to confess in word and deed that Jesus is indeed "the Christ," it is simultaneously warned against using that confession in the service of triumphalist religion. "The Christ of faith," when true, always leads again to the "Jesus of history"—that is, to him who "was crucified, dead, and buried," and whose anointing entailed a "descent into hell" before it could sit him down at the right hand of God.

DOUGLAS JOHN HALL

Pastoral Perspective

light for some. For most, they happen in the ordinary moments of our classrooms, boardrooms, and soup kitchens—any place where we make a space for the Holy to be present.

More subtly, the transfiguration offers the disciples the paradox that while there is nothing they can do to save themselves from suffering, there is also no way they can shield themselves from the light of God that sheds hope in their darkest moments. The mountain was the way for God to prepare a human band of companions for the sacred journey, to offer something to hold onto when they descend into the crushing reality of the world below.

An artist knows that everything he or she creates depends less on the subject matter and far more on the subject's relationship to the light. In sculpture, photography, painting, or drawing, the artist simply depicts the reflection of light off an object or an idea. The still life of an apple can be flat, dull, and uninspiring, or it can evoke emotion, reaction, and transcendence. What evokes that response is not the object; it is how the artist presents it in the light and how we respond to that reflection.

The moment of transfiguration is that point at which God says to the world and to each of us that there is nothing we can do to prepare for or stand in the way of joy or sorrow. We cannot build God a monument, and we cannot keep God safe. We also cannot escape the light that God will shed on our path. We cannot escape God, Immanuel among us. God will find us in our homes and in our workplaces. God will find us when our hearts are broken and when we discover joy. God will find us when we run away from God and when we are sitting in the middle of what seems like hell. So "get up and do not be afraid" (v. 7).

MARYETTA MADELEINE ANSCHUTZ

Exegetical Perspective

34:30). Instead, Peter offers to build shelters (booths), anticipating perhaps a lengthy meeting, a need for shelter, or an appropriate service for the feast of Tabernacles, which celebrates the harvest and God's redemption of Israel from slavery in Egypt (Lev. 23:33–43). The voice, however, drives the disciples prostrate to the ground (17:6), which is always appropriate posture before the Lord in the Old Testament (cf. Isa. 6:5; Ezek. 2:1; Dan. 8:17–18; 10:7–9). Jesus' teachings had also been replete with warnings of suffering and death (16:24–28), so there is little wonder they are overcome with fear (17:6–7). Jesus comes to his distracted and fearful followers, as he will one other time in Matthew following the resurrection (28:18), and he "touches" them. Just as he touched the diseased (8:3, 15) and the dead (9:25), he touches now these disciples and commands them to "rise" (*egerthēte*, v. 7) and not be afraid. The disciples now see only Jesus who alone is with them (17:8).

Anticipating the Resurrection (v. 9). Signs are often not easy to translate, especially when they are not fully understood (Mark 9:10). Even if the disciples do have a better grasp of the transfiguration's meaning, as Matthew suggests, how could anyone be prepared to face the suffering and death of God's Son, the Son of Man (cf. Deut. 21:22–23)? Thus Jesus commands the disciples not to share their "vision" of his divine sonship in the transfiguration until the "Son of Man has been raised from the dead," making God's judgment and the meaning of the transfiguration clear (17:9). The disciples will then be able to appropriate their experiences of the transfiguration through the risen Christ as they anticipate their own glorious resurrections to come. Moreover, this vision will help the disciples interpret the significance of John the Baptist (17:10–13). Ultimately for Matthew and his community, the transfiguration confirms Jesus' identity as the righteous Son of God, even as it signals hope for Jesus' followers of a glorious risen life without fear with Jesus.

ROBERT A. BRYANT

Homiletical Perspective

utterly extraordinary, that God consents to allow all that God hopes for us to be communicated in an ordinary human touch.

Most people have come to think of John Calvin as woefully austere, but listen how tenderly he explains that

> all thinking of God, apart from Christ, is a bottomless abyss which utterly swallows up all our senses. . . . In Christ God so to speak makes himself little, in order to lower himself to our capacity; and Christ alone calms our consciences that they may dare intimately approach God.[1]

This is the way that God comes into the world: not simply the brilliant cloud of mystery, not only a voice thundering from heaven, but also a human hand laid upon a shoulder and the words, "Do not be afraid." God comes to us quietly, gently, that we may draw near and not be afraid. God's glory is majestic and so far beyond our capacity to receive it that we can take just as much of God's glory as a human hand can hold.

God's glory and magnificence and power and majesty are unsurpassable, we say; but we must also declare that God's glory and magnificence and power and majesty are surpassed by God's willingness to shed them all in order that we might finally recognize God's love and gentleness. The measureless power that made the heavens and the earth concentrates in a hand reaching out to us.

Some would say that God is much too much to be contained within the walls of a church. Of course they are right. Some would remind us that God is so great that neither the earth below nor the heavens above can hold God. Certainly we must agree with them. God is certainly so great that God can never be contained in something as small as a crumb of bread or a sip of wine. We nod our heads, yes; but we must hasten to add: furthermore, God is so great, so majestic, so glorious, that God deigns come to us in a crumb of bread and a sip of wine, just as much of God as a hand can hold.

PATRICK J. WILLSON

1. John Calvin's commentary on 1 Peter 1:20, quoted in Ford Lewis Battles, "God Was Accommodating Himself to Human Capacity," *Interpretation* 31, no. 1 (Jan. 1977): 38.

Contributors

Charles L. Aaron, Pastor, First United Methodist Church, Farmersville, Texas

P. Mark Achtemeier, Associate Professor of Systematic Theology, Dubuque Theological Seminary, Dubuque, Iowa

Paul J. Achtemeier, Jackson Professor of Biblical Interpretation Emeritus, Union Theological Seminary, Richmond, Virginia

Harry B. Adams, Professor Emeritus, Yale Divinity School, Hamden, Connecticut

Joanna M. Adams, Retired Pastor, Morningside Presbyterian Church, Atlanta, Georgia

E. Lane Alderman Jr., Pastor, Roswell Presbyterian Church, Roswell, Georgia

Ronald J. Allen, Nettie Sweeney and Hugh Th. Miller Professor of Preaching and New Testament, Christian Theological Seminary, Indianapolis, Indiana

Maryetta Madeleine Anschutz, Founding Head, The Episcopal School of Los Angeles, and Priest Associate, All Saints Episcopal Church, Beverly Hills, California

Emily Askew, Associate Professor of Systematic Theology, Lexington Theological Seminary, Lexington, Kentucky

David L. Bartlett, Professor Emeritus of New Testament, Columbia Theological Seminary, Decatur, Georgia

Christopher A. Beeley, Walter H. Gray Associate Professor of Anglican Studies and Patristics, Yale Divinity School, New Haven, Connecticut

April Berends, Rector, St. Mark's Episcopal Church, Milwaukee, Wisconsin

Bruce C. Birch, Dean and Miller Professor of Biblical Theology, Wesley Theological Seminary, Washington, D.C.

Barbara S. Blaisdell, Pastor, United Community Church, Hilo, Hawaii

Dave Bland, Professor of Homiletics, Harding University Graduate School of Religion, Memphis, Tennessee

Ellen J. Blue, Mouzon Biggs Jr. Associate Professor of the History of Christianity and United Methodist Studies, Phillips Theological Seminary, Tulsa, Oklahoma

Matthew Myer Boulton, Associate Professor of Ministry Studies, Harvard Divinity School, Cambridge, Massachusetts

Robert A. Bryant, Associate Professor of Religion, Presbyterian College, Clinton, South Carolina

Drew Bunting, Musician and Homemaker, Milwaukee, Wisconsin

John P. Burgess, James Henry Snowden Professor of Systematic Theology, Pittsburgh Theological Seminary, Pittsburgh, Pennsylvania

Jason Byassee, Executive Director of Leadership Education at Duke Divinity and Director of the Center for Theology, Writing, and Media, Duke Divinity School, Durham, North Carolina

Cynthia M. Campbell, President, McCormick Theological Seminary, Chicago, Illinois

Greg Carey, Professor of New Testament, Lancaster Theological Seminary, Lancaster, Pennsylvania

Gary W. Charles, Pastor, Central Presbyterian Church, Atlanta, Georgia

W. Michael Chittum, Senior Minister, First Congregational Church, Salt Lake City, Utah

Kimberly L. Clayton, Director of Contextual Education, Columbia Theological Seminary, Decatur, Georgia

Andrew Foster Connors, Pastor, Brown Memorial Park Avenue Presbyterian Church, Baltimore, Maryland

Kate Foster Connors, Parish Associate and Youth Director, Brown Memorial Park Avenue Presbyterian Church, Baltimore, Maryland

Charles James Cook, Professor Emeritus of Pastoral Theology, Seminary of the Southwest, Austin, Texas

J. Blake Couey, Visiting Assistant Professor of Religious Studies, Millsaps College, Jackson, Mississippi

R. Alan Culpepper, Dean, McAfee School of Theology, Atlanta, Georgia

Michael B. Curry, Bishop, Diocese of North Carolina, Raleigh, North Carolina

William Joseph Danaher Jr., Dean, Faculty of Theology, Huron University College, London, Ontario, Canada

Lillian Daniel, Senior Minister, First Congregational Church, United Church of Christ, Glen Ellyn, Illinois

Linda Day, Independent Scholar, Pittsburgh, Pennsylvania

Carol J. Dempsey, Professor of Theology (Biblical Studies), University of Portland, Oregon

Steven D. Driver, Director of Formation, Immanuel Lutheran Church, Valparaiso, Indiana

Paul Simpson Duke, Co-Pastor, First Baptist Church, Ann Arbor, Michigan

Stacey Simpson Duke, Co-Pastor, First Baptist Church, Ann Arbor, Michigan

Noel Leo Erskine, Professor of Theology and Ethics, Candler School of Theology, Emory University, Atlanta, Georgia

Barbara J. Essex, Minister for Higher Education and Theological Education, United Church of Christ, Cleveland, Ohio

Judy Fentress-Williams, Associate Professor of Old Testament, Virginia Theological Seminary, Alexandria, Virginia

Lisa G. Fischbeck, Vicar, The Episcopal Church of the Advocate, Carrboro, North Carolina

Matthew Flemming, Instructor in Preaching, Columbia Theological Seminary, Decatur, Georgia

Greg Garrett, Professor of English, Baylor University, Waco, Texas; Writer in Residence, Seminary of the Southwest, Austin, Texas

Roger J. Gench, Pastor, The New York Avenue Presbyterian Church, Washington, D.C.

Alan Gregory, Academic Dean and Associate Professor of Church History, Seminary of the Southwest, Austin, Texas

Christopher Grundy, Assistant Professor of Preaching and Worship, Eden Theological Seminary, St. Louis, Missouri

Douglas John Hall, Professor Emeritus, McGill University, Montreal, Quebec, Canada

Jin Hee Han, Associate Professor of Biblical Studies, New York Theological Seminary, New York, New York

Douglas R. A. Hare, Wm. F. Orr Professor of New Testament Emeritus, Pittsburgh Theological Seminary, Pittsburgh, Pennsylvania

Daniel Harris, Associate Professor of Homiletics, Aquinas Institute of Theology, St. Louis, Missouri

John H. Hayes, Old Testament Professor Emeritus, Candler School of Theology, Emory University, Atlanta, Georgia

Susan Hedahl, Herman G. Stuempfle Chair of Proclamation of the Word, Professor of Homiletics, Lutheran Theological Seminary at Gettysburg, Gettysburg, Pennsylvania

William R. Herzog II, Dean of Faculty, Professor of New Testament, Andover Newton Theological School, Newton Centre, Massachusetts

Johnny B. Hill, Assistant Professor of Theology, Louisville Presbyterian Theological Seminary, Louisville, Kentucky

Geoffrey M. St.J. Hoare, Rector, All Saints' Episcopal Church, Atlanta, Georgia

David Holmes, Minister, McDougall United Church, Calgary, Alberta, Canada

Patrick J. Howell, Professor of Pastoral Theology and Rector of the Jesuit Community, Seattle University, Seattle, Washington

Paul Junggap Huh, Assistant Professor of Worship and Director of Korean American Ministries, Columbia Theological Seminary, Decatur, Georgia

Edith M. Humphrey, William F. Orr Professor of New Testament, Pittsburgh Theological Seminary, Pittsburgh, Pennsylvania

Joseph R. Jeter, Granville and Erline Walker Professor of Homiletics, Brite Divinity School at Texas Christian University, Fort Worth, Texas

Patrick W. T. Johnson, Pastor, Frenchtown Presbyterian Church, Frenchtown, New Jersey

Melanie Johnson-DeBaufre, Associate Professor of New Testament, Drew Theological School, Madison, New Jersey

L. Shannon Jung, Professor of Town and Country Ministry, Saint Paul School of Theology, Kansas City, Missouri

Aaron Klink, Westbrook Fellow, Program in Theology and Medicine, Duke University, Durham, North Carolina

Michael E. Lodahl, Professor of Theology, Point Loma Nazarene University, San Diego, California

Dwight M. Lundgren, National Ministries, American Baptist Churches USA, Valley Forge, Pennsylvania

Dean McDonald, Cathedral College of Preachers, Washington, D.C.

MaryAnn McKibben Dana, Pastor, Idylwood Presbyterian Church, Falls Church, Virginia

Jennifer Powell McNutt, Assistant Professor of Theology and History of Christianity, Wheaton College, Wheaton, Illinois

Allen C. McSween Jr., Pastor, Fourth Presbyterian Church, Greenville, South Carolina

Troy A. Miller, Associate Professor of Bible and Theology, Crichton College, Memphis, Tennessee

Robert C. Morgan, Fellow of Linacre College, Emeritus, University of Oxford, United Kingdom

Andrew Nagy-Benson, Senior Minister, Spring Glen Church, United Church of Christ, Hamden, Connecticut

Carmen Nanko-Fernández, Assistant Professor of Pastoral Ministry; Director, Ecumenical Doctor of Ministry Program, Catholic Theological Union, Chicago, Illinois

Rodger Y. Nishioka, Benton Family Associate Professor of Christian Education, Columbia Theological Seminary, Decatur, Georgia

Kathleen M. O'Connor, William Marcellus McPheeters Professor of Old Testament, Columbia Theological Seminary, Decatur, Georgia

Robert J. Owens, Professor of Old Testament, General Theological Seminary of the Episcopal Church, New York, New York

Stephanie A. Paulsell, Houghton Professor of the Practice of Ministry Studies, Harvard Divinity School, Cambridge, Massachusetts

Pheme Perkins, Professor of New Testament, Theology Department, Boston College, Chestnut Hill, Massachusetts

David Rensberger, Adjunct Professor of New Testament, Interdenominational Theological Center, Atlanta, Georgia, and Columbia Theological Seminary, Decatur, Georgia

Marcia Y. Riggs, J. Erskine Love Professor of Christian Ethics, and Director of the Th.M. Program, Columbia Theological Seminary, Decatur, Georgia

John D. Rohrs, Associate Rector, Christ Episcopal Church, Raleigh, North Carolina

Don E. Saliers, William R. Cannon Professor Emeritus of Theology and Worship, Candler School of Theology, Emory University, Atlanta, Georgia

Christian Scharen, Assistant Professor of Worship and Theology, Luther Seminary, St. Paul, Minnesota

David J. Schlafer, Homiletics Consultant, Author, and Conference Leader, Bethesda, Maryland

Timothy F. Sedgwick, Vice President and Associate Dean of Academic Affairs, The Clinton S. Quin Professor of Christian Ethics, Virginia Theological Seminary, Alexandria, Virginia

William L. Self, Senior Pastor, Johns Creek Baptist Church, Alpharetta, Georgia

John C. Shelley, Professor of Religion, Furman University, Greenville, South Carolina

Richard M. Simpson, Rector, St. Francis Episcopal Church, Holden, Massachusetts

Sheldon W. Sorge, Pastor to Presbytery, Presbytery of Pittsburgh, Presbyterian Church (U.S.A.), Pittsburgh, Pennsylvania

Barbara Brown Taylor, Harry R. Butman Professor of Religion, Piedmont College, Demorest, Georgia

Frank A. Thomas, Senior Servant, Mississippi Boulevard Christian Church, Memphis, Tennessee

James W. Thompson, Robert R. and Kay Onstead Professor of New Testament, Abilene Christian University, Abilene, Texas

David Toole, Associate Dean, Duke Divinity School, Durham, North Carolina

W. Sibley Towner, Professor Emeritus of Biblical Interpretation, Union Presbyterian Seminary, Richmond, Virginia

Martin G. Townsend, Bishop Retired, The Diocese of Easton, Springfield, West Virginia

Thomas H. Troeger, J. Edward and Ruth Cox Lantz Professor of Christian Communication, Yale Divinity School, New Haven, Connecticut

Steven S. Tuell, Associate Professor of Old Testament, Pittsburgh Theological Seminary, Pittsburgh, Pennsylvania

Edwin Chr. van Driel, Assistant Professor of Theology, Pittsburgh Theological Seminary, Pittsburgh, Pennsylvania

Carol L. Wade, Canon Precentor, Washington National Cathedral, Washington, D.C.

Paul Walaskay, Professor Emeritus of Biblical Studies, Union Presbyterian Seminary, Richmond, Virginia

Neal H. Walls, Associate Professor of Old Testament Interpretation, Wake Forest Divinity School, Winston-Salem, North Carolina

Richard F. Ward, Fred B. Craddock Professor of Homiletics and Worship, Phillips Theological Seminary, Tulsa, Oklahoma

Andrea Wigodsky, Chaplain, Saint Mary's School, Raleigh, North Carolina

Patrick J. Willson, Pastor, Williamsburg Presbyterian Church, Williamsburg, Virginia

Kevin A. Wilson, Adjunct Professor of Religion and Theology, Merrimack College, North Andover, Massachusetts

Lisa M. Wolfe, Associate Professor, Endowed Chair of Hebrew Bible, Oklahoma City University, Oklahoma City, Oklahoma

Charles M. Wood, Lehman Professor of Christian Doctrine and Director, Graduate Program in Religious Studies, Perkins School of Theology, Southern Methodist University, Dallas, Texas

David J. Wood, Senior Pastor, Glencoe Union Church, Glencoe, Illinois

Erica Brown Wood, Priest-in-Charge, St. Luke's Episcopal Church, Mount Joy, Pennsylvania, and Adjunct Professor, Lancaster Theological Seminary, Lancaster, Pennsylvania

Brett Younger, Associate Professor of Preaching, McAfee School of Theology, Atlanta, Georgia

Mark E. Yurs, Pastor, Salem United Church of Christ, Verona, Wisconsin

Scripture Index

Author Index

Numerals indicate numbered Sundays of a season; for example, "Advent 1" represents the First Sunday of Advent, and "Christmas 1" the First Sunday after Christmas.

Cynthia M. Campbell	Advent 1 E PP, Advent 2 E PP, Advent 3 E PP	Paul Simpson Duke	Advent 1 OT HP, Advent 2 OT HP, Advent 3 OT HP
Greg Carey	Epiphany 7 G EP, Epiphany 8 G EP, Epiphany 9 G EP	Stacey Simpson Duke	Advent 1 OT PP, Advent 2 OT PP, Advent 3 OT PP
Gary W. Charles	Christmas 1 OT PP	Noel Leo Erskine	Advent 1 OT TP, Advent 2 OT TP, Advent 3 OT TP
W. Michael Chittum	Epiphany 7 E TP, Epiphany 8 E TP, Epiphany 9 E TP	Barbara J. Essex	Epiphany 7 G PP, Epiphany 8 G PP, Epiphany 9 G PP
Kimberly L. Clayton	Epiphany 7 OT HP, Epiphany 8 OT HP, Epiphany 9 OT HP	Judy Fentress-Williams	Transfiguration OT EP
Andrew Foster Connors	Epiphany 4 OT PP, Epiphany 5 OT PP, Epiphany 6 OT PP	Lisa G. Fischbeck	Christmas 1 E PP, Christmas 2 E PP, Epiphany E PP
Kate Foster Connors	Epiphany 7 E PP, Epiphany 8 E PP, Epiphany 9 E PP	Matthew Flemming	Epiphany OT PP
		Greg Garrett	Epiphany 1 G HP, Epiphany 2 G HP, Epiphany 3 G HP
Charles James Cook	Epiphany 4 G PP, Epiphany 5 G PP, Epiphany 6 G PP	Roger J. Gench	Epiphany 4 E PP, Epiphany 5 E PP, Epiphany 6 E PP
J. Blake Couey	Advent 4 OT EP, Christmas Eve OT EP, Christmas Day OT EP	Alan Gregory	Epiphany 1 NT PP, Epiphany 2 E PP, Epiphany 3 E PP
R. Alan Culpepper	Christmas 1 G EP, Christmas 2 G EP, Epiphany G EP	Christopher Grundy	Transfiguration E HP
		Douglas John Hall	Transfiguration G TP
Michael B. Curry	Epiphany 7 PS PP, Epiphany 8 PS PP, Epiphany 9 PS PP	Jin Hee Han	Epiphany 7 OT EP, Epiphany 8 OT EP, Epiphany 9 OT EP
William Joseph Danaher Jr.	Transfiguration OT TP	Douglas R. A. Hare	Advent 4 G EP, Christmas Eve G EP, Christmas Day G EP
Lillian Daniel	Epiphany 7 OT PP, Epiphany 8 OT PP, Epiphany 9 OT PP	Daniel Harris	Advent 4 G HP, Christmas Eve G HP, Christmas Day G HP
Linda Day	Epiphany 1 PS EP, Epiphany 2 PS EP, Epiphany 3 PS EP	John H. Hayes	Epiphany 1 OT EP, Epiphany 2 OT EP, Epiphany 3 OT EP
Carol J. Dempsey	Epiphany 4 OT TP, Epiphany 5 OT TP, Epiphany 6 OT TP	Susan Hedahl	Christmas 1 G TP, Christmas 2 G TP, Epiphany G TP
Steven D. Driver	Epiphany 1 G TP		

William R. Herzog II	Advent 1 G EP, Advent 2 G EP, Advent 3 G EP	Jennifer Powell McNutt	Epiphany 1 OT TP, Epiphany 2 OT TP, Epiphany 3 OT TP
Johnny B. Hill	Christmas 1 E TP, Christmas 2 E TP, Epiphany E TP	Allen C. McSween Jr.	Transfiguration OT PP
		Troy A. Miller	Epiphany 1 G EP, Epiphany 2 G EP, Epiphany 3 G EP
Geoffrey M. St.J. Hoare	Advent 4 OT PP, Christmas Eve OT PP, Christmas Day OT PP	Robert C. Morgan	Advent 4 E TP, Christmas Eve E TP, Christmas Day E TP
David Holmes	Advent 1 PS PP, Advent 2 PS PP, Advent 3 PS PP	Andrew Nagy-Benson	Epiphany 1 PS HP, Epiphany 2 PS HP, Epiphany 3 PS HP
Patrick J. Howell	Advent 1 E TP, Advent 2 E TP, Advent 3 E TP	Carmen Nanko-Fernández	Epiphany 1 PS TP, Epiphany 2 PS TP, Epiphany 3 PS TP
Paul Junggap Huh	Epiphany 4 PS TP, Epiphany 5 PS TP, Epiphany 6 PS TP	Rodger Y. Nishioka	Epiphany 1 G PP, Epiphany 2 G PP, Epiphany 3 G PP
Edith M. Humphrey	Epiphany 4 E EP, Epiphany 5 E EP, Epiphany 6 E EP	Kathleen M. O'Connor	Advent 4 PS EP, Christmas Eve PS EP, Christmas Day PS EP
Joseph R. Jeter	Epiphany 7 E HP, Epiphany 8 E HP, Epiphany 9 E HP	Robert J. Owens	Christmas 1 PS EP, Christmas 2 A EP, Epiphany PS EP
Patrick W. T. Johnson	Advent 4 OT HP, Christmas Eve OT HP, Christmas Day OT HP	Stephanie A. Paulsell	Epiphany 1 OT PP, Epiphany 2 OT PP, Epiphany 3 OT PP
Melanie Johnson-DeBaufre	Epiphany 7 E EP, Epiphany 8 E EP, Epiphany 9 E EP	Pheme Perkins	Transfiguration E EP
		David Rensberger	Advent 4 E EP, Christmas Eve E EP, Christmas Day E EP
L. Shannon Jung	Christmas 1 PS TP, Christmas 2 A TP, Epiphany PS TP	Marcia Y. Riggs	Epiphany 4 G TP, Epiphany 5 G TP, Epiphany 6 G TP
Aaron Klink	Advent 4 G PP, Christmas Eve G PP, Christmas Day G PP	John D. Rohrs	Transfiguration PS HP
Michael E. Lodahl	Transfiguration PS TP	Don E. Saliers	Advent 4 OT TP, Christmas Eve OT TP, Christmas Day OT TP
Dwight M. Lundgren	Transfiguration E PP		
Dean McDonald	Christmas 1 PS HP, Christmas 2 A HP, Epiphany PS HP	Christian Scharen	Advent 1 PS TP, Advent 2 PS TP, Advent 3 PS TP
MaryAnn McKibben Dana	Epiphany 1 PS PP, Epiphany 2 PS PP, Epiphany 3 PS PP